Flight Lines

Flight Lines

ACROSS THE GLOBE ON A JOURNEY WITH
THE ASTONISHING ULTRAMARATHON BIRDS

ANDREW DARBY

PEGASUS BOOKS
NEW YORK LONDON

FLIGHT LINES

Pegasus Books, Ltd.
148 W. 37th Street, 13th Floor
New York, NY 10018

First Pegasus Books cloth edition November 2020

Library of Congress Cataloging-in-Publication Data is available.

ISBN: 978-1-64313-576-2

10 9 8 7 6 5 4 3 2 1

Printed in the United States of America
Distributed by Simon & Schuster
www.pegasusbooks.com

For Sally Johannsohn

In memoriam
Clive Minton
1934–2019

'For the song-men are the oral map-makers of the tribe, and the wanderings of the culture heroes are the roads across the land.'
Bill Harney, 'Roads and Trade'

'I had no nation now but the imagination.'
Derek Walcott, 'The Schooner *Flight*'

Contents

List of maps

One
Hunting on a no-good shore

Huff, huff. I'm running. Pretending I am agile, stomping on mounds of wet seagrass, trying to keep my feet. *Huff, huff.*

Forty metres has never seemed so far. Alongside me another runner, a young woman, trips and pitches into the seaweed. I keep running. For two hours I've waited with an instruction burning in my head: 'When the cannon fires, run as fast as you can to the front of the net.'

Huff, huff. I reach the net. The young woman, Emilia Lai, is there before me. She's already on her knees at the tideline. How did that happen?

'Move the net up the beach, but don't lift it. The birds might escape.'

So—with experienced catchers, local coastal workers, stray birders and hangers-on like me—I kneel and ease the net up out of the salt-water-and-seagrass soup.

Under the net are a few sodden grey-and-white rags of birds. So meagre. A bunch of wet tissues. Their swamped heads rise far enough for them to see us crowding around.

1

The birds do not struggle or cry out. Their amazed eyes speak for them.

Escape? There is no escape. People around them are jubilant, high-fiving each other.

I take a breath and watch as the catchers begin to disentangle the birds from the net. Lai is head down in concentration, her right hand holds a bird and her nimble left fingers work the net away from it, feather by feather. It is popped into a linen bag and disappears before I can properly look at it.

But I know it is a Grey Plover and this, of all birds, is the one I have come to see.

When it's over, I ask Lai, reserved and slight, why she has come all the way from Taiwan to do this.

'I fell in love with shorebirds from the first time,' she says. 'Because they are so tiny, and so strong.' She pumps her fist.

————

I've come to Thompson Beach, north of Adelaide in South Australia, to see these birds that are part of a group called 'migratory shorebirds'. I am looking for the little-known and exotic.

I had half a memory of something I may have seen when young; of a strange curve-billed bird standing on a sand-spit across the other side of a lagoon mouth. It has stayed on the rim of my mind ever since.

In talk with friends I keep disentangling them from other birds. They're not seabirds; they're *shorebirds*. People also call them *waders*. They don't feed at sea, or rest on the water like gulls or shearwaters. Many don't even float. Shorebirds scurry along tidelines of ocean beaches, they're the spindly stalkers of mudflats, the still and watchful birds of wetlands. Birds of an ephemeral, marginal world.

Their daily rhythm is driven by the tide. They are constant in their connection to it—for the food it exposes, or conceals. Many shorebirds are resident on coasts and wetlands. Migratory shorebirds are fleeting visitors, and often have a global domain. Some are born in the far Arctic north, and they migrate each year to escape impossible cold, bound to return there to breed. They routinely cross hemispheres.

We might expect glamour in such birds. Mostly they do it humbly. You have to look twice to distinguish them from mud or seaweed, and they are often 'out there', away from people. 'Waders typically are the "grey birds" that live far from the spectacle of human cause, human glory and human misery,' said the Dutch ornithologist, Theunis Piersma.

The greyest of these is the Grey Plover—a dovish wallflower at the shorebird dance. It spreads thinly around the world's margins and is often overlooked, not just by people who don't know shorebirds, but by those who do. For many it's a second-choice bird, and for that reason it interests me. In life there are many surprises to be found among the overlooked.

As well as the bird, I am out to discover shorebird study itself. I think it might stand as a beacon of the grind that makes good science; the kind to power biodiversity protection. This, at a time when it's often easier for the frightened to deny what science plainly tells us about our earth. So I am freighting this small, unknown bird with hope.

The first Grey Plover I glimpse on the shore of Thompson Beach stands taller among a group of sandpipers, and it has seen me. I get a quick look at a short-billed head, different in profile from the little long-bills around it. Even as I begin to emerge from the scrub it's gone. So fast! I keep track of it to a landing away in the distance, off the edge of a sandbar. It stands in water up to its knees, alone and dismissive, like Peter Pan on Marooners' Rock. I am intrigued.

Until recently the word 'plover' has mainly meant to me a noisy, common bird that is not very bright: a lapwing. The Masked Lapwing and its many relatives around the world have adapted well to living with people. On grass near my home, dozens gather to stand and study the ground, as if they are looking for the same lost car key. Pairs sometimes try to nest in our garden, and all of them willingly rasp out a grating alarm call.

Masked Lapwings do not push migratory boundaries. They might move from drying inlands to wetter coasts, but most live near where they were born, spreading out to claim nesting territories. I have seen lapwings collect in a protest vigil on a piece of new highway that was previously their ground. I've watched heart-in-mouth as newborn chicks try to follow their calling parents off a city traffic island. And I admit to waving a rake to discourage them from setting up their territory in mine. They are odd birds, but really, they are not so much plovers. Think of the lapwing as the gateway bird.

Lapwings are related to the Grey Plover the way that great apes are related to us. Truly but, we like to think, distantly. Both birds are from the family Charadriidae (waders or shorebirds); but the 25 global lapwings live in the sub-family Vanellinae, while the Grey Plover is in the parallel sub-family Charadriinae, and is one of just four species that make up the genus *Pluvialis*, the 'rainbirds'.

The Grey Plover is *Pluvialis squatarola*, the snub-faced rainbird—another claim against it. Its three closest relatives—the

Eurasian, Pacific and American Goldens—form with it an exclusive group called the tundra plovers.

To birders, a Grey Plover can quickly be distinguished in flight among a mixed flock of shorebirds because it's the one with the sweaty armpits. These are its black-feathered 'wingpits', visible in flight. In Americas—defiantly from the rest of the world—it is called the Black-bellied Plover.

For a second-choice bird it is held in curious regard. It's one of a handful of birds on the cover of the global standard text, *Shorebirds: An identification guide*. It turns up as the single bird chosen for wader study groups' own logos. It has a strong, historic place among the bird-hunting fraternity of the American south. At an auction in 2006, a world-record price of US$830,000, was paid for a wooden carved hunting decoy described as 'Black-bellied Plover in Spring Plumage'. The work is a flowing sculptural miniature, like something the great Henry Moore might have shaped as a maquette. The bird bends over and looks down to persuade others flying past that there's food below, within range of a shooter.

Standoffish even from other shorebirds, Grey Plover in Australia are elusive, usually far out of human sight, and reach. Except at times like this, at a beach in a corner of Gulf St Vincent, South Australia, where a net has just exploded over them.

———

On the first morning of the catching expedition I join the birders on early reconnaissance, and walk the dawning shore. Here, where the gulf's head pushes into the heart of the continent, the meadows are of seagrass. The Australian surf is away down south. There is no swell. The tide rises soundlessly from somewhere beyond the horizon, flooding over sand and seagrass piles, through mangrove clumps, up creek lines and into the marshland bogs. A flock of Australian Pelicans ease themselves off a seagrass bank into the water with their eyes on us. We startle a feral Red Fox nosing the weed. When we turn to retrace our steps, we find that, without notice, an empty creek has become thigh-deep. Later this water will leak back out.

Briny rot rises out of seagrass washed onshore. A squall rages in from the land behind and belts across the flats, lifting marine white caps. The wind subsides, mosquitoes and sandflies swarm in to bite, and bushflies drive me to arm-waving distraction. This is shorebird domain. It is a fertile tidal flat millions of years in the making.

The gash in southern Australia that is the St Vincent Basin emerged as the Australo-Antarctic Gulf expanded after the break-up of the Gondwanan super-continent around 50 million years ago. The shallow gulf alternately dried out and flooded as glacial maximums froze the water into ice, and then inter-glacial periods let it down. In the last maximum, about 20,000 years ago, this was a plain with a central salty lake.

Surrounded by semi-arid lowland, the northern gulf where we are is not river-fed. The only watercourse with that name, the Wakefield, is ephemeral with the seasons. The gulf is a rare 'inverse estuary'. Salinity is greater and the water temperature higher at its head than at its mouth.

Without river flow, marine life is nourished by ocean currents carrying in sediments to settle on the gulf floor. These currents deal with a tidal regime so restricted that in South Australia one set of tides has its own name: 'The Dodger'. This tide has almost no rise or fall.

Sediments drift up to settle as the foundation for the seagrass that covers more than half of the gulf's 4098-square-kilometre bed. In the northern gulf, 6000 years' worth of seagrass washed onshore has decayed to extend the shoreline several kilometres out into the water. A scattered mangrove woodland, more expected in tropical Australia, pokes out through this tidal zone.

What makes this habitat attractive for shorebirds is less appealing for most of us. Beaches of seagrass sponge, muddy sand to infinity, biting insects, bright hot sun flaring off the flat water. Stink.

Stores of shorebird food are hidden here—in the sediments, seagrass, shoreline and nearby inland. Worms, small shellfish, cockles and marine snails percolate through the sandy mud. Prawns and small fish hug mangroves. Birds probe the wet edge of the tideline and roost on floating islands of coagulated seagrass. They work up the creek lines and into the saltmarsh, or feed on algal mats in ephemeral clay pans behind the shore. Further down the gulf, towards Adelaide, there is bounty in brine life held in commercial salt fields.

There are stories of the Kaurna Aboriginal people using this waterway they call Wongajerla. Clans of the Kaurna people extended north along the eastern shore of Gulf St Vincent to its head, hunting waterfowl and fishing with reed nets. Archaeological scrutiny of Kaurna stone implements shows they lived here since well before the last Ice Age.

The gulf's first cautious European explorers tacked their way up in the 1802–3 Anglo–French race to explore Australia's coastline. The Englishman Matthew Flinders took the rowing cutter from his ship *Investigator* 'up to the head of this inlet to examine its termination' in April 1802. Even working around channels, they could not get the cutter closer than 800 metres to the shore. Squelching through the mud, Flinders' party made it to land: they walked up a ridge and confirmed they had reached the northern point.

Flinders, the mapmaker, named the waters after a British Admiral, the Earl of St Vincent, and barely noted the wildlife. 'Numbers of stingrays came round the boat whilst upon the flat, but being un-provided, we were not able to succeed in getting any.' His expedition naturalist, Robert Brown, said that on the excursion Flinders shot a hawk: 'Several kinds of small birds were seen but none shot.' They were there at shorebird migration time, but left no account of them.

Just twelve days afterwards, Nicolas Baudin, aboard the *Geographe*, surveyed the same coast for Napoleon's France. Pushed up the gulf by a south-easterly gale—a migration wind— the explorers became confused by shoals and Baudin had to keep all hands on deck through the night while they worked their way out. 'I gave this gulf the name of Golfe de la Mauvais [The Bad Gulf] because of the fatigue that it caused the whole crew.'

As white settlement expanded, farmers moved north from Adelaide onto the plains, using the gulf's waters for transport. They loaded their wheat onto boats at 'ports' that were nothing more than the end of a track where a flat-bottomed ketch was beached at low tide so bagged grain could be carted alongside. Over time, commercial fishers began to work the northern gulf, but to the government its greatest use came by default. A century ago, it began to operate an army proof range. This 'empty' shore was perfect for testing artillery fire and thought to be absolutely no good for anything else. Guns and ammunition could be tested for reliability by firing from a point of land, southward over a 25-kilometre length of sandy flat. Soldiers shot shells, sometimes hundreds of rounds each day, out over the birds.

At low tide, retrieval parties used horse and cart, and later vehicles, to drive out onto the flat, study a warhead's impact, and perhaps pick up remains.

Use of the proof range brought the first government acknowledgement of the existence of shorebirds in the upper gulf, though an official hand waved away any effects on their survival. Plans to enlarge the range for bigger and better explosions forced an environmental assessment. It was guessed that wildlife was not affected, and anyway: 'in time it is thought that the birds would adjust to the noise'. I am left to imagine how many birds learned to recognise the incoming whistle of bombardment and flee the danger, or instead disappeared in a sudden explosion of shrapnel, sand and water.

The range is still sometimes used for weapons testing but an expansion of its impact zone that would have razed 189 houses in coastal holiday-shack enclaves was rejected. That same decision gave a green light to a new subdivision at a place called Thompson Beach.

Hunched on a low dune between samphire marshland and wind-breaking scrub, Thompson Beach's houses raise themselves just high enough to cool down, and for people to be able to look through their living-room windows across the tidal flat and into the gulf.

To Australians used to ocean and surf, this is not the greatest coastal real estate. But generations have taken refuge or holidays in these off-track communities, and the hardscrabble shore has its enthusiasts. 'Thompson Beach. The Place To Be Beside The Sea. Because It's On The Coast That Has The Most' says a T-shirt. Sunsets across the gulf really do blaze the wide sky in dramatic reds and purples; otherwise there seems to be little to back this happy belief.

Without much water clear enough for swimming or deep enough for an outboard motor, choices of recreation are limited to a local tide-bound ritual. As it ebbs, people wearing wader overalls appear on shore. Their heads and faces are hidden from the glare in hats and bandanas. Keeping to the same prospectors' rhythm as the shorebirds, they go crabbing for Blue Swimmers. The crabbers fossick the seagrass with rakes that entangle the Swimmers' claws. They flip them into floating plastic boxes towed behind from the waist. Out on the wide flat, these spectral foragers trudge in slow motion to the horizon.

Such a modest coast for high ambition. The shorebird expedition came there wanting to chart new tracks in global migration: to the far north, and perhaps back again. The catching group were students of a retired Melbourne metallurgist; they were drawn there by a South Australian environmental bureaucrat and led by a former bookkeeper. Without these three, the South Australian Grey Plover's epic flights would never have been unlocked.

Clive Minton, a metallurgist who became a senior human resources executive, is the father of wader studies, a global figure in the field. He is also, in Australia, its general. Inside his square frame is a mind honed at Cambridge University in the 1950s, and he is still restless in his eighties.

'Yes, I have a thirst for knowledge,' Minton tells me. 'If there's a way not known of finding something out, then I'm challenged to do it. But I'm also a hunter by nature. I think all of us have probably got a little bit of it in us. I've got a lot of the hunter. I think that's one reason my unrest has been lifelong, 110 per cent.

I'm much more single-mindedly birds and shorebirds than anyone else I know.'

More often than many might admit, bird people are sub-limated hunters, separated only by degrees of passion or science. At the least-intense end of the spectrum are the watchers, who might spend a casual hour sauntering a pathway to squint through binoculars. There are 'listers', who seek out new birds and compile lists of different species sighted—over a single year or over a lifetime, with an eye on rivals. Listing can be a part of life, or it can take over: ruthless competition between extreme American listers is the stuff of birding folklore. People at that end, particularly in Britain, might be called 'twitchers'; they are driven birders whose lives are directed, sometimes consumed, by the need to see new and rare birds. Among these is a sub-species called 'togs'; heavers of massive camo-covered lenses, they are the photography army.

Then there are the banders, known in the old countries as ringers. These small groups of amateur and professional orni-thologists are drawn together to catch and band birds for research. They use hunting methods turned around for living science. For them, the prize is won when a freed bird tells a story of life and movement through its mark.

Cheshire-born Minton has been clipping metal bands on birds' legs since 1947, when he was twelve years old. He has led the Victorian Wader Study Group (VWSG) since he came to Australia in 1978. At last count, this small group of volunteers had caught and marked over a quarter of a million shorebirds—the great majority of them international migrants. Catching them around south-eastern Australia, and in north-western Australia jointly with the Australasian Wader Studies Group, this is the world's single largest banding operation.

As leader of the Victorian group, Minton reached actual mythic stature. A Sydney performance artist, Barbara Campbell, turned her imaginative eye on him as he orchestrated a catch at a favoured haunt—Melbourne's vast, bird-rich sewerage farm, the Western Treatment Plant. She likened him to an augur, the classical Roman figure who divined the will of the gods from the flight of birds. And in a real, scientific way, Minton does just that.

So when an Adelaide coastal conservation manager, Tony Flaherty, was looking for better protection for Gulf St Vincent's birds, he knew he would do well to involve Minton. Flaherty, who has spent a working lifetime on marine and coastal conservation in South Australia, practises politics as the art of the possible. 'I use shorebirds as a tool,' Flaherty says. 'Just another tool in the toolbox for trying to get people to change their thinking about stinking coast and mudflat.'

Shorebird counts had been underway in the gulf since 2008. They regularly notched up thousands of resident birds, like the dainty Banded Stilt, but also a dozen migratory species, including two of the best-known globally: the Bar-tailed Godwit and Red Knot. The soldierly godwit, with its long, thin bill, is a classic probing shorebird. The dumpy Red Knot scurries along tidelines, and is a global favourite to track. In 2012, when the Australasian Wader Studies Conference came to Adelaide, Flaherty thought it might be a chance to catch knot in the gulf.

Minton and his team hauled the Victorian group's catching equipment trailer over from Melbourne with them. The trailer carries the emblem of the VWSG: a Grey Plover in flight. I ask Minton: Why the choice of this particular bird? To him the reason is lost in the mists of time, so he calls: 'Pat? Pat?' His wife and inseparable intelligence appears. Pat suggests: 'Because it was a bird to aim for. It was so hard to get.'

On their first trip to Gulf St Vincent, Minton's folk were joined by Maureen Christie, who would eventually direct the Grey Plover catch. With her pale-blue eyes sharp under a floppy hat, Christie is a child of Victoria's western Mallee country. She went to university in Melbourne at a time 'when girls from the country who wanted a career were either teachers or nurses, and I knew I didn't want to be a nurse'.

She studied for an Arts degree in the early 1960s at the new and vibrant Monash University, discovered student activism and dropped out. She then lived an island life in Bass Strait for a while, married and became a bookkeeper, spending years counting figures. Retired and living near the ocean coast of South Australia at Carpenter Rocks, Christie came to the wader world when she noticed little birds running along the local shore. 'I knew birds as a child. I was a Brownie, and a Guide, and a member of the Field Naturalists. And I could identify this bird on the shore as a turnstone.'

With a local bird group, she watched the spring return of migratory Ruddy Turnstone and Sanderling, and their departure in autumn. Tough little scraps of mottled brown and white, turnstones fossick the rocky shore and seaweed as their name determines. The smaller Sanderlings use the same coast, but probe the beach sands.

When a Chinese-owned company proposed to take 10,000 tonnes of storm-tossed seaweed from the local coast each year using heavy machinery, Christie and her Friends of Shorebirds South-East (FoSSE) group took up the fight. 'We used science, networking and persistence,' she recalls.

State and federal approvals were appealed against and, after a two-year campaign, FoSSE won. Half the coast was closed, heavy machinery was banned and the seaweed harvesting company was told by a tribunal it had to live with much lower limits. Ulti-mately, according to Christie, the group's twenty-year shorebird record was vital in achieving this protection by the tribunal. Number-counting won, and this gave me my first lesson of shore-bird research. As Christie says: 'It requires good data to succeed.'

When the catching team first came to Gulf St Vincent they spent long days working the shore, chasing Red Knot and then godwit. 'It's the hardest place I've ever tried in the world to catch and band shorebirds,' Minton says. 'We could not catch more than one Red Knot, having tried for three years. We could not catch more than ten or twelve Bar-tailed Godwits.

'That was partly because the birds are extremely ephemeral. Here today and gone tomorrow. But the thing is, most of our catching is usually done when the birds are flooded off the flats by a spring tide and settle on a beach above the high-tide mark. What you've got in the gulf is great "wodges" of seagrass, hundreds of metres in diameter, which the birds can use as islands. So you can't do your normal process of setting a net to catch them.'

Accustomed to catching hundreds of birds on a single day, Minton's team came up with just 134 birds in four years of Thompson Beach expeditions.

Flaherty's aim was to have an international bird sanctuary proclaimed along the coast north of Adelaide; but to achieve this politically, he needed the team to identify an actual inter-national bird. Then a godwit marked at Thompson Beach in November 2012 was photographed at Nanpu, China, in April 2013, and back at Thompson Beach in 2014. Flaherty had his catch, his 'story bird'.

'That clicked with a lot of local people, to be able to see this bird that had just come from their beach,' Flaherty says. 'You can go on until the cows come home about migratory shorebirds and how far they travel. But to get a plot of a local bird up to China and onwards, for me *that's* awareness.'

Buoyed by this, the group hatched a much greater ambition: to use satellite tags to track some gulf shorebirds in near real time as they migrated. If this worked, it would give people a chance to travel 'with' the birds.

This is a great compulsion for people who band migratory birds: to bring tracks to life. They discover the birds' powers on odysseys that may traverse hemispheres over months; how they endure the physical costs of long distance flight, and avoid predators; what lies behind this other-worldly miracle of a single bird making its way through waypoints, 'home' to a breeding ground to renew its line and then back to where it started. If it all works, they are drawing lines of global ecology, 'flight lines' across the earth.

Two
Three letters will do

When I come to the gulf to watch the catch, Maureen Christie warns me: 'We may get nothing.' She shakes her head as she looks at the maps and records of this coast. 'One of the amazing things about this place is that we persevere,' she says. 'It's so hard, for so little return.'

For the first couple of years their target bird had been the glamorous godwit, but none were caught. They would keep trying for it, but as the group assembled for the first expedition to attach the costly satellite tags, Christie mulled over her options. She decided at the last minute that they should have a back-up bird. So she halted her dusty utility beside the highway on the way to Thompson Beach and made a phone call to the study group's ethics and permits officer. She was cleared to fit the satellite trackers to a second-choice bird: the Grey Plover.

Fossilised plumage records indicate the Grey Plover and its sister ancestor, the parent of the Eurasian, Pacific and American Goldens, arose around 1.8 million years ago, perhaps in the high mountains of Eastern Siberia. The authorities on these birds,

Ingvar Byrkjedal and Des Thompson, say: 'We shall probably never know the truth, but it is likely that the ancestral tundra plover lived before the Ice Ages, in the north of the Holarctic [the whole Arctic bioregion].' This ancestor left a mark on the Grey Plover that the later 'Goldies' lack: a remnant hind toe.

Grey Plover turn up sparsely on every continent north of Antarctica. The nature writer Peter Matthiessen saw it as 'wary, an indifferent formation flyer, with a liking for loose flocks, long-shore habitats, late coastal migration and the company of knots'. The American ornithologist Roger Tory Peterson thought that on the shore it stood out for its 'dejected, hunched posture'. I see a lapwing cousin there.

Clive Minton has had comparatively little to do with the Grey Plover, though he has known them since 1951, when it was a big deal for his British group to net one in their first week of shorebird catching in Northumberland, long before he came to Australia. He told me: 'In many places, they just occur in ones or twos around the shore. You don't get hundreds or thousands in flocks. And they don't mix with the other waders as readily as some birds do. They have been more difficult to catch and band. So they've never been one of our core species. The knowledge we have of them has accumulated slowly.'

It's always about the knowledge. Finding the most effective way to follow birds, and so discover their lives, has driven banders for more than a century. Benefit for the birds is not *the* reason they do it, Minton says: 'It's one of the reasons. But we start with a scientific quest. What's happening? How does it work?'

The origins of banding, or ringing, go back to the late nine-teenth century, and a Danish teacher, Hans Christian Cornelius Mortensen. Anyone who thinks birders an odd lot can find their historical baseline in the story of Mortensen. He was, disturbingly, known for his 'tiger-like' gait as he prowled the local village streets. He was also the man who in conservative Denmark thought it would be a good idea to try yellow eye shadow as a vision aid. Then, of all things, he began clamping rings on birds' legs.

He caught a European Starling in a nest-box trap, and fitted it with a zinc leg band inscribed: 'Ynglede i [Bred in] Viborg 1890 M'. That year Mortensen banded another 164 starlings and waited for replies. It was the first systematic use of the leg band to study bird movement patterns.

Tiger-prowling and yellow eye shadow failed to catch on, but banding did. Within 30 years, groups were operating through Europe and spreading around the world. Today in the United States, around one million bands are distributed annually, clipped on to flying creatures from hummingbirds to swans. Almost the same number of birds are ringed in Britain and Ireland, including 18,000 shorebirds. It's pioneering citizen science, a global big-data phenomenon governed by international protocols. Scientists and non-scientists, young and old, take part by the thousands. Banding was the first, and still is the most commonly used, tracking method.

Minton, at the age of fourteen, banded his own backyard birds and was hooked for life when he turned to shorebirds. 'I caught a beautiful Spotted Redshank, the first ever banded in Britain,' he tells me.

What a wonderful bird to start with. The Spotted Redshank is a supermodel of a shorebird. Slim and leggy, pretty even in non-breeding colours with finely speckled dark-grey plumage, orange-red legs and a lateral stripe down each side of its long grey bill. One walked into Minton's net at a reservoir near Birmingham: 'I was very pleased to see it in the hands, and put the band on it. I let it go, and thought, you know, that's it. Two weeks later it was shot in the south of France, by the Mayor of Perpignan.'

Dutifully, the mayor returned the band along with his explanation of its recovery. 'That sort of stimulating, unbelievable recovery, even though it's one in 500, or one in 1000, it still keeps you going, makes you tick,' Minton says.

Banding means much more than poking a message into a bottle and dropping it against all odds into the ocean, or spending hours in a raincoat on a drizzle-soaked rail platform waiting to spot a special train. It isn't just a hobby or a passion, though it can be both. It's a scientific method to make the unknown known. In ornithology there was Before Banding and After Banding. After, questions about birds' movements and survival could be asked and answered as never before.

Minton's formative Wash Wader Ringing Group adventured on the seaside mud of The Wash, north of Cambridge in East Anglia. In triumphant but impoverished post-World War Two Britain, these young birders could think themselves international pathfinders, making their own rules. A shared cunning in catching wild things fed a passion to invent new ways to catch more. In a world that did not yet know mass global air travel, let alone the reach of an internet, banding was a passport for the insatiably curious. They watched and waited for bands to return in the letterbox, for dots of light to illuminate a dark sky. An individual alpha-numeric code and a return address stamped on the ring meant a passport to the birds' world.

But first they had to catch their birds. In the late 1950s, when they began, there were already some contraptions in use. Tall, handheld bat-fowling nets and the Heligoland trap, a German-designed funnelling wire cage. Neither really suited nervous shorebirds, which moved around on open ground, always set to flee.

Borrowed hunting techniques helped. Shorebird students in the West learned from traditional East Asian net hunters how to catch their targets live. A US ornithologist in post-war Occupied Japan watched a skilled hunter lay his 15-metre-long silk net on a mudflat, tied to staked bamboo poles. The hunter set out decoys made from skins of his target birds, and then he sat inside a bulrush blind, waiting with the patience of centuries. When birds neared, the hunter blew a bamboo whistle to imitate the call of his quarry. As they flew down to the decoys, he jerked a trigger line that snatched the net over them.

'I have seen an expert netter sweep curlews and whimbrels out of the air as they circled low over the decoys,' H. Elliott McLure recounted with wonder in a 1956 article on bird netting in Japan. 'One of our netters disposed with the blind and sat quietly on his stool at the end of the net. He was so dexterous with his whistle that Wandering Tattlers or plovers would alight at his feet.'

The group at The Wash was among the first to adopt the use of these nets. With them, they caught the first Grey Plover to be banded in Britain, along with Ruff, Dunlin and Ringed Plover—all of them Arctic migrants.

The group moved on to try gossamer-thin mist nets, originally set out vertically in the woodland clearings and rice paddies of Asia. Birds that fly into mist nets are caught in a pouch of loose netting, to hang there at the hunter's pleasure. A line of 2-metre-high nets set on The Wash's mudflats on a moonless, windless night caught shorebirds that could not see the mesh. While a hunter might not care if these died overnight, the wader group needed them very much alive. So they had to navigate mud and The Wash's deep-draining creek lines in the darkness to extract and ring the birds.

Plunging into creek lines on winter nights was always going to have limited appeal and, with the war close behind them, the next logical step was to get explosive. For this they looked to the embodiment of British survival after heroic failure, Peter Scott. The son of doomed Antarctic explorer Robert Falcon Scott, Peter turned his passion for nature in the direction of waterfowl, and pioneered rocket-launched nets for ringing wild geese.

In a whimsical account for the *Severn Wildfowl Trust Annual Report,* Peter Scott wrote about his first rocket-netting expedition. He and his assistant Eunice Overend set the net before dawn on a frost-frozen field, aided by 'a nice little ferreting spade'. His rocket was adapted from the line-firing Schermuly Rocket Pistol Apparatus for Saving Life at Sea. Despite a last-minute hitch with a disconnected fuse wire, their initial shot caught 32 geese. They were 'all taffled up', Scott recorded. 'We had made the first great catch of geese alive for ringing.'

Banded and released, the flock settled in the fields again. 'A new game had been discovered—hunting the rings—and already at the first glance we were able to pick up four of the birds we had had in our hands only a few hours before . . . It is only the beginning, but it may well lead to a new understanding of the migration of wild geese.'

The Wash Wader Ringing Group coveted the Severn Wildfowl Trust's rocket nets. They knew of Peter Scott's links with The Wash from his years living in an old lighthouse at the Nene River mouth, fertile ground for *The Snow Goose,* written by Scott's visiting American friend, Paul Gallico. In this classic novella, the white Arctic migratory bird links an awkward friendship between a hermit artist and a stray girl. It is a parable about the sanctity of wild creatures, and on wartime sacrifice. It fits to find pioneering shorebird catchers on exactly the same ground as where this story is set, hard-wired as they were in the British tradition of discovering nature at forgotten edges of the realm, bound to the seasonal rhythms of migration.

In a memoir for the Wash group, Minton disclosed that Scott was wary about lending his rocket nets. Nearing the end of his Cambridge doctorate, Minton eventually managed to persuade Scott that a bunch of young men aged in their early twenties could handle his precious explosive equipment. Scott finally agreed and sent three staff to supervise.

The group fired the rockets over waders for the first time at The Wash in 1959, and in that single shot caught 1132 shorebirds. The next year 2893 birds were caught in rocket nets, and the group began to shine many more pinpoints of light into the global darkness of shorebird migration. Of these thousands they found fourteen Dunlin, small sandpipers, that had been ringed across Scandinavia as much as eight years earlier.

The group kept on rocket-netting for five years. They made good a promise of champagne all round if they caught a hundred Grey Plover, then scarce across Europe under hunting pressure. At one point they had to explain themselves to sceptical police who raided their isolated, borrowed cottage. The superintendent who led the raid was hunting for the 1963 Great Train Robbers. 'He was totally disbelieving of the reasons for our presence; even the local copper who accompanied him and who knew us, failed to convince him that we were genuine,' Minton wrote in his account, *My Memories of the Early Years*. 'The situation was not helped by the policemen surrounding the outside of the house finding a box marked "Arm" and "Fire" in one of our vehicles.'

Eventually Scott reclaimed the rockets for his geese, and the group had to find a different way of netting. So they turned to gunpowder and cannon.

Across the Atlantic, in Missouri, around the same time, two men at the Swan Lake National Wildlife Refuge were on their own mission to net geese. Instead of rockets, Herb Dill and Howard 'Hacksaw' Thornsberry came up with the cannon. The net would be hauled over the birds by steel projectiles blasted out of a metal tube, rather than behind a sputtering rocket. Herb and Hacksaw's first chronicler was a *Saturday Evening Post* reporter who recounted: 'the net whisked out like a banshee in a hurry'.

Cannon nets were tested on shorebirds at remote St George Island in the Arctic's Bering Sea, where turnstones gathered to feast on maggot infestation that erupted in the carcasses remaining after fur-seal hunts. There were tragic errors to begin with: in two firings, 229 turnstone were hit by the leading edge of a low-angled net, and killed.

In Britain, around the same time, the Department of Agriculture was developing a cannon net for oystercatchers, but the Wash Waders found it unsuitable. Minton's group made their own weapon in sometimes hair-raising trial and error. At a test firing of the first prototype, one of the projectiles pulling the net broke free. It sailed on towards the A38 highway.

'There was an almighty crash and a loud squeal of brakes,' Minton recalled. 'We rushed to the scene. No sign of a vehicle and no damage . . . just a large elm branch lying on the A38. The projectile was never recovered.' Their cannon worked though, and with these the group took the lead in a fundamental shift away from the once-only return of a band from a dead bird.

Shorebird science had, to this point, strongly relied on hunters like the Mayor of Perpignan. 'In those days quite a lot were shot in Europe and Africa, and you did get quite a high rate of ring recovery,' Minton tells me. His fellow Cambridge Bird Club members looked into the mortality of ringed starlings, and found that of 103 ring recoveries only fifteen were from live birds. In 31 cases the causes of death were described: fourteen shot, eight killed by cats, two by dogs, and the others by overhead wires, drowning or freezing to death. Even in the late twentieth century, a study of British Red Knots found 26 rings were recovered from birds illegally shot, and that knots shot in West Greenland were actually targeted because of their rings.

Net catching meant a change in the inevitability of this toll as researchers began to re-catch greater numbers of birds. At a peak, Minton marshalled a small army of 40 licensed ringers and at Morecambe Bay in north-west England they caught 4300 birds in one firing of the net, including 3354 of the target Red Knot. Among these were 30 knot ringed the previous summer at The Wash, confirming a hunch that these birds arrived from the Arctic to moult on one side of Britain and winter on the other.

And some of these birds then kept on telling their stories. A Red Knot ringed on The Wash as an adult in August 1968 was caught again by the group on 1 September 1992. This bird, weighing about as much as one and a half cups of flour, had survived the rigours of migration for a minimum 24 years.

This long-lasting record from individual birds is one of the reasons banding remains strong in countries like Britain, where intensive effort over a small area brings results. It's different in wide, sparse Australia. By the early 1990s, although 100,000 Australian shorebirds had been banded, just 222, or 0.2 per cent had been found and read in other countries. The step-change needed came in new techniques to gather information about a bird's movements without actually re-catching the bird—in leg ornaments that could be read from a distance. A set of brightly coloured plastic leg rings could be used to identify the 'bangle bunnies'.

Today the Wash Wader Ringing Group colour-bands four species, including Grey Plover, one of which is the group's symbol. Combinations can be a festoonery of leg bling that lets observers closely follow the dynamics of a single flock—say Redshank at the Firth of Forth in Scotland facing fierce predation from falcons and hawks. Each of 30 birds in the flock was given a unique identifier, a combination of six colour bands and a metal ring, tracking individual precarious lives.

Colour bands were followed by perky little plastic flags. The colour-coded flags stand out from a bird's leg, and can be read at a greater distance. In use on most shorebirds' global migratory paths, they are for the birding community their own set of internationally known pennants.

One or two flags are carried by each bird. For New Zealand, the flag is white. In Australia, Victorian shorebirds carry an orange flag; Queensland has dark green; waders banded in New South Wales carry a combined orange over green; and in South Australia, orange over yellow. Across the Americas in a different migratory path, or flyway, Canada has white and the United States is dark green.

In Europe where colour-use began, no national flag code was ever settled. 'Nobody recognised how it would take off,' explains Jim Wilson of the International Wader Study Group. 'By the time this was being thought about, it was too late . . . Thus there is no "system".' The 400 different projects in the European flyway are instead managed in a database. 'There are a few rogues, but not many,' Wilson says. But it does mean that instant identification is not as readily available in Europe as it might be for birds flying out of Australia, New Zealand or the United States.

'Say someone has seen a curlew feeding in Tokyo Bay on April 10,' Minton tells me. 'In the past they had no idea where it was from. As soon as they saw the orange leg flag they were able to say: "Right, a curlew that spent the non-breeding season in Victoria, Australia, is migrating northwards through Tokyo Bay." We got a flag sighting seventeen times more than we had a banding recovery. It was a very big step forward. Now it's happened to every bird species virtually from the north of Siberia to the south of New Zealand. When caught, they get a band and a flag on.'

This focus on knowing more about individuals has reached a point where a bird can be 'personalised' by a leg flag stamped with an engraved two- or three-letter code. If 'XYZ' bird is seen in another country, that sighting will filter back through national banding online systems or social media to its original bander, perhaps within hours. There are limits to this. First because of the total combinations available—to around 15,600 in three letter codes—and also because of the limited readability of letters on tiny pieces of plastic at a distance on muddy, or water-covered legs.

———

This is what the shorebird group in Gulf St Vincent had behind them. More than 60 years of evolution in catching and banding gave them the means to net these shy birds, to mark individuals and to release them to tell their own stories. The step they wanted to take was to bring this story to life in real-time.

They looked to a revolution in scientific-instrument design that at first had nothing to do with shorebirds. Over the past 30 years, wildlife technicians have made gradual changes in the power and miniaturisation of electronic tracking instruments. Technology that started on animals like Elephant Seals and birds like the Wandering Albatross has strengthened and shrunk to be useable on very small creatures. Among these instruments, two stand out for use with shorebirds: geographical locators (geolocators) and satellite transmitters.

Geolocators store daylight. Because daylight length varies according to where you are on earth, if an instrument has a light sensor, a clock and a memory, it can measure and store its position, accurate to around 150 kilometres. Basically, the sextant, chronometer and chart used by a mariner to fix latitude and longitude are replaced by a microchip. In the late 1980s, 'geos' were first used in instruments glued to the skin of Elephant Seals that migrated up the North Pacific coast. They revealed feeding grounds thousands of kilometres distant from the starting point.

At the same time, images of flights by the world's largest seabird were being revealed using some of the earliest satellite transmitters fitted to wildlife. The challenge of following a 3-metre wingspan Wandering Albatross across 10 million square kilometres of Southern Ocean was met with a Platform Transmitter Terminal weighing 180 grams, or about as much as a cup of sugar. Harnessed to this big bird, this battery-powered tag could send a location up to the Argos satellite receiver system anywhere on earth.

'I've seen this evolution in our marking systems so that, in terms of what they give us in information per bird, hour in the field, or dollar in catching, has gone up one thousand times,'

Minton says. 'None of those steps were anticipated long in advance. But if you put your toe in the water at the first opportunity, then it can be a very exciting ride using new techniques. And of course, sometimes they fall flat on their face.'

Webs of movement spun by geolocators and satellite tags have shifted wildlife science in the way that the first moving pictures changed our ideas of imagery. Records of wildlife travel that are turned into lines and pulses on maps can be assembled with transformative power. At a shorebird conference in Auckland I watched spellbound as a flock of 'geos' mounted on the legs of turnstones by Maureen Christie and many others left southern Australia, flew north to the Arctic, and returned.

But there is a catch: geos must be retrieved to download their treasure. And while satellite tags transmit as they go, they cost.

In South Australia, Tony Flaherty found money in a federal saltmarsh-conservation program. He bought tags that cost $5000 each, reduced in weight from the albatross's cup of sugar to barely a teaspoonful. A Teflon ribbon leg-loop harness holds the transmitter like a saddle on the bird's back. Fingernail-sized solar panels charge a signal that is sent up to the Argos satellite system, and then back down to a ground station, giving ready access to the bird's track. The signal transmits for ten hours before the battery sleeps and re-charges for 48 hours. That sleep would turn out to be a long couple of days' wait for Flaherty and Christie.

'I'm a hunter too—catching, which it is,' Christie says. 'I'm out to catch.' She marshals a Gulf St Vincent catch like a hunt, with all the tension of discovering quarry, preparing the trap, moving the right birds towards the right place, and firing the net over them. Given the right outcome, the aftermath is jubilant.

First they have to find the birds. 'I can't stress how important recce-ing is,' she insists. Along the gulf shoreline, days are spent by a local birder, Graham Parkyn, walking the seagrass banks and creek lines he has known since he was a boy, on reconnaissance to quietly find out which birds are currently roosting where at high tide.

Then, they set their trap. Based on the recce, Christie selects slightly different ground, perhaps a raised seagrass pile or the suggestion of a point of sand, that the target birds might choose as an appealing high-tide roost. 'I wouldn't go so far as to call it bird whispering,' she demurs. 'I make sure I know my beaches.'

Out of the VWSG trailer comes the catching gear—a set of cannon and net. They look both homemade and well-tried, not much changed in the decades since Minton began.

Three steel cannon tubes are each bolted to a base plate fitted with a gunpowder cartridge, and the plates are then set against lumps of scrap metal that Christie has scrounged, to anchor them in the loose gulf-weed pile. The tubes are set facing the sky at a carefully calibrated angle. If the angle is too high, the birds will escape. If it's too shallow, the net and projectiles are more likely to hit the birds—and yes, there are sometimes fatalities.

The 14-metre long net is furled in a line across the beach, with its ropes set on top of it. The back ropes are tied to pegs hammered deep into the weed pile to hold fast the rear of the net. Ropes at the net's leading edge are tied to heavy steel-rod projectiles inserted in the cannons' mouths.

The line of net is sprinkled with seagrass for camouflage, and two more lines are laid from it back into the scrub behind the beach. One is an electric wire rolled out to a hide where the shot-firers sit, and wired into a battery-powered firing box. The second is a string adorned with cloth scraps. This is called a 'jiggler'. It lies parallel to the net and in front of it and runs back to the firing position where, indeed, the shot-firers can jiggle it to gently encourage resistant birds into the net's safe zone.

Christie adds another touch—pieces of beach trash. Sticks or bits of plastic are carefully set out: some are 2 metres in front of the net, and others 12 metres away. They mark the safe zone. Inside these boundary markers, birds can be caught. Outside this area, the birds are either too close to a fired net's fatal leading edge, or too far away to catch.

Christie calls the shot from her vantage point, where she can sight the birds and the safe zone directly along the beach. It takes but a fraction of a second between her 'THREE-TWO-ONE-FIRE', the cannon shot and the landing of the net. What could go wrong?

———————

Along a 2-kilometre length of Thompson Beach and the nearby creek lines, Maureen Christie has been directing Tony Flaherty in the south and others at the north to raise the scattered birds they want, and cautiously encourage them to fly towards the catching zone. To lift, but not to frighten the wits out of a bird. This is the art of 'twinkling'.

There are no godwits about, and time and again we hear on the HF radio linking the catching group that the few distant Grey Plover have flown off as Flaherty walks the beach towards them. Instead of moving up the beach towards the net, he reports that the birds have circled out over the water behind him to alight further away from the net site. Sitting beside Christie, I don't even glimpse them.

'Maureen, do you want me to go down again?' he asks over the radio.

'Yes. Thanks, Tony,' she answers.

As the tide turns and time begins to run out, the only birds in front of the net are a few gulls, and a flock of Greenshank. Nervous and hard to catch in the gulf, the five lime-legged Greenshank are not satellite-tag target birds, but to Christie they are worth a cannon shot.

From her current position, lying on her side on the beach and watching the catching area, she orders it. Just then a slant of breeze comes in from the gulf, the net hangs for a fraction in the air and the Greenshank are gone. The gulls aren't.

'Oh bugger!' she says.

After all the hours the team has spent setting up the net and twinkling, or crouched in the scrub waiting to run to the net, they emerge with an embarrassment of a catch: five Silver Gulls, common and unwanted.

Relying on Parkyn's recce tallies, Christie decides to try further up the coast the next day, near Bald Hill, at the head of the army proof range, where dozens of Grey Plover gather at high tide. The net is set the night before, and we catchers meet before dawn in darkness, the inland scent of dewy, dry grass falling on us.

As the sun rises and the twinklers approach, 30 Grey Plover near the net suddenly flee. I am back in the scrub, and my second sight of this bird is of long-winged shards of silver-grey, lifting from the unseen beach and scattering in low dawn light. The tearaway bunch pipe high and briefly as they join up and head inland.

Most alight on a saltmarsh pan where an attempt to twinkle them back to the beach fails when a squall bursts over the shore. They disappear with the wind. Pressed again by the falling tide, and with birds from other species in front of the net, Christie orders a shot anyway. This time the catch comes up with nine turnstone, a Pied Oystercatcher, a Crested Tern and seven Caspian Terns.

The big Caspian Terns flounder under the net, dinosaur honks rasping out of their 7-centimetre-long dagger bills in angry forewarning. 'When they lock onto your hand, don't pull it away,' bander Peter Crighton recommends. 'You've got to resist the temptation. There are ridges in their bills that will tear your skin apart.'

As he works on the birds and they seize his hand, Crighton simply pushes it further into the red bill, slowly prying it open. A calm and methodical bander, his hands are scratched repeatedly in Caspian retribution, but they are not torn.

———————

Time and tide for our expedition is running out when Christie's team comes back to Bald Hill two days later to try again.

As the twinklers move in from the sides, a flock of about 30 Grey Plover settle helpfully in front of the catching zone. Then cormorants and Caspians land nearby, spooking the Grey Plover, which again lift and break into loose groups. But this time four peel off and decide to come back. They alight near the net.

Christie is on her knees, edging along the sand and twinkling inch by inch as the water seeps higher. 'There's one in front of the net,' she whispers over the HF radio. 'One Grey Plover in the catching area. The others are on slightly higher ground, maybe they don't want to go lower . . . I think they're almost in resting mode now.'

Back in the scrub, I wait with another ten people behind the shot-firers, poised to pelt down to the shore. There are mutterings from tired people who have waited like wound springs since before dawn. Christie shuffles closer to the net, her knees leaving a trail of 'turtle tracks' on the sand behind her.

'They're moving a bit now,' she says. 'We have a second Grey Plover moving into the catching area. Now it's in the danger area . . . coming back . . . We now have only one catchable, and I will be brave and wait . . . THREE-TWO-ONE-FIRE.'

CERRRACK!! The cannons fire like three shotguns at once.

We runners galumph over the seagrass piles to find four little grey-and-white scraps awash, spread-eagled under the net. Their eyes shine with amazement.

Christie raises her arms to the sky in a shout of relief. 'I was lying in the sand and the tide was coming up,' she laughs. 'I was in danger of getting my knickers wet!'

The more deft and experienced catchers, among them Emilia Lai, work each of the birds free of the net and settle them into keeping cages. These are cloth-walled boxes where the birds can calm a little and regain their senses before they are measured, banded, tagged and released. To my eye, on the weedy beach in the sun, this all looks like something between makeshift science lab and avian stockyard.

As the first bird is taken in hand from the keeping cage to be worked on, I see a Grey Plover up close. I am struck by its passivity. Unlike the Caspian, the Grey Plover does not struggle or stab, even though it is equipped with a sturdy black chisel bill. This is shorter than that of the other shorebirds it lives with, but I dispute the species name given it by that joker, Linnaeus. It's no snub-face.

The head is elegantly curved, and dominated by big dark eyes. We tend to think such eyes are a mark of greater intelligence. I am yet to appreciate that, but I can say straight away that it is a very careful watcher. I am some metres distant, but the eye shrinks from my camera lens's internal movement when I take a shot. Lai, as she holds one, tells me its heart is racing.

The Grey Plover seems not much bigger than a Common Blackbird until its wings are unfurled for measurement. They are long, much longer than the garden bird, and precisely pointed. The plumage at this time in its annual cycle is speckled grey and white around its neck. As each bird is handled it sheds down that floats off like dandelion heads in the breeze. I catch and bag some of these precious little pieces of DNA.

The climax comes with the fitting of the satellite tag. I watch Christie at work as Parkyn holds the bird, its tail pointed towards her. In readiness, this piece of technological wizardry has been temporarily tied onto a Diet Coke can and left by a window so as to help the solar cell and battery become used to cycles of warming and cooling. Christie takes the unit off the can. There is the harness, with loose leg loops that need to be eased over the bird. The tag nestles onto the centre of the back, and a wisp of aerial extends past the tail feathers. The critical decision is where to fix the leg loops, so that they are at exactly the right tension, using a sliding metal band. A millimetre too slack and it will slip off the bird; too tight and the plover could suffer when it gains weight. As the catching group's brains trust fusses with this decision, we crowd in.

'Clear off!' Christie orders.

The four Grey Plover each get a satellite tag, and an orange three-letter leg flag chosen from a bunch on a string. The birds become CAR, CAS, CAT and CAU.

Many wildlife researchers give their study creatures pet names, though the named will mostly never know them. It helps bind the worker to the bird, and the sponsoring money likes it as an aid in story-telling. The world's oldest known wild bird is Wisdom, a 68-year-old female Laysan Albatross. A Eurasian Cuckoo tracked from Beijing, east into Southern Africa was called, for heaven's sake, Flappy McFlapperson. In South Australia, this bunch of banders go for no such fripperies. Three letters will do.

With little ceremony, the Grey Plover are released on the sand. Several lift and fly quickly, but one limps wonkily away towards the receding tideline, and seems dazed. The banders watch with intense concern, and after about ten minutes it flies slowly away.

Within days, CAT's tag stopped transmitting. It was later seen on the shore at Bald Hill without a harness and identified by its leg flag. In the autumn, the three others headed north, drawn on the journey to their home tundra. One, CAU, made it to the Kimberley coast of Western Australia before turning around and coming back to Gulf St Vincent for the winter. Of the others, CAS's signal stopped over the Philippines, and CAR made it to South Sulawesi in Indonesia. Other than that, these birds' fates are unknown. None of the four tags was able to give more than a hint about their annual flights.

―――――――――

But a year earlier than the expedition I joined, Christie led Parkyn, Flaherty and others in another catch at Thompson Beach that was remarkable twice over. First, because it was so straightforward that no one who I later asked could remember many details. Second, because it would be an extraordinary success. The two Grey Plover from this catch would draw spectacular flight lines across the world.

I asked Christie to show me the site. She initially had a little trouble remembering it from others, but we ended up on a short footpath down through scrub at the northern end of Thompson Beach. There was a suggestion of a point of land among piles of seagrass near a boat ramp. It was an unremarkable stretch of coast; hardly the embarkation place for a great piece of science.

The day of the catch, 14 November 2015, was hot in the gulf, rising to over 40 degrees Celsius on the sand. Christie had overseen the twinkling and called the shot. At 9.15 in the morning when the net was fired, 28 birds were under it. They caught fourteen turnstones, eleven of the shoreline-scurrying Red-necked Stint, one little resident Red-capped Plover and two Grey Plover.

The team set up camp to process the birds in the scant shade of beachside scrub. As sandflies began to bite in the rising heat, all of the birds were leg-banded. The little plover, turnstone and stint were colour-flagged and released. The Grey Plover stayed behind to be fitted with letter flags and satellite tags.

Christie was, as always, worried about the harnesses. Images of this session show the team hunched on the ground in the scrub, deep in concentration as they tightened the tags onto the birds. Then each was held up to show its new outfit. The aerials trailed behind like long black hairs. Their leg flags were letter-coded CYA and CYB.

As the heat of a blue-sky Gulf St Vincent day intensified, the team walked down to the water's edge to release the birds. They flew off fast and clear. Flaherty and Parkyn were smiling. Christie, hands on her hips, looked pensive.

———

Curious about the epic flights undertaken by these overlooked little birds, I thought I would try to follow their paths when they were on migration. I wanted to touch the places CYA and CYB touched as they tracked across the planet. I hoped to find out about the shores that Grey Plover used, and the people who lived around them. Already I understood enough about the tools that science was using to unveil their lives. Now I might see what research had actually found out about the powers of migratory shorebirds, and the hazards they faced.

Worrying stories of the birds' current life trials told at night at the catchers' Gulf St Vincent camp rang alarms. Despite that, it was elating to begin to think deeply about their threads of flight, the weaving of enduring bonds between the far north and the south of our Blue Dot. And these shorebird people fascinated me; such an unlikely bunch of hunter-saviours. What was the thing about all these Brits?

So I began to lay out plans to follow the Grey Plover along the flyway from the far south of the globe, where I lived, to the Arctic, where they came from. Beyond the usual trials of travel, I had no reason to expect any great blight to afflict my journey.

Three
Tiny sparks

A shorebird flock sweeps onto a pile of wave-lapped rocks, their high-tide roost. The birds are a mix of Red Knot, Red-necked Stint and Ruddy Turnstone; there are a few Grey Plover outriders. Out of a dull sky they appear from nowhere, alight in sudden chatter, spill over limited roosting rock, and flare up for another cautious circuit. I am hidden in the scrub. And yet, the birds are nervous.

They are flying above Tasmania's Boullanger Bay, which is floored with fine sand, ruffled by Southern Ocean winds. Dotted with low islands, holding a labyrinth of tidal creeks, the bay feels to me as if little has changed since the first Aboriginal people lived here. It's quiet land and water: the shallows uncut by hustling boats, development limited to the slow-spinning ghosts of distant wind turbines.

Around 14,000 years ago, the Bassian Plain to the north became the Bass Strait. As an inter-glacial period arrived to raise the sea from the melting ice caps, the people were isolated from mainland Australia. They were left to their own stories of why some birds disappeared during the cold season, and where they went. Now this bay holds some of the farthest flying migratory shorebirds in the globe-spanning domain called the East Asian–Australasian Flyway (EAAF). And while I am here, their Southern-Hemisphere summer is nearing an end, and birders want to count them before they fly north—some of them, very far north.

This day 12,000 waders will be found on the shore. Just 39 will be Grey Plover, and many of these are in the small flock circling Knot Point on Robbins Island. It is this place—of all possible roosts at the wide southern end of the EAAF—they remember as their own. Year after year, small numbers of Grey Plover make the extraordinary decision to come back to this particular bay, and to roost at high tide on this point.

Approaching again over smooth sailing Black Swan, the shorebird flock sweeps in low circuits, with the plover still outermost. The flight is a lesson in avian unity. These birds differ in species and size, yet move as one. They silver as they catch the sun together, spread their wings to brake, and settle.

The Grey Plover reach one favoured rock momentarily ahead, leaving the rest of the flock to flutter complaining across to nearby outcrops. One of the Greys folds her wings, extends a black straw leg and tests the perch for a better stance.

She peers down. There. No, Not quite right . . . There.

Balanced, she turns her head, folds her bill into the plumage of her back, and closes her eyes under wrinkled grey lids. Against the sun-warmed rock, she and her companions blend in. The tide rises a little more and they move a few steps, ruffle up, and resume the head-turned resting pose. This is my first close-up chance to see the bird just being the bird. I see a sharply confident aerialist; a demure creature at rest.

A White-bellied Sea Eagle passes over on its rounds, low enough for the flock to take fright. They head for open sky over the water, circle for a few minutes, and settle again. The eagle has floated on. Nothing for it there.

A big Pacific Gull coasts onto rocks near them, and they lift once more. In between these rushes for the sky, the flock roosts for around an hour through high tide before they are up and off, back to feed. Such is the rest of the restless.

The shorebird riches here were discovered by Richard Ashby, who came to Australia from the UK as an assisted passage 'ten-pound Pom'. The tall, rangy Ashby became a radiographer in Tasmania, and took to kayaking the coastline in the 1980s. 'I landed one day, quite serendipitously, when several thousand were wheeling about.' He decided to look further. 'Much legwork and sloshing about in mud, water and darkness ensued.'

These Grey Plover were in north-west Tasmania. But they might have been at Gulf St Vincent, or Broome in Western Australia, across the Southern Hemisphere at Port Elizabeth in South Africa, or in the network of muddy *baia* (bays) that line the coast of tropical Brazil near the mouth of the Amazon.

At the same time of year, the species could also be seeing out the Northern Hemisphere winter at beaches in New Jersey, Florida or California, or at higher latitudes—say in Puget Sound, Washington State, around the medieval tower of Le Mont Saint-Michel in Normandy, or on the industrialised Tees Estuary of northern England.

When not on their Arctic breeding grounds, Grey Plover fly to niches in six continents. On these very different shores, the birds turn out to be highly adaptable to a range of temperatures and local conditions, and tough-minded about their own turf.

Most surprising, the sexes seem to do without each other in winter. That's what made the fussy-footed Grey Plover at Knot Point likely to be a 'she', just as CYA and CYB were.

More than other shorebirds, Grey Plover females fly further south than males. Ingvar Byrkjedal and Des Thompson found this when they searched the world for museum specimens and checked the data for latitude, age and sex in winter. 'These data confirmed that the proportion of males to females decreases to the south,' they reported.

Such a specimen lies lightly in my hand. It's the skin of a Grey Plover shot in 1960; one of the last ever to reach southern Tasmania, the farthest Australian end of the EAAF. Cotton wool fills her eye sockets; the black-ink script on a card label tied to her legs confirms with a symbol that she was female. Out of their breeding plumage, the sexes cannot be separated by sight. In 1960 this bird was necropsied to determine her gender. Today DNA tissue sampling lets researchers discover the same information—and the bird to be released alive.

A Victorian ecologist, Danny Rogers, advanced our knowledge about the females of the species using DNA sexing on blood samples taken from Grey Plover cannon-netted in Australia. Of more than 100 birds, 98 per cent were female. Wary of such an emphatic result, Rogers had the laboratory tests done again, with the same outcome.

'There is some literature on differential migration in other shorebird species,' Rogers says. 'But it's usually not so striking. Why would an average female Grey Plover migrate thousands of kilometres further than an average male? There's nothing else in the same league.'

Rogers believes the mating behaviour of the Grey Plover may explain it. Some shorebirds have exotic sex lives. Sandpipers of either sex can choose multiple partners at the breeding ground. Grey Plover are thought to be monogamous. That could mean pressure on males to stay closer to the breeding grounds in order to establish their territory year after year, if they are to be successful. 'The better the real estate, the better a chance of having that particular mate,' he explains.

There may also be no greater cost for females in flying the extra kilometres. In fact there may be benefits. Jane Turpie closely studied a Grey Plover population near Port Elizabeth in South Africa—not for their sexes, but for what and how they ate. In this far southern point of the Africa–West Eurasian Flyway she found these birds had high energy-intake rates, low body-heat costs, and low predation risk. 'This provides compelling evidence that the costs of migration are balanced by higher survivorship for birds migrating furthest south,' Turpie found. 'An original "necessity" of long-distance migration has probably evolved into an equally favourable "choice".'

In these southern refuges, migratory shorebirds live for months during what passes for the 'still' part of their lives. Through the southern summer, Maureen Christie and Tony Flaherty watched the satellite tracks of CYA and CYB sketch designs on the coastal margins of Gulf St Vincent. The tracks crossed often from the intertidal zone into saltpans and back lagoons, concentrated in quite small areas of the gulf.

At Teesside in England, closer observation of Grey Plover found tight control of 'plover patches' in a 140-hectare mudflat called Seal Sands. There, Durham University's David Townshend watched 301 colour-banded Greys come and go over nine years. In a benchmark study of shorebird behaviour called 'Decisions for a Lifetime', he found intricate division and control of territories by these birds.

The decision isn't always immediate. Some juveniles, after arriving on their first migration, may work a stretch of mud for months, then fly on further south, abandoning it for lack of food, or after being evicted by later-arriving adults. Townshend mapped the territories and saw one frantic young Grey Plover enter, and be evicted from, other birds' patches eleven times in just half an hour.

But other young birds did hold their ground. Through successive winters, Townshend kept watch as the same birds returned and stuck to a pattern set in that first year—of either returning to an old territory, or roaming Seal Sands without one. 'Lifetime patterns of defence of feeding space and adoption of a wintering site by most individual Grey Plovers were determined in the first autumn of life,' he reported.

Around one-third of adult Grey Plover that appeared on Seal Sands stayed to defend fixed feeding territories for several months, and they came back year after year. It's possible that this extended for decades. A juvenile ringed in December 1975 was seen again there in October 1997, aged 22, and they can live to 25.

Fidelity to a winter-feeding site, and defence of it, is distinctive in Grey Plover. They can seem as suburban about their boundaries as are the people looking at them. In North America, naturalist Chas Michael came down from Yosemite to balmy La Jolla, near San Diego, for the winter. He watched, perhaps with an eye to his own wealthy neighbours on the tightly held cliff top, as the birds worked the shore.

'Each bird had his own particular strip of shore-line [that far north, it was more likely to be 'he'] and each his favourite loafing ground,' wrote Michael. 'But let one of his neighbour Black-bellied Plovers [it is North America, so that's the name] come onto his domain and he at once declares war. He ruffles his neck feathers, crouches into a belligerent attitude and trots towards the enemy as though to butt him from the premises. His bluff always seems to work. No blows are ever struck.'

On the Swartkops estuary near Port Elizabeth, Grey Plover performed ritual sentry duty on their borders as Jane Turpie studied them. Birds in dispute would pace a boundary, beside each other. They would take turns at being in the lead, with the other one halting as if to consider the justice of this imaginary line. To dramatise the importance of this decision-making, they would erupt into bouts of display: fanning their tails, drooping their wings, or adopting low crouches or sitting postures— significant gestures in plover-speak.

Once their boundaries are settled, the birds go to work by the rhythm of the tides. Day or night seems to not make much difference. While there is mud to feed on, Grey Plover will use it. Image-intensifying devices and radio-transmitter tags found them hunting for worms, crabs and mud prawns. These electronics made up for what we can't see—but Grey Plover can. Dissection of its dark, soulful eye shows that among shorebirds it has highly developed vision.

In vertebrates, the eye's retina is lined with photoreceptors shaped like minute rods and cones. Rods pick out light, sometimes at low levels, while cones see colour. Their density and capacity vary between species, but they all catch images in the same way as a memory card does in a camera, and transmit these images to the brain.

In the coastal lagoons of Venezuela, three night-feeding shorebird species with different foraging strategies were 'collected'—that is, caught and killed—and their eyes microscopically examined. Grey Plover not only had the greatest density of night-vision rods, it had the greatest rod-cone ratio, exceeding the Greater Yellowleg and Short-billed Dowitcher that were also caught. These latter two are tactile foragers, using their bills to feel for prey in the dark. The Grey Plover, evolved with the short bill, aimed more at surface prey, and eyes that could watch day or night.

Often Grey Plover will be doing this on the fringe of a mixed flock of birds, a 'guild' such as alighted at Knot Point to rest together. Grey Plover don't seem to object to other species of shorebird on their feeding ground. They use different feeding methods, on different parts of the tidal flat, and gain the shared protection of the flock. While long-bills—knots and godwits—work the shallows of a receding tideline, Grey Plover might be found slightly further up the shore, waiting for surface movement.

It's the patience of the ambush predator. To watch a Grey Plover at work is to see a bird conserving energy, pausing until prey moves and catches its attention, stepping in to confirm, and then adroitly darting down.

Jane Turpie explains it this way: 'Plovers, while they are moving, are less able to see their prey than when they are stationary. They may use monocular vision in an attempt to improve visual acuity, although this would impair their ability to judge the distance to their prey.'

A 'stop-run-search' method of hunting prey lets them find and check a target, before closing on it. They tilt their heads thoughtfully to make a more accurate measure of distance. Then they pounce. Watch a lapwing at work on its patch of suburban grass, and you will see the same thing.

When the Grey Plover were in the hands of the banders in Gulf St Vincent, these complex birds had looked very vulnerable. Each of the tools the banders employed was alien to such small bones: the metal ruler held into their wings to measure length, the poly tube in which they were placed to be weighed, the gap-toothed pliers for crimping the band. Despite this, the Greys did not struggle; they seemed transfixed by their predicament. They were carefully restrained as their wings were gently fanned to assess primary feathers, as bands were fixed on their legs and they were harnessed with their satellite tags.

For CYA and CYB, that summer was likely to be at least the second they had spent in southern Australia. The banders aged them by the state of their plumage: they had shed their first-year flight feathers. At this age they may have already made their lifetime decisions about adopting a fixed southern territory—the one place where they would spend the longest period each year. Perhaps the small population of Grey Plover on the wide gulf sands meant they needed to spend less time on sentry duty; but the satellite tracks showed they were just as busy, day and night.

In tidal corners of both hemispheres, shorebirds by the million live little-noticed for months, resting from the hazards of their migratory corridors and the urgency of their breeding grounds. Most Arctic migrants to Australia and New Zealand spend six or so months of the non-breeding season in these southern corners.

In Australia, dozens of Sharp-tailed Sandpiper forage at a modest lake behind suburban houses near Point Lonsdale in Victoria, and swarms of Red-necked Stint gather at the Western Treatment Plant near Melbourne. Bar-tailed Godwit feed at night in a backwater reserve at Sydney's Port Botany, having

adapted to the container terminal's lights. Walk along the promenade at Cairns in Queensland and you might see Far Eastern
Curlew and Grey-tailed Tattler pressed close to the footpath,
overlooked by people who have eyes only for coral.

Across the Tasman in rural New Zealand's North Island, at
Pūkorokoro Miranda, it is part of a dairy farmer's day to see
Bar-tailed Godwit roost in the paddocks. Then when the tide
starts to lower, skeins of these birds lift from the grass, and
gradually funnel together in the sky. They circle in increasingly
dense numbers before pouring together onto the coastal mud,
like grain neatly spilling from the hand of God.

Each of these different Australasian flocks feeds for half the
year on the warm southern bounty. Then watched or unwatched,
at summer's end they migrate up through Asia to the coasts of
Siberia, Alaska and the Arctic Sea. Flyways like the EAAF are
global divisions of migratory birds' domains. They elastically
define parts of the world used by these species. For shorebirds,
the UN Convention on the Conservation of Migratory Species
of Wild Animals recognises five main flyways, fanning out
from the high-northern latitude breeding grounds. Around the
globe, they are the Central Asian, the Africa–West Eurasian,
the Americas, Central Pacific and the EAAF.

———

The greatest shorebird spectacle at the southern end of the
EAAF is in Western Australia, at Broome's Yawuru Nagulagun/
Roebuck Bay Marine Park and on nearby Eighty Mile Beach.
In late summer, despite the heat and occasional cyclone, birders
vie to join Minton's expeditions to band thousands of waders
on these shores. After the expedition and as the weather begins

to cool, attention shifts to these birds' departure for the north. That's when I go there.

The Yawuru Aboriginal people of the Broome district have lived for millennia with birds they know as *garmirda-garmirda*, the wader birds, at Yawuru Nagulagun. So I asked to talk to a Yawuru elder about shorebird stories, and started something. Community leaders decided to make this a cross-cultural learning time and carloads of people came to BirdLife Australia's Broome Bird Observatory.

Elders take charge of the gathering and talk about their land and sea while young Yawuru students shuffle and listen. Aunty Di Edgar describes the tidal movement in the bay as ocean cleansing. 'It's healing time,' she says. 'For us it's healing as well, because we are saltwater people.'

Aunty Di tells the children they are to hear about the 'frequent flyer' birds. 'They are interesting, because they open the door to the twitchers that come here and study the migration. All the environment, the movements, the eating habits, flight habits. It's good to see the study of what the birds are bringing across, because it may affect our fisheries, as well as the mud. So science is important. But cultural knowledge is important. So you have to have a balance.'

I could hug her. This is exactly what I wanted to learn on this journey.

As the Broome heat intensifies, elder Jimmy Edgar talks about the birds he knows as pipers and snipes. 'They are part of our customary diet,' he says. 'When shellfish get fat, the birds get fat, and we go and hunt for them. And they're really good tasting. We get fat too. We used boomerang and whatever to cull them. With the tide in, it was easy to hit them. We used to play with the little ones that run on the beach. There used to be thousands along the coast area. We're seeing now just a little bit of them.'

He says the Yawuru are now uncertain of the birds as food, and think they might carry pollution or disease across the world. The hunt on the bay shore has died out in favour of chilled chicken at the Broome supermarket: 'We don't need them anymore. We can go to Woolies.'

They then call on me to explain my story. I say I live on the land of the *palawa* in *lutrawita* country, Tasmania, and I have gone to the land of the Kuarna in Gulf St Vincent to learn about the birds that migrate north. After coming now to Yawuru country, I plan to go on to China, and to where the birds are born—to the lands of Arctic Indigenous people.

Nigel Jackett, warden of the bird observatory, hosts a slide show of bird species and explains their habits on the bay. Afterwards, Jimmy Edgar and Jackett speak under a tree. Edgar says the Yawuru have a song cycle of the bay that is private men's business. He says other local songs join with those sung by people from the Northern Territory desert, who live thousands of kilometres away and have never been to Yawuru country.

'Birds are like that,' Jackett says to him, recalling the slightly different versions of a song that are sung by the same species, but far apart. 'They'll sing something, and then that language changes as it moves.'

The birders at the observatory listen for language at migration time. On this coast-torn edge of the red outback, they hear the night-haunted cry of Far Eastern Curlew, the piping chatter of rising Grey Plover and godwit, the fainter cries of a startled Red Knot flock, the racket of Whimbrel.

At the eastern head of the bay lies the mouth of Man-galagun/Crab Creek. Emilia Lai, who has come back from Gulf St Vincent to assist at the observatory, guides me there. She manoeuvres the big Landcruiser through sand traps with ease, then we walk along the banks of the creek and out towards the birds feeding on the tidal flat. We are enclosed by mangroves, and the creek is tide-fallen several metres below the bank. Occasional wandering Saltwater Crocodile are seen laying up here, but the fiercest amphibians I see are little bug-eyed mudskippers.

The fine-grained grey-blue mud clings to me, as sticky and luminous as porcelain clay. Such rich sediments washed by 'ocean cleansing' make the tidal flats here among the most biodiverse anywhere. At the lowest tides, the exposed flats can extend for a dozen kilometres offshore. Staggering out over this ooze, and sometimes falling into it, a survey team led by Theunis Piersma found 368 different invertebrate creatures, including 167 different worms and 59 snails.

In close observation of these flats, Broome bird researcher Grace Maglio shot hours of video to analyse the birds' eating habits. She developed a good understanding of Grey Plover character: 'I see a stocky bird, bigger than the other shorebirds, hanging around in groups of two or three,' she says. 'It's a confident bird, not as vigilant for danger, interacts with other birds not so much.' She sums the bird up: 'Grey Plover have got it under control.'

She showed a shorebird conference a comical video of a young Grey Plover pulling a long sand eel out of a hole; then running around in excitement with this bonus, repeatedly tossing it to subdue it, and finally flying off with the prize. Mainly though, she found that the bird prefers slug-like sea cucumbers: 'High in protein, low in fat, whole lot of enzymes. I thought, yeah, if I was a shorebird I would probably eat sea cucumbers as well.'

As the evening draws near, the northern Australian heat and humidity abate and mosquitoes start to bite. The birders set up their camping seats and viewing equipment on the bay's low cliffs. Most of them have spotting scopes, the small high-powered telescope on a tripod favoured by birdwatchers the world over.

In front of them is the red sand and milky-blue water of this wide, flawless bay. Yawuru people using handlines fish noncha-lantly for threadfin salmon from a nearby point. After they catch a feed, they drive away. Agile Wallabies emerge from the bush to lope along the tideline, eating mangrove leaves and seeds. They take their fill and move off too as the sun lowers.

Chris Hassell, who works for Theunis Piersma's Global Flyway Network, is on the clifftop with partner Kerry Hadley, scanning Red Knot that are pinched into the shore along the high tideline.

Eye in the spotting scope, he calls out to her, 'Five-Blue-Yellow-Blue-Lime-Trace.' Hadley notes the call. Through the maze of bird legs, Hassell is confident he can see this knot's first band is on its left leg at position five, below the knee, and it is blue. Under that is a yellow band, while on the right leg the bands are blue and lime. I can decode this because Emilia Lai has given me a fast lesson in colour-band positions, drawn on a piece of cardboard she ripped off a box.

The knot has only a 'trace' of red breeding-plumage colour-ing, which at this time of year probably means it's female, and Hassell adds one more observation: 'body condition five'. This is his assessment of the bird's degree of fatness. He uses a system developed by Piersma and his colleague Popko Wiersma. As an aid to their typology of Red Knot body shape, these two Dutch ornithologists reference the Flemish old masters. The almost-too-lean condition—'one'—is Boschian, like a ghostly figure from the fantastic world of Hieronymus Bosch. A 'five' is fleshly Rubenesque.

As Hassell works his way through the flock, he is able to enter each bird into his database of thousands without touching it, and months or years after it was netted and banded. It's clear today there are no Boschs and many Rubens: 'We've got all of these down as migratory birds,' he says. 'They are about to leave.'

Hassell is a former Leicestershire farm worker who cycled the world and fetched up in Broome over twenty years ago. He joined expeditions led by Clive Minton, and learned cannon-netting and banding. Abandoning the idea of dairy farming in England, he stayed to watch over flyway flocks instead. Most days, if the tide is right, he will be out scanning them for coloured bands, flags or tags.

Like a farmer, he listens and watches for his charges' moods and habits: 'Oh Kerry, I've got Whimbrel J-something! Oh! Fish just leapt out of the water and landed at the feet of the Whimbrel. Made *it* jump! Ha-ha! Bird's got an aerial. I think it's JX. Very good. The bird looks absolutely fine.'

The bird Hassell judges as being in good health is one that was earlier in the year netted, leg-flagged with a two-letter code, and fitted with a satellite tag in an Australasian Wader Studies Group project.

For Whimbrel (a sort of half-sized curlew) and many other species of migratory shorebirds, Yawuru Nagulagun is home to more than the 1 per cent of their global population—the threshold for international significance of a particular location. This year the scannable numbers onshore are down. It's thought that a heavy Wet Season gave them rich feeding grounds in inaccessible country further up Crab Creek. Tens of thousands more are down the coast, at Eighty Mile Beach.

Still, there are more than enough around the bay for a new eye to shorebirds to draw in cameos, unguarded moments when the bird is just being a bird.

How does the world's biggest shorebird scratch the mud off its neck? For this task the 20-centimetre curved bill of the Far Eastern Curlew is just an obstacle. So it lifts its right foot and uses a claw, first on one side of the neck with a delicate scratch, then with the left foot on the other side. It fluffs its feathers in apparent satisfaction and resumes the food hunt. Head down, it plunges its bill down a crab hole until the mud is almost at eye level—and its chin gets muddy again.

Nearby a skirmish erupts between a Greenshank and a crab. The lime-legged Greenshank is trying to grab the crab, but avoids its upraised pincers as the pesky crustacean backs off towards a hole. The bird circles around, legs akimbo and with its bill poking at the crab, looking for all the world like Charlie Chaplin bowling along with a walking stick. Eventually it stabs, picks up the crab and waltzes away.

Grey Plover are working the mud close to the coast. A guest at Broome Bird Observatory, Heather Alexander, freezes with her camera the bird flying that I had seen only as a blur. At lift-off, the Grey Plover's black wing-pit feathers are lined up as neat as Issey Miyake pleats, its tail feathers spread like a scalloped white skirt.

As the light begins to fade into a tropical night, Hassell and Hadley move down the coast towards Crab Creek, and they again try to scan individual birds.

Hadley: 'They're coming out of the other side of the mangrove. Yellow–Green–Yellow–Red, I think . . . I'd only give him a three with that profile.'

Hassell: 'Would you? I'd give him a four.'

Hadley reconsiders the bird's fatness: 'I'd give the one behind him a four, but I wouldn't give him a four,' she says.

Hassell demurs and later says in an aside: 'She's harder than me on weights.'

Along the southern EAAF, the departure of most shorebirds on migration is unseen, adding to their mystery. Here in Yawuru Nagulagun, it is a reliable spectacle in March to April. Most curlew have already left when I arrive. Not many Grey Plover are around. This week is Bar-tailed Godwit week.

They assemble at Crab Creek's mouth and a flock of perhaps 200 rises, piping, swirls for a few minutes and drops down again onto the mud. Soon after, there is another rise, perhaps a little more determined and vocal. Are the birds recruiting more to join, issuing a call to fly?

'I don't think it's just excited chatter,' Hassell says. 'It's a heck of an undertaking. So the question is whether it's a "What do you think?" to the others.'

On the third rise, a decision is clearly made. A long skein of 180 godwit strikes out north, stretching and condensing through invisible dimensions of air current like a bicycle race peloton flowing on a curving road.

As if pressed by the oncoming tropical night, waves of godwit now lift and pass overhead. They're not in the classic tight V-formation said to assure the best wind assistance to those behind, but in a looser curve like a passenger aircraft's wings. United in purpose or not, these birds seem very small against the sky for the scale of their endeavour, the ceaseless wing-beats over thousands of kilometres.

Hassell offers reassurance: 'When I've got one in my hand, I can absolutely understand. It's a beautiful flying machine.'

He and Hadley are very much at home, hunched into their spotting scopes and swatting mosquitoes. Before them, out in the Yawuru sea country, Australian Snubfin Dolphin break the calm surface of water which is lit many colours by the sunset. The red cliffs glow. The air around us is windless, momentarily silent.

Unaccountably, in the distance someone hammers a sheet of metal for a few beats in a strange drum roll, and then stops. On the mudflat there are more excited godwit calls and two skeins lift up, one above the other.

'They're already looking reasonably determined, those guys,' Hadley says. 'They're off, I reckon.'

'That's a big call,' Hassell replies.

'Yes, I'll say it again,' she says. 'And there's more in the air somewhere.'

Quiet in their own piece of heaven, the couple listen intently for far cries. The sun sets quickly. As it lowers, they look for a hint of movement in the enveloping blue-black cloak above the bay.

There it is. A glint, way up, as the sunken sun catches birds.

Tiny sparks.

Gone.

Four
The undertone

About 50 billion of the world's total 200–400 billion birds migrate annually, and at least since the days of Aristotle scientists have worked to understand their journeys. The seasonal appearances of chimney-nest-building storks and rooftop-racing swifts were thought about in Europe long before anyone considered what shorebirds did or where they went. Even today the migrations of woodland and farmland birds are to be marvelled at. Like the Blackpoll Warbler, a little songbird weighing only about as much as three teaspoons of sugar. It was recently discovered to fly down the North-west Atlantic on migration from Nova Scotia through the Caribbean's Greater Antilles, on the way to South America.

In the Southern Hemisphere, we take particular pride in the feats of seabirds. The Short-tailed Shearwater, or Muttonbird, breeds in burrows on sea cliffs around south-eastern Australia. It forages from there far into the Southern Ocean, returning to its burrow to feed fat chicks before heading back north to the Bering Sea, the opening to the Arctic Ocean. These birds live an

endless Pacific summer. Arctic Tern have been tracked meandering from the North Atlantic around global oceans to the ice
floes of the Antarctic. Wandering Albatross spend years at sea in
the Southern Ocean between short, bill-clacking reunions with
mates—at the same island, same nest.

Land birds on exceptional journeys usually have a fallback
that long-distance migratory shorebirds lack: they mostly cross
terrain, on shorter journeys, giving them the chance to drop
down, feed and rest. Seabirds feed from the surface, and rest
on it, or along coastlines. And they soar, lifted by the updraft
of waves, saving energy. Long-distance shorebirds like the Grey
Plover fly in a netherworld: the land they cross may be alien,
with no useful food, and if they do come down at sea, they won't
float long before they sink. So instead they make epic flapping
flights, non-stop, without refuelling. But just how far are these
'superflights'? How do they do them, and where do they end?

When CYA and CYB flew out of Gulf St Vincent ten days
apart in March 2016 and headed north over Australia's desert
outback, no one saw them go. I pieced together their great
ambition using clues from Tony Flaherty's reports on their
satellite tracks, weather records, and other waders flying out of
Yawuru Nagulagun/Roebuck Bay. I also looked at work carried
out under the leadership of Theunis Piersma on Grey Plover
at Banc d'Arguin—muddy shores on the Atlantic coast of the
Sahara Desert.

As the sun lowered and turned Gulf St Vincent fiery, CYA
and CYB would each have called a high-pitched 'peeooowiii!' as
she flashed her black pleats, spread her tail skirt and took flight.
Choosing dusk as the most useful time of day to migrate, they
would have dodged the heat load of daylight; breezes at night
are often more constant, and offer important navigational clues.

At Banc d'Arguin, Piersma observed flocks of 30 or so Grey Plover leave, mostly all of their own kind. But nearly one in five flocks were mixed with others, such as godwit. At Yawuru Nagu-lagun/Roebuck Bay, Dutch ecologist Ingrid Tulp saw slightly larger Grey Plover flocks leave, fairly strictly in single species. At Thompson Beach a few dozen Grey Plover have been counted in recent summers, and around 110 godwit. Their company might have been sparse but it's very likely that CYA and CYB each left in a flock, whoever their companions were.

Grey Plover ascended most often in a loose V-formation at Banc d'Arguin. Following them with a distance-measuring rangefinder, Piersma's group saw them lift to 500 metres in a few minutes and then be lost in the Saharan sand-dusted sky. They did see one Grey Plover flock rise to nearly 1600 metres—higher than any of the other seven species they watched, lifting fast, their wings beating at a rate of around eight cycles each second—fast enough to be a blur to the naked eye. Piersma watched as they found their way through what he called 'an unmapped mosaic of rising and sinking air'.

To meet the risks ahead, an evolutionary armoury has been assembled for this bird. Their first and best asset is a shorebird shape: as migratory waders, they have an aerodynamic body. When Ingvar Byrkjedal watched a male Grey Plover attack a much larger buzzard, he was reminded of a Russian MiG-29 in flight. This is a jet-fighter buff's favourite plane, as much for its aggressive thrusting stance, as its abilities. Now look at a chicken laid out, breast side up, on a roasting pan, and compare what it lacks, or shares, with the plover. The chicken has nearly useless poultry wings and tail. The migrating bird has long, sharply pointed wings that allow a clean stroke through the air, and for drag to roll out at the tips; it also has a light build, a sleek tail, and skinny legs that will never make drumsticks. What the two share is a big pectoral breast, bred for food in the chicken and as the main muscular flight motor in the shorebird. They share that, and fat.

'Fat is the most energy-dense storable substance in the whole animal kingdom,' wrote the German ornithologist Peter Berthold in his *Bird Migration*. 'Most body tissues can burn fat, and muscle fibres that oxidise fat tire relatively slowly. This makes fat the optimal flight fuel for migrating birds.'

When caught, CYA was a touch smaller in bill and wing length than CYB, but at 246 grams she weighed 11 grams more. Each of them weighed about the same as Grey Plover banded in Victoria by Clive Minton's Victorian group, but more than Grey Plover caught at Broome.

CYA and CYB were not weighed before they left. If they were like their Victorian cousins, they may have put on almost 140 grams of extra fat, as Minton's team has reported, giving them a total weight equal to almost two cups of butter. They would have ballooned out to look less like the fleeting waifs that were banded, and more Rubenesque, as if they'd swallowed tennis balls.

Other changes were likely happening within them. Among long-distance migratory shorebirds, redundant internal digestive organs actually shrink before departure, or alter on the flight. A study of juvenile godwits killed hitting a radar defence dome in Alaska found that, fat as they were, their gizzards, liver, kidneys and guts had shrivelled before take-off. Researchers also compared the anatomy of Great Knot killed just before migration in north-western Australia with others at the end of their migratory leap. Only the brain stayed in equilibrium; the rest of their organs shrank.

One thing probably didn't change. Those plovers caught at
Gulf St Vincent when I was there were still just grey and had not
begun to colour up into breeding plumage.

The birds' next asset for migration is the wind—if they
handle it right. Studies of energy consumption by shorebirds
find that the longest fliers operate near the edge of the possible.
Favourable tailwinds may be essential for successful marathon
flights. To find them, they work through a labyrinth of breezes.

Standing on the roof of Lund University's Ecology Building in
Sweden, biodiversity researcher Martin Green used radar and telescope to track 888 geese and wader flocks mid-migration between
the Wadden Sea in the Netherlands and the Arctic. He identified
eight Grey Plover tracks among these, flying at a median altitude
of 1456 metres. They were coasting along with about 11 metres
per second wind assistance, at a spanking ground speed of
32 metres per second—or about 40 kilometres per hour.

'The waders seemed to be selective, and specifically chose to
depart on days with a better than average wind support,' Green
reported. They mostly chose tailwinds, but there is a risk to this.
Like a fast car that might miss a turn, flying with strong tailwinds raises the chance they will be blown off course; and the
longer they use a tailwind, the greater this risk.

The plovers' black eyes can always see their position among
flock-mates, as well as the sun, moon and stars. Below they
perceive the landscape, and even earth's magnetic field.

They need to orient, that is, to understand where they are
relative to the points of the compass. And they have to navigate—
choose and adjust a course. As American poet laureate W.S.
Merwin put it, they fly:

between the pull of the moon
and the hummed undertone of the earth below them.

CYA flew out first, leaving Thompson Beach on 14 March 2016 with steady south-east winds at about 350 metres altitude pushing her north. If the flock flew higher—to, say, 1500 metres—they would have encountered a more difficult easterly crosswind.

I have tracked these birds' odyssey in these winds approximately using the US National Weather Service's Global Forecast System reproduced online in EarthWindMap. Amazingly to me, it gives historical data for wind direction and speed at different altitudes, adjustable to local time, around the globe.

Ahead for CYA was a flight in air rising from the hot ground of the outback, first across the Simpson Desert's hundreds of parallel dunes, where she appears to have been in the more difficult easterlies. As she reached the centre of the continent, winds were being spun down out of a low deep in the Gulf of Carpentaria, and CYA's track veered west over the flat and sparse Great Sandy Desert. This was not a helpful course. After a while, the bird turned back north-east into headwinds before taking another dogleg turn to regain her course due north. With the remains of the low now assisting from behind, CYA crossed the coastline about 2500 kilometres north-west of her starting point. There, at the mouth of the Ord River, a resting place and smorgasbord of mud below was ignored. She flew on, out over the coast.

Ten days after CYA left, when CYB lifted up at Gulf St Vincent, a low-pressure system ran through from the Great Australian Bight in the south-west, pushing winds up through the outback that turned into a steady south-easterly tailwind between 1500–3000 metres. A couple of days after this, CYB exited Australia near Darwin, having flown north over Alice Springs and the Tanami Desert, her path from Thompson Beach an uncomplicated and economical direct line. For CYB, leaving was literally a breeze.

A million wing-beats behind each of them, the Grey Plover flew on. In Adelaide, Tony Flaherty logged in to Argos to check the signals, and found the flights had begun. 'I guess the birds have been doing it for millennia, so they get an idea of opportunity,' Flaherty says. 'I used to sail a bit, and you know that over the centuries sailors worked out where to go through trade-wind routes. You've got a long journey, you try everything to make it easy.'

Everything, including adjusting flight directions to compensate for those easterly winds that would otherwise have taken them off the Western Australian coast and out into the Indian Ocean. Like sailors on trade routes, CYA and CYB needed to know where they were, and where they wanted to go.

To make it to their breeding grounds, these small birds not only had to orient themselves to the earth, they had to navigate in a preferred direction. Each bird in their flock had to make a similar choice; to show the kind of avian unity I saw in the guild landing in Boullanger Bay, or the godwit flock striking out from Yawuru Nagalagun.

In a migratory bird's head, probably in the eye, is an extraordinary sixth sense that gives it the means to know where it is, and the basis for it to navigate anywhere. Birds can 'see' earth's magnetic field. To accept the invisible power of the magnetic compass is to step through the looking glass towards grasping the magic of bird migration.

This power's existence was revealed by the University of Frankfurt's Wolfgang Wiltschko in the 1960s when he used magnetic coils to alter the field around caged migratory European Robin and watched them re-orient to the artificial pull. Since then, he and his wife Roswitha have worked to understand the phenomenon, which is widespread among birds.

'The number of species tested for magnetic compass orientation is so high because researchers initially found it hard to believe that birds should possess a sensory quality that we humans apparently lack,' Roswitha Wiltschko wrote drily.

Earth's magnetic field is best known to us through the standard compass and its north-pointing needle. The field is highlighted by the auroras, australis and borealis, the light displays created when particles from solar wind are attracted to the south and north magnetic poles. The field's lines, invisible to us, leave the earth in the Southern Hemisphere and are drawn in again at the North.

Curved around the earth by gravity's pull, the lines incline at an angle to the surface—from 90 degrees at the poles to a flattened zero degrees above the equator. When birds are migrating north or south, the lines offer a kind of grid map. They show birds the direction towards, and away from, the equator. Field lines are like the staves on a blank music sheet. They are the 'hum of the earth', ready for these birds to write the song of their own travels.

The strongest candidate currently for enabling this feat of recognising the magnetic field is a protein called cryptochrome 4 (Cry4), which exists in the cones of a bird's retina. It's likely that in response to the magnetic pull, this protein causes the bird's eye to become more or less shaded—in effect, the bird has a basic head-up display like the instrument display on a fighter pilot's helmet visor.

Certainly, something must already be present to enable young shorebirds' first migratory flights. In contrast to the great Arctic flocks of geese and swan, shorebirds do not migrate in family groups; there are less likely to be experienced adults to show the route to first-time travellers. As a rule, the adults leave the breeding ground early. Juveniles learn to fly alone, and to make their own way to the safety of warm feeding grounds far beyond the Arctic winter. When CYA and CYB made their initial journeys south at a few months of age, their directions were hard-wired; they had genetic insurance against a leap into the unknown.

'Apparently migratory direction is inherited as an additive trait, the expression of which is probably controlled by a number of genes,' Peter Berthold concluded.

'Possibly,' wrote the Wiltschkos, '. . . when some (ancestor) birds began to migrate and undertake increasingly long flights, they already had a compass mechanism available which they could use to orient in specific directions.'

What juvenile migrant birds can use is vector navigation— the ability to follow a specified course to a goal. In aviation terms, they follow a predetermined flight plan. What they may *not* be able to do is navigate independently, as a pilot would around a squall, to reach the same goal.

The gift of vector navigation was confirmed when Dutch Professor Albert Perdeck caught thousands of northern European Starlings near The Hague on their southward autumn migration, and had them flown by plane to Switzerland for release. His team recovered 354 rings and from them he could map where both adults and juveniles had gone, after being displaced 800 kilometres to the south-west of their normal flight path. Adults would backtrack to their original wintering areas in northern France or southern England. Juveniles kept on going towards southern France or Spain. The direction and distance of their first migratory flights were pre-determined.

The scale of the great shorebird flights makes it harder to accept that juveniles are pre-set on their intrepid first migration from their Arctic birth nest, eventually to cross the Australian outback and aim for Gulf St Vincent, or Boullanger Bay, where they will likely arrive long after the adults. Yet that is exactly where these birds end up, leaving us to work out why they choose to fly farthest.

As CYA and CYB flew north across the Australian coast and headed into the tropics, their magnetic compasses' limitations became apparent. Field lines are horizontal at the equator, and so probably are less of an aid. To refine their course in an around-the-clock flight, migratory birds need to use other reference points: the sun, and the heavens at night.

Another German scientist, Gustav Kramer, again using starlings, found that if caged during their normal migration period, they would orient themselves in the same direction as free starlings, just as long as the sun shone and they could see it. Dunlin caged in Iceland and tested for their movements near sunset, wanted to head straight towards the magnetic south, a course that would have taken them to their usual destination in Portugal. There is even evidence of migratory shorebirds using a sun compass to employ the navigator's short cut, the Great Circle route. Lund University's Thomas Alerstam watched flocks of American Golden Plover and three sandpiper species take the shortest track across a sphere at a point in the Arctic, where converging magnetic field lines are probably of little help.

At night, long-distance migratory shorebirds fly on across the hemispheres, gradually seeing stars above them change position, or drop out of sight behind, as others rise above the horizon. Their view includes both the Southern Cross and the North Star. Caged birds tested inside a planetarium have oriented to a star pattern, and the Wiltschkos believe that birds' ability to calibrate celestial cues, particularly from the stars, is tied to the magnetic field.

We might think that the moon, our close night-time friend, must be of value, but it seems to remain only the master of their daily tidal movement, and a poet's symbol in their flights. CYA flew out from Gulf St Vincent with the new moon, a waxing crescent growing from a fingernail. CYB's great leap was taken in a full moon, waning gibbous to a last quarter. Such different phases speak of no obvious link, and Berthold believes birds hardly ever use the moon for orientation.

As scientists burrow deeper into migratory birds' command of the world, they are finding connections with polarised light, barometric pressure and low-level infrasound. Most obvious to us would be the landscape passing below—waypoints of mountains and coasts, straits and capes. Clearly these shorebirds know local geography; they return to the same small points of land to roost and feed each day and year. But how do they assemble land and sea unfurling beneath them into milestones on long migratory maps? We can only speculate.

Alerstam, an evolutionary ecologist, warns bluntly to think of the answers as an agnostic scientist, and I hold to his caution as a constant in a changing world. 'There is of course no purpose in evolution—only selection effects, mutations, genetic inter-actions and constraints,' he says. 'So the path towards adaptive explanations must be trodden with great care and humbleness.'

———

However assembled in body and mind, our two birds indis-putably flew on. Their satellite tracks showed them steady in their determination. Beyond the north coast of Australia, many Indonesian islands passed below them in the Timor, Banda and Molucca seas. The 1500-kilometre length of the Philippines

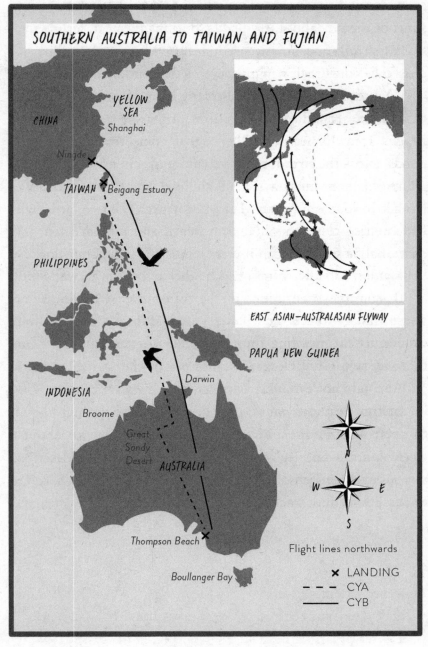

SOUTHERN AUSTRALIA TO TAIWAN AND FUJIAN

CHINA

YELLOW
SEA

Shanghai

Ningde ✕

TAIWAN ✕ Beigang Estuary

PHILIPPINES

EAST ASIAN–AUSTRALASIAN FLYWAY

PAPUA NEW GUINEA

Darwin

INDONESIA

Broome

Great
Sandy
Desert   AUSTRALIA

N

W   E

S

Thompson Beach ✕

Boullanger Bay

Flight lines northwards

✕   LANDING
- - - CYA
—— CYB

Sources: Flight Data, Victorian Wader Study Group and Friends of Shorebirds
South-East; Flyway, BirdLife International

rolled away. Each bird beat on without pause through a week of sunrises, sunsets and starry nights, burning their fat, feeling their bodies shrink and adjust, negotiating tricky winds, rolling air resistance out at their wingtips, eyeing the comfort of flock-mates.

CYA touched down at the Beigang Estuary, on the west coast of Taiwan, around seven days after lifting off from Thompson Beach. Tony Flaherty saw her signal come from aquaculture ponds across the river from a wetland park built for birds. After a flight of about nine days, CYB alighted near the coastal city of Ningde in southern China's Fujian Province. The two birds, who had been so close on Thompson Beach and migrated ten days apart, had flown through different winds and in separate flocks to land within 350 kilometres of each other across the Taiwan Strait.

Despite the frustrations of the transmitter's ten hours 'on' and 48 hours 'off' cycle, Flaherty and Maureen Christie were excited by the tracking they managed to receive. They found that the two Grey Plover, wallflowers of the shorebird world and second-choice tracker carriers, each flew more than 7000 kilometres. Without pause, they beat their way through the air to cover around 1000 kilometres every 24 hours for about a week. On the first leg of their migration, their lines described a new benchmark in distance. They outflew any other shorebird to carry a satellite tracker on a non-stop flight from Australia.

Five

The treasure map

In a Bangladeshi scooter taxi, a tall man was bent nearly double as he rattled towards the steaming Ganges delta, south of the capital, Dhaka. He tried to avoid being brained by the cabin roof, or taking a punch to the chin from the telescope tripod between his legs. Beside him was his guide and, filling all remaining space, their packs. Over 40 kilometres of rough road, Mark Barter's hope of a little mobile birding turned into an excruciating view of his bouncing driver's back. 'We got out physical wrecks,' he recalled.

But he made it to a fishing village in the delta, determined to hire a boat and push on through mud-braided islands little visited by Westerners. Here he was: a mad-keen birder pioneering new ground, scouting the delta where the holy Ganges deposits billions of tonnes of silt carried down from the mountains of Nepal and China, and along the people-clogged plains of India and Bangladesh.

'There was plenty of evidence of the erosion/accretion cycle which operates in the delta, with many metres of the northern shores of islands being removed each year and the equivalent amount being deposited in the southern ends,' Barter wrote. 'Bad for people, good for birds.'

It mattered not that a boat they hired had a crewman whose constant job was to bail out water at a greater rate than it entered; that he was heckled by small children on the banks who laughed at the European scanning for birds; or that he narrowly made it back to workday reality from the trip, after the crew, poling the boat through mud-channel labyrinths, became lost in the dark.

Just west of where he was birding, the Sundarbans swamp forest held swimming Bengal Tigers and Saltwater Crocodiles. Still, at the first wader roost they could find, Barter and his guide left the boat. 'Rashid and I waded through thigh-deep water, and knee-deep mud, to the shore and had an excellent start to our bird-watching, with an estimated 15,000 birds roosting and feeding around us ... Mongolian Plover, Curlew Sandpiper, Golden and Grey Plovers.'

But the Bangladesh expedition yielded no other flocks as large as this, and to add a few more birds to his list Barter had to pick his way past an aggressive bull water buffalo, 'who was rather protective of his large harem'.

Barter was in his element, on the loose in Asia, discovering shorebird haunts. A tall, charming English-Australian, he wore the weekday suit of a metals marketing expert who advised manufacturers in expanding developing economies. At weekends, or when he could borrow time—any time—he went birding.

'Don't mention Bangladesh to me,' his wife Terry says. 'When the Gulf War broke out, he'd taken a fortnight's holiday because they wanted some bird survey or other done there. The company rang up and said, 'Where's your husband? We want to bring him home.' And I hadn't a clue. I thought *they* were keeping track of him. There was no phone, no e-mail. He would just go, and then he'd come back.'

As he roamed birding hotspots, Barter was becoming absorbed in the Asian passage of migratory shorebirds, searching for the places that long jumpers like Grey Plover critically relied on to refuel. It was work that would come to define his shortened life, and leave a legacy for the whole flyway. His passion shone through short memoirs published in the *Victorian Wader Study Group Bulletin*.

In the few scattered bird reserves of Southeast Asia, Barter found plentiful migrants. More often he scouted accidental feeding grounds, like the leftover shore next to a four-stack coal-fired power station at the Dadu River mouth of western Taiwan, or the military-owned Bangpu pier near Bangkok.

Barter went to 'one of the nicest spots you'd ever want to watch waders', Olango Island in the central Philippines. 'Apart from the tropical climate, the cooling sea breezes, coconut palms and the smiling people, the most memorable feature of Olango is the freedom to walk around on the coralline sand among feeding birds. The waders co-exist very happily with the villagers, who are constantly walking through the foraging flocks, and they don't seem to mind visiting birders either.'

The shorebird death traps of Asia caught his attention early: 'For me, it's always an experience to make a pilgrimage to recovery sites of birds that have been banded by the group.' This duty took him to Cirebon, on the north coast of Java, where Indonesian hunters plied a trade in shorebirds for snacks. Six Victorian bands had been found on their legs and miraculously returned. Snipe, plover and sandpiper were trapped in mist nets at night and delivered to market next morning in flapping bunches, tied by the legs.

'It's a pitiful sight to see them lying in a heap on the ground, unable to find a comfortable or dignified position,' he wrote. 'The objective is to keep the birds alive, as little is paid for dead ones due to the possibility of meat spoilage.'

Cheaply priced to an Australian, but a luxury food for impoverished Indonesians, these birds were sold plucked, split and wok-fried for an equivalent of 12 cents apiece. 'I chose Pintail Snipe and found it to be very tasty,' Barter recalled. 'Tender, with a good flavour.'

Tens of thousands of shorebirds were being caught for food in many countries across Asia. But much greater numbers were still landing at the southern end of the flyway every southern spring and making the trip north to reach their breeding grounds again in the autumn.

These birds had to be staging somewhere. Barter had travelled southern Asia from Pakistan to Taiwan, but not found any great refuge. There were pointers, but no clear evidence, not the many flocks of tens of thousands such as lived at Eighty Mile Beach. As he thought about the next step along this trail, he went to work at the far southern end of the flyway, in Tasmania.

On the shore of the Derwent River in Hobart stands a zinc works, a sprawling pile of grey conveyors and chimney stacks, yellow sodium lights and steam. Owned in Barter's time by the Electrolytic Zinc Company of Australia, the smelter poured metal ingots, and sold them to manufacturers of consumer goods, toys and widgets. His job for nearly twenty years was to give technical advice to EZ's customers, the diecast factories.

'If you just sell great big slabs of zinc, you're a price-taker,' former colleague, Mike Newman, explains. 'If you add value with alloys, particularly zinc and aluminium, then it's got a specialty market. How do you differentiate yourself from your competitors? The way we did it was to provide technical support to the product. Mark might go out to a customer in Asia, they would say their extrusions were showing defects, say getting bubbles in the metal, and we would troubleshoot them.'

In an intriguing confederacy, Barter, Newman and a prickly EZ senior technologist named David Thomas were all British-born metallurgists, like Clive Minton, who came to Australia to run Imperial Metal Industries. All became expert on the EAAF. Why metallurgy should be a common foundation for pioneering work on migratory shorebirds eludes me.

I suggest to Newman that at EZ, birdwatching might have given these scientists an imaginative escape from the hellish industry around them. He is a bit more down to earth. 'Our conditions weren't exactly infernal,' he says. But EZ's managers did not keep a very close eye on the metallurgists' use of the working day. 'It was about time management—and how you absolutely filled the cup. I'm just saying there was excess intellectual capacity. The fact that we did all that shows how unfulfilled and under-employed we were.'

Too often to be a coincidence, I again come across this British wader diaspora, almost as if these people were being pumped out of some secret Hogwarts School of Shorebirdery. I begin to quiz them, but find no college hidden somewhere in the Scottish Highlands. Instead these were young and clever people, instilled by parents or luck in the British nature traditions. Children of *Wind in the Willows* and Christopher Robin's Hundred Acre Wood; intellectual descendants of Isaac Newton and Charles Darwin, of Geoffrey Chaucer's *Parlement of Foules*, and Ralph Vaughan Williams' *Lark Ascending*. They were steeped in close examination of the nature around them; bred to the calling. The British saw bird study, whether by professional or amateur, as a

much more acceptable ordinary pastime than many Australians
did—or perhaps still do. In Britain anyone could put a ring on
a bird if they wanted. No one had to pass a test. Chasing long-
distance migratory shorebirds was a logical extension of this.
They didn't have to go on an unaffordable African safari to see
exotic wildlife. It was on the local mud.

And they became emigrants too. They left their homeland,
usually permanently, for the Far East, Australia and New Zealand.
It can't be a coincidence that, displaced to the other side of the
earth, they spent so much of their time trying to answer questions
about the lives of birds born in far reaches of the Northern Hemisphere and committed to life in the south. When they flew back
'home', what routes did these birds actually take? How far could
they fly non-stop before they burned all their available energy
and fell from the sky? Where were their refuges on the way? And
exactly where in the vast cold north did they actually breed?

Mark Barter brought zinc-alloy products back from Asia to EZ
to David Thomas for scrutiny. When Thomas wasn't sectioning
toy cars for inspection in the basement of EZ's research building,
he was pulling shorebird data sheets out of his desk drawer and
writing up reports. Late in the 1960s, he drew together sparse
knowledge to calculate that more than one million migratory
shorebirds spent the southern summer in Australia and New
Zealand. He guessed, correctly, that the unsurveyed north-west
Australian coast would be their stronghold, and he began to
calculate the extent of their flights.

Thomas thought small waders easily capable of continuous flights in excess of 2900 kilometres—the distance between

Tasmania and the Gulf of Carpentaria. 'They certainly cross Australia, possibly in numbers,' he wrote in 1970. Studying the Curlew Sandpiper, he thought about how it might tackle the 14,000 kilometres from Tasmania to the Arctic, and decided it might take 24 days, including stops along the way. Much more work was needed to unravel the routes they took.

Impatient with the trickle of evidence from banding, ornithologists looked at formulas to estimate a bird's flight range based on the weight of its fat. Combined with a species' known flight speed, and multiplied by the energy value of a gram of fat, a fair hypothetical range emerged. In South Africa, Ron Summers led the task of assembling fat measurements for twelve migrant species. Building on a formula proposed by the Canadians Raymond McNeil and Francoise Cadieux, Summers' study in 1978 came up with remarkable range estimates, including a 3800-kilometre flight by the Curlew Sandpiper on just 27 grams of fat (equivalent to two tablespoons of butter) and a potential 6500 kilometres super jump by the Grey Plover fuelled by 120 grams of fat.

Barter began tinkering with some of the possibilities on the EAAF. In papers he wrote for the Tasmanian Shorebird Study Group, he looked at potential ranges for local Curlew Sandpiper and Red-necked Stint that allowed each a single flight to reach northern Australia. Others used the formulas to plot arcs of distance for flights from southern Australia by many of the waders. They figured that the beautifully balanced physiology of the Grey Plover and Red Knot meant they might make it as far as the Philippines.

For analytical problem-solvers like these metallurgists, pulling these facts together was intriguing desktop detective work. They could use the new yield of data from cannon-netting catches: not just the numbers of birds banded and weighed, but their basic biometrics. The counts by wader study groups of the weights, wing and bill lengths of birds were by now in the thousands. Together with the ability to age a bird by its plumage, comparisons could be made with birds caught by others, say at their northern breeding grounds.

In Moscow, just off Red Square at Lomonosov State University Zoological Museum, a researcher named Pavel Tomkovich was looking at the Arctic end of the shorebird migration. Making one of the early wader biometric studies, Tomkovich looked at 118 Red Knot skins gathered from all the main museums in the USSR. He found slight differences in the bill- and wing-length combinations of knots collected at different breeding locations. Variations of just a few millimetres were enough to tie sub-groups to four different Siberian breeding grounds.

By comparing Tomkovich's data with local measurements, Barter was able to discount a belief that Australian Red Knot bred at Wrangel Island, a fabled Arctic Sea wildlife stronghold. Instead, Red Knot data in both southern and north-western Australia tallied with Russian work showing that they bred in the far-eastern reaches of Siberia, on the Chukchi Peninsula. Nuggets like this mounted up for waders, though not often for Grey Plover—it was still not known where in the wide tundra these birds flew from southern Australia to nest.

And despite all this evidence—band returns, fat-to-distance sums and biometric data—many sketch maps of the time could only join data points with hemisphere-sized dotted lines. Their calculations clearly told them there had to be limits to flights. It seemed impossible that any shorebird could fly the planet non-stop between nest site and southern summer mud. But where were the staging grounds?

On his travels in Southeast Asia, Barter had rarely seen the longer-distance fliers: Far Eastern Curlew, Great Knot, Red Knot, Grey Plover and Bar-tailed Godwit. So he turned his mind further north.

Much earlier than most, he stuck his neck out in his calculations of flight prospects for the Great Knot. Greater only when compared to the Red Knot, this sandpiper's global wintering stronghold is in northern Australia. Based on measurements from more than 2000 birds caught at Broome and nearby Eighty Mile Beach, Barter figured that Great Knot of average weight could fly 4500 kilometres, and at their peak might make 7300 kilometres without refuelling.

'Great Knot at the maximum weight of around 250–260 grams could comfortably reach Shanghai, where two banded in north Western Australia in recent years have been re-trapped,' he ventured.

And so the arc of possibility was being drawn further north, to reach southern China, Japan and the Korean Peninsula.

———

As China's export consumer-goods economy began to open up, and their need for zinc products grew, Barter could go there too. When he did, he woke the Chinese to their shorebird riches. Early on he made contact in Shanghai with a Chinese ecologist, Tian Hou Wang, who had done his PhD at Queensland's Griffith University and studied wader habitat at the nearby mouth of the Yangtze River. 'Among birds, shorebirds are less known in China,' Wang wrote in his 1987 book, *Shorebirds in the Yangtze River Estuary and Hangzhou Bay*. 'And this is the first monograph of China which covers ecological and biological aspects of shorebirds during the non-breeding season.'

His work had been a long time coming. In the early ornithology of China, it had been a British tea merchant, Frederick William Styan, who catalogued the birds of the Yangtze delta at the end of the nineteenth century. He counted different species of migratory waders, including Red Knot and Curlew Sandpiper, by checking Shanghai food-market stalls.

The bedrock of China's attitude to nature lies in the Confucian tradition, which leans towards nature's mastery by people. In Styan's time, towards the end of the Qing Dynasty which preceded modern China, a person could confirm their high status by 'bird-walking'—strolling in a park with a caged songbird. Even today in China, a wise use of natural resources means taming ecosystems for the good of society. There is an ingrained notion of conquering nature, inherent from ancient legend to Maoist command.

When former president Jiang Zemin spoke at a ceremony for part of the transformational Three Gorges Dam project, he recalled the Chinese people's struggle to reform nature and the traditional story, *Jingwei Fills the Seas*. In this myth, a beautiful girl drowns and is reincarnated as a bird committed to revenge against the ocean. She flies between sacred Mount Jiuhua in the mid-Yangtze to the sea, each time carrying a few stones or sticks to drop there. For the Chinese President the point was not her futile quest to fill the sea, but the tenacity of the bird: 'From old, the Chinese people have had a brave history of carrying out activities to conquer, open up and utilise nature,' he said.

Taken literally, this belief gave permission to harm birds most grievously. In Mao Zedong's Great Leap Forward of 1958–60 he named sparrows as one of 'Four Pests'. Along with flies, mosquitoes and rodents, they were to be eliminated by the Chinese people. Sparrows were targeted because they ate grain. Their eggs were broken and their nestlings destroyed; poisons were laid and they were shot out of the air. Millions of people were mobilised to bang pots, gongs or drums in a din that frightened birds from landing until they dropped from the sky in exhaustion.

Of course, countless other birds once plentiful around Chinese villages and towns suffered the same indiscriminate fate. Only when insect numbers exploded, and famine increased, were sparrows removed from the Four Pests list. Even today this great loss of local birds shadows Chinese life. Birders prize a local 'Magic Wood'. It's that strip of remnant trees, along an old roadway or on a dyke between rice paddies, where woodland birds hang on, and still sing.

The fate of shorebirds under Mao's regime was not described. It's possible they were overlooked, out on the mud. But in the war against nature, and the battle against famine, it is hard to imagine none were targeted with nets when they flew in to feed in the coastal fish and shrimp ponds.

After Mao, as China opened up in the 1980s, more conventional scientific values began to take hold instead. Tian Hou Wang's pioneering shorebird surveys near Shanghai with Gouzhen Qian showed they clearly valued the lives of these passing birds. Their detailed bilingual publication carefully describes the species, down to evoking their calls. To a Chinese ear, the Far Eastern Curlew sang 'kou-liu, kou-liu', and the Grey Plover a melodic 'ti-wu-wei, ti-wu-wei'.

Much of their work was done at survey points along the Hangzhou Bay coast, south of Shanghai. Wang also looked downstream of the city, where the Yangtze's wide mouth holds a long tongue of island called Chongming Dao. It was here that he and Barter began to work together.

Chongming Dao is formed, and is still forming, from silt washing down the Yangtze. Its birds' lives are likewise re-shaped by China's growth. As Wang summed it up for me, the: 'beach was reclaimed seriously as the land [was] too small for the human population explosion in the district of the estuary of the Yangtze River, which interfered with the structures of the wader community.'

Here, at that time, artisanal hunters still exploited shorebirds for food. As the birds circled, looking for company, the hunters called them in by blowing bamboo whistles to mimic their high-pitched cries. In the manner of Japanese hunters, they set decoys to lure the birds within reach of a pole net, which was first laid flat on the mud and then heaved in quickly over the catch using a hand-pulled line. Many days and years these hunters had sat under an umbrella or a rudimentary brush hide on the mud, smoking and scanning the sky for quarry.

The devastation of Mao's famine lived in current memory on Chongming Dao. Catching a bird for food was a matter of necessity. Under the pressure of an exploding human population, the level of hunting worried the scientists, particularly when they found that up to 35 hunters were taking up to 38,000 wader birds each northern spring. 'Hunters consider that waders are a natural resource, like fish and plants,' Wang's colleague, Sixian Tang, reported. 'Hunting has been undertaken for many years and they did not believe that the activity would result in a decline in numbers.'

Still, these hunters were useful for their skills. They knew how to catch and handle live shorebirds, at least to the point of preserving them for market. So Wang and Tang asked the hunters to bring in birds for weighing and banding, so they could be released to fly on.

Out of 100 Great Knot, Red Knot and Bar-tailed Godwit, they found four birds that already had been banded in north-western Australia just seven to twelve days earlier, and whose condition gave stark evidence of the hunters' needs. These were not the fat *garmirda-garmirda* brought down with a boomerang as they were about to migrate from Yawuru Nagulagun; they were drastically thin—so starved that their fat reserves were all gone and they must have been burning muscle in flight.

The physical condition and timing of their capture led Barter and Wang to conclude there was no way these birds could have refuelled between their Australian departure points and Chongming Dao. They must have flown directly, and not just from Broome. 'It seems quite possible that south-east Australian Great Knot and Bar-tailed Godwits also make non-stop flights to the Asian mainland, and to do so fly at least 8000 kilometres,' they wrote in 1990.

This was an ambitious finding for the time, for what it implied of bird endurance and survival along the flyway. Ultramarathon flight was proposed in what Barter said was the longest heavily used shorebird-migration stage in the world. It provoked in-triguing next questions. How critical was this particular Yangtze River mud for replenishing these birds? Were there other similar sites, as yet unknown, across Barter's arc along the Chinese coast and Korean Peninsula? The possible routes opened out in front of him.

Six
The treasure house

Around seven days after lifting off from Thompson Beach in South Australia, the Grey Plover CYA made her first landfall, touching down in the Beigang Estuary of densely populated western Taiwan. It was a 7270-kilometre flight, counting the wind-blown dogleg she took over northern Australia. She landed just south of the Dadu River mouth that Barter had visited years before. Tony Flaherty, watching the satellite plots back in Adelaide, contacted Taiwanese birders and they began to look for her. Finding a satellite-tagged bird would mean not just publicity, but a chance to eyeball the bird to see how it was managing the burden.

'CYA was right next to this beautiful wetland park which had been built on a reclaimed site, and provided wonderful facilities for bird lovers,' Flaherty says. 'But she was on the other side of the estuary, in the aquaculture ponds, away from the Taiwanese Wader Study Group people who tried to get a glimpse.'

As CYA spent time resting and refuelling, CYB overflew Taiwan a little further to the north, passing directly over the

Dadu River and landing 350 kilometres beyond CYA on the Chinese mainland at Ningde, having taken a straighter 7090-kilometre flight line.

Despite the great distance flown, the initial landing proved to be a brief rest halt for CYB. The bird used the Ningde mud for only a few days before taking a 450-kilometre hop to Hangzhou Bay, Wang's original study area, just down from Chongming Dao.

Each Grey Plover was an adult when caught at Thompson Beach, aged by the plumage, and so was very likely to have made at least one previous full migration. CYA was slightly shorter, though heavier when measured. Maybe a little more wisdom lay in CYB's head. Having taken a useful ten extra days to fatten up before leaving Gulf St Vincent, there was fuel to fly further, even though the passage took longer. She also didn't need to correct her course.

In early April, the time of year when CYB landed there, I stand on the Hangzhou Bay seawall for my first sight of Chinese coast. I had flown out of Broome, where it was too hot to think, to Darwin via Kununurra. The pilot did a go-around there to avoid a passing rain wall, letting me see the Kimberley's red gorges and canyons. It was a reminder at altitude of the harsh weather these birds must negotiate. In Darwin, I met the environmental scientist Stephen Garnett, lead author of the benchmark *Action Plan for Australian Birds*. I wanted guidance on flyway shorebirds from someone with his long view, and Garnett had thoughts on both persistence and folly. He had faith in the capacity of birds to evolve against challenges, but he called international management of them 'insipid'.

In a cab on my way to see Garnett, I had chatted with an inquisitive Indian taxi driver about my journey. A survivor of emigration battles himself, he grasped the idea of migratory shorebirds straight away: 'So they are global citizens, yes? They don't know any country, any government, any border?'

I keep these benchmarks from northern Australia in my mind as I look out at the other world of Hangzhou Bay, estuary of the Qiantang River. The birds have left behind the wide, hot blue skies and clear waters of Australia for a grey-brown murk, with cold haze eddying above.

As tide and fog ebb, a strange contraption looms. It's a fishing machine rising high above the reedy mud. Rickety scaffolding holds wires and a jib used for lowering a wide fixed net. With its cabin shuttered and net held above the water, it looks like an idle siege engine, a symbol of Chinese fishing determination. Behind the seawall, a Yellow-bellied Weasel picks its way across waste ground. Nearby, a few Greenshank make the best of pickings among the reeds. A flight of godwit shoot past low and disappear into fog over the water. Where in the far south have they just come from?

Next day I meet a small group for a tour organised by Chinese shorebird advocates to travel up the coast of Jiangsu Province, north of Shanghai. We begin at the tip of Chongming Dao's tongue, where there are multitudes of birds. On a rising tide, and in the same cold grey haze, thousands of shorebird dots forage across an ink wash of mud, spiked by reeds. The birds lift in waves to flow across a grey-black landscape. The sight makes me think of the romantic flow of inked Chinese characters on paper—it's a living canvas.

Sharper eyes than mine spot among the many Great Knot one with a yellow flag on its leg, denoting its arrival from north-west Australia. There are similar numbers of Dunlin, the Northern Hemisphere sandpiper that holds an eager 'Forward march!'

posture. As the tide rises the birds settle in a half circle radiating away from us. It's a humbling display of flock wariness. Thousands of small birds reach an agreement between themselves that the optimum roost is a line about 50 metres away from that bunch of humans. Beyond the sandpiper cordon, Redshank patrol. I glimpse Grey Plover in distant silhouette, outermost and alone again.

The presence of flocks like this, right here at this highly symbolic marine gateway to China, encouraged a belief over the years that this was *the* critical staging habitat for migrating shorebirds. After all, Wang counted 9519 waders of 32 species on one day in May. An exhaustive count led by Barter at nine sites on Chongming Dao, together with likely evidence of others, confirmed to him 'the critical significance of the Yangtze estuary' for wader conservation.

When Barter had time to do more work and reflect, he realised that the fit was too neat. The real story was being confused by an over-reliance on too little evidence. 'Many Australian bands had been recovered there, and the indications were that the extensive intertidal areas at the eastern end of the island supported very large numbers of waders,' he said.

'Not so! It seems that the area rarely holds more than 15,000 waders at peak times. Band recoveries are good at locating hunting activity, and flag sightings at pinpointing affluent telescope-owning birdwatchers, but they can be misleading when trying to find important bird-watching sites.'

He contemplated the further possibilities as he stood among the domestic water buffalo on the mudflats of Chongming Dao, and on the banks of crab-farming ponds. Barter watched small flocks rising and calling in the evening, the way departing birds did over Yawuru Nagulagun/Roebuck Bay. He saw echelons and

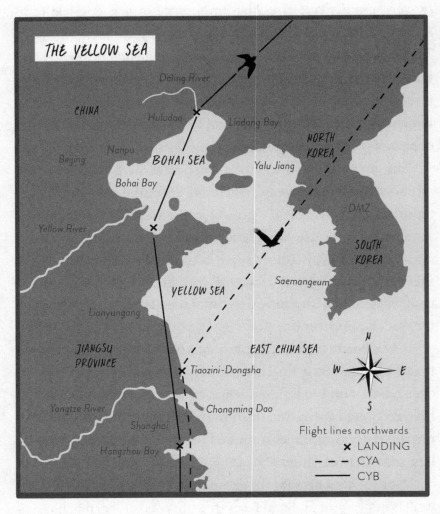

Sources: Flight lines, Victorian Wader Study Group and Friends of Shorebirds
South-East; Flyway, BirdLife International

V-formations of Grey Plover and Far Eastern Curlew lift, and in
a light following wind, head north. Yes, the Yangtze delta *was* a
gateway. It signposted the path to the discovery of the EAAF's
shorebird treasure house, the Yellow Sea.

In northern Jiangsu, on a fishing boat out of the old port of Lianyungang, the Yellow Sea is grey, its surface dotted white, and the air above slashed by red. The spring haze shrouds water pockmarked by plastic trash, and around us fishing boats of many kinds fly the Chinese national flag. Wooden skiffs ferry mum-and-dad crews to their fields of seaweed. Aboard polystyrene-hulled catamarans, deckhands pull in fine gillnets. Further out, steel offshore vessels trawl the sea and drag its floor.

We pull alongside one of the steel boats and for little money buy a bucket of seafood as the fishers extract it from the net. Mainly the bucket holds sea-floor mud prawns; there are a few whelks, a large mid-water prawn, and a single trigger fish barely the size of my hand. Rinsed and cooked, the mud prawns are eaten slowly and sociably. There is far more shell to peel than there is flesh, and it is still rankly silty.

As we head further out to sea, a ship appears. It is sunken; a token oil-spill boom floats freely around it and there is no sign of life. The North Korean flag is painted on its smoke-smeared funnel. Carrying coal from the closed state, the *Kum San* was turned away from Lianyungang a month earlier because of UN sanctions. At night it collided with a Chinese fuel tanker and sank within two hours, according to Reuters. All 27 crew were rescued and the tanker steamed on, claiming not to have suffered any damage.

Only the ship's funnel and derricks are visible above the surface. It rests out of a shipping lane and on the shallow sea floor, a symbol of the tense politics of this 458,000-square-kilometre embayment of the north-west Pacific.

Traversed clockwise, the Yellow Sea coast rises north from the Yangtze, indents towards Beijing at the Yellow River mouth in the Bohai Sea, turns east to a corner where China meets

North Korea, and descends along the west coast of the mountainous Korean Peninsula.

Mostly the sea is no more than 80 metres deep, and along the Chinese side of the 4000-kilometre coastline where the *Kum San* sat, very shallow water predominates. A 10-metre depth contour is drawn far offshore and tides range from 2 to 6 metres, exposing vast areas of sea-floor mud and sand. In the bays of its Korean Peninsula coast, where the tidal range can be 8 metres or more, there are similar broad shallows. By the time our boat trip ends the tide has fallen around 3 metres, leaving one wooden fishing vessel high and dry across a rock bank on a makeshift dry-dock.

A vast flotilla of fishing boats constantly sails out from Chinese ports to use the Yellow Sea. Many fly the red flag of China, and the throb of their diesels in the distance is an undertone to outdoor life. But people do not fish only by boat; they trudge out onto the flats at low tide to disentangle snared fish from labyrinthine net fences, and to dig bounty from the mud.

On the seawall near Lianyungang, a woman—wearing thigh-length rubber boots, belted blue jacket and yellow headscarf—parks her electric scooter. She nods her weather-beaten face at me, picks up a heavy hand rake and an empty white poly box with a rope handle; then she clambers down the wall. A small group are at work already on the mud, backs bent low, hacking away. She joins them, heaving the curve-tined rake and picking up revealed shellfish.

Later, a truckload of small bivalves in mesh bags passes by, a work crew riding on top of the bags. And later still, I walk among brick shanties of old Lianyungang, past a small seafood restaurant, its aerated tanks filled with snails, clams and winkles, seaweed, small crabs and sea slugs.

Around the hillside from this stall, China's romance with the sea is on vivid display at a sandy beach. Five white-gowned brides are being photographed with their grooms. Each couple occupies their own territory, a stretch of sand. One dressed in red, the traditional Chinese bridal colour, is arrayed on a rock shelf oblivious to waves splashing her dress. Beside the beach in a car park, souvenir stalls offer for sale romantic dreams of pure tropical waters far distant: sprigs of white coral, and big Baler shells.

The Yellow Sea and its mud is also home to Koreans, who use the term *Getbol* to describe the intertidal zone and its workday use (*Get* means coast and *bol* an open field). They employ similar rakes and hooks to capture shellfish, in what the Koreans describe as 'bare-handed' fisheries.

All of this marine wealth is created by two phenomena: nutrient-laden silt flowing down the major rivers, and the confluence of warm and cold currents offshore, which encourages fertilisation at the base of the food web. In their 'natural' state a thousand years ago, before China's deforestation and intensive agriculture, the Yangtze and Yellow rivers are thought to have delivered between them around 340 million tonnes of silt to the sea each year. This is just one-fifth of the level that poured down at the turn of this past millennium.

The river mouths themselves are constantly moving. The Yangtze's estuary progresses relentlessly east. Over the course of 6000 years (the blink of a shorebird's evolutionary eye), the Yellow River's delta has shifted up and down across more than 250 kilometres of coast, building up swathes of land as it discharges into the Bohai Sea, the north-western lobe of the Yellow Sea.

In winter, as cold winds howl down from the far north-west, pushing the sea with them, the Yangtze's seasonally low sediment discharge runs south. In summer this sediment turns up and across the Yellow Sea, under the influence of weak southerly winds and a warm current from Taiwan. The fertility of the Yellow River dominates the shape of the Bohai Sea. This river has been estimated to carry an average of 23.5 kilograms of silt *per cubic metre*, nearly all of it deposited in the Bohai rather than drifting out and south. Around the whole of the Yellow Sea's coast, more than 60 smaller rivers, having travelled across the plains of China or down the valleys of the Koreas, add their loads to the tidal shallows.

These days we can see this in easily accessed satellite imagery on the internet. Just as we can zoom in from above to check the shadowed shapes of our homes, we can follow the course of these rivers and see the mud swirling out from their mouths. But Google Earth only became available in 2001. Before then, the hunt for the best shorebird feeding grounds in all of Asia meant looking at paper maps.

———

'Two things were obvious to me when I arrived in Australia and started studying the spring migration on the East Asian–Australasian Flyway,' says engineer Jim Wilson, a British wader specialist who came to Canberra to live in the 1990s. 'Firstly the shorebirds on northward migration "disappeared" for a month. And secondly, although very few waders had ever been recorded along the north coast of the Yellow Sea, from a geographic consideration that is where they had to be.'

An early assessment of China's Yellow Sea possibilities was made in 1993 when the Asian Wetland Bureau's Taej Mundkur drew together scattered information on a dozen potential shorebird sites and found three potential super-sites of more than 200,000 birds.

When Wilson wanted to know more, he walked down to the National Library of Australia in Canberra, and asked to see maps of China and the Korean coast. Some were compiled by the US Army Map Service in the Korean War era. 'They were stamped "Secret", and so I had to sign the Official Secrets Act,' Wilson recalls. 'Then I spent the most exciting five days of my birding life, studying the maps and measuring the areas of mudflats. I couldn't believe what I found. It was obvious to anyone studying waders that here on the north coasts of the Yellow Sea must be the world-class staging areas as yet undiscovered. The whole area of tidal flat I measured in the Yellow Sea was twice the area of the European Wadden Sea, and the biggest area of mudflats in the world.'

Maps might show habitat, but they don't show birds. Proving their existence meant surveying the coast—actually walking the hundreds of kilometres of shoreline.

Tian Hou Wang began this pioneering work, painstakingly making his way up from Shanghai, along the coast of Jiangsu Province towards Lianyungang in the north. It was here that Wang and Barter came to see the Tiaozini–Dongsha mudflats. This is a vast intertidal zone in a corner of the Jiangsu Province coastline about 180 kilometres north of Shanghai. The onshore Tiaozini and offshore Dongsha shoals cover 266 square kilometres, enough space for a shorebird city. Here Wang and Barter found numbers that dwarfed the flocks of Chongming Dao.

At Tiaozini, Chinese birders led by Tian Hou Wang once counted over a period of two days 72,584 waders on northward migration, and 244,000 waders going south in the autumn. Birds are seldom counted on the hard-to-reach Dongsha, but have been seen there in great numbers.

CYA made a 1000-kilometre flight from Taiwan in early April to use Dongsha for nearly two months, sometimes venturing towards the Tiaozini coast.

We have been driven in a minibus to the edge of the Tiaozini seawall with expert Chinese bird guides to work the rising tide. The hard mudflats run out to a heat-shimmered horizon where, inevitably, fishing boats are at work. So flat and grey-brown are sky, mud and sea that the division is indeterminate. It's almost as if the boats are sailing across the flats.

We step down the seawall onto the flat and walk out half a kilometre. Between the boats and us, the bird clouds are gathering: Grey Plover, Bar-tailed Godwit and Dunlin by the thousand; Great Knot and Red-necked Stint in the hundreds, along with many smaller plovers. Among these flocks that rise and settle there is one species the birders are scanning and hoping for—a needle in these haystacks.

'I can see a Spoonie! I can see a Spoonie!' sings Nigel Pleass, a bank security specialist from Swindon in England. It is a 'mega-tick' for him, a bird he wants on his life-long list, and has spotted. Bubbling with excitement, he shares the sighting.

'On the right—three Kentish Plover. Further left, standing— one Sanderling. So he's just in a triangle formed by the three

Kentish Plover. He's got his head under his wing now with his back to us . . . There he is! Hopping on one leg now!'

Pleass offers his spotting scope to me just as the Spoon-billed Sandpiper unfolds a resting leg and busies itself around a puddle. It's impossibly cute. A tiny wind-up toy of a bird with a smiling spatulate black bill, jauntily rocking on bandy legs. At any moment it seems the clockwork might run down and the bird will gently roll over onto its side, revealing the winding key in its belly.

Spoonies once flew the length and breadth of Southeast Asia from their far-eastern Russia breeding grounds. Now they are rare, threatened and carrying the hopes of ornithologists that they might cut through to the public as a symbol of shorebird conservation, the way Giant Panda did for animals. The group counts eleven Spoonies out of the 30,000 or so birds on Tiaozini this day.

For me, a 'dude', a birding novice, it's the sheer numbers that leave me open-mouthed. The birds have settled far from us but as the tide rises they seem to feel hemmed in and take flight repeatedly, back and forth in front of us. This isn't a panicked rise, more of a precautionary lift, and its scale is immense.

These are great mixed-species flocks, in which the birds form a sweeping geometry of movement, silvering like light photons as they turn together. At one point they take on a flowing dragon shape as they fly along the waterline. At another moment they spread to fully occupy the wide sky in front of my eyes. After they land, I turn around to see that we are ringed at a distance by shorebirds. It is extraordinary to have so much fast-moving life settle around me, like breathing the heady oxygenated air that rises from a waterfall.

I wonder what Barter and Wang may have seen and felt decades before. Unlike us in our minibus, these pioneer birders not only had to walk long distances through watery plains before they reached the mud, they had to overcome layers of officialdom in order to unveil the shorebirds of the Yellow Sea.

When Tian Hou Wang made the first foray northward, beyond Jiangsu Province, he led a team from East China Normal University to survey the soft new mud gushing out of the Yellow River delta. Wang's group checked five sites in Bohai Bay, one of the three bays that comprise the Bohai Sea. This represented about 2 per cent of the total potential shorebird habitat in a delta that was itself expanding at the rate of 27 square kilometres each year.

Sloshing out as far as they could, they counted 80,905 birds in a limited area, meaning that across the delta there could be many more. Because of the difficulties of walking the mud, they could not often get down to individual species. I felt for Wang's team as I watched Shanghai's master bird guide, Lin Zhang, click a digital tally counter in each hand through thousands of look-alike birds at Tiaozini. Zhang is an expert in the art of counting multitudes of shorebirds fast, during the brief minutes when they are settled on the flat. He must sort one species from the other, and count thousands, or tens of thousands. I watch him rattling his tally counters like they are dice. That's 10 Grey Plover, 100 of them, ten times 100 of them! Now do that for another species. The concentration is superb.

———————

On the day in 1995 that Mark Barter turned 55 and became eligible for early retirement, he quit his job marketing zinc. From then on he devoted himself to shorebirds, and particularly to China. Finding the wader El Dorados meant walking the long and inaccessible coasts of the northern Yellow Sea, a task not only beyond him, but not his alone to do. So he went to work training the Chinese.

Twice a year, around peak migratory times, Barter and other foreigners led workshops to train Chinese students and birders to identify and survey local waders. They made sure to always include a complete count of the area. Starting at Chongming Dao, the teams worked their way around the Yellow Sea coast in a broadly clockwise direction to the border with North Korea, tallying the main shorebird sites as if time was ticking against them.

'He was a tall, thin guy, with very good legs,' Clive Minton says. 'So 20 or 30 kilometres of seawall in a day was no problem. I don't think I could have done that, even then.'

Sometimes Barter brought the Chinese back to his home in Melbourne, where his wife Terry remembers having five nationalities sleeping on the lounge-room floor at a time. 'They would come out and learn techniques of surveys and record keeping,' she says. 'A lot of them were young university students who weren't necessarily doing waders. He would teach them how to identify birds. He was very focused on techniques, because he believed that you should only collect data if you could use it.'

When Barter began on this ambitious new phase in his life with the Chinese, he first decided to follow Wang's tantalising early work and head for the Yellow River delta. He and Melbourne colleague Dale Tonkinson led a Chinese team slogging through swamps and reed beds to reach ten counting sites over 165 kilometres of coastline. They had to give up on some of the target areas because deep mud and extensive channel networks made it impossible to get through.

Still, they were able to count around 130,000 shorebirds over a two-week period. Calculating that these birds were likely to have halted on passage and be replaced by others, and that the survey covered only half of the available terrain, Barter thought the delta might support half a million shorebirds on northward migration.

'It is possibly the single most important site in the flyway in terms of numbers,' he concluded in a paper published in 1998. So rapidly were they finding important sites, it seems, that they were revising these conclusions about what mattered most even as they went.

He and Jim Wilson made it to the farthest north point of the Yellow Sea, the mouth of the Shuangtaizi River, western distributary child of northern China's 'Mother River', the Liao. Logically, they thought, this might be a gathering point for shorebirds readying themselves for the most expedient next 'long hop', to the Arctic.

The terrain was slightly easier, the mud firmer and access smoother. They found plentiful Great Knot, Dunlin, Bar-tailed Godwit and Grey Plover in the estuary, which was covered by the Shuangtaizihekou National Nature Reserve, established for the disappearing oriental symbol, the Red-crowned Crane. East of there, the Bohai coast ran south to the Liaodong Peninsula, and then around towards the North Korean border, where shorebird knowledge was nearly blank.

After the Shuangtaizihekou survey, the pair called in to the Beijing office of the NGO, Wetlands International, originally formed in Britain to protect waterbirds and newly expanding into wetlands biodiversity. In their office was a map of the known Chinese national nature reserves, including one that was hard up against the border with North Korea at the mouth of the Yalu River. 'Wetlands International knew little about this reserve at Yalu Jiang,' Wilson remembers. 'There were apparently no staff there. There were no records of any waders from there.'

He had already noted this area for attention, with a hunch there could be a great find there. And so it turned out to be. 'The first morning at Yalu Jiang, the air was filled with clouds of godwits. The next eight days' survey work showed us that we had discovered one of the major shorebird staging sites in the world.'

With a big tidal range on very flat ground, the fast-moving tide enlivens the mud at Yalu Jiang, and shorebirds were counted along a 60-kilometre length of coastline. Most were close to the river mouth where Great Knot, Bar-tailed Godwit and Far Eastern Curlew raced to feed. They found perhaps one-quarter of the total world breeding population for each of these species on these flats, which had gone unnoticed by China and unknown to the world until this count was made.

For Wilson, that was enough. 'I did not return to China after 1999,' he says. 'The surveys were great fun, but China was too polluted and crowded for me—and I never liked the crazy drivers. Also, the hypothesis of the 1998 paper was proved.'

Mark Barter kept on going, leading teams that drilled down into other corners of Bohai Bay, and re-counted the Jiangsu flats north of Shanghai. He was building a picture for his legacy publication, *Shorebirds of the Yellow Sea*, which gave detailed accounts of nearly 30 staging grounds on the Chinese coast and Korean Peninsula in a holistic survey of the sea and its birds.

He estimated two million shorebirds migrated northwards through the Yellow Sea, or around 40 per cent of all the birds on a flyway that stretches from Pakistan to the Philippines, and southern New Zealand to the Arctic Sea. Among them were 90 per cent of the breeding population of six species, including the Great Knot, Bar-tailed Godwit and Grey Plover. For these birds, the Yellow Sea was their most vital migratory sanctuary.

Barter died in 2011, taken by cancer to the grief not only of his family but of shorebird people around the world. Lei Cao, of the University of Science and Technology in Heifei, wrote that she and her group held their own thanksgiving day in his memory at their lab. 'We thank God for creating Mark to love the water birds of China! We thank Mark for what he has done for birds and wetlands for us, for China and the planet!'

Barter wrote in the foreword to his monograph: 'I've often asked myself the question: "Why do shorebirds fascinate me so much?"—especially when there's a gale blowing and I'm up to my ankles in mud. The best answer I've come up with is because they are such free spirits, living in some of the most beautiful places on earth; moving endlessly to feed and roost as the moon dictates the ebb and flow of the tide, and migrating from one side of the earth to the other to breed, in harmony with the sun.'

———

After the Hangzhou Bay halt near Shanghai, CYB is tracked flying up the Chinese coast again, past Tiaozini to the southern side of the Yellow River delta, where she stays a week before crossing Bohai Bay, and flying as far north as it is possible to go in the Yellow Sea—to the head of Liaodong Bay, at the Daling River mouth, next to Shuangtaizihekou Nature Reserve. She settles in for six solid weeks of fat-building. Tony Flaherty tracks her movements back and forth across the mud, and then inland across fish ponds, to a roost on the edge of a swamp.

In the Yellow Sea, Grey Plover will usually feed near, but not with, other birds. Here there is species regimentation in the mixed flock's progress down the tideline. I watch at the

Linhong River mouth as the ebb begins, and wave upon shimmering wave of birds fly in, silvering in the morning light like shoals of fish. They stretch and condense as an elastic, malleable organism. Avian liquid. They form into super-flocks, tear apart into smaller ones, break off into tiny groups and then all become absorbed into the mass again.

The haze, grey mud and low sun make it another sepia, monochrome day. Brighter colours are flattened, but nevertheless such a life-filled sight is overwhelming. As I stand on the bank, transported, I am brought back to earth by the sight of another tidal-flat fisherman. He walks out along the seawall and sits nearby smoking, waiting for the tide to fall so that he can tow out onto the mud a wooden sled with his gear.

In front of us, settling first into knee-deep water is the godwit advance party, bayonet-bills probing. Red Knot and Great Knot keep up, staying a little shallower. Greenshank and the beautiful Spotted Redshank roam constantly. There appears to be almost no dispute over ground between the different species. No pecking or wing-waving. Everyone is too busy feeding, except perhaps for the Far Eastern Curlew, which goes wherever it damn pleases, though not into another curlew's space.

Most of the birds flow down with the fast-receding tideline. Grey Plover tend to hunch and wait for these masses to move on, leaving clear ground. Their habit makes for slow birdwatching. Patient and distant, they spread out ready for prey to become apparent on clearer patches of mud. Poised, taking a tentative step and freezing, one knee crooked with the leg held up, and then darting in with chisel-billed certainty.

With the northern spring turning to summer and the sea warming, CYA at Tiaozini and CYB at Liaodong are 900 kilometres apart. But like most shorebirds in the Yellow Sea they undergo a common, synchronised transformation. This time it's not just fat they gain—it's plumage. Within striking distance of their birth grounds the Arctic breeders metamorphose.

The indistinct Curlew Sandpiper of southern Australia is barely recognisable now with its fresh chestnut head, breast and matching mottled back. The Red-necked Stint at last fulfils its descriptor. The Bar-tailed Godwit's previous grey-brown now colours up to a russet. The belly of the Great Knot mottles black-and-white, like a thrush's does. Red Knot vary between sub-species: the *piersmai* sub-species of north-western Australia turn a brick red, while the *rogersi* of eastern Australia and New Zealand become a paler fawn.

I see the change happening to Grey Plover. Their black wing-pits join as a band across the belly, and their dark plumage spreads up the throat. The sexes then diverge, most luxuriantly in the males. Their grey heads transform to hold an extravagant swathe of ermine-white feathers, carefully arranged like a close-fitting judge's wig. This finishes at the eye-line, where it sharply contrasts with blackened faces and chests. Female colouring is more silvered: the white mixed with grey, and less dark around the head. They are harder to notice, but still a very different bird. Slightly regal now, *Pluvialis squatarola* is almost ready for its other, Arctic life.

Seven
Perfectly suited

M-m-m-my turn now . . . I'm clinging to the door handle as the hair-raising Chinese traffic that repelled Jim Wilson comes at me.

Chinese minivan driver, Xiao Liu, with fierce, gritted teeth, expertly negotiates his way from Tangshan train station down a long highway chicane of tyre skid marks, black evidence of helter-skelter traffic, towards Nanpu.

'Ha-ha,' Liu chuckles, as we pass trucks that have crashed, one on top of the other, down an embankment. 'Two!'

Then more horn-hooting and weaving before Liu threads our path to a halt in an urban laneway between dust-covered apartment blocks, their windows barred. Liu seizes my case and races up flights of stairs to a steel door that opens to the wide grin of Chris Hassell.

Last seen on the shore of wild Yawuru Nagulagun/Roebuck Bay watching twinkling migrants head off through an indigo sky, here is Hassell counting as many of the same birds as possible amid the full force of Chinese industrialisation on the northern coast of Bohai Bay.

To get here I have left behind the Jiangsu coast and travelled north by train to the Global Flyway Network's Nanpu study site. Across inland Jiangsu Province, the 300 kilometres per hour express train sped through a rural past towards today's China. In blurred rice paddies, farmers still walked village paths, and small cemeteries stood in field corners. Anywhere there was a pond, a fisher, usually old, dipped a line into the water. It was a timeless meditation on the hopeful unknown below the surface as we rushed into the future.

Between the inland Tangshan railway station and Nanpu near the coast the impatient upward economic shift unfolded. Along the highway, Liu's van passed abandoned and crumbling peasant houses, decaying beside the more recent two up-two down village homes. These in turn had been emptied in favour of incarcerating apartment blocks nearer to the worksites. Small factories stood derelict, superseded by larger ones. A six-lane highway was half complete and closed, its concrete pylons untroubled by any bridgework, a row of street lights had nothing to illuminate. All this progress marched relentlessly towards the coast.

Next door to Nanpu is Caofeidian, a sprawling monument to the pace of early twenty-first century China. Originally there was a 5-square-kilometre island before dredges covered 142 square kilometres of the Yellow Sea with an economic development zone. So rapid and chaotic was Caofeidian's development that it became a poster-child for China's outpaced, failed investment: a 'rotten tail' project. Weeds grew in roadways; shops and services were absent for people living in unfinished apartment buildings.

Still there was industrial movement. Iron-ore ships unload at Caofeidian's port having travelled, like the birds, from north-western Australia. In a new growth phase, other ships would pump out liquefied natural gas piped in from the north-west too.

————

Caofeidian's port cranes rise to the east as Liu drives down to the shore as I ride along beside Hassell and his workmate, Adrian Boyle. A professional bird guide and field researcher, Boyle first came to shorebirds working with Maureen Christie in South Australia. He was excited, at the age of seventeen, by the tense spectacle of cannon-netting. Not so much now.

The two Australians will spend 55 days on end peering through the cold murk of northern Bohai Bay, searching each day for flags and coloured bands on birds' legs. Xiao Liu will be their reliable marshal and driver, like his father before him.

Down the road from Nanpu town to the coast, the Liu minivan bounces past a network of earth- or brick-walled shrimp-and-salt ponds stretching to the horizon. Here and there are state prisons, whose inmates must work on these ponds in a part of China where ice covers the sea rim from December to March.

At a corner of the road there is a shop dummy dressed as a uniformed cop—cap, red flag and all. Boyle scans for birds as we drive, and takes a verbal note: 'Godwits flying from Fake Policeman towards Prison Pond.'

The dummy has lasted for years but each time Hassell and Boyle have come back there has seemed to be a new set of real officials to deal with. Wrapped up in dark outdoor clothing and shouldering their spotting scopes, these two purposeful non-Chinese men do look strange enough to attract the attention of local security.

'When we first came in 2007, we were carted off by the police,' Hassell recalls. 'They couldn't work out what we were doing.' It took several hours of roughly translated questions, the discovery that their bird survey work coincided with a visit by a Chinese government minister, and a call to a Beijing university, to resolve their detention.

Hassell points out a fenced pond, white with alkali waste from a chemical factory. 'It comes in a pipe from the plant in town, and then gently leaks out onto the mudflat. Yesterday, with the wind from the sea, there was a cloud of white stuff blowing back into town.'

In past attempts to reach birds, the pair edged around the waste pile's fence, which is criss-crossed with barbed wire. 'A guy came along on his moped and we were like, "Yeah, the birds fly over there,"' Hassell says. 'A couple of days later another guy came, a policeman, and he said: "You've got to go." We said, "Yeah, yeah." Next time we came, a policeman appeared and said, "You've got to go," again. We said, "Yeah, yeah," and turned around. There was a police car with four policemen and a big Alsatian dog. So we went: "Oh, yes!"'

They don't go that way much anymore, but they are still commonly met with suspicion. I watch from the van as Boyle, squatting at his spotting scope and under tide-time pressure, is questioned by two port security guards while a twitchy third man dressed in military camouflage paces nearby. The officials eventually leave after giving a mild warning; they appear leery of Boyle's denial that he has any interest in the land installations of the offshore Jidong Nanpu oil and gas field that surround him.

Hassell and Boyle have climbed out of the van to survey an 8-kilometre stretch of seawall at their main Nanpu study site, their pace urged on by the tide. Instead of rising or falling straight out from the shore, the tide here helpfully washes through at an angle. Helpful, for those who are fit. I am quickly outpaced, struggling for energy.

The pair reminds me of the run-stop-search life of a feeding plover as they tag team along the seawall to keep up with the birds' movements over the wide mudflat. At low tide the birds are too far out and their bands and flags are undetectable; at high tide they are too close, and there is every chance they will take flight and move inland to roost on some remote wall in the labyrinth of salt ponds.

So each man jogs a few hundred metres and then stops, sets up the spotting scope and hunches into it, absorbed in the search for marks, while his companion runs past to take up a fresh position further along the wall. When they find a colour-banded or flagged bird, they must concentrate on *that* pair of legs among hundreds, a pair of legs that can easily become hidden in water, or by wind-blown feathers or mud, in air that is dusty, foggy and shiveringly cold.

It's intense work that doesn't end when the birds fly inland to the ponds. Then the Liu van will thread the network of bund-wall trails looking for roosts and high-tide feeding areas. Back in their flat at night, the pair then read out their findings in the same coded chant used by Hassell and Kerry Hadley in Broome.

Boyle: 'Chrisso, I have a Red.' That is, Knot. 'Yellow, lime, red, yellow, rog.' The leg band colours and the sub-species, *rogersi.*

Hassell, works through his laptop spreadsheets: 'Great Knot. Two, Yellow, Red, Blue, Yellow. Saw it very well. It was banded [in Australia] in 2007. You saw it here in 2014, I think, Ady. It was an easy bird today, right in front of me. That bird has had flags and bands on for ten years and it's been seen here twice. Whereas we've got birds that we've seen 60 or 80 times in Broome.'

At Nanpu, this is mostly the way they eke out the data. Something like a Spoon-billed Sandpiper is exciting. And occasionally a single day's work can dramatically show how critical the Bohai is to shorebirds.

In 2013, as they checked through the salt ponds, they came upon one impoundment with an astounding number of birds feeding on an explosion of brine shrimp and worms. They ran separate counts by samples—of total bird numbers and of species. In a flock estimated at 95,883, they counted 61,891 Curlew Sandpiper. That's something like one-third of this bird's known total flyway population, gathered at one time in a 3-square-kilometre pond.

But it is the critical value of this piece of coast to the Red Knot of the EAAF that is confirmed most strikingly when they do a count. Across their research area on a single mid-May day in 2018, they counted 48,630 Red Knot, or nearly half the total flyway population.

———

Shorebird science first came to Nanpu when Mark Barter led a team to survey the entire Bohai coast just after the turn of the century. He estimated the 300-kilometre rim might support 250,000 shorebirds, and found strong numbers in the bay's north, including at Nanpu.

Barter, always the bird science Pied Piper, took the chance to find young Chinese scientists eager to work on their home mud.

Students like 'Nicky' Hong-Yan Yang. 'Mark Barter! He's my guide, my star!' she says, holding his memory aloft years after his death. 'I love shorebirds. So cute!'

A Beijing-based biology school teacher and birder, Yang met Barter by chance at a conference on banding, and he later found work for her as a part-time Masters student. Her field work was at Nanpu, where she began counts from 2003, and four years later she started PhD work on Red Knot foraging under Theunis Piersma. This meant getting onto, and into, the soft mud.

'I am a tomboy!' she says. 'That's why I am a field-work woman. I have to go out exactly after the ice-cover period. It's really freezing cold. Sometimes we do the penguin movements to walk, sometimes riding a surfing knee-board, [so] we can 'fly' over the mud. I love the mud, because the whole benthic community is amazing. If you walk in the mud, it's so full of life. So dense. For every square metre there are maybe five crabs, and of course there are worms. But the whole Nanpu mudflat is shellfish.'

Only the top 4 centimetres of mud is accessible to a Red Knot's bill. In the absence of a feast, like that of the Horseshoe Crab spawning of Delaware Bay on the Atlantic Americas Flyway, this bird must find another high-energy food to process quickly if it is to make the flight up the EAAF to its breeding ground.

The Red Knot's life in Nanpu, and probably that of other shorebirds, depends on one particular morsel: the 2- to 7-millimetre bivalve *Potamcorbula laevis*. At Nanpu these can live in densities of many thousands of shellfish per square metre.

Under the guidance of Piersma, Yang worked on the role of 'Pot' in shorebird diets. She found that, at Nanpu, tiny Pot are so abundant and within reach that the Red Knot, when eating as fast as it could, can process them through their tough, shell-crushing gizzard three times faster than was previously predicted for this species. It is a neat energy bonanza.

Red Knot have pressure-sensitive corpuscles clustered in their bill tips and they use these to locate Pot. Piersma found that when a knot probes the mud, these sensors can feel the resistance of sediment that lies against a shellfish a few centimetres away, and then move in on it.

Hassell has watched fishers on the same mud taking a leaf out of the knots' book with bigger shellfish. The fishers poke a stick into the mud and feel for Razor Clams, before inserting a hooked wire to haul them up.

At Nanpu, as we watch, shell-fishing crews alight from a shallow-draft wooden boat and fan out to trudge through frigid thigh-deep water and sediment, each hauling a small rubber raft mounted with a suction pump. Yang believes the removal of larger shellfish by fishers lets the smaller Pot flourish, and benefits the Red Knot, known in Chinese as *Hóng fù bīn yù.* 'This is a very fragile balance with humans, but is very good for Red Knot,' she says.

In the course of 55 days of observation at Nanpu and nearby flats and ponds, Hassell and Boyle will sight, among a total of 669 known individual shorebirds, 265 Red Knot colour-banded in north-west Australia. A few of these birds will have multiple re-sight histories that tell of far travels through the flyway. A Red Knot, flagged YVA and banded in Yawuru Nagulagun/ Roebuck Bay, was seen over a few years in New Zealand, back in Yawuru Nagulagun/Roebuck Bay, then at the Nanpu study site, in New Zealand again, back at Nanpu, and lastly near the remote Russian coastal hamlet of Meinypil'gyno on the Bering Sea.

This kind of pinpoint data, together with repeat counts led by Nicky Yang, has found that nearly half of all Red Knot on the EAAF pass through Nanpu. And the driver of this phenomenon is a single, perfectly suited, high-energy shellfish.

Roused by Xiao Liu at 4 a.m., we drive down for a dawn scanning session on the Nanpu seawall. Again I gaze out upon the confounding Yellow Sea, at once vivid and indistinct. Ghosts of tankers and ore carriers loom in the early haze, as do Caofeidian's dockside cranes. Nearby, someone's business folly, a tropically themed two bungalow 'resort', is slowly sliding down the seawall. Trucks thump across a road bridge. Before us an incoming tide is bringing the birds close and they are nervous, lifting with each thump. They quickly settle again, working fast to take all they can out of the mud.

When the birds rise, I can hear them rustle in the still air, like wind-blown leaves. As the Red Knot flock wheels, their plumage is brightly lit by the sunrise, their rufous chests aglow. By turns, the different shorebird species depart the engulfed mud for the ponds behind us. Over my head pass four Eurasian Curlew, powerful with their broad white backs and deep speckled chests. A Grey Plover joins them for no discernible reason, except that often I seem to find my bird as outrider to others. Black wing-pits caught in the early light, long thin primary feathers comfortably astir, it heads inland. Sooner or later, it will then turn far north.

Eight

The white bear bird

With a sense of timing I find hard to grasp, CYA and CYB fly out of the Yellow Sea for the Arctic within a day of each other, although they are 900 kilometres apart. A summer solstice signal would still be weeks away. But in late May, the cold had given way to helpful warm breezes from the tropical south.

The satellite tag's beam, caught in Flaherty's computer in Adelaide, shows that at Tiaozini, furthest from the breeding ground, CYA joins birds picking an initial course across the sea towards North Korea. CYB, at the more efficient jumping-off point on the Daling River mouth, is in a flock striking out directly north. EarthWindMap shows CYA has an easterly abeam of her, but CYB has a southerly tailwind most helpful at around 1000 metres.

Each bird has had to build up enough fat in the Yellow Sea for another non-stop flight of a week or so if they are to reach their breeding grounds. Being female, they also need to gain enough nutrients at some time or other to produce offspring.

In female birds, microscopic eggs form, and are held, in their ovaries before enlarging just prior to laying. Big migratory geese may take on extra nutrients before their shorter flights to breeding grounds. They have these in store already as 'capital' for egg-laying when they land. Smaller, more finely calibrated shorebirds must rely on 'income'—that is, on food eaten after they arrive.

How do we know this? Tundra-based nutrients have a different signature from those of temperate-zone estuaries. The Dutch migratory bird ecologist, Marcel Klaassen, decoded stable-isotope ratios in the eggs and plumage of Grey Plover and other birds to show where in the world the birds had been eating.

Like millions of shorebirds closing on the Arctic around this time of year, the Greys' flight is timed to maximise their use of the breeding ground. Ideally, they will get there very soon after the snow has melted, in order to court and mate. A halt on the way, whether for food or storm-forced, might be to their cost. Just as CYB was preparing to leave Bohai, a Black-tailed Godwit, satellite-tagged there by Beijing Normal University's Bingrun Zhu, was shot near Yakustk on the Lena River, the great artery to the Arctic Sea. Zhu found this out thanks to a local naturalist, who made contact via Adrian Boyle, and eventually sent a photograph of a grandfatherly Russian hunter, proudly holding up the dead bird so that its transmitter and aerial were visible.

'Hunting may be common or traditional, but I don't see how much meat you could get from such a long-distance, tiny bird,' Zhu said in a Facebook post. 'Seeing a healthy bird released from my hand and dead in another's hand really upset me. I have nothing to say but tears.'

When I eventually cross paths with Zhu in the Nanpu apartment, he is still upset. 'That was me! So sad.'

Nor is this isolated. A few years earlier, a Sanderling migrating from South Australia was shot on the shore of Russia's Sakhalin Island as it headed north along the Pacific rim. We know because the hunter found a geolocator attached to the bird's leg, and eventually it was returned. I can only guess how many of the others were hunted down, and their bands and tags never sent back, the shooters and netters perhaps wary of officialdom, perhaps ashamed.

A few days after leaving the Yellow Sea, the Grey Plover are each still on widely separate courses. Having crossed North Korea, CYA is being pushed along by strong southerlies as she flies inland and parallel to the Sikhote-Alin Mountains of Russia's Pacific coast, stronghold of the Siberian Tiger. CYB is further ahead, flying into light headwinds inland in the Sakha Republic and closer to the course taken by the shot godwit—perhaps using the Lena River as a mark while she crosses the taiga forest, a vast country of itself.

'Sib Ir', the sleeping land, as the Tatar people called it, holds in the taiga a rolling blanket of pine, spruce and fir and on a scale only matched on these birds' flights by the stretches of Australian deserts. Each expanse is nearly desolate of towns and highways; they are natural landscapes, but hostile to shore-birds. In this way these birds, replenished on the rim of the industrialised world, leave that imprint behind and fly into the wild. As they travel, daylight grows longer. Through whatever darkness they encounter, Polaris, the North Star stands ever higher above them with the rising latitude, as do the magnetic field lines.

CYA turns north-east over the taiga near the Sea of Okhotsk. Flying on for several days, she crosses CYB's path as their flocks thread the 3000-metre Verkhoyansk and Chersky mountain ranges, ramparts of the Russian Far East. The birds of hot Australian summers now overfly unmelted snow cover on these mountains for hundreds of kilometres. They traverse deciduous larch forests, greening with the spring as the altitude lowers, and then fading away before the polar wind's onslaught into treeless tundra. Dicing now with the thaw, the two birds halt near the coast of the Arctic Sea. Their flight lines, begun in far distant southern Australia, now sing of home.

CYA alights from her Tiaozini flight on a mosaic of spongy sphagnum bogs and pools divided by low ridges, inland and south of the Arctic Sea's New Siberian Islands. The closest human habitation is the small village of Yukagir, 100 kilometres to the north-east on the frozen shore of Laptev Sea.

The Yukaghir people, ancient Indigenous hunters and reindeer herders of the Kolyma River region, are animists. In their world, 'persons' can take a variety of different animal forms, of which a human being is only one. Even objects such as sleds may be accorded lives.

A Danish anthropologist, Rane Willerslev, lived and hunted with the Yukaghir. 'An elderly Yukaghir hunter, Vasili Shalugin, told me that animals, trees, and rivers are "people like us" because they move, grow and breathe, but they are distinct from inanimate objects such as stones, skis and food products, which he claimed are alive but immovable.' Like many northern cultures, they pay particular attention to 'certain species of birds, most notably the raven [which] may be thought of as persons'.

Now much reduced, the Yukaghir once lived across lowland tundra and into the forests across thousands of kilometres from

the Lena River to the Pacific coast. Those still living traditionally hunt birds like the hen-sized ptarmigan, ducks, geese and
swans. Probably the greater danger to shorebirds lies in Yukaghir
reindeer herds. Browsing the tundra moss, these may step on
nests and will relish a snack of an egg or unfledged chick.

CYB, having taken a more easterly bearing after crossing
the mountains, first comes to ground inland and south of CYA.
Then, after a pause, CYB flies off to low-shrub moss tundra
near the mouth of the Kolyma River, which drains most of
eastern Siberia.

Across Kolyma Gulf at Ambarchik stands a ghostly relic of
the twentieth century. In the eons of migratory bird history it is
a mere wing flick, a transient curiosity. It's the decaying remains
of a Soviet Gulag-era forced-labour transit camp, a coastal port
for prisoners before they were transported inland up the Kolyma.
Today there's an automatic meteorological station at Ambarchik and its records show that a day or two after CYB lands,
warm air from the south brings a sunny 22 degrees Celsius day,
doubling the temperatures of the previous week.

The two Greys, depleted though they must be, do not stay
to breed on this coast. A westerly wind blows up and as the
enthralled Flaherty and Christie watch the satellite tracks, first
CYA and then, about a day later, CYB, take flight again. They
head out over hundreds of kilometres of Arctic Ocean ice to the
unpeopled last home of the extinct Woolly Mammoth. Wrangel
Island is their final destination.

So these two Grey Plover are birds of extreme shores. Their
paths have been parallel, and each stretches from exactly the
same place in the far south of Australia to its counterpart far
north in the Arctic. Just as there is the Southern Ocean below
South Australia, there is no land between Wrangel and the

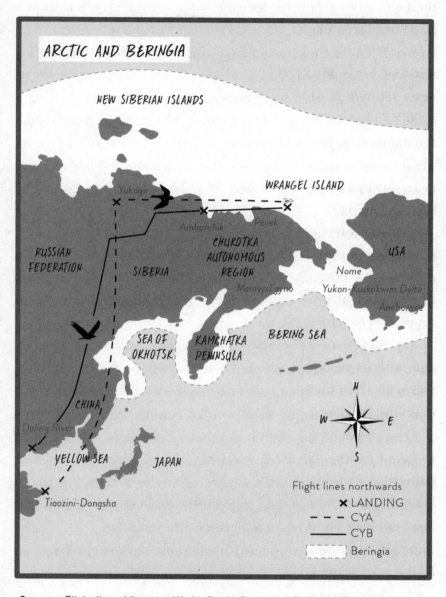

ARCTIC AND BERINGIA

NEW SIBERIAN ISLANDS

Yukagir

WRANGEL ISLAND

Ambarchik   Pevek

RUSSIAN
FEDERATION   SIBERIA   CHUKOTKA
AUTONOMOUS
REGION   USA

Nome
Meinypil'gyno   Yukon-Kuskokwim Delta

Anchorage

SEA OF
OKHOTSK   KAMCHATKA
PENINSULA   BERING SEA

CHINA

Daling River   N

YELLOW SEA   JAPAN   W   E

Tiaozini-Dongsha   S

Flight lines northwards
✖ LANDING
– – – CYA
——— CYB
Beringia

Sources: Flight lines, Victorian Wader Study Group and Friends of Shorebirds
South-East; Flyway, BirdLife International; Beringia, *The Beringian Land and Bridge*,
S. Elias and B. Crocker

North Pole. In this way, does the web of ultramarathon shore-bird travel bind us.

For CYA, the long jump from the Yellow Sea across Russia has been a sapping 6140 kilometres. CYB hints again that she is more efficient, with a more conservative 4835-kilometre flight. Satellite fixes of these dates are inexact, but probably each landed around 5 to 6 June. After flying separately all that way from the weedy shores of Thompson Beach, which they left months before, the two birds likely fold their wings at Wrangel within a day of each other.

To my greater amazement, only a few days earlier the island is released from the grip of snow. NASA Worldview satellite records show the land turning brown. What knowledge can these birds have that their unseen breeding ground, still surrounded by sea ice, will be ready for them?

In many recent years, Wrangel has still been mostly snow-covered at this time of the year. Perhaps the summer air signal back on the Siberian shore was decisive. Maybe the birds have the confidence of evolution, of countless failures before success, implying an ingrained genetic judgement. Or are they programmed to dice with survival? In any case, this tracked journey is the first direct evidence of any bird from Australia ever flying to Wrangel, and powerfully shows the breakthrough satellite telemetry gives to migratory bird science.

'This was one of the most memorable days in 40 years of wader migration studies in Australia,' Clive Minton concluded.

Previously, researchers had relied on morphometrics, the study of a species' dimensions, to assemble a possible link for Grey Plover between Wrangel Island and far-distant south-eastern Australia. The case of these birds is a cautionary story on the value of morphometrics—one about denying potential overreach.

Its first chapter was compiled over decades of bird-skin collecting for museums. Its second was a landmark analysis of geographical variation among shorebirds. Dutch ornithologists Meinte Engelmoer and Cees Roselaar measured the skins of 264 Grey Plover, from all of their circum-Arctic breeding ranges, and found enough differences between them to suggest they should be split into three sub-species. The main type was *Pluvialis squatarola*. But they thought there were enough differences in birds from two particular breeding grounds to make of them distinct sub-species: *Pluvialis squatarola cynosurae* (the eye-catching beauty) from Northern Canada and *Pluvialis squatarola tomkovichi* from Wrangel. The latter was found to have a slightly shorter bill and leg length, and a noticeably longer wing.

Though honoured with the name, Russia's Pavel Tomkovich warned against too much reliance on the use of morphometric tools for reaching conclusions about birds' homes. 'There is a long way to go before it can be used reliably for a sound identification of wader origins,' he had said.

It was here that the study of Australian Grey Plover breeding grounds lay until Clive Minton and Italian researcher Lorenzo Serra took it on. This time, examining the measurements of 399 live birds caught with cannon nets, they found bill and wing lengths of many Grey Plover from north-western Australia were distinctly different from those of the south-east. Enough south-eastern Australian birds had the slightly shorter bills and longer wings to suggest some kind of link with Wrangel.

The island's remoteness meant it was years before Tomkovich could reach Wrangel, where few shorebirds had ever been measured or banded. In 2007, after waiting a month in the bleak port of Pevek for an on-again, off-again helicopter flight, he made it. Tomkovich's primary focus was the Red Knot, but he and Alexei Dondua caught and measured 30 Grey Plover adults at their nests. They confirmed, in an admittedly small sample, that Wrangel's Grey Plover had an average wing length several millimetres longer than usual for the bird.

They also managed to fix a total of 232 shorebirds, including 63 Grey Plover, with leg bands and Wrangel's own pale-blue-over-white leg flags. The first sightings off the island of any of these flags fitted the evidence that pointed Wrangel's shorebirds towards the Pacific Americas Flyway. In the following year, two flagged Red Knot were seen at Grays Harbour, Washington State, and at a lagoon in Baja, California. As for the Grey Plover, six years passed before a signal flung out into the dark from Wrangel bounced back.

A deeply experienced EAAF specialist, David Melville, was standing on a seawall south of the Jiangsu fishing port of Lianyungang in 2013, scanning birds that were using a shell bank as a high-tide roost. He glimpsed a Grey Plover wearing light-blue-over-white leg flags, probably on its right leg. The bird flew off soon after it was sighted. Because of the likely leg position—Wrangel shorebird chicks were tagged on the right tibia—Tomkovich was able to say this bird was caught and tagged on the high Arctic tundra in Wrangel's central north, near the Neizvestnaya (Nameless) River. That brief sighting by Melville was the only one of a Wrangel flag ever seen on a Grey Plover away from the island. It backed up the morphometrics, but at that stage remained just a tantalising suggestion.

Now there was proof of the tracked flights of two birds, from the same southern summering ground, reaching the same remote breeding ground at the same time. And the cautionary note? When measured at Thompson Beach, neither CYA nor CYB had longer than usual wings.

'Those Grey Plovers in South Australia, they were almost an accident,' Minton reflects. 'It was a second-choice bird. But science is like that. You ask a question, you get an answer to it. So you ask another question. If you are flexible and pragmatic, you can read the signs, you know which way to follow.

'And they gave us a wonderful ride. They kept going and stopping, going and stopping, and finally at the northern Siberian coast you think, 'Right, this is just where many others went.' Then two or three days later, they tootle off to Wrangel Island! That, of course, is what lit this whole thing up.'

It also lit me up. A journey to a place as distant, and as hard to reach, as Wrangel spoke for itself. I resolved to try to see it.

I found a small tour company that runs a few voyages to Wrangel late each summer in a small icebreaker out of the Chukotkan port of Anadyr. The tour company agreed to give me a berth in return for newspaper travel stories if I could reach Anadyr. I booked to fly via Moscow where the Russian shorebird patriarch, Pavel Tomkovich, would see me.

The reading of runes from satellite plots and weather data might be overtaken: this way I could have a ground truth at the nest.

About the same time of year that the Grey Plover began their flight from the Yellow Sea to Wrangel, just after I came back from China, I went to my city hospital's emergency department. The back pain I had put down to travelling on uncomfortable bus seats had intensified to take hold of my chest on the left side. I was cleared of heart attack and began taking antibiotics. Perhaps I might have a respiratory disease picked up in China.

My inability to keep up with Chris Hassell and Adrian Boyle on the seawall had not just been poor fitness after all.

A series of follow-up tests ruled out respiratory problems, and a blood clot, but led to the discovery of a small primary cancer at the top of my right lung. Then a truly terrifying positron emission tomography (PET) scan showed many secondaries. The largest was eating its way into my spine, sending nerve pain around my chest. They collectively shone inside my torso from groin to collarbone like baubles on a spectral Christmas tree. I was at stage four of lung cancer.

'Andrew, you have an incurable disease,' the respiratory physician told me, as he showed the scan to me and my wife, Sally. 'Statistically, you have 12 to 18 months,' he said. 'But no one is a statistic. Andrew, can you hear me? Can you hear me?'

I descended into a dark winter, falling for months into a haze of mortal pain and painkillers. If there was any time that I needed science to work for *me*, for hard-won life-giving data to be joined together, this was it.

I kept my sanity, thanks to Sally's love and the close kindness of many, while science began to answer my call. I thanked my luck to be living in a world of freely available first-class health care; near a city just big enough to have the best, but not so big as to have lost the collegial eye of personal medical networks. I was encouraged by medical friends to break a taboo, and went straight to palliative care. Here my pain was managed with scientific diligence, finely balancing my needs with drugs. Delayed for weeks by circumstances, I anxiously waited for treatment against the cancer.

'Think about your birds,' Sally said. And so for solace, I sought them out. Through wakeful, fearful nights, I lay remembering the mesmerising flocks in the Yellow Sea. I reconstructed the flights I had seen; their living freedom. I rewound the ritual of the godwits' excited departures, striking out over Yawuru Nagulagun/Roebuck Bay Marine Park in their awesome flights north. Further back I went, to recall details of the catches at Thompson Beach, to the stillness in the human hand of the Grey Plover, those most wild, faraway birds.

I held onto my first sight of a Grey Plover, of the Peter Pan bird standing off from others near a sand bar at Thompson Beach, its feet in the water. There was always something in that moment of J.M. Barrie's story that resonated for me. Peter is a careless, mischievous boy. His power of flight is lost to injury, and he stands on Marooners' Rock as it submerges on a rising tide. With the water lapping around him, he is defiant, ambivalent; but decides: 'To die will be an awfully big adventure.' Then he is rescued by the Never Bird.

I looked to the profound migratory power of my bird, the Grey Plover, to inspire my survival.

———————

Shorebirds migrating from Australasia converge in the Yellow Sea with birds flowing in from a flyway that stretches between India and the Philippines. They are like iron filings, all drawn to a magnet. Then the seasonal polarity switches and they scatter north into a near-hemispheric array of nesting grounds. The great flocks radiate out to ever smaller groups spanning the broad head of their flyway, as if trying to escape most of their kind.

Some don't fly as far as the Arctic, but this is not apparently a matter of size. The biggest migratory wader of Australia, the Far Eastern Curlew, has been caught summering at Inverloch in Victoria, and again when laying eggs near the Amur River in north-eastern China. The 75-gram Greater Sand Plover that lives through a Broome summer prefers another hot land, the Gobi Desert of Mongolia, for breeding.

But the elfin Australian shoreline runner, the Red-necked Stint, flies to the mountain slopes of the Chukchi Peninsula on the Bering Strait. One was also shot 2500 kilometres west, near the riverside settlement of Saskylakh in the Sakha Republic, inland of where CYB alighted on the shore of the Arctic's Laptev Sea.

Other shorebirds nearly as small as the stint have a surprising appetite for travel. A Curlew Sandpiper banded at Melbourne's Western Treatment Plant was trapped again mid-breeding season on the Taimyr Peninsula of north central Siberia. Sanderling from the ocean beach at Canunda, South Australia, have been followed to the Arctic Sea's greatest river delta, the 29,000-square-kilometre mouth of the Lena. Other Sanderling land in an apparent shorebird mecca, the New Siberian Islands, where Red Knot of the *piersmai* sub-species also breed, as do Ruddy Turnstone from Tasmania's King Island.

The glamour bird of EAAF migration, the Bar-tailed Godwit, ranges far across the Arctic. Bar-tails of the *menzbieri* sub-species fly between Broome and the north Siberian coast. The *baueri* sub-species prefers tracking between New Zealand, eastern Australia and Alaska. Many of these *baueri* birds use the Yukon Delta, which flows into the North Pacific; but one, banded in 2002 at Corner Inlet in Victoria, was trapped with a hand net 1200 kilometres past the Yukon, near the Ikpikpuk River of Alaska's North Slope.

Geolocator and band recoveries, together with flag sightings, make up most of the evidence for these journeys. Not as much data has come yet from satellite transmitters, limited as they have been by the inability of smaller birds to carry them, their finite battery life and technical faults like inaccurate positioning. But more and more tracks are coming and, as they do, there is a growing strength to this scribing of lines on Google Earth, to our godly watching from above. There is a magnetic immediacy to it.

'When you can see a bird moving around on the tundra on Wrangel Island, as it's doing it, and you're sitting in Melbourne or Adelaide or whatever, it's just something that I find especially exciting,' Minton says. 'And I think many people around the world do too.'

For me, who has been riveted over the decades by the tracks of Wandering Albatross, Great White Shark and Minke Whale, the Grey Plover tracks mean much more. I am not just seeing their line of a journey. Remote sensing now means I can look into the detail of their lives even as they fly. It's like being the only person in a crowd to know there is a special sight in front of us all; a privileged knowledge of the earth.

Through an Adelaide winter, in the evenings after work, Tony Flaherty turns to his two birds' daily movements in the emerging summer on Wrangel. CYA chooses moist tundra near the Tundrovaya River, not far from Pavel Tomkovich's study site. This ground was the first to clear of snow. Her transmitter's fixes quickly show close faithfulness to the nest site, as she settles amid the very low grasses and mosses of a gentle slope facing north to the pole.

As for CYB, her fixes show something close to panic. The wiser flier is having great trouble settling down. At first she reconnoitres valleys and mountains in the south-west of the island, testing the limits of its coastal margins but always coming back to one particular tundra valley. Then she suddenly takes off for Wrangel's north-east and dithers there in the still snowy uplands, before flying back again to where she started in the south-west. Nearly two weeks after arriving, she finally settles near the Gusinaya River. Driven perhaps by a search for a mate, by rivals for sites, or by predators, CYB now lags in the seasonal race to breed.

———

These are the wildlife moments of Wrangel. The tilted ovoid island stands astride Eastern and Western hemispheres at exactly 180 degrees longitude—here the International Date Line is displaced to the east so it does not bisect the island. Wrangel is a 7600-square-kilometre relict of Beringia, the enigmatic landmass that connected Siberia with Alaska in the last glacial era. As the ice melted and the sea level rose around 10,000 years ago, the island separated, and an ecosystem stayed with it.

On the mainland at this time, Pleistocene-era animals like the Woolly Rhinoceros and Woolly Mammoth were disappearing. The latest rhinoceros found on Wrangel are 30,000 years old, but mammoths survived on its plant life until as recently as 4389 years ago. They became the last of their species on earth before succumbing, not to lack of food, or hunters, but to genomic meltdown—they were too inbred. As they dwindled, genetic damage was signalled by their particularly shiny, satin coat of translucent hairs. It was inferior to the thick, rough hair that a mammoth needed. Pavel Tomkovich wondered whether the danger of narrow island genetics might also face Grey Plover on Wrangel when he found that 17 per cent of eggs had dead embryos or were infertile.

Some 700 years after the mammoth era, the first people to arrive on the island, Paleo-Eskimos, probably worked their way out over the sea ice. They were hunters of walrus, seal and waterfowl. Russian archaeologist Nikolai Dikov uncovered their stone knives and blades, and a walrus-tusk harpoon head dated at 3360 years ago, on rocky headland at Devil's Gorge in the island's south-west. In this dig there was evidence of human occupation for about 500 years; then the Indigenous record went silent. It's since been partly reconstructed by linguist Michael Krauss. He thinks the island was used into the nineteenth century as a waypoint by Chukchi and Iñupiat peoples, who travelled over the sea ice between Siberia's Chukotka and far northern Alaska, and spoke a common language.

To Russian and European explorers of the north, Wrangel had about it the kind of fabulousness held by Terra Australis Incognita in the south. Relying on local stories, repulsed by ice and fog, they tried to get through to a rumoured land. The Russian Baron, Ferdinand von Wrangel was repeatedly driven back, as was the British Vice Admiral, Henry Kellett, who sighted what he named Plover Island, after one of his ships. It fell to the revered Scottish–American naturalist, John Muir, founder of its national parks, to describe the first landing upon what he called the 'Land of the White Bear'.

In August 1881, the US Revenue Cutter, *Corwin*, made several attempts to break through the sea ice past roaming Polar Bears, including three that were shot from the ship for sport, to Muir's clear anger. 'How civilized people, seeking for heavens and angels and millenniums, and the reign of universal peace and love, can enjoy this red, brutal amusement, is not so easily accounted for,' he wrote. 'Of all the animals, man is at once the worst and best.'

Briefly ashore in 'Wrangel Land' and under threat of the *Corwin*'s besetment in the ice, Muir collected some nearby coastal plants: a short grass, some golden and white star saxi-frages. Mostly, in the small area he examined, Muir described a 'feeble' tufted tundra vegetation of mosses and lichens. If he had been granted time to wander the island, Muir would have found himself nearer heaven. Wrangel's 417 different vascular plants are double that of any comparable Arctic tundra territory. Set as it is in a zone of climate collisions, the island encounters the Siberian continental wind, which aided our migrants, but it also receives cold and dry Central Arctic airs from the north, plus wet, warmer cyclonic air masses that invade through the Bering Strait from the Pacific.

The *Corwin*'s ornithologist, Edward Nelson, hurriedly counted bird life, including Pacific Golden Plover, on what he called the 'dreary shore'; but the expedition arrived late for many shorebirds. In fact, 62 bird species nest on Wrangel.

Half-hearted attempts at settlement were made later by Canadian and American colonists until the Soviet Government moved in and stayed through to the mid-1990s, when the new Russian Federation could no longer support access. Few people alive today have lived a year there, let alone watched its birdlife. One is a Queensland marine scientist, Katya Ovsyanikova. At the age of twelve she went to Wrangel with her wildlife-biologist parents, and they stayed isolated through the polar winter, her mother working on Snowy Owl, her father on the bears.

'In the autumn, those that can leave, all leave, like the birds,' Ovsyanikova says. 'As a young person it was a bit of a shock because we were very isolated, just stuck with each other for winter months. But I did fall in love with the island, surely.'

During her family's isolation they moved between research-ers' huts, watching out for occasional wolves that follow reindeer to the island, and for the bears, of which Wrangel has the highest natural density anywhere.

'We were encountering Polar Bears all the time, so I wouldn't say I had any fear of them,' she says. 'The rules of behaviour are just showing the bear in the body language that you are more dangerous. Never run away. Never even walk away. Stand your ground, be confident. Even a bear spray—in twenty years, Nikita, my father, has had to use it three times. It's the ultimate final resort, which always works.'

In the spring, when the birds came back, Ovsyanikova recalls seeing many waders: Ruddy Turnstone, Red Knot and Dunlin, and the shorebird that to her was big by Wrangel's standards: Grey Plover. Rare among people, she was there when the birds first arrived for courtship and egg-laying.

I am excited at the prospect of what she may have seen of this ritual step in renewal of the line, but she does not recall it. 'I was a young teenager,' she explains.

———

Arctic shorebird discovery is a narrative of fortitude, failure and rivalry as romantic as any other polar exploration. One of its prizes was the nest of the Grey Plover, which I wanted to see for myself. It's one thing to imagine remotely what's happening at the centre of radiating satellite plot lines. It's another to be on the tundra, to feel the landscape, and to see the hope of its future in front of my eyes.

The day I'd been due to fly out for Anadyr, I was instead lying on a bench looking up through cherry-blossom branches at a blue sky. It was an image on the ceiling of the radiotherapy room at the hospital. As I lay flat and still, with spots newly tattooed on my chest to line up the target, the x-ray zeroed into the secondary tumour on my spine.

Treatment, and its physical costs, spooled out after that. The first chemotherapy infusion was followed by a multiple pulmonary embolism, a shower of blood clots that left me hospitalised and gasping. For months I was addled by pain medication. When these effects began to abate, and the chemotherapy took hold, I started to research who had been to the Arctic before, and to imagine that I might still be able to touch some of the same ground.

Inevitably, these foreign explorers relied on the skills of Indigenous guides, who saw these birds as a naturally regarded part of their world, and named them so. The music of the Indigenous names for birds resonates across the Arctic, often interchangeably between First Nations, many of which had no use for a detailed written language. Instead, descriptive terms are lyrical approximations of the birds' calls, or of their plumage. A few broadly describe all tundra plovers, but most are distinct to a species.

North American First Nations' names have been most assiduously collected, and similarities between them stretch from Hudson Bay across the breadth of the continent to the Yukon Delta. Among Arctic 'Esquimaux' of the far north-east in the mid-eighteenth century a plover was called *Atuudlack*. Soon after, the Inuit of northern Hudson Bay used a cheery *Toolee-areeoo* or *Tooglee-aiah* to describe our bird. More recently, further down the bay at Chesterfield Inlet, they referred to the Black-belly as *Tull'iuk*. Across the continent at its north-west corner, Point Hope Iñupiat people called it *Tuligaq*. Further north at Utqiagvik/Barrow, a mid-twentieth century schoolteacher recorded the Iñupiaq language's *E-lak-tal'lik*. Down the Bering

Strait coast of Alaska, King Island Iñupiat have a similar name for it: *Ilik-taat-tuqhiq*—the scorched feathers bird. Further south on the Yukon Delta, a series of the Central Yup'ik peoples' names have been transcribed: *Tulee-huk*, *Tuyik* and *Tuligaq*.

So much more attractive than the bird's plain English name, these Indigenous words circle enticingly around my tongue. Who wouldn't want to hear *Toolee-areeoo* on the tundra, or search out *Ilik-taat-tuqhiq* on its nest?

Lighting up my imagination is one more name. In the late eighteenth century, a Hudson's Bay Company fur trader, Andrew Graham, collected a description attributed to 'the Indians'—either the Cree people or, more likely, the more northerly Chipewyan who fought with the Iñuit. This name speaks of the bird's true home, the domain of the great Arctic predator. They called it *Wapuska-Apeth-ey-shish*—the White Bear Bird.

From his fort at the southern end of the bay, Graham described seeing large flocks in the marshes in May and again in September, before the White Bear Bird left entirely: 'They build no nest only making a hollow in dry moss on barren ground,' he wrote in his *Observations on Hudson's Bay*. 'They fly only a short distance at a time.'

Around the same time, another Hudson's Bay Company explorer, Samuel Hearne, said 'plovers' were commonly called Hawk's Eyes. He was most interested in their use as food. 'They generally feed on insects, and are at all times good eating, but late in the Fall are most excellent,' Hearne wrote. 'I am informed that at Albany Fort, several barrels of them are annually salted for winter use.'

Whichever tundra plover these birds were, Hearne knew of their migration. He reached their breeding grounds on an overland snowshoe journey to the Arctic Sea at the mouth of the Coppermine River in July of 1771, apparently after their chicks hatched and too late to describe a nest. 'This bird during summer resorts to the remotest northern parts, though in those dreary regions only in pairs. The young of those birds always leave their nests as soon as hatched, and when but a few days old run very fast; at night, or in rainy weather, the old ones call them together and cover them with their wings, in the same manner as a hen does her chickens.'

Back at the fort, Andrew Graham encouraged the Cree and Chipewyan to bring in bird skins with their furs, to be sent to the Royal Society in Britain. As many young scientists discover, work they might call their own can sometimes be claimed by others with little apparent regard. In Graham's case, observations on north-eastern Canada's shorebirds turn up in the 1785 books, *Arctic Zoology I & II*, drawn together by Thomas Pennant, a wealthy Welsh naturalist who never reached the Arctic.

Pennant's portrait by Thomas Gainsborough is of a relaxed and enlightened man in a sylvan setting, holding his book in the crook of his arm, and with the hint of an icy mountain behind him. 'Multitudes of birds retire to this remote country [Hudson Bay], to *Labrador*, and *Newfoundland*, from places most remotely south, perhaps from the *Antilles*, and some even of the most delicate little species,' Pennant wrote. 'Most of them, with numbers of aquatic fowls, are seen returning southward, with their young broods, to more favorable climates. The savages, in some respects, regulate their months by the appearance of birds.'

Pennant knew the Grey Plover already from its non-breeding life in Britain, and had first described it in his book, *British Zoology II*, published in 1776. 'These appear in small flocks in the winter time. Their flesh is very delicate.' In *Arctic Zoology*, he dressed it in breeding plumage, and added: 'very common in *Sibiria*; and appear in autumn in flocks after breeding in the extreme north.'

Sorting the tundra plovers from each other, and from birds like lapwings, took early ornithologists some time. The Scottish–American, Alexander Wilson, who was a forerunner to John James Audubon, in 1808 found the Black-bellied Plover, as North Americans by then preferred to call it, 'abounding on the plains of Long Island in the Fall . . . They have a loud, whistling note; often fly at great height, and are called by many gunners along the coast the Black-bellied Killdeer.'

Wilson favoured its Hudson Bay nickname of Hawk's Eye, 'on account of its [visual] brilliancy', and he introduced a new claim: 'it seems particularly attached to newly-ploughed fields, where it forms its nest of a few slight materials'.

If Wilson is right, the ultimate Arctic native once bred in more temperate agricultural lands. But surely it's a mistake. There is no small resident lapwing to be confused with in North America, but there is the widely distributed Killdeer, a roughly similar-sized plover with the piercing cry of its name.

Audubon himself thought along the same lines as Wilson. 'I have traced this species along the whole of our eastern coast, and beyond it to the rugged shores of Labrador [Newfoundland]', Audubon wrote in *The Birds of America*, 'where my party procured a few, on the moss-covered rocks, although we did not then find any nests, and where some young birds were obtained in the beginning of August. Individuals of this species spend the summer months in the mountainous parts of Maryland, Pennsylvania, and Connecticut, where they breed.'

Regardless of this, Audubon's painting of the bird is a fluid and masterly family romance, instantly appealing to the

ordinary heart as is so much of his art. In the background, a
female is alert in non-breeding plumage. At centre is a breeding
male with scallop-feathered back and jet-black belly, bowing
low in a broken-winged predator decoy posture. Ahead of both
is their future: a dun-coloured fledgling, all legs and smile.

Grey or Black-bellied, for me, there is more revelation in the
extraordinary breadth of Indigenous names for this bird. They
speak of an appreciation of its special character across its wide
northern domain. Today's accepted common names tell only of
stubborn parochial scientific divisions.

The search for the little grail—for the first discovery of a Grey
Plover nest—was won by the Russian naturalist, Alexander von
Middendorf. He went to the Taimyr Peninsula of central Siberia,
aided by nomadic Nenet reindeer herders, and nearly perished
when he struck out alone in the cold. On the endless tundra
plains south of the peninsula, beside the Boganida River, he
found Grey Plover 'on the 26th of June [1843], still sitting on
its nest of lichen and leaves, in which there were four eggs'. He
knew this had not been described before by a naturalist, so
he measured the eggs to the millimetre, described their colour as
'yellowish-grey, now brown-yellow', and moved on.

The modern authority on Arctic birds, Richard Vaughan,
was in no doubt Middendorf was the first to discover the Grey
Plover's nest. Vaughan rejected claims made 32 years after
Middendorf by the British ornithologists Henry Seebohm and
John Harvie-Brown. But Middendorf's is such a dry description,
and others are larger than life.

In the line of dauntless British Empire explorers of the earth, the rich steelmaker Seebohm and his sidekick Harvie-Brown fitted right in. Seebohm rousingly described the tribulations of trial-and-error tracking through clouds of mosquitoes, and the pair's blithe shotgun-birding. In the Pechora and Yenisei river basins, north-east of Moscow, they brought down many Grey Plover and emptied eleven nests of what Seebohm called 'these rare birds'. Clearly they were hunters by inclination, keen to claim discovery. Seebohm's record of the journeys showed little interest in the ecology around them, except for what it meant to the hunt and in trophies.

'The results of our somewhat adventurous journey exceeded our most sanguine hopes,' he claimed. 'Of the half-dozen British birds, the discovery of whose breeding grounds had baffled the efforts of ornithologists for so long, we succeeded in bringing home identified eggs of three—the Grey Plover, the Little Stint and Bewick's Swan.'

Well, yes . . . His lifetime collection did eventually amount to 17,000 birds. Seebohm was a conqueror, alright.

I'm drawn more to others who were moved by the Arctic: the Australian, Robert Hall, and Briton, Maud Haviland. They too were shooters—as are a long line of ornithologists. But these two adventurers were uplifted by the High North, and by wildlife on the tundra.

Hall was a naturalist from Lal Lal in country Victoria who became a tea merchant in Melbourne. He joined an expedition to the Kerguelen Islands in the sub-Antarctic before heading to Siberia to collect specimens and eggs of birds that he knew migrated to Australia. Early in the twentieth century, he was one of the first to explore migratory shorebirds up what is known today as the East Asian–Australasian Flyway.

In the far north, he was enchanted by what we rarely see in the south: the switch made by these birds into breeding plumage. 'Australia does not know these living birds in beautiful colours of black and gold, with variation,' Hall wrote for the ornithological journal, *Emu*, in 1919. After a 4800-kilometre journey along the Lena River, he found himself among the birds on the tundra: 'The sandpipers of different species fly separately, and yet the air is full of their voice, as if there was a vast multitude. It is a tender sight to see these individual, gentle birds in graceful flight.'

Hall's epic journey climaxed with just a couple of hours at the head of the Lena's vast delta, where he was able to take his fill of shorebird magic before he had to turn back. He made the most of it. 'Nature in those two hours gave us a compensation in a magnificent mirage, showing us the whole delta and some outside islands ... It showed us the Polar Sea, and impressed us with gratitude. It was a great uplifting, and I felt as a guest in the birthplace of Australian migratory birds, in their mile upon mile of the greatest moss plain in the world, and its mile upon mile of feathered life.'

Soon after Hall, Maud Haviland, who grew up in the enclosed countryside of rural south-east Ireland, made her trip down the Yenisei River of eastern Siberia. Haviland loved birds, wrote nature books for children, and at the age of 23 joined an anthropology expedition led by a Czech, Maria Czaplicka, to the Tungusic people of the Yenisei.

Haviland walked in the footsteps of Seebohm, but with much lighter feet. 'To us, whose maps are speckled all over with the names of hills and rivers and townships, there is something arresting in the blankness of the map of Northern Siberia,' she wrote in *A Summer on the Yenesei*.

'Here and there a hair streak of river wanders up into the Arctic Ocean. The rest is emptiness. But ... sometimes ... as you trudge across a sphagnum bog and believe yourself to be all alone except for the Golden Plover, you hear a long, low 'ai-aie', and over the ridge comes a little sledge, drawn by one of the little tundra men ...

'You realise that where you are standing is not really a solitary place at all. It is part of a country, which is as exhaustively mapped and charted as any in the world. And each day, as you look at its shrouded, quivering horizon, you want to thrust it back farther from the limit of your knowledge, and long to learn a portion, however meagre, of its secrets.'

I would be drawn on like Hall to the far northern edge of Australian birds' lives, and like Haviland to search its horizon, learn of the tundra, and find the nest.

Nine
Beringia

In the summer an ice age ago, people would come to Bluefish Caves, on the edge of the cold sanctuary, Beringia. Their visits were short, just enough time to cut up a hunted beast and eat it, sheltered from the weather. But they kept coming back to these three shallow rock shelters in a limestone ridge above a tributary of the Yukon River, over a period of 12,000 years.

When people were absent, bears, wolves and foxes used the caves and, further down the predatory line, birds too. The rich bone litter they left behind is a diorama of life on this grassland refuge against an ice age. The pony-sized Yukon Horse, long-horned Steppe Bison and the Woolly Mammoth—pieces of all of them ended up on the floors of these three caves above the Bluefish River. So did the bones of dozens of smaller mammals and birds, including the Black-bellied Plover.

The caves' discoverer, Canadian Jacques Cinq-Mars, fought established views for decades before the bones were accepted as the oldest evidence of human occupation in North America. Recent radiocarbon dating work has confirmed that human

cut marks on some bones were made between 24,000 and
12,000 years ago. They strengthen what's known as the Beringian Standstill Theory: that ancient people did not move in a
steady stream from Siberia to populate North America. Instead,
during the last ice age, a small number of people, perhaps no
more than a few tens of thousands, lived in bands who roamed
across the grasslands, tundra and mountains, isolated by
surrounding ice sheets.

'Bluefish Caves . . . may have been located at the easternmost
extent of the standstill population's geographical range,' Laurian
Bourgeon, who led work to confirm the dates, wrote. Blocking
their progress further east was the Laurentide Ice Sheet, which
covered much of today's northern Canada.

I have seen an ice cap appear on the horizon, in the Antarctic. Approached by ship, it stretches and rises to make its own
weather, holding cold sway over all. As the sun rose over the
Laurentide each day, it loomed as another impassable weather
generator, too hostile for most animal life to approach except at
the height of summer.

But in the other direction—4000 kilometres to the west
of these caves and far into Russia—the uplands of the Beringian land were covered by rolling meadows and steppe-tundra,
a low grassland mixed with lichen and moss. Shrub thickets
grew on the flood plains and a little meagre woodland gained
a toehold amid snowbanks. Megafauna depended mostly upon
forbs—herbaceous plants, including thyme, vetch and anemone,
colouring and scenting a wide, wild landscape.

All of this has been reconstructed from samples of ancient
pollens. These show that the larch trees of Siberia did not cross
the bridge, and neither did the spruce of Alaska. The central
windswept plains were nowhere forested.

Beringia stretched across today's Siberia and Alaska, and spread north and south into the Arctic and Pacific oceans. This is a fantastic land for the imagination, a lost world named— along with sea and strait that now cover its heart—after Danish seafarer, Vitus Bering.

Here the sea repeatedly lowered over geological time as ice was formed, creating mountain ranges out of places like Wrangel Island. During the Pleistocene epoch, from two million to 11,000 years ago, Beringia's land mass was exposed at least nine, and possibly as many as twenty, times. It came and went with the cycle of glacial and interglacial periods.

The last of these cycles marked the beginning of the current Holocene, the 'whole, new' epoch. These were historic millennia for humans. For the first time as anatomically modern people, we faced the challenges of living through an ice age.

When all around was frozen, Beringia was the kind of place where Arctic migratory shorebirds could hang on and breed. Perhaps their generational succession was made easier by mega-fauna cropping the landscape low, hungering for herbaceous plants, or by the seasonal rush of snow melt, which created pools ripe for insect hatches.

The surrounding ice walls contrasted with life at the other, non-breeding end of the birds' flyways. During the last glacial maximum there was more coastal mud and relatively little ice over Southern Hemisphere continents. At that end lay easier sanctuaries, encouragement for long flights.

Bluefish Caves' bone trove tells us that this flourishing landscape was summer home to a rich bird life and that many of the species seen in today's Alaska and Yukon were there then; inconspicuous woodland birds, like the Olive-sided Flycatcher and Say's Phoebe, the eye-catching Harlequin Duck and Snow Goose, owls and hawks, and an array of shorebirds. As well as the Black-bellied Plover, the land was used by the American Golden Plover, sandpipers, and the now probably extinct Eskimo Curlew.

The story of Beringia reminds us of the shorebirds' resilience, their endurance over time. The ancestors of tundra plovers pre-date the Cretaceous–Tertiary boundary 65 million years ago, a time when Europe was yet to join the Asian continent and Australia was much closer to Antarctica. Though dinosaurs went extinct, probably as the world darkened under the dust of an asteroid strike, molecular dating shows that these birds were able to survive this catastrophe. Along with curlews and sandpipers, *pluvialis* found enough on the edges to sustain themselves.

To someone facing a suddenly uncertain life, these birds' longevity is a comfort of continuity to me. Small though my place is in the world, and brief my existence, evolutionary splendour rolls on. I fill my mind by looking into their lives—into their perils at the climax of their year. I remember the precious value of each day, and how these birds ceaselessly fill it. I hold to the Roman poet Virgil, who wrote in his epic poem, *The Georgics*: '*Sed fugit interea fugit irreparabile tempus.*' Fast flies meanwhile the irreparable hour.

———

The story of Beringia tells of the freedom of shorebird movement, and of our own constricted concept of the wild, blinkered as we are by our land-bound limits. These birds are driven to be restlessly, globally, mobile. They possess the innate ability to do so, and are supreme travellers. Unlike early tribal people, or the megafauna lumbering across their landscape, these birds needed no land bridge. Ancestry, whim and weather chose routes to renew their line.

'Beringia is a very dynamic place,' says Bob Gill, doyen of Alaskan shorebird biology. 'You've got this link for them between Wrangel and Australia, but I'm not going to be surprised if some of those Siberian Black-bellies go all the way down to South America. There is so much to be discovered in that sense.'

A wealth of exchange is rapidly being found between Australian and New Zealand shorebirds in the south, and Alaska in the north. There are connections between today's Russia and the broader United States that few knew existed. Beringia is the ground that EAAF birds share with others of their species, who migrate instead along the American flyways; their shared evolutionary cradle.

My mind was first opened to this on the red cliffs of Yawuru Nagulagun/Roebuck Bay. I was watching Chris Hassell and Kerry Hadley as they scanned for re-sights, picking their way through a distant mixed flock of Whimbrel and Great Knot. Though the birds were huddled, as they eyed raptors floating along the clifftop, individuals in the flock were sharply outlined in the scopes by a red rock-shelf backdrop.

Hassell's booming Leicestershire voice suddenly gurgled with excitement. 'That one down there! The Great Knot just behind those two Whimbrel! To the right of the boulder near the water. Can you see it? That bird there! Six–Red–Red–Blue–Red!' And from the tidily compartmented archives of his mind, the would-have-been livestock farmer pulled the records of this particular charge of his.

The bird was first caught at Broome in October and fitted with 6RRBR leg bling, as well as a satellite tag. After six months on the bay, it flew non-stop for around 4570 kilometres over about four days, directly to the Mai Poi marshes in Hong Kong. There it happened to be seen by Hassell's Global Flyway Network colleague, Ginny Chan, and photographed. Plotting its satellite track, Hassell saw the bird move on in short hops up through the Yellow Sea, and then migrate to Far Eastern Chukotka to breed.

'What you would expect is that the bird would then turn around and come back again,' Hassell said. 'Not this bird. It went right to the coast of the Bering Sea—and then it went to Alaska!' There it spent some time exploring Safety Sound on the vast, wild Seward Peninsula, which thrusts out like a fist into the sea. Against the odds it was photographed again before taking off back across the Bering Sea for Kamchatka Peninsula—and Australasian Wader Studies Group volunteers on the mudflats snapped it once more. By this time 6RRBR was gaining some fame.

'It left Kamchatka, flew to Sakhalin Island, to North Korea, and we lost contact with it when it was about 50 kilometres from Rudong on the Jiangsu coast. I then got a photograph of this bird from Rudong!' The picture was taken by the master bird guide of the Jiangsu coast, Lin Zhang. It showed that the harness had loosened, and the tag had slipped below the left wing-pit.

'We thought, oh man, that's bad,' Hassell said. 'The tag's broken. What's going to happen to the bird?' Then 6RRBR's signal disappeared. The bird literally fell off the radar. Until six months later when it was photographed again, by a Broome Bird Observatory guest a few days before us on the coast where we now stood.

'It's cutting-edge technology, and birds die, and all that,' Hassell said. 'But that bird survived. And it went to Alaska! Effing amazing East Asian–Australasian Flyway!'

The deeper I delve, the more extensive are the cases of Beringian crossover. And, of course, while these birds may be individually tracked, they are likely not lone-fliers and part of a flock that takes these routes.

A Ruddy Turnstone from Flinders, on the coast south-east of Melbourne, was geolocator-tracked twice on successive great-loop migrations that took it from Siberian nesting grounds back south via Alaska's Aleutian Islands. Others seem to spill over from the Russian Arctic to breed in North America. The little Red-necked Stint is usually thought of as a pan-Siberian breeder, but it has been found repeatedly by Alaskan researchers on mountain nests, also on the Seward Peninsula.

Most intriguing is the Sharp-tailed Sandpiper, a small wader of Australia and New Zealand adept at finding useable interior or coastal wetlands in flood or drought. I watched four of them follow each other in a tight quadrille as they fed in a small saline lake near Point Lonsdale in Victoria. 'The intensity!' I thought. BirdLife Australia calls the Sharpie 'the most dinky-di' of all migratory shorebirds, because of is adaptability to the vagaries of the continent. But the young arrive in their southern summer land with an American accent.

Sharpies favour breeding grounds in the Arctic coastal tundra strip, where CYA and CYB first landed before going to Wrangel. Their time at the nest is brief. Male adult Sharpies fly south by early July, and females later that month, both sexes heading down the Asian coast.

A month or more later, the new fledgling Sharpies leave the breeding grounds by themselves. Instead of following the adult route, the juvenile flocks fly 1000 kilometres east over the Bering Sea to Alaska's Yukon–Kuskokwim Delta, a wetland labyrinth the size of England. This is thought to be an ancestral Beringian route, still hard-wired into the birds for their first flight.

They reach the delta with very little fuel. But in an average twelve days on this rich autumn mud, where there are few predators to deplete their energy, young Sharpies nearly double their weight. This supercharges them as they head back to the EAAF.

Of course, American shorebirds go west over Beringia too. The closely related Pectoral Sandpiper breeds from far-western Siberia to eastern Canada, but mainly uses American flyways so as to winter in South America. I was once walking on the wide dark sands of Chesterman Beach, near Tofino in British Columbia, when I noticed a trim wader almost at my feet. It was feverishly probing the contents of a tidal pool and took no notice of me, even as I bent down and snapped close-ups with my pocket camera.

'Pectoral Sandpiper,' adjudged Tofino bird guide, Adrian Dorst, when he took a look at my snap. I dragged Dorst away from his work hand-carving a wooden bowl to take a closer look, but of course the bird was gone, headed south, running late after a summer on the breeding grounds of Chukotka or Alaska.

'Pecs' migrate along a broad front through the Americas. One band recovery linked a bird marked in Kansas with Chukotka, where it was shot two years later on its way further north.

Pavel Tomkovich put together scattered scraps of banding and sighting information to assign shorebirds on the Chukotka side of the Bering Sea to their broad migratory paths. He found eleven species, mainly sandpipers, crossed through Beringia to use the American flyways on migration. Even the very specifically named American Golden Plover has been found at a nest in the maze of creeks and ponds that make up the delta of the

Ekvyvatap River, which runs into the Arctic Sea just below Wrangel.

I thought about these birds, about the great flow of migratory shorebirds across Beringia, and of how I might grasp the lives of Grey Plover on the breeding ground at Wrangel. How were the seasonal climaxes of life unfolding for CYA and CYB?

Few scientists have seen this ultimate Arctic shorebird through a single breeding season, let alone repeated the achievement long enough to build a picture of its character. I searched for accounts along the Russian Arctic coast, and found a useful study over six years conducted on the Yamal Peninsula by V.K. Riyabitsev. At much the same time, Tomkovich spent three summers on the northern Taimyr Peninsula and later he made his first flight to Wrangel in that short summer of helicopter delays. These Russian accounts shed chinks of light on Grey Plover habits, but for answers to my questions about their lives I went to the other side of Beringia.

Trawling through reports by the Alaskan Shorebird Group, I came across notes by a Hawaiian biologist, Phil Bruner, and his wife Andrea. He was bemused when I phoned and put it to him that they probably had been studying the same tundra plovers on the same grounds longer than any other scientists.

'Well, we did start back in 1988,' Bruner said. 'We headed up to Alaska with our tent, and some not very adequate equipment. Fish and Wildlife had a beat-up GM Suburban and they ran us out, and just left us. Turned out, we had set up our tent in Plover Central. Fortunately we had no issues. A grizzly bear came by. We poked our head out of the tent, in the fog, and saw the bear with a reindeer in its mouth. So we just edged on back into the tent until it left. That's how we got going.'

The Bruners, based at Brigham Young University in Hawaii, selected a study site below the western end of the sawtooth Kigluaik Mountains, on the Seward Peninsula west of Nome. In the winter this gold-mining town is snow-bound, the sea beside it frozen. The beginning of the end of its annual isolation is marked by the arrival from Anchorage of the first musher in the 1000-mile (1609 kilometres) Iditarod Sled Dog Race.

The next wave of seasonal incomers includes droves of serious early-summer birders, chasing migrants and rarities. They use the three gravel roads that fan out from Nome; each of these runs for up to 130 kilometres before stuttering to dead-ends in the otherwise road-less Seward, a wilderness twice the size of Wales.

The Bruners' site is on the land of the Ukivokmiut, the King Island Iñupiat, who take this name from the offshore rock stack that was for centuries their precipitous home. King Islanders' mainland possessions centre on Woolley Lagoon, one of the long waterways that fringe the Seward, parallel to the sea, separated from it by grey storm-washed strands. Just along the coast in the other direction lies Safety Sound, where Great Knot 6RRBR paused for its Alaskan holiday before heading back, eventually, to Broome.

The King Islanders are part of the Iñupiat First Nation, whose lands stretch over much of far north-west Alaska. They are familiar with the Black-bellied Plover, which they know as *Ilik-taat-tuqhiq*, the scorched feathers bird; they see it commonly as they move across the coastal tundra. Under Alaskan law, Iñupiat can hunt shorebirds and their eggs, including *Ilik-taat-tuqhiq* or, as it is known further south on the Yukon coast, *Tuligaq*.

In the Yukon delta earlier last century, local people traditionally scoured the low ridges on open ground in late May looking for *Tuligaq* eggs. 'Among the Eskimos the eggs of this plover, as food, are considered superior to any bird in this region,' American dogsled adventurer Herb Brandt wrote.

He was clearly entranced by my bird: 'Only those who have met this lordly plover on his native heath can appreciate how he seems to rule with a martial air the domains under his control,' Brandt wrote. 'He is the mentor and monitor of the tundra, always alert to potential danger. Powerful of wing stroke, trim of form as a greyhound, and erect of carriage, this, the largest of our common plovers, is the speedster of the wild birds of the north.'

These qualities were held up by the Iñupiat. At Utqiagvik/ Barrow in the far northern tip of Alaska, earlier nineteenth century US expeditioners found our bird was regarded as a source of power and good fortune. 'The natives are perfectly familiar with the bird, and use the dried skins as amulets or talismans to secure good luck in deer hunting,' expedition leader John Murdoch recorded. They wanted its swiftness to carry them to success.

Few Black-bellied Plover, or their eggs, are taken today from a land with multitudes of more profitable ducks and geese. Alaskan wildlife researcher Liliana Naves estimates that waders amount to less than 1 per cent of the total subsistence bird harvest of 400,000 birds per year.

I peer at images of the Bruners' study site, a piece of tundra about 1.5 kilometres by a few hundred metres, bisected along its length by a gravel track beside a creek that leads down to King Islanders' fishing huts at Woolley Lagoon. On this gently sloping tundra, rare among these birds, three species nest: the Black-bellied, the Pacific and American Goldens.

About eight months after my initial diagnosis, the cancer has abated under treatment and my head is sufficiently clear of painkillers and chemotherapy for me to again form whole meaningful sentences. I feel rocky, but I am on my feet. I decide to try for the tundra, to see the birds.

Wrangel stays out of reach. On the voyage that I would have joined, they saw 200 Polar Bears gathered on the island's shore, gorging on a washed-up whale carcass. Global publicity of this unparalleled sight meant that all the cabins on their upcoming trips were fully booked. Instead, I thought it might be possible to get to Woolley Lagoon.

I am taking two chances: that some of my birds will actually be there, and that I can manage the journey. I have some confidence in finding the bird after discovering Phil Bruner. My strength to make the trip relies on my new treatment: the breakthrough of immunotherapy.

Evolutionary principles that explain the marvels of bird migration also help to understand the growth and spread of cancer. As Thomas Alerstam and Anders Hedenstrom said about migration: 'Adaptation leaves its inescapable and pervasive signature on living nature.' Genetic mutations are another manifestation of evolution's trial-and-error adaptation at work in our bodies.

My cancer resulted from a particular gene mutation known as the K-RAS, and this was my good fortune. As immunotherapy rapidly develops, treatment of the K-RAS mutation in some lung cancers is one of the early responders to treatment.

In 2018 the American, James Allison, and Japan's Tasuku Honjo were jointly awarded the Nobel Prize in Medicine for their pioneering immunotherapy work. They independently found ways to unlock the body's own immune system to engage and fight cancers.

'One of the things we have learned since the war on cancer started is that trying to target a single cause of mutation . . . always essentially leads to relapse after response,' Allison said in his Nobel Lecture. 'That's because there are so many mutations, by the time you target one there's already a resistant mechanism which your tumour can use after selection to bypass it.'

In most infections, be they septic cuts or common colds, our immune system's inbuilt T cells can focus on an infected cell and provide overwhelming defence against it. Cancer hides from the immune system. Allison said that given the opportunity, the immune system 'is easily a match for cancer'. So he worked on ways to treat the immune system and not the cancer. He and Honjo separately developed means to take 'blinders' off the immune system, so the T cells could *see* the cancer and get to work on it.

In the months before I go to the Arctic, I grow confident that I will be well enough to travel because I trust the way my oncologist, medical friends and family retain their strong belief in science. I am a son of generations of doctors, and in a working life as a journalist, I came to love scientists' dogged construction of knowledge. We live in an era of noisy, self-interested science deniers, and hucksters selling unhelpful alternative therapies. I have the potential to prove what can be done thanks to the power of evidence-based medicine. Also I am lucky. The very costly immunotherapy drug came onto the government subsidy scheme just weeks after my initial diagnosis.

According to Honjo, about 20 to 30 per cent of cancer patients currently respond to immunotherapy. That means the great majority still don't. It makes the luck of those who do even more valuable—however long it lasts. 'Some day, 2030 or not, cancer may not completely disappear, but it will be controlled by immunotherapy,' Honjo said in his Nobel speech. 'Cancer may become one of the chronic diseases.'

Allison, in his speech, thanked the 'several thousand' patients who in recent years had been through trials of quickly proliferating immunotherapy drugs, in what the *New York Times* calls 'Desperation Oncology'. For many of those people it was not a success. It is to them too that I owe my continuing life, just as I am contributing to others who follow. We are ultimate 'data points' in this research.

I can't help being reminded of Clive Minton's words, as he and the hundreds of other people in many nations gather their facts on migratory birds from this and other flyways. Ask a question, devise a way to find an answer, gather the results. If that's good for birds, fine. The point is to keep exploring.

When the immunotherapy breakthrough was first becoming apparent, Allison gave a self-deprecating speech in Houston, in which he said that he decided to be a scientist rather than a medical doctor like his father. People in that profession could not afford to be wrong, he said, while 'to be a scientist you could be wrong a lot. All you have to be is just right occasionally on something that's important.'

As an afterthought, he said of the breakthrough: 'all of this came out of basic science, not any attempt to cure cancer. It came out of understanding how the immune system works.' The point was: he kept exploring.

Ten
A portion of their secrets

In a dusty back street where I have strayed, a husky breaks its worn chain and comes at me. I had not seen the dog, and it is close and fierce. But I know, like Ovsyanikova with the bears, that to run would make me prey. So I make myself big as it barks in confected fury; I command it to back off in what I hope is a powerful voice; and as I hold its eye, I keep taking slow steps away. Finally it turns with a sneer and stalks back inside its territory.

Welcome to Nome.

I am on the way to see Brandon Ahmasuk, who manages subsistence hunting for the Iñupiats' Kawerak Corporation. We talk about local hunting traditions. He knows the Black-bellied Plover.

'If I go hunting, I notice them all along the coast. You don't have to go to Woolley Lagoon to see them. Myself, I don't go after plover. Sometimes I go after snipe, sandpiper, but it means you have to get a few of these to make a difference. We go for swans and geese.' Nevertheless, there is my bird, on the permitted-target species list in a brochure in the hallway rack.

To connect with the traditional owners of Woolley Lagoon, Ahmasuk directs me to the King Island Native Corporation. Along another dusty back street in Nome—which I carefully scan—I find their office. A courteous manager wordlessly hands me a ten-page application form to fill out in order to speak to someone. I see it as suitable revenge for a century of abuse under white bureaucracy, and the freeloading expropriation of Indigenous culture. I fill it out and hear no more.

To get my bearings, I have joined a small group tour led by a former Californian clinical psychologist, Forrest Davis. On the sands and hills around Nome, the migratory shorebird invasion is under way. A flock of phalarope bounces across Bering coast wavelets as they dash after fish eggs, oblivious of people, like seagulls after chips. Atop a wooden pole, a small sandpiper shrills his presence fit to explode. A wing of Bar-tailed Godwit jets over Safety Sound and disappears into mountains. Up on a distant hill, a wary Bristle-thighed Curlew, migrant from Polynesia, allows a side-on approach. Near it, an American Golden Plover courteously leads a 'follow-me' path away from his nest. A Golden Eagle stands silhouetted on a ridge, as if it is stone on a castle parapet.

In the evening, birders trade sighting tips at Milano's Pizzeria and these leave me worried for the birds. As a highlight of the day, we had stood beside a stream watching from a hillside a Gyrfalcon on its nest, built atop the pier of a road bridge. We were 40 metres away using scopes, but the splendid silver-white Arctic raptor looked immediately vulnerable, sitting as it was underneath the bridge's road surface and almost within arm's reach. At Milano's, a birder at the next table eagerly suggests to others that they just lie down on the bridge and look at the bird 'right there'.

Davis initially drives me out to Woolley Lagoon. He is cautious about seeing my bird. Its numbers there have been in decline, he says. We take an SUV along the Teller Road through gently rising Alaskan mountains, shedding their snow into blue streams. We pass small raptors and bands of Musk Ox, a beaver dam. The air is finely iced, pure. The Seward wilderness has opened to spring life, and after my long dark months it is quickly elating.

At the mile-forty mark on the road we are at last in the presence of Singatook, the rampart mountain and weather-maker at the western end of the Kigluaik Range. Reindeer rest on a lower-slope snow patch, preferring it to the insect-riddled clear ground. Singatook's snows feed the stream that runs to the lagoon, and we turn off down the track beside it. Offshore in the distance, King Island looms in fog like an Arctic acropolis.

Davis points out other birds. Predatory Long-tailed Jaegers which he cheerfully despises, and a common songbird, the Lapland Longspur. On a rise up the slope, a Pacific Golden Plover gives me a start—my naïve eye wishes it to be my bird. Overhead flaps an Arctic Tern, the world's longest-travelling bird.

Then halfway down to the lagoon, on stony tundra between the road and the stream, Davis draws to a halt. 'There's your bird,' he says.

A pair are working the streamside ground—the male distinc-tive, the female needing a careful look to discover. I had expected his regal black and whiteness, and he stands on the tundra as a boast, everything I wished for. She takes me by surprise. Her plumage is a mottled silver, a pewter, and its shimmer makes her harder to see until she moves. I breathe out. It has been a long way for me from Thompson Beach to the tundra. Now here are my surrogates, at home in their Arctic space.

She keeps to a particular piece of ground; but he roams around, much keener at run–stop–peck. He calls, perhaps to her. His voice is thin, crystalline and persistent. Later that day we watch as they mate by the stream. A quick flurry on top of her and he is away, while she stays bowed and quiet.

The Bruners' study looked at some of the questions about these birds I have long wondered as I try to understand their character. How faithful are they to their mates and breeding sites; to possible partners among thousands, and to these pinpoints in the tundra? Are they instead faithless? Do females take more than one partner, or is it the males who spread their genes around the neighbourhood? How many fledglings make it through the initial year of turbulent life to return to their birthplaces?

These things we see as fundamental to us. To birds that navigate through precarious, vast migrations, answers to the imperative of passing on genes may be quite different.

Working through early Alaskan summers, the Bruners use small circular spring nets set over the nests and triggered by a string, to catch and individually colour-band adults and young. They mark out nest locations using a cryptic code of found stones, laid out just *so*. One of these stones will have dates and a bird species code written on the underside.

Phil Bruner, amiable and instructive, meets me in Nome the day after he lands. He drives me out to the site and shows me the stone code. 'What we learned is that rocks are your friend,' he says. 'Bushes die. Rocks stay. You can flip a rock over and other people won't know what's marked beneath, but *you* will know. And some of these nests are good year after year.'

They focused first on Pacific and American Goldies, which back then were only just being teased apart as separate species. Working with Oscar 'Wally' Johnson, they tracked the Pacifics' migrations. Amazingly, a Pacific tagged at Woolley Lagoon turned up on parkland down the road from the Bruners' Oahu home.

They also drew up some individual histories that hinted at complex lives on the breeding ground. 'A male Pacific Golden Plover banded in 1988 was once again on his territory in 1998,' they reported in their published annual summaries. 'We know of only three seasons in the past eleven when this bird was successful in attracting a mate, and hatching a clutch.'

Persistence in folly? What made this bird so unlucky, unattractive? Hard times, anyway. Not so much for a female Black-bellied Plover banded initially in 1993, and watched over the following twelve years: 'After her initial capture she retained the same mate for nine subsequent years but has paired with a different mate each of the last three years.'

Fog, late snow melts and unusual cold over the years dogged the Bruners at Woolley Lagoon, but they became immersed in life on the wild tundra. In almost continual daylight, they could see last year's desiccated vegetation rapidly replaced by green shoots and tiny wildflowers. Ground squirrels popped out of holes. Musk Ox and Moose lumbered along, and an occasional Grizzly held the rest of life in pause as it passed by. Over the hill from their study site is the Feather River valley, locally known as Bear Alley. 'They [the Grizzlies] move down to the coast, feed on dead whales,' Bruner tells me. 'It can be quite spooky around there when it's foggy.'

Through the years the Bruners have seen the birds through from mating to the early weeks of their offspring's life, from the male's highly stylised 'butterfly flight' to the chicks scattering out across the tundra, starting lives of their own.

Males, first to arrive, return to their territories to proclaim their fitness and their ground's riches with song flight overhead. Anyone who has heard a lark whistle over a field will recognise this enthusiasm. For our plover it is a sky ballet, repeated yearly as a ritual offering. 'It's usually trying to convince the female that it's the right spot—and she's not easily convinced,' Bruner says.

Looking every inch the Tundra Boss as he stands alert on ridge or rock, the male lifts for the start. At low height, he levels off and slows. Flight becomes a stiff exaggeration. His wings flap up to touch tips above his head, and then down below his belly, like a slow-moving butterfly's. At the same time he sings in apparent joy.

Tundra plover experts Ingvar Byrkjedal and Des Thompson wrote: 'the pure whistling songs with their bubbling trills used during their song flight are surely the paeans of the north in early spring. To our ears, the Grey Plover is the master.'

They rendered its trill as *pee-rrrrrrwit-poo-plluuueee-poolee-pooooeee*. As I try this on my tongue, it sings out as bright as the Arctic air.

The butterfly flight ends with a swoop downward to the claimed ground. The Bruners have worked hard to understand what it is in a piece of tundra, almost featureless to our eye, that makes it preferred by the bird.

'We did 50 metre transects, random and deliberate, over the ground looking at the substrate,' Phil says. 'It's pretty clear that for the Black-bellied Plover, it's based on the right mix of lichens. They go for that. And they will re-use the same nest cup, sometimes for several years.'

The nest sites may be on slightly raised, drier ground, and have a good 360-degree view. Out on their territory around the nest, the pair mates repeatedly over about six days for the issue of four eggs. These neat capsules of promise are speckled dark brown, grey and black, about bantam-sized but more pointed. For a wild bird, they are big in comparison to the female. The clutch totals about 70 per cent of her body weight.

After some time with Phil he has my measure, and he invites me to walk up to a nest cup, to reach my little grail. I remember the Gyrfalcon, and am diffident about disturbing the plover. Bruner is confident it will return afterwards. He instructs me that to walk up is not going to be so easy. I need to keep an eye exactly on where the bird has been sitting, and to stay on two feet amid boggy tundra. Also I mustn't step on any egg, of any kind, anywhere.

We select a nest. The female leaves it. As I walk up I keep in my mind a tuft of greenery and a larger stone near the nest. I glance down to hop over a rivulet. As I look up again, the stone reappears, I take a few more steps and I am there.

For all of its fragile and subtle beauty, my breath catches and my heart fills. Surrounded by the buds of wildflowers and moss scraps, the small bare cup is distinct from the tundra only by its few extra lining strands of a white lichen. In it are three intricately camouflaged eggs, their tips pointing down, with a space waiting for a fourth. Here is the essence, the vulnerable beginning of global lives. I close my eyes and bow my head for a few seconds in order to hold the memory. My breath, so recently in doubt, tingles with the wild Arctic around me.

———

For the Bruners, a clutch was laden with questions. Who exactly were the parents? The different shorebird species, or some-times just sub-populations, choose exotically different mating systems: polygamy (more than one mate), polygyny (more than one female mate), polyandry (more than one male) and the many choices of promiscuity. There is also plain vanilla monogamy.

Early on, the Bruners supervised tests of the birds' determina-tion to incubate, a question that might point towards certainty of parentage in the Black-bellied Plover. Females proved willing to sit on decoy eggs briefly slipped onto a nest, but males disdained them. To these males, the identity of an egg was more important than urgency to breed. As DNA techniques improved, so the Bruners were able to nail down another answer. Sampling three years of broods and adults, they found each clutch was totally fathered by the male at that particular nest.

In a species with mate retention, this bespeaks a thoroughly committed faithfulness in *Pluvialis squatarola*, despite their long separations away from the breeding grounds. Only one example of mate-switching was found, and that happened when the female of one pair and the male of another failed to return to Woolley Lagoon. The surviving mates made the best of it. They formed a pair.

At the same study site, Ruddy Turnstone had hectic sex lives. A third of turnstone chicks were the result of polyandry, with nineteen out of 55 not fathered by the male attending the nest. Few turnstones held a mate beyond a single season.

Nests need constant defence until the chicks hatch after about four weeks. At Woolley Lagoon, male Black-bellies tend to take most of the day shift and females settle in during the polar summer twilight. A non-incubating partner will stand sentinel, and an incubating bird's first and best tactic is to leave the nest before discovery. On many Arctic breeding grounds, it will secretively leave the nest though a human is far distant. Early ornithological adventurers spent frustrating days trying to find nests, so well do they fit into the land.

This thorough defence helps not only save the Grey Plover's young, the bird is also seen as a guard species, the kind that others choose to nest near for its promise of protection against predators. A study on the Taimyr found that, within 100 metres of the typical Grey Plover nest, there was a greater number of smaller shorebirds nesting than near those of other bigger birds.

Curlew Sandpipers and Pectoral Sandpipers, Dunlin and Little Stint sheltering close to the 'Hawk Eye' could rely on its early call to warn of the presence of a predator, and for this alarm often to be followed by an attack on the intruder. Pacific Golden Plover or the larger Bar-tailed Godwit were far less inclined to offer this sort of defence.

As a last resort, all tundra plovers use distraction displays, feigning an injury to entice danger away: the crouched run with outspread 'broken' wing, feeble calls, whatever it takes. Still, the odds against shorebird breeding success at times seem overwhelming, given that they are persecuted from above by predatory birds and on the ground by foxes.

The Bruners see a constant struggle between predatory jaegers and breeding plovers at the study site. Twice the size of a tundra plover, the Long-tailed Jaeger courses low, harassing other birds into revealing or deserting their nests, and then it seizes eggs or chicks.

I drive out to Woolley Lagoon alone to get a fill of Beringia's drama by myself. Using the hired SUV as a hide I watch, gripped, as a pair of Black-bellied Plover defend their nest. It took me an hour or two to find the pair though the nest is just

20 metres from the road. The jaegers, on the other hand, sit on the tundra seeking no cover.

I first see the male plover's ermine head in profile on a low ridge next to a melt stream. The rest of him is tucked down into the cup. After I stop the vehicle and turn the engine off, the head subsides. Minutes later he rises sharply, crying out at a Long-tailed Jaeger approaching from behind.

'Tood-lee-oo! Tood-lee-oo!' the plover shrills, hotly chasing the jaeger, which slides away. The male plover then alights 30 metres from the nest, pecks at nothing, and works its way back circuitously to the nest, settling again in the sun.

On the shore near the lagoon, waves break white on dark sand. A raven coasts over, then three Sandhill Crane flap gently past in close formation. Further up the slope a Pacific Golden Plover male is in courtship flight, lifting high above its territory, calling and slow-flapping.

I reflect on the spooked Moose that galloped out of the Feather River valley and across the road in front of my car, and on two tundra Grizzly Bears glowing gold on a hill a couple of nights before. Around me the great spread of the Beringian land is quietly ancient.

The jaeger appears again, the plover takes straight off from the nest and swings after it, the two wheel away. The chase lasts split seconds, but carries them 200 metres before the male peels off and settles on the ground beside the stream to feed. The female appears. She zig-zags a course towards the nest, lowers herself to scuttle the last few metres through the grass, and her pewter feathers melt into the tundra. A short distance away stands the jaeger.

After a while the scavenger comes for a third time, directly over the top of the nest. This time the plover pair give chase and see the intruder off, before the female creeps back once more to sit on her cup. Each time, the jaeger has come closer to a good look at what is in the nest. Are there enough eggs yet to make a grab? Perhaps not.

Jaegers don't have it all their own way. The blink-of-an-eye sprinting ability of this plover, and its tough chisel bill, can even the contest. 'We had a male Black-belly kill a Long-tailed Jaeger,' Bruner says. 'He hit it hard with his bill and stunned it. Knocked it right out of the sky. Jaeger broke its neck when it fell on the tundra.'

Nesting Snowy Owls rim the high Arctic and are known to take Grey Plover chicks at Wrangel to feed their own. But at Woolley Lagoon, foxes, both Red and Arctic, are the more dangerous shorebird predators.

'The Reds are very bold,' Bruner says. 'They'll trot around 10 feet behind you and wait for you to stir up a bird. Then they'll come back for it. So you just have to stop and wait until they go away.' One year the Bruners counted at least three active dens around the study site.

Halting at a river further along the Teller Road, I see a Red Fox. Disturbed from an afternoon nap, it turns to assess me. Healthy and thick-coated, the animal is barely recognisable as related to the rangy feral Red I saw on Thompson Beach. It trots away calmly, sits down to watch me, and then scampers a few more steps. Finally deciding that I present no useful opportunity, it delicately steps out of view.

It's common around the Arctic for many shorebirds to lose their nests to foxes and predatory birds. For some time it's been thought there is a pattern to this that relates to the waxing and waning of the storied rodent, the lemming. The work suggests that when the lemming numbers are up, shorebirds are buffered because of the availability of this food for predatory birds and foxes. Conversely, when lemming numbers are down, the birds suffer.

In early shorebird research there was evidence that every three to four years Grey Plover, Sanderling and turnstone numbers increased; in a good year they migrated in greater numbers to Swartkops estuary in South Africa. More recently, it's been learned that some lemming cycles are fading out, and in their absence the predators are choosing the nests of plentiful larger birds like ducks and geese. Wader chicks may be a second-choice prey. It's possible that warmer Arctic summer temperatures might be affecting lemmings, and this links to poor or successful shorebird breeding years.

A critical moment in the predation of plovers, the hatch, happens over a few days of early summer when chicks 'pip'— fracture the eggshell from within. As impossibly frail little balls of life, they break into a world that some of them will grow up to span.

'When they emerge they are all legs, and a puff of feathers on top,' Bruner says. 'But they are very precocial. They are able within 24 hours to run, and feeding is instinctual—not like a hen teaches chickens. They learn pretty much by trial and error. Essentially anything that moves is fair game. On our site there are lots of little ponds with fly and mosquito larvae. But if there is a blade of grass waving in the wind, they'll try that.'

Chicks are born with an external yolk sac that provides nourishment for the first day or so; then the sac shrivels and the chicks' ability to feed on insects takes hold. Mosquitoes, flies, beetles and bugs should be flourishing on the tundra by then, to the point of forming dense swarms, and the chicks are able to run after them.

'There are big, aggressive mosquitoes at Woolley Lagoon and, if you don't have a head net on after around the third week of June, they'll practically sting you to death,' Bruner says. 'The proboscis goes right through my pants. If there's a breeze it can be OK. If it's a windless day, sometimes it's better to go back to Nome and wait for a better one.'

In the early days of the chicks' lives, both adults may brood them at the nest; but then they desert the cup and the chick is a sitting meal for a predator. Soon after that, adult females usually leave the breeding ground and head south, having spent only a couple of months at the home they flew so far to reach. It's up to the less-travelled males to watch over the progeny.

As the chicks spread out seeking food, the male stays sentinel with his vigilant eye so appreciated by other shorebirds, and his piercing high-note alarm. The fluff balls do not always make for the parent at a sign of danger. Instead they crouch motionless, relying on the patterns of their tawny down to camouflage them in the tundra's dun mosaic. Males will stay with the chicks for several weeks before they too head south.

There is no evidence that the Seward Peninsula Black-bellied Plover fly down the EAAF. Instead Woolley Lagoon birds have been tracked along the Pacific American Flyway. Satellite tags fitted to the plover by the Smithsonian Migratory Bird Center show them flying out to the Yukon Delta, and pausing there before heading over the North Pacific, to cross land again along the west coast of the Lower Forty-Eight. The tags lasted long enough to show one female spending time on wetlands upstream of San Francisco Bay, and two birds reaching down to the Baja Peninsula.

Left behind on the tundra, the chicks must grow fast enough to fly south without adult guidance before the Arctic winter closes in. There is little rest in the sun for these young. Survival means feeding up and fledging. If all is synchronous, then they will be able to fly short distances around the time that the male usually leaves. All depends on the growth of feathers.

Little work has been done anywhere on this bird at this precarious stage of life, when it is quickly developing wings that will enable it to migrate, and the rest of its body is attempting to catch up with its legs. The most detailed observations were made on the Truelove Lowland, a lush polar oasis on Canada's Devon Island, near Greenland. Over four summers in the late 1960s, David Hussell and Gary Page watched the birds, sometimes up very close, and collected specimens in a classic work of observation of an Arctic migrant on their breeding ground.

The study tells of things that can only be seen from a close hide—the 'quiet quivering trill' of a brooding parent to call back a stray chick, and the initial struggle for life in a noticeably weaker bird. 'By the time it was thirteen hours old, it was definitely feeding,' they reported, indicating the concentration of their watch.

They also detailed that strange phenomenon of the natural world, the eruption from a bird's skin of feathers. The third day after hatching, the translucent sheaths of feathers were starting to appear on the backs and chests of chicks. By six days, wing primaries and the tail feathers began to emerge and grow, though the bird still looked downy all over. The first juvenile feathering was noticeable over the bird at twelve to thirteen days, prominent by eighteen days, and one of the chicks could fly 150 metres at 23 days.

'The entire cycle, from laying of the first egg to fledging of the last young occupies about 55 days for a single nesting,' they said.

These birds on Devon Island lost five of seventeen nests to predators during incubation, and the surviving chicks showed a wide variation in growth rates, hinting at trouble ahead for some low-weight juveniles as they attempted their first migration. At Woolley Lagoon, after many dozens of colour bands and 30 years of observation, the Bruners have an answer to the question, 'How many Black-bellied Plover fledglings return to their birthplace?'

The answer is none. Despite all the work, there has been no return of a banded chick. Phil Bruner has a stark view of their fate: 'Probably most of the juveniles never make landfall on migration. They just drop into the water. Otherwise we'd be up to our ears in plovers.'

Eleven
Now south

On Wrangel Island in early July, the usual time of the Grey Plover hatch, Bob Gill saw an Arctic unlike any other part of the north-polar world: a rainbow-coloured wildflower landscape. He went there in 1994 as part of a big Swedish-mounted tundra ecology expedition. He shakes his head now as he remembers wandering the island alone without defence against bears, assigned to trap and band shorebirds.

'Wrangel has this quality of land before time,' he says. 'You walk down a stream bed, and here is the femur of a mastodon sticking up, and there's its tusks. We camped at one spot where the Russians dug out a 12-foot-long tusk. Musk Ox, Snow Geese— foxes everywhere. And while it didn't have the quality of the Galapagos in terms of tameness and exposure, you had a sense that a lot of these critters were seeing a human for the first time.'

In 2007, the year that Pavel Tomkovich was there, egg-laying began in early June and chicks began hatching in the first week of July. He thought they took around 30 days to begin flying, longer than on Devon Island.

For CYA and CYB, breeding patterns revealed by satellite-tag data make a study in contrasts. It's almost certain that each of them mated, and it's possible they connected with a previous mate. The origin of the males is an intriguing unknown: perhaps they flew up the EAAF too. But long before CYA and CYB landed there, Tomkovich suggested there was a 'normal' shorebird migration route from Wrangel to the American continent. As Gill says, Beringia is full of secrets to be revealed.

When CYA arrived at Wrangel she flew straight to her nesting area, chose ground that was snow-free, and stayed in that spot for 57 days. After that she left only to fly to upland tundra 10 kilometres distant, perhaps within sight of the nest territory. She returned to it two days later for a visit of a few hours, and then flew out of Wrangel on 4 August. This extended loyalty to the nest is not only unusual for female Grey Plover, it might have meant that the brood was carefully guarded by both parents through to their first flights.

The timeline for CYB tells of a much sketchier season. Maybe she needed to find a mate, spurring her to try across the island. After the lost initial ten days, she spent at most 30 days on her eventual breeding ground before leaving on 19 July. Mating, laying and incubation over that period could have been possible. She might have seen chicks through to a hatch—just. She would also have rapidly left those chicks behind. With such an abrupt end to the season, her brood may have been taken.

'From the middle of July only birds with broods remained at the nesting sites,' Tomkovich wrote. He and Alexei Dondua found signs of predation pressure on Grey Plover at Wrangel. The birds were extremely cautious, much warier of approach than continental birds. 'As a rule we had to leave at least a distance of 200 to 300 metres or more from the nesting area and hide there in a long wait for the birds to return . . . Such unique behaviour . . . is most likely an adaptation to the considerable density of foxes on the island.'

The final phase in the Grey Plover's breeding season, the departure of new fledglings, came after their parents had left. In early August, Wrangel is at its least hostile. Sea ice has cleared around it and the snow has melted from the mountains. At this time offspring gather in small flocks, moving between the shores of northern tundra lakes and then flying to Wrangel's southern coast before migrating in early September.

That August when Tomkovich was there, the skies on Wrangel were mostly socked in with cloud. In September they cleared. There was a week or so of the kind of cloudless days that might encourage young birds taking their first migration, starting out on a journey unknown, except for what is genetically programmed into their heads.

Do the first-year migrants take a sideways hop, like the Sharp-tailed Sandpipers, which cross Beringia to the Yukon Delta? What is known, thanks to CYA, is that adult Grey Plover can fly further before flying south. They may head from Wrangel to a rich feeding ground far off the obvious path.

When CYA left Wrangel in a helpful south-easterly breeze, she at first retraced the direction of her inward flight but then veered high in the Arctic to alight on another island 1200 kilometres westward: Great Lyakhovsky. This is part of the New Siberians, the uninhabited island group magnetic to Australian shorebirds.

It was on Great Lyakhovsky that the holotype—the benchmark specimen—of a Red Knot sub-species was collected. Tomkovich later recognised it as distinct and named it *piersmai* in honour of the Dutchman 'most deeply devoted' to the bird.

The *piersmai* Red Knot are the birds that Chris Hassell sees in north-west Australia, and counts through Bohai Bay along with the East Australian/New Zealand *rogersi*. *Piersmai* breed across the New Siberians, as do most of the Sanderling that fly to Australia, and at least half of its Ruddy Turnstone.

Other birds head for these islands after they leave their breeding grounds, to feed up on what Tomkovich believes to be a summer bounty of long-legged crane flies. In July 2017 a Bar-tailed Godwit of the *menzbieri* sub-species, which had been satellite-tagged near Broome, flew another 1000 kilometres north-east from her breeding ground near Chersky, Siberia, to spend sixteen days feasting at the New Siberians.

It's hardly a holiday. It's a risk to head further north in order to build condition ahead of a long flight south, and underscores these birds' need for a full breadth of the Arctic. By early August weather is at its warmest on the wet New Siberians, encouraging a flush of insect hatches. But CYA's few days on Great Lyakhovsky coincided with the passage of a deep low-pressure system that swept the island with strong winds from the south. By 6 August the low had passed, and left lighter tailwinds from the north in a brief lull. The next day CYA began her southward migration.

She flew back to the Siberian coast and, with a south-westerly now blowing at her head, took an uncertain, zig-zag course about 280 kilometres inland. Then near a tundra pond, where she had briefly halted on her northward migration, CYA's signal disappeared. After all those months of knowing her movements, on 7 August her pinpoint of light went dark. Her flight line was done.

We can only guess why. At best, she dropped her harness just as the Great Knot 6RRBR had done. At worst, the rig finally entangled her and she perished. Perhaps her condition suffered under the extra-long duty she served at the nest, and she wasn't able to make up the weight in bad weather on Great Lyakhovsky. Did that strange course show she was in trouble? Weakened, was she taken by a waiting Gyrfalcon?

We did learn something of her character. CYA was first to leave South Australia and took a longer, harder, route north. She seemed eager, perhaps less experienced. More certainly than CYB she bred, showing extraordinary faithfulness to a single nest site on Wrangel, poignantly visiting it briefly again before her departure. In this she differed from the usual profile of early-leaving females. If a measure of a successful life is the production of the next, CYA likely did it.

I imagine her, shimmering in silver female breeding plumage. Quickly pairing with her mate. Spending weeks on twilight incubation. Carefully lifting out of the nest her brood's tell-tale broken eggshells and disposing of them. Calling a come-to-me trill to her chicks. Seeing off jaegers. Finally striking out for Australia again. There is a surviving image of CYA taken at Thompson Beach: she's running in the seagrass shallows, head up, dark eye watchful, set to take flight.

It can be a fluky business, this satellite tracking of shorebirds. Of a total ten Grey Plover to leave from Thompson Beach with trackers over three years, only two made it to the Arctic. Apart from the Thompson Beach birds, another four Grey Plover were sent off from Broome. Two of them reached the Yellow Sea, and then northern Siberia; but neither of them left a trace beyond that.

Battery life is questionable in some transmitters. Harness design and the fit to the bird constantly worry people who put them there. Of this Australian cohort, CYB now remains the only one still able to carry discoveries of Grey Plover further south, still holding potential to close the loop.

————

When CYB left the nest site, she flew to tundra near a coastal lagoon at Yuzhny Bay on the south-west of Wrangel. A Russian Polar Bear naturalist, S.M. Uspenski, noticed Grey Plover gathering in pre-migratory flocks on the southern side of the island in late July. Through summer the birds had kept clear of each other, but now they were flocking for the shared strength in long flight.

With a helpful south-easterly breeze, CYB launched her attempt at a return migration across the globe on 24 July, much earlier than CYA. Flying west from Wrangel across the still-frozen East Siberian Sea, she retraced her inward path nearly to the Gulag port of Ambarchick. Then she turned south over the mainland coast.

Within a day, a slight tailwind became a strong headwind at 1500 to 3000 metres altitude as the flock worked up above the tundra hills and low mountains of western Chukotka, over the headwaters of the Kolyma River and south to the Magadan region. Beneath her, the Arctic fell behind; steppe meadows and larch forest grew between the bare granite peaks of the Kolyma range.

CYB was far to the east of her efficient northward path. Day and night she was beating into headwinds. Reaching the North Pacific's Sea of Okhotsk, she crossed it, and then appeared to have had enough of this particular flight. The bird took a hard right turn away from the ocean, and flew west to land in an obscure corner of this sea called Ul'banskiy Bay.

At that time of year, Ul'banskiy Bay's river estuaries are alive with Pink and Chum Salmon running to spawn. Beluga Whales gather by the hundred for this feast. In turn, Orcas hunt the white Belugas which surf inshore to escape.

This kind of raw, intact ecosystem survives along much of the coastline of the 1.6-million-square-kilometre Sea of Okhotsk. It is bounded on the east by the volcanic line of the Kamchatka Peninsula and the Kuril Islands, by Sakhalin Island and Japan's northern Hokkaido, and to the west by sparsely inhabited taiga forest. Around 30 shorebird staging areas are known in the sea, but there are big holes in our knowledge of their use of its tidal flats. Estuaries tens of kilometres wide are unsurveyed.

Where the flats are accessible, researchers have found heavy autumn shorebird traffic. Many birds will be juveniles on their maiden long hops, taking the first chance to rest after crossing the Russian Far East. A survey of Ul'banskiy Bay's 5-kilometres-wide flats in early August counted around 5000 shorebirds. They were mainly Great Knot, Terek Sandpiper, Wood Sandpiper and Redshank. Further east lies the mouth of the Amur River, a large estuary of lagoons and islands, where an estimated 250,000 shorebirds passed south—nearly ten times the number seen there on northern migration.

On the northern side of the Sea of Okhotsk fly autumn shorebird clouds. There in Penzhina Bay the highest tidal range anywhere in the Pacific sluices down 12.9 metres to open swathes of ground for feeding. The total number of birds on southern passage in this estuary probably exceeds one million. At the mouth of the Penzhina River itself around 500,000 shorebirds have been counted through, mainly Dunlin, Red-necked Stint, and Red-necked Phalarope.

These birds come in waves over the Sea of Okhotsk. We know from the work of Aleksey Antonov and Falk Huetmann at Schastya Bay on its southern coast that first the non-breeding birds and females turn up in mist nets; then come the males and, later, juveniles. By counting re-traps, these two researchers have estimated that the birds spend only two or three days there before flying on. They saw hints of destinations in a few leg-flagged Australian birds— Great Knot flagged in the north-west and stint from the Victorian Wader Study Group's (VWSG) south-east.

Antonov also saw some Grey Plover come through Schastya Bay in mid- to late September 2002, most likely juveniles. Others have been seen in autumn transit on Sakhalin, but the bird is uncommon in most areas of the sea. It usually prefers the longer hop, which makes CYB's arrival unusual, a sign of a radical change of plan. She settled down on the flats into August, tundra life behind her, once more joining the rhythm of the tides.

———

In the great winter migration down the north-western Pacific coast of the EAAF, the Sea of Okhotsk offers some of the earliest riches. Dozens of sites fringing Japan are also targets for birds that do not wait for the Yellow Sea. But for one Beringian migrant there is no such choice. To it, the ocean is a highway south, though it cannot settle. Instead it makes the longest non-stop flight by any land bird.

Bob Gill was new to Alaska and out on the Yukon–Kuskokwim Delta in the 1970s when he first saw this bird. He thought of it then as an almost mythical Asian–Alaskan creature that somehow showed up in Australia and New Zealand.

'I have one vivid recollection of waking up, in post-breeding season, and suddenly there's a flock of thousands of Bar-tailed Godwits right in front of me. I'd never seen them before. Big storm comes, we hunker down in a cabin, we wake up next day and they're gone. Not only are they gone, but these guys were fat. Unbelievably fat.

'Now if you're going over the coast to Asia, which is just a hop, step and jump, why are you carrying all this fat? It's counter intuitive. Then you start looking at the storms. Well these birds left when they had a massive tailwind that would take them right south in the Pacific. So that was my first exposure, and things just went from there . . .'

The work Gill led, first with Mark Barter but mainly in a long collaboration with New Zealand researchers, stands as a landmark in global understanding of shorebird powers. As new techniques emerged, these scientists often used them most dramatically to illuminate the exceptional feats of the Bar-tailed Godwit's *baueri* sub-species. From this comes a vivid under-standing of many shorebirds' long migratory flights.

The *baueri* godwit's breeding grounds spread widely along terrain inland from the coast of Alaska, from the delta up the Bering Strait and around the North Slope to the Arctic Sea. Gill has found nests buried in dense shrubs, and others out in open grassland. In general they are cryptic breeders, hard to study. But no matter how far apart they nest, it appears they all gather at the Yukon–Kuskokwim in the late summer and autumn to feed up before their southward migration. They arrive there in waves, the most northerly birds last.

Like their flyway counterparts—the *menzbieri* godwits that I saw disappear into indigo north-west Australian evening skies—these *baueri* birds coalesce into excited, chattering flocks

when they are in the delta. To the Yup'ik people of the Yukon–
Kuskokwim, the bird is *Tevatevaaq* (*de-vaah-dev'aahq*).
Emblematic of the godwit cry, this name is collected in an
absorbing study of Alaskan natives lives with shorebirds by
Department of Fish and Game researchers Liliana Naves and
Jacqueline Keating. They found *Tevatevaaq* is also *Sugg'erpak*
(*sooggh'erh-buck*), one of a group of long-billed shorebirds. As
these birds gather and swirl in flocks, they become *Puyunaq*
(*boo-yoo'naq*)—like smoke in the sky.

Naves and Keating spent years in face-to-face research
discovering Indigenous knowledge of shorebirds, and assessing
the level of hunting. By the way they emerged with a story that
resonates across cultures, and carries an Alaskan bird to the
heart of European thought. It involves what appears to be
the only surviving traditional ceremonial artefact of a shorebird made by an Alaskan people—a Yup'ik dance mask of
a bird believed to be a godwit.

The dark wooden mask has at its base a small head, and
from this a long, thin bill extends downwards. Narrow wings
fly out to the sides. Stick thin legs and unwebbed feet point up.
At the mask's centre, emerging from the bird's back, is a broad,
smiling human face. It's the visage of a Yup'ik.

'The faces in the mask are the spirits,' Naves tells me. 'They
are part of a story. These masks are used in dance festivals,
usually done over winter, in prayers for the abundance of
animals. Arriving migratory birds in spring were often the food
that alleviated starvation. Famine in late winter was common.
So these birds can have cultural and emotional value, because
they saved people many times.'

There was a rich flowering in the tradition of Yup'ik
mask-making around the end of the nineteenth century, when

a fur trader-naturalist, Adam Hollis Twitchell, came to live at Bethel on the Kuskokwim. Out of the long winter nights, carvers would emerge carrying grotesque human and spirit masks, as well as images of their food: reindeer, salmon, and birds like loons and guillemots.

The godwit mask was one that Twitchell collected and sold to the American, George Gustav Heye. From there it made its way to New York, to gather dust until in the mid-twentieth century it was swept up in an artistic passion. Exiled European surrealists seized on these masks as if they were kin.

The French writer André Breton, painter Max Ernst and others from the surrealist school were World War Two refugees in the United States. Burnt by the dark politics of Europe, their art and writing often reflected the hellish and bizarre. In New York, their lives collided with French philosopher, Claude Lévi-Strauss. A founder of anthropology, Lévi-Strauss developed a basis for studying all societies on equal footing, not as the previously divided 'primitive' or 'civilised'.

How these tumultuous European minds must have leapt at a chance to own these hair-raising, cultish masks when they found them in a Bronx warehouse. How could they *not* go on to provoke the imaginations of these creative artists?

Among the group was Robert Lebel, a writer who would later become Marcel Duchamp's friend and biographer. Lebel left the warehouse having bought the godwit mask. From there it went back to post-war France and later passed to Lebel's artist son Jean-Jacques, who sold his collection at auction earlier this century.

'It seems the godwit mask sold for US$360,000,' Naves wrote. 'It now resides at the Musée du Quai Branly, in Paris.'

Indeed, there it is, clearly visible in the online catalogue for this grand public museum of Indigenous art and culture on the banks of the Seine. The mask is labelled on the back: 'Surrealism-Eskimo Mask 190'. Awkwardly, however, the museum describes the object as '*figurant l'inua d'un huitrier nageant à la surface de l'eau*', or 'depicting the soul of an oystercatcher swimming on the surface of the water.'

There are problems with this label. The Black Oyster-catcher has been hunted further south in the Aleutian Islands, but not by the Yup'ik. No oystercatcher ranges near the central Yukon–Kuskokwim Delta, where the mask originated. It's not a tundra bird.

Naves has already disentangled this mask from another repre-senting a guillemot, a confusion resulting from a handwritten note of Robert Lebel's. She is careful: 'The characteristic bill shape and proportions and non-webbed feet allow recognition of the bird represented in the mask as a godwit.'

If I could reach back to the carver, circa 1900, I could ask. In his absence I see a godwit's noble, narrow-chiselled head, much sharper than an oystercatcher's. In any case, this mask's extra-ordinary story tells of the marginal lives of these birds, and of what has been lost in their traditional meaning to us. As I try to get a grip on our shared existence with super-flying shorebirds, this diversion to Europe underscores how little they are known to the world.

The Yup'ik, alone among Alaskan natives, do continue to hunt the *baueri* godwit, taking perhaps 1000 a year, a consider-able number of this sub-species' global population. The human need to prevent spring starvation may have reduced by now, but delta-fattened *Tevatevaaq* can carry 200 grams of fat on a bird weighing around 485 grams.

Yup'ik traditional knowledge of the birds' arrival, their favoured grounds and their physical condition is sought by Bob

Gill when he goes into the field. 'I make first for the elders,' he says. 'They are such keen observers. They may not know what's behind the biology that drives a certain observation. They don't need to. But boy, they are so spot-on as to where that critter fits into their lifestyle.'

So too have been the people at the other end of the flyway over the centuries; their folklore hints at the bird's great ocean crossing. Ancient Polynesians had noticed *Kuaka*, the *baueri* godwit, flying from their islands. These were probably 'fallouts'— birds that halted on land to recover after a storm or days of adverse winds. They were obviously not seabirds and, when they lifted off again, they always headed south. Legend says the first Maori followed them to settle Aotearoa/New Zealand, around 700 years ago.

Both the *menzbieri* and the *baueri* godwits migrate north through the Yellow Sea route. For contemporary researchers, an early hint that they took a different course back from the Arctic came when Barter noticed *baueri* birds banded in south-east Australia and New Zealand were not among the band returns along the Asian coast on southward migration.

Before there were satellite trackers small enough to use on godwits, Bob Gill and others gathered lines of evidence, including sightings throughout Oceania. 'There ought to have been records of them out there,' Gill says now. 'Not every one is going to be able to make this flight, especially the juveniles. You think they might stop in Hawaii or the Tuamotus. But no. There were just a handful of records given the population size.'

A breakthrough, pointing towards a more likely ocean-spanning flight, came with a study of the energetics of the bird—when their weights were translated into fuel. 'There are a lot of models you can use,' he recalls. 'We had something on the fat, and thought, lo and behold they could probably fly there to New Zealand. But still, you go: "That's just too much, to be in the air for eight or nine days non-stop."'

Then the satellite tags showed that they could do this. Godwits were netted in the Yukon–Kuskokwim and in New Zealand. Trackers were surgically implanted in twelve females, and leg-harnessed to eleven males. Nine of these eventually returned southward tracks, departing from the delta. Among them, the shortest flight was by a male, H6. He made landfall at Tarawa in the Gilbert Islands after flying 7008 kilometres in five days. Other tracks petered out over the ocean. One female, E5, last signalled near New Caledonia but was later seen on tidal sands at Broken Bay, just north of Sydney.

The title of Long-Haul Queen went to another female, E7, who was originally implanted with a tag at Miranda, near Auckland. Her flight from Alaska back to the same New Zealand shoreline covered 11,680 kilometres in 8.1 days, the longest known non-stop flight by any land bird, ever.

Only in a current human lifespan have we developed machines sophisticated enough to undertake this sort of journey. These godwits probably have been managing ultramarathon flight for millennia. We are puny.

In profile, the godwit looks close to nature's perfected distance flier. The long, slightly upturned wind-breaking bill and aerodynamically smooth head lead into an elongated tube of a body. This slims down with weight loss, losing resistance in long flight. The wings are broad, spanning about twice the bird's total length. On migration a 4-gram heart keeps pumping as the body burns fat at eight to ten times resting intensity for nine days on end.

Gill believes this to be an unprecedented feat in the animal world. He thought about how these godwits use this physique to thread Pacific air. And he started by looking at the storm into which the godwits vanished the first time that he saw them.

The Aleutian Low Pressure system is one of the most reliable features of North Pacific weather. 'It waxes and wanes seasonally in storm intensity, but when the godwits are leaving it's really ramping up, the cyclones are bigger and moving further north,' Gill says. Matching the passage of the cyclones with known godwit departures, he saw that they picked moments when storm winds swung around to their tails.

It isn't random. Nearly all satellite-tracked birds leaving Alaska choose the best wind days in a two-week period. They probably sense a change in the barometric pressure and wind direction that will provide favourable air for 1000 kilometres to come. Out over the Pacific they fly, as if connecting to a highway system.

After taking the Yukon on-ramp, they ride the Aleutian freeway to an off-ramp across a zone of Pacific westerlies. That might drift them a little east of a direct line. But next comes a turn into the north-easterly trade wind ring road that brings them back on line.

'They might make a big loop, but they'll get back in and compensate for it. And then you leave the Trades and you're in an Equatorial zone with a tremendous uplift of warm air.' Up the flyover they go.

'You come out of that, and in the Southern Hemisphere it's just a mirror image of what you just flew.' South-east trade winds flow into Queensland, and westerlies across south-eastern Australia and New Zealand bring direct or quartering tailwinds. Straight on to morning.

Gill shrugs. 'It's very structured,' he says.

Defined route it may be, but not all godwits read it successfully all of the time. 'I'm not implying that these birds have it hard-wired and that there are not any failures. Not at all. I guess, to extend the analogy, you could suddenly see a roadblock, an atmospheric detour zone.'

Pacific air movement is invisibly complex. Winds vary during the day with heating and cooling, by altitude as it rises and falls, weekly and monthly with pressure systems, and between years when giant events like El Niño take control. Work on godwit air management has found out how they make careful choices about the best place in the sky to fly.

Using GPS trackers on Black-tailed Godwit flying between North Africa and Northern Europe, conservation ecologist Nathan Senner discovered that the birds routinely fly up to 5000 metres altitude. This is above the height that an oxygen mask would trigger for us in an aircraft cabin if it were to lose pressure.

The birds do not fly to a single level and stay there, but frequently change height, not in response to wind support, but to find cooler air. The trick for them is to keep up their bodily fluids. 'Godwits may fly at high altitudes in order to minimise the potential for hyperthermia and, ultimately, water loss during their long non-stop flights,' Senner wrote.

Senner's work also went to the heart of godwit flight: wing-beat. Accelerometers on the trackers showed that, at no point, did the godwits soar or glide as they made their way on long migrations. Instead their wing-beats averaged 6.30 hertz (that is, beats per second). The sum is frightening. If something like that pace transferred to Bar-tails, then hypothetically—just hypothetically—it would mean E7 beat her wings around 4.5 million times on end.

Known peak long-distance shorebird flight skills lie with the godwits; but, as the technology miniaturises, there are signs that the ability is more widespread. New Zealand Red Knot may fly a 10,100-kilometre route to the Yellow Sea, and Pacific Golden Plover take a 9794-kilometre flight from Alaska to American Samoa. One of these plovers, tagged at Nome, chose to winter in Queensland's Fraser Island as it made a 26,700-kilometre round-trip.

Gill has no hesitation in saying that wind-reading refinements possessed by godwits apply to other trans-Oceanic long-haul migrants. 'They have to have figured this out. Those that spend multiple days in the air. Otherwise it's a crap shoot, and you know how the odds are in favour of the house.'

So come southern migration season, the skies of the Pacific are a web woven with unseen shorebird life making directly for their resting grounds, evolved for superflights as the best fit to reach their shores of need. In a south-west corner of this ocean's rim, far from Beringia, I can reliably see godwits—just a few dozen. Bar-tails hang out near a road causeway outside Hobart. They are very likely *baueri* birds from Alaska, wearing the dowdy non-breeding disguise, huddled on the causeway's rocks to roost, or on a small finger of sand near a sewage pumping station. Local birders await their return and treasure these few, but the birds are unremarked and their feats unknown to almost all who drive by.

With this little Bar-tail flock have been seen a single Black-tailed Godwit, and a Hudsonian Godwit of the American flyways. Maybe they are not confused about where they choose to spend time in their Pacific domain. Maybe we are.

Twelve
A flick of the dragon's tail

The sweet air of the Russian taiga conifer forest, pure streams feeding into unpeopled Ul'banskiy Bay, easy foraging across broad tidal flats. Why leave this? The cold Arctic hand that compels shorebird migration reaches down the Pacific coast. Refuelled, CYB lifts and turns south again.

Migration theory says these birds are retracing routes of ancestral spread. They always have to follow light and warmth for the life it enables; they would never survive a polar winter. Their breeding and non-breeding shores might have been closer during glacial periods, but each year they inevitably go.

For Arctic-nesting shorebirds the distance they fly seems to matter much less than maintaining a route across barriers like seas or forested mountains to reliable feeding grounds. Exactly how these routes arose is still mysterious. 'With many shore-birds, migrations probably developed so far back in time that it is impossible to tell from current patterns how they evolved,' British ornithologist Ian Newton wrote. Birds must have taken many wrong flights and failed. The survivors were the ones who made the small step-changes that achieved evolutionary fitness. Passed on to progeny, it was that amazing genetic knowledge of the first-year migrant. Knowing the direction.

Fresh from the predatory dramas of the tundra, I might have thought that the critical factor limiting the population growth of these birds was losses at the nest. Or, as in Phil Bruner's grim aside, that many young birds get their weight or direction wrong and just drop into the water. But Newton says it's likely their numbers are capped by the availability of food outside the breeding ground. Locked by evolution into migration, they can make small adjustments to their routes, but not radical shifts. If they lose access to places offering critical food supplies, that's what will knock them over.

Around 7 August, as an early whisper of the approaching winter steals down the western side of the Sea of Okhotsk, CYB takes off. The following breeze allows a traverse along the valley of the Amur. The pioneer Russian surveyor Vladimir Arsenyev watched, spellbound, as swirling, undulating flocks of birds headed south on autumn passage in 1902 at nearby Lake Khanka. He saw Grey Plover 'holding to the marshy lowlands, flying along ponds of standing water, perhaps using them as landmark'. Within a day or two, though, the massed passage turned to panic, 'a wall of chaos', as the birds sought to escape an early blizzard howling in from the north. Arsenyev survived being caught in the blizzard, thanks to a reed-grass shelter built by his guide, a man of the animist Gold people called Dersu Uzala. When they woke next day, the guide told him: '"Last night many people die." I understood that the "people" Dersu was referring to were the birds.'

CYB leaves behind the taiga forests and the wild rivers, and crosses into northern China. At this stark divide, there is forest

on the Russian side and agriculture pressing to the very border
of China.

The breeze helps the bird fly an inland route parallel to the
path she took north a few months earlier. She navigates over
collective farms and low mountain ranges, passes the regional
town of Hailin, and flies onto the broad Manchurian plain, with
its many rivers gathering yellow-grey loess soil sediments the
way they have for centuries of Chinese farming. In only a few
days CYB completes the 1800-kilometre flight and she lands
where one of these rivers enters the Yellow Sea.

It's exactly the place she used on the northward flight. She is
on the mud again at the mouth of the Daling River.

Uncounted generations of shorebirds have sought out
ground among the estuaries of the four rivers that run into the
100-kilometre wide head of Liaodong Bay. It's that clear prize—
the shore furthest north in the Yellow Sea, the first shore for
birds flying south. But in a Grey Plover lifetime, Liaodong Bay
has changed from ancestral sanctuary to dangerous ground.

This stark shift reverberates out into the greater Yellow Sea,
into the rest of the flyway and beyond to many shores. These fleet
flocks murmuring on the edges of our world, the air's super fliers,
are fading to black. Migratory shorebird numbers are sliding
away, worst of all in this East Asian–Australasian Flyway.

The Daling River rises north-east of Beijing and flows east in a
long half circle through Liaoning Province to reach Liaodong
Bay. Shortly before turning for the sea it meanders through
an unrivalled trove of ancient bird history. Here, survival and
extinction are written in fossils.

A flock of around 40 crow-sized birds with clawed fingers at the leading edges of their wings were gathered near a lake millions of years ago where today the farming village of Sihetun stands. They are the oldest-known beaked birds, called *Confuciusornis* by today's Chinese discoverers, with a hat tip to the timeless philosopher. They lived in the company of dinosaurs, insects and plants, part of a rich, temperate ecosystem known as the Jehol Biota, 125 million years ago in the Cretaceous period.

These birds likely used fingers on their wings to help climb conifer trees before launching into the air. *Confuciusornis*'s flight was clumsy compared to today's migratory birds. Their bone structure did not allow them to raise their wings high. Perhaps they were more like today's Australian lyrebird, a clumsy short distance flapper, and accomplished forest-floor runner.

On the day when their Armageddon came, they may have been startled into flight, they may have been caught on the ground, but they made no distance at all. The 40 died together, falling in an area 10 metres by 10 metres. The flock was caught by a pyroclastic blast.

Vulcanologists prefer the passionless term 'pyroclastic density currents' for these, the most devastating type of eruptions. They are made of ash, gas and pumice, and come as avalanches, when a rising explosive column collapses, or as a jet blast when the mountain bursts its side. They can travel at 500 kilometres per hour and are very hot. All life enveloped by the pyroclastic current at Sihetun that day, plant and animal, was extinguished. The flock fell as one, possibly instantly gassed, into a shallow lake where their carcasses settled on its floor to be covered by sediments.

Over 10 million years and through different volcanic explosions, many of the dinosaurs in the Jehol Biota were preserved in three-dimensional form. 'The hyper-extended spine, in which the skull and neck are re-curved over the back, and with strong extension of the tail . . . arose at the time of death, and not afterwards, and they attribute it to poisoning of the central nervous system,' observed the British palaeontologist Michael Benton.

The Jehol birds, on the other hand, tend to be found lying flat, their remains left in little more than two richly-detailed dimensions. Their bodies are outlined in the rock down to tiny bones. Feathers and even colour-banding are clearly visible. Some were eating at the time they were struck down. A chicken-sized *Yanornis martini* died with one fish in its gullet and another in its stomach.

More than 1000 *Confuciusornis* fossils have been retrieved from Jehol shale sediments. The number of birds and their extraordinary state of detailed preservation make them the most important and diverse fossil-bird fauna known to science. Yet until recently no fossil specimen had been found anywhere to show us a direct ancestor of CYB, despite their territory being just downstream on the Daling River mouth.

The American paleo-ornithologist Alan Feduccia proposed 'transitional shorebirds' were survivors of the Cretaceous–Tertiary (K–T) mass extinction and indeed could be primary ancestors of all modern birds. Somehow these birds, living on the margin of water and land, were adaptive enough to survive the long-lasting reverberations around the planet likely caused by a giant asteroid impact.

The new science of DNA genome sequencing came along to tease out this possibility. It's been able to reconstruct evolutionary pasts in roughly the same way that it can tell each of us in which part of the world our own genetic family 'tree' is rooted. Canadian geneticist Tara Paton traced back the DNA of eighteen different birds, among them the Ruddy Turnstone, Emu and Rook. She produced an evolutionary tree linking the birds far back to the DNA of the alligator and an African turtle. Her skills enabled her in 2002 to give an estimate of the origin of modern birds at 123 million years, which coincides with the Jehol fossils.

On this tree, shorebirds diverged from ancestral birds of prey between 79 and 99.5 million years ago. This is still well before the K–T holocaust at 65 million years. Later, in 2007, Paton revised her own work in collaboration with avian evolutionary scientist, Allan Baker. They spread the DNA net wider and pushed back the age of the ancestral shorebird to 93 million years. Their work confirmed that the ancestors of many shorebird species—including sandpipers, curlews and the forebear of tundra plovers—predated the K–T boundary.

Then, eight years later, along came another Jehol stone bird to propose an extraordinary age. Out of 130.7-million-year ash-grey siltstone at Sichakou near Inner Mongolia emerged two fossils of a bird species little bigger than a sparrow. It was toothed like the oldest known bird, *Archaeopteryx*, which lived 150 million years ago. The difference is that *Archaeopteryx* died without descendants. The Sichakou bird's anatomy meant its discoverers could claim it as an ornithuromorph—a bird from which almost all modern birds are descended.

Borrowing from the oldest bird, and paying credit to a Chinese palaeontologist, they called it *Archaeornithura meemannae*. It has the relatively longer un-feathered legs and wider feet that indicate it was a specialised wader of ancient shores. *Science* magazine reported that the second-oldest known bird was 'similar to today's plovers'.

I look at artists' impressions and fossil images of these ancient birds. I compare them not just with the Grey Plover, but

with the Hooded Plover of Australian beaches, the Piping Plover
of the US Great Lakes, the Ringed Plover of the UK's shingle
banks, and I wonder: How many evolutionary steps were taken
between *Archaeornithura* and these birds, doing the same thing
on shores 130.7 million years later?

This breadth of existence, of change or constancy through
time, is nearly too much to comprehend. But it stands as a measure
of the antiquity of shorebirds in our precarious era. Yet the Daling
River, as it flows downstream and into the sea, past Grey Plover
CYB, a descendant of the K–T holocaust survivors, enters a new
moment: the Anthropocene, time of a sixth extinction.

As scientists struggle to wake us to the multiple threats the
planet and humanity face, the concept of an Anthropocene
is being rapidly embraced to crystalise the magnitude of our
power. Proposed by the Dutch geoscientist Paul J. Crutzen, the
word suggests our changes to the planet are so profound they
impact on the geological record.

It's not a settled term. So far its advocates have been unable
to convince the arbiter on geological time, the International
Commission on Stratigraphy. The concept persists though, as
threats magnify and our actions rival great forces of nature. The
strongest candidate for the start of this period is the mid-twentieth
century, and a formal case will be put to the commission by 2021
by its Anthropocene Working Group. They are considering the
evidence of accelerated industrial production, use of agricultural
chemicals, atomic bomb blasts—all of them indelible marks on
earth's timescale. So is the total loss of living species.

Previous mass extinctions showing up on the geological record
began at the Ordovician–Silurian boundary around 439 million
years ago. The worst, the Great Dying, came 250 million years
ago in the Permian–Triassic era, with the loss of 95 per cent of all

living species. The last came at the 65 million year K–T boundary. Now we must contemplate our own era of 'defaunation', where we are witnessing the rapid loss of whole populations, and of species themselves.

In 2019, a UNESCO committee on global biodiversity reached the shocking conclusion that around one million animal and plant species face extinction, many within decades, if changes aren't made to reduce the intensity of loss. The number of species already lost, particularly of invertebrates such as insects, comes as a jolt.

'Of a conservatively estimated 5 million to 9 million animal species on the planet, we are likely losing 11,000 to 58,000 species annually,' the Stanford University evolutionary ecologist, Rodolfo Dirzo, found. 'Across vertebrates, 16 to 33 per cent of all species are estimated to be globally threatened or endangered, and at least 322 vertebrate species have become extinct since 1500.' Dirzo uses comprehensive threat categories prepared by the International Union for the Conservation of Nature (IUCN) to record vertebrate losses. Among these are 130 bird extinctions, 50 of them since 1900.

The record for birds is more dramatic when looking back into the era of global exploration. In the widely scattered Pacific islands of Oceania, up to 1800 bird species are estimated to have gone extinct in the 2000 years of its human colonisation. Ground-dwelling pigeons and parakeets, rails and crakes dominate lists of birds gone, most of them leaving only the trace of bone remains. And this is a clue to what makes for precipitous losses. A species confined to an island, and in small numbers, stands a poorer chance if something like European rats make it to shore. It's also a warning of a greater problem: extirpation, or the complete loss of a species' local population.

A Mexican ecologist, Gerardo Ceballos, worked with Paul Ehrlich and Dirzo to look at the whole world in 10,000-square-kilometre blocks, and map each block's decreasing species. Most went in tropical regions, but losses were global. In the worst block, a total of 296 different birds were falling away. 'The true extent of this mass extinction has been under-estimated, because of the emphasis on species extinction . . . overlooking the accelerating extinction of populations.'

In Liaodong Bay and further out around the whole Yellow Sea, the Anthropocene is rapidly unfolding, threatening this flyway most starkly with the sixth extinction. It howls at these birds' tails like an Arctic blizzard, a 'wall of chaos'. But the Yellow Sea is also a crucible that burns with the means of understanding, in fast time, what has been done to these birds of many shores. Their study is shifting from an era of movement discovery to give us sentinel warnings about the ecological state of the places we populate most: our coasts. I take courage from the forewarning of the shorebird people, and see their work for the spearhead it is.

———

When today's birders first pushed down towards the mouths of rivers like the Daling into Liaodong Bay, they were breaking new ground. The East Asian bird specialist author, Mark Brazil, went there in 1991 to run a survey for the World Wildlife Fund, and said, 'It appears the ornithological importance of the once vast wetlands at the head of Bohai Bay and their significance for both breeding and migratory birds has been quite overlooked.'

On foot and by bicycle, Brazil managed to find dozens of species new to the Shuangtaizihekou National Nature Reserve, next door to the Daling River mouth. Many of the birds on his list are eye-rolling to me, steeped as I am in the colours of Australian parrots, finches and robins. A Zitting Cisticola is just too small, brown and obscure. But to these birders this was precious ground, particularly as the home of the revered Red-crowned Crane and rare Saunders's Gull.

When Brazil and his WWF colleague, David Melville, first went, they were looking particularly for this gull's black balaclava head, rather than shorebirds. Their forays into the heads of Liaodong Bay's several river mouths largely found tidal flats spreading as they long had done. Traditional crops held sway. Commercial reed beds were hand-harvested for paper-making in a below-zero winter. Industry was largely upstream, where it had been set up by occupying Japanese forces in the Manchuria of the 1930s.

Shorebird riches began to be counted a few years later when Mark Barter and his local teams loped out onto the northern Liaodong. He walked the Daling River mouth and found strong numbers of Grey Plover and Great Knot, then moved to the next-door Shuangtaizihekou. Tens of thousands of Arctic shorebirds were working mud there. Further east, more of them used the tidal flats around the cities of Yingkou and Gaizhou. Barter thought perhaps a quarter of a million shorebirds could funnel northward through Liaodong Bay.

Counts by the Chinese birders who Barter mentored underscored the bay's value over both seasonal migrations. Big flocks of Grey Plover can be found there in August, before they split wide along the flyway in their flights to their own warm souths. On a single day during northward migration, volunteers at Shuangtaizihekou counted 80,000 Great Knot, half of the species' total global population.

Over the years, David Melville has checked on Liaodong Bay, and has drawn international attention to it. A tall, greybeard epitome of the British-born shorebird diaspora, this ecologist has threaded his way through the vagaries of East Asian culture in the name of these birds for most of his working life, and is not easily taken aback.

But in 2013 that changed when Melville travelled around the entire Yellow Sea coastline. 'I came home emotionally damaged,' he tells me. 'I had been coming and going from there for years. I knew that there was development. I had no idea it was so bad. It was so unrelenting around the whole coast.'

In China, particularly since the late 1990s, there has been a rapid ecological shift so fundamental as to entrap these global birds in local change. Their lives on Arctic tundra or Australian tidal sand have come to depend on how China treats the Yellow Sea, upon a flick of the dragon's tail.

One of the bargains China's rulers made for economic growth was to restrict the loss of cultivated land, so as to defend food supplies for its giant population. This drove people and industry seaward. As a whole, the coastal region of China is little more than a tenth of its area. But four in ten of its people live there, and they produce 60 per cent of its GDP. In Liaoning Province there's been a 50-fold increase in GDP over a single generation.

A national government 'Five Points and One Line' development strategy for Liaoning listed a legion of industrial clusters, all in coastal cities. At its launch, local mayor Huaming Zhao promised land to spare for Chinese pressing seaward. 'Our 120 square kilometres of wasted seashore and salty land will prove to be valuable resources for industrial use,' Zhao said. Pity anything that stands in the way.

On the bay coast today there is not as much mud, but everywhere there is industry. The oldest is to the west of the Daling River at Huludao, where the largest zinc smelter in Asia has been a heavy-metals polluter since the 1950s. In the haphazard world of Chinese environmental monitoring, this plant's uncontrolled pollution outfall was calculated at 33,000 tonnes of zinc and 8000 tonnes of other metals over a 30-year period. Next door to the zinc plant there is an oil refinery and chemical plants. Nearby there's a shipyard that builds supertankers and atomic submarines, and a nuclear power station is under construction.

Off Huludao the sea-floor sediments are thick with heavy metals that spread into Liaodong Bay, just as the mud once did. In 2012 the Chinese ecologist, Xiaoyu Li, called it a 'highly polluted area in the world', where the sea floor is 'extremely contaminated due to many years of random dumping of hazardous waste and free discharge of effluents'. A single oyster might contain 100 times more zinc than the recommended daily allowance.

Excessive copper levels flow down the Daling and Shuangtaizi to join the Liaodong Bay trace-metal pool. With this comes the discharge of waste water from millions of homes and intensively farmed land. Nitrogen and phosphorus run into the bay, supercharging toxic algal blooms. Summer in Liaodong Bay is a time of brown tides as planktonic diatoms mix with dinoflagellates that produce neurotoxins. In 2013, when China's central government found the bay officially had 'poor' quality water, environmental scientist Wenquin Cai said 'it was impossible to find pristine areas or sites in Liaodong Bay, because it is severely disturbed'.

It has one unrivalled seafood resource: the Flame Jellyfish. Liaodong Bay has the most important jelly-fishery in China. Surviving fin-fish have largely left the bay, and in the absence of these predators, jellyfish larvae can grow unimpeded. Is this our Anthropocene seafood future?

Damage to the marine ecosystem extends further out into the Bohai Sea. Its rim holds 5.4 per cent of China's land area, but 17.5 per cent of its population who produce a US$1 trillion GDP. 'The sea itself is being rapidly degraded and has basically lost its function as a fishing ground,' concluded Xuelu Gao of the Yantai Institute of Coastal Zone Research in 2014. 'Many scholars have claimed that the Bohai Sea would turn into a dead sea sooner or later if no appropriate and effective measures were taken as quickly as possible.'

When I went to Nanpu to see Chris Hassell at work, I leaned on a bridge rail to watch as a wooden fishing boat returned to port from the Bohai. It flew the red flag, carried a red star on the cabin roof, and another painted on its blunt bow. On board, three deckhands were pulling the last of their catch from grimy gillnets. This amounted to a couple of hand baskets full of mantis shrimp. A hopeful third basket stood empty on the deck as the boat passed beneath me.

The *Red Star* swung around a mudbank scattered with shorebirds to putter along a creek leading to Nanpu Ercun (Nanpu Second Village), where outside every shanty a small boat is tied up. Such wooden boats exist in their hundreds of thousands along the Chinese coast and they bring with them a cost in pollution that worries David Melville: DDT.

The old pesticide enemy of wildlife was officially banned in China in 1983, but somehow kept on being used in agriculture until 2000. Long after that, it has been used in anti-fouling paint to keep woodworm out of fishing boats.

'Chinese fishermen paint their boats for anti-fouling twice a year, and around 250 tonnes of DDT a year leaches out of the paint and into the sea,' Melville says. 'If you think about DDT in the Bohai, you've got residues in the sediment, shellfish absorbing it, and them being eaten by shorebirds. Okay, DDT is bound up in fat. But as the bird migrates, it burns the fat, and the DDT gets into the system.'

Migratory songbirds laden with agricultural pesticide have been shown to lose their ability to find their way, but the classic evidence of DDT's destructive power up the food chain is the near-loss of the Peregrine Falcon's reproduction. Melville's words make me wonder: What if the high nest failures Pavel Tomkovich saw among Grey Plover on Wrangel was not a case of in-breeding, but of hitchhiked poison?

Work was carried out and reported in 2003 on chemical contamination of Arctic migratory shorebirds in the densely populated Red River delta of Vietnam. The birds there all carried DDT contamination, worst of all Great Knot and Red-necked Stint, both hurrying mud-peckers. Grey Plover, choosers of prey, had levels about half as bad.

There is also a Korean study that found chronic lead contamination in Terek Sandpiper and Great Knot, and acutely toxic levels of lead and cadmium in Red-necked Stints. The study was published in 2010, many years after the samples were collected, and the authors suggested brightly that the contamination must have happened in breeding or wintering grounds.

These harms are rarely counted among shorebirds as they needle and pick at China's ancestral Yellow Sea sediments. That country's newly hatched shorebird science makes a priority of numbers and ecology. Melville says he knows of heavy metals and DDT studies that have been forbidden from publication. 'They weren't allowed to publish in Chinese, let alone internationally.'

Out in the haze from Nanpu's fishing villages stood the silhouette of another uncounted hazard: an oil-production platform. The Bohai oil basin has 165 marine platforms and, inevitably, there are leaks. In June 2011 the Penglai 19-3 oilfield in the central Bohai Sea twice sprung leaks, which were undisclosed for days. Within a month these wells, jointly owned by the US's ConocoPhillips and China National Offshore Oil Corporation, had driven a slick over 840 square kilometres of water. Losses to fisheries and marine aquaculture were estimated at ¥12.56 billion (US$1.87 billion).

A production-rig gas flare stands off the Daling River mouth. Ashore at Liaodong Bay, pump-jacks are spread through the Shuangtaizihekou Reserve, which has the third largest onshore oilfield in China. These 'nodding donkey' derricks stand as a symbol for what is permitted inside a Chinese national nature reserve—of the vast gap between notion and fact.

'When they declared the reserve, no one actually produced a map of it,' Melville tells me. 'That's the first problem.' The Shuangtaizihekou Reserve contains a profusion of villages supporting tens of thousands of people who work on the reed beds and the oilfield. The newer businesses chipping away at its edges are aquaculture ponds.

'It started with shrimp ponds in the 1980s,' Melville says. 'There was a gold rush, where the locals would basically get a backhoe, fling up a pond, and fill it with shrimp. Then along came white spot disease, and wiped a lot of it out.

'At Shuangtaizihekou they started more recently on sea-cucumber ponds. With the growing wealth in China there was a sudden demand for sea cucumbers and another gold rush. A local developer built these ponds, which need to be much more solid than shrimp ponds because the sea cucumbers don't like muddy water. He then on-sold them to operators. But the bottom fell out of that market when President Xi Jinping brought in his ban on banquets.'

These are the boom-and-bust vagaries of the mammoth Chinese market. Throughout it all, the bureaucracy that enables it sails on.

Shuangtaizihekou's story of a flexible border was reprised at the Daling River's Linghekou Wetland Protection Zone. Here, the struggle over its boundary turned into a wrestle between state authorities.

When Mark Barter first went to the area he gleaned that a 'proposed' reserve on the Daling estuary would cover 140,000 hectares, including 20,000 hectares of tidal flat. By the time it was set up in 2009, the reserve area had been near halved, and it was to contain 21,000 hectares of housing, and 5000 hectares of 'beach'.

A wind-farm developer liked the site too, and set up a 74-turbine project. This shaved another block off the boundaries, but raised the hackles of the state forestry bureau, which manages it. When a swan was killed by a turbine blade, Linghekou reserve's director, Peng Liu, saw a chance to prosecute the power company. He claimed the farm had been illegally built; maybe the single dead swan might add its weight to a workable prosecution.

At first Peng won a ¥5.59 million (US$880,000) fine, which he hoped would go towards wetland protection. Then he ran up against the local municipal council, which said the wind farm developer was right to build on 'wasteland'. With local taxes from an eventual ¥3.3 billion (US$552 million) project at stake, the power company said bluntly, 'We will not pay any fine.' The bold Peng Liu was transferred into a paper-shuffling job.

The turbines spun on, as they do around the Yellow Sea.
When Melville took his road trip, the vast extent of wind-farm
development was one of his biggest shocks. I glimpsed it in
Jiangsu, where their hum was an ever-present bass reverb track
behind the piping shorebird flocks on CYA's Tiaozini mudflat.

Birds wanting to roost inland had to work their way past
these blades in often hazy air. I shuddered at the thought of a
tightly bunched flock scythed out of the sky, but little is known
about whether this happens. Surveys of shorebird deaths as
a result of wind farms are few globally. In the Yellow Sea, a
reckoning of bird strikes is even less likely. It would take the
witnessing of an undeniable catastrophe.

Horrifying industrial accidents in China are already known
in the cataclysmic explosions that still happen with an awesome
destructive power over people, and any other life. Because of
the breakneck pace of coastal industrial development, many
of the worst accidents are on the Yellow Sea rim.

At the port of Dalian on the tip of the Liaodong Peninsula,
a refinery explosion in 2010 led to the release of thousands of
tonnes of crude oil. The destruction was symbolised by the
sight of a brave young emergency worker sinking to his death
in crude, as people rushed to clean up the spill by hand. The
slick spread for 430 square kilometres; blackened shellfish were
held out by grim-faced aquaculture farmers, and a warning was
issued of threats to seabirds. For shorebirds at least, it was lucky
that this was a July accident—most migrants along that coast
would likely have been north in the Arctic.

It was August, the month of returning birds, when a chain of
ever-more powerful explosions at a chemical factory near Nanpu
sent up fireballs large enough to be recorded in weather satellite pixels. Censored reports of these 2015 Tianjin explosions

admitted an official death toll of 179, another 800 injured and thousands made homeless.

Melville looked at this man-made pyroclastic blast, and wondered what it might mean for shorebirds. Red Knot and Curlew Sandpiper had used the mud and salt pans of Tianjin in globally significant numbers. There were thousands of Grey Plover; ranks of the careful watcher. Stockpiles at the dockside chemical factory site at the time of the explosion included hundreds of tonnes of illegally stored sodium cyanide. Within a week there were reports of a mass fish kill near the port.

'Industrial pollution, whether from accidents or chronic discharge is a serious problem for waders and other wildlife, as well as people along the Chinese coast,' Melville said.

He warned that the Jiangsu coast was in just as precarious a state. It had the highest numbers of both hazardous chemical enterprises and known pollution accidents in China, which has had no rigorous reporting rules, and where publicly known accidents only hint at the actual number.

When I went to the Yellow Sea, I had driven past the tanks, stacks and catalytic crackers of Yangkou Chemistry Industrial Park near the shorebird-rich Tiaozini tidal flats in Jiangsu. The size of an Australian suburb, Yangkou was China's first industrial park devoted solely to making pesticides. In April 2019, the official *China Daily* disclosed that at last count there were 7372 'chemical enterprises' in Jiangsu. This count was only released after a massive explosion at Chenjiagang Zhen, further up the coast from Tiaozini, that killed 78 people and injured more than 600. The explosion at the Tianjiayi chemical plant left a crater the size of a city block. In the nearby Guanhe River estuary, highly elevated levels of precursor chemicals for plastics were reported.

The output of many of these Chinese chemical factories *is* plastics—our plastics—and these are a wide scourge of the Yellow Sea. The Yangtze and Yellow rivers are reckoned to be respectively the largest, and second largest, plastic-debris conveyors in the world. Currents that sweep the Jiangsu coast carry rafts of polystyrene. Broken off from fishing floats and boxes, scum-browned foam pieces line the shore in jarring counterpoint to the beauty of wild birds. In their search for a geological marker in sediments, the Anthropocene Working Group might do worse than measure the earth layer pock-marked with polystyrene beads.

In Liaodong Bay, sampling of its few beaches found more than a hundred pieces of microplastic per kilogram of sand. Out in the wider Bohai, floating microplastic debris was collected every time a survey net was towed. Many of these floating pieces were fine threads broken off from fishing nets, and it is these nets, fixed on the flats, that are proving fatal for the birds too.

At falling tides I saw local fishing folk on the Yellow Sea mud, working like the wader birds themselves to the daily rhythm of the revealed food. The fishers' backs were bent, wearing harnesses with which they dragged wooden sleds out from the seawall. They cleared nets that were set on bamboo poles and running as long fences, to trap small fish on the high tide. It was hard, low-reward work. Peter Crighton—that Australian bird bander whose hands were scarred by Caspian Terns back at Thompson Beach—went to join the trudging fishers on a shorebird expedition in 2016. He was hunting for their catch of birds.

Crighton had seen shorebird flocks fly clear of the nets during the day, but found dozens trapped after the night-time's falling tides. In checks at Tiaozini during southward migration, he had most often come upon trapped Kentish Plover; sometimes

Red-necked Stint or a Grey Plover. He also discovered three Spoon-billed Sandpiper. He noted bleakly that these few deaths took out 0.5 per cent of the Spoonies' total population. Fishers told him the shorebirds were a net-snarling nuisance—usually they just left them to rot.

David Melville thinks tens of thousands of shorebirds tangle and die each year in nets around the Yellow Sea. Far worse is deliberate shorebird hunting by mist net in Southern China. 'It's always been bad, now it seems to be a complete slaughterhouse,' he says. 'Parts of it are plastered wall to wall with mist nets.'

This is a story of those people left behind by China's economic boom—subsistence villagers, who never made it to the cities—and of those who did go and became wealthy there. 'In Hong Kong, where I worked as an authorised officer, I cut all the nets down,' Melville says. 'Then the economy changed, and people went away from wild food anyway, wanting the mass consumer foods. Now people are richer, they are coming back to wild food as a luxury.'

After all, this is a country where the very concept of protecting edible wildlife is a novelty introduced from the West. Beijing Normal University's Professor Zhang Li put it this way: 'From a traditional Chinese perspective, the same as many other countries, wildlife (is) a resource to be exploited, not something to be protected for its intrinsic value.' In today's China, he said, 'Robust market demand gives a huge drive to money-oriented smugglers.'

In pursuit of this craze for wild food, a small grassland bird called the Yellow-breasted Bunting is near to becoming a second Passenger Pigeon, the once superabundant North American bird that was hunted to extinction. Until China's economic boom began, an estimated 100 million of the buntings ranged and bred between Eastern Europe and Chukotka. They funnelled down the same bottleneck as EAAF shorebirds, the eastern Chinese coast, to winter further south in Asia. The bird's habit of migrating and roosting in swarms heightened its vulnerability. By 2013 trappers were catching a hair-raising 8.6 million yearly of these 'rice sparrows', and up to 95 per cent of the population was gone, the victim of a food fad.

So it is that poor southern Chinese fishers and aquaculture labourers will supply shorebirds as 'live game birds'. How about paying one of these part-time hunters ¥30 (US$5) for a Spoonie, a distinctively different bird that will look a quaint curiosity on a high-end plate? Shorebirds' habit of roosting in close flocks leaves me nervous for their fate should the food lovers of Guangdong lock onto them.

Thirteen
Lost flocks

I study the satellite data points of CYB's movement across the grey-brown Daling River mouth's mud. They show her working the upper shore, occasionally bouncing onto the coastal edge to roost. But she and the birds with her are walled in. Around them is the worst peril shorebirds face in the Yellow Sea: land claim. The birds are losing the ground beneath them.

In the dynamic language of last century, when all engineering was viewed as pure progress, it is known as 'reclamation'. This implies human endeavour to turn the bad into good. In fact it's doing nothing of the sort. It's nearly always wetland theft, which usually worsens and becomes sea-enclosure. Natural intertidal margins disappear to make more land that is then pushed out below the low-tide mark.

I agree with shorebirds authority Tony Prater, who says 'reclamation' should only describe the recovery of land actually lost to the sea. 'Virtually no intertidal flats fall into that category, except on a geological timescale. The correct definition is really the claiming of land. There should be a different philosophical approach to taking something one never had, from recovering that which was lost!' It grates, in the same way that old-growth forest loggers talk about taking a 'harvest' as if they had planted the trees 400 years ago and looked after them ever since.

The grab for coastal land in the Yellow Sea began after Mao Zedong proclaimed the one-party People's Republic of China in 1949, and it has exponentially gained pace in recent decades. More than half of China's coastal wetlands have gone, a total loss of 1.2 million hectares. The Daling's intertidal zone is today at the epicentre of this landscape reshaping.

Even until the mid-1980s, early Landsat images showed the Daling meandering on its silty bed unhindered, out to the Yellow Sea. Intertidal flats were just beginning to be marked by what appeared to be lines. The shore gained on the sea only by around 8 metres each year as wetland was dyked and the water allowed to evaporate. Over the next decade there was actually a coastal retreat as dredging began to pump the easily worked sandbanks back, to top up the dyked ground. Then the assault on the sea escalated.

At a rate of 69 metres a year through the 1990s, and 211 metres a year through the early 2000s, the coast stepped out. The river mouth was forced to veer a more-useful east. At the furthest point of the new coast, a 7-kilometre advance was made into the sea—all within the lifetime of a Grey Plover.

The natural world of the estuary was all but gone. The fluid roiling of coastal waters on sand was replaced by human geometry. Some salt marshes and reed swamps were left along the riverbank, but aquaculture ponds covered the tidal flat almost completely in ordered ranks on a squared coastline.

Snowballing Yellow Sea land claim began after paramount leader Deng Xiaoping in 1988 commanded that coastal areas should accelerate the economic opening-up to the outside world. If China was to trade, clearly the coast had to be the meeting place. For years the pace of development exceeded capacity to regulate. As he later reflected on those times, a State Oceanic Administration director, Haiqing Li, spoke of the serious abuse of the sea. 'Referred to as the "three noes", namely "no order" in marine development, "no control" on the extent of marine development and "no fee" paid for any sea-use activity.'

Eventually a law on the management of sea use was brought in to confirm national ownership of the coastal zone and, in theory, rein in land claim under control of the ruling State Council. But fenced at the rear by the agricultural-land 'red line', and emboldened by low sea-use fees, developers and local governments saw great profit in making more land claims.

At Tianjin port, site of the devastating 2015 chemical factory explosion, the engineering and sea-use cost for new land totalled ¥295 million (US$43 million) per square kilometre. It sold for ¥738 million (US$110 million) per square kilometre, split between local government and the developer. Advanced sand-blowing technologies made it possible to reclaim one square kilometre of land in about twenty days.

'It has to be recognised that illegal reclamation is widespread,' David Melville says. 'Many projects are broken into units smaller than 50 hectares, thereby avoiding the need for State Council approval.' In theory, illegal projects were liable to fines of five to fifteen times the cost of the construction. In fact, the State Oceanic Administration said that 61 of 62 illegal cases in a single year were the work of other state-owned entities.

Overlooked in the shadow of this rush is a marine environmental protection law, which itself does no more than attempt to prevent pollution and give compensation to fishers. A ¥1.4 billion

(US$207 million) land claim in Shandong, between Jiangsu and the Bohai Sea, was slated to pay compensation for the loss of fishery resources at 0.5 per cent of budget. Coastal wetlands became classified as 'unused' lands—destruction of this brought negligible penalties, reserve boundaries were flexible and meant little in practice anyway.

There was every encouragement to cover the mud and to build. Besides, it was grand. 'China strides forward where Europe hesitates to tread,' proclaimed Han Vrijling, professor of hydraulic engineering at Delft University in the Netherlands, a champion of dykes. 'They make great plans and execute them with speed and precision.' As the Dutch showed the world, if you are to move out beyond the intertidal zone against the sea, dykes are needed. 'Great Walls', in other words. This became an exhortation.

I saw a young woman pushing a small boy in a cart at Lianyungang's fishing-boat harbour. The cart was a bright plastic mash-up of toy box and spaceship; the young master of China's future was being perambulated past a wall topped by blue tiles. Each wall panel was painted with a coastal mural: a sandy beach and islands, a promenade with waving old folk, bright dockside cranes, a ferry boat cutting through blue water.

Beyond the wall, the grey-watered boat harbour was alive with red flags, and above the wall stood two signs lettered in Chinese *and* English. The first pronounced: 'Coastal Defence Management Area', and the second commanded: 'Construct the Firm Coast Defence as Great Wall. Ensure the Healthy Development of Economy.'

Dykes and seawalls built to cope with a 1-in-1000 year wave on coasts threatened by typhoons—these were constructions of engineering magnificence. No wonder Professor Vrijling cleaved to China and its march seaward. Walling the coastline was a duty of national protection for the economic future. Comrade Xie Shileng, the Communist Party People's Congress representative and revered designer of dykes, told a coastal engineering conference that China's achievement was 'amazingly magnificent'. 'The coastlines with relatively favourable natural conditions have been almost developed and utilised,' he said. He claimed that no effort had been spared to find the equilibrium between beach *reclamation* and wetland protection, 'that they complement each other in order to realise the optimal coordination between human and nature'.

Around the Yellow Sea, even far north of the typhoon danger, most of the coast became bordered by seawalls. The rest was already rocky shore.

We might think that in a shallow sea, more mud would eventually settle outside the wall. But at the same time as the coast was being driven into deeper water, less sediment was being issued from the great rivers because more dams were being built upstream.

Using historic satellite imagery, a Queensland geospatial scientist, Nick Murray, zoomed out to map the entire 4000-kilometre Yellow Sea coastline. Up to two-thirds of its tidal flats had vanished since the 1950s. 'Our analysis indicates that tidal flats along the Yellow Sea are declining at a rate comparable to many other at-risk ecosystems, such as tropical forests, seagrass meadows and mangroves.'

Compounding the loss of access for shorebirds, an exotic North American cordgrass, *Spartina alterniflora*, is invading the Yellow Sea. A rich seed producer, spartina flourishes in that stretch of once-clear flat from high-tide mark to mid-tide so hungrily sought by refuelling shorebirds.

At Tiaozini, we had driven out on the seawall past rampant spartina. Spotting scopes and camera gear shouldered, we stepped gingerly down a trash-littered 20-metre concrete slope (a Xie design perhaps) and walked out over the flat for a kilometre to watch the birds come in with the tide.

As the flocks grew into those dazzling bird clouds, Grey Plover, Bar-tailed Godwit and Dunlin were so numerous that on the sightings list that day they were just designated '###'. Many numbers.

At one stage a nature reserve had been created on the Tiaozini shore. It even had a watchtower. But in an act of bureaucratic bloody-mindedness, a guide told me, the tower was built a kilometre inland so it could watch little. And then came the largest land-claim project ever to receive one-step approval from China's State Council.

The first phase captured 6750 hectares of mudflat, but the overall plan proposed to encompass 26,600 hectares, covering the Dongsha shoals, the offshore flats out from Tiaozini that CYA used on her flight north. A dyke ring would circle far over the low-tide mark. Inside this ring, smaller dykes would catch water flowing in at high tide, trapping sediment and building new land. Long bridges would access the shoals, little surveyed for bird riches, but to CYA and many others sought-after ground.

The Tiaozini flocks were great, but as often happens, smaller details tell the story. We were standing on another Jiangsu seawall where the sea had washed a thin beach into a corner. A flock of Great Knot flew in at high tide, chattering constantly while they worked the water's edge, going without usual shorebird rest. Beside them the remains of a wooden boat resigned itself to final decay in the mud. Spartina was clumping, though it had not yet choked the sand. Out of the haze, a tug emerged hauling a freight barge to catch high water through an open barrage, and steam inland up a canal. Onshore at a steel fabrication plant, the din of clashing metal cracked the air.

Usually on the Yellow Sea, Great Knot would take flight at the slightest human approach. Even at their peaceful Australian wilderness home, Yawuru Nagulagun/Roebuck Bay, they were wary of anyone in distant view. Not this time. I watched from within a stone's throw while the birds hunted the tideline as if famished. They jumped at a clang from the factory, circled and flew back to the same little beach. Twice more they lifted in alarm and rushed down again. They had nowhere else to go.

———

The plan to claim Tiaozini for industry is part of an unrivalled reach worldwide by giant projects into the sea. In this, the scale of China's ambitions exceeded all others. There was Caofeidian, that 'rotten-tail' complex next to Nanpu. The battered and exploded Tianjin port. The world's largest offshore airport being built on a 2100-hectare artificial island at Dalian in Liaodong Bay. In Yalu Jiang the fingered docks of Dandong port dividing Godwit Central.

All that wetland obliteration. The coast reshaped on a scale unseen before and at the deadly expense of intertidal life; seawalls stretching past the horizon. But the most dramatic illustration of how things went very bad for the birds actually happened not in China, but across the Yellow Sea in South Korea.

On ideal ground, Great Knot find themselves working a wide, fast-washed flat. Rarely are they found at a place like that Jiangsu seawall corner. They closely follow the waterline in and out, probe the loosened mud to locate shellfish by bill touch,

tweeze prey free and swallow it whole to be crushed through a
nutcracker gizzard. *Repeat, fast.*

The highest-value feeding ground anywhere in the world for
Great Knot once existed on the tidal flats at the junction of the
Dongjin and Mangyeong rivers, where sediments washed out
of the Sobaek mountains, the spine of South Korea. This bird
treasury was long unknown to Koreans. The flocks had stayed
out there, on the mud, with only shell-fishers for company.
When the first shorebird surveyors went there in the 1990s,
they found Great Knot by the tens of thousands, as part of a
shorebird aggregation richer and more diverse than any other
single place in the Yellow Sea.

Mark Barter thought perhaps a quarter of a million shorebirds used it on northern migration. 'It was at the time the most
important site on the flyway,' David Melville says. 'The numbers
were so big that at the time, people couldn't believe it.' These
birds, particularly the Great Knot, were likely to have been
faithful for many generations to this estuary complex. That mud
was their own evolutionary best fit.

The twin estuaries first fell under the eye of South Korea's
leaders towards the end of its extended period of military rule.
But as the country embraced democracy, the grand 'Saemangeum Reclamation Project' to close the estuaries became a
vote-catcher. 'The SRP began as an election-time pledge given
by unpopular authoritarian elites,' said Yonsei University's
Tae-soo Song. 'Astonishingly, this enormous state-led project
was implemented without an elaboration or budget plan, and
despite strong public and government opposition.'

Construction of the seawall linking islands with the
mainland was already under way when Nial Moores came to
South Korea in 1998 and began to pour his birding passion

into earnest opposition to the SRP. To understand the depth of this shorebird missionary's vocation in this flyway, we do well to appreciate a story from his childhood.

Moores was a child living near Liverpool, deaf until the age of four. Then he underwent a simple operation to alter the position of his adenoids and he could hear. The first sound he remembers was the horrifying roar of traffic. His first-remembered *best* sound came when he was in bed on a still, cold night.

'I was lying there and I could hear what sounded like music,' Moores tells me. 'I thought it was angels playing trumpets. It was wonderful, really wonderful. They were Pink-footed Geese, flying over our house to the marshes in the Ribble estuary. The sound absolutely captivated me. And I realised, of course unconsciously at first, but by the age of seven or eight, that birds had opened up the world to me. They came into my space, which had been very tiny and dark, and expanded it heavenward. It was an amazing connection.'

When Moores grew up and left Britain for the world, he first went to Japan to look for birds, and saw Spoonies and the equally rare Nordmann's Greenshank. He encountered the tail end of Japan's land-claim rush. 'When people tell the story of reclamation now, many rightly focus on the Yellow Sea. But they forget this kind of tragedy happened in Japan through the 1960s to the 1990s. By the time I left for South Korea, I had already seen the loss of wetland where I saw my first Spoon-billed Sandpiper. I saw areas of Tokyo Bay destroyed, and Nagoya threatened with a garbage dump.'

Many initial shorebird band returns to Australia came from Japan, where the birds were more closely monitored early on by local birders, who could afford to spend more time looking, had high-quality binoculars and scopes, and held to fond folk memories. 'When people in Japan gave names to birds, they were also describing abundance,' Moores says. Australian and New Zealand shorebirds still fly through Japan, but the passage of big flocks is largely a thing of the past.

Moores joined local Japanese activists to save an 80-hectare tidal flat. At this time he met Koreans who told him of threats to mudflats that were ten, or 100 times bigger on their coast; so he moved there, and began to campaign. 'It was extremely chaotic, extremely buttock-clenching,' he says. The SRP had already been under construction for five years. Dumping dug-up mountains into deep water with strong tides was a very slow process.

In its natural state the Saemangeum area had supported the livelihoods of over 20,000 people, who worked the mud, as well as the several hundred thousand shorebirds. But the South Korean Ministry of Forest and Agriculture waved away concerns. 'The reclamation invites more migratory birds to the area,' they said. 'Furthermore, snipes and plovers easily move their habitat . . .'

The project was stopped under legal challenge over its adverse effect on water quality, then started up again and protests against the destruction of local community life increased. Moores is a believer in the power of honest data but, as opposition to the SRP grew, he became involved in a most unscientific way.

He supported a Buddhist Samboilbae protest, an ordeal in which clerics objecting to the project led a ritual procession, taking three steps and then making a low bow, prostrating themselves to the ground. They did this for 320 kilometres, from Saemangeum to Seoul.

'The smell of the road and the ground, hands stinging with contact, legs shaking as they straighten out incompletely before the next drop and bow,' Moores wrote. 'After only a couple of kilometres performing Samboilbae . . . my body could take no more.'

Moores contacted the Australasian Wader Studies Group and Danny Rogers, the Victorian scientist, who had been working on Great Knot at Broome. They developed a plan to bear witness in a different way—by counting the effect of the seawall on migratory shorebirds. In this they set a benchmark for describing the destructive power of land claim.

The 33 kilometres Saemangeum wall, the world's longest, was completed in April 2006. It enclosed an area of around 400 square kilometres, just as the birds landed from the south on spring migration and AWSG volunteers stepped off the plane to count them. 'People arrived and said, "Well what time does the tide come in?"' Moores recalls. 'And I explained, "No, there are no more tides. This is the end of it. Ten thousand years of tides in this particular bay are finished. It's all over."'

Before, the tidal rise and fall across a shorebird mudflat wonderland had been around 6 metres. Sluice gates now allowed a rise and fall of less than a metre. The mud began to dry out.

That summer the birds were still there. Danny Rogers was used to the big flocks of Yawuru Nagulagun/Roebuck Bay, and Eighty Mile Beach, but Saemangeum's flocks that year were an order of magnitude greater. 'We could see 80,000 birds in one flock,' Rogers recalls. 'They were just like a dark cloud that suddenly changes to a light cloud in an instant. The rush of wing-beats was something you could hear from a kilometre away. There was nothing like it.'

Initially the birds gorged on easy pickings. David Melville joined the count and saw the mud covered with myriad white dots. 'Loads of clams and other shellfish came to the surface, gaping and dying as the mud dried,' Melville tells me. When the easy pickings were done and the remains rotted, Great Knot had to try substitutes.

'Great Knot have this big muscular gizzard for crushing clams. But after a while they were turning to eating sea snails, which have a hard corkscrew shell. The birds have to regurgitate pellets of these, which you could see on the mud. Clearly now, in hindsight, these birds were in trouble. The intake rate of protein drops hugely when you have to eat snails.'

At the time of the initial seawall construction they counted 181,000 shorebirds at Saemangeum in peak northern migration, and expected many more to fly south through the autumn. Around half of these birds were Great Knot. Within two years, these were reduced to 12,000, and by 2013 they were gone. The same ground had been the most important known staging area anywhere for Spoon-billed Sandpiper. In 2008 the surveyors searched exhaustively and found exactly three.

Ingenious crab feeders like Whimbrel and Far Eastern Curlew hung on in lower numbers. That didn't happen for Great Knot. More than 92,000, a quarter of the estimated global population at the time, was lost at a stroke. Continuing counts show that more than 300,000 shorebirds have gone from South Korea during northward migration. Thirteen different species halved their numbers.

Just two plover tried to dodge the trend. The little Kentish Plover, never numerous, took advantage of new sand islands. And a few Grey Plover, the quiet survivor, lingered on. 'Reclamation impacts take years and years to work their way through the ecosystem,' Moores says. 'I understand Grey Plover as very territorial. Specialist shellfish-eating and crab-eating species disappear very rapidly, but those species that are more territorial

tend to linger. We've lost most of them. But they are more persistent. Grey Plover may be staying around for longer.'

Where did the Great Knot go? There was no mass mortality
on the exposed mud. A few corpses were found, of undetermined
cause. They weren't struck down like the Jehol fossil birds, or
wrecked by the thousand like shearwaters that periodically wash
up on the Australian coast in early summer after failing to make
the journey home.

At the time that the seawall at Saemangeum closed, there
was no contemporary count further north at the Great Knot's
Chinese stronghold, Yalu Jiang. Before and after though, their
numbers at Yalu Jiang were on a slide. No place turned up where
the birds might comply with the South Korean government's
belief that they could 'easily move'.

To Melville it was a question of whether a Great Knot, with
only a quarter of a tank of fuel instead of a full tank, flies for
its Siberian breeding ground anyway, driven by the calendar of
reproduction that says it's time to go. 'Does it still set off on that
journey, or does it stop off at the Sea of Okhotsk, take on more
and then keep going? The fact that there was a huge reduction of
the birds in north-west Australia suggests that they did die. But
where that happened, we have no idea.'

Nial Moores still goes back to Saemangeum. 'You can now
drive along the seawall, and it's quite a barren landscape out
there, with bulldozers picking away. They don't have enough
money to build the inner dykes. There's about a 10-centimetre
tidal range and a mini inland sea with poor water quality
in the deeper part of the system. The higher tidal flats have
all dried out. There are maybe 100 shorebirds on a reclamation pond. So, from several hundred thousand birds, to
virtually none.'

At least in South Korea, the flowering of democracy meant this calamity could be clearly recorded. Attempting to illuminate the Yellow Sea shorebird black hole has meant drawing together scattered pinpoints in carefully controlled China—and in North Korea, which is even more closed. But it is a global flyway, so data can come from elsewhere.

Near the far southern end, Clive Minton's teams gathered these dots for decades at a remote embayment of shifting sands and islands hooked into Wilsons Promontory in Victoria. Since the early 1980s, VWSG volunteers have taken small boats out for annual counts on favoured roosts at Corner Inlet.

When Minton looked back through the count's trends, he found birds known to pass through the Yellow Sea were nearly all declining. More worrying, he also saw the crunches of step-falls. Grey Plover numbers at Corner Inlet halved at a stroke in the mid-1990s, then flattened out, but did not recover. Ruddy Turnstone, Great Knot and Red Knot all fell away.

At the inlet itself nothing had changed to affect the birds. The low islands and healthy waters swirling over bright-yellow sand had always been rich in shorebird diversity and number. Neither were these the bumps of good and bad Arctic breeding seasons. It was population loss.

Did the Corner Inlet birds rely on a particular Yellow Sea staging ground, now suddenly gone? Melville thought this might be one possible explanation, but raises another awful possibility. 'One thing somebody should look at is the severe famines in North Korea, and whether or not any of those mid-90s losses were tied to that.'

For four years from 1994, North Koreans suffered famines driven by natural disasters and economic mismanagement following the loss of subsidised imports with the collapse of the Soviet Union. It was known in Pyongyang as the 'Arduous March'.

Melville says, 'A friend of mine was in North Korea at the time, not doing bird work, doing something else. He said that at low tide, the mudflats were just covered with people desperate for food. So everything would have gone. Everything.'

After Saemangeum and the counting of the Yellow Sea birds, the alarm of the shorebird community grew rapidly. But the task of scientifically proving losses on the much more extensive Chinese side of the Yellow Sea depended on finding an internationally convincing case. This crystallised in the fates of the flyway's two Bar-tailed Godwit sub-species.

Apart from a slight difference in bill length, these godwit are essentially of the same physique. *Menzbieri* breeds inland from the Arctic coast in northern Chukotka and Yakutia. It prefers to spend the non-breeding part of the year on the red coastal sands of north-west Australia. *Baueri* is the bird that breeds in Alaska, then takes the Pacific superhighway to New Zealand and eastern Australia for the southern summer. On their migratory flights north, both species spread throughout the Yellow Sea. *Menzbieri* leans more to the Chinese coast, and *baueri* to the Korean side. The best single refuelling station for both sub-species lies along the Yalu Jiang coastline, hard up against the border of North Korea.

Land claim on the Yalu Jiang reserve reduced the wetland's extent. Then the construction of a long barrier seawall for ship navigation altered the flow of the river sediment that fed the mud fauna, that fed the birds. The little shellfish 'Pot' once dominated this mud, along with the Ghost Shrimp. Coinciding with the wall's completion, the abundance of each collapsed in 2011 to 2012. In the absence of this high-quality prey, the total food intake rates by godwits dropped by around half. As people scanned for increasingly scarcer leg flags, it became clear that both sub-species were on a slide.

Jesse Conklin, a shorebird movement specialist, found the greatest risk to these birds stemmed from their dependence on very few high-quality staging sites in the Yellow Sea. But the *baueri* birds still had the advantage of the wild, unspoiled Yukon–Kuskokwim before they took their great leap over the Pacific. *Menzbieri*, on a more direct route south, flew back through badly compromised Yellow Sea grounds again.

The Queensland tidal flat analyst Nick Murray mapped the entire extent of lost ground for each sub-species, and drew together counts of their abundance. *Menzbieri* birds had lost twice as much Yellow Sea tidal flat as *baueri*, and were declining at three times the rate. There was no doubt. For *menzbieri* birds, double exposure to the perturbed Chinese side of the Yellow Sea meant more trouble. Some shorebirds tried to cope with the loss of ground by crowding together. Over just a few years, most of the flyway's Red Knot likely abandoned places like industrialised Tianjin and shifted to the Nanpu area in spring, and so did many Curlew Sandpiper. But they could not 'just move'. Populations of these birds were in free-fall.

———

As we live through the sixth extinction, our focus is often local and fragmentary. The shorebirds' flyway passes over Australian woodlands from which the Paradise Parrot is gone. They fly to the mouth of the Yangtze River, where the Baiji, a whitefin dolphin known as 'Goddess of the Yangtze', has not been seen since 2007. Our birds, CYA and CYB, flew the ranges where people despair of saving the Siberian Tiger.

These are all natural-heritage dramas. What makes the migratory shorebird crisis on this flyway distinct is its breadth and depth. These birds are part of many lands and people, and more species are at risk.

Grey Plover are relatively few. But they are there, in all their humble fortitude, if you look. Like Great Knot, they are part of the sea country of the Yawuru people of north-west Australia, as are *menzbieri* godwit. The *baueri* godwit, or the *Kuaka* to the Maori, are also known to the Yup'ik of the Yukon–Kuskokwim. The Great Knot, 6RRBR, bred on Chukchi land in Russia before touring North Pacific coasts and eventually flying back to the Yawuru. That is to barely begin a reckoning of these birds' places in the lives of people in 22 countries.

At the turn of the century, Mark Barter estimated two million migratory shorebirds used the Yellow Sea during northerly migration, and about one million went south. Within a few years it was clearly time to re-calculate. The crash that had been forecast was now happening.

Theunis Piersma confirmed that the simultaneous declines of Red Knot, Great Knot and the Bar-tailed Godwit *menzbieri* signalled the flyway was at risk. He ranked this a potential extinction wave as dangerous as any among migratory animals. The bell tolled in *Nature Communications* for more species. An analysis led by Colin Studds made plain the effect on the birds. 'Population declines are driven by low survival during or soon after staging in Yellow Sea mudflats, likely because the birds are unable to refuel enough to meet the energetic demands of migration.'

In work at the University of Queensland, Rob Clemens found twelve out of nineteen migratory shorebird species were decreasing through their Australian range, and five more at the

edge of the flyway in southern Australia. Curlew Sandpiper—
a third of whose population was crowded into one Nanpu salt
pond—topped Clemens' list with precipitous losses. 'Eastern
Curlew and Grey Plover were declining more rapidly in regions
where they are more abundant. These species are highly sensitive to interference competition, and one might expect more
rapid declines in more densely populated sites.'

The EAAF had more threatened shorebirds than any other
of the world's flyways. So stark was the evidence becoming that
by 2016, four shorebirds were suddenly listed by the Australian
Government as critically endangered. The Curlew Sandpiper,
Far Eastern Curlew, Great Knot and Bar-tailed Godwit *menzbieri* joined just a handful of the 828 Australian bird species to
be given this extreme-warning status. Each shorebird had lost
more than 80 per cent of its population within three generations.

———

Still and all, it should be a time of hope.

These listings were made, and Clemens and his 21 co-
authors reached their conclusions, because of countless hours
of shorebird surveys, decades of cannon-netting expeditions, of
banding and flagging, and late nights at the computer unspool-
ing tracker paths. Hundreds of people had collected the data.
They had done the science. They did not have to guess what was
happening, or worse, actually miss seeing it. What they had to
do was shift these underpinnings into change for the better.

'I was in Mongolia last year, banding passerines, and every
Yellow-breasted Bunting got an individual colour combination,'
Melville says. 'But what is the chance of any of those birds being
seen again? Infinitesimal. With forest birds we just don't have

data sets. By the time you reach a crisis point, it's much further down the line.'

Shorebirds, he thinks, have a natural advantage that might see them better candidates for survival. 'Away from the breeding grounds they are concentrated in fairly well-defined habitats. It's easier to see what's going on. You can count them. And because people have liked counting them for years, we've got a relatively long-term data set to show us what's happening. So in that sense they have been lucky.'

Fourteen
A spoonful of hope

Super Typhoon Meranti was born in the North Pacific near the island of Guam only a few days after a timely warning on these destructive weather systems. Climate scientists had found that in recent years typhoons were becoming more intense in East and Southeast Asia. Those in the most damaging categories of Four and Five had tripled in frequency as sea-surface temperatures rose.

At first notification by the US Navy's Joint Typhoon Warning Center on 8 September 2016, Meranti was a breezy 37 kilometres per hour. By 10 September it was picking up speed, blowing at around 65 kilometres per hour. Alarms sounded in Taiwan and southern China. On its path westward towards land, meteorologists saw it building dangerously. Around the evening of that day, after a month's replenishment at the Daling River mouth, CYB flexed her wings, flew to migratory altitude in calm weather, and headed south towards the typhoon.

As they begin long flights, migrating birds probably have little inkling of the vagaries of weather thousands of kilometres away.

Yes, they can time departures to achieve a local boost, and know the broad wind patterns of a flyway. But in encounters with tumultuous weather their survival is more likely to be a matter of fitness and fortune. Already this bird had aborted her initial flight from Wrangel in the face of constant headwinds across the Sea of Okhotsk. How would the feather-scrap manage Meranti?

Seeking an answer, there is little data available for the EAAF except that the typhoon season does coincide with southward migration and there are dozens of tropical cyclones each year, some of which intensify into typhoons. But there is useful precedent available across the world in the Atlantic Americas Flyway where southward migration coincides with the height of the hurricane season and birds are frequently forced to tackle them.

It's become a part of the US Weather Channel's hurricane-watching to see what meteorologists call 'biological returns'. These are satellite images of large numbers of birds and insects, flying in the eye of the hurricane. Trapped, or taking refuge, they circle in the netherworld of the eye. There, they are out of the worst of the wind, clear of pelting rain that might cast them down.

Satellite tracking of migratory shorebirds has also begun to reveal their ability to survive the edges of these intense storms. 'Until recent years it was a generally accepted theory that most birds migrating into large hurricanes over the open Atlantic perished,' said Fletcher Smith, of the US Center for Conservation Biology (CCB). 'We now know that at least some types of birds are able to navigate directly through these storms and beyond.'

The evidence has come from Whimbrel, a bird slightly larger than the plover. Nine Whimbrel satellite-tagged by the CCB have been followed in near real-time across the paths of big

Atlantic storms. Some skirted the systems, but six were tracked through them. The centre's scientists saw one Whimbrel spend a persistent 27 hours pushing into a tropical storm's headwinds in the North Atlantic at 14 kilometres per hour before sliding back to Cape Cod at 140 kilometres per hour on a tailwind. Another flew directly through headwinds in the north-east quarter of a 177-kilometres-per-hour hurricane, in at least its second encounter with a tropical storm.

In 2018, Smith satellite-tagged six Black-bellied Plover, which had an easier time of the very damaging Hurricane Michael. Already at their staging or wintering grounds, all survived, presumably on the ground, some shifting inland. The plover has on its side its enviable status as an aerialist. As Peter Matthiessen watched it over Long Island wetlands, he thought, 'In time of storm, it seems to be sometimes the only bird aloft.'

Meranti doubled in strength within hours on 11 September and built to Category Five Super Typhoon status, with sustained winds in excess of 240 kilometres per hour as it began to close on land. CYB was riding towards it on a tailwind that poured down from the Sea of Japan, drawn in by Meranti's rotation. By 12 September, when Tony Flaherty took a fix, the bird was east of Taiwan's southern coast and running into what the South Australian wryly called 'this lovely weather system'.

Wind and rain likely beat on the bird as she tried to thread past the advancing Meranti. With the outer spiral blowing at her tail she skated across the front edge of the system as it bowled through the Luzon Strait. Flaherty described CYB as stoic, and indeed she picked a successful, boosted course. A matter of hours after she passed by, Meranti's eye intersected the route that CYB took. Just outside the eye, the wind, by now screaming at 295 kilometres per hour, must have shot rain like bullets.

The super typhoon went on to graze southern Taiwan and barrel into China. Damaging downpours hit several provinces as it swung north in an arc on the mainland, to dissipate and exit as a rain storm in the Yellow Sea near Tiaozini, leaving an estimated ¥31 billion (US$4.7 billion) damages bill. By this time, CYB was flying over the coast of West Papua. Which was just as well. Hard on the heels of Meranti, Tropical Cyclone Malakas emerged from the same waters a few days later to circle north, driving headwinds up against the course she had taken.

———

Killer weather always has been a natural hazard for migratory shorebirds. But the number of intense typhoons on the EAAF is probably a more recent phenomenon. Wei Mei, a climate specialist who highlighted this change for the worse in the East Asian region looks ahead with a warning. Ocean surface warming under projected greenhouse gas emissions is likely to intensify even further typhoons boiling out of the Pacific to strike this part of the world. 'It is a very substantial increase,' he wrote in *Nature Geoscience*. 'We believe the results are very important for East Asian countries because of the huge populations in these areas.'

Sustaining wildlife like migratory shorebirds seems to pale in the face of such a climate challenge. How can we keep our own lives, let alone those of obscure birds? And this question underscores the odds against them, not just on this flyway, but globally. At a time of multiple ecological challenges, our attention is often elsewhere.

This is where we miss out. The way that migratory shorebirds can or can't thread the world holds a mirror to our ways of living, particularly on the coasts. But we have to look. Grey, out there on the mud, they are often so little noticed. Their losses—like a slow leak from a bucket, leading to extirpation or even extinction—may go unseen.

The fisheries scientist Daniel Pauly coined the term 'shifting baseline syndrome' to describe how succeeding generations in his discipline tended to base their understanding of changes in fish stocks on those measurements taken at the start of their careers. As a result of these shifts, they missed seeing gradual losses of fish found in historical, even anecdotal, data.

So it is with our grasp of the wildlife that we encounter first-hand. We are tempted to base our understanding of population trends on our own direct lifetime knowledge. At my local Arctic shorebird wintering ground in Tasmania, Orielton Lagoon, there have never been Grey Plover for me to see and few Far Eastern Curlew. That was, and is, just the state of things, I might think.

In fact, one of the last Grey Plover to be seen at Orielton was that bird specimen I held in my hand, shot in my lifetime, in 1960, by the Tasmanian Museum director, J.R. Cunningham. Earlier than that, the curlew were plentiful and hunted for food, as shorebird researcher Priscilla Park discovered when she sought out anecdotes.

She was told by older local residents, 'The sky was black with curlew as they flew over the Orielton causeway where we would hide to shoot them . . . At the end of summer they were so fat that when shot they would burst on hitting the water . . . Taste much nicer than wild duck.'

Park's shooters were describing pre-migration hunts in the first half of the twentieth century. The decline in curlew numbers since then has been measured at Orielton over decades of counts by volunteers from BirdLife Tasmania and its predecessors.

Today a handful of the birds is sometimes glimpsed, far out on the flats. Never are they seen within range of a shotgun.

Though the current focus of international concern is the Yellow Sea, we should take account in our short memories of global precedents. Land has been claimed from the sea in Britain from at least the time of the Roman Empire, when early advantage was taken of The Wash's saltmarsh. The country with the most notable mastery of sea enclosure, the Netherlands, intensively manages grasslands on this claimed ground where for 50 years the Black-tailed Godwit has been in steep decline. In Queensland, a developer is currently wrestling with BirdLife Australia over a 40-hectare wetland claim at Toondah, Brisbane, which is sought for a 3600 apartment and marina development on shrinking Far Eastern Curlew habitat. On Tasmania's Robbins Island, where I saw some of the EAAF's furthest flung Grey Plover, there are plans for the largest wind farm in the Southern Hemisphere.

Neither is pollution of the coast a new thing. At least 1300 Dunlin were among birds killed by eating lead-contaminated prey in outfall from a fuel-additive works on the Mersey Estuary in northern England in 1979. The Deepwater Horizon spill in the Gulf of Mexico exposed many tens of thousands of migratory shorebirds to oil during the 2010–11 non-breeding season. Months after the event, nearly 10 per cent of shorebirds caught in mist nets were visibly oiled at this, their first feeding ground south on their long hop from the Arctic.

As for hunting, in sophisticated France today the list of permitted quarry includes *Pluvier Argenté*, the Silver Plover— our bird. I saw a video that young hunters took of themselves shooting shorebirds on the Bay of Biscay coast. They displayed their kills to the camera, including a colour-banded *Pluvier*

Argenté. Pathetically floppy, it seemed a trivial amusement for well-fed Frenchmen.

The video was posted online, and I learned through Twitter that the bird had been banded further north near Caen. It survived two round trips to the Arctic before falling to the hunters.

Globally there is now a good understanding of shorebird losses, based on carefully assembled numbers, even if we don't know the exact state of many species, nor their extended populations. In these widely travelled and distant birds, that task is not complete, but there is a good grasp on trends.

Around half of all migratory shorebird populations have been declining globally, at least since the turn of the century. Then, as now, many more populations were dwindling rather than growing, according to estimates by Wetlands International. In North America, long-distance migratory shorebirds have lost on average 70 per cent of their populations since 1970.

Some estimates of losses are only broadly indicative. In the vast African–Eurasian region, for example, the sandpiper family, *Scolopacidae*, has been assessed as having 22 declining populations among its different species.

But the exceptionally thorough UK Wetland Birds Survey shows nearly all of its Arctic shorebirds are in decline. Counters covered 2771 wetlands in Great Britain and Northern Ireland in 2018 and found that over the past decade a third of Golden Plover had gone, Turnstone were down by a quarter, and there were one in six fewer Grey Plover on British tidal flats. Godwits were improving. Not so the Eurasian Curlew.

Globally, Grey Plover is thought to be managing—just. Its numbers are likely decreasing, but the bird is of 'Least Concern' in the IUCN Red List of Threatened Species, with a total population around the world estimated in the high hundreds of thousands. It's comfort against the toll; evidence of our bird's perseverance.

For hope against any real hope, look to the curlews, who have fared poorly longer than most. Belief still officially exists in the survival of the tiny Eskimo Curlew of North America, though the last of its millions was verified when one was shot in Barbados in 1962. Loss of grassland and insect life, worsened by persistent hunting, took this bird away. It's a sign of the broader politics of final extinction that even now the US and Canadian endangered species committees refuse to give it this classification. An extinct bird is a badge of shame. It may mean a loss of some already scarce government resources—and it could be professionally scarring to make the wrong call too early.

In the meantime a tribute exists to this little bird with a 6-centimetre curved bill in an abstract sculptural painting by the New York master, Frank Stella. It forms part of his 1976 series, *Exotic Birds*, an examination of flight and endangerment in three-dimensional metal-relief paintings. At the centre of Stella's *Eskimo Curlew* are three floating, energetically curling shapes, restrained by boxes.

Across the Atlantic, the Eskimo Curlew's counterpart is just as remarkably not present. The Slender-billed Curlew had a range from Siberia through Europe to North Africa. It was last seen at a breeding ground in 1924 on a marsh island in taiga forest in Omsk Province, and the most recent sighting of the bird was from Hungary in 2001. Its call, a short and tremulous rising whistle, survives in a sonogram archive. If it lives, there are fewer than 50.

Researchers have tried to narrow down the potential breeding area of the Slender-billed Curlew by studying the atomic structure of its feathers in museum specimens. Hydrogen atom ratios can indicate latitude, and the study pinpointed the stronghold of the specimens in the steppes of Kazakhstan. Those who hold out hope for the Slender-bill's survival take heart from a re-sighting of the Steppe Whimbrel, erroneously declared extinct in 1994, but found wintering in Mozambique in 2016.

———

Survival is a rich story. In the faraway world of migratory-shorebird work, hope does a good trade. So does sadness at the losses.

Social scientists talk of concepts of Ecological Grief, or Environmental Melancholia, as natural responses to the loss of species and ecosystems. I read of a Dutch shorebird researcher, Egbert van der Velde, who felt aged in his thirties, so long had he been trying to save Black-tailed Godwit nests and nestlings from meadow-harvesting machines. 'I can hear it when Godwits have lost their chicks,' he told a local newspaper columnist. 'They cry, they search, they sound an alarm . . . You see that there is nothing to defend. Yes, then what? Then I want to leave.'

I recall David Melville's shellshock at discovering the scale of Yellow Sea coastal change, and the choking voice of the University of Queensland's Richard Fuller. Deeply immersed in clear-eyed analysis of flyway problems, Fuller nevertheless broke up as he recalled to Australian broadcaster Ann Jones the 'incredibly depressing' losses at Saemangeum. 'Literally I just burst into tears . . . I'm going to do it now. I just couldn't . . . '

But these people keep working on shorebirds. They strike the better part of the bargain offered by American naturalist–philosopher, Aldo Leopold: 'One of the penalties of an ecological education is that one lives alone in a world of wounds,' he wrote.

'An ecologist must either harden his shell and make believe that the consequences of science are none of his business, or he must be the doctor who sees the marks of death in a community that believes itself well, and does not want to be told otherwise.'

It's taken but a single human lifetime for our knowledge of the EAAF to move from almost complete ignorance to a deep understanding of the birds and their movements. Troubles they face are now more known than unknown. Barter's tribute to their free spirits, crossing the earth in annual harmony with the sun, is not an elegy. Instead, work on migratory shorebirds often has the whiff of resistance, of a quietly spinning underground web of conservation.

At a time when we are numbed by the scale of global environmental damage, among these people, on this flyway, there are signs of a hopeful Anthropocene. As they work on this ecosystem, many are choosing to be the doctor, and to tell the community. Taking a cue from their birds, they are working inconspicuously through a miasma of bureaucracies to fashion means for change.

Emblematic of this is the campaign for the wind-up bird, the Spoon-billed Sandpiper. There are nearly as few Nordmann's Greenshank as there are Spoonies. But the Nordmann's is just a slightly different version of the Common Greenshank. The little Spoonie with the spatulate bill has Pixar movie appeal, and a very dire future. Perhaps 210 breeding pairs stand between continuation of a line unique to this flyway, and extinction.

Pavel Tomkovich warned early that the state of this bird must be a matter of urgent international concern. No migratory shorebird has yet gone extinct on the EAAF. But this is the very obstacle: the flyway. Many deeply threatened species—the Amur Leopard, Mountain Gorilla, Orange-bellied Parrot—are creatures of one or two countries. Cross-border collaboration is as hard as it gets. The more that was learned about the Spoonie and its life, the more was discovered about the spread of international obstacles confronting anyone wanting to save a highly migratory bird.

To begin with, the best knowledge came from Russian scientists, who found it trilling mating music from its tiny clarinet of a bill on breeding grounds along the coasts of Chukotka and Kamchatka. Tomkovich led a survey across these widely scattered grounds in search of a sparrow-sized bird that was probably always rare.

At the back of his mind was the first person to describe the Spoonie in Chukotka, Adolf Nordenskiold. The Finnish polar explorer found it so common in spring that it was served at the ship's dinner table. Tomkovich said, 'In light of current knowledge, we can state that the local population was completely destroyed by the expedition.'

His team concentrated their searches on crowberry-strewn tundra on lagoon spits. After decades of belief that the bird was fine, they found that at the turn of the millennium its global population was probably half of the previous estimate. There were perhaps 1000 breeding pairs, implying a total of 3000 birds. When they went back and looked again over the next few years, they halved the estimate again. Spoonies had completely disappeared from more breeding grounds.

German zoologist Christoph Zöckler was working with the Russians, and well-connected in the world of international conservation organisations centred on Cambridge, when he came upon the Spoonie. 'From the beginning we realised that something is not quite right here,' Zöckler tells me. 'Maybe because of the very rare occurrence of the bird or its fragile position on the outer edge of the Arctic Ocean we realised it's in peril, and we rang the alarm bells, in actually 2000. Also, with my Russian friends, they were not really hoping enough that there will be international support for this little bird. Nobody was listening then. So for many years I was on my own.'

This began to turn around when the Spoonie was taken in a Russian bear hug by Evgeny Syroechkovskiy, an Arctic ornithologist who worked alongside Zöckler. By 2003 these two were becoming desperate for an international response. At a shorebirds conference in Canberra, Syroechkovskiy scolded conservationists' inertia. 'In spite of the fact that warning information on status and trends of SBS has been known for several years, no real action for conservation at the flyway level is going on,' he said. 'In our opinion, the key problem . . . is the lack of recognition and attention to the species from international conservation bodies.'

In fact on this flyway, at that time, there was little internationally co-operative protection work on any migratory shorebird at all. Zöckler and Syroechkovskiy began to change that for the Spoonie. If it was to be saved, its advocates had to move beyond careful peer-reviewed scientific papers and into the shape-shifting world of conservation politics.

On the sidelines of a waterbirds conference in Edinburgh they formed a Spoon-billed Sandpiper Recovery Team. 'I think the ingenuity of my Russian friend has well helped us,' Zöckler says. 'He is a chameleon in the conservation world. Without that you cannot survive or adapt in the constantly changing environment.'

Their early work was supported by the UN-backed Convention on Migratory Species (the CMS), which gave Zöckler and Syroechkovskiy the official imprimatur to draw up an 'action plan' for Spoonies.

At the time, the Saemangeum seawall was being completed, and at a stroke the main Spoonie staging ground lost. The joint CMS/Birdlife International action plan named the destruction of intertidal mudflats as the greatest threat to the Spoonie's survival. It also made the apparently quixotic call for all major reclamation projects along the flyway to be put on hold. Quixotic not least because China, and for that matter nearly all of Asia, do not belong to the CMS.

David Melville believes hopes were held that the CMS convention agreed in Bonn in 1983 might do more for these birds. 'But there's no interest in CMS at all in East Asia,' he says. 'And I don't think that will change in the foreseeable future.' Japan rejects the CMS because of its potential effect on whaling and fisheries. South Korea follows suit. China, like Russia, and for that matter the United States, don't see the need for another UN-linked overseer.

Zöckler and Syroechkovskiy moved ahead with their science to probe the causes of Spoonie decline. They found there was high predation by foxes on the breeding ground, but they decided that wasn't the total answer. Trouble lay in recruitment—the return of young birds to join the breeding adult population after their first migration.

Like many other migratory shorebirds making maiden flights, young Spoonies may choose to stay on their southern grounds through their first year, or make a partial migration north, not returning to their original breeding grounds until the second northern summer. If banded young fail to return there at all, then clearly their peril lies further south.

The Spoonie's next breeding and staging ground away from Chukotka is in Kamchatka, with its great, mountainous peninsula running down from the north coast of the Sea of Okhotsk.

Syroechkovskiy led a survey there, in Karaginskiy Gulf. This turned up one breeding bird where once there were 50, plus a big bunch of hunters.

He surveyed the hunters as best he could. 'We think it was close to random, as we had been requesting all adult men villagers who were sober and willing to communicate,' he wrote drily. The threat from hunters was real, Syroechkovskiy concluded, since most Spoonies migrated through the region both ways. 'It is clear several SBS could be shot each year by hunters of Karaginskiy region only.'

Zöckler looked to the other end of the Spoonie's migration path. He was treading little-known shorebird ground when he worked around the coastlines of Southeast Asia to Myanmar, where he found both good numbers of wintering birds and more hunters.

Spoonies move about tidal flats in the company of other small shorebirds. These mixed flocks, and not Spoonies in particular, were being targeted by mist-netters. 'Use of fishing nets to catch waders is common among fishermen in Myanmar when the fishing is bad,' Zöckler says. 'Most fish caught are tiny, so even a 20 gram Red-necked Stint provides a substantial amount of food.' He determined around 60 per cent of the Spoonie's population wintered in Myanmar, at least another 20 per cent in next door Bangladesh. Hunting in these countries could be the main cause of its slide towards extinction.

Not far away along the Spoonie migratory corridor also lie the nightmare flats of southern China. There at a single location, Maoming, two investigators from the Hong Kong Birdwatching Society counted 235 mist nets. Add Peter Crighton's find of net-killed Spoonies at Tiaozini, and the picture worsens. Then of course there was the exploding Yellow Sea land claim.

Bird advocacy organisations were waking to the Spoonie. But in the absence of any international structure like the CMS, there was nothing to make governments own the problem, no forum dedicated to the flyway.

Doug Watkins, a Western Australian drawn by the shore-bird magnet when young, has spent most of his life building links between people and governments on the EAAF. He has a long memory and few illusions. For decades flyway countries including Australia have had bilateral migratory bird conservation agreements. These helped to build networks, and to give advocates a place at an international table. But Watkins adds, 'Don't look for a lot of benefit on the ground from the bilateral agreements.'

What did grow out of the Japan–Australia agreement was an international meeting at Kushiro in 1994 that assembled the bones of what, twelve years later, became the East Asian–Australasian Flyway Partnership (EAAFP). Watkin's became its chief executive in September, 2019.

It's a hybrid of national governments, inter-governmental organisations like the CMS, advocacy groups, even the odd multi-national corporation. Its headquarters are hosted by Songdo, a new city in South Korea built on tidal flats and in need of green credentials. China was unhappy with the Korean location, I'm told, and did not join until 2008.

For the EAAFP, the Spoon-billed Sandpiper quickly became an emblematic species. Syroechkovskiy and Zöckler's recovery team morphed into a taskforce under the partnership just as the bird was listed as critically endangered by the IUCN. They had an international framework to help, even if it was a compromise.

'The EAAFP is supposed to be a national partnership as well,' Watkins told me before his appointment. 'But national governments usually don't get around to creating international accountability mechanisms. They prefer to focus on their own country, and they find it difficult to collaborate. What the flyway partnership has done is create a forum where relationships can be struck up, with varying levels of success. Spoon-billed Sandpiper is a success. It's great to have Evgeny and the Russians very much in there. But other governments have not really engaged a lot in this bird so far. It's really left to those completely fanatical, dedicated people to reach out and encourage others.'

Saving the Spoonie did become a passion for many, and it has along the way transferred gains to other shorebirds. In Myanmar and Bangladesh, Zöckler worked with local environmental advocates to start a fundamental cultural shift by local villagers away from shorebird hunting and towards their conservation. In the UK, a highly ambitious attempt has been made to breed the bird in captivity. And on the Chukotka breeding grounds a 'head-starting' project for wild chicks was mounted to ensure greater survival.

Zöckler shifted his passion for the Arctic into understanding the people of the tropical Gulf of Mottama in southern Myanmar. He and local scientists from the Myanmar nature charity BANCA tracked down individual hunters to discover the extent of the shorebird catch. They found it included Grey Plover, Bar-tailed Godwit and Red Knot in catches that might be sold in local markets for 400–500 Kyat (26–33 US cents) each. So they came up with an extraordinary alternative.

The bird hunters agreed in front of their community to give up the hunt. Instead of being admonished or punished, they were paid out and their status was raised in their villages. In Buddhist Myanmar, the killing of animals is generally seen as a last resort of the hungry. The hunters were offered a better life.

Myanmar zoologist Tony Htin Hla explained that in some villages each man deemed to be a 'professional' hunter was given a new livelihood worth the equivalent of US$500—perhaps in the form of a boat and fishing nets. 'Opportunistic' hunters were given US$150 worth of goods.

With their agreement to give up the hunt came new duties. 'The village leaders assigned the former bird hunters the role of *seheinhmu*, which is the person in charge of ten households,' Hla reported. 'This is an honour which makes their behaviour more visible and accountable, increasing the likelihood they will no longer hunt.' In Bangladesh a similar method was employed, instead offering micro-credits.

All for the sake of a quaint little bird.

Securing protection in the Gulf of Mottama also meant heading into the labyrinth of international agreements, this time through Ramsar. 'The Ramsar Convention on Wetlands of International Importance especially as Waterfowl Habitat', to give it its full title, is named after a city in Iran where it was first agreed. It is one of the oldest global conservation agreements. It's also one of the most widely adopted on the flyway, partly because its demands are few. It's a soft convention that requires 'conservation and wise use' of wetlands, and carries no enforcement stick. Still, it comes with advice and technical support to signatories, and can be a very useful tool if it can be embedded in national environment law.

Zöckler said, 'It's highly valued among Asian countries, and hence a powerful conservation instrument.'

Under Ramsar, if a wetland contains a measured 1 per cent of the global population of any species, that makes it internationally important. This standard has become a universal benchmark of shorebird survey reports. Globally, Ramsar sites cover 252 million hectares. The Myanmar Government, after deep consideration, agreed to list the north-east corner of the Gulf of Mottama in 2017, worthy for its 'large and diverse populations of waterbirds including threatened and charismatic species like the Spoon-billed Sandpiper'.

Speaking after visiting the upper gulf in 2019, Zöckler bubbles with the success for shorebirds generally brought by the limiting of hunting. Where ten years ago, flocks totalled around 30,000 birds, they have become too great to reliably count. 'It's utterly impressive,' Zöckler says. 'I am trained and expert in counting waterbirds but there's too many flying around in all sorts of directions in bigger and different flocks. It's at least 60,000 and may well be up to 200,000 birds.'

Also because of the Spoonie, bridges are being built between different cultures. Zöckler describes the sight of flocks moving with the tide on the deep Mottama mud. 'We had fantastic back-light, we were scoping through, and we found five Spoon-billed Sandpiper in a flock of 6000 birds. My Bangladeshi colleague said to the Myanmar guy, 'Now you see the result of your work.' And that was so nice a thing to say, and so true as well, I was very touched by that.

'Bangladesh and Myanmar, you know, countries who are, if you look at the political scene from an Australian or European perspective, they are big enemies. But these guys were sharing this awesome moment where we were almost speechless, when 40,000 birds were taking off slowly, in these masses.'

If only this shorebird revival had actually happened for the Spoonies too. In the upper Gulf of Mottama, while other birds prospered, Spoonie counts fell by about half. It became clear that if it was to be saved from extinction, people needed to go to extremes.

Breeding in captivity a bird genetically programmed to fly twice a year between the Arctic and the tropics is a great ask. 'It was an absolute last minute "ark" attempt,' David Melville recalls. 'Nobody really wanted to do it.'

The project was seeded with Spoonie eggs collected in Chukotka and transferred through Moscow to the Wildfowl and Wetlands Trust at Slimbridge in Gloucestershire. This incidentally rounded a circle of EAAF life that began when the Slimbridge Trust's founder, Peter Scott, loaned rocket nets to a young man who would become the flyway's first father, Clive Minton. Now a new generation was taking on the survival of its most endangered species.

It took time at Slimbridge to understand the life cycle of these birds; four years of adjusting habitat, light and food before two short-lived chicks were produced. Then in 2018 two more hatched and one survived to fledge. This proved the young female's undoing. In what was called a fluke 'night fright' accident, she apparently flew, hit something and died. 'It is heart-breaking, and we all feel with the team,' Zöckler says.

The Slimbridge team themselves saw even one chick's survival to fledging as a great breakthrough consolidated the next year when two chicks fledged. Outside their intense roller-coaster of commitment, Melville was cooler. 'I think by now it's clear that captive breeding is not going to mean a rapid increase in the population,' he says. 'But it's clearly been a huge help in techniques for the head-starting program.'

Each summer as the snow is melting, the head-starting team meets at a remote Russian field base called Meinypil'gyno on the Chukotka coast. They set up a temporary bird-breeding outfit: incubators, disinfected aviary, food and all. To succeed, they must find and collect the earliest possible clutches of eggs laid by Spoonies on return to their breeding grounds.

Whether their nests are robbed by people or predators, Arctic breeding shorebirds may lay a replacement clutch. If the Spoonies do, this might double that pair's benefit to the population.

The eggs taken are incubated at Meinypil'gyno and chicks moved to the temporary aviary where they are fed through to fledging. Their minders make sure the birds do not attach to people. Instead people may make sacrifices for the chicks—more than one arm has been bared to collect Arctic mosquitoes. After fledging, the aviary is opened and the young birds flap their way out to join the wild, wide flyway. There are casualties here too, but in excess of 160 Spoonies have been head-started this way, resulting in hundreds of sightings in nine countries. One by one, they add to the precious population.

As Zöckler scans the horizon he sees more to worry about. 'After the hunting, the head-starting, artificial breeding, where the main problem with Spoonies lies I think we're not quite clear, really,' he says. 'For me, on overall glancing at all the issues, I still have a nagging void that we are missing something.' Among his worries are increased predation and the question of population viability. 'Although I'm quite optimistic, there is a pessimistic note that the species is already beyond a threshold genetically. It has so many perilous genes that it is very difficult to get out of this.'

At the same time he recognises the bird he has devoted twenty years to saving has the power to command attention and do good for other shorebirds. 'It's definitely a flagship species for our world, and it triggers other work, which is exciting.'

Fifteen
Navigating the possible

Evgeny Syroechkovskiy crouched on the tundra near Meinypil'gyno, his brow creased. Between his hands he held a male Spoonie, glowing russet in breeding plumage. Opposite Syroechkovskiy, an eagle ecologist from Scotland, Ewan Weston, was intent on gluing a fingernail-sized satellite tag weighing less than a gram to the back feathers of the bird, leg-flagged Lime 07. The tag would drop off when the feathers did. But before that happened, Lime 07 would open up new possibilities for Spoonie movement.

When the satellite track unfolded, what stirred the Wildfowl and Wetlands Trust's Spoon-billed Sandpiper team manager Baz Hughes was Lime 07's flight to a wintering halt in Indonesia. This country has the greatest extent of tidal flats in the world: 14,416 square kilometres. Yet Indonesia's use by flyway shorebirds is largely unknown, and the stop in northern Sumatra was a first for Spoonies.

Lime 07's flight seized Christoph Zöckler's attention for another reason. It, and several other satellite-tagged Meinypil'gyno birds, staged further north in the Yellow Sea at Yonan, North Korea, beside the highly sensitive Demilitarised Zone with the South. Zöckler thought again about the cultures of the people living along the flyway and how their differences affect his bird. He hopes that one day he might be at the DMZ, flagging a Spoonie in symbolic truce. If he does, he will be following in the tracks of a very unlikely handful of birders from New Zealand.

Shorebird workers on this flyway, as a matter of course, encounter international barriers that deter most of us. To them, Valdimir Putin's Russian Federation or Xi Jinping's One Party China hardly seem hurdles to tracking their birds at all. The Russians have a saying for it, 'They can pass unseen'. This capacity can't just be because study of the birds themselves is as near as possible to being apolitical. Maybe these folk, with their pocketed safari vests and binoculars are more likely to be officially dismissed as a harmless lot. But certainly they think, like the birds they follow, that borders exist only as things to be crossed.

This is the case with the most unlikely Asian diplomatic bridgehead to be built since Ping-Pong Diplomacy thawed relations between Mao-era China and Nixon's United States in the 1970s. And the envoy of hope for migratory shorebirds was a wiry Auckland house builder named Adrien Riegen.

Inevitably another transplanted Briton, Riegen was part of a survey at Yalu Jiang in China, watching the great flocks of New Zealand wintering godwit move across the estuary to the east, to the North Korean side. 'You couldn't help wondering that, as the rest of the Yellow Sea had been surveyed, there was an awfully big gap,' he recalls. So he asked how it might be possible to go to North Korea and was told to forget it. 'And of course, me being me, that was just like a red rag to a bull.'

The opportunity came in 2007 when the equally uncon-
ventional New Zealand politician, Winston Peters, announced
that as Foreign Minister he would visit North Korea. Riegen
and Keith Woodley, who runs the Pukorokoro Miranda Shorebird Centre south-east of Auckland, decided to write to Peters
suggesting that he might ask the North Koreans whether the
New Zealanders could go there and count some birds. 'It's
the sort of wacky thing that Winston Peters wouldn't be ashamed
to ask,' Riegen says. Indeed Peters did, and several months
later the North Koreans said they were very happy with the idea.

It took months of negotiations, and reluctant New Zealand
government funding, but they went, flying in from Beijing in
2009 to survey a nature reserve at Mundok, near Pyongyang.
'We were able to show the North Koreans a Dunlin banded in
Barrow, Alaska, and a Godwit banded in Invercargill—the two
completely opposite ends of the flyway. The North Koreans saw
that they were part of a global network, that they weren't as
isolated as we tend to make them.'

It was some years before the New Zealanders were able to
go back. 'The problem was cost,' Riegen says. 'A lot of companies don't want anything to do with North Korea. As soon as
you say you're asking for money to go there they say, "Woah!
Uncle Sam won't like that."' Eventually the big New Zealand
dairy co-operative, Fonterra, agreed to help. Since 2014, New
Zealand–North Korean teams have systematically surveyed the
country's Yellow Sea wetlands during northward migration.

Surveys in the hermit kingdom take months to organise. The
New Zealanders' counterparts from the North Korean Nature
Conservation Union have no internet access, cannot even receive
posted prints of satellite images. Nor can they access GPS. But
they can accept paper maps marked with suggested locations.

They discuss these with the security forces, and then central, local and township level government officials.

'You are quite restricted in North Korea,' Riegen says, showing a shorebird conference a picture of the New Zealand–Korean team, sitting and waiting for high tide, with a loose-slung rifle's muzzle poking into the corner of the image. 'You can't just wander about wherever you like. But we don't do too badly.'

The days are long. The surveyors stay in accommodation that often lacks running water or electricity, and they take grinding drives on bumpy roads to the coast. They need to arrive three hours before high tide to watch the birds fly in to roost and to find an agreeable place to count—agreeable to the security. Then they count, scan for bands and flags, and drive back just in time to snatch some sleep before doing it all again.

To their frustration, they are not allowed out onto the tidal flats to check on the birds' food. But they have surveyed many important North Korean flats from the shore, including the coast that Riegen first looked at ambitiously, east of Yalu Jiang. There they found a hidden inlet at Elephant Island Bay where 13,000 Bar-tailed Godwit roosted, nearly 5 per cent of the flyway population. They scanned flags of godwit from New Zealand and Victoria, a Far Eastern Curlew from Broome, and Grey Plover from Thailand.

David Melville is often a member of the surveys and he also thinks of the mudflats close to the DMZ with longing. 'One can only take from those tagged Spoon-billed Sandpipers stopping for a month or so, that the birds will go and moult there. So this is very important in their lives.' In the 2019 survey they managed to get within 11.5 kilometres of the border. 'But we were only allowed to stand on one small bit of the seawall.

We didn't see any Spoonies, but were able to confirm that the flats are still, for the time being, very extensive.'

North Korea's Yellow Sea coast is comparatively undeveloped, but it has not proven to hold a trove of great undiscovered shorebird numbers, nor is it a secure refuge from other habitat losses in the Yellow Sea. Though Pyongyang has signed up to both Ramsar and the flyway partnership, none of the birders is under any illusion about the vulnerability of its coast to land claim.

Nial Moores, who has made repeated visits to North Korea, tells me its people have embedded in their culture the system of *Juche*, or self-reliance. 'There are many slogans in party conventions and in propaganda signs all over the countryside about self-reliance, natural resources and environment.

'On the one hand self-reliance teaches people in that nation they have to cherish natural resources. The director-general of the Ministry of Land and Environment Protection, she loves shorebirds. When she sees them, she's really excited. But she is in a nation that for 60 years has used reclamation as a way of making their territory bigger.

'So I don't know. Is it really going to be a hidden refuge? Is it? Only in the last two months they have announced projects of 8000 hectares. They only have 110,000 hectares of wetland. It's a big loss in the short term. I'm actually more encouraged by what's happening in China.'

———

Jing Li prowled the Tiaozini mudflat with the two pieces of gear seemingly ever-present in her life: a mobile phone planted to her ear, and a spotting scope over her shoulder. The former Shanghai businesswoman has taken a path highly unusual in

China—to advocate for a bird. Family and friends advised her against such unrewarding work, potentially at odds with the government. But for her the challenge of turning a hobby into action was too great to ignore.

She says she wanted to work with an amateur team who were interested in shorebird conservation. 'We felt we could do something, or change something,' she tells me. 'It is because the Spoonie is such a high-profile species, we get extra benefit and become important.'

As she guided our small group along the Jiangsu shore she spoke with some frustration at the sight. 'All along the coast is factory, docks, factory, docks.'

That day we would be interviewed by a local television crew she organised to promote the value of shorebird-watching tourism. We would stay at a hotel whose owner had been persuaded to adopt the Spoonie as a mascot, built a giant Spoon-billed Sandpiper mosaic in the hotel grounds and hosted us to dinner. Li would give away soft-toy Spoonies made for school students' art prizes. On the mudflat she unfurled for the camera a handheld red banner bearing the cute bird logo of her group, 'Spoon-billed Sandpiper in China'.

The simple goodness of all of this seems likely to be crushed without notice under China's juggernaut. And yet, as her work shows, China is changing.

This is a country that now has half a billion middle-class people, who are well educated and have disposable income for things like travel and gadgets. When a group of giggling young friends in smart clothes trips out onto the flats at Tiaozini to investigate us, our guide, Lin Zhang, welcomes them, and encourages them to use the scopes. He says later, 'They were alright. They were educated.'

Migratory shorebirds are now studied at several Chinese universities, including Beijing Forestry University, which hosts a new flyway partnership science unit. The appetite of Chinese bird photographers for rarities is becoming the stuff of legend. A European Robin has twice turned up in a Beijing Park, to be surrounded by a cannonade of lenses. Fudan University's shorebird professor, Zhijuan Ma, found that birdwatchers increased from 600 to 20,000 in the first ten years of this century, and their growth was closely linked to the wealthier provinces. At that pace, by 2020 half a million Chinese might call themselves birders.

This bottom-up growth is reflected in top-down China. Nial Moores looked across the Yellow Sea from South Korea at President Xi's embrace of the concept of ecological civilisation. 'When I first heard it I thought, oh my gosh, what an awful expression. But when you think about it, it puts the science of ecology at the heart of civilisation. That is such a powerful twinning of these words.'

First promoted by Xi's predecessor, Hu Jintao, it's since been added to the Communist Party Congress's constitution and overall development plan for China. Crucially for the birds, in 2015 the party's Central Committee and State Council published an ecological progress reform plan that included protecting all wetlands, and developing a system of restoration.

In careful synchronicity, a Coastal Wetland Blueprint appeared. It was prepared as a collaboration between Chinese geographers, the government and the Beijing office of the influential Paulson Institute. This is a non-partisan, independent 'think and do tank' founded in 2011 by former US Treasury Secretary, Henry Paulson, with the aim of fostering US–China relations. A long-standing Sinophile and an avid birder (as too is his wife, Wendy), Paulson knows the Tiaozini flats. Jing Li helped to organise their second trip onto the mud there a week after we left it.

'The Paulsons saw several Spoon-billed Sandpipers in good light with clear visibility,' an institute staffer blogged of their visit. 'More impressively they stood amid tens of thousands of other migrating shorebirds. They were amazed.' Paulson has written of the importance of wetlands, not just to him but to China's paramount leader. 'As President Xi commented to me in a meeting in April 2103: "we have to build more wetlands, which will be the kidneys of Planet Earth".'

The Coastal Wetland Blueprint mapped 180 priority conservation sites, among them eleven migratory bird habitats including Nanpu in Bohai Bay, Panjin next to the Shuangtaizi River mouth in Liaodong Bay, and Tiaozini. The same Tiaozini where there had been grand plans to expand land claim onto the offshore Dongsha shoals.

After the loss of its main known staging ground at Saemangeum in South Korea, if the Spoonie was to survive, it would need Tiaozini. Jing Li wrangled logistics and helped a survey led by Guy Anderson, from the UK Royal Society for the Protection of Birds, of the 2018 autumn migration. Using cannon nets, the Anglo–Chinese team caught and flagged 33 Spoonies among 1891 shorebirds. They estimated the flats were used by around 200 of the species. Anderson called Tiaozini 'the single most important site for SBS, certainly in Jiangsu, and possibly in the world'.

Gradually, the ship of Chinese national government began to turn in favour of the birds. National reform orders came to the Yellow Sea like a lifeboat for castaways.

First the authority controlling coastal land, the State Oceanic Administration, called a halt to land-claim projects 'approved but not started and do not comply with the current policy'.

The SOA's director, Shanqing Li, said projects that did not concern the national economy and people's livelihoods would not be approved in future. 'Using reclaimed land for commercial real estate development is prohibited and all reclamation activities in the Bohai Sea area will be banned,' he said.

The January 2018 ruling was followed six months later by the handing down of a stone tablet, a circular from China's highest executive, the State Council. In the preamble, the circular noted: 'Coastal wetlands . . . are important habitat breeding sites and migration stations for birds. They are precious resources with important ecological functions.'

The circular reinforced and detailed the SOA's earlier ban. It anchored the changes to a guiding ecological ideology that made wetland reform a new national environmental goal, fitting China's attempts to clean up the broad-scale damage of its exploding economic growth. The unrestrained land-claim rush was over.

Only 'major national strategic projects' might still continue, but not if they were on ecologically vulnerable shores including Bohai and Liaodong bays. Illegal reclamations would be wiped out. New wind farms were banned in 'migrating areas of birds'. The circular's fillip for flyway shorebirds was the recognition of five wetlands for protection, including Jiangsu Rudong, which covers Tiaozini, and Jiangsu Yancheng National Nature Reserve, where 314 square kilometres of aquaculture farms were to be shut down. Instead these were to be held inside Ecological Red Lines of protection around the country.

———

In a country stretched to capacity, an Ecological Red Line is a reminder of that other red line protecting agricultural land, which did so much to drive expansion into the sea. Migratory shorebird advocates in the Yellow Sea needed China to make an *international* commitment. This meant walking a high wire, and risking failure, to inscribe them on UNESCO's World Heritage List.

On the face of things, it seemed straightforward. China already had 54 sites registered on the World Heritage List—a measure of the riches of culture and nature still intact there. Adding Yellow Sea sites would be in line with the governing ecological civilisation theme. It would tighten national protection and had the potential to light ordinary people's imagination: 'Oh, so this mud is *that* important.'

This path is also well-trodden by global conservation advocates keen to ring-fence precious assets before they are destroyed. The World Heritage Committee can keep a careful eye on its properties and, among its powers, embarrass countries that fail to protect them by listing them as 'In Danger'. Australia fought an expensive campaign to avert the adding of the Great Barrier Reef to this list of ignominy.

But the committee of 21 elected nations has strict rules about how a nomination comes forward, which is then subject to intense political lobbying at inscription time. Outcomes can be far from the expected.

China was encouraged by IUCN to mount a nomination for more than a dozen Yellow Sea coastal sites to be inscribed on the list as a hub for one of the world's most threatened flyways in a three phase serial nomination. If successful it would throw a protective fence not only around places like Tiaozini, but also Nanpu and Yancheng. Looking at a map of the planned nomination was like seeing Mark Barter's wish list within tempting grasp.

Good fortune meant that the IUCN's President happened to be the former Chinese Vice-Minister for Education, Zhang Xinsheng. It's hard for an outsider to know exactly who, in the opaque Chinese corridors of power, is able to pull strings. But clearly Zhang *would* know. He is a senior mandarin, and he nailed his colours to the shorebird mast.

'Iconic mammals, such as Panda, Tiger, Polar Bear and many others are playing an important role in conservation of the planet,' he wrote. 'In recent years iconic bird species have come to our attention, and now we are witnessing the rise of one such species on the East Asian–Australasian Flyway—the Spoon-billed Sandpiper.'

The speed with which China took up the idea of a Yellow Sea nomination surprised David Melville, who gave advice on it. 'I was at a meeting in Beijing in December 2017, the nomination had to be in the following February, and it just seemed too tight, but they did it.'

World Heritage listing is a gold standard for conservation. To be listed, a property needs to have Outstanding Universal Values, and the initial Tentative Nomination for the Yellow Sea as the world's largest mudflat complex relied strongly on migratory birds for that. In Tiaozini's case, Spoonies were high on the reasons. Melville encouraged the Chinese also to highlight the importance of the Dongsha shoals, spiralling out from the mainland, as a significant landform perhaps once linked to the Yellow River.

Beijing's further refined push was explicitly about the birds. The 'Migratory Bird Sanctuaries Along the Coast of Yellow Sea and Bohai Gulf of China' nomination contracted to two phases. The first to come forward in 2019 covered 268,000 hectares of shorebird tidal flats on the Jiangsu coast—homes to those swelling and ebbing bird clouds. It had that most important thing missing from Chinese wetland nature reserves: lines on a map.

Tiaozini–Dongsha squeaked in to this phase. When at first it was not included, a Chinese environmental advocacy NGO made noises to get it there. Jinfeng Zhou, of the China Biodiversity Conservation and Green Development Foundation, insisted on the inclusion of 'this most precious place'. Zhou recounted how he even used the forum of a Ramsar meeting to lobby for it, irritating 'relevant parties' until they agreed, and told him to stop 'messing around'.

Late in 2018, the local Yancheng City Government announced its support for the inclusion of Tiaozini–Dongsha in the nomination in front of an audience that included IUCN President Zhang. 'It will truly turn Xi Jinping's ecological civilisation thought and the idea of "lucid waters and lush mountains are invaluable assets" into practice on the Coastal Wetlands of Yellow Sea,' Acting Mayor Lubao Cao said.

So far so good. The run-up to a successful nomination seemed smooth. Then out of the blue, it hit a hurdle. The World Heritage Committee takes its official advice on the values of natural sites from an expert unit of the IUCN—a unit fire-walled from the rest of the organisation. Never mind that the IUCN President was Chinese, nor that Beijing was supercharging the process. Experts in the World Heritage Unit were not convinced. They advised that the nomination be deferred. The property as a whole suite of sixteen sites around the Chinese Yellow Sea coast had the potential to meet World Heritage criteria, the experts said. But at that point, the nomination didn't.

In their view it was likely the Jiangsu coast was already too far gone. The IUCN expert advice said the Phase One nomination was so compromised it could not make the grade under the criteria of 'outstanding ecological processes', nor was it a 'most important' habitat for migratory shorebirds—it was too small. The experts suggested China come back another time with a whole Yellow Sea nomination.

The dragon was unimpressed. 'What was absolutely clear was that for China to continue with the whole nomination, this (first) inscription had to happen,' Nicola Crockford, of BirdLife International tells me. 'There were some very tense meetings in Beijing . . . Eventually they agreed to proceed, but they needed certainty that it *would* proceed.'

Crockford marshalled 62 advocacy groups calling on China to hold the line. When the committee's open meeting rolled around in Baku, Azerbaijan, it was up to Australia to champion the case for nomination. Under meeting protocols China had to take a back seat. The bargain that Australia struck was to drop the criteria requiring 'outstanding ecological processes' from the Phase One nomination. It would only go ahead as most important habitat for the birds. It sailed through, to applause, along with a set of guidelines for the Phase Two nomination of another 460,000 hectares across fourteen sites.

Slices of the Nanpu coast, beleaguered bastion of the Red Knot, and Godwit Central at the Yalu River estuary would be protected under Phase Two, which Crockford is convinced will happen rapidly. 'Without a doubt it will be delivered by 2022,' she says. 'I have absolute faith.'

The World Heritage bandwagon may also be joined by South Korea, though irony fills this bid. The country of Saemangeum is turning itself towards a nomination of tidal flats on each side of the great failed sea enclosure, and further south. The pin-up

Spoonie, the same bird that lost its stronghold at Saemangeum, is being used in promotion for it too.

———————

China's delivery of wetland protection is still to unfold. On the Nanpu shore after the State Oceanic Administration ban on further development was imposed, Chris Hassell and Adrian Boyle were back for another season surveying Red Knot. What they found was a state of uncertainty.

With the help of the Paulson Institute and WWF, local authorities had agreed to establish a provincial nature reserve specifically to protect migratory birds at Nanpu, one of the Coastal Wetland Blueprint's key sites. But by their 2019 survey, evidence of it was little more than a large signboard portraying local bird species. Just north of the study site, say ten minutes in the air for a Red Knot, a sprawling new By-port Economic Zone was being built. Hassell believes it will host five steel companies, each moved from its current urban location.

'We drove past the construction site during our fieldwork season and it is a sight to behold, with all construction seemingly going on at once,' he reported. 'In addition to the steelworks, a port will be developed.'

Another signboard showed that much more mudflat and shallow sea would be squared off and covered by landfill and concrete. Bohai Bay already contains Tianjin port and Caofeidian. Massive construction between these two would start to leave the Red Knot with the kind of space I saw in Jiangsu for that little flock of Great Knot, jostling for their vital mud in a tiny corner of natural coast.

Surely this new 'by-port' is just the sort of project, not yet advanced into the bay, that will be scrapped under the State Council's edict? Generally wary of what he calls 'Gov-speak', Hassell says, 'Let's see what they actually do.'

As Jing Li looks at the changes from the stance of a small advocacy group, she doubts that enough has yet happened to benefit Spoonies. 'Well, I don't think we could save the species with the current situation in China,' she says. 'Everything is still on paper.'

Despite the mention of migratory shorebirds high in China's decisions to protect wetlands, her caution is shared among most of the flyway's scientists. Christoph Zöckler says he doubts that their Spoonie work has triggered broad changes in China. 'I think that would be exaggerating,' he said. 'But we certainly contributed to that.'

To Melville, it would be nice to think that by now the great weight of shorebird science published in high-quality peer-reviewed journals has helped to shift policy. 'To be honest, I'm not sure that happens anywhere—let alone China,' he says. 'I'm sure, particularly through the Paulson Institute with their very high-level contacts in the Chinese Government, there has been advocacy for coastal wetlands and shorebirds. Equally, there are many internal economic and political reasons. I think a lot of stars have just ended up aligning, resulting in something which is good for shorebirds.'

Bob Gill, reflecting from Anchorage on his birds of Asia, says scientists have become desperate for solutions. 'We were just stalled, in terms of writing white papers saying you need to do this, and they would just disappear into the wherever. Then the China thing turned around. I'm not sure, I would like to think our constantly beating the drum about what's going on opened some eyes, but probably, when it gets down to it, there were one or two key individuals, whether it was the provincial governor, or whoever, who liked to see a flock of godwits in April, and suddenly: "No more filling in mudflats".'

As for me, I think people winning protection for migratory shorebirds on this flyway are selling themselves short. Breakthroughs can't happen in a void. They see the marks of death, and they tell of them. Volunteers band birds. Scientists gather the evidence and publish it. Their advocates offer strategic solutions to decision-makers. Often in the rush and grind of government, good solutions are lost. Just occasionally their timing is perfect.

This time the shorebird shepherds have made their charges literal World Heritage, the adornment of many countries, an example offered to earth's threatened biodiversity. To find the Yellow Sea a safer place for shorebirds would encourage belief that survival for them is possible. If change can happen there, it can be done anywhere.

———

Such a shift of ground as China's stands as hope in the face of our most existential threat: climate change. In this our own, very coastal, lives shadow those of the birds. Their disappearance would show our own troubles have increased; their reactions now are signals we can heed, overwhelmed as we are by the scale of the emergency.

Early warnings of profound ecosystem change are already part of Arctic life. Katya Ovsyanikova, the Brisbane PhD student who lived as a teenager on Wrangel Island, returns there often as a tourist guide. She finds obvious landscape-scale change.

'You see it in just about everything,' she says. 'By the end of July we can get to Wrangel with a non-icebreaker ship. Originally it would have been much later. You have more open seas, stormy weather and generally warmer temperatures. There's melting permafrost, so the tundra just erodes and sort of drops off. We never used to have rain and now it rains. Species not on the island before have arrived. For instance, Tufted Puffins. They are becoming more and more common.'

Along the High Arctic, the story is the same. When CYA left Wrangel to top up ahead of her flight south, she detoured west to Great Lyakhovsky in the New Siberian Islands where Australian turnstone breed. Along Great Lyakhovksy's coastline at the mouth of the Eterikan River a mammoth calf was extracted from the ground, intact even to the fur. Frozen for 24,700 years, but no more. The permafrost of the New Siberians is being lost. The dark, shiny soils of the island are sliding into the Arctic Sea in smooth portions, like melting chocolate.

Oksana Lipka, a lead author for the Intergovernmental Panel on Climate Change (IPCC), says until recently it was thought the New Siberians had the fastest pace of shore erosion in Russia—and the world. The coast was stepping back by 5 to 15 metres each year—20 metres in some places after a storm. That title of quickest disappearing island has since passed on to Vize, further west.

In both cases, the loss of coastline is attributed not just to warming temperatures, but to increased wave energy on the shorelines. The waves come more often, and more intensely, because the sea-ice dampener around these islands is gone for longer. This is a fast-acting climate feedback loop at work.

The Arctic has been warming more than twice as rapidly as the rest of the world for the past 50 years. Before the middle of this century it will have increased by 4–5 degrees Celsius above temperatures there late last century, according to advisers to the eight-nation Arctic Council. 'These changes are locked in, whatever cuts in emissions are made,' their report said. Losses in the extent of sea ice bounced around, but there have been no annual gains on the summer minimum since 2002. In 2018, that meant 1.63 million square kilometres less ice over the water than the 1981–2010 average.

Around the turn of the century, Indigenous observations of Arctic change were collected in an Alaskan anthology. The title of the book came from a Yup'ik elder of St Lawrence Island in the Bering Sea. Mabel Toolie told her nephew, Caleb Pungowiyi: 'The earth is faster now.'

She did not mean time or events were moving more quickly, as they might seem to all older people. She was talking about the weather. Once, people could predict it for a few days in advance. 'Now, those predictions cannot be made anymore,' Pungowiyi said. 'The weather patterns are changing so quickly, she could think the earth is moving faster now.'

Birds of the flyway must live faster too. In a study in south-eastern Australia, geolocator-tagged Ruddy Turnstone were found to leave for the Arctic two days earlier each year, and to arrive in the High Arctic one day earlier. Meijuan Zhao of Deakin University concluded rapid evolution was at work: 'They're adapting to make sure they reach their breeding grounds in time to find food, and give their offspring the best chance of survival,' Zhao said. 'If they arrive too late, the food has already declined, so the timing is crucial.'

Arctic spring—as marked by the thaw, the greening of plants and the arrival of birds—is many days earlier than it was even a decade ago. Turnstone, and all other long-distance migrants, must time their arrival and breeding on the tundra finely to maximise use of the hatch of insect life. I recall the intense patrols by plover at Woolley Lagoon over snow-browned vegetation newly revealed by the melt, waiting for a flicker of movement to betray a beetle or fly. Each day of a lost patrol would count.

There is underway a worldwide decline in insect life, largely driven by habitat loss to agriculture and artificial chemicals. Climate change is playing a role in this collapse too. Insect loss is most dramatic in the tropics; nevertheless evidence of a disconnect has begun to assemble in the Arctic, where bountiful insects are crucial to shorebird survival.

In a study in the Canadian Arctic, Baird's Sandpiper mis-matched the timing of its breeding and peak cranefly-larvae supply, and the chicks raised outside this period of food abundance grew more slowly. At Utqiagvik/Barrow in Alaska, an invertebrate hatch got out of whack because of an earlier melt, and as a result, across eight shorebird species fewer than half the broods had sufficient food for average growth in the first ten days after their chicks hatched.

The potential for damage came into sharp focus in a study that linked Arctic warming to body shrinkage of Red Knot. This was a forced, rapid, evolutionary change, and it would not help the birds survive.

The Dutch Red Knot specialist, Jan van Gils, found that over 33 years, snow melt happened earlier on the Taimyr Peninsula sixteen times. In these years, 1990 juvenile Red Knot from the Taimyr were caught on southward migration at Gdansk Bay, Poland and measured. During summers with a much earlier melt, the insects were smaller and fewer. Consequently birds were smaller too: they weighed less, and, most worryingly, had shorter bills.

In these birds' wintering grounds at Banc d'Arguin in West Africa, a shorter bill means the knot has much reduced access through the mud to its target shellfish. They have to make do with poorer prey. In turn, birds with shorter bills have lower survival rates as juveniles. 'This mechanism may be one of the drivers of the steep and ongoing population decline of the *Calidris canutus* Red Knots,' van Gils concluded.

Van Gils thought the same problem might extend to other Arctic migrants. Bob Gill says the study has led to a much wider examination of the problem. But he says it has not been confirmed in work on Dunlin on Alaska's North Slope, which did not change body size at all. 'It's got a long ways to go before you can hang the dogma sign on it, and say this is how it is,' Gill concludes.

The wider tundra habitat is under examination, with predictions that shrubs and trees will move north with warming, reducing opportunities for shorebirds to breed on their preferred open ground. 'There's already some studies coming out saying habitats for godwits and curlews are going to change, and not for the better,' Gill says. 'I'm not in that camp yet.'

I wonder about the Grey Plover's preference for slightly elevated real estate, and whether it will have to see off more rivals seeking an escape from lower, damper tundra. 'Your bird is a generalist,' Gill replies. 'If we see problems with it, there'll be a lot of other stuff happening too.'

His deeply experienced insight is a calming balance at a time when it is becoming a preoccupation to understand which birds will manage Arctic climate change and which will lose. Some hypothetical models for their future are very worrisome. Looking at 24 birds that nest above the tree-line, the University of Queensland's Hannah Wauchope found that up to half, including Grey Plover, could lose much of their climatically suitable breeding conditions. Some birds that use specialised niches, such as the Stilt Sandpiper and Curlew Sandpiper, face 'dire consequences'. Only two American species gained in future scenarios: the stint-like Western Sandpiper and the Hudsonian Godwit.

Beringia, that refuge during past glacial eras, and now species-rich with shorebirds, will be largely bereft of climatically suitable breeding conditions for them, Wauchope found. 'Remaining suitable area for most species shifts and contracts, becoming almost exclusively limited to northerly islands, the vast majority in the Canadian Arctic.'

Think also of the Spoon-billed Sandpiper, not part of that study, but out among the crowberries on its preferred—likely vulnerable—lagoon spits in Chukotka. There, climate change becomes part of another chain linked to shorebird demise— increased predation. At the Meinypil'gyno site, as they collected precious Spoonie eggs, researchers shot a particularly trouble- some fox. Killing one predator was not a lasting solution, they readily admitted, but it did highlight a problem.

'If you look at the changes in the past twenty years, I would say that it must be related to the changes in the lemming and vole cycles that has a knock-on effect on the predators,' Christoph Zöckler says. 'It is a pattern which might be related to the warming of the Arctic, that does not give these birds a respite from a predator.'

There is a hot debate between scientists over whether shorebirds, particularly in the Arctic, are suffering from more nest predation. Czech ecologist Vojtech Kubelka led a study joined by Pavel Tomkovich that found predation had increased three-fold, so that 70 per cent of Arctic shorebird nests were losing their eggs. Why? For a mix of reasons linked to climate, the Arctic might be turning into an 'ecological trap'. Lemming abundance cycles may have been disrupted by faster snow melt, and predators like the Red Fox are without doubt making inroads northward, with increased vegetation perhaps giving them ambush cover. An argument on these findings played out in the journal *Science*, with Kubelka insisting there is clear evidence in the Arctic.

Time on the tundra, more dangerous though it may be, is only part of the disturbance of flyway life in a perturbed climate. The Siberian taiga and North American boreal forests are burning more often. The birds are exposed to increased weather hazards of the kind seen in CYB's threading of Super Typhoon Meranti. The sea's uptake of excess carbon increases ocean acidification and makes it harder for shellfish to build shells. Profound changes occur as the sea-level rises over the tidal flats.

If governments achieve drastic emission cuts, sea levels are still predicted by the IPCC to rise by up to 54 centimetres on pre-2005 heights by the end of the century. If emissions continue their rise, that figure will be more like 82 centimetres—and these estimates are conservative.

Already tidal flats can change rapidly according to the ebb and flow of sediment, of structures around them, or local weather. 'There are real natural dynamics to intertidal flats,' says the University of Queensland's Richard Fuller. 'They are not static habitats like a patch of forest, that you can stick a boundary around and say, "job done".'

Satellite mapper Nick Murray worked with Fuller and others, including Google, to produce a searchable map of tidal-flat change over time around the world. It's revealing for EAAF shorebirds, not least because it shows that the three countries with the world's largest tidal flats extents are Indonesia, China and Australia.

'This gives us eyes and ears in places where we haven't had them before,' Fuller says of their work. They found that globally we now have 127,991 square kilometres of tidal flat; but, working back to the earliest Landsat records 33 years ago, we appear to have lost 16 per cent already. Coastal development and the damming of rivers played large roles in this. So did erosion, and sea-level rise.

The consequences for flyway shorebirds can worsen, depending upon where the rise happens. Tidal-flat loss to sea-level rise at Nanpu, for example, could affect nearly half of all flyway Red Knot. The perilous reliance by this species on few, but vital, staging grounds is already known from the crash in the United States of the Atlantic Flyway's Red Knot, *Calidris canutus rufa*. Its population was around 67,000 in the 1980s, and fell to a fraction of that before a halt to the over-fishing of Horseshoe Crab, which provides spawn as vitally timed food at Delaware Bay on the US's east coast.

These knot numbers have partly recovered, but not enough to prevent their listing as 'threatened' under the US Endangered Species Act. The designation includes concerns about sea-level rise, making it the first US bird to be listed as threatened explicitly because its existence is imperilled by climate change.

In Australia, sea-level rise is flagged for its potential impact on all four EAAF shorebirds now counted as critically endangered. Whether you have the small legs of a Curlew Sandpiper, or the longer legs of the Far Eastern Curlew, when the mud once exposed as tidal flat stays too far under water, it's gone.

Estimates of the loss of intertidal shorebird habitats on the EAAF show a sea-level rise of a metre would eliminate one-fifth of the Yellow Sea flats, where the tidal range is wide, and about half of southern Australia's, where it is narrower. Fuller's Queensland colleague, Takuya Iwamura, looked at 163 sites across the flyway and found that, depending on the magnitude of the rise, 13 to 64 per cent of habitat could be lost. 'We could witness dramatic collapses of population flows caused by inter-tidal habitat loss for at least some of the migratory shorebird species within a few decades,' Iwamura wrote.

On some low-lying, unhardened coasts, tidal flats may move inland. The ephemeral saltmarsh behind Thompson Beach on Gulf St Vincent, perhaps. But not at Tiaozini or the Daling River mouth. These are now hardened shores. And the flats may not move out quickly enough to meet already conservative time-frames of the IPCC's predicted rises.

The cost of tearing down hard coasts and re-establishing lost wetlands would be astronomical, as some attempts are showing. At Medmerry, on the West Sussex coast in the UK, a 183-hectare wetland was built to manage sea-flooding and incidentally give waterbirds a new home. To do this they imported 60,000 tonnes of boulder rock by barge from Norway in a project that cost £28 million (US$45 million). One unexpected gain was the introduction of a valuable new term for the climate-change era: as opposed to 'Land Reclamation', this project was for 'Sea Surrender'.

If we are to maximise conservation gains under sea-level rise, the Yellow Sea stands out clearly as the single most-important target for investment to protect flyway shorebirds. But Southeast Asia is emerging as a valuable region. Among causes for hope, there are signs that already the birds are making adjustments to these less-developed tropical coasts. Melville says it seems some migration routes and strategies are changing. 'Possibly more use

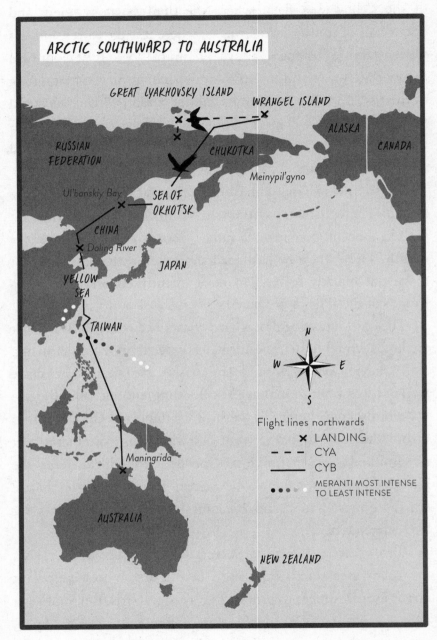

ARCTIC SOUTHWARD TO AUSTRALIA

GREAT LYAKHOVSKY ISLAND

WRANGEL ISLAND

ALASKA

CANADA

RUSSIAN
FEDERATION

CHUKOTKA

Meinypil'gyno

Ul'banskiy Bay

SEA OF
OKHOTSK

CHINA

Doling River

JAPAN

YELLOW
SEA

TAIWAN

N

W   E

S

Flight lines northwards

✕   LANDING

– – –   CYA

——   CYB

●●●●   MERANTI MOST INTENSE
TO LEAST INTENSE

Maningrida

AUSTRALIA

NEW ZEALAND

Sources: Flight data, Victorian Wader Study Group and Friends of Shorebirds
South-East; Flyway, BirdLife International; Typhoon Meranti's path, H. Gu et al.,
The Impact of Tropical Cyclones on China in 2016

is being made of Southeast Asia now than we thought—or that the birds were doing 30 or 40 years ago.'

So many of the shifts made by these birds chime with our own existence: the realities of shortened or changed seasons, different numbers or species around us, increased weather havoc, a warming sea that has trouble producing shells. But their fortune under climate change is not the only lesson they offer.

The genius of migratory shorebirds is that they have survived many ice ages, navigating their way around the edges of the possible. They are a reminder to us to measure our lives by the persistence of wildlife on the fringes of daily existence. We should value tidal wetlands as a mark of our own coastal health; learn to read its vibrancy at a glance by the presence, or absence, of the grey birds out there. Their dauntless superflights across the planet join far-distant people, who once could only wonder at these mysterious travellers coming and going with the turn of the seasons.

Now after the shorebird people's lifetime of work, we know much more. We know these birds are so like us. Flung out into the world, capable of great feats, destined to make the best of our fates. The earth is always faster for shorebirds. They fly, ahead of us.

Sixteen
In harmony with the sun

I am in a sturdy launch, in the hands of the Bawinanga Djelk
Rangers of Arnhem Land in Australia's Northern Territory. We
are riding up the wide Liverpool River investigating the loss of
CYB. The tropical heat is held at bay by the speedboat's breeze.
Seasonally it is the Build-up, the time before the Wet, when the
migratory birds are flitting in from the north. I have made sure
to be here at exactly the time of year of our bird's last fix, in the
hope of finding her kind.

The boat is helmed by William Dennis and the deckhand is
Jonah Ryan, but the skipper is Joyce Boehm, leader of the Djelk
Women Rangers. She is lifeblood of the Aboriginal community
at Maningrida, a town of 2000 mainly Kunibidji people on the
mouth of the Liverpool. She made sure that Jack Marilain, a
traditional owner of lands bordered by the river, gave his permission for this journey, and he is with us. All of these people are
here to help me complete my journey, and I hope in return that
I have a worthy story for them.

I think about the travels that led me here. It's months since I touched the Arctic, over a year since my treatment began. My hopes have been jolted by the revival of the primary, and more secondaries, before each is deterred under radiotherapy, the cancer put back in its box under immunotherapy's guard once more.

I hold onto this journey as a vital point in my life. More than anything, I had to come to Maningrida. The journey has become for me a proof of the science that keeps me alive, and of the science that traced the loss of the bird. Our twin odysseys. And now here I am, amazed, inside the heart of an Aboriginal community.

I flew in from Darwin two days ago, over Kakadu National Park and across flattened dark granite hills, squarely segmented like a crocodile skin: ancient country, full of ancient life. Banking to land, I saw the afternoon sea breeze from the Arafura Sea kick up white caps on the mouth of the Liverpool. Around its edges, mangrove-lined creeks wound their way down from low coastal plains.

I walked out of the airport and across the road to check in at the visiting-workers' lodge. Then I wandered the Maningrida streets in a heat-dazed state looking for the local Bawinanga Aboriginal Corporation's office. There, I was scooped up and driven to the rangers' station where Joyce Boehm took me under her wing.

We agreed we would try to take the boat down the river the next day, and I came back in the morning to find that over-night the world at Maningrida had changed. We stepped into a four-wheel drive and she drove me around the community.

She picked up a child here, dropped another there, stopped to chat with folk, collected a cigarette from one person, gave it to another. Then we drove to the airport and joined a hundred people who were gathered for a funeral.

At no time was I, such an outsider, ever made to feel I should not take part in this event in whichever way I wished. So I stayed with Joyce as she explained that we were waiting for a light aircraft to bring back to the community a sixteen-year-old girl, a Djelk Ranger cadet, who had passed away at her own hand.

Most of the Maningrida school was there. As the plane taxied in, there were grieving cries and a distraught young woman shook the wires of the airport gates. The cries intensified as the coffin was unloaded and ferried into the rear of a Landcruiser wagon, to the earnest call of didgeridoo and clapping sticks. From this makeshift hearse's bull-bar fluttered a blue flag slashed with the outline of a white bird, the flag of Maningrida.

The hearse drove in slow procession from the airport through the heat of the day with the musicians' dirge in front of it, and silent schoolchildren walking on each side. Occasionally people dashed for garden hoses and taps to quench their thirsts. Two girls walking close to the hearse wore T-shirts emblazoned with 'Last Run FJ'. Black kites circled overhead.

When the funeral stopped at the Maningrida church, I waited at a distance under the shade of a tree while a service was held and speeches were made.

I was full of thoughts. Of life's fragility and the often profound injustice of its loss. The connection I felt for the demure Grey Plover, their uplifting journeys, and the wish we have in our hearts for completion, for neat resolution. I thought of the untimely end of things. I felt my own cancer. It weighed but little in the balance of such a tragic early death as this in Maningrida.

So much future had been taken; from this young woman, from her family, young friends and community, all forced to comprehend too much, far too early.

It became clear there would not be a boat trip that day. Asked whether I would like to go to the family's house for ceremony and vigil, I decided to leave the grieving to their bereavement.

Next day, her eyes dry, her voice firm, Joyce Boehm rounded up the rangers, Jack Marilain and me. Already, she told me brightly, I was the 'Bird Man' to local people. She had told the story again and again, of the travels of 'this little Gik-Gik', flying all the way from South Australia to China, Russia and back to Australia at Maningrida. I was relieved to know the story was spreading. We launched the boat and drove up the river just in time to make the most of the high tide.

In the bow of the boat, I unfold an image of CYB's local satellite track and talk about the path that the bird took. On the flight from the Yellow Sea, onward past the super typhoon, she flew out over the Pacific, east of the Philippines, and crossed the Bird's Head Peninsula of West Papua to land from her long hop on Yilan beach, east of Maningrida. After a day or so CYB then flicked over the town and down the Liverpool River, where her signal centred on open ground up one of the mangrove creeks near Bat Island.

We will try to reach that place.

Marilain, whose dreaming is the Magpie Goose, knows this country as a place for camping. 'We get mussels and yams, everything, food is there,' he says. 'Lots of birds gather there.'

We come to Mulgari Creek, and motor quietly up its mouth past a shrieking fruit bat colony and under flocks of lorikeet. A Brahminy Kite drifts overhead and an Azure Kingfisher eyes the water severely. We surprise a small flock of Terek Sandpiper, birds arrived from Arctic Chukotka via the Yellow Sea. Their clownish upturned bills make them seem permanently amazed, and they put on a show for us. Staring at the boat from their mangrove-branch perch, they cry alarm, and take off further up the creek to land on another branch. Again and again they take flight in front of us, disbelieving that we are following.

Some way up, when we can press no further, we step ashore. Marilain contemplates the ground without comment. There is a clearing, but it is not the right place. So we climb back into the boat, retrace our way back to the Liverpool, and drive further down to try again, entering Bungarnim Creek.

A sandbar near this creek's entrance is crowded with Far Eastern Curlew and Greenshank. Still I see no Grey Plover. This creek is wider and more promising, but the ebb is under way and with it will go our access.

William Dennis helms the boat with concentrated ease through opaque grey waters, past mangrove roots and swirls of Barramundi, as Jonah Ryan tells me a crocodile story. At one time, the Djelk Rangers decided to try crocodile farming, and needed to collect eggs from a wild nest. Ryan was designated as first-time collector. He describes being dropped out of a helicopter and told to use a strong stick to fend off the female Saltwater Crocodile while he took her eggs. That worked initially, but the crocodile started snapping closer and the stick was proving ineffective. He jumped around for a while among the mangroves, all the time trying to save the eggs, until the helicopter returned to pull him—and them—out. He laughs a big infectious laugh at the memory.

We see a Whimbrel shoot over the mangrove tops, a tall white egret raise its neck to regard us, and then we come to a fork in the creek. The mud banks here are deeply ploughed by feral buffalo crossing the water at the shallowing fork. Over 10,000 buffalo inhabit the Djelk Indigenous Protected Area, and a big task of the Bawinanga Corporation is to cull them, which they do by helicopter with semi-automatic rifles.

The land is rising above us now as the tide drops, and there's not much time; but as we check the creek fork on the satellite image it's clear we have found the right place. Beside us is a wide, nameless flood plain, the central point of CYB's signal transmissions for three weeks before the last fix, on 12 September 2016. She disappeared on this ground cut up by buffalo, fringed by the creeks and trees of the savannah, a roost far apart from people.

After the weed-wash of Thompson Beach, the press of people against the Yellow Sea, the Arctic space of Wrangel Island, and again the Daling River mouth; across 25,000 kilometres of the earth, this was where we lost touch with her. The end of her flight line. I look out across the plain. There is no sign of any bird.

CYB died, or maybe she didn't. For Tony Flaherty, it is the nagging unanswered question: 'Are we having a massive mortality from satellite telemetry or do we just not see our Grey Plover back at their study sites? I don't know.' There is but a sliver of hope she shed the tracker harness and flies still, drawn by the turn of the seasons, following the lines of the earth.

————

The fearless Australian poet, A.D. Hope, turned his mind to migratory birds once. In 'The Death of the Bird' he writes of her going away also being a coming home, and of the loss of her guiding instinct, a spark gone.

And the great earth, with neither grief nor malice,
Receives the tiny burden of her death.

We motor back down the creek with little conversation and speed up along the river, hugging a bank to stay out of the rising chop. Boehm is thoughtful. She decides we should do some more birding. She will drive me out to Rocky Point, along the coast to the east of Maningrida.

'I've seen a lot of birds out there,' she says. 'Maybe we'll see something.'

So we climb into the vehicle and wind our way out along tracks to a beach near where CYB first landed. It's low tide now and she is disappointed—the birds are few and far away. An Australian Pelican works the tide edge. A Far Eastern Curlew prowls among rocks. Two elfin Black-naped Tern fly close past us, to lead our eyes across the beach as they land on wide sand between fingers of tumbled rock.

That bird between them. What's that?

It's close enough for me to see with binoculars. The plumage is mottled, silvery grey and white, splashed with black. It's part-moulted, looking out across the Arafura Sea at the direction it has come from—the far north. Surviving.

'Joyce,' I say as I hand her the glasses. 'Remember what I said about how to identify it for sure.' As she settles her gaze on it, the bird flicks its wings and flies, fast and free, away from us to disappear.

'Black wing-pits,' she says.

Next day before I leave we go to see Jack Marilain again. He seems a serious man, of measured words. I had given him some copies of the satellite maps and tried as best I could to fill in the bird's story. Her path was so different from his world, but I hope now part of it.

He smiles and murmurs, 'I thought about it all night.'

Author's note

This story rose on the shoulders of many. Some are described in the text and more in the reference notes that follow. But behind the note abbreviation 'et al.', or otherwise unacknowledged, are dozens who shared their research, stories and inspiration, kindly and freely.

Here I mean people like Phil Straw, Alison Russell-French and Ken Gosbell of the Australasian Wader Studies Group, whose depth of knowledge gave me a path to tread. And Eric Woehler, Hazel Britton and Denis Abbott of BirdLife Tasmania, working in the local shorebird field long before I came to the scene. Or Graham Appleton, the British celebrator of shorebirds online at *Wadertales*.

I found many generous people around the world only too happy to share their images when they understood what the book was attempting. These include Roy Lowe, Richard Chandler, Tony Flaherty, Imogen Warren, Chang Yong-Choi, Adrian Boyle, David Young, Daniel Ruthrauff, David Melville, Peter Crighton and Wyatt Egelhoff.

And I cannot let this moment pass without counting those guiding me through life with cancer. Medical protection has been wrapped around me by Louise Nott, Raef Awad, John Kruimink, Guy Bannick, Rob Ware, John Farmer, Adrian Barber and Claire Darby Champness. Friends John Coomber, Robert Wilson, Ian Moore and Robert Mitchell stepped up to support instinctively, as have my family. I have been able to have a purpose thanks to them all. My wife, Sally Johannsohn, lovingly ensured that I achieved it.

In the end I can only provide the goods, and it is the publisher who makes a book. Like countless Australian journalists and writers before me, I owe a start with *Flight Lines* to Richard Walsh. His patience and encouragement through to manuscript completion validated both it, and me.

Since then it has navigated the turbulence of book publishing today thanks to Elizabeth Weiss and Rebecca Kaiser. Elizabeth's determination for the book to succeed is its rock. Among Rebecca's quiet feats, she cleared the thickets to pluck its title from the text.

It has been through the diligent copy editing of Lauren Finger, and Julia Cain's close proofreading. Mika Tabata's maps bring the birds' realm alive, and cover designer Peter Long made the hard task of joining a few simple elements look easy.

Finally, I thank you, the reader. I hope that *Flight Lines* has given you a warmer place in your heart for these wild birds, and for the powers of science.

Notes

For the song-men are the oral map-makers . . . Harney, W., 'Roads and Trade', *Walkabout*, 1 May 1950, vol. 16, no. 5, p. 43

I had no nation now . . . Walcott, D., 'The Schooner *Flight*', in Baugh, E. (ed.), *Selected Poems—Derek Walcott*, Farrar, Straus and Giroux, New York: 2007, p. 129

Chapter One: Hunting on a no-good shore

'Waders typically are the "grey birds"' . . . Piersma, T., 'Red Knots and the Red Square', *Wader Study*, 2015, vol. 122, no. 3, pp. 169–70

It's three closest relatives . . . Byrkjedal, I. & Thompson D., with Halvorsen, G., *Tundra Plovers*, T & AD Poyser, London: 1998, p. 35

Hayman, P., Marchant, J., Prater, T., 'Shorebirds: An identification guide,' Houghton Mifflin, New York, 1986

At an auction in 2006 . . . Anon., 'Record price for decoy of $830,000 established at Guyette and Schmidt's', *Antiques and the Arts Weekly*, 5 December 2006, www.antiquesandthearts.com/record-price-for-decoy-of-830000-established-at-guyette-and-schmidts/

The gash in southern Australia that is . . . McGowran, B. & Alley, N., 'History of the Cenozoic St Vincent Basin in South Australia', in S. Shepherd et al., *Natural History of Gulf St Vincent*, Royal Society of South Australia, Adelaide: 2008, pp. 13–16

In the last maximum about 20,000 years ago . . . Harbison, P., et al., *Gulf St Vincent: A Precious Asset*, Friends of Gulf St Vincent, Adelaide: 2009, p. 3

Sediments drift up to settle . . . Edyvane, K., 'Macroalgal biogeography and assemblages of Gulf St Vincent' in S. Shepherd et al., ibid, p. 248

Stores of shorebird food are hidden . . . Benkendorff, K., et al., 'Intertidal ecosystems' in S. Shepherd et al., ibid, p. 130

Further down the gulf, towards Adelaide . . . Purnell, C., et al., *Shorebird Population Monitoring Within Gulf St Vincent: July 2014 to June 2015, Annual Report*, BirdLife Australia, Melbourne, 2015, pp. 17–20

Stories of the Kaurna Aboriginal people . . . Bryars, S., Foreword in Shepherd et al., ibid, p. 2

Archaeological scrutiny of Kaurna stone . . . Tindale, N., 'The wanderings of Tjirbruki', *Records of the South Australian Museum*, 1987, vol. 20, p. 11–12

Flinders, the mapmaker, named the waters . . . Flinders, M., *Journal on HMS 'Investigator'*, vol. 1, 1801–1802, State Library of New South Wales, Sydney

His expedition naturalist, Robert Brown . . . Vallance, T.G., et al. (eds), *Nature's Investigator: The diary of Robert Brown in Australia 1801–1805*, Australian Biological Resources Study, Canberra: 2001, p. 171

Just twelve days afterwards, Nicholas Baudin . . . Cornell, C., (tr.), *Journal of Nicolas Baudin*, Friends of the State Library of South Australia, Adelaide: 2004, p. 282–3

A century ago, it began to operate an army proof range . . . Bell, P., *History of the Port Wakefield Proof Range*, Historical Research P/L, Adelaide: 2004

Plans to enlarge the range . . . Anon., *Proposed Extension of the Proof and Experimental Establishment, Port Wakefield. Assessment*

Report, Department of Environment and Planning, South Australia, Adelaide: May 1986

The range is still sometimes used for weapons testing . . . Beazley, K. 'Decision on proof and experimental range extension', Minister for Defence, Media Release, 22 August 1986

Chapter Two: Three letters will do

Fossilised plumage records . . . Byrkjedal, I. & Thompson D., with Halvorsen, G., ibid, p. 91

The nature writer Peter Matthiessen saw it as . . . Matthiessen, P., *The Wind Birds*, Chapters Publishing, Shelburne: 1994, p. 86

The American ornithologist Roger Tory Peterson . . . Peterson, R., *A Field Guide to Western Birds*, The Riverside Press, Cambridge: 1942, p. 104

The origins of banding, or ringing . . . Preuss, N.O., 'Hans Christian Cornelius Mortensen: Aspects of his life and of the history of bird ringing', *Ardea*, 2001, vol. 89, no. 1, pp. 1–6

Today in the United States, around one million . . . Smith, G., 'The US Geological Survey Bird Banding Laboratory: An Integrated Scientific Program Supporting Research and Conservation of North American Birds', USGS, Reston, Virginia: 2013

Almost the same number . . . Anon., *Summary of Ringing Totals for Britain & Ireland in 2015*, British Trust for Ornithology, https://app.bto.org/ring/countyrec/results2015/ringBI2015.htm

'I have seen an expert netter sweep curlews' . . . McLure, H., 'Methods of bird netting in Japan applicable to wildlife management problems', *Bird-banding*, 1956, vol. 27, pp. 67–73

The group at The Wash was among the first . . . Standen, R., 2015, *The Father of Wader Studies: Tales of C.D.T. Minton*, Victorian Wader Study Group, Melbourne: p. 22

Peter Scott wrote about his first . . . Scott, P., *Severn Wildfowl Trust Annual Report*, 1948, pp. 43–8

Minton disclosed that Scott was wary . . . Minton, C., 1998, 'My memories of the early years', *Wash Wader Ringing Group 1997–8 Report*, pp. 5–11

The next year 2893 birds were caught . . . Minton, C. in *Cambridge Bird Club Report*, 1960, p. 29 and p. 32

'He was totally disbelieving of the reasons' . . . Minton, C., 1998, ibid, p. 7

Herb and Hacksaw's first chronicler . . . Anon., 'A look back . . . Herb Dill and Howard Thornsberry', *Refuge Update*, US Fish & Wildlife Service, November/December 2015

Cannon nets were tested on shorebirds at remote . . . Thompson, M. & DeLong, R., 'The use of cannon and rocket-projected nets for trapping shorebirds', *Bird-Banding*, 1967, vol. 38, no. 3, July, pp. 214–18

'There was an almighty crash' . . . Minton, C., 1998, ibid, p. 7

His fellow Cambridge Bird Club members . . . Cutbill, J. & Evans, P., *Cambridge Bird Club Report*, 1959, p. 26

Even in the late twentieth century . . . Boyd, H. & Piersma, T., 'Changing balance between survival and recruitment explains population trends in Red Knots "calidris canutus Islandica" wintering in Britain, 1969–1995', *Ardea*, 2001, vol. 89, no. 2, p. 306

By the early 1990s, although 100,000 Australian shorebirds . . . Barter, M. & Rush, M., 'Leg-flagging waders in Australia: Why and how?' *Stilt*, 1992, vol. 20, pp. 23–6

A set of brightly coloured plastic leg rings . . . McGraw, K., et al., 'Ultraviolet reflectivity of colored plastic leg bands', *Journal of Field Ornithology*, 1999, vol. 70, no. 2, p. 237

Today the Wash Wader Ringing Group . . . Creswell, W., et al., 'Ringing or colour-banding does not increase predation mortality', *Journal of Avian Biology*, 2007, vol. 38, no. 3, p. 31

This focus on knowing more about individuals . . . Clark, N., et al., 'The production and use of permanently inscribed leg flags for waders', *Wader Study Group Bulletin*, 2005, vol. 108, December, pp. 38–41

Geolocators store daylight . . . Stewart, B.S. & DeLong, R.L., 'Post-breeding foraging migrations of northern Elephant Seals', in *Elephant Seals: Population ecology, behaviour and physiology*, J. Burney., et al. (eds), University of California Press, Berkeley: 1994

At the same time, images of flights ... Nicholls, D.G., *Satellite tracking of large seabirds—a practical guide,* Department of Conservation, Wellington: 1994

Chapter Three: Tiny sparks

Around 14,000 years ago, the Bassian plain ... Lamback, K. & Chappell, J., 'Sea level change through the last glacial cycle', *Science,* 2001, vol. 292, p. 684

This day 12,000 waders will be found ... Woehler, E. & Drake, S., 'Summer and winter wader counts 2015' in Webber, W. (ed.), *Tasmanian Bird Reports,* 2015, vol. 37, pp. 53–9

When not on their Arctic breeding grounds ... Byrkjedal, I. & Thompson, D., ibid, p. 216; Galbraith, C.A., et al., *A Review of Migratory Bird Flyways and Priorities for Management 2014,* UNEP/CMS Secretariat, Bonn: 2014, p. 14

More than other shorebirds, Grey Plover females ... Byrkjedal, I. & Thompson, D., ibid, p. 217

Grey Plover are thought to be monogamous ... Whitfield, D. & Tomkavich, P., 'Mating systems and timing of breeding in Holarctic waders', *Biological Journal of the Linnean Society,* 1996, vol. 57, pp. 277–90

'This provides compelling evidence' ... Turpie, J., 'Comparative foraging ecology of two broad-ranging migrants, Grey Plover *Pluvialis Squatarola* and Whimbrel *Numenius Phaeopus*', PhD thesis, University of Cape Town, Cape Town: 1994

At Teesside in England, closer observation ... Townshend, D.J., 'Decisions for a lifetime: Establishment of spatial defence and movement patterns by juvenile Grey Plover *pluvialis squatarola*', *Journal of Animal Ecology,* 1985, vol. 54, p. 267

A juvenile ringed in December 1975 ... M. Blick, *Birds of Cleveland,* Tees Valley Wildlife Trust, Saltburn: 2010

[A]nd they can live to 25 ... Anon., *Longevity Records for Britain and Ireland in 2017,* British Trust for Ornithology, https://app.bto.org/ring/countyrec/results2017/longevity.htm

'Each bird had his own particular strip' ... Michael, C., 'Feeding habits of the Black-bellied Plover in winter', *Condor,* 1935, p. 169

Grey Plover not only had the greatest ... Rojas De Azuaje, L., 'Comparison of rod/cone ratio in three species of shorebirds having different nocturnal foraging strategies', *The Auk*, 1993, vol. 110, no. 1, p. 143

Jane Turpie explains it this way ... Turpie, J., 'Why do plovers have a stereotyped behaviour?' *Wader Study Group Bulletin*, 1994, no. 75, p. 39

Staggering out over this ooze ... Piersma, T., et al., 'Anna Plains and Roebuck Bay benthic invertebrate mapping 2016,' Field Report, Global Flyway Network and Broome Bird Observatory, Broome: 2016, p. 3

He uses a system developed by Piersma ... Wiersma, P. & Piersma, T., 'Scoring abdominal profiles to characterize migratory cohorts of shorebirds: An example with Red Knots', *Journal of Field Ornithology*, 1995, vol. 66, no. 1, pp. 88–98

For Whimbrel (a sort of half-sized curlew) ... Anon., *Information Sheet on Ramsar Wetlands, Roebuck Bay 2003, updated 2009*, Department of Conservation and Land Management, W.A., 2009

Chapter Four: The undertone

About 50 billion of the world's total ... Berthold, P., *Bird Migration: A general survey,* second edition, Oxford University Press, Oxford: 2009, p. 10

Like the Blackpoll Warbler ... DeLuca, W., et al., 'Transoceanic migration by a 12g songbird', *Biology Letters*, 2015, vol. 11, p. 2

Arctic Tern have been tracked meandering from the North Atlantic ... Fijn, R., et al., 'Arctic Terns *sterna paradisaea* from the Netherlands migrate record distances across three oceans to Wilkes Land, East Antarctica', *Ardea*, 2013, vol. 101, no. 1, p. 3

Wandering Albatross spend years at sea ... De Roy T., et al., *Albatross: Their world, their ways*, Bloomsbury, London: 2008, p. 28

Choosing dusk as the most useful time of day ... Piersma, T., et al., 'Behavioural aspects of the departure of waders before long-distance flights: Flocking, vocalizations, flight paths and diurnal timing', *Ardea*, 1990, vol. 78. pp. 157–84

At Yawuru Nagulagun/Roebuck Bay, Ingrid Tulp saw . . . . Tulp, I., et al., 'Migratory departures of waders from north-western Australia: Behaviour, timing and possible migration routes', *Ardea*, 1994, vol. 82, no. 2, pp. 201–21

At Thompson Beach a few dozen Grey Plover . . . Purnell, C., et al., *Shorebird Monitoring in Gulf St Vincent: 2014–15 Annual Report*, 2016, BirdLife Australia, Carlton: p. 68

[L]ifting fast, their wings beating . . . Piersma, T., et al., 'Climb and flight speeds of shorebirds embarking on an intercontinental flight', *Ibis*, 1997, vol. 139, pp. 299–304

'Fat is the most energy-dense storable substance' . . . Berthold, P., *Bird Migration: A General Survey*, Oxford University Press, Oxford: 2001, p. 91

If they were like their Victorian cousins . . . C. Minton & L. Serra, 'Biometrics and Moult of Grey Plovers, *Pluvialis squatarola*, in Australia', *Emu*, 2001, vol. 101, p. 15

A study of juvenile godwits killed hitting a radar defence dome . . . Piersma, T. & Gill, R., 'Guts don't fly: Small digestive organs in obese Bar-tailed Godwits', *The Auk*, 1998, vol. 115, no. 1, pp. 196–203

Only the brain stayed in equilibrium . . . Battley, P., et al., 'Empirical evidence for differential organ reductions during trans-oceanic bird flight', *Proceedings of Royal Society B.*, 2000, vol. 267, pp. 191–5

Favourable tailwinds may be essential . . . Butler, R., et al., 'Wind assistance: A requirement for migration of shorebirds?' *The Auk,* 1997, vol. 114, p. 457

'The waders seemed to be selective' . . . Green, M., 'Flying with the wind: Spring migration of Arctic-breeding waders and geese over South Sweden', *Ardea*, 2004, vol. 92, no. 2, pp. 145–60

As American poet laureate W.S. Merwin put it . . . Merwin, W.S., 'Shore Birds', *The River Sound*, Knopf, New York: 1999. Copyright, used by permission of the Wylie Agency (UK) Limited

I have tracked these birds' odyssey in these winds . . . C. Beccario, *Earth Null School*, https://earth.nullschool.net

The number of species tested . . . Wiltschko, R. & Wiltschko, W., 'Avian navigation: A combination of innate and learned mechanisms', in Brockman, H., et al. (eds), *Advances in the Study of Behaviour*, Academic Press, Amsterdam: 2015, p. 244

The strongest candidate currently . . . Gunther, A., et al., 'Double-cone localization and seasonal expression pattern suggest a role in magnetoreception for European Robin cryptochrome 4', *Current Biology*, 4 January 2018, DOI, https://doi.org/10.1016/j.cub.2017.12.003

'Apparently migratory direction is inherited' . . . Berthold, P., ibid, p. 146

'Possibly,' wrote the Wiltschkos . . . Wiltschko, R. & Wiltschko, W., ibid, p. 244

What juvenile migrant birds can use is vector navigation . . . Bingman, V. & Cheng, K., 'Mechanisms of animal global navigation', *Ethology, Ecology and Evolution*, 2005, vol. 17, p. 296

The gift of vector navigation . . . . Perdeck, A.C., 'Two types of orientation in migrating starlings, *sturnus vulgaris* and chaffinches, *fringilla coelebs*, as revealed by displacement experiments', *Ardea*, 1958, vol. 46, August, p. 33

Another German scientist, Gustav Kramer . . . 'Orientierte Zugaktivat gevafigter Singvogel', *Naturwissenschaften,* 1950, vol. 37, p. 188

Dunlin caged in Iceland . . . Sandberg, R. & Gudmundsson, G., 'Orientation cage experiments with Dunlins during autumn migration in Iceland', *Journal of Avian Biology,* 1996, vol. 27, pp. 183–8

There is even evidence of migratory shorebirds using a sun compass . . . Alerstam, T., et al., 'Migration along orthodromic sun compass routes by Arctic birds', *Science*, 2001, vol. 291, p. 300

Alerstam, an evolutionary ecologist . . . Alerstam, T. & Hedenstrom, A., 'The development of bird migration theory', *Journal of Avian Biology*, 1998, vol. 29, p. 343

Chapter Five: The treasure map

'There was plenty of evidence' . . . Barter, M., 'Birding on the cheap in Bangladesh', VWSG Bulletin, no. 14, August 1990, pp. 11–16

Barter went to 'one of the nicest spots' . . . Barter, M. 'A wandering metallurgist', VWSG Bulletin, no. 13, July 1989, pp. 6–12

'It's a pitiful sight to see them lying in a heap on the ground' . . . Barter, M., 'Running the gauntlet in Java', VWSG Bulletin, no. 12, July 1988, pp. 23–8

Thomas thought small waders easily capable . . . Thomas, D.G., 'Wader migration across Australia', *Emu*, 1970, vol. 70, no. 4, pp. 145–54

Studying the Curlew Sandpiper . . . D. Thomas & Dartnall, A.J., 'Moult of the Curlew Sandpiper in relation to its annual cycle', *Emu*, 1971, vol. 71, no. 4, pp. 153–8

Impatient with the trickle of evidence from banding . . . Summers, R.W. & Waltner, M., 'Seasonal variations in the mass of waders in southern Africa with special reference to migration', *Ostrich*, 1978, vol. 50, pp. 21–37

Barter began tinkering with some of the possibilities . . . Barter, M., 'Weight variations and migration of Curlew Sandpiper (*Calidris ferrugginea*) wintering in Tasmania' and 'Weight variations in Red-necked Stint (*Calidris ruifcollis*) whilst wintering in Tasmania', *An Occasional Stint*, 1984, no. 3

They figured that the beautifully balanced physiology . . . Starks, J & Lane, B., 'The northward migration of waders from Australia, February to April 1985', *Stilt*, April 1987, no. 10

In Moscow, just off Red Square . . . Tomkovich, P., 'An analysis of the geographic variability in knots, *Calidris canutus*, based on museum skins', *Wader Study Group Bulletin*, 1992, vol. 64 supp., pp. 17–23

'Great Knot at the maximum weight' . . . Barter, M., 'Great Knots partly undone', *Stilt*, 1986, no. 9, pp. 5–16

In Styan's time, towards the end of the Qing Dynasty . . . Ma, Z., et al., 'The rapid development of bird watching in mainland China: A new force for bird study and conservation', *Bird Conservation International*, 2013, vol. 23, pp. 259–69

For the Chinese President the point . . . Shapiro, J., *Mao's War Against Nature*, Cambridge University Press, Cambridge: 2001, p. 205

Taken literally, this belief gave permission . . . Dikotter, F., *Mao's Great Famine*, Bloomsbury, London: 2010, pp. 186–8

After Mao, as China opened up in the 1980s . . . Wang, T.H. & Qian, G., *Shorebirds in the Yangtze River Estuary and Hangzhou Bay*, East China Normal University Publishing House, Shanghai: 1988

'Hunters consider that waders are a natural resource' . . . Barter, M., 'Hunting of migratory waders on Chongming Dao: A Declining Occupation?' *Stilt*, 1997, vol. 31, appendix, p. 22

'It seems quite possible that south-east Australian Great Knot' . . . Barter, M. & Wang, T.H., 'Can waders fly non-stop from Australia to China?', *Stilt*, 1990, no. 17, pp. 36–9

Chapter Six: The treasure house

Garnett, S., Szabo, J., Dutson, G., *The Action Plan for Australian Birds*, CSIRO Publishing, Collingwood, Vic. 2010

An exhaustive count led by Barter . . . Barter, M., 'Wader numbers on Chongming Dao, Yangtze Estuary, China, during early 1996 northward migration and the conservation implications', *Stilt*, 1997, vol. 30, pp. 7–13

When Barter had time to do more work, and reflect . . . Barter, M., 'The Yellow Sea—a race against time', *Wader Study Group Bulletin*, 2003, vol. 100, pp. 111–13

He contemplated the further possibilities . . . Barter, M. & Tonkinson, D., 'Wader departures from Chongming Dao (near Shanghai, China) during March/April 1996', *Stilt*, 1997, vol. 31, pp. 13–18

At night it collided with a Chinese fuel tanker . . . Anon., 13 March 2017, 'North Korean cargo ship sinks off China', www.reuters.com/article/us-china-northkorea-ship/north-korean-cargo-ship-sinks-off-china-all-crew-rescued-idUSKBN16K17S

In the bays of its Korean Peninsula coast . . . Li, X., et al., 'Low frequency variability of the Yellow Sea cold water mass identified from the China coastal waters and adjacent seas reanalysis', *Advances in Meteorology*, vol. 2015, pp. 2–15. Article ID 269859

The Yellow Sea and its mud is also home to Koreans . . . Koh, C. & Kim, J., 'The Korean tidal flat of the Yellow Sea: Physical setting, ecosystem and management', *Oceans & Coastal Management*, 2014, vol. 102, pp. 398–414

All of this marine wealth is determined by two phenomena . . . Saito, Y., et al., 'The Huanghe [Yellow River] and Changjiang [Yangtze River] deltas: a review of their characteristics, evolution and sediment discharge during the Holocene', *Geomorphology*, 2001, vol. 41, pp. 219–31

In winter, as cold winds howl down . . . Naimie, C., et al., 'Seasonal mean circulation in the Yellow Sea—a model-generated climatology', *Continental Shelf Research*, 2001, vol. 21, pp. 667–95

An early assessment of China's Yellow Sea possibilities . . . T. Mundkur (ed.), *A Status Overview of Shorebirds in the East Asian–Australasian Flyway*, Asian Wetland Bureau, 1993, Bangkok: p. 73

Sloshing out as far as they could . . . Wang, T., et al., 'Survey of shorebirds and coastal wetlands in yellow river delta, Shandong Province, autumn 1991', East China Waterbird Ecology Study Group, East China Normal University, Shanghai

Twice a year, around peak migratory times . . . Barter, M., 'The Yellow Sea—a race against time', *Wader Study Group Bulletin*, 2003, vol. 100, pp. 111–13

'It is possibly the single most important site in the flyway' . . . Barter, M., et al., 'Shorebird numbers in the Huang He [Yellow River] Delta during the 1997 northward migration', *Stilt*, 1998, vol. 33, pp. 15–26

With a big tidal range on very flat ground . . . Barter, M. & Wilson, J., 'Yalu Jiang National Nature Reserve, North Eastern China: A newly discovered internationally important Yellow Sea site for northward migrating shorebirds', *Stilt*, 2000, vol. 37, pp. 13–20

'We thank God for creating Mark' . . . Gosbell, K. & Watkins, D., 'A tribute to Mark Barter', *Stilt*, 2011, vol. 60, pp. 1–4

'The best answer I've come up with' . . . Barter, M., *Shorebirds of the Yellow Sea*, Wetlands International, 2002, p. vi

Chapter Seven: Perfectly suited

So rapid and chaotic was Caofeidian's development . . . Wu, W., 'What happens when Chinese investment goes really bad, and is there any way out of the hole?' *South China Morning Post*, 22 June 2016, www.scmp.com/news/china/economy/article/1978543/what-really-happens-when-chinese-investment-goes-bad-and-there

That's something like one-third of this bird's known . . . Hassell C., et al., *Global Flyway Network Bohai Report*, Global Flyway

Network, 2013, pp. 25–7; Anon., Species Profile and Threats database, *Calidris ferruginea*, Curlew Sandpiper, SPRAT, Environment Australia profile, www.environment.gov.au/cgi-bin/sprat/public/publicspecies.pl?taxon_id=856

Across their research area on a single mid-May day in 2018 . . . Hassell C., et al., *Global Flyway Network Bohai Report*, Global Flyway Network, 2018, p. 17

He estimated the 300-kilometre rim . . . Barter, M., et al., 'Shorebird numbers in Bohai Wan During Northward Migration, 2003', *Stilt*, 2004, vol. 44, pp. 3–8

It is a neat energy bonanza . . . Yang, Hong-Yan, et al., 'Economic design in a long-distance migrating molluscivore: How fast-fuelling Red Knots in Bohai Bay, China, get away with small gizzards', 2013, *Journal of Experimental Biology*, vol. 216, pp. 3627–36

This kind of pinpoint data . . . Rogers, D., et al., 'Red Knots (*Calidiris canutus piersmai* and *C.c rogersi*) depend on a small threatened staging area in Bohai Bay, China', *Emu*, 2010, vol. 110, pp. 307–15

Chapter Eight: The white bear bird

The Dutch migratory bird ecologist, Marcel Klaassen . . . Klaassen, M., et al., 'Arctic waders are not capital breeders', *Nature*, vol. 413, 25 October 2001, p. 794

A few years earlier, a Sanderling migrating from South Australia . . . Livovski, S., et al., 'Movements patterns of Sanderling (*Calidris alba*) in the East Asian–Australasian Flyway and a comparison of methods for identification of crucial areas for conservation', *Emu*, 2016, vol. 116, pp. 168–77

The birds of hot Australian summers . . . Anon., *NIC IMS Data Archive*, US National Ice Center, Naval Ice Center, www.natice.noaa.gov/ims/gif_archive.html

CYA alights from her Tiaozini flight . . . Lappo, E., et al., *Atlas of Breeding Waders in the Russian Arctic*, Institute of Geography, Russian Academy of Sciences, Moscow: 2012, p. 41

A Danish anthropologist, Rane Willerslev, . . . Willerslev, R., *Soul Hunters: Hunting, animism and personhood among the Siberian Yukaghirs*, University of California Press, Berkeley: 2007, pp. 73–5

Now much reduced, the Yukaghir once lived across lowland tundra
. . . Jochelson, W., *The Jesup North Pacific Expedition, vol. IX,
Part III, The Yukaghir and the Yukaghized Tungus*, Memoir of
the American Museum of Natural History, New York: 1926

To my greater amazement, only a few days earlier . . . Anon.,
Worldview, National Aeronautics and Space Administration,
https://worldview.earthdata.nasa.gov/

Its first chapter was compiled over decades . . . Engelmoer, M. &
Roselaar, C.S., *Geographical Variation in Waders*, Luwer,
Dordrecht: 1998, pp. 72–86

Though honoured with the name, Russia's Pavel Tomkovich . . .
Tomkovich, P. & Serra, L., 'Morphometrics and prediction of
breeding origin in some Holarctic waders', *Ardea*, 1999, no. 87,
pp. 289–300

It was here that the study of Australian Grey Plover breeding grounds
lay . . . Minton, C. & Serra, L., 'Biometrics and moult of Grey
Plovers, *Pluvialis squatarola*, in Australia', *Emu*, 2001, vol. 101,
no. 1, pp. 13–18

Tomkovich's primary focus was the Red Knot . . . Tomkovich' P.
& Dondua, A., 'On peculiarities of the Grey Plover (*Pluvialis
squatarola*) population on Wrangel Island, the Arctic Far East of
Russia', *Ornithologia*, 2011, vol. 36, pp. 103–13

They also managed to fix a total of 232 shorebirds . . . Tomkovich, P. &
Dondua, A., 'Red Knots on Wrangel Island: Results of observations
and catching in summer 2007', *Wader Study Group Bulletin*,
2008, vol. 115, no. 2, pp. 102–9

He glimpsed a Grey Plover wearing light-blue-over-white leg flags . . .
Tomkovich, P., et al., 'Observation on the East Asian–Australasian
Flyway of a Grey Plover *Pluvialis squatarola* originating from
Wrangel Island', *Wader Study Group Bulletin*, 2014, vol. 121,
no. 1, pp. 51–2

The great flocks radiate out to even smaller groups spanning the broad
head of their flyway, as if trying to escape most of their kind . . .
Lappo, E., et al., *Atlas of Breeding Waders in the Russian Arctic*,
Institute of Geography, Russian Academy of Sciences, Moscow:
2012; Minton, C., et al., 'New insights from geolocators deployed

on waders in Australia, 2013', *Wader Study Group Bulletin*, 2014, vol. 120, no. 1, pp. 37–46; Lisovski, S., et al., 'Movement patterns of Sanderling (*Calidris alba*) in the East Asian–Australasian Flyway and a comparison of methods for identification of crucial areas for conservation', *Emu*, 2016, vol. 116, pp. 168–77; Anon., 'ABBS database—FAQ—Greatest movement by species', Australian Bird and Bat Banding Scheme, 2019, www.environment. gov.au/cgi-bin/biodiversity/abbbs/abbbs-faq.pl?proc=top_distance

Remote sensing now means . . . Piersma, T. & Bairlein, F., 'Using the power of comparison to explain habitat use and migration strategies of shorebirds worldwide', *Journal of Ornithology*, 2010, vol. 148, no. 10, S45–S59

On the mainland at this time, Pleistocene-era animals . . . Rogers, R. & Slatkin, M., 'Excess of genomic defects in a Woolly Mammoth on Wrangel Island', *PloS Genetics*, 2017, vol. 13, no. 3, pp. 1–16; Vartanyan, S, et. al., 'Collection of radiocarbon dates on the mammoths (*Mammuthus primigenius*) and other genera of Wrangel Island, northeast Siberia, Russia', *Quaternary Research*, 200, vol. 70, pp. 51–9

Pavel Tomkovich wondered whether . . . Tomkovich, P. & Dondua, A., ibid, 2008, p. 107

He thinks the island was used into the nineteenth century as a waypoint . . . Krauss, M., 'Eskimo languages in Asia, 1791 on, and the Wrangel Island–Point Hope connection', Etudes/Inuit/ studies, 2005, vol. 29, no. 1–2

It fell to the revered Scottish–American naturalist, John Muir . . . Muir, J., *The Cruise of the Corwin*, 1917, Chapter XV, 'The Land of the White Bear', https://vault.sierraclub.org/john_muir_exhibit/ writings/cruise_of_the_corwin/

If he had been granted time to wander the island . . . Anon., *Natural Reserve System of Wrangel Island, World Heritage Nomination*, Russian Federation, 2004, https://whc.unesco.org/en/list/1023/

The *Corwin's* ornithologist, Edward Nelson . . . Wilson, E.W., *Report of the Natural History Collections Made In Alaska Between the Years 1877 and 1881*, Government Printing Office, Washington: 1887, p. 88

North American First Nations' names have been most assiduously collected, and similarities between them stretch from Hudson Bay to the Yukon Delta . . . Williams, G. (ed.), *Andrew Graham's Observations on Hudson's Bay 1767–91*, The Hudson's Bay Record Society, London: 1969, p. 238; Swainson, W. & Richardson, J., *Fauna Boreali-Americana, Part Second, The Birds*, John Murray, London: 1832, p. 370; Hohn, E., 'Eskimo bird names at Chesterfield Inlet and Baker Lake, Keewatin, Northwest Territories', *Arctic Journal*, 1969, p. 75; Nelson, R., *Hunters of the Northern Ice*, University of Chicago Press, Chicago: 1969, p. 167; Richards, E., *Arctic Mood: A narrative of Arctic adventures*, Caxton, Idaho: 1949, pp. 264–5; Nelson, S. & the Elders of King Island, *Guide to the Birds of King Island*, unpub., 2010, pp. 47–8; Naves, L., *Central Yup'ik Shorebird Names*, unpub., Alaska DF&G, Anchorage: 2018, p. 7; Brandt, H., *Alaska Bird Trails*, Bird Research Foundation, Cleveland: 1943, p. 144

'They build no nest only making a hollow' . . . Williams, G. (ed.), *Andrew Graham's Observations on Hudson's Bay 1767–91*, The Hudson's Bay Record Society, London: 1969, p. 59

Around the same time, another Hudson's Bay company explorer . . . Hearne, S., *A Journey from Prince of Wales's Fort in Hudson's Bay to the Northern Ocean in the Years 1769, 1770, 1771, 1772*, The Champlain Society, Toronto: 1911, p. 427

As many young scientists discover, work they might call their own . . . Williams. G., 'Andrew Graham & Thomas Hutchins: Collaboration and plagiarism in 18th century natural history', *The Beaver*, Spring 1978, pp. 4–14

'Multitudes of birds retire to this remote country' . . . Pennant, T., *Arctic Zoology, Volume I, Hudson's Bay*, Henry Hughes, Printer, 1784–85, p. 193

Pennant knew the Grey Plover already from its non-breeding life in Britain . . . Pennant, T., *British Zoology, Class II Genus XVIII &c., Birds*, Benjamin White, London: 1776, p. 362–3

In *Arctic Zoology*, he dressed it in breeding plumage . . . Pennant, T., ibid, 1784–85, p. 48

'I have traced this species along the whole of our eastern coast . . .' Audubon, J., *The Birds of America*, 1827–1839, Audubon Society, 2019, www.audubon.org/birds-of-america/black-bellied-plover

The search for the little grail—for the first discovery of a Grey Plover nest . . . Middendorf, A., *Th. Sibirische Reise, vol. 2 Saughtethiere, Vogel und Amphibien*, 1875, pp. 209–10

The modern authority on Arctic birds, Richard Vaughan . . . Vaughan, R., *In Search of Arctic Birds*, T & A.D. Poyser, London: 1992, p. 208

'The results of our somewhat adventurous journey' . . . Seebohm, H., *The Geographical Distribution of the Family Charadriidae*, Henry Sotheran & Co. 1887, pp. 103–4; and Seebohm, H., *The Birds of Siberia*, John Murray, London: 1901, p. 237

In the far north, he was enchanted by what we rarely see in the south . . . Hall, H., 'The Eastern Palaearctic and Australia', *Emu*, 1919, vol. 19, pp. 82–98

Soon after Hall, Maud Haviland, who grew up in the enclosed countryside . . . Haviland, M., *A Summer on the Yenesei*, Edward Arnold, London: 1915, p. 204

Chapter Nine: Beringia

The caves' discoverer, Canadian Jacques Cinq-Mars, fought established views . . . Cinq-Mars, J., 'Bluefish Cave 1, A Late Pleistocene Eastern Beringian cave deposit in the Northern Yukon', *Canadian Journal of Archaeology*, 1979, no. 3, pp. 1–32

'Bluefish Caves . . . may have been located at the easternmost extent' . . . Bourgeon, L., et al., 'Earliest human presence in North America dated to the last Glacial Maximum: New radiocarbon dates from Bluefish Caves, Canada,' *PLOS One*, 6 January 2017, pp. 1–15

This is a fantastic land for the imagination . . . Hopkins, D., et al. (eds), *Palaeoecology of Beringia*, Academic Press, New York: 1982, pp. 425–44; Willerslev, E., 'Fifty thousand years of Arctic vegetation and megafaunal diet', *Nature*, 2014, vol. 506, pp. 47–51; Pringle, H., 'Welcome to Beringia', *Science*, 2014, vol. 343, pp. 961–3; Colinvaux, P. in West. F., (ed.), *American Beginnings: The prehistory and palaeoecology of Beringia,* University of Chicago Press, Chicago: 1996, pp. 14–15

The last of these cycles marked the beginning of the current Holocene, the 'whole, new' epoch . . . Steffen, W., et al., 'The Anthropocene: conceptual and historical perspectives', *Philosophical Transactions of the Royal Society A,* 2011, vol. 369, pp. 842–67

Bluefish Caves' bone trove tells us that this flourishing landscape was summer home to a rich bird life . . . Harington, C. & Cinq-Mars, J., 'Bluefish Caves: Fauna and context', *Beringian Research Notes,* no. 19, Yukon Tourism and Culture, 2008

The story of Beringia reminds us of the shorebirds' resilience . . . Baker, A., et al., 'Phylogenetic relationships and divergence times of Charadriiformes genera: Multigene evidence for the Cretaceous origin of at least 14 clades of shorebirds', *Biology Letters,* 2007, vol. 3, pp. 205–9

I hold to the Roman poet Virgil . . . Publius V., *The Georgics,* Georgic III, *The Internet Classics Archive,* MIT, http://classics.mit.edu/Virgil/georgics.mb.txt

A Ruddy Turnstone from Flinders, on the coast south-east of Melbourne . . . Minton, C., et al., 'Geolocator studies on Ruddy Turnstones *Arenaria interpres* and Greater Sandplover *Charadrius leschenaultii* in the East Asian–Australasian Flyway reveal widely different migration strategies', *Wader Study Group Bulletin,* 2011, vol. 118, no. 2, pp. 87–96

The little Red-necked Stint is usually thought of as a pan-Siberian breeder . . . DeCicco, L., et al., 'History of the Red-necked Stint breeding in North America', *Western Birds,* 2013, pp. 273–8

This is thought to be an ancestral Beringian route, still hard-wired . . . Handel, C. & Gill, R., 'Wayward youth: Trans-Beringian movement and differential southward migration by Juvenile Sharp-tailed Sandpipers', *Arctic,* 2010, vol. 63, no. 3, pp. 273–88

But in an average twelve days . . . Lindstrom, A., et al., 'A puzzling migratory detour: Are fuelling conditions in Alaska driving the movement of juvenile Sharp-tailed Sandpipers?', *The Condor,* 2011, vol. 113, no. 1, pp. 129–39

Pavel Tomkovich put together scattered scraps of banding and sighting . . . Tomkovich, P., 'List of wader species of Chukotka, Northern

Far East of Russia: Their banding and migratory links', *Stilt*, 2003, no. 44, pp. 29–43

Even the very specifically named American Golden Plover ... Arkhipov, V., et al., 'Birds of Mys Schmidta, North Chukotka, Russia,' *Forktail*, 2013, no. 29, p. 27

'Only those who have met this lordly plover on his native heath' ... Brandt. H., *Alaska Bird Trails*, The Bird Research Foundation, Cleveland: 1943, pp. 142–5

These qualities were held up by the Iñupiat ... Murdoch, J., *International Expedition to Point Barrow, Alaska 1881–1883*, US Army/Smithsonian Institution, 1885, p. 109

Few Black-bellied Plover, or their eggs, are taken today from a land ... Naves, L., et al., *Shorebird Harvest and Indigenous Knowledge in Alaska*, Research Paper, USGS/ADF&G, Anchorage: 2018

Evolutionary principles that explain the marvels of bird migration ... Alerstam, T. & Hedenstrom, A., 'The development of bird mnigration theory', *Journal of Avian Biology*, 1998, vol. 29, p. 343

'One of the things we have learned since the war on cancer started' ... Allison, J., 'Immune Checkpoint Blockade in Cancer Therapy: New insights, opportunities and prospects for cures', *Nobel Lecture*, 7 December 2018, Nobel Media AB, 2019, www.nobelprize.org/prizes/medicine/2018/allison/lecture/

According to Honjo, about 20 to 30 per cent of cancer patients currently ... Honjo, T., 'Serendipities of acquired immunity', *Nobel Lecture*, 7 December 2018, Nobel Media AB, 2019, www.nobelprize.org/prizes/medicine/2018/honjo/lecture/

Allison, in his speech, thanked the 'several thousand' patients ... Kolata, G., '"Desperation Oncology": When patients are dying, some cancer doctors turn to immunotherapy', *New York Times*, 26 April 2018, www.nytimes.com/2018/04/26/health/doctors-cancer-immunotherapy.html

As an afterthought, he said of the breakthrough ... Allison, J., 'Acceptance speech for the 2015 Lasker Debakey Clinical Medical Research Award', Albert and Mary Lasker Foundation, 12 April 2016, www.youtube.com/watch?v=19FaraPilXI

Chapter Ten: A portion of their secrets

Persistence in folly? What made this bird so unlucky, unattractive? ... Bruner, P. & Bruner, A., Alaska Shorebird Group Annual Summaries 1994 and 2004, www.fws.gov/alaska/mbsp/mbm/shorebirds/working_group.htm

'To our ears, the Grey Plover is the master' ... Byrkjedal, I. & Thompson, D., ibid, pp. 163–5

At the same study site, Ruddy Turnstone had hectic sex lives ... Bruner, P. & Bruner, A., 'Extra pair paternity in Black-bellied Plover and other observations at Woolley Lagoon, Seward Peninsula', Alaska Shorebird Group Annual Summaries, 2011, www.fws.gov/alaska/mbsp/mbm/shorebirds/working_group.htm

This thorough defence helps not only save its young ... Larsen, T. & Grundetjern, S., 'Optimal choice of neighbour: Predator protection among tundra birds', *Journal of Avian Biology*, 1998, no. 28, pp. 303–8

In early shorebird research there was evidence that every three to four years Grey Plover ... Martin, A. & Baird, D., 'Lemming cycles: Which Palearctic migrants are affected', *Bird Study*, 1988, no. 35, pp. 143–5

More recently, it's been learned that some lemming cycles are fading out ... Aharon-Rotman, Y., et al., 'Loss of periodicity in breeding success of waders links to changes in lemming cycles in Arctic ecosystems', *Oikos*, 2015, no. 124, pp. 861–70

Satellite tags fitted to the plover by the Smithsonian Migratory Bird Center ... Harrison, A.L., *Migratory Connectivity Project*, Smithsonian Migratory Bird Center, 2018, www.migratoryconnectivityproject.org/BBPL-AK.html

The most detailed observations were made on the Truelove Lowland ... Hussell, D & Page, G., 'Observations on the breeding biology of Black-bellied Plovers on Devon Island, N.W.T., Canada', *The Wilson Bulletin*, 1976, vol. 88, no. 4

Chapter Eleven: Now south

It was on Great Lyakhovsky that the holotype—the benchmark specimen ... Tomkovich, P., 'A new subspecies of Red Knot

Calidris canutus, from the New Siberian Islands', *Bulletin of the British Ornithologists Club*, 2001, vol. 121, no. 4, pp. 257–63

Other birds head for these islands after they leave their breeding grounds ... Chan, Y.G., et al., 'Migration of the Bar-tailed Godwit Y5RBRL', *Global Flyway Ecology: Team Piersma*, 23 August 2017, https://teampiersma.org/2017/08/23/migration-of-the-bar-tailed-godwit-y5rbrl/

At that time of year, Ul'banskiy Bay's river estuaries are alive ... Solovyev, B., et al., 'Summer distribution of beluga whales (*Delphinapterus leucas*) in the Sea of Okhotsk', *Russian Journal of Theriology*, 2015, vol. 14, no. 2, pp. 201–15

Where the flats are accessible, researchers have found heavy autumn shorebird traffic ... Pronkevich, V., 'Migration of waders in the Khabarovsk region of the Far East', *International Wader Studies*, 1998, vol. 10, pp. 425–30

Further east lies the mouth of the Amur River ... Antonov, A., 'A shorebird census of Schastya Bay and the Amur Estuary, Sea of Okhotsk, Russia from 6 August–21 September 2002', *Stilt*, 2003, no. 44, pp. 52–5

On the northern side of the Sea of Okhotsk fly autumn shorebird clouds ... Gerasimov, Y. & Huettmann, F., 'Shorebirds of the Sea of Okhotsk: Status and overview', *Stilt*, 2006, no. 50, pp. 15–22

These birds come in waves over the Sea of Okhotsk ... Antonov, A. & Huettmann, F., 'Observations of shorebirds during the southward migration at Schastya bay, Sea of Okhotsk, Russia: July 23–August 8 2006 and July 25–August 1 2007', *Stilt*, 2008, no. 54, pp. 13–18

Antonov also saw some Grey Plover come through Schastya Bay ... Antonov, A., 'A shorebird census of Schastya Bay and the Amur Estuary, Sea of Okhotsk, Russia from 6 August–21 September 2002', *Stilt*, 2003, no. 44, pp. 52–5

They arrive there in waves, the most northerly birds last ... Conklin, J., et al., 'Breeding latitude drives individual schedules in a trans-hemispheric migrant bird', *Nature Communications*, 7 September 2010, vol. 1, no. 67

Emblematic of the godwit cry, this name is collected in an absorbing study of Alaskan natives' lives with shorebirds ... Naves, L. & Keating, J., *Shorebird Subsistence Harvest and Indigenous Knowledge in Alaska, Draft Report,* Alaska Department of Fish and Game, Division of Subsistence, Anchorage: 2018

She is careful: 'The characteristic bill shape and proportions' ... Naves & Keating, ibid, p. 33

The title of Long-Haul Queen went to another female, E7 ... Gill, R., et al., 'Extreme endurance flights by landbirds crossing the Pacific Ocean: Ecological corridor rather than barrier?' *Proceedings of the Royal Society B,* 2009, no. 276, pp. 447–57

The birds do not fly to a single level and stay there, but frequently change ... Senner, N., et al., 'High altitude shorebird migration in the absence of topographical barriers: Avoiding high air temperatures and searching for profitable winds', *Proceedings of the Royal Society B,* 2018, vol. 285, http://dx.doi.org/10.1098/rspb.2018.0569

... there are signs that the ability is more widespread ... Tomkovich, P., et al., 'Pathways and staging areas of Red Knots *Calidris canutus rogersi* breeding in southern Chukotka, Far Eastern Russia', *Wader Study Group Bulletin,* 2013, vol. 120, no. 3, pp. 181–93; Johnson, O., et al., 'New insight concerning transoceanic migratory pathways of Pacific Golden Plovers (*Pluvialis fulva*): The Japan stopover and other linkages as revealed by geolocators', *Wader Study Group Bulletin,* 2012, vol. 119, no. 1, pp. 1–8

Chapter Twelve: A flick of the dragon's tail

For Arctic-nesting shorebirds the distance they fly seems to matter much less ... Newton, I., *The Migration Ecology of Birds,* 2007, Elsevier, London: pp. 639–73

The Pioneer Russian surveyor Vladimir Arsenyev ... Arsenyev, V., *Across the Ussuri Kray, Travels in the Sikhote-Alin Mountains,* Translated with annotations by Jonathan C. Slaght. Indiana University Press, Bloomington: 2016

A flock of around 40 crow-sized birds with clawed fingers at the leading edges of their wings . . . Benton, M., et al., 'The remarkable fossils of the early Cretaceous Jehol Biota of China and how they have changed our knowledge of Mesozoic life', Presidential Address, Proceedings of the Geologists Association, 2008, no. 119, pp. 209–28; Jiang, B., et al., 'New evidence suggests pyroclastic flows are responsible for the remarkable preservation of the Jehol Biota', *Nature Communications*, 4 February 2014; Williams, R., 'Deadly volcanic flows: Understanding pyroclastic density currents', *The Geological Society's London Lectures*, 2016, www.geolsoc.org.uk/DeadlyFlows16

The American paleo-ornithologist Alan Feduccia proposed 'transitional shorebirds' . . . Feduccia, A., 'Explosive evolution of tertiary birds and mammals', *Science*, 1995, vol. 267, 3 February, pp. 637–8

DNA genome sequencing came along to tease out this possibility . . . Paton, T., et al., 'Complete mitochondrial DNA genome sequences show that modern birds are not descended from transitional shorebirds', *Proceedings of the Royal Society B*, 2002, vol. 269, pp. 839–46

Later, in 2007, Paton revised her own work in collaboration with avian evolutionary scientist, Allan Baker . . . Baker, A., et al., 'Phylogenetic relationships and divergence times of Charadriiformes genera: Multigene evidence for the Cretaceous origin of at least 14 clades of shorebirds', *Biology Letters*, 2007, vol. 3, pp. 205–9

Borrowing from the oldest bird, and paying credit to a Chinese palaeontologist . . . Wang, M., et al., 'The oldest record of ornithuromorpha from the early Cretaceous of China', *Nature Communications*, 2015, vol. 6, art. no. 6987, www.nature.com/articles/ncomms7987

Science magazine reported that the second-oldest known bird was 'similar to today's plovers' . . . Balter, M., 'Feathered fossils from China reveal dawn of modern birds', *Science*, 5 May 2015, www.sciencemag.org/news/2015/05/feathered-fossils-china-reveal-dawn-modern-birds

The strongest candidate for the start of this period is the mid-twentieth century ... Subramanian, M., 'Anthropocene now: Influential panel votes to recognize Earth's new epoch', *Nature*, 21 May 2019, www.nature.com/articles/d41586-019-01641-5?utm_source=twt_nnc&utm_medium=social&utm_campaign=naturenews&sf21 3117945=1

Previous mass extinctions showing up on earth's geological record began ... Wake, D. & Vredenburg, V., 'Are we in the midst of the sixth mass extinction? A view from the world of amphibians', *Proceedings of the National Academy of Sciences*, 2008, vol. 105, pp. 11466–73

In 2019, a UNESCO committee on global biodiversity ... Diaz, S., et al., 'Summary for policymakers of the global assessment report on biodiversity and ecosystem services of the Intergovernmental Science Policy Platform on Biodiversity and Ecosystem Services', UNESCO, 6 May 2019, p. 3, http://whc.unesco.org/en/news/1967

Dirzo uses comprehensive threat categories ... Dirzo, R., et al., 'Defaunation in the Anthropocene', *Science*, 2014, vol. 345, issue 6195, pp. 401–6

A Mexican ecologist, Gerardo Ceballos, worked with Paul Ehrlich ... Ceballos, G., et al., 'Biological annihilation via the ongoing sixth mass extinction signalled by vertebrate population losses and declines', *Proceedings of the National Academy of Sciences*, 2017, www.pnas.org/content/114/30/E6089

The East Asian bird specialist ... Brazil, M.A., 'The birds of Shuangtaizihekou National Nature Reserve, Liaoning Province, P.R. China', *Forktail*, 1992, vol. 7, pp. 91–124

Barter thought perhaps a quarter of a million shorebirds ... Barter, M., et al., 'Northward migration of shorebirds in the Shuangtaizihekou National Nature Reserve, Liaoning Province, China in 1998 and 1999', *Stilt*, 2000, no. 37, pp. 2–9

Counts by the Chinese birders who Barter mentored went on to underscore ... Bai, Q., et al., 'Identification of coastal wetland of international importance for waterbirds: A review of China coastal waterbird surveys 2005–2013', *Avian Research*, 2015, pp. 6–12

This drove people and industry seaward ... Tian, B., et al., 'Drivers, trends and potential impacts of long-term coastal reclamation in

China from 1985 to 2010', *Estuarine, Coastal and Shelf Science*, 2016, no. 170, pp. 83–90

At its launch, local mayor Huaming Zhao promised land to spare . . . Lijun, S., '"Five Points, One Line": Strategy guiding light for Liaoning', *China Daily*, 9 March 2007, www.chinadaily.com.cn/cndy/2007-03/09/content_823163.htm

Off Huludao the sea-floor sediments are thick with heavy metals . . . Li, X., et al., 'Integrated assessment of heavy metal contamination in sediments from a coastal industrial basin, NE China', *PLOS One*, 2012, vol. 7, no. 6, pp. 1–10

A single oyster might contain 100 times more zinc . . . Gao, M., et al., 'Metal concentrations in sediment and biota of the Huludao Coast in Liaodong Bay and associated human and ecological health risks', *Archives of Environmental Contamination and Toxicology*, 2016, vol. 71, pp. 87–96

Excessive copper levels flow down the Daling and Shuangtaizi . . . Gao, X., et al., 'Pollution status of the Bohai Sea: An overview of the environmental quality assessment related trace metals, *Environment International*, 2014, vol. 62, pp. 12–30

'[I]t was impossible to find pristine areas or sites in Liaodong Bay, because it is severely disturbed' . . . Cai, W., et al., 'Assessing benthic ecological status in stressed Liaodong Bay (China) with AMBI and M-AMBI', *China Journal of Oceanology and Limnology*, 2013, vol. 31, no. 3, pp. 482–92

It has one unrivalled seafood resource: the Flame Jellyfish . . . You, K., et al., 'Study on the carry capacity of edible jellyfish fishery in Liaodong Bay', *Journal of Ocean University of China*, 2016, vol. 15, issue 3, pp. 471–9

'The sea itself is being rapidly degraded' . . . Gao, X., et al., ibid

The old pesticide enemy of wildlife was officially banned in China . . . Hu, L., et al., 'Occurrence and distribution of organochlorine pesticides (OCPs) in surface sediments of the Bohai Sea, China', *Chemosphere*, 2009, vol. 77, pp. 663–72

Migratory songbirds laden with agricultural pesticide . . . Eng, M., et al., 'Imidacloprid and clorpyrifos insecticides impair migratory ability in a seed-eating songbird', *Nature Scientific Reports*, 2017, vol. 7, Article no. 15176

Work was carried out and reported in 2003 on chemical contamination ... Tanabe, S., et al., 'Persistent organochlorine residues and their bioaccumulation profiles in resident and migratory birds from North Vietnam', *Osaka University Knowledge Archive*, 2003, https://ir.library.osaka-u.ac.jp/repo/ouka/all/13058/

There is also a Korean study that found chronic lead contamination ... Kim, J. & Koo, T.H., 'Acute and/or chronic contaminations of heavy metals in shorebirds from Korea', *Journal of Environmental Monitoring*, 2010, vol. 12, pp. 1613–18

Losses to fisheries and marine aquaculture were estimated at ¥12.56 billion (US$1.87 billion) ... Pan, G., et al., 'Estimating the economic damages from the Penglai 19-3 oil spill to the Yantai fisheries in the Bohai Sea of northeast China', *Marine Policy*, 2015, vol. 62, pp. 18–24

By the time it was set up in 2009, the reserve area had been near halved ... Cheng, Q. & Zhou, L., 'Monetary value of the Linghe River Estuarine Wetland Ecosystem service function', *Energy Procedia*, 2012, vol. 14, pp. 211–16

The bold Peng Liu was transferred into a paper-shuffling job ... Wu, Q., 'Official sidelined for fining wetlands wind developer, *Windpower Monthly*, 1 September 2012, www.windpower monthly.com/article/1146984/official-sidelined-fining-wetlands-wind-developer

The slick spread for 430 square kilometres; blackened shellfish were held out ... Watts, J., 'China's worst-ever oil spill threatens wildlife as volunteers assist in clean-up', *The Guardian*, 22 July 2010, www.theguardian.com/environment/2010/jul/21/china-oil-spill-disaster-wildlife

'Melville looked at this man-made pyroclastic blast' ... Melville, D., 'Tianjin's tragic explosions highlight risks to the coastal environment from China's expanding chemical industries', *Wader Study*, 2015, vol. 122, no. 2, pp. 85–6

Red Knot and Curlew Sandpiper had used the mud and salt pans of Tianjin in globally significant numbers ... Barter, M., et al., 'Shorebird numbers on the Tianjin Municipality coast in May 2000', *Stilt*, 2001, vol. 39, pp. 2–9

The output of many of these Chinese chemical factories *is* plastics . . . Schmidt, C., et al., 'Export of plastic debris by rivers into the sea', *Environmental Science and Technology*, 2017, vol. 51, no. 21, pp. 12246–53

In Liaodong Bay, sampling of a few beaches found more than a hundred . . . Yua, X., 'Occurrence of microplastics in the beach sand of the Chinese inner sea: The Bohai Sea', *Environmental Pollution*, July 2016, vol. 214, pp. 722–30

Out in the wider Bohai, floating microplastic debris was collected . . . Zhang, W., et al., 'Microplastic pollution in the surface waters of the Bohai Sea, China', *Environmental Pollution*, 2017, vol. 231, pp. 541–8

Crighton had seen shorebird flocks fly clear of the nets during the day . . . Crighton, P., 'Bird mortality in fish nets at a significant stopover site of the Spoon-billed Sandpiper *Calidris pygmaea* in the Yellow Sea, China', *Stilt*, 2016, vol. 69–70, pp. 74–6

After all, this is a country where the very concept of protecting edible wildlife . . . Li, Z., 'Wildlife consumption and conservation awareness in China: A long way to go', *Biodiversity Conservation*, 2014, vol. 23, pp. 2371–81

By 2013 trappers were catching a hair-raising 8.6 million . . . Kamp, J., et al., 'Global population collapse in a superabundant migratory bird and illegal trapping in China', *Conservation Biology*, 2015, vol. 29, no. 6, pp. 1684–94

So it is that poor southern Chinese fishers and aquaculture labourers will supply shorebirds . . . Martinez, J. & Lewthwaite, R., 'Rampant shorebird trapping threatens Spoon-billed Sandpiper *Eurynorhynchus pyegmeusi* in south-west Guangdong, China', *BirdingASIA*, 2013, vol. 19, pp. 26–30

Chapter Thirteen: Lost flocks

I agree with shorebirds authority Tony Prater, who says 'reclamation' . . . Prater, A.J., *Estuary Birds of Britain and Ireland*, T & A.D. Poyser, Calton: 1981, p. 98

Even until the mid-1980s, early Landsat images showed the Daling meandering . . . Yan, X., et al., 'Monitoring wetland changes both outside and inside reclamation areas for coastal management of the Northern Liaodong Bay, China', *Wetlands,* 2017, vol. 37, pp. 885–97

As he later reflected on those times, a State Oceanic Administration director, Haiqing Li, spoke of serious abuse of the sea . . . Li, H., 'The impacts and implications of the legal framework for sea use planning and management in China', *Ocean and Coastal Management,* 2006, vol. 49, issue 9–10, pp. 717–26

At Tianjin port, site of the devastating 2015 chemical factory explosion . . . Wang, W., 'Development and management of land reclamation in China', *Ocean & Coastal Management,* 2014, vol. 102, Part B, pp. 415–25

In fact, the State Oceanic Administration said that 61 of 62 illegal cases . . . Anon., 'State firms, govts behind illegal sea reclamation', *China Daily,* 23/6/2009, www.chinadaily.com.cn/china/2009-06/23/content_8311114.htm

'China strides forward where Europe hesitates to tread,' proclaimed Han Vrijling . . . Vrijling, J.K., 'Delft University of Technology. Tiaozini Land Reclamation. Preliminary Port Area Design', 2012, Foreword, p. iii

'The coastlines with relatively favourable natural conditions have been' . . . Xie, S., et al., 'The advance on China coastal engineering: Keynote address', *Proceedings of 32nd Conference on Coastal Engineering, Shanghai, China, 2010,* Mckee Smith, J. & Lynette, P. (eds), at https://icce-ojs-tamu.tdl.org/icce/index.php/icce/article/view/1437

Using historic satellite imagery, a Queensland geospatial scientist . . . Murray, N., et al., 'Tracking the rapid loss of tidal wetlands in the Yellow Sea', *Frontiers in Ecology and the Environment,* 2014, vol. 2, no. 12. pp. 267–72

'The SRP began as an election-time pledge given by unpopular authoritarian elites,' . . . 'The Saemangeum Reclamation Project and politics of regionalism in South Korea', *Ocean and Coastal Management,* December 2014, vol. 102, pp. 594–603

'The reclamation invites more migratory birds to the area,' they said . . . Moores, N., 'The Ministry of Agriculture and Forestry's

Defence of the Saemangeum Reclamation: Credible science or wishful thinking?' *Birds Korea Blog*, 2003, www.birdskorea. org/Habitats/Wetlands/Saemangeum/BK-HA-Saemangeum-MAFrebuttal.shtml

'After only a couple of kilometres performing Samboilbae ... my body could take no more.' ... Moores, N, 'East meets West: A meeting of minds to help save Saemangeum', *Birds Korea Blog*, 2004, www.birdskorea.org/Habitats/Wetlands/Saemangeum/ BK-HA-Saemangeum-Samboilbae-for-Saemangeum.shtml

More than 92,000, a quarter of the estimated global population at the time, was lost at a stroke ... Moores, N., et al., 'Reclamation of tidal flats and shorebird declines in Saemangeum and elsewhere in the Republic of Korea', *Emu*, 2016, vol. 116, pp. 136–46

Grey Plover numbers at Corner Inlet halved at a stroke in the mid-1990s ... Minton, C., et al., 'Trends of shorebirds in Corner Inlet, Victoria, 1982–2011', *Stilt*, 2012, vol. 61, pp. 3–18

Jesse Conklin, a shorebird movement specialist, found the greatest risk ... Conklin, J.R., et al., 'Declining adult survival of New Zealand Bar-tailed Godwits during 2005–2012 despite apparent population stability', *Emu*, March 2016, vol. 116, no. 2, pp. 147–57

There was no doubt. For *menzbieri* birds, double exposure to the perturbed Chinese side ... Murray, N., et al., 'The large scale drivers of population declines in a long-distance migratory shorebird', 2017, *Ecography*, vol. 40, pp. 001–009

Populations of these birds were in free-fall ... Yang, H-Y., et al., 'Impacts of tidal land reclamation in Bohai Bay, China. Ongoing losses of critical Yellow Sea waterbird staging and wintering sites', *Bird Conservation International*, 2011, vol. 21, pp. 241–59

Theunis Piersma confirmed simultaneous declines of Red Knot, Great Knot and Bar-tailed Godwit *menzbieri* signalled the flyway was at risk ... Piersma, T., et al., 'Simultaneous declines in summer survival of three shorebird species signals a flyway at risk', *Journal of Applied Ecology*, 2016, vol. 53, pp. 479–90

The bell tolled in *Nature Communications* for more species ... Studds, C. E., et al., 'Rapid population decline in migratory shorebirds relying on Yellow Sea tidal mudflats as stopover sites',

Nature Communications, 2017, vol. 8, art. no. 14895, www.nature. com/articles/ncomms14895

[T]welve out of nineteen migratory shorebird species were decreasing through their Australian range ... Clemens, R., et al., 'Continental-scale decreases in shorebird populations in Australia', *Emu*, 2016, vol. 116, pp. 119–35

The EAAF had more threatened shorebirds than any other ... MacKinnon, J., et al., 'IUCN situation analysis on East and Southeast Asian intertidal habitats, with particular reference to the Yellow Sea (including the Bohai Sea)', *Occasional Paper of the IUCN Species Survival Commission*, 2012, no. 47, IUCN Gland, Switzerland & Cambridge, UK

Chapter Fourteen: A spoonful of hope

Climate scientists had found ... Mei, W. & Xie, S-P., 'Intensification of landfalling typhoons over the north-west Pacific since the late 1970s', 2016, *Nature Geoscience*, vol. 9, pp. 753–7

[T]here is little data available for the EAAF except that the typhoon season... Bushnell, J. & Falvey, R., *Annual Tropical Cyclone Report 2016*, Joint Typhoon Warning Center, pp. 6–26

Satellite tracking of migratory shorebirds has also begun to reveal ... Anon., 'Scientists track shorebird into Hurricane Irene', Center for Conservation Biology, 2011, https://ccbbirds.org/2011/08/25/scientists-track-shorebird-into-hurricane-irene/

'In time of storm, it seems to be sometimes the only bird aloft.' ... Matthiessen, P., *The Wind Birds*, Chapters Publishing, Shelburne: 1994, p. 22

The super typhoon went on to graze southern Taiwan and barrel into China ... Anon., 'Member report (2016) China', *ESCAP/WMO Typhoon Committee*, World Meteorological Organisation, 2017, p. 14

Killer weather always has been a natural hazard for migratory shorebirds ... Carrington, D., 'Asian typhoons becoming more intense, study finds', *The Guardian*, 6 September 2016, www.theguardian.com/environment/2016/sep/05/asian-typhoons-becoming-more-intense-study-finds

Mei, W. and Xie, S-P, 2016, 'Intensification of landfalling typhoons . . .'

The fisheries scientist Daniel Pauly coined the term 'shifting baseline syndrome' . . . Pauly, D. 'Anecdotes and the shifting baseline syndrome of fisheries', *Trends in Ecology and Evolution,* 1995, vol. 10, no. 10, p. 430

She was told by older local residents, 'The sky was black with curlew . . . Park, P., 'Orielton Lagoon and Sorell Wader Areas', *An Occasional Stint,* 1983, no. 2, pp. 15–33

Land has been claimed from the sea in Britain from the time of the Roman Empire . . . Brew, D. & Staniland, R., *Coastal Change Around The Wash: Literature review'*, English Nature, 2004

The country with the most notable mastery of sea enclosure, the Netherlands . . . Kentie, R., et al., 'Estimating the size of the Dutch breeding population of Continental Black-Tailed Godwits from 2007–2015 using re-sighting from spring staging sites', *Ardea,* 2016, vol. 104, no. 3, pp. 213–23

At least 1300 Dunlin were among birds killed by eating lead-contaminated prey . . . Osborn, D., et al., 'Mersey estuary bird mortalities' in Osborn, D., (ed.) *Metals in Animals,* NERC, Cambridge: 1984

The Deepwater Horizon spill in the Gulf of Mexico exposed many tens of thousands of migratory shorebirds . . . Henkel, J.R., 'Large scale impacts of the Deepwater Horizon oil spill: Can local disturbance affect distant ecosystems through migratory shorebirds?', *Bioscience,* July 2012, vol. 62, no. 7, pp. 676–85

Around half of all migratory shorebird populations have been declining globally, at least since the turn of the century . . . Anon., *Waterbird Population Estimates, Fifth Edition. Summary Report,* Wetlands International, Wageningen: 2012

In North America, long-distance migratory shorebirds have lost on average 70 per cent . . . Anon., *The State of North America's Birds 2016,* Environment and Climate Change Canada, Ottawa: 2016

In the vast African–Eurasian region, for example, the sandpiper family . . . Nagy, S., et al., *Sixth AEWA Report on the Conservation Status of Migratory Waterbirds in the Agreement Area,* Wetlands International, Wageningen: 2015

[T]he exceptionally thorough UK Wetland Birds Survey . . . Frost, T., et al., *Waterbirds in the UK 2016/17: The wetland bird survey*, BTO, RSPB and JNCC in association with WWT, British Trust for Ornithology, Thetford: 2018

Its call, a short and tremulous rising whistle, survives in a sonogram archive . . . Gretton, A., 'XC398794 Slender-billed Curlew *Numenius tenuirostris*', www.xeno-canto.org/398794

If it lives there are fewer than 50 . . . BirdLife International, *Numenius tenuirostris: The IUCN Red List of Threatened Species*, 2018, www.iucnredlist.org/species/22693185/131111201

Researchers have tried to narrow down the potential breeding area . . . Buchanan, G., et al., 'The potential breeding range of the Slender-billed Curlew *Numenius tenuirostris,* identified from stable-isotope analysis', *Bird Conservation International*, 2018, vol. 28, issue 2, pp. 228–37

. . . the Steppe Whimbrel, erroneously declared extinct in 1994, but found wintering in Mozambique in 2016 . . . Allport, G., 'Steppe Whimbrels, *Numenius phaeopus alboaxillaris* at Maputo, Mozambique, in February–March 2016, with a review of the status of the taxon', *The Bulletin of the African Bird Club*, 2017, vol. 24, no. 1, pp. 27–37

Social scientists talk of concepts of Ecological Grief, or Environmental Melancholia . . . Cunsolo, A. & Ellis, N., 'Ecological grief as a response to climate change-related loss', *Nature Climate Change*, April 2018, vol. 8, pp. 275–81

I read of a Dutch shorebird researcher, Egbert van der Velde, who felt aged in his thirties . . . de Boer, J., 'Researcher Egbert van der Velde: "Meadow bird management must come from the heart"', *Leeuwarder Courant*, 23 June 2018

Deeply immersed in clear-eyed analysis of flyway problems, Fuller nevertheless broke up . . . Jones, A., 'Flying for your life: China's new great wall', ABC Radio 'Off Track', www.abc.net.au/radionational/programs/offtrack/flying-for-your-life-2/7479994

'One of the penalties of an ecological education is that one lives alone in a world of wounds' . . . Leopold, L. (ed.), *Round River: From the journals of Aldo Leopold,* Oxford University Press, New York: 1993, pp. 156–7

Perhaps 210 breeding pairs stand between continuation of a line unique to this flyway, and extinction . . . Clark, N., et al., 'First formal estimate of the world population of the critically endangered Spoon-billed Sandpiper *Calidris pygmaea,*' *Oryx,* 2018, vol. 52, no. 1, pp. 137–46

'[W]e can state that the local population was completely destroyed by the expedition' . . . Tomkovich, P., in Zockler, C., et al., 'International Single Species Action Plan for the conservation of the Spoon-billed Sandpiper *Eurynorhynchus pygmeus,*' *CMS Technical Report Series no. 23,* 2010, Foreword, CMS, Bonn

His team concentrated their searches on crowberry-strewn tundra . . . Tomkovich, P., et al., 'First indications of a sharp population decline in the globally threatened Spoon-billed Sandpiper *Eurynorhynchus pygmeus*', *Bird Conservation International,* 2002, vol. 12, pp. 1–18

At a shorebirds conference in Canberra, Syroechkovskiy scolded conservationist groups' inertia . . . Syroechkovskiy, E., 'The Spoon-billed Sandpiper on the edge: A review of breeding distribution, population estimates and plans for conservation in Russia', in Straw, P. (ed.), *Status and Conservation of Shorebirds in the East Asian–Australasian Flyway,* 2003, pp. 169–74

'It is clear several SBS could be shot each year by hunters of Karaginskiy region only' . . . Syroechkovsky, E. & Zöckler, C., 'Breeding Season 2009: Preliminary results and conclusions of the Spoon-billed Sandpiper Survey in Kamchatka and Chukotka', *Spoon-billed Sandpiper Recovery Team News Bulletin,* December 2009, no. 3

'Most fish caught are tiny, so even a 20 gram Red-necked Stint provides a substantial amount of food' . . . Zöckler, C., et al., 'Hunting in Myanmar is probably the main cause of the decline of the Spoon-billed Sandpiper *Calidris pygmeus*', *Wader Study Group Bulletin,* 2010, vol. 117, no. 1, pp. 1–8

Hunting in these countries could be the main cause of its slide towards extinction . . . Zöckler, C., et al., 'The winter distribution of the

Spoon-billed Sandpiper *Calidris pygmaeus*,' *Bird Conservation International*, May 2016, pp. 1–14

... investigators from the Hong Kong Birdwatching Society counted 235 mist nets ... Martinez, J. & Lewthwaite, R., 'Rampant shorebird trapping threatens Spoon-billed Sandpiper *Eurynorhynchos pygmaeus* in Guangdong, South West China' *Birding Asia*, 2013, vol. 19, pp. 26–30

Myanmar zoologist Tony Htin Hla explained ... Htín Hla, T., et al., 'Reports from Nan Thar Island and Bay of Martaban, Myanmar', *Spoon-billed Sandpiper Recovery Team News Bulletin*, 2011, no. 5, p. 13

If only this shorebird revival had actually happened for the Spoonies too ... Pyaephyo, A., et al., 'Recent changes in the number of Spoon-billed Sandpipers *Calidris pygmaea* wintering on the Upper Gulf of Mottama in Myanmar,' *Oryx*, September 2018, DOI 10.1017/S0030605318000698

Then in 2018 two more hatched and one survived to fledge ... Hughes, B., et al., 'World first! Rare Spoon-billed Sandpiper fledges in captivity—leading to new hope it can be saved from extinction', *Spoon-billed Sandpiper Task Force News Bulletin*, 2018, no. 19, pp. 24–6

Chapter Fifteen: Navigating the possible

This country has the greatest extent of tidal flats in the world: 14,416 square kilometres ... Murray, N., et al., 'The global distribution and trajectory of tidal flats', *Nature*, 2018, no. 565, pp. 222–5

They scanned flags of godwit from New Zealand and Victoria, a Far Eastern Curlew from Broome, and Grey Plover from Thailand ... Riegen, A., et al., 'Coastal shorebird survey in the Province of North Pyongan, Democratic People's Republic of Korea, April 2018', 2018, *Stilt*, vol. 72, pp. 21–6

Fudan University's shorebird professor, Zhijuan Ma ... Ma., Z., et al., 'The rapid development of birdwatching in mainland China: A new force for bird study and conservation', *Bird Conservation International*, 2013, vol. 23, pp. 259–69

Crucially for the birds, in 2015 the party's Central Committee and State Council published an ecological progress reform plan . . . Anon., 'Full Text: Integrated Reform Plan for Promoting Ecological Progress', *Xinhua*, 22 September 2014, http://english. gov.cn/policies/latest_releases/2015/09/22/content_28147519 5492066.htm

In careful synchronicity, a Coastal Wetland Blueprint . . . Anon., Coastal Wetlands Blueprint Project, Paulson Institute, 19 October, 2015, Beijing

'The Paulsons saw several Spoon-billed Sandpipers in good light with clear visibility' . . . Shi, J., 'Hank and Wendy Paulson: Working for China's endangered wetlands', *Paulson Institute Conversations*, 2017, www.paulsoninstitute.org/paulson-blog/2017/05/18/hank-and-wendy-paulson-working-for-chinas-endangered-wetlands/

'As President Xi commented to me in a meeting in April 2103: "we have to build more wetlands . . . Paulson, H., *Dealing with China: An insider unmasks the new economic superpower*, 2015, Hachette, New York: p. 300

[I]f the Spoonie was to survive, it would need Tiaozini . . . Anderson, G., et al., 'SBS survey and flagging in Jiangsu, China, September 2018', *Spoon-Billed Sandpiper Task Force News Bulletin*, 2018, no. 19

'Using reclaimed land for commercial real estate development is prohibited' . . . Yu, L., 'China introduces toughest ever regulation on land reclamation', *Xinhuanet*, 18 January 2018, www.xinhuanet.com/english/2018-01/18/c_136903321.htm

The January 2018 ruling was followed six months later by the handing down of a stone tablet . . . Anon., 'Circular of the State Council on Strengthening the Protection of Coastal Wetlands and Strictly Controlling the Reclamation', translated at Hassell, C., et al. in *Red Knot Northward Migration through Bohai Bay, China, Field Report April–June 2018*, 2018, Appendix 1, http://globalfly waynetwork.com.au/bohai-bay/reports-and-papers/

New wind farms were banned . . . Anon., Construction of wind farms banned in important areas of ecological function, CCTV News, Beijing, 29 March 2014

Jiangsu Yancheng National Nature Reserve, where 314 square kilometres of aquaculture farms were to be shut down ... Gao, J., 'How China will protect one-quarter of its land', *Nature,* 23 May 2019, vol. 569, p. 457

'In recent years iconic bird species have come to our attention' ... Zhang, X., 'Guest editorial' in Zöckler, C. (ed.), *Spoon-billed Sandpiper Task Force News Bulletin,* 2018, no. 18, p. 4

Zhou recounted how he even used the forum of a Ramsar meeting to lobby for it ... Zhou, J., 'CBCGDF's efforts to add Tiaozini Wetland to the World Heritage Nom List have been successful!', www.cbcgdf.org/English/NewsShow/5007/6850.html

Late in 2018, the local Yancheng City Government announced its support ... Anon., 'The world hears Yancheng! The wetland protection "2018 Yancheng Initiative" releases to the public!' *Yanfu People's Daily,* 19 November 2018, http://m.ycnews. cn/p/392973.html?from=singlemessage&isappinstalled=0)

Frozen for 24,700 years, but no more ... Maschenko, E., 'Mammoth calf from Bolshoi Lyakhovskii Island', 2005, *Russian Journal of Theriology,* vol. 4, no. 1, pp. 1–10

... until recently it was thought the New Siberians had the fastest pace of shore erosion in Russia—and the world .... Anon., 'Alarming erosion in Russian Arctic', *WWF News,* 10 August 2016, http://wwf.panda.org/wwf_news/?275471/Alarming-erosion-in-Russian-Arctic

The Arctic has been warming more than twice as rapidly as the rest of the world for the past 50 years ... Arctic Monitoring and Assessment Programme Secretariat, *Snow, Water, Ice and Permafrost in the Arctic: Summary for Policy-makers,* 2017, AMAP, Arctic Council, Oslo

In 2018, that meant 1.63 million square kilometres less ice over the water than the 1981–2010 average ... Anon., *State of the Cryosphere: Sea ice,* 2018, National Snow & Ice Data Center, https://nsidc.org/cryosphere/sotc/sea_ice.html

Around the turn of the century, Indigenous observations of Arctic change ... Krupnik, I. & Jolly, D., (eds), *The Earth is Faster Now: Indigenous observations of Arctic environmental change,*

Arctic Research Consortium of the United States, Fairbanks: 2002, p. 7

Meijuan Zhao of Deakin University concluded rapid evolution was at work ... Thompson, K., 'New study shows climate change impacting shorebird migration', Media Release, Deakin University, 12 June 2017, www.deakin.edu.au/about-deakin/media-releases/articles/new-study-shows-climate-change-impacting-shorebird-migration

Arctic spring—as marked by the thaw, the greening of plants ... Post., E., et al., 'Acceleration of phenological advance and warming with latitude over the past century', *Nature Scientific Reports,* 2018, vol. 8, no. 3927

There is underway a worldwide decline in insect life ... Sánchez-Bayo, F. & Wyckhuys, K., 'Worldwide decline of the entomofauna: A review of drivers', *Biological Conservation,* 2019, vol. 232, pp. 8–27

In a study in the Canadian Arctic, Baird's Sandpiper mismatched ... Butchart, S., et al., *The Messengers: What birds tell us about threats from climate change and solutions for nature and people,* BirdLife International and National Audubon Society, Cambridge, UK and New York: 2015

At Utqiagvik/Barrow in Alaska, an invertebrate hatch got out of whack because of an earlier melt ... Saalfeld, S. & Lanctot, R., 'Phenological mismatch in Arctic-breeding shorebirds: adaptability to earlier summers and impacts on chick growth, 2017', Presentation, Alaska Shorebird Group Meeting

In these birds' wintering grounds at Banc d'Arguin in West Africa, a shorter bill ... Van Gils, J.A., et al., 'Body shrinkage due to Arctic warming reduces Red Knot fitness in tropical wintering range', *Science,* 13 May 2016, vol. 352, no. 62, pp. 819–23

Some hypothetical models for their future are worrisome ... Wauchope, H., et al., 'Rapid climate-driven loss of breeding habitat for Arctic migratory birds', *Global Change Biology,* 2016, vol. 23, no. 3, pp. 1085–94

Czech ecologist Vojtech Kubelka led a study ... Kubelka, V., et al., 'Global pattern of nest predation is disrupted by climate change in shorebirds', *Science,* 2018, vol. 362, no. 6415, pp. 680–3

An argument on these findings played out in the journal *Science* ... Kubelka, V., et al., 'Response to comment on "Global pattern of nest predation is disrupted by climate change in shorebirds"', *Science,* 2019, vol. 364, no. 6445

If governments achieve drastic emission cuts, sea levels are still predicted ... Church, J., et al., 'Sea level change' in Stocker et al., (eds), *Climate Change 2013: The Physical Science Basis Contribution of Working Group 1 to the Fifth Assessment report of the Intergovernmental Panel on Climate Change,* Cambridge University Press, Cambridge: 2013

Satellite mapper Nick Murray worked with Fuller and others ... Murray, N., et al., 'The global distribution and trajectory of tidal flats', *Nature,* 2018, vol. 565, pp. 222–5

... before a halt to the over-fishing of Horseshoe Crab, which provides spawn as vitally timed food ... Smith, D.R., et al., 'Conservation status of the American horseshoe crab *Limulus polyphemus*: a regional assessment', *Reviews in Fish Biology and Fisheries,* 2017, vol. 27. pp. 135–75

These knot numbers have partly recovered, but not enough to prevent their listing as 'threatened' under the US Endangered Species Act ... Parramore, L., 'Service protects Red Knot as threatened under the Endangered Species Act', News Release, US Fish & Wildlife Service, Falls Church, Virginia: 2014

[M]aking it the first US bird to be listed as threatened explicitly because of climate change ... Cramer, D., 'Red Knots are battling climate change: On both ends of the earth', *Audubon,* May–June 2016, www.audubon.org/magazine/may-june-2016/red-knots-are-battling-climate-change-both-ends

'We could witness dramatic collapses of population flows caused by intertidal habitat loss' ... Iwamura, T., et al., 'Migratory connectivity magnifies the consequences of habitat loss from sea-level rise for shorebird populations', *Proceedings of the Royal Society B,* 2013, vol. 280, issue 1761, https://doi.org/10.1098/rspb.2013.0325

At Medmerry, on the West Sussex coast in the UK, a 183 hectares wetland was built ... McGrath, M., 'Sea surrender plan to ease flood fears on south coast,' *BBC News*, 4 November 2013, www.bbc.com/news/science-environment-24770379

But Southeast Asia is emerging as a valuable region . . . Iwamura, T., et al., 'Optimal management of a multispecies shorebird flyway under sea level rise', *Conservation Biology*, 2014, vol. 28, no. 6, pp. 1710–14

Chapter Sixteen: In harmony with the sun

'And the great earth' . . . Hope, A.D., 'The Death of the Bird' in *The Wandering Islands*, Edwards & Shaw, Sydney: 1955. By arrangement with the licensor, The A.D. Hope Estate, c/-Curtis Brown (Aust) Pty Ltd

Index

The Smart
Investor's Guide
to Real Estate

The Smart Investor's Guide to Real Estate

Big Profits
From Small Investments

Robert Bruss

New, Updated Fourth Edition

Crown Publishers, Inc.   *New York*

Library of Congress Cataloging in Publication Data

Bruss, Robert.
  The smart investor's guide to real estate.

  Includes index.
  1. Real estate investment. I. Title.
HD1382.5.B78   1985   332.63'24   85-4208
ISBN 0-517-55854-8

Design by Camilla Filancia
10 9 8 7 6 5 4
Updated, Fourth Edition

Contents

Introduction

Why invest in real estate? That is a question which is often asked but rarely answered. In a nutshell, the answer is, there is no better long-run investment.

But real estate is cyclical. Whether you are buying your first home or investing in a multimillion dollar commercial property, the value and resalability will fluctuate with economic conditions. In the long run, however, virtually every sound, well-located property goes up in value. Most of this appreciation in value is due to inflation. But it is also due partly to real estate's unique characteristic of rising demand (from increasing population) and scarcity of supply in good locations.

This book is about "insider's secrets" of buying property wisely, how to hold it for maximum tax and income advantages, and how to sell it for the biggest profits. Along the way, many topics are explained.

Practical "nuts and bolts" information about real estate is the theme of this book. Tips on the right and wrong ways to handle real estate transactions are explained, especially in the question and answer section of each chapter. These questions and answers, edited from my syndicated "Real Estate Mailbag" newspaper columns, add to the basic content of each chapter.

The field of real estate attracts some of the finest investors, sales agents, and others that you will ever meet. But because real estate offers opportunities unmatched elsewhere, it attracts a few of the worst people too.

Fortunately, these "crooks" are a tiny minority in the real estate industry, but it is essential to protect against becoming their victim. This book explains how to avoid being swindled in real estate, as well as how to gain maximum benefits from real estate without taking unfair advantage of anyone. It is known as the "win-win" strategy.

That is what this book is all about—how to profit from real estate by using insider knowledge.

The Smart Investor's Guide to Real Estate

1.

Why Real Estate Is the Best Investment in the World

Real property, when properly bought, managed, and sold, offers the greatest economic return of any form of investment in the United States. That may sound like a broad, oversimplified statement, but it is true.

Whether you are buying your first home or your umteenth investment property, always look at your realty purchase as an investment. If the property gives extra "pride of ownership" benefits, that is great. But never, never, never buy just for emotional benefits. If you follow this strategy, you will never buy a bad property.

Homes purchased for personal use, unfortunately, often are bought with the heart instead of the head. Emotional decisions have no place in real estate, even in home purchases. If a home is not purchased as an investment first, and as a place to live second, it can easily turn into a losing proposition.

Consider all the overpriced, unique one-of-a-kind homes that have been bought or built for prices far above what rational buyers will pay for homes. Many owners of these "white elephant" homes find they can get their money out only by waiting many years for inflation to bail them out. It is known in real estate as the "greater fool" or "latest sucker" strategy. Avoid being its victim by purchasing wisely according to the insider principles spelled out, for the first time, in this book.

Andrew Carnegie said, "Ninety percent of all millionaires become so through owning real estate. More money has been made in real estate than in all industrial investments combined." The reason Carnegie was right is real estate values do not depend upon emotions but upon the hard facts of supply and demand.

Unlike the stock or commodities markets, which are a form of legalized gambling, real estate market value is under the owner's control. If he thinks a particular property is worth a certain amount, he waits until he can get his price from a buyer. But buyers and sellers of common stocks and commodities are at the mercy of the "marketplace" which may or

1

may not reflect the owner's opinion of the asset's value. If you do not believe this, check the per share book value of stocks selling on the New York Stock Exchange.

Many stocks are selling for less than their corporation's per share book value. Why? Because the marketplace is not placing as high a value on that stock as do the shareholders.

In other words, the real estate owner sets the value for his property. If buyers do not agree, no sale takes place. The result is the realty owner controls what happens to his property. He can let it run down, hence it loses value. Or he can improve it, thus increasing its market value if he makes the right improvements.

INCREASING DEMAND FOR REAL ESTATE

"Every person who invests in well-selected real estate in a growing section of a prosperous community adopts the surest and safest method of becoming independent, for real estate is the basis of wealth." When Teddy Roosevelt made that statement, our nation's real property was worth far less than it is today. Before Roosevelt's time, and certainly after, real estate has appreciated in value—far beyond the expectations of even the most optimistic, knowledgeable real estate experts.

Much of this market value appreciation, of course, is due to inflation. But part is also due to the increasing demand for well-located property, brought about by shifting and increasing population pressures. The best realty usually increases in market value at a rate either equal to or greater than the inflation rate. Good times or bad, real estate continues to be a safe, consistent hedge against inflation.

REAL ESTATE BETTER
THAN BUSINESS INVESTING

Of course, not all real estate goes up in market value. The secret is to anticipate which property will increase in worth. This is done by selecting only well-located realty. That means buying real estate where people want to live and work, even though that property costs more than poorly located property.

One of the great retailing empires of this century was built by Marshall Field of Chicago. Although he was an extremely successful businessman, he recognized the importance of real estate when he said "Buying real estate is not only the best way, the quickest way, and the safest way, but the only way to become wealthy." Unfortunately, after Marshall Field passed away, his successors in the department store business, which he built by selecting good locations and offering merchandise people wanted, forgot this principle. They made some serious errors which have hurt the profitability of the Marshall Field department store chain.

In the short run, business profits can be excitingly large. But for the long term, real estate profits can be not only large, but also consistent. Real estate values do not change overnight, as can the fortunes of a business operation. Witness the formerly financially sound W. T. Grant chain which became bankrupt a few years ago. Even though that firm was insolvent, in the bankruptcy proceedings its major assets turned out to be its real estate leases and owned property. Another example is the Penn Central Railroad. Its vast real estate holdings turned out to be the only profitable part of the business.

While there is nothing wrong with business profits, and no investor should give up a going business or a good job to switch into full-time realty investing until he can safely afford to do so, real estate profits are, over the long term, far more assured than are unpredictable business profits.

THE INGREDIENTS FOR SUCCESSFUL REAL ESTATE INVESTING

There are two key factors in successful real estate investing: (1) understand the inherent value of land and the added value of improvements constructed on that land and (2) understand how the dynamic tax consequences of real estate ownership lead to profit. Land plus tax benefits are the first secrets to unlocking the door of real estate profits.

Contrary to what a few people think, profit is not a dirty word. Without profit our nation would not have the highest standard of living in the world. Capitalistic profits benefit everyone. Those who become rich benefit from the incentives offered by our profit-motivated system. And the poor benefit too by having the availability of profit opportunities and jobs if they want to improve their lives.

Unfortunately, many of the poor have little or no desire to improve themselves. So they remain poor. But in our nation even the poor are pretty well off, compared to the "have nots" in more socialistic nations.

Profits from real estate have made more people wealthy than has any other source. Contrary to popular myth, it does not take money to make money in real estate. Many ways to acquire realty with little or no cash will be discussed later.

How are real estate profits earned? One way is from the inflationary increase in property values which have done better than most other investments in keeping ahead of inflation. Many realty investments, especially single-family homes, have appreciated in market value faster than the inflation rate. As a result, most home owners realize their residence is their best investment. If one house is a good investment, two, three, or more would be better.

THE SECRET OF CREATING REAL ESTATE WEALTH

Creating wealth by owning real estate is simple. Realty wealth is created by increasing the property's market value. Although inflation helps increase market value of most real estate, smart property investors do not rely on inflation alone. A real estate wealth creator is a person who improves real property at a cost that is less than the marketplace will pay for the increased value of those improvements.

"Improvements" mean not only new construction but also renovation of existing structures and creating a new use for underutilized buildings or underused land.

For example, if a person spends one dollar to improve his or her home and, as a result, that home's market value goes up by two dollars or more, real estate wealth has been created. Thousands of real estate investors are creating realty wealth this way in virtually every town in the United States. The person who spends $10,000 adding a bedroom to his home may be adding $20,000 to its market value if there is a demand in that community for larger homes.

WHY LOSSES OCCUR IN REAL ESTATE

No one should get the idea that losses never occur in real estate. They do. Some of the most successful real estate developers have lost everything by making foolish realty investments. The famous William Zeckendorf is the best known example of a highly successful real estate investor who lost virtually everything. Why?

Because he was in the riskiest part of the real estate business— development. He underestimated costs of developing his properties, including construction and financing, and he overestimated market demand for what he was constructing. Further, he was a victim of real estate cycles because he needed financing money when it was not available or was prohibitively costly.

When a real estate developer, sometimes called a promoter, loses money in real estate, it is usually because he went wrong in his estimates, as William Zeckendorf did. Property development is the riskiest way to make real estate profits. The potential for both high profits and high losses is great. Novice investors should stay away from development, especially since there are so many better and easier ways to earn profits in real estate. The secret is stay away from real estate development unless you can afford to lose everything.

Most real estate profits do not come without work and careful planning. Even buying vacant land, sitting back, and waiting for population pressures to increase its value takes time, money, and work (to earn the money elsewhere to pay the carrying costs for property taxes and mortgage payments while awaiting possible land resale profits).

WHY RAW LAND IS USUALLY NOT A GOOD INVESTMENT

Although many property profits have been made investing in vacant, raw land, chances of earning high profits are slim. The reasons are inflation and carrying costs.

Just to break even, vacant land must appreciate in market value at least 30 percent per year. The reason is the owner must pay property taxes (usually 1 to 3 percent of value), mortgage interest (perhaps 12 percent, usually financed by the seller because banks and other mortgage lenders regard land mortgages as too risky), real estate sales commission upon resale (5 to 10 percent of the sales price), lost income on the down payment cash investment (10 to 15 percent per year), and inflation (pick your own figure for this).

Land ownership is so risky that even home builders (the biggest real estate risk takers of all) try to avoid buying land until just before they start construction of a new housing development. Instead, home builders buy options to purchase land, a neat financing trick which gives the builder control of the land with only a minimal cash investment until construction is ready to begin.

But if raw, vacant land is not a good investment, what is a sound realty investment? The answer to that question will have to wait until the four key variables of any investment are discussed. As you read the following section, apply these variables to any investment you wish, including real estate. Consider land, homes, apartments, shopping centers, warehouses, or whatever interests you.

THE FOUR VARIABLE FACTORS IN ANY INVESTMENT

Any monetary investment involves four key variables that are related to each other. They are (1) safety, (2) potential for change in market value, (3) yield, and (4) liquidity.

SAFETY

The primary factor most people consider when making any investment is safety. The investments considered safest by most people are U. S. Savings Bonds, bills, notes, and other federal government obligations. These securities offer virtually 100 percent safety of principal because the chances of the U. S. government failing to repay these debts when due is practically nil. But such obligations rarely show any increase in value, other than accumulated interest (which is rarely as high as the inflation rate).

Although the safety of U. S. government obligations is excellent, there are discounts and fees charged for early redemption before maturity. Many U. S. obligations now owned by banks, if the banks had to sell them today, could only be sold at deep discounts from their book value. The reason is the low interest rate on these government obligations reduces their value.

After considering the loss of purchasing power on the invested dollars (due to inflation) and federal income taxes (but not state income taxes) on the interest income, U. S. government instruments in recent years have consistently shown losses to investors. Their only redeeming factor is high safety of the principal, even if that principal has lost value due to inflation.

Next in order of safe investments are the various types of insured savings accounts and certificates of deposit offered by savings and loan associations and banks. These accounts are now insured by federal government agencies up to $100,000. If there were a serious run on these depositories, the government printing presses would work overtime to pay off the investors (in inflated dollars, however). The U. S. treasury would probably come to the rescue, but it is not now legally obligated to do so.

THE BIG DRAWBACK OF SAVINGS ACCOUNTS

Even though it is considered admirable to save money in savings accounts and similar savings instruments, the big drawback for savers is these accounts offer no appreciation in value. In fact, the dollars in those accounts depreciate in value after considering the lost purchasing power of the dollars sitting idly in savings accounts losing value because of inflation.

Since the interest rates paid on savings accounts and certificates are usually below the inflation rate, savings instruments can be very expensive investments for the investor. Most people cannot afford the luxury of losing money on their savings. But they do not realize it. The banks and savings associations, of course, do not want people to know what foolish investments savings can be in times of high inflation rates.

For example, suppose you earn 12 percent interest on a savings certificate. If you are in a 20 percent tax bracket, income taxes will eat up about 2.4 percent of the interest earnings, reducing the yield to about 9.6 percent. If the inflation rate exceeds this after-tax yield, the saver loses purchasing power on his dollars kept in savings.

In fairness, however, the big liquidity advantage of savings accounts should be emphasized. Or at least that is what savers think. Although savings account withdrawals are customarily paid upon demand, if you read the fine print it says up to thirty-days advance notice can be required by the bank or savings association before your withdrawal request is honored.

Some eastern savings banks have refused to allow early withdrawals on savings certificates even though the saver is willing to pay the interest penalty for early withdrawal. So savings account liquidity really is not what the banks and savings associations lead their customers to believe.

THE SAFETY OF REAL ESTATE INVESTMENTS

Since this book is about real estate, the safety of realty investments should be discussed. Because each property is unique, unlike any other, the safety of real estate investments varies with each specific property.

Well-located, sound real estate is the safest investment in the world. It is not going to disappear, as can the value of dollars put into savings accounts. Neither will real estate values be lost because of inflation. In fact, property values tend to increase at a pace at least equal to the inflation rate. Most homes have appreciated at a rate greater than the inflation rate (due mainly to strong buyer demand and insufficient supply of newly constructed homes).

When was the last time you heard of a real estate investor selling his property for less than he paid for it? Exclude developers who have more in common with Las Vegas gamblers than with investors. Would you sell your home today for the price you paid for it? Probably not, if you are like most homeowners who have large profits in their homes.

Most real estate owners know their property is increasing in market value year by year. They feel perfectly safe continuing to hold on to it. Real estate holds its value and increases in market worth far faster than most other investment alternatives and with much less downside risk.

The reason real estate holds its value and is not subject to wild value fluctuations is it is a scarce commodity in limited supply. To be more precise, well-located real estate is limited. As population increases, value of well-located land increases too. This result is not true for most other investments, such as common stocks, bonds, or savings accounts.

Unless a real estate owner must sell his or her property very soon after purchasing it, assuming the owner did not pay more than its fair market value, it is a very rare situation where money is lost on realty investments.

Because of all the safety factors in real estate, mortgage lenders will loan a higher percentage of value on real property (usually 70 percent to 90 percent of market value, sometimes more) than on most other investment security.

The federal government will even go so far as to guarantee GI home loans for qualified veterans for 100 percent of the purchase price. And real estate lenders will loan money secured by real property for a longer term, usually twenty-five to thirty years, sometimes forty years, than on any other security. Since these lenders are notoriously conservative, real estate must be a safe investment.

POTENTIAL FOR CHANGE IN MARKET VALUE

If you offer to sell me your passbook savings account, if I am in a good mood, I will probably pay you the amount of your account's balance. I would be a fool to pay any more. The reason is a savings account is worth only its value in dollars, never any more.

But real estate is different. It offers both upside and downside potential for change in market value. Fortunately, most good real estate goes up in value. But there are a few exceptions, such as poorly located property that is away from growing areas or located in high-crime areas where buyers are few and far between. Another way realty can lose value is by neglect. It must be properly maintained to avoid a loss in market value.

The market value of every specific real estate parcel depends on the demand for such property as well as the available supply of similar parcels. Since well-located land is in limited supply, values go up as demand increases. The better the location, the greater the potential for appreciation in a property's market value.

Of course, the safety of real estate investments is a factor in market value changes, usually upward, but other considerations also apply. The two major factors tending to force property values up are (1) increasing demand from an increasing population for a limited supply of well-located land and improvements, and (2) inflationary cost increases for new construction that make existing properties more valuable than their original construction cost.

The availability of mortgage financing also enters into the picture. If mortgage money is easily available, this tends to allow property values to rise rapidly. But if mortgage money is tight and expensive, property values do not rise rapidly. However, when hard money lenders (such as banks and savings associations) cut off mortgage money, a new source develops. It is the seller. Property sellers often finance their buyer's purchases if the buyer is willing to pay the seller's price for the property. This financing development, especially during times of tight mortgage money, tends to keep property values rising even when normal mortgage lenders are out of the market.

Real estate values traditionally rise at least 3 percent per year, good times or bad. But due to runaway hyperinflation in the late 1970s, property value increases of 20 percent to 30 percent per year, especially for well-located homes, became commonplace.

Unimproved land values, however, usually increase at a much slower pace unless the land is located on the very fringe of development. That is why it is essential for real estate land investors to check market value trends for the immediate area before any vacant property is bought. Real estate agents usually have ready access to statistics on recent sales prices in the local vicinity.

But watch out. Just a block or two in distance can make a big difference in the rate of market value appreciation. Do not be fooled by statistics. Location is the key to successful realty investing. If a property is offered at what looks like an especially cheap price, there is probably a very good reason. Find out why before, rather than after, you buy.

YIELD

The third factor of any investment, yield, means the annual return from the purchased asset. For example, a passbook savings account might earn 5½ percent annual interest. This is that investment's yield.

Sound real estate investments far surpass any other type of equity investment for consistent total yield, commensurate with safety and liquidity. However, the yield in real estate is not a fixed amount. Rather it is the sum of at least two components.

These components of real estate yield are (1) the net income (or loss) produced by the property and (2) the income tax dollar savings resulting from the tax deductions for the property. Income tax dollar savings often increase the investor's annual real estate yield by 3 percent to 20 percent, sometimes more, depending on the owner's income tax bracket.

Most professional real estate investors will not even consider making a property purchase that will not yield at least 20 percent to 30 percent total annual yield. Some investors include market value appreciation as part of their annual yield. But most do not because it is an uncertain amount until reduced to possession at the time of reselling the property. Probably the safest and most conservative approach is to consider market value appreciation as "bonus yield" that will most likely be realized upon sale of the property.

LIQUIDITY

The fourth factor to consider when making any investment is liquidity. It is defined as the time delay required to convert an asset into cash.

For example, common stocks listed on the New York Stock Exchange are considered relatively liquid since they can be sold and converted into cash within three or four days at most. But the "cost" of that liquidity is that the stock is sold at its market price on the day of the sale, and the investor has no control over what that price will be. Other examples of highly liquid investments are savings accounts and U. S. Savings Bonds, which can usually be converted quickly into cash. However, the dollars received from the sale of such highly liquid assets are usually worth less than when they were invested. This is due to the dollar's constantly declining purchasing power caused by inflation. Most highly liquid investments, such as savings accounts and common stocks, offer little or no inflation hedge.

Many people think real estate's biggest drawback is its lack of easy liquidity. Real estate certainly is not as liquid as a savings account. But most good property can be sold within thirty to ninety days for its true market value. However, due to unrealistic pricing by many sellers who often take longer to try (and sometimes succeed) in getting top dollar for their property, realty sales often take a long time. This inflationary property price squeeze to wring the last dollar of profit from properties contributes to rising property sales prices in a neighborhood.

But there is another aspect to real estate liquidity. It is the refinance bonus. Except in times of extremely tight mortgage money, which real estate experiences cyclically, most good property can be refinanced to produce liquid cash. A major advantage of refinancing a mortgage, instead of selling the property, is this refinancing cash is tax-free to the property owner. Since it is a loan, there is no tax due on the cash produced from mortgage refinancing.

Mortgage refinance liquidity is an advantage most other investments lack. For example, it is possible to borrow on the security of common stocks, bonds, and personal property such as autos. But the loan-to-value ratio is usually not as high as for real estate. And the payback term, normally thirty years for real estate mortgages, is much shorter for other investments.

So real estate is really more liquid than most people think. But there are times when real estate liquidity suffers, such as during mortgage crunches when mortgage money is either very expensive or unavailable. This slight disadvantage, however, is more than compensated by the bonus advantages of real estate, such as refinancing and the special income tax savings benefits.

ADDITIONAL ADVANTAGES OF REAL ESTATE INVESTING

So far we have discussed the four variable factors to consider when making any investment. Real estate came out pretty good, but not perfect.

No investment will ever come out perfect when applying these four variables, so do not waste time looking for the "perfect investment." It just does not exist. But real estate comes pretty close.

There are additional advantages offered by real estate investment that most alternative investments lack. Real estate offers these bonus advantages that many potential investors do not completely understand. It is important to comprehend at least the concept, if not the details, because property evaluation can be intelligently made only after considering all its advantages and disadvantages.

1. HIGH LEVERAGE OPPORTUNITIES IN REAL ESTATE

Leverage means investing the least possible amount of the owner's cash when buying investment assets in order to earn the maximum percentage return on those invested dollars. In other words, leveraging means borrowing money. Real estate investors call those borrowed dollars OPM (other people's money).

In real estate, thanks to leverage, the property owner controls his entire property even though his own cash dollars invested may be only 10 percent to 25 percent of the purchase price. The ultimate leverage, of course, is no cash down payment at all.

The balance of the purchase price is usually financed with a first mortgage and possibly also with a second mortgage. Even a third or fourth mortgage can be used too.

No alternative investment asset allows such a low down payment percentage without corresponding disadvantages. Real estate leverage lets the investor get the entire benefit from the property's appreciation in market value with only a small cash investment (the down payment).

If the property should lose value (which rarely happens in sound, well-located real estate investments), the investor's loss is limited to his dollars invested if there is no personal liability on the mortgage.

Especially in highly leveraged property purchases, in case the property should lose value due to some unexpected event, it is important that the investor not have personal liability on the mortgage. The property alone should be the security for the mortgage loan.

If the investor does not have personal liability on the mortgage, and a foreclosure loss results, the lender cannot sue the investor for the deficiency loss. Several states, such as California, automatically bar such deficiencies if foreclosure is at a trustee's sale (rather than a court judicial sale).

Leverage is the insider's real estate secret that maximizes the smart investor's return on his investment. For example, suppose you buy a $100,000 income property, such as a commercial store building or perhaps a small apartment house. You can pay 100 percent cash down payment or possibly as little as 5 percent or 10 percent. The variables are infinite as to the relationship between the amount of the down payment and the mortgage(s) and the investor's return on dollars invested.

There is no one best leverage alternative for all real estate investors. Variables include the amount of cash the investor has available, his or her income tax bracket, the need for tax shelter, the desire for cash flow from the property, the seller's need for cash, and the buyer's need to conserve cash for later expenses such as improvements to the property.

What is the best leverage ratio? How much cash down payment and how large a mortgage is best?

As the next chart shows, the higher the leverage (lowest cash down payment, maximum OPM borrowed funds), the higher the total percentage return on the invested dollars.

While it is not always possible to get 90 percent high leverage financing, even using first and second mortgages, this is usually a good objective to try to achieve if the property can comfortably carry itself from its rental income produced. Many professional real estate investors regularly achieve 100 percent financing by combining various financing techniques.

Even home buyers can achieve 100 percent financing by using a GI home mortgage. FHA home loans achieve about 95 percent financing. If the government encourages maximum leverage when buying a home, there is no reason properties purchased without government financing cannot be bought the same way. With the aid of a seller-financed mortgage, high leverage is usually possible.

Note that while the annual spendable cash increases as the amount of cash down payment increases, the percentage total return on invested dollars decreases. Also, the tax shelter is highest with the largest equity and tax shelter is lowest with the smallest equity. In summary, the following leverage chart says:

1. Lowest Leverage (Highest Cash Investment) = Highest Tax Shelter and Highest Cash Flow
2. Highest Leverage (Lowest Cash Investment) = Lowest Tax Shelter and Lowest Cash Flow

But the overall total return on investment is about the same, approximately 12 percent in this example, regardless of whether or not maximum leverage was used.

Using a hypothetical $100,000 income property investment, such as apartments, stores, or offices, here are some possible leverage alternatives to illustrate the dramatic results:

1. Cash Down Payment	$100,000	$50,000	$40,000	$25,000	$10,000
(Equity)	100%	50%	40%	25%	10%
2. Annual Mortgage Payment					
(30 years, 12% interest)	0	6,172	7,406	9,258	11,109
3. Minus: Annual Interest					
(Tax Deductible)	0	6,000	7,200	9,000	10,800
4. Annual Equity Mortgage					
Build-up (First Year)	0	172	206	258	309
5. Annual Net Operating Income	12,000	12,000	12,000	12,000	12,000
6. Annual Net Cash Spendable					
Income After Loan Payments	12,000	5,828	4,594	2,742	891
7. Depreciation (18 Years)					
$80,000 Building Value,					
175 Percent Method (First					
12 Months)	7,200	7,200	7,200	7,200	7,200
8. Taxable Income (or Tax Loss)					
(Line 5 minus 3 minus 7)	4,800	(1,200)	(2,400)	(4,200)	(6,000)
9. Tax Sheltered Tax-Free Income*					
(Line 7 minus 4, or 6 minus 8)	7,200	7,028	6,994	6,942	6,891

RETURN ON CASH DOWN PAYMENT IN RELATION TO

Annual Net Spendable Cash	12%	11.6%	11.5%	11%	8.9%
Annual Equity Buildup as					
Percent of Down Payment					
(First Year)	0%	.4%	.5%	1%	3.1%
Total Return on Investment	12%	12%	12%	12%	12%

Plus Income Tax Dollar Savings Due to Tax Losses

*Tax shelter is the same as (1) depreciation minus equity buildup or (2) the amount by which annual net cash spendable exceeds taxable income. These amounts are always identical. The difference between the equity buildup on the mortgages and the depreciation is tax sheltered, but it does not require any cash outlay since depreciation is a noncash bookkeeping tax deduction.

$$\frac{\text{Depreciation}}{\text{Minus: Equity Buildup}} = \frac{\text{Cash Spendable After Payments}}{\text{Minus: Taxable Income}}$$
$$\text{Tax-Sheltered Income} = \text{Tax-Sheltered Income}$$

More about the "tax magic" of depreciation will be discussed later. For now, all that is important is to understand depreciation is another of the benefits of owning depreciable real estate. It contributes to the owner's total return from his or her real estate investment.

2. TAX-DEFERRED EXCHANGES

Many of the benefits of owning real estate are a creation of the tax laws written by Congress. Without the unique tax breaks given to realty owners, much of the incentive to own property would be gone. Although a real estate investment should never be made for the tax benefits alone, they are a powerful investment incentive.

Perhaps the reason real estate tax breaks are so good is so many congressmen own realty. This investment continues to be the tax-favored investment, far exceeding the tax advantage of owning oil, gas, timber, coal, common stocks, bonds, commodities, gems, and other investment alternatives.

Tax-deferred exchanges are just one of the many tax benefits of owning real estate. Although such exchanges are more fully explained later, at this point exchanges must be listed as a major tax break for real estate investors. Thanks to the tax deferral rule of Internal Revenue Code Section 1031, it is possible to pyramid one's wealth from a small beginning into millions of dollars of net equity—all without paying one dollar of profit taxes.

Such property swaps are often referred to as "Section 1031 exchanges." Some real estate agents, when discussing realty trades, erroneously refer to them as "tax-free exchanges." This gives clients the wrong impression that such property trades are a way to completely eliminate tax on their profit when disposing of one property and acquiring another. This is not true!

A qualified real estate exchange is a way to *defer* the tax on a profitable real estate trade. This tax postponement, however, can last forever because it is possible to make a continuous chain of trades, never paying profit tax as the investor goes from a small property to a multimillion dollar one.

Only if the investor makes an outright sale, will the deferred profit tax become due. And, thanks to a new technique called a "Starker exchange," it is now possible to make an outright sale and still defer the profit tax. Starker exchanges will be more fully discussed later.

Tax-deferred exchanges can be used for both owner-occupied principal residences and investment or business property. When exchanging your personal residence for another, use Internal Revenue Code Section 1034. Other exchanges come under Internal Revenue Code Section 1031.

The details of Internal Revenue Code 1034's "residence replacement rule" will be discussed later.

The term "tax-deferred exchange" primarily refers to deferring profit taxes when disposing of one investment property or business property and acquiring another. This tax rule of Internal Revenue Code 1031 cannot be used if the owner's personal residence is involved (then IRC 1034 should be used).

To qualify for an IRC 1031 tax-deferred exchange, both properties must be "held for investment or for use in a trade or business." That means just about any property can qualify, except one's personal residence.

For example, vacant land may be traded for apartments, a warehouse can be traded for a hotel, or an office building can be exchanged for industrial property, all without paying any profit tax. It is all due to the special tax-deferred exchange rule of IRC 1031.

WHY TRADE?

Frankly, most investors who want to dispose of one property and acquire another do not want to trade. But the tax law requires the myth of an exchange if the profit tax is to be deferred. However, the real result is the investor disposes of his first property and winds up with one he wants more.

The intermediate step of a trade is well worth the slight inconvenience since the investor's profit is not eroded by income tax if a trade is used. A deferred tax is always better than one paid today.

Investors have many reasons for using tax-deferred property swaps. For example, many want to use their equity in a small property, such as a two-family duplex, for trading as the down payment on a larger property such as a fourplex. Other reasons for making tax-deferred exchanges include (1) disposal of an otherwise hard-to-sell property, (2) acquisition of a larger property that is easier to manage, (3) increasing depreciation tax benefits, and (4) consolidation of several small properties into a larger one.

THREE-WAY EXCHANGES

After making a tax-deferred exchange to a larger "like-kind" property, the "up trader" has completed his part of the trade. He accomplished what he wanted, namely (a) avoidance of tax payment and (b) acquisition of a larger property. But the party disposing of the larger property in the trade usually does not want to keep the smaller property offered by the "up trader."

So the "down trader" usually sells the smaller property so that cash will be received for it. This is known as a "cash out sale." It will not disqualify the tax-deferred exchange for the up trader. Such a cash out sale accomplishes the result the owner of the larger property wants, namely to sell his property and receive cash. These are called "three-way exchanges" because there are three parties involved, the up trader, the down trader, and the cash buyer for the smaller property sold after the exchange is completed.

3. INSTALLMENT SALES DEFER PROFIT TAXES

Another major tax benefit of real estate is installment sale tax deferral. This type of tax deferral, unlike the exchange's indefinite tax postponement until the acquired property is disposed of without exchanging again, spreads out the tax over the years the buyer makes payments to the seller.

Many property sellers, especially retirees, use installment sales to minimize their profit tax by spreading it out over several years to avoid being thrown into a high tax bracket in the year of the property sale. Also, the excellent interest earnings on the buyer's unpaid debt to the seller produce extra income for the seller. Security for installment sales can be a mortgage, deed of trust, land contract of sale, long-term lease-option, or other security device.

Property installment sales often result in doubling the total amount received from a realty sale. For example, suppose you sell a property for $120,000 with $20,000 down and take back a $100,000 installment sale mortgage at 12 percent interest. That note would produce $1,000 monthly interest. The principal balance could either be amortized or there could be a balloon payment due in perhaps five or ten years. If it is a ten-year mortgage note, for example, the total interest income for ten years will be $120,000, equal to the sale price.

The basic requirements for installment sales were greatly simplified by the 1980 Installment Sales Revision Act, which became effective October 20, 1980. Now any deferred payment sale profits are taxable (as long-term capital gain if the property was owned over six months) after June 22, 1984, in the year the seller receives the profit payment from the buyer. Of course, interest earned on the unpaid balance is taxed in the year of receipt as ordinary income.

To qualify for an installment sale today simply requires that at least some part of the profit payment from the sale be deferred into a future tax year. There is no longer any 30 percent limitation on payments received in the year of the sale, nor must there be at least two installment payments in different tax years.

Even if a property has an existing mortgage on it, an installment sale can be used to spread out the profit tax payments. Major installment sale benefits of offering "easy financing" mean the seller can usually (a) get top dollar for the property and (b) make a quick sale without outside financing.

Each installment sale payment from buyer to seller, whether received in the year of the sale or in a future tax year, is allocated to (a) nontaxable return of the seller's capital investment, (b) profit (taxed at low, long-term capital gain rates if the property was owned over twelve months before sale), and (c) interest (taxable as ordinary income).

If the installment sale seller needs cash, either right after the sale or later on, he can usually hypothecate or collateralize his note as security for a loan to produce tax-free cash. Or the mortgage note can be sold to an investor, often at a discount, but this will involve payment of tax on the remainder of the profit.

4. SPECIAL CAPITAL GAINS TAX BENEFITS

How many investments, other than real estate, can be sold for the same price as the original purchase price, and yet produce a profit which is taxed at the lowest capital gain tax rates? Thanks to the tax magic of depreciation, real estate has this unique advantage which permits conversion or ordinary income from rents into long-term capital gains at the time of the property's sale.

THE TAX MAGIC OF DEPRECIABLE REAL ESTATE

Suppose an income investment property is purchased for $100,000 and $20,000 is allocated to the nondepreciable land value (because land never wears out and loses value) with $80,000 allocated to the depreciable building improvements. Using an eighteen-year estimated useful life, if it is an older structure, the straight-line depreciation method gives a $4,444.44 annual depreciation deduction ($80,000 divided by eighteen years).

If the property is held for just three years, that means $13,333 of its rental income will have been received tax-free thanks to the $13,333 ($4,444 for three years) depreciation deduction which "shelters" rent income from taxation. Depreciation is a noncash bookkeeping expense, so it requires no actual cash payment to be entitled to this tax deduction.

After three years of ownership, if the property only sells for its $100,000 purchase price, since the owner's basis is depreciated down by $13,333 to $86,667, the $13,333 profit ($100,000 sales price minus $86,667 basis) is taxed as a long-term capital gain (since the property was owned over six months). Long-term capital gains are only 40 percent taxable and are 60 percent tax free.

The tax result is that only 40 percent of the $13,333 profit ($5,333) is added to the seller's other taxable income and the remaining $8,000 escapes tax. Thus, ordinary income (rents) are converted to long-term capital gains, which are the most lightly taxed of all profits.

That is how the "tax magic" of depreciation works. While it is very rare to not sell a depreciable property for more than its purchase price, due to appreciating property values in most areas, there is still a profit for the owner if he or she sells for only the amount that was paid to acquire the property.

Long-term capital gains profits are lightly taxed because Congress wants to encourage investment. As of this writing, only 40 percent of such profits are taxed; the remaining 60 percent are tax-free.

For example, suppose you sell a property for $100,000 long-term capital gain profit. Only $40,000 (40 percent) will be taxed. This $40,000 will then be added to your other ordinary taxable income, such as job salary. Even if you are in a 50 percent bracket, the tax on this $40,000 would be no more than $20,000. That is only 20 percent of the total $100,000 profit. Most people would gladly pay $20,000 tax to net $80,000. By contrast, if $100,000 of wages are received and the taxpayer is in a 50 percent income tax bracket, he will owe $50,000 tax and get to keep only $50,000.

But the best part of real estate capital gains taxation of income property is that it is the tenants who buy the building for the owner. Their rent pays the expenses. After making the initial down payment, the owner should not need to put any more of his own cash into the property. But if the building needs improvements, most banks and savings associations gladly make improvement loans that, again, are paid off with the tenant's rent payments.

5. SPECIAL INHERITANCE BENEFITS

The tax law gives special benefits to persons inheriting realty. Unfortunately, to take advantage of this tax break, someone has to die—a rather extreme and irreversible action!

The general rule is a person inheriting property receives it at its fair market value on the date of the decedent's death. All untaxed capital gains are forgotten.

For example, suppose you inherit some land worth $100,000. The decedent paid only $10,000 for it years ago. If he had sold it the day before he died, he would have owed capital gain tax on the $90,000 profit. But that potential capital gain is forgotten upon death. If you sell the inherited property for $100,000, you owe no profit tax since your basis is the $100,000 fair market value on the day the decedent died.

In the case of joint tenancy, property received by a surviving joint tenant, this stepped-up basis rule applies only to the portion received from the decedent.

To illustrate, suppose husband and wife own land worth $100,000 on the day the husband dies. They paid $10,000 for the land. So each joint tenant has a $5,000 basis for each half interest in the property. After the husband's death, the wife's basis for the property as surviving joint tenant will be $5,000 (for her half interest) plus $50,000 (fair market value of the half received from the decedent joint tenant), a $55,000 total. If she sells for $100,000 she has a $45,000 taxable capital gain ($100,000 minus $55,000).

If you live in a community property state, your attorney should be consulted because there are certain tax benefits of owning real estate as community property rather than as joint tenants.

6. THE BEST BENEFIT OF ALL—TAX-FREE REFINANCING CASH

The best advantage real estate has over most alternative investments is it can be refinanced to produce tax-free cash for the owner.

Real estate's acknowledged inflation hedge is universally recognized. As the market value of good property keeps pace with inflation, lenders will increase the amount of their mortgage loans secured by a property. For example, suppose you buy a home for $100,000 and obtain an $80,000 first mortgage. Most homes appreciate in market value 5 percent to 15 percent per year, sometimes more. Suppose in a few years your home has appreciated in market value to $150,000. Using the traditional lending standard, most lenders will loan up to 80 percent of its appreciated value. That is $120,000 in this example. The $40,000 cash received from the refinancing is tax free (because it is a loan, and loans are nontaxable).

Many investors live off tax-free cash received from refinancing. By doing so they legally never pay income taxes. In case of an emergency, by keeping their mortgages at maximum levels they resell easily because properties with big assumable mortgages generally sell quickly.

SUMMARY

After considering the four factors of any investment (safety, potential for change in market value, yield, and liquidity) plus the special benefits of real estate, property ownership comes out far ahead of alternative investments. Investors planning real estate purchases, however, should analyze these benefits as applicable to the specific property under consideration for purchase.

No other investment offers the flexibility of real estate to meet each investor's specific requirements such as cash flow, tax shelter, resale profits, or just plain old pride of ownership. With the aid of qualified real estate agents, tax advisers, and attorneys, realty investors can find the right property and buy it in the right way to maximize its benefits. Now that you know real estate is the world's greatest investment, use this insider's knowledge to accomplish your investment goals.

QUESTIONS AND ANSWERS

HOW REAL ESTATE CAN PROVIDE
YOUR RETIREMENT INCOME

Q. I am forty-four and my wife is forty-six. Our children will soon graduate from college. I have a secure job with the phone company, but it doesn't pay too well. We're now starting to think about our retirement years as I realize social security and my pension won't be enough to live on if 10 percent annual inflation continues. In another seven years we'll own our home free and clear. It's worth at least $85,000 today. Our only major asset is our home. We think owning real estate is the best way to beat inflation. For retirement income, what kind of property would you recommend? —*Joseph Y.*

A. Congratulations on planning your retirement now. You will never be dependent on relatives, friends, or welfare (as are many retirees) if you invest in sound income property now.

Depending upon how much time you have available to manage property, you may wish to buy apartments (except in rent control areas), rental houses, commercial property, offices, or industrial buildings. But before you buy, spend a few months looking at investment properties to find out which type is best in your community.

By purchasing income property, the rent paid by your tenants will pay the mortgage and operating expense payments. Avoid buying vacant land as it usually produces little or no net income. The only hope of profit from vacant land is resale or development profit, both highly speculative. After considering carrying costs and inflationary loss of purchasing power for dollars invested, land must appreciate in value at least 30 percent per year just to break even. It is too risky an investment for most people.

When you become too old and feeble to manage your income property, then you can sell it on installment sales which should provide at least twenty-five or thirty years of secure retirement income. While you are young, buy income property. Refinance it every few years to create tax-free cash with which to buy more property. When you are older, then you can sell and use the installment sale earnings for safe, extra retirement income.

HOW TO GET OFF THE SALARY TREADMILL

Q. Your articles about how to make money in real estate fascinate me. As I have about $25,000 to invest, do you recommend I quit my job to buy good income property? It seems every time I get a pay raise, it's eaten up by withholding tax or social security increases. How can I best invest in real estate to get off my salary treadmill? I don't want to give up my job. —*Vickie M.*

A. You do not have to quit your job to profit from real estate. In fact, it is advisable to keep your job, as it helps you establish credit with which to buy realty.

There is no reason you cannot invest in real estate while you continue your job. Unless you buy a huge income property, such as a large apartment house or office building, real estate will not provide the cash flow your job gives you.

However, your long-range goal should be to invest so your job will be just a supplement to your real estate income. After a few years of real estate ownership, you will have built up a steady source of tax-free income.

The secret is to buy at least one income property per year for at least five years. As soon as mortgage conditions are good for refinancing, refinance the mortgage on at least one property each year. Cash received from mortgage refinancing is tax-free.

For example, suppose you buy a $100,000 income property today, and it has $90,000 of mortgages against it. In other words, you pay $10,000 cash down payment. In five years, at 10 percent average annual appreciation in market value, your property will be worth at least $160,000. If you then get a new first mortgage for 75 percent of $160,000, which is $120,000, you will pocket the $30,000 excess tax-free cash after paying off the $90,000 old financing. If you do this often enough, you can quit your job and get off the salary treadmill.

WHY HOUSING PRICES WILL KEEP GOING UP

Q. We were going to wait for six months or so to buy our first home. But I'm pretty discouraged, as I just read a magazine article which says home prices will keep going up even if we have a recession. That doesn't make sense does it?—*Bayless J.*

A. Yes, it does. Even if we have a recession, home prices in most communities will continue rising. Of course, there will be a few local exceptions, such as areas where the major employer closes a factory, thus creating a temporary oversupply of homes for sale.

Except for local situations like this, prices of new and resale homes will keep going up. Part of the reason, of course, is inflation. New construction becomes more costly every month, due to rising material and labor costs. The result is increasing prices of new homes. Sellers of used homes then find their homes in greater demand, so they can get higher prices.

Another factor is rising demand for housing due to increased number of family formations. Part of this demand comes from more people living in smaller living units, such as single people and divorced people. Another portion of this demand comes from the rising number of young, first-time home buyers who are reaching the home-buying ages of twenty-five to thirty-five.

The number of these first timers will increase about 10,000,000 in the 1980s over the number of potential first-home buyers in this age group in the 1970s. To satisfy this demand, we need about 2,000,000 new homes each year, but we are building far less than this number. The result is and will continue to be rising home prices even if we have a recession.

THE BEST INFLATION HEDGE OF ALL

Q. I am disgusted with the way our economy is being run. When I put my money in the bank, they only pay me 5.5 percent on a passbook account. If I had $10,000 I'd put it into Treasury Bills. But even those higher-yielding T-Bills are a rip-off when you consider that inflation is at about the same rate those bills pay. I used to invest in the stock market until I discovered it really is the "world's biggest casino" as you often say. As I am sixty-eight and too old to buy real estate, where should I put my money? Where is the best place for an old man like me to invest to keep ahead of inflation?—*Byron A.*

A. I could not have explained the dilemma elderly people face better than you did. Everything you said is correct. Savings accounts are losers today. It is best to keep only money for emergencies there. Keeping idle money in a savings account today is very costly. Even putting money in the higher-paying money market funds is not profitable because they usually yield about the same as T-Bills (but without tying up your cash for long time periods).

You knew I would suggest buying good income property, such as rental houses, apartments (in non-rent-control areas), offices, or stores. If you cannot manage such property, hire professional management. I know many active real estate investors, much older than you, who are profiting from their properties far more than they could earn any other place.

Do not ever say you are too old to invest in good real estate. If other people, older than you, can succeed in property investing, you can too.

NO INFLATION PROTECTION IF YOU DO NOT INVEST IN REAL PROPERTY

Q. I am 64, one year away from retirement, and have about $20,000 excess funds to invest. I own my home free and clear and am a widow. My son suggests I invest my $20,000 in several second mortgages. What do you think?—*Laura M.*

A. I think you should first decide what your investment goals are. Income? Inflation protection? Pride of ownership? Tax shelter? Leaving a big estate to your heirs?

All of these above can be accomplished in real estate. But usually not at the same time in just one investment. If you invest in second mortgages, for example, you will probably maximize your income yield. That is why so many retirees invest in second mortgages. But there is no inflation protection and no tax shelter for the excellent interest earnings of second mortgages.

If you buy a small income property, however, it will probably appreciate in market value at least as fast as the inflation rate. But such property will not give you immediate cash income equal to what you can earn on second mortgage investments.

To help decide which form of real estate investment is best for you, consult a real estate counselor. If you do not know such a person, you can find one through your local board of realtors. For a reasonable fee, you will be objectively counseled and guided into the best real estate investment for your circumstances.

2.
The Importance of Understanding Real Estate's Tax Benefits

Never buy real estate for the tax benefits alone. That is the first message of this chapter. The second point is: maximize the tax advantages of real estate ownership by understanding tax angles that further enhance ownership benefits.

In other words, real estate's inherent advantages are increased by the tax incentives of ownership. But if you own a lousy piece of property, its tax advantages will not make it into a great investment.

Many so-called real estate investors have gone wrong buying real estate just for its tax advantages. This is the way most limited partnership syndications are sold, often by stockbrokers who know little or nothing about real estate. The promoters of syndications know that 98 percent of the limited partner investors could care less about the property—all they want is the income tax savings resulting from ownership.

But tax savings alone are never a sound reason to buy real estate. That motivation can lead to losses if the property is not inherently good.

Truly professional realty investors buy property first for its basic benefits, such as investment safety and potential for increased market value. Secondarily, they buy for the bonus income tax savings.

An example will illustrate how to combine real estate's inherent advantages with its bonus income tax savings advantages.

Several years ago I bought a three-bedroom rental house in San Mateo, California, for $103,000. Today that house is worth at least $150,000, probably more. Why has it proven to be a sound investment? There are several reasons.

First, it is in a good neighborhood not far from a freeway, a bus line, and shopping. Second, the house is in basically sound condition, although it needed about $1,500 of painting and fixing up to get it in presentable rental condition. Third, much of that home's increase in market value is due to inflation. If inflation had not been 15 percent in 1980, that home probably would have gone up in market value only about 5 percent instead of over 17 percent.

Real estate insiders understand these concepts. But there is another one which is even more important. It is leverage. Leverage means borrowing other people's money (OPM) to make more money.

That house was purchased for $20,000 cash down payment—not especially high leverage, rather conservative in fact. But its $47,000 value increase is a 46 percent annual return on the $20,000 investment. The nice thing is that "profit" is not taxable until the house is eventually sold. Better yet, it will probably be traded so the profit tax can be deferred indefinitely. More about tax-deferred exchanges in Chapter 10.

To summarize, this basically good property offered not just a substantial increase in market value each year, but it also produced 46 percent annual return on the $20,000 invested dollars. In addition, last year I refinanced it and netted about $24,000 tax-free from the new loan.

THE BONUS ADVANTAGE OF REAL ESTATE INVESTING

But the bonus advantage of investing in this property is its income tax savings. That is right. In addition to the return on invested dollars from appreciation in market value, income tax savings add even more yield.

Here is a quick summary of how the income tax savings on that house work. These tax benefits will be discussed in greater detail in Chapter 4.

First, the $103,000 purchase price must be allocated between the nondepreciable land value and the depreciable building value. If a significant portion of the purchase price was for acquisition of personal property, such as furniture or appliances, a three-way allocation is necessary to include the personalty. Most owners use the local tax assessor's land-to-building ratio shown on the property tax bill for making this allocation, but there are other ways to make the allocation.

Let us suppose this allocation comes out $3,000 for personal property, $20,000 for land value, and $80,000 for building value. It is up to the taxpayer to make the allocation, using any rational method such as the tax assessor's bill. Some taxpayers hire a professional appraiser, but this usually is not necessary. Other investors use their fire insurance agent's replacement cost estimate, allocating the balance to land value.

Of course, do not use the tax assessor's land-to-building ratio if it does not fairly reflect the true valuations. For example, if the ratio was 60 percent for land value and 40 percent for building value, the owner might get an independent appraisal that, hopefully, will show a more favorable allocation.

The higher the allocation to the value of the depreciable building and to the depreciable personal property the better. Taxpayers seek to minimize the allocation to the land value because, since land never wears out, it is not depreciable and yields no income tax savings.

Second, these allocated values for the depreciable building and any personal property must be depreciated over their estimated remaining useful economic lives.

The 1984 Tax Act set the useful life for depreciable buildings "placed in service" after March 15, 1984, at eighteen years, except manufactured housing (pre-fabs), which can be depreciated over ten years. Buildings placed in service between January 1, 1981, and March 14, 1984, have a fifteen-year depreciation schedule. No longer will taxpayers have to argue with IRS auditors about their buildings' depreciable useful life.

WHAT IS DEPRECIATION?

Depreciation is strictly a bookkeeping or paper-entry tax deduction allowance for wear, tear, and obsolescence. It is purely an estimate. In most cases, while the building and personal property are theoretically wearing out, the land value is actually going up. The end result is the owner's market value for his property is rising while his book value for income tax purposes is dropping. Illogical as this seems, the tax laws require taxpayers to depreciate their buildings owned for investment or for use in their trade or business. Isn't Uncle Sam wonderful?

HOW DEPRECIATION DEDUCTIONS SAVE
INCOME TAX DOLLARS

The 1981 Economic Recovery Tax Act really should have been called the real estate investor's tax bonanza law. The reason is it cut to just fifteen years the depreciable useful life for commercial and residential rental buildings acquired between January 1, 1981, and March 15, 1984. However, the old twenty, thirty, forty and sometimes longer useful lives still apply to buildings acquired before 1981.

In addition to reducing depreciable useful life to fifteen years for most buildings, the 1981 Tax Act added a new category of 175 percent accelerated depreciation. This means that if a taxpayer elects to do so, he can take an extra 75 percent depreciation deduction beyond the normal annual straight-line depreciation deduction. The 1984 Tax Act lengthened the depreciation schedule from fifteen to eighteen years, not a major change.

For example, suppose you buy a $100,000 investment property and allocate $80,000 of its purchase price to the depreciable building. Using the straight-line depreciation method yields an annual $4,444 ($80,000 divided by eighteen years) depreciation deduction for the next eighteen years. But if you elect the new 175 percent rapid depreciation method instead, during the first twelve months of ownership you can deduct $7,200 depreciation. This amount is determined from the official IRS 175 percent accelerated depreciation chart found in Chapter 4 (where depreciation is explained more completely) on page 86.

If the owner of the building in this example is in a 30 percent income tax bracket, the $4,444 straight-line depreciation deduction saves him about $1,333 of income taxes; a 50 percent tax bracket taxpayer will save about $2,222.

But if the taxpayer elects the 175 percent accelerated depreciation method (also known as "Accelerated Cost Recovery System" or ACRS), if he is in a 30 percent income tax bracket the tax dollar savings will be about $2,160. A 50 percent tax bracket investor will save approximately $3,600 of income taxes he will not have to pay to Uncle Sam.

WATCH OUT FOR NEW DEPRECIATION "RECAPTURE" RULES

Needless to say, most taxpayers will elect the 175 percent rapid depreciation method because of the maximum income tax dollar savings. However, when a property that has been depreciated using this 175 percent rapid method is sold, special "recapture" rules apply.

This means that Uncle Sam, at the time of sale, wants to tax the accelerated depreciation deducted. The rules are as follows:

1. If the property is used for residential rentals, at the time of sale the difference between the accelerated depreciation deducted and the straight line depreciation that could have been deducted is taxed as ordinary income. To illustrate, if you deducted $20,000 of accelerated depreciation during ownership and $15,000 would have been allowed at straight line rates, the $5,000 difference will be taxed as ordinary income at the time of sale. Since you had the use of the tax dollars saved, however, this result really is not so bad.

2. If the property is commercial or industrial, and accelerated depreciation deductions were claimed during ownership, *all* depreciation deducted is recaptured at the time of sale and taxed as ordinary income. For most taxpayers, this means they should avoid the 175 percent rapid depreciation of commercial buildings.

NEGATIVE CASH FLOW IS NOT A TAX BENEFIT

A big problem with investment properties today is that rents have not kept pace with inflation. The result is many such properties do not produce enough rent to pay the mortgage interest, property taxes, and maintenance costs.

Some owners think that negative cash flow really is not bad because it saves them from paying income taxes to Uncle Sam. These owners reason that it is better to pay out cash from their pocket to meet negative cash flow than it is to pay Uncle Sam income tax dollars which are gone forever.

But what good does it do to pay out one dollar to get a one dollar income tax deduction that may save only twenty cents, thirty cents, or even fifty cents in income tax dollars? The answer is it does not do any good *unless* the property is appreciating more in market value than the negative cash flow is costing the owner.

For example, the $103,000 house discussed in this chapter has a negative cash flow of about $200 per month. Negative cash flow, of course, does not include the paper depreciation tax deduction. Yet the house is going up in value at least $400 per month. Clearly, it pays to have a $200 per month negative cash flow to earn $200 net monthly appreciation in market value, plus the income tax shelter savings.

Many prospective investors shy away from negative cash flow properties. Such acquisitions should be avoided only if (1) the property is not reasonably expected to appreciate in market value at least as much per month as the negative cash flow costs and/or (2) the owner cannot afford to pay out the monthly negative cash flow dollars.

Of course, the way to invest in potentially negative cash flow properties is to structure the purchase on terms which avoid any monthly deficit. This can be done with creative finance techniques. An example would be getting the seller to carry back a purchase-money second mortgage that provides for the payments to be added to the principal amount, with the total amount due in perhaps ten years (when the property's first mortgage can be refinanced to pay off the second mortgage).

Negative cash flow is definitely not a tax benefit of owning a deficit property. But if that cash loss enables the taxpayer to earn more than the negative cash flow costs, assuming the owner can afford to make the negative payments, then it is an ownership benefit that permits the taxpayer to take advantage of the property's other attributes.

To summarize, do not be afraid of negative cash flow. But accept it only if you can afford the deficit and the property is appreciating in value more than the negative cash flow costs in cold, hard cash.

A simple calculation will show when this occurs. First, multiply the monthly negative cash flow by twelve. Second, estimate the annual market value appreciation for the property plus any appreciation in value that will be created by new capital improvements (such as a room addition) exceeding the cost of these improvements. If the negative cash flow is less than the annual estimated increase in the property's value, it is probably a good investment property.

A WORD ABOUT THE BENEFITS OF OWNING YOUR HOUSE OR CONDOMINIUM HOME

Recently, I sold a house to two of my tenants for nothing down. Their monthly payments to me are about $420 per month higher than it cost them to rent that same house. They said to me that their primary reason for wanting to buy and pay these high amounts was "We're tired of paying Uncle Sam and would rather take the tax deductions instead."

They were buying for the wrong reason. Not wanting to get into an argument, I did not explain that it really does not do any good taxwise to pay out one dollar for mortgage interest or property taxes to get a one dollar itemized income tax deduction that may save twenty cents, thirty cents, or even fifty cents in income taxes, depending on the taxpayer's income tax bracket.

My tenants did not realize it, but they should be buying because that property promises to be an excellent inflation hedge. It has appreciated at least 10 percent per year, usually more, in the twelve years that I owned it. There is no reason to believe that will not continue in the future. The real reason those tenants should buy, and the reason I let them buy, is inflation protection, not income tax deductions.

In other words, never buy real estate just for the tax deductions. Buy only because you expect the property to hold its value safely and to probably appreciate in value. In a nutshell, that is why smart real estate investors buy property. The tax benefits are just an additional bonus for owning real estate.

QUESTIONS AND ANSWERS

WHAT ARE THE BEST REAL ESTATE TAX SHELTERS?

Q. Please explain how realty tax shelters work and what are the best real estate tax shelters? I heard that apartments used to be best but that now commercial buildings offer the biggest tax loopholes. Please explain. —*Meri T.*

A. A "tax shelter" means the taxpayer gets a bigger income tax deduction than what he had to pay out in cash. In other words, a tax shelter "shelters" ordinary income from being taxable.

But please do not confuse a tax shelter with an itemized income tax deduction. For example, your home mortgage interest is a dollar for dollar itemized income tax deduction. If you pay $1,000 in mortgage interest, you get a $1,000 itemized interest tax deduction. Such a deduction is *not* a "tax shelter" because you have to pay out one dollar for every one dollar of such a tax deduction.

But a tax shelter means you get more than one dollar of tax deductions for each one dollar you pay out.

Suppose you own a small rental property which earns $10,000 annual gross rents and has $4,000 of operating expenses. If annual mortgage interest is $5,000, you would have $1,000 of net income. Mortgage principal amortization payments, incidentally, are not tax deductible as is interest.

Owners of income-producing buildings get an annual bookkeeping tax deduction allowance for wear, tear, and obsolescence. This is a noncash tax deduction expense called depreciation.

For example, if your building is entitled to an annual $4,000 annual depreciation tax deduction (which, remember, requires no actual cash payment), your building would show a $3,000 "tax loss" or "paper loss" ($1,000 net income minus $4,000 depreciation deduction).

This $3,000 paper or tax loss can shelter $3,000 of your other ordinary income as job salary which would otherwise be taxable. In other words, the $3,000 tax or paper loss shelters $3,000 of your ordinary income from taxation. If you own enough depreciable property, all your income will be tax-sheltered.

Today's best real estate tax shelters are probably commercial buildings which have not been remodeled for at least thirty years. The reason is costs of renovating such buildings qualify for the 15 percent investment tax credit in addition to the normal depreciation deductions. Larger tax credits are available for older buildings. Ask your tax adviser for details.

HOW INFLATION AND TAX DEDUCTIONS MAKE HOME OWNERSHIP COST-FREE

Q. We've been putting off buying our first home for over a year now in hopes that mortgage interest rates will come down. But it seems prices continue to go up, even though we understand mortgage interest rates might drop. How soon do you think mortgage interest rates will drop? —*Corry M.*

A. I do not think we will see 10 percent interest rate home loans for a very long time, perhaps never. The reasons include inflation and the ever-rising cost of funds for mortgage lenders.

When you consider the income tax savings from home ownership, plus the likely appreciation in market value of good homes, even if you pay 12 percent or more interest on a home loan, your home will cost you little or nothing in net expense.

For example, suppose you buy a $100,000 home with $10,000 cash down payment and get a $90,000 mortgage at 12 percent interest. If you are in a 30 percent income tax bracket, after the itemized deduction for mortgage interest, that loan will cost you only about 8.4 percent (30 percent of 12 percent is 3.6 percent; 13 percent minus 3.6 percent is 8.4 percent). Since most homes appreciate in value each year, that home mortgage is virtually cost-free in the long run. Buy now before home prices go higher.

HOW TO COMPUTE TAX BENEFITS OF BUYING YOUR HOME

Q. Several times you've mentioned the tax benefits of buying a home. Please explain more. I know mortgage interest and property taxes are deductible. But I would like to know how much this saves me in actual tax dollars.—*Peter M.*

A. Your question gives me an opportunity to show how to evaluate a contemplated home purchase to compute your true after-tax housing cost.

For illustration, let us assume you are buying a $100,000 home with a $20,000 cash down payment and a $80,000 mortgage at 12 percent annual interest for 30 years. I am also going to assume the annual property taxes are $1,000 and that you are in a 30 percent combined federal and state income tax bracket.

1. Your monthly mortgage payment on the $80,000 loan will be $822.90 of which about 99.6 percent or $819.61 per month will be first-year, tax-deductible interest. The monthly property tax will be $83.33 ($1,000 divided by 12 months).

   So your total monthly mortgage and property tax payments are $906.23 ($822.90 plus $83.33) of which $902.94 ($819.61 plus $83.33) are itemized income tax deductions. If you are in a 30 percent income tax bracket these deductions save about $270.88 (30 percent of $902.94) per month in income tax dollars, thus reducing your net monthly housing cost to approximately $635.35 ($906.23 minus $270.88).

2. Each month you will be paying off your mortgage balance slightly. In the first year, this payoff only averages about $3.29 per month, but the monthly principal payment gradually increases so the loan will be paid off in thirty years. This principal payoff is like a forced savings account in which you gradually build equity. $635.35 minus $3.29 is $632.06 which is your net housing cost after income tax savings and equity buildup.

3. Next, estimate your home's probable appreciation in market value.

As you know, homes are considered an outstanding inflation hedge because they usually appreciate in market value at least at the inflation rate.

Let us be conservative and presume your home will go up in market value only 5 percent per year on the average.

Five percent of $100,000 is $5,000 value appreciation per year. That is $416.66 per month. Subtracting $416.66 per month from $632.06 gives an estimated net housing cost (after income tax savings, mortgage equity payoff, and market value appreciation) of $215.40. Of course, there will be nontax consequence expenses for maintenance and fire insurance to consider too, perhaps $200 or so per month.

But after calculating your income tax dollar savings, the mortgage equity buildup, market value appreciation of the home, and upkeep costs, it is usually more profitable to own your home than rent, even at today's high mortgage interest rates.

HOW TO COMPUTE TAX ON PROPERTY SALE PROFIT

Q. We just closed the sale of our home. The buyer, a veteran, got a new VA mortgage for which we had to pay the mortgage company a 4 percent loan fee. Our sale price was $93,000. We also paid a $5,500 real estate sales commission. How do we compute our sale profit? Our cost was about $22,000 for the house, but we have added about $12,000 of improvements such as landscaping, new roof, new garage, and kitchen remodeling.—*Conners M.*

A. Congratulations on your all-cash sale which is difficult to achieve in today's home sale market. Most sellers have to help finance their buyer's purchase.

That 4 percent VA loan fee of $3,720 to get a cash sale was expensive, but probably worthwhile if you have a good use for the money received.

Your profit is the difference between the "adjusted sales price" and the "adjusted cost basis" of your home.

"Adjusted sales price" means the home's gross sales price minus selling expenses. Your $5,500 real estate sales commission and the $3,720 loan fee paid for the buyer's VA mortgage appear to be your only selling expenses. So $83,780 ($93,000 minus $5,500 and $3,720) is your adjusted sales price.

"Adjusted cost basis" is your purchase price (including closing costs that were not tax deductible at the time of purchase), plus capital improvements added during ownership, minus any depreciation and casualty loss tax deductions taken during ownership. So your adjusted cost basis is $22,000 plus $12,000, a total of $34,000.

Your profit is $83,780 minus $34,000 which is $49,780, which qualifies as a long-term capital gain. That means only 40 percent of $49,780 ($19,912) is taxable. The other 60 percent ($29,868) is tax-free. The $19,912 taxable portion is added to your other ordinary taxable income and taxed at regular income tax rates. For example, if you are in a 40 percent tax bracket, the tax on $19,912 would be $7,965. That is only about 16 percent of your total $49,780 sales profit.

Of course, if you are eligible for one of the special home sale tax rules, then you can avoid taxation on your profit. If you buy a more expensive replacement principal residence within twenty-four months before or after the sale you must defer paying your profit tax. Or, if you are fifty-five or older and qualify for the $125,000 home sale tax exemption, you may wish to use your once-in-a-lifetime tax-free benefit. Ask your tax adviser for details.

DOES UNCLE SAM REALLY SUBSIDIZE HOME BUYERS?

Q. You've said that Uncle Sam subsidizes home buyers in the form of income tax savings due to itemized deductions for mortgage interest and property taxes. This isn't entirely correct as any single person can take a $2,300 standard deduction and married couples get a $3,400 zero bracket tax deduction. So taxpayers who buy a home and pay less than $2,300 or $3,400 for their itemized deductions don't get any extra tax benefit.— *Michael M.*

A. You are partly correct. However, it is pretty hard to buy a home today and pay less than $2,300 to $3,400 per year total for property tax and mortgage interest. Since most homeowners pay more than these amounts, it pays them to itemize their income tax deductions.

For example, suppose you are in a 30 percent income tax bracket and you are buying a home with a 30-year mortgage for $50,000 at 12 percent interest. The itemized interest deduction will be about $5,976 per year, resulting in income tax dollar savings of about $1,792.

Another way to look at it is the true interest rate is only about 8.4 percent (12 percent multiplied by 30 percent is 3.6 percent; 12 percent minus 3.6 percent is 8.4 percent).

DO NOT CANCEL PROFITABLE SALE JUST TO AVOID TAX

Q. Six months ago I contracted to sell my apartment house which I've owned for many years. The sale will yield me over $200,000 profit. I wanted a long closing time, so I could find a larger property to trade up to, so I could defer my profit tax. But I haven't been able to find a suitable property to exchange up to. What is the best way to get out of this sale so I won't have to pay that big profit tax?—*Reid M.*

A. Do not cancel your profitable sale just to avoid paying a little tax to

Uncle Sam. While it would be nice to defer your profit tax by means of a "like kind" tax-deferred exchange, since you cannot find a suitable property to exchange for, paying the profit tax will not be so bad.

As you may know, on November 1, 1978, the long-term capital gains tax rates were reduced. The 1978 reduction means only 40 percent of your long-term capital gain is taxable; the other 60 percent escapes tax. The result puts the long-term capital gain tax rate in the range of 5.6 percent minimum to 20 percent maximum, depending on your income tax bracket.

Do not fear paying a little tax. It is better than being sued by the buyer if you fail to deliver the apartment house as agreed in the sales contract. P.S. Read Chapter 10 to learn about new Starker "delayed" tax-deferred exchanges.

THE INHERITANCE TAX LOOPHOLE

Q. My mother is very ill and is expected to die shortly. I am her sole heir. But it worries me if I inherit all her properties, which she has owned for many, many years. During the Great Depression she bought many properties for nothing down and now they are worth a fortune. What worries me is the tax I fear I'll owe on these properties. Is there any way to avoid the capital gain tax?—*Richard W.*

A. Your mother's estate will pay the estate tax on the value of all her estate assets, minus the generous estate tax exemptions. Estate tax is levied by the federal government on the net assets left by decedents.

When you receive the properties, however, you will not owe any estate or capital gain tax. The reason is the estate, not you, pays any federal estate tax due. If necessary, the estate's executor can sell some of your mother's properties to raise cash to pay the estate tax.

However, you may owe state inheritance tax on the value of the assets you inherit. The inheritance tax rates vary widely by state and the blood relationship of the decedent to the heir.

Thankfully, there is a big tax loophole which saves capital gain tax on inherited property. Even though your mother has a very low-cost basis for her properties, your inherited basis will be the value of the properties on the day of your mother's death. In other words, the difference between her low-cost basis and the market value on the date of death completely escapes capital gain tax. Congress made this tax rule permanent in the 1980 Oil Windfall Profits Tax Act.

DO NOT FORGET UNCLE SAM, YOUR PARTNER, WHEN BUYING A HOME

Q. Home buying is looking more and more impossible for us, and it's getting my wife down. We live in an apartment with our two kids. But my wife is expecting our third, so we've got to find a home soon. Do you think we should wait until interest rates come down? A few weeks ago a realtor found us a home we could buy, but the monthly payment would have been $745.95 at 10 percent interest (the seller would finance the sale). Property taxes are extra. I have a good job, earning over $2,000 per month. What should we do?—*Keith Y.*

A. Buy that home. Finding a low 10 percent interest rate mortgage is not easy in today's market. You passed up a "good deal" without knowing it.

While $745.95 per month for the mortgage payment seems high, it really is not when you consider your silent partner, Uncle Sam, who wants to help you. Your interest is tax deductible, of course. So are your property taxes.

In the early years of the mortgage, most of your payments go toward tax-deductible interest. For example, if you are in a 30 percent income tax bracket, you will save about $223 per month in income tax dollars for that $745.95 monthly mortgage payment. This reduces your after-tax mortgage interest cost to about $523. The same tax savings apply to your property tax payment too.

Instead of wasting money on rent, you will be building equity in a home. And I will bet your family will be much happier with more space and the security of building equity instead of a pile of worthless rent receipts.

3.

How to Get the Greatest Income Tax Savings from Your Home

The first real estate purchase for most taxpayers is their home. A home may be a single-family house, a condominium or cooperative apartment, a mobile home, or even a houseboat. To qualify for home ownership income tax benefits, the land underneath the residence need not be owned. It can be leased. The only criteria for eligibility for the major tax savings of home ownership is that the owned residence be the taxpayer's principal residence.

This chapter is divided into two major sections. The first deals with the tax benefits of owning a home. The second discusses the tax savings available when selling a home.

PART 1   TAX BENEFITS WHILE YOU OWN YOUR HOME

Home ownership can be a source of major income tax benefits. Some of these deductions are well-known to most taxpayers. Others are known only to a few tax-wise homeowners. Smart homeowners take advantage of these tax benefits if circumstances qualify. Some tax deductions, such as the casualty loss deduction, apply only in very special situations. But wise homeowners need to know about such conditions so they can recognize a tax-saving opportunity if and when it occurs.

TAX SAVINGS FOR LOAN INTEREST PAID

The general rule for itemized deductions is it is tax deductible if the interest was paid in connection with an indebtedness or forbearance. Of course, interest paid on your home's mortgage (or other obligation secured by the residence, such as a deed of trust, contract for deed, installment sale contract, land contract, or long-term lease-option) is a major income tax deduction if the taxpayer itemizes personal deductions on Schedule A of IRS Form 1040.

These rules apply to all loans secured by real property, such as first and second mortgages, improvement loans, deeds of trust, and land contracts. Of course, the taxpayer cannot itemize the interest deductions if he or she uses the standard deduction available to all taxpayers ($2,300 for single taxpayers and $3,400 for married taxpayers filing joint returns for tax years ending in 1979 and thereafter).

With the high cost of interest, few homeowners come out better using the standard deduction. Therefore, most homeowners elect to itemize their deductions if their total itemized deductions exceed the $2,300 or $3,400 standard nonitemized deductions.

However, some taxpayers who use part of their home for business purposes (discussed later) elect to take the standard nonitemized deduction, but they can still deduct the business use allocation of their home interest expenses as a business cost on Schedule C or E of their income tax returns.

A word of caution is in order if the purpose of the borrowing, secured by your residence, is for business purposes. Examples would include refinancing your home mortgage to use the cash to buy or start a business. Then the mortgage interest, even though the security for the loan is your personal residence, qualifies as a business expense rather than a personal itemized tax deduction. Such a business expense interest deduction should be listed on Schedule C or E and subtracted from the gross income of the business.

In such a situation, the interest is fully deductible as a business expense even if you elect to not itemize your personal income tax deductions and take the standard $2,300 or $3,400 deduction instead. It is the *use* of the borrowed money, not the specific property which secures the debt, that determines whether the interest is a personal itemized deduction or a business expense deduction.

MORTGAGE LOAN INTEREST DEDUCTIBILITY

If you are on the cash basis of reporting your taxable income, as most taxpayers are, mortgage loan interest is deductible in the tax year paid. Repayments of the loan's principal amount, of course, are not tax deductions. Most mortgage lenders provide their borrowers with an annual allocation of payments to nondeductible principal and to deductible interest.

PREPAID INTEREST

Until 1967, a cash-basis taxpayer could deduct, in the year of payment, all interest paid in advance of its due date. But in 1968, in response to growing abuse of the prepaid interest deductions, IRS Revenue Ruling 68–643 said prepaid interest deductions greater than for the current tax year, plus up to twelve months in advance, would be disallowed as "material distortions of income."

In 1976, the Tax Reform Act eliminated even this twelve-month advance prepaid interest allowance. Now only interest paid during the current year, and earned by the lender for the current tax year, is deductible. In other words, *no more prepaid interest deductions are allowed.* Of course, interest can be paid in advance, but such a prepayment is not allowed as an income tax deduction until the tax year when the lender earns the interest (even if the lender received the interest in the year before it was earned).

TAX DEDUCTIONS FOR "LOAN FEES," "POINTS," AND "LOAN-PROCESSING FEES"

Most savings and loan associations, banks, and mortgage brokers making home loans charge "points" or a "loan fee" for granting a mortgage. No matter what the name, if the charge is for use or forbearance of money, it is interest and is tax deductible. If the loan is secured by your personal residence, and the purpose is to buy or improve the home, such a loan fee is fully tax deductible as interest in the year paid.

But loan fees paid to obtain a loan on any other property, such as land, apartments, or commercial property, must now be amortized (deducted) over the life of the loan. The 1976 Tax Reform Act made this important law change. This means, for example, if you pay a $1,000 loan fee to obtain a 30-year mortgage on your commercial building, for the next 30 years you will have a $33.33 annual interest expense deduction for that loan fee. If the property is sold before the loan fee is fully amortized, the unamortized portion is capitalized and added to the book value basis of the property. Remember, however, the amortization of loan fees only applies to property other than your personal residence.

However, VA loan points or processing fees, whether paid by the home buyer or seller, are "service charges" and are *not* tax deductible as interest (Revenue Rulings 67–297 and 68–650). Such fees, which are paid by the home seller, are a selling cost that should be subtracted from the home's gross sales price. By law, the buyer is limited to paying a maximum one point VA "loan-processing fee" (which is *not* tax deductible as interest). Of course, the buyer can deduct the interest portion of his monthly payments on his VA mortgage.

To summarize, loan fees or points (one point equals one percent of the amount borrowed) are tax deductible as interest in full in the year paid if the purpose of the loan was to buy or improve your personal residence and if it is not a VA home mortgage. Loan fees paid to obtain a loan secured by any other type of property, or by your personal residence if the purpose was not to buy or improve it, must be amortized (deducted) over the life of the loan, even though the entire loan fee was paid in the year the loan was obtained. VA loan fees paid by the seller qualify as sales costs to be subtracted from the home's gross sales price. Such fees are never deductible as interest by either seller or buyer.

TAX SAVINGS FOR LOAN PREPAYMENT FEES AND PENALTIES

If you prepay your mortgage, whether secured by your home or other property, any prepayment fee or penalty is tax deductible in full in the tax year in which it is paid to the lender.

HOME IMPROVEMENT LOAN INTEREST

The cost of home repairs and maintenance, of course, is not tax deductible for your personal residence (unless it qualifies as a business expense if you use part of your home for an office or shop or for rental to tenants). The cost of capital improvements, such as room additions and remodeling, should be added to your home's purchase cost book value. Save the receipts forever.

But interest paid on a loan used to pay for home improvements is tax deductible in the year the interest is paid. If the improvement loan is of the discount type (rather than simple interest), the next paragraph on discount loan interest explains how to compute your interest deduction.

DISCOUNT LOAN INTEREST

FHA loans, home improvement loans, and some bank mortgages are of the discount type. This means interest is charged in advance at the time the loan is granted. Such interest is "discounted" or subtracted from the amount of funds actually given to the borrower.

EXAMPLE: Jim took out a three-year, $5,000 home improvement loan at 5 percent discounted interest (the true annual interest rate is about 10 percent) to pay for kitchen remodeling in his home. He signed a promissory note for $5,750 payable in 36 monthly payments. He receives $5,000 cash to pay for the improvements. $750 is his total interest cost, discounted in advance. The interest is $\frac{1}{36}$ or $20.83 each payment. If Jim made seven loan payments in this year, he would deduct on his Schedule A $145.81 or 7 times $20.83 as itemized interest.

GROUND RENT

A little-known income tax deduction is ground rent for homes located on leased land. Annual or periodic payments on redeemable ground rents may be deductible as interest. To qualify, the lessee-homeowner must have a lease of at least fifteen years with the right to eventually buy the lessor's ownership interest in the land by paying an agreed sum.

The lessor's ground lease is a security interest to secure the rental payments due to him, much like a mortgage is security for future payments. For more details, see Internal Revenue Code Sections 163C and 1055.

If the ground rent is for the mere use of the land, such as farm land rented to a farmer, with no eventual right to buy the land, such a lease does *not* include a redeemable ground rent. There is no interest deduction in such a situation (although there may be a business expense deduction if the land is used for business purposes). Of course, principal payments to buy redeemable ground rent property for a home are not tax deductible.

PENALTIES AND INTEREST ON LATE PROPERTY TAX PAYMENTS

Penalties for late payment of property taxes are *not* tax deductible. However, interest paid on late property tax payments qualify as itemized interest deductions.

TAX SAVINGS FOR REAL ESTATE PROPERTY TAX PAYMENTS

As a general rule, state and local real estate taxes paid on your personal residence are deductible as itemized income tax deductions. Property taxes are deductible in the year they are actually paid to the local tax collector. The date the tax accrues is immaterial to cash basis taxpayers.

The date of the actual payment determines the tax year of the deduction. Payments to a collection agent, such as a bank impound escrow account, are *not* deductible until the tax year such property taxes are remitted to the tax collector.

NO LIMIT ON PROPERTY TAX PREPAYMENTS

Property taxes may be prepaid to the tax collector without limit and fully deducted on your income tax returns in the year paid. However, most tax collectors will not accept advance property tax payments beyond the current property tax fiscal year.

PROPERTY TAX BUSINESS DEDUCTIONS

If part of your residence is used for business purposes, such as an office or shop, or for rental to tenants, then a proportionate share of the real estate taxes paid are deductible as personal itemized deductions on Schedule A. The balance qualifies as a business expense.

Although the entire amount of the property tax is deductible, it must be apportioned between the personal and business use. Such a taxpayer can use the standard deduction (and not itemize his personal tax deductions) and still deduct the business portion of his real estate taxes.

EXAMPLE: Martin paid $600 for annual property taxes on his home. He uses ⅓ of his home for his insurance sales business. So he can deduct $200 of his property tax on his business tax return (Schedule C), even if he elects not to itemize his personal income tax deductions on Schedule A and uses the standard deduction instead.

REAL ESTATE TAXES PAID
IN THE YEAR OF PROPERTY SALE

When real estate is sold, unless the parties agree to the contrary, the property taxes must be prorated between buyer and seller according to the number of days in the property tax fiscal year each owned the property.

EXAMPLE: Albert bought a house from Victor. The transfer was on April 1. Victor had already paid the property tax of $800 which, under local law, pays the property tax for the fiscal year which ends on June 30. The $800 property tax is apportioned $254/365$ to Victor because he owned the property 254 out of 365 days of the property tax fiscal year which runs from July 1 to June 30 in that state. So Victor can deduct $254/365$ (69.6 percent) or $556.80, providing he actually paid all the tax. If he paid part in the previous year, only the part he paid this year is deductible on this year's income tax returns. Albert, the buyer, can deduct the other $243.20 or $91/365$ of the total property tax paid, even though Victor actually paid the money to the tax collector. Tax bills are usually prorated as part of the closing settlement for most property transfers.

Even if the property tax has not yet been paid to the tax collector before title transfers to the buyer, the property tax must be apportioned between buyer and seller at the closing settlement so the seller can deduct his share. IRS Regulation 1.164.6 gives the details.

EXAMPLE: Jane sold her home to Mary on December 1. The property tax in their state is due on January 10. It covers the fiscal tax year from July 1 to June 30. Although the Internal Revenue Code says a cash-basis taxpayer can deduct taxes only for his income tax year in which the property taxes are actually paid to the local tax collector, this is the *only exception* to the rule. Here, Jane can deduct $185/365$ of the property tax (July 1 to December 1), even though the tax was not paid this year. The theory is that Jane "paid" her tax share to Mary, the buyer, at the title transfer closing, and Mary paid the tax collector on January 10.

SPECIAL ASSESSMENT OR BENEFIT TAXES

Taxes assessed against your home for local benefits which will increase the value of your home are *not* tax deductible.

> EXAMPLE: Sidewalk or street paving assessment taxes are capital improvements (nondeductible) and should be added to the cost basis book value of your home. But if all or part of such a special assessment tax is for maintenance of civic improvements, then the tax *is* deductible as a property tax. Or if part of such a special assessment tax is for interest, the interest portion is tax deductible as an interest expense.

TRANSFER AND RECORDING FEES AND TAXES

Many local and state governments impose transfer or recording taxes and fees on the sale of a home or upon the recording of a new mortgage loan against a property. Such taxes are tax deductible only if connected with operation of a trade, business, or income property. So if part of your home is used for business or rented to tenants, then part of your transfer and recording taxes or fees will be deductible.

All transfer taxes and recording fees or taxes should be added to the purchase cost basis or book value of your home. Then, if you are entitled to a depreciation deduction for business use or rental of your home, you will automatically deduct a proportionate share of such transfer and recording taxes and fees. If you are not entitled to such a depreciation deduction, the transfer fees and taxes will remain part of the cost basis of your home.

If the home seller paid the transfer tax, he or she should subtract that tax as a sales expense from the gross sales price of the home. But transfer taxes paid by home buyers must be capitalized and added to the cost basis of the home.

EFFECT OF LIEN DATES OR PERSONAL
LIABILITY PROPERTY TAX DATES

In some states, property taxes become a lien against real estate on a certain date (usually called the lien date) each year. In other states, realty taxes become a personal liability against the property owner as of a specified date.

For cash-basis taxpayers, unless the property tax is actually paid on the lien date, *these lien dates are irrelevant* and have no effect on the income tax deductibility of the property tax.

The important rule is to deduct the property tax in the income tax year when it is actually paid to the tax collector. This rule applies even if the property tax is paid after it became due. No payment, no income tax deduction!

The *one exception* to this rule, discussed earlier, occurs when the property is sold during the year but before the property tax is paid to the tax collector. Of course, accrual-basis taxpayers deduct property tax in the year the liability accrues even if it has not yet been remitted to the tax collector.

TAX SAVINGS FOR BUSINESS USE OF YOUR HOME

To qualify for income tax deduction of normally nondeductible home operating expenses, such as repairs, fire insurance premium, heating, garbage, and other expenses, part of the residence must be used for business purposes. Qualified renters can deduct part of their rent if they use a portion of their apartment for business use. There are several strict tests that must be met to qualify for the business-at-home tax-saving deductions.

THE EXCLUSIVE BUSINESS USE TEST

If you use part of your residence for an office or shop, or if you rent part of your home to tenants, you are entitled to tax deductions for the expenses of operating that business use portion of your residence. This is a legitimate income tax deduction, which, unfortunately, has been abused by some taxpayers. So in recent years the IRS has become overly tough about allowing such deductions. But if you are qualified, use this deduction to maximize your income tax savings from your home business use.

The "exclusive use test" requires that the business portion of your residence be used *only* for business purposes. Part-time use of the same area for business and personal use disqualifies entitlement.

A separate room used only for business, full or part time, clearly qualifies. Use of part of a room for business, however, may qualify. Clearly, use of a chair in your living room in the evenings to read business reports or magazines will not qualify.

EXAMPLE: Margaret has a desk in one corner of her living room from where she manages her properties. These investments produce a major portion of her income. Margaret uses the desk to keep records of rents, purchases, and sales as well as to make busines phone calls. The rest of the living room is used for television viewing, pleasure reading, and entertaining guests. If Margaret's "business area" is used exclusively for business purposes, she can qualify for the home business use tax savings deductions.

EXAMPLE: Susan is an outside sales representative for a cosmetics company. She uses a spare bedroom in her home for storing supplies, writing orders, arranging deliveries, and contacting clients by phone.

She uses the bedroom-office exclusively for an office. Susan concludes this business space occupies one-fifth of her home's square footage. So she deducts one-fifth of household expenses for utilities, insurance, maintenance, mortgage interest, and property taxes as business expenses.

If part of your home is used for both personal (nondeductible) and business (deductible) uses, then allocation of business expenses on the ratio of time used for each purpose is no longer acceptable, according to the 1976 Tax Reform Act.

EXAMPLE: George manages apartment houses. He spends about two hours each morning doing bookkeeping, calling managers, etc., from a desk in his den. The rest of the day the den is used by George and his family for television viewing and reading. Since this area is used for both business and pleasure, George gets a business deduction only for the desk space. Of course, George can also deduct his business telephone cost and any other direct business expenses.

THE BUSINESS LOCATION TEST

If you meet the "exclusive use test," in addition, your residence must be either (1) your principal place of business or (2) a place of business used to meet patients, clients, or customers.

EXAMPLE: Tom is a salesman for ABC Supply Company that furnishes him with a desk at its offices. But Tom frequently entertains customers at his home and sometimes writes up their orders in his home. If Tom meets the exclusive business area test, he can also meet the test of using his home to meet customers there. But he cannot qualify on the basis of his home being his principal place of business since his employer furnishes his desk space.

THE EMPLOYER'S CONVENIENCE TEST

While the two previous tests apply to all taxpayers desiring to claim deductions for home business expenses, an additional test applies to persons who are not self-employed, such as Tom in the example above. If an employee is to claim business deductions for home use, such use must be "for the convenience of the employer."

Frankly, this is a gray area of tax law. In the earlier example involving Susan, the cosmetics sales representative, although she is an employee she can easily meet the home use test if her employer does not furnish her with any desk space or is located in a distant city. But Tom, in the example above, would have a hard time meeting the "employer's convenience test" since the employer furnishes desk space for Tom.

However, there have been several tax court decisions involving school teachers allowing them to claim office at home deductions. These occurred where the teachers were ordered to leave the school after classes because of security problems. In such a situation, the teacher has little alternative to taking student papers and other classroom work home. Of course, such a teacher would have to meet the "exclusive business area test" and the "business location test" too.

WHAT OFFICE-AT-HOME EXPENSES ARE DEDUCTIBLE?

Self-employed persons should report their expenses for a qualified home office or shop on Schedule C of IRS Form 1040. Employees using part of their residence for their employer's convenience use IRS Form 2106 for Employee Business Expenses.

Part of all ordinary residence expenses affecting the "business area" are tax deductible. Examples include a portion of home utilities, insurance, mortgage interest, repairs, and property taxes. In addition, the "business area" can be depreciated.

Depreciation is a noncash bookkeeping estimate of wear, tear, and obsolescence of the "business area." To arrive at a depreciation estimate, your home's cost basis (the lower of original purchase price plus capital improvements added during ownership or market value on the date business use began) must be allocated between nondepreciable land value and building value (partly depreciable). Use the new eighteen-year, 175-percent rapid depreciation for home business use begun after March 15, 1984.

EXAMPLE: Dave paid $40,000 for his house which is now worth $100,000. The $40,000 cost is Dave's basis for depreciation. He estimates the land value cost was $10,000. So he allocates $30,000 to the value of the house and uses an eighteen-year useful life. Dividing $30,000 by 18 years is $1,666 per year. If Dave uses one fourth of home for business, $417 is his annual depreciation deduction.

The IRS constantly revises its rules in the field of home business use because this tax area has, in the past, been abused by taxpayers. Recent IRS proposals, for example, tried to ban home business deductions if the taxpayer has a full-time job and seeks to deduct expenses for a part-time home business. But Congressional opposition to such IRS regulations is so strong the IRS had to back down on this subject.

MOVING EXPENSE TAX DEDUCTIONS SAVINGS

If you bought or sold your personal residence during the tax year, or if you moved from and/or to an apartment, you may be eligible for the generous moving expense tax deduction. Both renters and homeowners are eligible for this often overlooked tax break.

But this tax-saving benefit applies only when the taxpayer changes his job location. If the move is for personal reasons, unconnected with a job site change, the moving expense deduction is not available.

If qualified, taxpayers can claim the moving expense deductions even if their other income tax deductions are not itemized. IRS Form 3903 is the place to claim your eligible moving cost deductions.

ELIGIBILITY FOR MOVING COST DEDUCTIONS

To qualify for moving cost tax savings, both the distance and time tests must be met.

A. The Distance Test

Moving expenses are tax deductible if your new job site is over thirty-five miles further away from your old home than was your former job location.

EXAMPLE: If your old job location was ten miles from your home, your new job location must be at least forty-five miles (ten plus thirty-five) away from your old home to qualify.

B. The Time Test

If the distance test is met, the taxpayer must continue employment in the vicinity of the new job site at least thirty-nine weeks during the twelve months after the move. Self-employed persons must work at their new location at least seventy-eight weeks during the twenty-four months following the move to the new location.

Either husband or wife can qualify for these two tests. If, at the time your tax return is due, you have not met these thirty-nine or seventy-eight week tests, you can either (a) take the moving expense deduction and amend your tax return in the future if you fail to qualify, or (b) file an amended tax return after you meet the test and claim a tax refund at that time.

NO LIMIT ON DIRECT MOVING COSTS

No dollar deduction limit applies to direct moving expenses for (a) transporting the taxpayer and household members from the old home to the new one, (b) moving household goods, and (c) meals and lodging en route. Careful records of these expenses should be kept to document the deductions. Deduction for auto transport costs can be either actual expenses or nine cents per mile en route, plus actual tolls and parking during the move.

A LIMIT ON INDIRECT MOVING COST DEDUCTIONS

Although there is no limit to the amount of direct, actual moving costs which can be tax deductible, there is a $3,000 limit on some indirect moving costs. Examples of expenses in this category include (a) up to thirty days temporary housing at the new job site location, (b) cost of house-hunting trips from the old home to find a new one, and (c) expenses for sale, purchase, or lease of a residence (including attorney fee, title fee, real estate sales commission, and other sales costs). Not over $1,500 is deductible for temporary housing and house-hunting travel.

Even if you defer paying your profit tax on the sale of your old residence (using the "residence replacement rule" of Internal Revenue Code Section 1034, described later in this book) or if you use the "over-55 rule" $125,000 home sale tax exemption of Internal Revenue Code Section 121 (described later in this book), it usually pays to deduct home sale and purchase costs up to the $3,000 limit for indirect moving costs.

The reason is moving expense deductions offset income that is otherwise taxable. But merely subtracting home sale costs, such as real estate sales commission, from the old home's gross sales price will probably not produce as big a tax saving, if any. It is always better to take a tax deduction today rather than one in the future. The reason is that a future tax deduction will be worth less than one today, due to inflation.

EMPLOYER REIMBURSEMENTS FOR MOVING COSTS

Many employees obtain moving cost reimbursements from their employers. Such payments are additions to the employee's gross income, just like wages, and are subject to withholding tax unless corresponding moving expense deductions can be shown. However, active duty United States armed forces personnel do not have their moving expenses, which are paid by the federal government, included in their gross income.

HOW TO CLAIM MOVING COST TAX DEDUCTIONS

Eligible moving costs, both direct and indirect expenses, are subtracted from the taxpayer's gross income, rather than being a less desirable itemized deduction. Full details are available in IRS Publication 521, available free at your local IRS office.

TAX SAVINGS FOR CASUALTY AND THEFT LOSSES

If you itemize your personal tax deductions on Schedule A of IRS Form 1040, you can deduct any property casualty loss (over $100 for nonbusiness casualty losses), minus any insurance recovery. However, beginning in the 1983 tax year, only casualty losses over 10 percent of gross income are deductible.

As mentioned earlier, insurance premiums for home casualty insurance are *not* tax deductible. They are personal living expenses without any income tax significance. But, if part of your insurance premium is allocable to a portion of your residence used for business or rented to tenants, then that portion is of tax significance as a business expense deduction.

WHAT IS A CASUALTY LOSS?

A casualty loss income tax deduction, *not* incurred in your business or involving your tenants (which would be fully tax deductible as a business expense), can be deducted from your taxable income if the event was *sudden, unexpected,* or *unusual.* Those three key words are vital to eligibility for the casualty loss deduction. Losses due to steady deterioration of your property are *not* casualty loss tax deductions.

> EXAMPLES OF DEDUCTIBLE CASUALTY LOSSES: Fire, flood, storm, theft, sonic boom, smoke, land sinking, broken pipes, blast, vandalism, accidents, and freezing.
> EXAMPLES OF NONDEDUCTIBLE LOSSES: Rust, well contamination, termite damage, moth damage, dry rot, carpet beetles, rat infestation, and tree disease damage. The reason these causes are not tax deductible as casualty losses is they are not sudden, unexpected, or unusual.

THE SUDDEN, UNEXPECTED, OR UNUSUAL TEST

To be tax deductible as a casualty loss, the event must be rapid and not normally to be anticipated. The difficulty is usually one of proving the speed of the loss. For example, a sudden attack on trees by insects might be allowed as a casualty loss, but not one that took many months to produce any noticeable damage. An accident, such as an uninsured car hitting your house, would usually be considered a sudden and unexpected event, and thus, it would qualify for the tax deduction.

Termite damage generally is too slow to qualify for casualty loss status. However, there are several tax court decisions approving casualty loss deductions. But in those cases, the facts presented by the taxpayers showed their termites were especially fast working. For example, if you bought your home and got a termite inspection report clearance at that time, and three months later noticed termite damage, that might qualify. But most termites work too slowly to qualify for the casualty loss tax deduction.

HOW TO COMPUTE THE CASUALTY LOSS DEDUCTION

Although most taxpayers will not have a casualty loss each year, when one occurs it pays to know how this tax deduction is calculated. In these days of unexpected events, such as a burglary of your home, the casualty loss tax deduction can at least partially compensate for your loss of any uninsured items. Or if insurance pays for only part of your loss, the other portion can be deducted as a casualty loss.

IRS Form 4684, Casualties and Thefts, should be used to report your casualty loss. This is a favorite audit topic of the IRS, so be prepared to document the casualty loss claims if your tax return is picked for audit.

The deductible casualty loss is computed as follows:

1. The lesser of (a) decrease in value or (b) adjusted cost basis
   of the property $___
2. Minus: Any insurance recovery award $___
3. Minus: $100 per destructive nonbusiness event $___
4. Your tax-deductible casualty loss deduction $___

"Decrease in value of the property," real or personal, means the difference in its fair market value just before the casualty and just after the event. An appraisal may be necessary. Deduct the cost of the appraisal under miscellaneous deductions.

"Adjusted cost basis" means the cost of the property to the taxpayer, plus capital improvements added since purchase, minus any previously deducted casualty losses.

If the damaged property is used partly for business and partly for personal use, the $100 floor per event only applies to the personal loss portion. The $100 casualty loss floor does not apply to the business loss allocation since it is fully deductible as a business expense.

EXAMPLE: Suppose your house was damaged by a fire. You paid $20,000 for your home several years ago. A year ago you spent $1,000 on remodeling. Just before the fire, your home's appreciated fair market value was $50,000. After the fire it is worth $14,000, as determined by your appraiser. All the furniture, which cost $4,000, was destroyed. Insurance paid only $6,000 of the loss to the house since you failed to increase your fire insurance coverage as inflation drove up the replacement cost of your home. The insurance company refused to pay for loss to your furniture which was very old and practically worthless. Your tax-deductible casualty loss is computed as follows:

1. Value before the fire $50,000
2. Value after the fire   14,000
3. Decrease in fair market value   36,000
4. Adjusted cost basis ($20,000 cost + $1,000 improvements)   21,000
5. Loss: (the lesser of line 3 or 4)   21,000
6. Minus: Insurance payment received   6,000
7. Casualty loss on the house (net)   15,000
8. Plus: Loss on furniture   4,000

9. Minus: Insurance payment received	0
10. Casualty loss on the furniture (net)	4,000
11. Total casualty loss (lines 7 + 10)	19,000
12. Minus: $100 per nonbusiness destructive event	100
13. Casualty loss deduction on Schedule A of IRS Form 1040	$18,900

YEAR OF THE CASUALTY LOSS DEDUCTION

Casualty losses should be deducted in the tax year when the loss occurs, minus any expected insurance or other payment to be received in the future. If the exact loss amount is unknown at the time of filing your tax returns, the casualty loss deduction can be amended anytime within the three-year statute of limitations.

Should the insurance or other payment later received turn out to be more or less than the expected amount, an adjustment can be made on the next year's income tax return rather than amending the previous year's return.

THEFT LOSS CASUALTY LOSS DEDUCTIONS

Net losses due to theft are deductible as casualty losses whether the theft occurs on or off your residence premises. Theft losses are deductible in the year of the loss discovery, not necessarily the same year as the actual theft (which may never be exactly known).

Larceny, embezzlement, and robbery are included in this theft loss category. However, losses due to misplacing or losing articles or money are not tax deductible. The $100 per event floor applies to each theft loss event. The amount of the loss is the property's actual value on the date of loss. That means its depreciated value. This is usually the original cost minus decline in value due to wear, tear, and obsolescence (depreciation). The amount of loss is *not* what it would cost to replace the stolen item (except cash would not be subject to depreciation, of course).

THE TAX CREDIT FOR SAVING ENERGY

A little-known part of the 1978 federal tax legislation was the Energy Tax Act. It enables homeowners, renters, and business owners to take a credit against federal income taxes owed if they installed energy-saving devices after April 19, 1977. Tax credits are better than tax deductions because a tax credit results in dollar for dollar income tax savings.

TWO TYPES OF ENERGY TAX CREDITS

Most home energy tax credits involve installation of conservation devices. But a more generous tax credit applies to costs of "renewable energy sources," such as devices using or transmitting (1) solar energy, (2) geothermal energy, or (3) wind energy.

TAX SAVINGS FOR HOME ENERGY CONSERVATION

A 15 percent tax credit against income tax due applies for up to $2,000 of energy conservation costs. $300 is the maximum tax credit for this category.

Examples of qualifying conservation items at your principal residence include (a) insulation for walls, floors, and ceilings, (b) new energy-efficient furnace burners, (c) storm or thermal windows and doors, (d) automatic clock thermostats, (e) exterior door and window caulking or weatherstripping, and (f) electrical or mechanical devices replacing gas pilot lights. Qualifying equipment must be new and have at least a three-year expected life.

Examples of nonqualifying devices include heat pumps, airtight wood stoves, and replacement of oil, gas, or coal furnaces. More nonqualifying items include carpets, drapes, fluorescent lights, swimming pool conservation devices, wood paneling, and exterior house siding.

BIGGER TAX CREDITS FOR RENEWABLE ENERGY DEVICES

A bigger credit of 40 percent of the first $10,000, up to a $4,000 maximum tax credit, is available for devices to transmit solar, geothermal, or wind energy. But swimming pool connected devices cannot qualify.

WHO GETS THE ENERGY TAX CREDIT?

These energy tax credits apply to both renters and owners of houses, condominiums, cooperatives, or rental apartments who install conservation devices between April 19, 1977, and the end of 1985.

The energy credits up to $300 for conservation devices and up to $4,000 for renewable energy devices are available to the taxpayer each time he moves to a new principal residence. They are allowed even if the previous owner or renter used these tax credits.

HOW TO CLAIM THE ENERGY TAX CREDIT

Use IRS Form 5695 filed with your income tax returns to claim the energy tax credit. These credits apply only to your principal residence, not to your vacation or second home or to investment property. However, special energy tax credits for business property are allowed for devices such as heat exchangers, recycling equipment, solar or wind energy devices, and heating equipment modifications which save at least 25 percent oil or gas fuel.

SUMMARY OF HOMEOWNER TAX BENEFITS

This survey of tax deductions and credits for homeowners is not intended to make anyone an expert. But its purpose is to alert homeowners to the opportunities to save income tax dollars for the tax advantages offered by home ownership. Consultation with a tax adviser or attorney is suggested to apply this tax knowledge to the specific facts of your circumstances.

The next section, one of the most profitable in this book, explains the tax angles of selling your principal residence. Taken together, the tax benefits of home ownership and at the time of sale, all these tax breaks add up to additional reasons why your home is probably the best investment you will ever make.

PART 2   TAX BENEFITS
WHEN YOU SELL YOUR HOME

In the first part of this important chapter, we looked at the major tax-savings sources during home ownership. Now the focus shifts to the time of residence sale and how to avoid paying tax on the sale profit.

Selling your principal residence, whether it is a single-family house, condominium, cooperative apartment, mobile home, or even a houseboat can be an emotional experience. To compound the trauma of moving and selling, Uncle Sam is waiting patiently for his tax on the profit. Smart home sellers keep Uncle Sam waiting forever.

There are right ways and wrong ways to sell your primary residence if you wish to avoid paying tax on your profit. On the next few pages will be found the simple and perfectly legal techniques for tax avoidance when selling your home. Few real estate agents and attorneys fully understand these methods for avoiding, deferring, and even cancelling the home sale profit tax.

Since this is just an outline of the tax angles of selling your home, consultation with a local tax adviser or attorney who thoroughly understands real estate is advised *before you sell,* so these methods can be applied to your specific situation.

HOW ARE HOME SALE PROFITS TAXED?

Before finding out how to avoid profit taxes, smart home sellers compute the amount of their gross sales price that is potentially taxable. They then can figure how to avoid paying tax on that amount. Remember, tax avoidance is perfectly legal and admirable. But tax evasion is illegal!

LONG-TERM CAPITAL GAIN TAX

Most home sale profits qualify for the long-term, capital gain tax rates, the lowest available. To be eligible for this low tax category, the capital asset (such as your residence) must have been owned for over twelve months, or over six months if acquired after June 22, 1984. If it was not owned this minimum time period before you sell, the profit is fully taxed as ordinary income. The profit is then short-term, rather than long-term, capital gain.

HOW TO COMPUTE THE LONG-TERM CAPITAL GAIN

The 1978 Tax Act reduced the portion of long-term capital gains which are taxable. Only 40 percent of long-term capital gain profits are taxable. The other 60 percent is untaxed (except for the alternative minimum tax which affects only a few wealthy taxpayers).

The 40:60 taxable-untaxed ratio applies to long-term capital gains received after October 31, 1978. Even if you sold property before this date, if you received the payment after October 31, 1978, the new, lower tax ratio applies. Thus, if you sold property in 1975 on an installment sale and are still receiving installment payments, the 40:60 ratio applies, even though at the time of the sale the former law taxed 50 percent of long-term capital gains.

EXAMPLE: On December 1, Larry and Stella sold their home for $75,000. Their adjusted cost basis (discussed later) was $25,000. They paid a $4,500 real estate sales commission but had no other sales costs. So $70,500 ($75,000 minus $4,500) is their adjusted sales price. Their long-term capital gain is therefore $45,500 ($70,500 minus $25,000). Larry and Stella report this amount on IRS Form 1040, Schedule D, if they are not eligible for any of the tax avoidance rules discussed later. Of their $45,500 long-term capital gain, however, only 40 percent ($18,200) is taxable. The $18,200 would be added to other taxable income received by Larry and Stella. The remaining 60 percent ($27,300) profit escapes tax. If Larry and Stella are in a 30 percent income tax bracket, they would pay about $5,460 extra income tax (30 percent of $18,200). On their overall profit of $45,500, this tax of about 12 percent is quite reasonable.

Long-term capital gains are taxed within a range of 5.6 percent minimum to 20 percent maximum, depending on the taxpayer's overall income tax bracket as determined by his ordinary income.

For example, the highest tax which could be paid by a high tax bracket taxpayer on a $100,000 long-term capital gain would be $20,000 (20 percent of the $100,000 profit). For comparison, tax rates on earned income (such as job salaries) range from 14 percent to 50 percent.

The 1978 Tax Act eliminated the so-called 15 percent "minimum tax" as it applied to long-term capital gains. However, a new "alternative minimum tax" may apply to a few wealthy taxpayers who have long-term capital gains from capital asset sales. But long-term capital gains on the sale of one's principal residence are exempt from this new alternative minimum tax.

HOW TO CALCULATE YOUR HOME SALE PROFIT

Now that you understand long-term capital gains taxation, it is important to become knowledgeable on calculating the profit on the sale of your home. Then we will show how to avoid tax payment on this profit.

To compute your potentially taxable profit, subtract the "adjusted cost basis" of your principal residence from its "adjusted sales price."

ADJUSTED SALES PRICE

The adjusted sales price is simply the gross sales price of the residence, minus sales expenses such as the real estate sales commission, transfer fees, advertising costs, escrow fee, attorney fee, title fee, FHA or VA loan points paid by the seller, and other sales expenses.

ADJUSTED COST BASIS

The adjusted cost basis is the purchase price of the residence, plus purchase or closing costs which were not tax deductible at the time of the purchase. Examples of such nondeductible purchase closing costs include legal fees, title fees, and escrow charges. Added to this basis are costs of any capital improvements added during ownership, such as cost of a room addition or new swimming pool. Subtracted from this total amount are any tax deductions claimed during ownership for casualty losses or depreciation for business use or rental of the residence to tenants.

EXAMPLE: Carla bought a house for $100,000. At the time of purchase she paid a $250 attorney fee, $300 escrow charge, $350 title fee, $400 prorated interest on the mortgage she assumed and $450 prorated share of the annual property taxes. During ownership Carla paid $4,000 for a room addition, deducted $1,000 for an uninsured casualty loss, and depreciated $2,000 for rental of a spare bedroom to a college student. Carla's adjusted cost basis is $100,000 plus $250, plus $300, plus $350, plus $4,000, minus $1,000, minus $2,000, which is $101,900. Notice that Carla's down payment and mortgage are irrelevant to calculating her adjusted cost basis. Interest and property tax do not affect basis either.

EXAMPLE: After several years of ownership Carla's house appreciated in market value to $140,000. She sold it for this amount, paying a $8,400 real estate sales commission to her realty agent. In addition she had the following sales closing costs: $450 prorated property tax, $1,000 local transfer fee, $3,000 VA loan fee paid for the buyer's new VA mortgage, and $300 attorney fee. Her adjusted sales price was $140,000 minus $8,400 minus $1,000, minus $3,000, minus $300, which is $127,300.

EXAMPLE: Carla's long-term capital gain is the adjusted sales price of $127,300 minus the adjusted cost basis of $101,900 which is $25,400. Please notice that the prorated mortgage interest and property taxes did not enter into the profit computation because mortgage interest and property taxes are itemized tax deductions that do not affect the adjusted cost basis or the adjusted sales price.

HOW TO AVOID TAX ON THE SALE OF YOUR HOME

Internal Revenue Code section 1034 contains a very important tax rule for persons who sell their principal residences. This rule does not apply to any other type of property, just the taxpayer's primary residence.

THE RESIDENCE REPLACEMENT RULE

This tax rule, called the "residence replacement rule" applies to home sellers of any age who sell their principal residence and buy a qualifying replacement principal residence. Vacation or part-time second homes and other types of property, such as land, office buildings, or warehouses, cannot qualify.

Determination of your principal residence, however, is not always easy. Factors such as time spent living in the dwelling, voter registration location, length of ownership, business and community involvement, and other considerations can enter into the determination if there is question whether or not the residence sold was the taxpayer's principal residence.

HOW TO AVOID TAX AND PUT TAX-FREE CASH IN YOUR POCKET WHEN SELLING YOUR RESIDENCE

To qualify for total profit tax deferral, the taxpayer must sell his old principal residence and (1) buy and occupy within twenty-four months before or after the sale another principal residence (2) that has an adjusted cost basis higher than the adjusted sales price of the former principal residence.

EXAMPLE: Emily sold her condominium for a $100,000 adjusted sales price. Her adjusted cost basis was $60,000 so she had a $40,000 long-term capital gain. Within twenty-four months before or after the sale, Emily bought a single-family house for $125,000. Since the adjusted cost basis exceeds the adjusted sales price, and Emily met the twenty-four-month time limit, she must defer paying tax on her sale profit.

A LOOK AT THE TIME LIMITS

As shown by the following illustration, the qualifying replacement principal residence can be bought anytime within a forty-eight month time period starting twenty-four months before the sale of the old home and ending twenty-four months after the sale of the old home.

← 24 months before sale →	← 24 months after sale →

SALE
DATE

If the replacement residence costs less than the sales price of the former principal residence, then the seller's profit is taxable, but only on the difference between the two prices.

EXAMPLE: Jack sold his house for $80,000 and bought a $50,000 condominium. Jack's adjusted cost basis was $45,000. So his profit on the sale was $35,000 ($80,000 minus $45,000). Since Jack's replacement principal residence cost less than the $80,000 adjusted sales price of Jack's old house, his profit is taxable up to the difference in the two prices. $80,000 minus $50,000 is $30,000, so $30,000 of the $35,000 profit is taxable now. Tax on the remaining $5,000 of profit must be deferred until Jack sells his replacement principal residence without buying another qualifying replacement.

The residence replacement rule can be used over and over again without limit as to the number of times. For example, it is possible to start out with a modest $50,000 home, sell it and buy a $75,000 residence, sell it and buy a $100,000 home, and so on, and defer all the profit tax along the way. In fact, Internal Revenue Code 1034 is a mandatory law requiring tax deferral in qualifying situations. Isn't Uncle Sam nice?

Use IRS Form 2119 to report the sale and replacement, even if the tax is deferred. This form shows how to establish the adjusted cost basis on the replacement principal residence.

LIMIT ON FREQUENT USE

Although there is no limit to the number of times the residence replacement rule can be used, there is a limit on frequency of use. The rule cannot be used more often than once every twenty-four months. However, one exception exists. If the sale and replacement is part of a job location change that qualifies for the moving expense tax deduction, discussed earlier, then the rule can be used more often than once every twenty-four months.

> EXAMPLE: On January 1, 1980, Tom bought a $75,000 condominium. On April 1, 1983, Tom sold his condo for a $79,000 adjusted sales price and bought a $100,000 replacement principal residence. This situation qualifies for tax deferral using the residence replacement rule. On September 1, 1983, Tom's job location was moved 200 miles away, so he sold his house for a $125,000 adjusted sales price and bought a replacement principal residence costing $130,000. Even though Tom had just used the residence replacement rule tax deferral in April, he can use it again in September since his move qualified for the moving expense tax deduction, explained in Part 1 of this chapter.

BASIS FOR THE REPLACEMENT PRINCIPAL RESIDENCE

One difficulty that arises with the replacement residence rule is computing the adjusted cost basis of the replacement principal residence.

In the example above, Tom sold his first principal residence and bought a qualifying replacement costing more than the sales price. Although Tom paid $100,000 for the first replacement, this is *not* his adjusted cost basis for it.

Rather, it is the price he paid minus his deferred profit from his previous sale on which tax is deferred. His first-sale profit was only $4,000 ($79,000 minus $75,000). To determine his adjusted cost basis for the first replacement, he subtracts this $4,000 deferred profit ($100,000 minus $4,000) to arrive at a $96,000 adjusted cost basis.

When Tom sold that house for $125,000 his gain was $29,000 ($125,000 minus $96,000). Although his second replacement principal residence cost $130,000, Tom's adjusted cost basis is determined by subtracting his $29,000 deferred profit ($130,000 minus $29,000) to arrive at a $101,000 adjusted cost basis for the house which cost Tom $130,000. If Tom eventually sells this house, his profit will be his adjusted sales price minus the $101,000 adjusted cost basis.

WHAT HAPPENS TO DEFERRED PROFIT UPON DEATH?

Suppose further that in the above example Tom dies while owning that second replacement house for which his adjusted cost basis is $101,000. At the time of death, perhaps it is worth $140,000. If Tom sells one day before he dies, he will owe tax on $140,000 minus the home's $101,000 adjusted cost basis, a $39,000 taxable profit. But if he instead dies, his heirs receive that house with a basis of its $140,000 market value on the date of death. The potential $39,000 profit is forgotten by Uncle Sam.

Of course, the $140,000 market value of the house will be included in Tom's estate for federal estate tax purposes (subject to the generous exemptions). But no capital gains tax will be due. If Tom's heirs decide to sell the house at its $140,000 market value, they will not owe any profit tax. This is called "stepped-up basis."

HOW TO POCKET TAX-FREE CASH
WHEN SELLING YOUR HOME

Several pages ago reference was made to deferring tax and putting tax-free cash in your pocket. Although the residence replacement rule tax deferral has been thoroughly explored, the tax-free cash angle has not.

Please notice that the residence replacement rule says nothing about mortgages or having to reinvest any or all of the cash received from the sale of the old residence into the replacement principal residence.

Smart residence sellers therefore make a minimal cash down payment on their replacement residence and use the rest of their sale cash to pay other expenses or, better yet, to buy more property as a further hedge against inflation.

EXAMPLE: Jim and Joan sell their old home for $75,000 cash. They buy a $100,000 replacement principal residence, using a new VA home loan (100 percent financing, no down payment). The result is total tax deferral plus Jim and Joan have $75,000 cash to spend as they please. Of course, they must pay off any old, existing mortgage on their former residence which was not assumed or bought "subject to" by their buyer.

THE REPLACEMENT RESIDENCE LOCATION LOOPHOLE

A special loophole in the residence replacement rule is worth attention. It involves the location of the replacement principal residence. The law does not require the replacement to be located in the United States. So if your replacement residence otherwise qualifies for tax deferral, its location outside U.S. borders will not stop the taxpayer from deferring his profit tax, even if he never returns to the U.S.

EXAMPLE: Cora sold her modest $75,000 home and bought a luxurious $100,000 qualifying replacement principal residence in Mexico. If Cora sells her Mexican home at a profit in the future, she owes tax on that profit back in the U.S. But if Cora never returns to the U.S., chances of the IRS collecting tax are not too great.

THE MYTH OF HOME SALE FIX-UP COST TAX DEDUCTIONS

There is a popular tax myth, perpetuated from one generation to the younger one (probably by real estate agents), that if you spend money to fix up your home for sale those costs are tax deductible. This is incorrect.

The only situation where tax is saved by home fix-up payments is when the principal residence seller buys a less expensive replacement.

It is true that fix-up costs to prepare your home for sale take on tax significance if certain requirements are met. Those requirements are that sale preparation costs must be incurred within ninety days before the signing of the sales contract and paid for within thirty days after the close of the sale.

Examples of home sale fix-up costs include painting, repairing, and cleaning. But items of a major capital improvement nature, such as a new furnace, new built-in appliances, or a new roof, should be capitalized and added to the cost basis of the residence.

Whether your expenditures are for major capital improvements or for just getting the house in shape for sale, save the receipts because they may save tax later on.

Qualifying fix-up costs, which normally have no tax consequence because they are normal home maintenance, become subtractions from the home's gross sales price when arriving at the adjusted sales price. But the only time such fix-up costs save tax dollars is if a less-expensive replacement principal residence is purchased.

> EXAMPLE: Dave sold his home for $110,000. He had $6,000 of sales expenses and $4,000 of qualified fix-up costs. Thus his adjusted sales price becomes $100,000. If he buys a replacement principal residence costing more than $100,000, his total profit tax must be deferred. But if he buys a less-expensive replacement, he pays profit tax only on his profit up to the difference in the two prices. So if he had a $30,000 sale profit and buys a $90,000 replacement, $10,000 ($100,000 minus $90,000) of his profit is taxed. Tax on the remaining $20,000 of Dave's profit is deferred. Without the $4,000 of fix-up costs, the difference in prices would be $14,000 ($104,000 minus $90,000) so Dave's fix-up costs saved him from paying tax on $4,000. But he spent $4,000 to do so.

SUMMARY

The residence replacement rule allows total profit tax deferral when selling one principal residence and buying a qualifying replacement. Partial tax is due if the replacement costs less than the adjusted sales price of the former principal residence.

This tax deferral rule can be used over and over again to build a tax-deferred estate. But it is only a tax deferral rule. Tax must be paid if the final home in the chain of tax-deferred sales is sold without buying another qualifying replacement. But there is a way to avoid all that deferred tax when selling the final principal residence on the deferral chain. It is called the "over 55 rule" and is the subject of the next section.

THE BIG "OVER-55 RULE"
$125,000 HOME SALE PROFIT TAX EXEMPTION

If a taxpayer cannot qualify for the residence replacement rule of Internal Revenue Code section 1034, usually because he is not buying a qualified replacement principal residence, his next best tax break is the "over-55 rule" contained in Internal Revenue Code Section 121.

This tax bonanza is available to qualified principal residence sellers who are at least age fifty-five on the day they transfer title.

WHO QUALIFIES?

To qualify for the $125,000 home sale profit tax exemption, the principal residence seller must be fifty-five or older on the day title to the residence is transferred to the new owner. It is immaterial what day the sales agreement was signed. It is not sufficient if the seller became fifty-five in the year of the sale. He or she must actually be fifty-five or older on the day of title transfer.

> EXAMPLE: Norman, on September 1, sold his principal residence. On December 15, he became fifty-five. He does *not* qualify and cannot use the over-55 rule $125,000 tax exemption on this sale. But if Norman is married and his wife is fifty-five or older on the title transfer date, then they can qualify if both spouses file a joint income tax return for the sale year *and* if the spouse who is fifty-five or older (the wife, here) is a title holder of the property in joint tenancy, community property, or tenancy by the entireties. It will not disqualify eligibility if title is held with a spouse who is not yet fifty-five if one spouse co-owner is fifty-five or older.

WHAT IS THE $125,000 EXEMPTION?

The $125,000 home sale tax exemption is elective, not mandatory as is the residence replacement rule. It applies to post-July 20, 1981, sales of the taxpayer's principal residence.

(For sales closed on or before July 21, 1981, the old, less generous "over-55 rule" allowed only a tax exemption on up to $100,000 profit from the principal residence's sale.

By the way, if a taxpayer used the old, now repealed "over-65 rule" before the July 27, 1978, effective date of the $100,000 "over-55 rule," he or she can use the "over-55 rule" on any post-July 26, 1978, principal residence sale.

The $125,000 exemption applies to both profits on the sale of the qualified taxpayer's current principal residence and deferred profits from sales of earlier residence sales where the "residence replacement rule" was used to defer profit tax.

THE OWNERSHIP AND OCCUPANCY TEST

In addition to the age requirement, the $125,000 home sale profit tax exemption requires the seller to have owned and lived in his principal residence at least three of the five years before the sale. Any three years will do. They need not be consecutive. Nor must they be the last three years before sale.

EXAMPLE: Florence bought her condominium on December 1, 1977. She sold it on December 2, 1980. Florence has met the three out of five year ownership and occupancy requirement. She need not have owned her principal residence for five years before the sale, just the last three years are sufficient if she also occupied the condo as her primary residence during those three years.

EXAMPLE: Ken and Mary have owned and occupied their house for many years. They are considering moving to a retirement community but they are not certain they will like it. The three out of five year rule allows Ken and Mary to move to the retirement community to try out living there for up to two years without losing their $125,000 home sale tax exemption if they decide to sell their former principal residence.

EXAMPLE: Jane, age seventy-five, is in poor health. Her family insisted she move to a convalescent hospital where she could receive proper care. If Jane has owned her principal residence for at least three years, she could remain away from her home for up to two years without losing her $125,000 home sale tax exemption. But if she does not live in her principal residence at least three of the five years before she sells it, she loses the $125,000 tax-free profit exemption.

Of course this "over-55 rule," like the residence replacement rule, only applies to the sale of the taxpayer's principal residence. Such a home can be a single-family house, condominium, cooperative apartment, mobile home, or even a houseboat. The land need not be owned; it can be leased.

But the rule can be used by sellers of investment property if the seller resides in one apartment as his principal residence. To illustrate, suppose you own a four-unit apartment house and reside in one apartment. You could use the "over-55 rule" to make yourself exempt from profit tax up to $125,000 profit on the sale of the apartment where you reside. Profit on the sale of the other three apartments will not qualify. In other words, selling such a building is like selling two separate properties. One is your personal residence. The other is the three rental apartments.

The purpose of this "over-55 rule" (Internal Revenue Code Section 121) is to enable taxpayers aged fifty-five or older to sell their primary residence without having to buy a replacement principal residence (as younger home sellers must do to defer their profit tax payment). But sellers aged fifty-five or older who buy a principal residence replacement should use the residence replacement rule of Internal Revenue Code section 1034 to defer their profit tax. Also, it is possible to combine the "over-55 rule" and the residence replacement rule in one sale, as will be illustrated later.

THE ONCE-PER-LIFETIME TEST

This "over-55 rule" can be used only once per lifetime. Any unused portion cannot be saved for future use.

EXAMPLE: Grace sold her house for a $75,000 net profit. If she is eligible and elects to use her "over-55 rule" $125,000 home sale tax exemption, she cannot save the unused $50,000 for future use.

Even though each person can use this rule once, if a married couple elect to use this tax break, they get only one $125,000 exemption per marriage.

EXAMPLE: Henry age sixty-six, and his wife Dora, age sixty-four, sell their home for a $150,000 profit. They get only one $125,000 exemption so they will owe tax on the extra $25,000 of profit (a long-term capital gain if the home was owned over twelve months).

EXAMPLE: Frank, age fifty-five, and his wife Margo, age fifty-four, sell their home which they own in joint tenancy. Since Frank meets the age requirement, this is sufficient. ONLY ONE OWNER-SPOUSE NEED BE FIFTY-FIVE OR OLDER. No additional tax savings are available if both spouses are fifty-five or older. There is no extra tax saving for waiting to sell until Margo becomes age fifty-five because there is only one $125,000 exemption per married couple.

But if two qualified co-owners, not married to each other, sell their principal residence, then each can receive up to $125,000 of tax-free profits.

EXAMPLE: Mabel, age seventy, and Emily, age sixty-seven, are joint owners of the house where they have each resided for three of the five years before the sale. When they sell their home, *each* can take a tax exemption for up to $125,000 of her share of the sale profit. This means each co-owner who meets the age, ownership, and occupancy requirements can qualify for up to $125,000 of tax-free profits. In this example, if the sale profit is $250,000 and Mabel and Emily split it equally, the entire $250,000 profit is tax exempt. It may seem unfair to give a married husband and wife only one $125,000 exemption while unmarried joint co-owners each get a $125,000 tax exemption, but who said tax law is fair?

However, if a husband and wife *each* meet the age and time requirements, but are divorced before the transfer date of their principal residence, they can each take one "over-55 rule" $125,000 home sale tax exemption.

EXAMPLE: Bill, age fifty-six, and his wife Carole, age fifty-five, lived in their jointly owned house at least three of the five years before its sale. They decide to get a divorce. After receiving their final divorce decree, they sell their home and split the sales proceeds. In such a situation, Bill and Carole *each* can get up to $125,000 tax-free profits, just as Mabel and Emily did in the previous example. This means no profit tax will be due if the home sells for under $250,000 profit in this situation.

Of course, if a married couple get a divorce, sell their former principal residence, each claim their "over-55 rule" $125,000 tax exemption, and then remarry, the IRS will probably attack the proceedings as a sham.

This once-per-lifetime rule can be especially important to persons who remarry. If a taxpayer who has used his $125,000 exemption marries someone who has not used his exemption, this bars future use of the rule for both persons.

EXAMPLE: Clara and John used their $125,000 exemption when they sold their home. John died a few years later. Clara married Victor. They lived in Victor's house which he owned before the marriage. When Victor sells that house, the $125,000 exemption is not available since Clara used up her once-per-lifetime exemption previously. This prohibits Victor from using this tax break even though the house is his separate property in his name alone. If Victor planned to sell the house, he should have done so before marrying Clara.

HOW TO CALCULATE YOUR TAX-FREE EXCLUSION AMOUNT

To calculate the tax-exempt "over-55 rule" profit which is excluded from federal income tax, subtract the principal residence's adjusted cost basis from its adjusted sales price. The first $125,000 of this amount is tax-free. IRS Form 2119 must be filed with your federal income tax return to claim this exemption. Of course, any profit over $125,000 is taxable, and any unused part of the $125,000 exemption is lost forever.

EXAMPLE: Jerry, age sixty, and otherwise qualified for the "over-55 rule" sells his condominium for a $95,000 adjusted sales price. His adjusted cost basis is $25,000. Jerry's $70,000 long-term capital gain ($95,000 minus $25,000) is tax-free since it is below $125,000. But the unused $55,000 portion of his exemption is wasted.

HOW TO COMBINE THE "OVER-55 RULE" WITH OTHER TAX-SAVING METHODS

The "over-55 rule" can be combined with other tax deferral rules if the $125,000 exemption is insufficient to shelter all the sale profit from tax.

THE RESIDENCE REPLACEMENT RULE

This rule, discussed earlier, is available to home sellers of any age who sell one principal residence and buy a replacement within twenty-four months before or after the sale. Combining this rule with the $125,000 exemption can result in both tax exemption and tax deferral. Of course, if you buy a more expensive replacement residence, you will not be using the $125,000 exemption, so the $125,000 exemption and the residence replacement rule are only used if a less-expensive replacement residence is purchased.

EXAMPLE: Larry, age fifty-five, and his wife Mary, age fifty-three, sell their primary residence, which has an adjusted cost basis of $35,000, for an adjusted sales price of $175,000. They buy a $45,000 condominium replacement principal residence. Using the "over-55 rule" $125,000 home sale profit tax exemption, $125,000 of their $140,000 profit ($175,000 minus $35,000) is tax-free.
   Larry and Mary then subtract this $125,000 exemption from their $175,000 adjusted sales price to get their $50,000 "revised adjusted sales price." If they buy a replacement principal residence costing more than this $50,000 revised adjusted sales price, then tax is deferred on the remaining $15,000 of their sale profit (using the residence replacement rule) until they sell that replacement home without buying another qualifying replacement. But Larry and Mary

cannot ever again use the $125,000 home sale tax exemption.

However, Larry and Mary are buying a *less-expensive* replacement principal residence, the $45,000 condo. So their remaining $15,000 profit will be taxed up to the difference in the two prices ($50,000 minus $45,000), which is $5,000. Tax on the remaining $10,000 must be deferred. This $10,000 is subtracted from the $45,000 purchase price to give Larry and Mary a $35,000 adjusted cost basis for their condo. This adjusted cost basis is the same as the adjusted cost basis on their former principal residence which they sold.

THE INSTALLMENT SALE RULE

Many home sellers use installment sales to minimize their profit tax and to provide excellent interest earnings from the mortgage, trust deed, or land contract they take back to finance their buyer's purchase. By spreading out the buyer's payments over future years, sellers of any property can avoid being boosted into a high tax bracket in the year of sale.

An installment sale (discussed further in Chapter 8) can be combined with the $125,000 exemption and/or the residence replacement rule to hold the capital gains tax down or defer it entirely. At the same time, secure installment sale interest earnings are provided by the buyer's installment obligation to the seller.

In late 1980, Congress passed major installment sale rule changes. Most are retroactive to property sales made after January 1, 1980. For installment sales made after that date, there is no minimum or maximum down payment required in the year of sale (the old installment sale law allowed the seller to receive only a maximum of 30 percent of the gross sales price in the year of sale).

Another major installment sale rule change eliminated the requirement of installment payments in two or more tax years. Now it is possible to sell a property on an installment sale with no down payment in the year of sale.

For installment sales made after October 20, 1980, the installment sale election is automatic. If the taxpayer wants to pay his tax in the year of sale and not spread it out over the years of the buyer's payments, he must "unelect" the installment sale tax deferral.

To combine the installment sale tax deferral with the $125,000 home sale tax exemption is easy. It is best illustrated by an example.

EXAMPLE: Betty, age sixty-five, sold her home and qualified for the $125,000 exemption. The adjusted sales price was $200,000 and her adjusted cost basis was $50,000, giving her a $150,000 sale profit. Her $125,000 exemption reduced the taxable profit to $25,000. Betty carried back an installment sale second mortgage to spread out her tax on this

$25,000 over the future years the buyer will make payments to her. In addition, the interest on the buyer's unpaid balance to Betty gives her safe, high-interest income.

INCOME AVERAGING

Any taxable profit on a real estate sale is eligible for income averaging. This includes long-term capital gains. If your taxable income, including capital gains, exceeds by 40 percent your average income over the past three tax years, income averaging will probably save you income tax dollars.

SUMMARY

Tax savings opportunities for principal residence sellers can be substantial. But the law's requirements must be met exactly because no exceptions are allowed. Consult an experienced tax adviser *before* selling your principal residence to take advantage of all the tax exemptions and deferrals available.

QUESTIONS AND ANSWERS

HOW TO GET MORE THAN $125,000
HOME SALE PROFIT WITHOUT PAYING TAX

Q. We have been very fortunate as we only paid about $24,000 for our home years ago. It is worth at least $160,000 today. I will retire soon. We are thinking of selling and moving to Florida. But as I read your explanations of that new $125,000 "over-55 rule" tax break, we would owe tax on about $11,000 of our $136,000 profit. Is that correct?—*Joel M*.

A. Not necessarily. You may be able to exempt from tax all $136,000 of your profit.

To qualify for the "over-55 rule" of Internal Revenue Code Section 121, I will assume you or your spouse will be fifty-five or older on the day you transfer title to your home to the buyer. In addition, you must have owned and occupied it at least three of the five years before sale and never have used this $125,000 tax exemption before. If qualified, up to $125,000 of your profit is tax-free using this law.

Subtracting the $125,000 exemption from the $160,000 sale price (which I assume is net after paying sales costs), gives a $35,000 "revised adjusted sales price." If, within twenty-four months before or after the sale, you buy a principal residence replacement costing at least this $35,000 amount, you must defer paying tax on the remaining $11,000 of your profit.

This tax rule, called the "residence replacement rule" of Internal

Revenue Code Section 1034, is available to home sellers of any age who sell their principal residence and buy a more expensive replacement. If you buy a Florida condominium, for example, costing over $35,000 (your "revised adjusted sales price"), you can qualify. For details, see your tax adviser.

WHEN A HOME BECOMES A HOUSE FOR TAX PURPOSES

Q. We just bought a run-down house, as you suggested. Frankly, it was all we could afford. Since it is in a pretty good neighborhood, with some fix-up I think it will turn out to be a profitable investment. I'm interested in the tax angles. Will the money we spend on new plumbing, wiring, and repairs be tax deductible?—*Bettina McG.*

A. Congratulations on buying a house in need of repairs. I think such properties, if in basically sound condition and in good locations, are the best buys in today's market.

If you are going to occupy the structure as your principal residence, then all your fix-up costs are additions to your original purchase price basis. Those improvements are not tax deductible.

But if you do not plan to occupy the dwelling as your home, and you plan to rent it to tenants, then the tax picture changes. Costs of capital improvements, such as the new plumbing and wiring, are added to the purchase price cost basis and are depreciable on your tax returns along with the value of the house. Repair costs, however, can be deducted as expenses if the house is rented to tenants. In addition, you can deduct costs of maintenance, fire insurance, and operating expenses. Your tax adviser can further explain the tax benefits of owning rental property.

NO TAX BREAK FOR SALE
AND REPLACEMENT OF SECONDARY HOME

Q. We just sold our Florida house for $47,500. Our primary home is near Washington, D.C. The profit on our sale was about $13,000. Next spring we plan to buy a Florida condominium for $67,000. Will we have to pay any tax? I heard it's possible to sell one property and reinvest the money in another property, thereby avoiding any profit tax.—*Goldie M.*

A. Sorry, but your situation will not qualify for profit tax deferral.

The only type of property sale on which profit tax can be deferred when a more expensive replacement is purchased is your principal residence. To qualify, both properties must be your principal residences, and the replacement must be bought within eighteen months before or after the sale. No other type of property can qualify for this tax break. Your tax adviser has further details.

THE KEY QUESTION
ELDERLY SHOULD ASK BEFORE MARRIAGE

Q. I am sixty-six, and I just married a beautiful young lady of fifty-six. Before we got married last September, she sold her home and used that $125,000 profit tax exemption since her sale profit was almost $88,000. Now I want to sell my condominium so we can buy a house together. My profit will be about $75,000. My CPA told me my profit will be taxed, even though I've never used that $125,000 tax break because my new wife has already used up her once-in-a-lifetime exemption. Please tell me this bad news isn't true.—*Charlie K.*

A. I am sorry to report that your CPA's bad news is correct. Your new wife's use of the $125,000 exemption "over-55 rule" stops you from also using this tax benefit because the law allows only one such exemption per lifetime. This may seem harsh, since your condo is your separate property, but Congress apparently did not think of this bad result when the law was written.

If you each had sold your homes before you married, then you each could have taken up to $125,000 of tax-free profits from your home sales. But since your wife already used her exemption, that stops you from doing so. The key question elderly people should ask their new mate, before they march down the aisle to get married, is "Honey, have you used your $125,000 home sale tax exemption yet?"

HOME TAX DEDUCTIONS ONLY FOR OWNERS

Q. We own our home, but our son pays our mortgage payments and property taxes as we are disabled. Can he deduct these costs on his income tax returns?—*Josie H.*

A. No. To be entitled to deduct property taxes and mortgage interest on a personal residence, the person paying those costs must be the owner. You might wish to make your son a co-owner so he can deduct future property tax and mortgage interest payments.

NO LIMIT FOR MULTIPLE HOME SALE TAX DEFERRALS

Q. Several years ago when we sold our home in New York and bought our present one, we deferred paying our profit tax. Now we will be selling our present home and buying a larger one. Will we owe tax on our deferred profit as well as on the profit from our current home's sale? —*Harold L.*

A. Maybe. It depends on the purchase cost of the replacement principal residence you buy.

There is no limit to the number of times you can use the residence replacement rule of Internal Revenue Code Section 1034 to defer profit tax when selling one principal residence and buying a more expensive replacement.

But you cannot use this tax deferral rule more often than once every twenty-four months unless you change job locations and qualify for the moving expense deduction.

To qualify for the residence replacement rule tax deferral you must buy a replacement principal residence costing more than the adjusted sales price (that is gross sales price minus sales costs) of your former principal residence. If the replacement costs less, your profit is taxed up to the difference in the two prices. The replacement must be bought within twenty-four months before or after the sale.

HOW TO GET MAXIMUM INCOME TAX SAVINGS FROM YOUR HOME

Q. You often explain tax breaks for people who are selling their homes. But what about the rest of us who aren't selling? Are there any ways we can squeeze some extra income tax savings from our homes? —*Homer S.*

A. Yes, there are many tax savings breaks for homeowners. Some are well-known, such as tax deductions for mortgage interest and property taxes. Others are often overlooked, such as deductions for mortgage loan fees and prepayment penalties, business use of part of your home, moving expense deductions, casualty losses for thefts, fires, floods, broken pipes, roof leak damage, and even ground rent if your house is on leased land with an option to buy.

Of course, not every homeowner qualifies for all these tax breaks. While you may not be eligible this year, it is important to be aware of these benefits so that if you qualify, or you have a friend who does, you will know of the income tax dollars you can save.

INHERITED REAL ESTATE IS A TAX BONANZA

Q. My aunt died last September, leaving me most of her property. The two major assets are her home, worth at least $75,000, and a twelve-unit apartment house worth at least $300,000. Both are free and clear. She inherited these properties from my late uncle. As I live about 450 miles away from the house and apartments, I am considering selling them. (1) If I sell, will I owe a big capital gains tax? (2) Do you think I should sell or keep these buildings?—*Kurt R.*

A. (1) No. You will owe little or no tax if you sell the buildings after inheriting them. The 1978 Tax Act restored the old tax rule that inherited property is valued at its market value on the date of the decedent's death.

Your profit will only be any appreciation in market value between the date of your aunt's death and the day you close the sale. Of course, the estate pays the federal estate tax, and there may be a state inheritance tax too.

But no tax is due on the difference between your aunt's low basis for the properties and their market value on the date of her death. This is a big tax bonanza for you.

(2) The general rule is the more property you own, the better off you will be. But it can be difficult managing small properties from 450 miles away. If you sell, reinvest the money in good investment property closer to home.

USE $125,000 TAX EXEMPTION FOR
DEFERRED PROFIT TAXES TOO

Q. In 1972, we sold our home and purchased a more expensive one, so we deferred our profit tax. If we sell the second home, can we use that $125,000 tax break to avoid tax on both profits?—*Harold P.*

A. Yes. To qualify for the $125,000 home sale tax break, you or your co-owner spouse must be fifty-five or older on the title transfer date. You must also have owned and lived in your principal residence three of the five years before its sale.

This tax benefit can be used to exempt from tax not only the profit on the sale of your current home, but also any deferred profits from previous home sales when you used the "residence replacement rule" of Internal Revenue Code Section 1034.

THE THREE-YEAR RESIDENCY
FOR $125,000 HOME SALE TAX BREAK

Q. Does the three-year residency requirement for the $125,000 home sale tax exemption mean three continuous years?—*Evan F.*

A. No. Any three of the five years before sale is sufficient.

CAN UNUSED HOME SALE TAX EXEMPTION BE SAVED?

Q. If we sell our present home, we will have about $40,000 profit. When we use that $125,000 tax exemption, can we save the other $85,000 of our exemption for future use?—*Conwright M.*

A. No. You can use the $125,000 home sale tax benefit only once per lifetime. Any unused portion is wasted.

CAN MARRIED COUPLE
GET TWO $125,000 HOME SALE TAX EXEMPTIONS?

Q. I am fifty-seven, my wife is fifty-four. If we wait to sell our home

until my wife is fifty-five, will up to $250,000 of our profit be tax-free?
—*Paul T.*

A. No. It will not pay to wait until your wife becomes fifty-five to sell
your home, since only one $125,000 home sale tax exemption is allowed
per married couple.

ARE HOME IMPROVEMENTS TAX DEDUCTIBLE?

Q. We recently installed new air conditioning and a new furnace in our
home. We're considering installing new copper pipes. Are these expenses
tax deductible?—*Robert W.*

A. No. The cost of capital improvements should be added to the
purchase price cost basis of your home. Neither repairs nor capital
improvements to your principal residence qualify as itemized income tax
deductions. But save the receipts forever for those capital improvements.

CAPITAL IMPROVEMENT COSTS SAVE TAX
AT HOME SALE TIME

Q. We recently sold our home for $89,750. The realty sales commission
was $5,385 and various closing costs totaled $1,250. We bought the house
many years ago for only $27,500. Since then we've spent about $6,000 for
a room addition, about $550 for a new roof, $55 for a water heater, about
$200 for landscaping, and around $350 for a fence. Also, we replaced the
old wood windows with new aluminum ones which cost about $700. I
don't have the receipts for any of these costs. How do I compute my home
sale profit?—*Mr. W. W.*

A. Your home sale profit is the difference between the "adjusted sales
price" (gross sales price minus selling costs) and the "adjusted cost basis"
(original purchase price, plus closing costs which were not tax deductible
at the time of purchase, plus costs of capital improvements, minus any
casualty loss or depreciation deductions taken during ownership).

Computing your adjusted sales price is easy. That is $89,750 minus the
$5,385 and $1,250 costs, or $83,115. But computing your adjusted cost
basis is more difficult. Since you do not have receipts for the capital
improvement, the IRS will often accept reasonable cost estimates. But
repair costs are personal expenses and are not additions to your cost basis,
nor are they itemized tax deductions.

A repair maintains the property, but a capital improvement improves,
adds value, or extends the property's useful life. Sometimes it is hard to
tell the difference between a repair and a capital improvement.

After consulting your tax adviser, you might calculate your cost basis by
adding the $27,500 purchase price, plus the $6,000 room addition, plus the
$550 roof, plus the $200 landscaping, plus the $350 fence, and the new

$700 windows. But the $55 water heater was probably a repair cost rather than a capital improvement addition to your home's cost basis.

Your sale profit would be the $83,115 adjusted sales price minus the $35,300 adjusted cost basis. The result is $47,815 profit.

YOU HAVE TWENTY-FOUR MONTHS TO DECIDE ABOUT HOME SALE TAX DEFERRAL

Q. Last month we closed the sale of our home at a profit of almost $52,000. We moved into a luxury apartment house that we like very much. But then I read your article about the "residence replacement rule" that says a home seller can defer paying his profit tax if he buys a more expensive replacement house or condo. We have just learned the apartment house where we are renting will soon be converted to condominiums. Would this qualify, and how long do we have if we want to defer our tax?—*Sheri T.*

A. The "residence replacement rule" gives you up to twenty-four months before or after the sale of your principal residence to buy a more expensive replacement and defer paying the profit tax.

When a less-expensive replacement principal residence is bought, then your sale profit is taxed up to the difference in the two prices.

If you buy your condominium apartment, and it costs more than the sale price of your old home, and if the sale closes within twenty-four months of the sale of your old home, you must defer paying profit tax.

PROFIT TAX DEFERRAL NOT LOST BY TEMPORARY RENTAL

Q. We used that "residence replacement rule" you often write about to defer profit tax on the sale of our old home. We've lived in our current house about eleven months. I am being transferred to New Mexico on a one-year assignment. If we rent our home during our absence, will we have to pay the deferred profit tax?—*Walter M.*

A. No. Since you have not sold your replacement principal residence, no taxable event has occurred. Conversion from personal residence to rental status is not a taxable event.

But if you fail to return to your house as your principal residence, it thereby is permanently converted to rental status and you would lose the opportunity to again use the residence replacement rule if you decide to sell it.

TAX DEDUCTIONS FOR SOME HOME LOAN FEES

Q. Please clarify for me when loan fees paid to get a home mortgage are tax deductible. As a real estate agent, I'm often asked if loan fees are tax deductible. Also, what about FHA and VA home loan fees?—*Dan F.*

A. Loan fees paid to obtain a home mortgage on your personal residence, to either purchase or improve it, are tax deductible as itemized interest deductions. But VA home loan fees are never tax deductible.

Loan fees paid to get a mortgage on any property other than your personal residence must be amortized (deducted) over the life of the mortgage.

VA loan fees are special. Lenders usually charge VA loan discount points to raise the low, government-set interest rate up to market levels. Each one point loan fee raises the lender's yield about ⅛ percent. By law, the VA home buyer cannot pay such fees. So if the seller pays, the loan fee is a sales cost subtracted from the home's gross sales price.

But the VA home buyer can pay a one point "loan processing fee" to the lender. However, this processing fee is not tax deductible as interest for the buyer. FHA loan fee "points" paid by the home buyer are now tax deductible as interest, just like loan fees on conventional loans.

WHAT IF BUYER AND SELLER CANNOT AGREE ON INSTALLMENT SALE?

Q. We want an installment sale of our home, but the buyer wants to pay all cash. The realty agent suggests putting the money in escrow trust which would pay us over twenty years. Will this work?—*Robert A.*

A. No. Nice try, but IRS Revenue Ruling 77–294 rejects the idea of a seller getting installment sale benefits when the buyer deposits installment sale money into a trust account for payment to the buyer.

4.

Why Income Property
Is Your Second Best Investment

The previous chapter explained the tax benefits of owning your principal residence. Smart real estate investors make their first realty purchase a home for their personal use. The pride of ownership, inflation hedge, and tax benefits of owning one's home are unequalled. Of course, such a home may be a single-family house, condominium, cooperative apartment, mobile home, or even a houseboat. But the important thing is to make your home purchase your first real estate investment.

After buying your own home, your next investment should be income-producing real estate. Just as your home can take many different forms, income property comes in lots of shapes and sizes too. Some investors prefer apartments. Others like shopping centers. A large number specialize in industrial income property such as warehouses and industrial parks. Still others buy single-family investment houses, as I do.

Each type of income property offers special advantages and disadvantages. Professional realty investors often argue the merits of each type of income property. But it is vital, before deciding which type of income property is best for you, to understand the all-important tax aspects of income property ownership.

NEVER BUY FOR TAX GIMMICKS ALONE

One basic rule of investing in income property is never, never, never buy for tax benefits alone. If a property is not inherently sound without the tax gimmicks, it probably is not a wise investment.

The tax breaks of owning income property should be viewed only as a "bonus advantage." However, these bonus tax benefits are a major reason for buying income property rather than vacant land. Raw land offers practically no tax benefits. And, since most raw land produces little or no income, the costs of holding such property almost always outweigh the possible future advantage of resale profit.

Even farmers have come to realize, in many areas, that their major source of profits now comes not from crops which can be raised on their land but from probable future land sale profits. Unfortunately, having to sell raw land to make a profit is not as advantageous as making a profit while owning it, as income property investors do.

PROFIT DURING OWNERSHIP AS WELL AS AT RESALE TIME

Smart real estate investors count resale profits as another bonus of investing in real estate, just as the tax benefits are an ownership bonus. Why invest if you cannot make a profit while owning a property? If a property does not produce an overall profit during ownership, maybe it should not be bought (unless you can afford the risk of making your only profit dependent on resale profits).

Property investors who admit their only hope of profit will come at the time of resale are not investors. They are speculators. Speculators count on some fortuitous event, such as continued runaway inflation, for profits. But true investors create their own profits, both during ownership and at the time of eventual resale.

INVESTORS VS. SPECULATORS

In the next chapter we will look at how to find the best properties. That chapter discusses what smart investors want in a property that offers the best profit opportunities during ownership and at resale time. But before that discussion, it is vital to understand the tax benefits of property investing because the tax angles are important to understanding why it pays to buy income property rather than raw land.

An investor is a property owner who contributes something to the property, such as good management, physical improvements, or cash so someone else can use the property for their benefit. But a speculator is a quick-buck artist who contributes little or nothing to the property and is betting he can resell the property relatively quickly for more than he paid.

Characteristics of investors are (1) reasonable property management policies which are fair to tenants as well as to themselves, (2) expert financing techniques to use other people's money to purchase and improve the property (discussed in Chapter 6), (3) savvy use of ownership tax aspects to maximize their return from the property, (4) improvement and good management of the property to increase its market value (discussed in Chapter 8), and (5) creation of value by combining all these characteristics.

Indications of speculators include (1) shrewd management techniques that take advantage of the weaknesses of other people, such as property sellers and tenants, (2) little or no contribution of increased value due to physical improvements or efficient management of the property, (3) quick purchase and resale, (4) lack of concern for the long-run aspects of the property and its effect on the neighboring community, and (5) desire to maximize operating and resale profits (greed) without considering the long-term effect on the property itself.

An example of the latter is allowing deferred maintenance to accumulate and then selling the property just before major work becomes necessary. However, this can create profit opportunities for the next owner, who will hopefully be an investor rather than a speculator. A property that has two speculator owners in a row is easily recognizeable— usually with minimal cosmetic improvements such as cheap paint, least expensive carpets, and poor grade materials used throughout.

HOW TO UNDERSTAND THE MAJOR ADVANTAGES OF OWNING INCOME PROPERTY

How many times have you heard someone say "If only I had bought that property years ago I'd be wealthy today," or something similar? Today is yesterday's tomorrow. If you do not get busy investing in good real estate, you will be saying "If only I had bought" too.

While most investors believe real estate investing is the best way to keep up with and get ahead of inflation, too many potential realty buyers just talk about investing and do not take the first step of buying an investment property. Perhaps, if you are one of those lazy investors as I once was, you need a little friendly pushing. Please consider me your friendly realty "pusher"!

START BY SETTING YOUR INVESTMENT GOALS

Real estate can help investors realize many goals. Some are increased after-tax cash income, a hedge against inflation, providing a job from owning or managing property, opening up profit opportunities to upgrade property for profitable holding or resale, and many others.

But some types of properties meet investment goals better than others. For example, if you want maximum cash flow, buying vacant rural land obviously is not very smart. Investing in second mortgages would provide a higher cash flow (10 percent to 30 percent returns are not unusual for buyers of discounted second mortgages). Similarly, if you need to shelter your job earnings from income taxes, buying vacant land is not wise because it offers no tax savings from depreciation.

UNDERSTANDING REAL ESTATE OWNERSHIP BENEFITS

In Chapter 1 we looked at the four variables of any investment: (1) safety, (2) yield, (3) liquidity, and (4) potential for market value change. Although real estate did not come out perfect, overall it topped just about every other possible alternative investment.

This chapter takes a closer look at the advantages of owning real estate, specifically income properties. The term "income property," of course, refers to property which produces net, overall income for its owner. Examples include apartments, stores, and office buildings. "Nonincome property" includes vacant land, farmland, motels, boarding houses, and other property that requires personal labor to produce income from the property. As many investors in motels have found out, for example, some properties are merely real estate oriented businesses which offer the owner a full-time job. If you want to buy such property, and a full-time job, go ahead but do not think you are investing in income property because you are not. You are buying yourself a business first and a real estate investment second.

HOW TO LEGALLY CUT YOUR
INCOME TAX TO ZERO

In addition to all its inherent advantages, one of real estate's major attractions is its ability to shelter the owner's ordinary income, such as job salary, from income taxes. For example, an apartment house produces rents from its tenants. The owner uses that rent money to pay operating expenses (such as property taxes, repairs, utilities, and insurance) for the property. After paying all these costs, plus mortgage interest, he is left with either a positive or a negative cash flow from the property into his pocket.

EXAMPLE:

$ 20,000—Annual gross rental income from apartment rents
 − 8,000—Annual operating costs *(40 percent of gross for most apts.)*
$ 12,000—Annual net operating income
 − 10,000—Annual interest on mortgage
$ 2,000—Annual net income cash flow into owner's pocket

But a major expense has been left out! That is the noncash tax deduction for the building's depreciation. Income tax depreciation is a bookkeeping estimate for wear, tear, and obsolescence. It requires no cash payment to be entitled to this deduction.

Let us suppose our hypothetical building (not including the non-depreciable land value which never wears out) cost $80,000, and we elect to use an 18-year estimated remaining useful life with straight-line depreciation (these terms will be explained later in great detail).

EXAMPLE:
$ 2,000 —Annual net income cash flow into owner's pocket
    4,444 —Annual depreciation *($80,000 divided by 18 years)*
$ (2,444)—Annual tax or paper loss from this income property

In this example, mortgage payments were considered to be mostly tax-deductible interest expense. In the early years of most mortgages, this is correct because only about 1 percent of the mortgage payments go toward equity buildup (loan principal payoff). The other 99 percent is tax-deductible interest.

But as the years go by, the deductible interest portion of the mortgage payment decreases and nondeductible principal amortization payoff increases. When the amortization becomes so great that a tax loss no longer results, that is the time to refinance to increase the mortgage interest tax deduction. Contrary to the thinking of most homeowners, income property owners rarely want to own their property free and clear, due to the tax disadvantages.

A tax or paper loss from income property is good. The owner of the property in the example above can subtract his $2,444 loss from his other taxable income, such as job salary.

If the owner of the building above has $20,000 taxable income, thanks to his building he will pay tax only on $17,556 (due to the $2,444 tax loss), thus saving about $489 in income taxes if he is in a 20 percent tax bracket. Yet he still can receive that $2,444 cash in the example and put it in his pocket tax-free. If this owner owns enough depreciable income properties, they can shelter all his otherwise taxable income from taxation.

HOW THE "TAX MAGIC" OF DEPRECIATION CAN SAVE YOU TAX DOLLARS

To understand how depreciation works and how it can save you income tax dollars requires some work. You may want to reread the next few pages several times because they are so important for real estate investors to fully comprehend.

Smart investors do their own income tax returns. Then they take them to their tax adviser to see if any tax deductions were missed. But without an understanding of important tax concepts, such as depreciation, you cannot do your own income tax returns for review by a specialist.

NO ONE HAS AS GREAT AN INTEREST IN SAVING YOUR TAX DOLLARS AS YOU DO.

The reason depreciation works "tax magic" is that it requires no cash payment to be entitled to this tax deduction. Other tax deductions, such as interest and property taxes, require the payment of hard, cold cash. But not depreciation.

That is why depreciation is the best tax deduction of all! It is even better than a tax credit (which is a subtraction from the income tax you owe). Although it is said "There's no such thing as a free lunch," the income tax deduction for depreciation comes pretty close.

INTRODUCTION TO DEPRECIATION

Any owner of business or rental real estate must deduct an allowance on his income tax returns for the theoretical loss in value of the improvements on his land due to the passage of time. Depreciation is a mandatory income tax deduction to compensate the owner for loss in value caused by wear, tear, and obsolescence of the improvements' value.

The value of the land on which the improvements rest, however, is *not* depreciable. That is because land is theoretically indestructible and never wears out. After the building becomes obsolete and is demolished, the land will still be there without any decline in its value due to wear, tear, or obsolescence.

WHAT IS AND IS NOT DEPRECIABLE PROPERTY?

There are three major classes of real estate that are *not* entitled to any tax deduction for depreciation.

A. Land Value

The value of land, whether it is raw, vacant land, improved farmland, or land with buildings resting on it, cannot be depreciated. While it is arguable that some land loses value, such as farm cropland which loses minerals each year, that argument is not recognized for income tax purposes.

Some land is subject to a depletion allowance, however, such as for oil or mineral removal. But depletion is not the same as depreciation and is beyond the scope of this book.

B. Personal Residences

Owners of single-family houses, cooperative apartments, or condominiums who reside in those structures are not entitled to any depreciation of those buildings. One exception exists, however, if the personal residence is used for rental to tenants or if part is used for a home office or shop. Then the personal residence qualifies for business use depreciation, as discussed in Chapter 3.

The reason personal residences are not depreciable is they are not held for investment or for use in a trade or business. This is the basic test for depreciable real estate.

However, an owner who resides in one apartment of a multi-unit apartment house can depreciate all of the building except his personal residence unit.

C. Property Held for Sale (Dealer Inventory)

Property which would otherwise be depreciable cannot be depreciated if it is held solely for sale to others. Such property is usually owned by a real estate dealer whose business is selling his inventory to others. Examples include homes constructed by a home builder for sale to customers or a new shopping center constructed by a developer for sale to investors.

WHAT IS DEPRECIABLE PROPERTY?

Just about any building, structure, or personal property used in the owner's trade or business or held for investment is depreciable. This includes buildings, sidewalks, fences, parking lot improvements, and other installations involving a "profit-inspired use." Depreciation is allowed even if the investment operation produces a loss, if there is a long-term profit intention. Even vacant buildings must be depreciated if they are held for investment or for use in a trade or business.

Orchards, orange trees, lemon groves, and other fruit and nut bearing trees are depreciable too. The *key test* for the depreciation deduction is DOES THE ASSET HAVE A DETERMINABLE LIMITED ECONOMIC USEFUL LIFE? If it does, it is depreciable!

HOW TO APPLY THE DEPRECIATION TEST

Using this test, land is not depreciable because it has no determinable limited economic useful life. For example, unless replenished by fertilizers, farmland will eventually lose its ability to produce crops. But this time period cannot be determined with any accuracy.

However, a fruit tree on nondepreciable land has a determinable useful life beyond which it will not produce a worthwhile crop. Similarly, land under a building is not depreciating due to wear, tear, or obsolescence. It just sits there, unaffected by what happens to the building that is resting upon it.

Interestingly, Revenue Ruling 74–265 held that landscaping adjoining a depreciable building can be depreciated if the owner can show the landscaping will most likely be destroyed at the end of the useful life of the building. In such a case, trees and landscaping shrubbery have the same useful life as adjoining building. The cost of planting annual flowers, of course, would be deductible as a current expense and would not qualify for depreciation.

HOW TO APPORTION THE COST BASIS

Upon acquisition of a depreciable property, the owner is required to allocate his cost basis among the (1) nondepreciable land value, (2) the improvement value, and (3) the value of any personal property.

THE CONSERVATIVE, NONCHALLENGEABLE METHOD

Allocating the cost basis of a property among its components is, at best, guesswork. It is far from a scientific procedure. Most owners start the process by looking at their local tax assessor's ratio among the depreciable assets such as building, personal property, and nondepreciable land value, as shown on the annual property tax bill. In most states, the tax assessor's bill shows his assessed value for the land, improvements, and, sometimes, the personal property. Owners who consider the assessor's ratio to be reasonable then apply that ratio to their purchase price of the property. The IRS will not challenge an allocation made by this method.

> EXAMPLE: Curt bought an apartment house for $200,000 (the amount of his cash down payment and mortgage(s) have nothing to do with depreciation deductions). The tax assessor's bill, although the assessed value is usually lower than the price paid for the property, shows 70 percent of assessed value is for the building, 20 percent for the land, and 10 percent for the personal property (refrigerators, stoves, and furniture). Curt feels this ratio is reasonable. So he allocates 70 percent of his $200,000 cost, or $140,000, to the depreciable building value, 20 percent or $40,000, to the nondepreciable land value, and 10 percent, or $20,000, to the depreciable personal property value.

Cost basis (purchase price) of the property acquisition of a depreciable property should be apportioned among land, buildings, and any personal property in proportion to their market value on the acquisition date. If the owner feels the local tax assessor's ratios are not realistic, he should use some other objective method for apportionment of the purchase price.

One way is to get a professional appraisal. Another is to obtain evidence of sale prices of nearby vacant land and then apply that square foot value to the land under the building purchased by the taxpayer, with the remainder allocated to improvements.

As will be explained later, the second safest method after using the tax assessor's ratio, is probably the professional appraiser's valuation. The third safest method is to use your insurance agent's estimate of the building's replacement cost.

ACQUISITION WITH INTENT TO DEMOLISH THE STRUCTURE

If property is bought with intent to demolish the building within a short time, then the owner cannot make any allocation of his purchase price to the building value. The entire purchase price must then be allocated to the nondepreciable land value. The cost of razing the structure must also be added to the land value, less any salvage collected. Demolition costs are not tax deductible in such a case.

Even if the owner intends to eventually demolish his building, if he rents it or uses it in his trade or business temporarily, he is then entitled to deduct depreciation for the limited use period. The depreciation basis of the building would be its present value at the time of acquisition (less land value, of course).

But if the building is not promptly demolished, any initial intent to destroy it must be ignored. When the building is later demolished before it is fully depreciated, a loss deduction is not allowed for the undepreciated basis of the structure. The 1984 Tax Act requires capitalizing the undepreciated basis by adding it to the nondepreciable land value.

BASIS ALLOCATION BY CONTRACT IS WORTHLESS

Sometimes a buyer and seller of depreciable real estate, in an arm's-length contractual negotiation, will allocate the purchase price among land, improvements, and personal property. If such an allocation makes no real difference to the seller—that is, all his profit is taxed as capital gain—the IRS will usually disregard any such allocation.

But if the seller has part of the gain taxed as ordinary income instead of as long-term capital gain due to the allocation, then the IRS will usually accept such an allocation of the purchase price. Since it is very rare to have a real estate sales profit taxed as ordinary income, this limited exception does not apply very often.

HOW TO MAXIMIZE DEPRECIATION BENEFITS UNDER THE 1981 TAX ACT

The 1981 Tax Act, also known as the 1981 Economic Recovery Tax Act (ERTA), greatly simplified the depreciation rules for real and personal property acquired after December 31, 1980. The old depreciation rules apply to property acquired before this date. These old, now outdated depreciation methods are fully explained in the 1981 first edition of this book (available from public libraries or local bookstores).

The law's Accelerated Cost Recovery System (ACRS) must be used for all depreciable real and personal property "placed in service" after December 31, 1980.

ACRS DEPRECIATION PERIODS

Depending on the type of depreciable real or personal property, you have a choice of useful life "recovery periods":

PROPERTY	USEFUL LIFE
Vehicles	3, 5, or 12 years
Other personal property	5, 12, or 25 years
Manufactured housing (mobile homes)	10, 25, or 35 years
Real property	18*, 35, or 45 years

*15 years if "placed in service" before March 15, 1984.

Investors desiring to maximize their depreciation benefits will select the shortest possible useful life in each category. It does not matter whether the real or personal property acquired is new or used; the same useful life applies.

These new depreciation useful-life time periods will stop the hassles taxpayers often encountered with IRS audit-agents. Now the taxpayer can select the eighteen, thirty-five-, or forty-five-year useful life for his depreciable buildings and the IRS auditor cannot challenge the selection. However, these rules only apply to federal income tax returns, not state tax returns. Unless the states conform their depreciation tax rules, a taxpayer might need two depreciation schedules—one federal and one state.

END OF COMPONENT DEPRECIATION

However, in return for establishing shorter useful lives for assets, the 1981 Tax Act removed the taxpayer's election to use the component method of depreciation. This technique permitted the property owner to depreciate separately the costs of various components such as plumbing, wiring, roof, and building shell.

Since these components usually had shorter useful lives than the composite whole, the owner maximized his depreciation deduction by using component depreciation. However, the 1981 Tax Act eliminates use of component depreciation except for depreciable property acquired before 1981.

HOW MUCH DEPRECIATION IS ALLOWABLE?

The depreciation deduction for depreciable real and personal property is limited by its cost to the owner. If the property was inherited, the owner's basis is the property's market value on the date of the decedent's death. However, if the property was a gift, the donee's basis is the lower of (1) the property's adjusted cost basis to the donor or (2) the property's fair market value on the date of the gift.

The cost of any capital improvements added after acquiring the property should be added to its basis. Salvage value need not be considered for property acquired in 1981 or later years.

The basis of depreciable real or personal property must be reduced by its allowable depreciation deduction each year under the schedule the owner adopts during the first year of ownership. Even if such depreciation reduces the owner's book value and gives him no income tax savings benefit in a particular tax year, he must reduce his book value by the allowable depreciation amount. In other words, he cannot make up in a future tax year for his loss of tax benefit in a previous tax year when the depreciation deduction gave him no tax dollar savings.

EXAMPLE: Laura's annual depreciation deduction for her three-family triplex resulted in a $2,500 tax loss on that property last year. Unfortunately, Laura's income from her other businesses also showed a loss last year. Since Laura had no other taxable income from which to deduct her $2,500 paper or tax loss from her triplex, she must reduce her book value "adjusted cost basis" on the triplex for the required depreciation even though no income tax shelter saving resulted.

USEFUL LIFE OF THE DEPRECIABLE ASSET

Two factors determine how much income tax depreciation is allowed: (1) the estimated useful life of the depreciable asset and (2) the depreciation method selected by the property owner.

For depreciation purposes, "useful life" of an asset means how long its economic life will be in the owner's trade or business or how long it will produce investment income. *Useful life does not mean physical life* unless that time is the same as useful economic life.

Under the pre-1981 law, Revenue Ruling 62-21 established "guideline" useful lives for average quality brand-new construction of various types of buildings. For example, these old guidelines suggested useful lives of forty years for new apartments, fifty years for bank buildings, forty-five years for factories, forty years for hotels, and sixty years for warehouses.

The new law abolishes these categories for buildings "placed in service" in 1981 or later years. The owner can now select an eighteen-, thirty-five-, or forty-five-year useful life for his structures regardless of the building's use or its current age.

To maximize depreciation tax deductions, 99 percent of all building owners will probably select the eighteen-year useful life. Owners selecting the thirty-five- or forty-five-year useful life would be those taxpayers who have no use for maximum depreciation deductions.

DEPRECIATION METHODS

The 1981 Tax Act allows only two depreciation methods: straight line and 175 percent accelerated.

THE CONSERVATIVE STRAIGHT-LINE DEPRECIATION METHOD

Most taxpayers use the straight-line depreciation method because (1) it is the easiest to use, (2) it eliminates any "recapture" problems (discussed later) when the property is sold, and (3) it gives easily predictable results rather than annually changing results of accelerated methods.

To use the straight-line depreciation method, the asset's basis is divided by its estimated useful life in years. The result is its annual depreciation deduction. But if the asset was not owned for the full tax year, it can be depreciated only for the number of months it was owned. In other words, prorations must be made for less than a full year of ownership.

The straight-line depreciation method can be used for all new and used depreciable real and personal property.

> EXAMPLE: Warren allocates the $400,000 purchase price of his shopping center to $300,000 for the depreciable building and $100,000 for the non-depreciable land value. He selects an eighteen-year useful life for depreciation. Dividing $300,000 by eighteen gives an annual $16,667 straight-line depreciation deduction. However, since Warren bought the shopping center in November 1984, he only deducts ²⁄₁₂ or $2,778 depreciation for the building on his 1984 federal income tax returns.

THE NEW 175-PERCENT ACCELERATED DEPRECIATION METHOD

The only other depreciation method now available for depreciable real property "placed in service" after December 31, 1980, is the new 175 percent accelerated depreciation method. This method uses the eighteen-year useful life but allows an additional 75 percent of the straight-line depreciation deduction. It can be elected whether the building is brand-new or used. However, before selecting this depreciation method, consider the "recapture" consequences at the time the building is sold (discussed later). Accelerated depreciation recapture can be very disadvantageous for commercial property owners but not so bad for residential rental property investors.

The following chart gives the annual depreciation deduction as a percent of the taxpayer's cost basis for the property. Please notice that the amount of deduction depends upon the month in which the depreciable real estate is purchased.

ACRS Cost Recovery Tables for 18-Year Real Estate

All Real Estate (Except Low-Income Housing)
"placed in service" after March 15, 1984

If the
recovery
year
is:

18-Year Real Property (18-year 175% Declining Balance)
(Assuming Mid-Month Convention)

The applicable percentage is:

If the recovery year is:	Jan	Feb	Mar	Apr	May	Jun	Jul	Aug	Sep	Oct	Nov	Dec
1	12	11	10	9	8	7	6	5	4	3	2	1
2	10	10	11	11	11	11	11	11	11	11	11	12
3	9	9	9	9	10	10	10	10	10	10	10	10
4	8	8	8	8	8	8	9	9	9	9	9	9
5	7	7	7	7	7	7	8	8	8	8	8	8
6	6	6	6	6	7	7	7	7	7	7	7	7
7	6	6	6	6	6	6	6	6	6	6	6	6
8	6	6	6	6	6	6	5	6	6	6	6	6
9	6	6	6	6	5	6	5	5	5	6	6	6
10	5	6	5	6	5	5	5	5	5	5	6	5
11	5	5	5	5	5	5	5	5	5	5	5	5
12	5	5	5	5	5	5	5	5	5	5	5	5
13	5	5	5	5	5	5	5	5	5	5	5	5
14	5	5	5	5	5	5	5	5	5	5	5	5
15	5	5	5	5	5	5	5	5	5	5	5	5
16	—	—	1	1	2	2	3	3	4	4	4	5

EXAMPLE: Suppose you buy a small apartment house for $125,000, allocating $100,000 to the depreciable building's value and $25,000 to the nondepreciable land value. Using the chart, if you bought in January you can deduct 9 percent of the $100,000 building's cost ($9,000) the first year, 9 percent ($9,000) the second year, 8 percent ($8,000) the third year, etc.

But, again using the chart, if you buy this same building in May (the fifth month of the year), you can only depreciate 6 percent of the building's cost ($6,000) in the year of purchase, 9 percent ($9,000) the second year, 8 percent ($8,000) the third year, etc.

Whether you acquire the depreciable real property early or late in the year, however, using this 175 percent accelerated depreciation method will still result in full depreciation of the building within eighteen years. But the big advantage of using this 175 percent accelerated depreciation method is maximization of tax shelter from the depreciation tax deduction in the early years of ownership. This depreciation method helps implement the smart real estate investor's motto: A tax deduction this year is better than a tax deduction in the future.

HOW "DEPRECIATION RECAPTURE" WORKS
AND WHY IT CAN BE EXPENSIVE

Depending on when a depreciable property was bought and when it is sold, all or part of the eighteen-year, 175 percent accelerated depreciation deducted may be "recaptured." Recapture, in tax language, means taxed as ordinary income.

Here are the new recapture rules for eighteen-year, 175 percent rapid depreciation:

1. If the property is used as a residential rental, at the time of the property's sale, the difference between the 175 percent accelerated depreciation deducted and the allowable eighteen-year straight-line depreciation is taxed as ordinary income.

EXAMPLE: Suppose you deducted $20,000 of eighteen-year, 175-percent accelerated depreciation before you sold the property. If the eighteen-year straight-line method would have allowed only a $15,000 depreciation deduction, the $5,000 difference will be "recaptured" and taxed as ordinary income upon resale.

2. If the property is used for any purpose other than residential rental, at the time of its sale the *entire amount* of 175 percent accelerated depreciation deducted will be recaptured and taxed as ordinary income.

EXAMPLE: Using the amounts in the previous example, but now presuming the property is commercial (such as offices, stores, or warehouses), the entire $20,000 eighteen-year 175 percent accelerated depreciation deducted will be taxed as ordinary income at the time the property is sold.

Obviously, Congress wants to discourage commerical property owners from using the new 175 percent accelerated depreciation method since *all* such depreciation is recaptured and taxed as ordinary income. So unless the taxpayer saves a huge amount of income tax dollars by using 175 percent accelerated depreciation on his commercial property, in most cases it will pay to use straight-line eighteen-year depreciation on commercial buildings acquired after March 15, 1984.

Although it may seem disastrous to some property investors to have part of their resale profit recaptured and taxed as ordinary income tax rates, it should be remembered that the taxpayer has the tax-sheltered use of that profit money from depreciation (actually, the income tax dollars saved) until the property is sold.

For residential property owners electing the 175 percent accelerated depreciation method, it is also important to note that the longer the property is owned before sale, the less the recapture amount will be because the difference between accelerated and straight-line depreciation declines annually. By the eighteenth year, both methods fully depreciate the building.

HOW TO AVOID DEPRECIATION RECAPTURE

Smart taxpayers who own either residential or commercial property, however, can forget the recapture problem if they never sell. Another way to avoid recapture of depreciation deductions as ordinary income is to make a tax-deferred exchange.

Internal Revenue Code Section 1031 approves property trades as a continuous investment, rather than a sale and reinvestment in a second property. The happy result for traders is avoidance of accelerated depreciation recapture if the easy requirements of IRC 1031 are met.

As explained in Chapter 9, tax-deferred exchanges are virtually the only method of pyramiding your wealth without paying income taxes as you do so. Such exchanges allow a smart investor, for example, to start out with a small property (such as a two-family rental), build some equity in it, and later make a tax-deferred trade of that equity for a larger property to be held for investment or use in a trade or business.

BEWARE OF THE NEW ANTI-CHURNING RULES
FOR TAX-DEFERRED EXCHANGES

Although tax-deferred exchanges are a great way to avoid depreciation recapture and profit taxation when disposing of one property and acquiring another, the 1981 Tax Act has an exchange pitfall to avoid. It is called the "anti-churning rule."

If you own investment or business real property acquired before 1981, you probably would like to dispose of it and acquire other property so you can take advantage of the 1981 Tax Act's generous depreciation deductions. So you might think you can exchange your pre-1981 property (thus deferring the profit tax) for post-1981 property (to use the new depreciation rules).

But Congress anticipated this desire because it did not want taxpayers to both defer profit tax upon disposal of property and be able to take advantage of the new generous depreciation rules for the replacement property.

Greatly simplified, the 1981 Tax Act's anti-churning provisions say that if you make a tax-deferred exchange of business or investment real estate for another such property, your old basis and its old depreciation method carry over to the newly acquired property. The new eighteen-year, 175 percent accelerated depreciation methods can only be used on the increased depreciable basis of the property acquired in the exchange.

EXAMPLE: Suppose you own a $100,000 depreciable building which you have depreciated down to $20,000. If you sell it, you will owe long-term capital gains tax on your $80,000 profit. So you decide to trade for a $300,000 property. The anti-churning rule requires you to use your old depreciation method on the $20,000 basis carried over to the $300,000 property. But the new eighteen-year, 175 percent accelerated depreciation methods *can* be used on any increased depreciable basis in the acquired property.

However, if the owner of property acquired before 1981 has a depreciated book value adjusted cost basis only slightly less than the property's market value, he might be better off selling his old property, paying a small long-term capital gains tax on his small profit, and reinvesting in another property that can fully qualify for the new rapid depreciation.

EXAMPLE: Suppose you own a $100,000 depreciable building which you have depreciated down to $90,000 adjusted cost basis (book value). If you sell, you will have a $10,000 long-term capital gain with a maximum 20 percent tax of about $2,000. You can reinvest the $8,000 remaining into another depreciable property and use the new depreciation method on the new acquisition's entire depreciable basis. But if you make a tax-deferred exchange instead, the 1981 Tax Act's anti-churning rule requires you to carry over your old $90,000 adjusted cost basis and its old depreciation method (perhaps a twenty-five- or thirty-year useful life) to the acquired property.

To maximize tax shelter from the new depreciation rules, and to avoid the adverse results of the anti-churning rule in the 1981 Tax Act:

1. If you own low basis pre-1981 property, use an IRC 1031 tax-deferred exchange to defer your large profit tax and carry over your old, low basis and old depreciation method (but just on the old basis amount) and use the new eighteen-year depreciation rules for the amount of the increased basis.
2. If you own a high basis pre-1981 property, consider selling it, paying the long-term capital gain tax on your profit, and acquiring another property which can be fully depreciated using the new eighteen-year depreciation rules (with no carry-over of your old basis and old depreciation method).

A SPECIAL TAX BONANZA—NEW PERSONAL PROPERTY
DEPRECIATION RULES

In addition to the new eighteen-year depreciation rules for depreciable buildings and other real property improvements, the 1981 Tax Act improved the rules for depreciating personal property used in a trade or business.

The tax law requires depreciation of business personal property such as equipment and furnishings. In real estate, examples include apartment house furniture and appliances used by the tenants of the apartment rentals.

EXAMPLE: Howard bought $10,000 of furniture and appliances for his apartment house. Using the new ACRS depreciation method, he can select a five-, twelve-, or twenty-five-year useful life for this personal property. Like most realty investors, Howard selects the five-year useful life because he then maximizes his depreciation tax deductions and this depreciation bookkeeping write-off will approximate the rate at which the furniture and appliances drop in actual market value as they wear out.

ACCELERATED DEPRECIATION ALLOWED FOR PERSONAL PROPERTY

The 1981 Tax Act allows taxpayers to select either straight-line or accelerated depreciation for personal property. The accelerated depreciation tables provided in the new tax law are equivalent of 150 percent declining balance accelerated depreciation. It does not matter if the personal property is new or used.

Further note should be made of the so-called "half-year convention." Regardless of whether you acquire depreciable personal property in January, July, or December, in the year of acquisition you get a prorated depreciation deduction as if you had bought the personal property on July 1. But this half-year convention applies only to personal property using accelerated depreciation. All real property and personal property depreciated on the straight-line basis does not use the new half-year convention provided for in the following ACRS depreciation chart.

150 PERCENT RAPID DEPRECIATION FOR PERSONAL PROPERTY

YEAR	3-YEAR VEHICLES	5-YEAR PERSONAL PROPERTY
1	25%	15%
2	38%	22%
3	37%	21%
4		21%
5		21%

However, this chart only applies to business personal property *after* the allowable first-year write-off (up to $5,000) has been first subtracted from the cost. Also, please note that it is not necessary to consider any salvage value for business personal property.

INVESTMENT TAX CREDIT

Although the investment tax credit will not apply to personal property acquired by most real estate investors for use in their properties, the investment tax credit does apply to vehicles (such as a car used in supervising your properties). This tax credit is a direct subtraction from your income tax liability as follows:

Vehicles	6% credit
Other personal property	10% credit

The reason the investment tax credit does not apply to most real estate investors is that the tax law specifically excludes from eligibility personal property used in connection with lodging facilities unless used by transients more than half the time (IRC 48(a)(3); Reg. 1.48-1(h)). However, nonlodging commercial facilities open to the public, such as coin-operated laundry machines or vending machines in an apartment house, qualify for the investment tax credit.

If the personal property, on which an investment tax credit was claimed, is sold before it is fully depreciated, the taxpayer can keep 2 percent for each year the property was owned.

EXAMPLE: Betty claimed a 6 percent investment tax credit on her new car acquired in 1984. She keeps it two years and disposes of it in 1986 before it is fully depreciated. Betty can keep 4 percent of her investment tax credit but the remaining 2 percent will be recaptured on her 1986 tax returns.

SUMMARY

The 1981 Tax Act was a tax bonanza for real estate investors who understand how to take advantage of its provisions. The rapid eighteen-year, 175 percent accelerated depreciation useful life methods will further enhance real estate's inherent advantages, which are unmatched by alternative low-risk investments. But what Congress giveth, Congress can take away. The sooner you acquire depreciable real estate, the sooner you can benefit from these tax benefits of owning depreciable property.

SUMMARY OF THE "TAX MAGIC" DEPRECIATION APPLICABLE TO INVESTMENT REALTY

The goal of tax-wise property investors should be to own total holdings which at least break even on a cash basis. After deducting the paper loss from depreciation, the properties should lose money to give the owner "tax shelter" for his other ordinary income, such as job salary. If your real estate produces an after-tax profit, rather than a paper loss, it is time to trade up to larger properties which will give higher depreciation deductions and, hence, tax shelter.

Depreciation tax magic occurs when the building's cash flow is exceeded by its depreciation deduction. The result is a tax loss. A tax loss should be every investor's goal!

But the best news is that while the building is depreciating in book value, in the real world it should be appreciating in market value. When the owner sells his building, the difference between his net sales price and depreciated book value is profit (taxable at the low, long-term capital gain tax rates ranging from 5.6 percent to 20 percent of the total profit, except for any recaptured depreciation taxed as ordinary income.).

A footnote should be added, however. Another advantage of owning depreciable real property is *it is just about the only investment that can be sold at a profit even if the price attained is the same as the investor paid for the property*. It is all due to the *tax magic of depreciation that converts ordinary income into long-term capital gains*.

For example, suppose your $100,000 building is depreciated down to $80,000 book value when you resell it for $100,000. That $20,000 difference between the adjusted sales price and the adjusted cost basis is profit. During ownership, the $20,000 depreciation deduction sheltered $20,000 of ordinary income (such as rents or job salary) from income taxes. At resale time, that profit is taxed at the lowest possible rates for long-term capital gains.

The happy result is conversion of ordinary income (taxed at the highest income tax rates) to long-term capital gain (taxed at the lowest rates).

There is nothing wrong with paying income taxes. But smart investors pay those taxes at the low, long-term capital gains rates. This is made easy for investors who understand the tax benefits of owning depreciable real property.

HOW SMART INVESTORS USE NEW EQUITY-SHARING RULES TO SAVE INCOME TAXES

Parents who want to help their adult children purchase a first home can now get tax deductions for doing so. The Black Lung Benefit Revenue Act, passed by Congress in late 1981, contains a little-known amendment to Internal Revenue Code Section 280A that clarifies equity-sharing tax deductions.

This law applies to equity-sharing plans for all investors, not just those between parents and their adult children. For example, many investors use equity-sharing plans to cut or eliminate negative cash flow when investing in single-family rental houses. Other investors use equity-sharing plans to acquire properties but eliminate the management time usually involved with rentals.

To illustrate, suppose a young couple want to buy a $75,000 house that requires a $15,000 cash down payment that they don't have. So they ask dear old mom and dad to put up the $15,000 down payment in return for an equity-sharing co-ownership agreement.

Such an equity-share contract might provide for a fifty-fifty home ownership and an equal split of resale profits in five years when the house will be sold. The couple get to occupy the residence (and make the mortgage, property tax, and repair payments), and the parents get to depreciate their half of the house, which is technically rented to the young couple who own the other half of the house. Everyone wins, except Uncle Sam.

A relatively new idea, equity sharing is becoming popular among real estate investors (who have the cash for a down payment) and occupants (who lack down payment money but who can afford the monthly payments). Equity sharing means the investor usually buys the residence and then sells half the house to the co-owner occupant for nothing down. The occupant makes the payments and gets income tax deductions for his share, such as half, of the mortgage interest and property taxes. The nonresident investor receives rent for his portion of the house but has tax deductions for his share of the mortgage interest, property taxes, and depreciation for part of the house.

After perhaps five years of ownership, the equity-sharing contract between the nonresident investor and the resident co-owner usually provides for sale or refinancing of the house, with the profits then split equally between the investor and occupant.

To qualify for equity-sharing income tax deductions, the occupant co-owner must pay fair market rent to the investor for use of the investor's share of the house. The investor gets depreciation tax shelter from his ownership share. He can use the new eighteen-year depreciation deductions, including 175 percent accelerated depreciation, on his share of the property.

The new equity-sharing tax law doesn't bar these deductions even if the co-owners are related, such as parents and children.

Other possible co-owners with the occupants can be an employer or an investor. Due to this recent tax law change, the nonoccupant co-owner can claim deductions exceeding rental income received from the occupant co-owner, thus sheltering some of the nonresident's income from other sources from income tax.

At the time of the agreed resale of the property, such as in five or ten years, the resale profits will be taxed as long-term capital gains. If eligible, the resident occupant should be able to use the "residence replacement rule" (IRC 1034) tax-deferred rollover if another residence of equal or greater cost is purchased within twenty-four months before or after the sale, or the "over 55 rule" $125,000 home sale tax-exemption benefit on his profit share.

However, this new tax law sets two equity-sharing qualification rules: (1) two or more persons acquire the residence together and (2) one or more of these co-owners occupies the dwelling as a principal residence and pays rent to the nonoccupant co-owner. A real estate attorney should be consulted to draw up the written equity-sharing co-ownership agreement between the resident and nonresident co-owners.

QUESTIONS AND ANSWERS

UNLOCK HOME EQUITY TO BUY DEPRECIABLE INVESTMENT PROPERTY

Q. We sold our stocks at a substantial loss. After reading your newspaper articles about how it costs money to keep cash in a savings account, after considering inflation and income tax on the interest, we decided to buy an apartment house. The first agent showed us a ten-unit building we saw advertised in the newspaper. When we told him we had about $25,000 to invest, he asked if we would like to buy a twenty-seven-unit building instead. Of course, we told him we were interested (because we want to maximize our tax shelter from the depreciation) but that we have only $25,000 to invest. He suggested we "create" a second mortgage on our home equity for the rest of our down payment. This sounds like a good idea. Is it?—*Charles R.*

A. Yes. By giving the seller of the twenty-seven-unit building a second mortgage on your house for part of your down payment, in addition to your $25,000 cash investment, you are unlocking your idle home equity.

Most homeowners should unlock their home equities. The more property you control, the better protected you will be against inflation. If you buy that twenty-seven-unit building, you will own two properties (your home and the apartments) which are probably going up in value at least as fast as the inflation rate. In addition, that apartment house should give you a "tax loss" or "paper loss" to shelter the rents and some of your other ordinary taxable income from income taxation.

WHERE TO GET CASH TO BUY INVESTMENT PROPERTY

Q. I own my home, valued at $55,000. My mortgage at 7 percent interest rate is about $13,500. I have over $6,000 in my savings account. To buy income property, probably apartments, should I take the $6,000 for my down payment, or should I refinance my home mortgage to raise the cash for the down payment? I want to acquire as much income property as possible. I have heard that to get a mortgage on income property, you must live in the building. Is that true? Does FHA make apartment-house mortgages?—*Mr. D. K.*

A. To raise cash for your down payment, instead of refinancing that beautiful 7 percent mortgage, consider adding a second mortgage instead. Weigh both alternatives before deciding. Unless you have good borrowing power, keep adequate cash in savings for emergencies.

No, you do not have to live in the apartment house to get a mortgage on it. But FHA mortgages on one- to four-family buildings require owner occupancy of one apartment. FHA loans on over four units do not require you to live in the building.

However, your best finance source is the property's seller. In your first purchase offer, provide for the seller to carry a first or second mortgage to help finance your purchase. Many sellers will do so. Also, please remember to make as small a cash down payment as possible to maximize your leverage yield per dollar.

DO CONDOS MAKE GOOD HOMES AND INVESTMENTS?

Q. Last winter we visited Florida for a month. We are thinking of retiring there. While we were there, we looked at several new developments of retirement houses and condominiums. The condo idea appeals to us, as we can just lock the door and drive away without having to worry about maintaining the property while we're gone. But we are two years away from retirement. Would it be smart to buy a retirement condo now, rent it for two years, and then move into it as our retirement home? I guess what I really want to know is whether or not condos make good homes and investments?—*Marty R.*

A. Yes, condominiums can be excellent homes and investments. But they can also be lousy if you buy the wrong one.

Before you buy, talk to current residents of the development. Find out what they like most and least about it. Ask if they would buy there again.

Some condos are well built and extremely satisfactory. Others are cracker boxes. Personally, I have done well with condo investments. But I strongly suggest you double-check the soundproofing before you buy. Lack of adequate soundproofing is the number one complaint of condo owners.

As investment property, condos can be extremely profitable due to their high building-to-land ratio. Unless the condo development has lots of open space, you may be able to depreciate up to 90 or 95 percent of the purchase price for the cost of the condo unit (land value is nondepreciable). Your tax adviser can further explain the tax benefits of condo investing.

VACATION OR SECOND HOMES
ARE RARELY GOOD TAX SHELTER INVESTMENTS

Q. We bought a second home in a vacation area. The summer season lasts about sixteen weeks, and there is winter ice fishing and some skiing too. The realty agent will try to rent it to tenants as much as possible except when we use it for about three weeks each July. Will we be able to take depreciation on this property so we can get some tax shelter from it? —*Woody M.*

A. For income tax purposes, if your personal use of your second home exceeds fourteen days per year or 10 percent of its rental period, it cannot qualify as "investment property." That means no tax shelter benefits for you.

Your mortgage interest and property tax are always deductible on your income tax returns even if they exceed the second home's rental income. But if your personal use time exceeds the limits above, then your tax deductions for the second home cannot exceed the rent received.

Suppose your house earns $4,000 annual rent and $3,000 is the total of the annual mortgage interest and property taxes. If your personal use exceeds the time limits above, you can then only deduct up to $1,000 of other expenses, including any depreciation.

In other words, no "tax loss" is allowed on second homes if your personal use exceeds the fourteen-day or 10 percent limits. But you can get tax loss benefits for your vacation home if your personal use time is below these limits since the cabin then qualifies as investment property.

NO INFLATION PROTECTION IF YOU
DO NOT INVEST IN REAL ESTATE

Q. I am sixty-four, one year away from retirement, and have about $20,000 excess funds to invest. I own my home free and clear and am a widow. My son suggests I invest my $20,000 in several second mortgages. What do you think?—*Laura M.*

A. I think you should first decide what your investment goals are.

Income? Inflation protection? Pride of ownership? Tax shelter?

All these goals can be accomplished with real estate. But usually not at the same time with just one investment. If you invest in second mortgages, for example, you will probably maximize your income. That is why so many retirees invest in second mortgages. But there is no inflation hedge protection and no tax shelter for the excellent interest earnings.

If you buy a small rental property, however, it may appreciate in market value at least as fast as the inflation rate. But such property will not give you immediate cash income equal to what you could have earned investing in second mortgages.

To help decide which form of real estate investment is best for you, consult a local real estate counselor. If you do not know such a person, you can find one through your local board of realtors. For a fee, you will be objectively counseled and guided to the best type of realty investment for you.

YOUR PROPERTY CAN PROVIDE
YOUR RETIREMENT INCOME

Q. In 1975, when you first started writing your newspaper articles in Washington, D.C., I said to myself "There's a guy who knows what he's talking about." This was long before real estate obviously became such a good inflation hedge. In 1976, my wife and I took $10,000 of savings and bought a run-down house which we fixed up. We bought it to live in. But a real estate agent dropped by while we were working on it and offered us such a fantastic price we couldn't refuse to accept. To make a long story short, we followed your ideas. Today we still live in our bargain-rent Washington apartment where we pay only $325 per month rent, but we have over $750,000 in equities in various properties. Keep up the good work telling people what a great investment real estate can be.—*Jess R.*

A. Thank you for sharing your success story. I believe that reader comments like yours do more to motivate people to invest in good property than I ever can. When you are ready to retire, you can gradually sell off your properties to provide your retirement income security.

To illustrate how vital it is to buy good property while you are young, let me tell a personal story. I recently bought a rental house being sold by an elderly lady who now lives with her children. I offered to buy it with $15,000 cash down payment and a mortgage for the balance payable at $1,030 per month. That house was the major asset the seller owned. Thanks to its sale, she will receive money to live comfortably for the rest of her life. Clearly, you are in a much better position for your retirement in a few years since you own several properties.

WOULD GOLD, SILVER, OR REAL ESTATE
BE A BETTER INVESTMENT?

Q. We have saved about $6,000. My husband wants to invest it in gold or silver, but I think we should put it as down payment on a small rental house. Which investment do you think will offer the greatest long-run security?—*Frannie M.*

A. Gold and silver market values can fluctuate wildly, but home values are relatively stable. Homes are necessities; gold and silver are not.

Gold and silver prices are subject to market fluctuations beyond your control. On the other hand, people must have homes to live in. For this reason, only a tiny fraction of homes are sold in any one year so this stabilizes their value.

If you want long-run security, without worry, invest in rental houses whenever you get a little extra cash to invest. In addition to the joy of ownership, you will probably benefit from the house's market value appreciation which, in recent years, has averaged 10 to 15 percent per year on a nationwide average. Gold and silver investments are for speculators. True investors buy good real estate for long-term security.

INVEST, DO NOT SPECULATE, IN REAL ESTATE

Q. I would like to speculate in rental house investments. Being a salaried insurance company clerk, I can spare up to $200 per month to make up any negative cash flow for up to one year. Do you think I should speculate in rental houses even though they won't produce enough rent to cover the mortgage payments, property taxes, insurance, and maintenance?—*Joseph M.*

A. Don't speculate. Invest. Buyers who will have to sell in a year or so can get themselves in a jam if the local home sale market is slow when they have to sell.

A better approach is to buy property in need of upgrading. After you improve the property, thereby raising its market value, you can almost surely resell for more than you paid. The result is you have turned yourself from a speculator, depending upon inflation to give you a profit, into an improver who raises the property's value regardless of what happens to inflation.

LIFETIME PROPERTY PLAN PROVIDES FOR
COLLEGE, RETIREMENT COSTS

Q. I sure wish our newspaper had been running your articles when we first started investing in real estate back in 1968. We could have used your advice, but somehow we got over the hurdles. As a result we now own twelve properties, all bought as a result of a $6,000 initial investment. Today, due to inflation, I think it would take about $10,000 to get started, however. Perhaps our experience can help others. Our goal was to buy one investment property each year. By refinancing our existing holdings, we've managed to do that. We sold one small duplex apartment to give us cash for our son's college tuition. Next year we'll sell another building to pay for more tuition. In four years we'll sell another building on an installment sale to provide for our retirement income. Then we'll sell off buildings as we need the cash. That's not too bad for a taxi driver with a ninth-grade education is it?—*Claude R.*

A. Thank you for your marvelous letter. It shows how wise property investment can provide long-term security. Your example should be an inspiration to others to get busy in real estate investing.

DEPRECIATION RECAPTURE EXPLAINED

Q. What does "depreciation recapture" mean? When we did our last year's income tax returns, our accountant told us not to take accelerated depreciation on a fourplex we bought. He gave his reason as "depreciation recapture."—*Amos M.*

A. Depreciation recapture applies only when you sell your property held for investment or for use in a trade or business. Recapture means the difference between accelerated depreciation deducted and the lower amount you could have deducted using the straight-line depreciation method, and it is taxed as ordinary income at the time of sale.

To illustrate, suppose when you sell your fourplex you have deducted $20,000 of accelerated depreciation, but you could have deducted only $15,000 using the straight line depreciation method. The $5,000 difference will be "recaptured" and taxed as ordinary income. This really is not such a "bad deal" since you had the use of the tax savings until the time of the resale.

IS IT BEST TO SELL OR RENT FORMER HOME?

Q. In November 1979, we bought a $50,800 house with an 11.5 percent interest rate mortgage. The Air Force has advised my husband he is to be transferred to Alaska for a minimum of three years. Would it be best for us to sell or rent our house? The monthly payment is $609. Realtors tell us it will rent for about $400 per month. We fear that if we sell we may not be able to afford to buy another house when we return to the continental U.S. What do you advise? Our realty agent says "sell," but I think he wants the sales commission?—*Barbara M.*

A. Your house can be an excellent investment if you do not sell. If you can afford the $209 monthly negative cash flow, after considering your income tax dollar savings from the deductions and depreciation, plus the home's probable future appreciation in market value over the next three years, it can be very profitable for you to keep that house. As rents go up in future years, your negative cash flow will probably decrease.

Your biggest problem will be management of the house. Do you have someone who can rent it when it becomes vacant? Is someone available locally to arrange repairs? Many realty agents are glad to do so for a nominal fee.

If you sell your house now, after ownership for such a short time, you may have little net profit after paying the sales expenses. A home sale within a year or two after purchase generally is not very profitable unless home values have risen rapidly in your neighborhood.

ARE VACATION HOMES GOOD INVESTMENTS?

Q. Do you think investment in a vacation home would be profitable? I am considering buying a cabin on a lake that is also near a winter sports area. I can buy it for just $23,000 down payment. The agent says he can rent it when I'm not using it.—*John N.*

A. Never, never, never buy recreational property with any hope of resale profit. Buy such property only for personal use. Your chances of keeping the cabin rented year around are very slim. The tax advantages are not good either if you make considerable personal use of the vacation home.

If you have $23,000 to invest, you will probably do much better investing in depreciable income property close to your home. Rental houses, commercial property, or rental condos usually make much better investments than risky vacation property.

5.

How to Find
the Best Properties to Buy

Up to this point, we have looked at why real estate (including your home and income property) is your best investment opportunity, the tax benefits of home ownership, and reasons why income property is so profitable.

Now the focus changes. This important chapter gets down to the nitty gritty of how to find the best properties.

If this chapter had to be summarized in one word, it is "persistence." Do not give up. The right property for you will not have a flashing neon sign saying "This is it!" Instead, each successful property buyer has to work to locate and sometimes create the bargain properties. If it was easy to buy the best properties, everyone would be doing so. Since it is not always simple to locate good properties, this limits your competition. In fact, if you are competing with another buyer for the same property, it is usually smart to walk away because competition makes the purchase terms less desirable.

HOW TO START YOUR PROPERTY SEARCH

Before rushing off to look at homes for sale or income properties offered by local realty brokers, take at least one hour to analyze your personal financial situation. *Do this alone—be 100 percent honest with yourself.*

Do not let your spouse or friends see what you write down.

First, list all your financial assets and their true market value today if you had to sell them to raise cash. For example, your gas guzzler car which cost $8,000 last year may only be worth $4,000 as a used car today.

Next, list all the ways you can raise cash. Although not part of your financial statement, your cash-raising ability is an important asset. Include your credit card lines such as Visa and MasterCard, bank credit lines, and department store charge cards (which are handy for property improvements).

Lastly, list the liabilities you owe. Examples might include your auto loan, your charge account balances, and any college tuition debts.

The difference between the value of your assets and what you owe on your liabilities is your net worth. Add to your net worth the amount of cash you can raise within thirty days. This total is the maximum amount you can afford to invest (although you will probably invest something less than this sum).

Here is a quick summary of this procedure of financial self-analysis:

ASSETS	$__
Cash in checking and savings accounts	$__
Accounts receivable	$__
Mortgages owned	$__
Marketable securities owned	$__
Cash surrender value of life insurance policy	$__
Real estate owned (today's market value)	$__
Automobiles (today's market value)	$__
Personal property (today's market value)	$__
Other assets	$__
TOTAL ASSETS	$__
LIABILITIES	
Accounts payable within thirty days	$__
Notes payable beyond thirty days	$__
Income taxes payable	$__
Loans on life insurance policy	$__
Mortgages or liens on real estate	$__
Installment loan total balances	$__
Auto loan	$__
Other liabilities	$__
TOTAL LIABILITIES	$__

To arrive at your net worth, subtract your total liabilities from your total assets:

Total assets	$__
Minus: Total liabilities	$__
NET WORTH	$__

Add to this amount the amount of cash you can raise within thirty days by borrowing. This is the maximum amount you can invest, although you should probably invest less. As you acquire more properties, your net worth and borrowing power will increase, allowing you to acquire still more properties.

Next, check your income and expenses to see if you can afford to make the payments on your realty acquisitions.

ANNUAL INCOME $___
Job salary—gross income from employment $___
Interest income $___
Dividends $___
Rental income (net after expenses and mortgage payments) $___
Alimony, child support, separate maintenance $___
Other income $___
TOTAL ANNUAL INCOME $___

ANNUAL EXPENDITURES $___
Housing costs: mortgage payments or rent $___
Property taxes $___
Income and other taxes $___
Loan payments $___
Insurance payments $___
Living expenses $___
Alimony, child support, separate maintenance $___
Charity donations $___
Other expenses $___
TOTAL ANNUAL EXPENSES $___

The excess income over expense is the "savings" in your budget. This is the amount you can set aside for your real estate investments. Of course, keep a cash reserve or, better yet, an emergency borrowing credit line at the bank.

WHAT CAN YOU OFFER A PROPERTY SELLER?

Your financial analysis was probably very revealing. If you did not fully complete your self-survey, stop now and do it. It is always a surprise to find out how little or how much your net worth really is. But without this basic knowledge of your current financial position, you are not ready to start acquiring real estate.

Now consider what you can offer to a property seller besides your charm and good looks. Property sellers know they own something valuable. The reason they are selling is they think they will be better off after the sale than before. This may or may not be true.

But if you get nothing else from this book, remember:
SMART PROPERTY BUYERS OFFER THEIR SELLERS A WAY TO IMPROVE THEIR SITUATION WHILE, AT THE SAME TIME, IMPROVING THE BUYER'S POSITION TOO.

Normally, the way most buyers improve the situation of the seller is to offer a cash down payment. But this is not always what the seller wants. If you are a multimillionaire, for example, more cash is not always what you want.

In other words, smart property buyers offer sellers the benefit the seller is seeking from the property sale. Usually, this benefit is cash and the buyer makes a down payment to satisfy the seller's need. But smart buyers look beyond the seller's obvious or stated needs. Many sellers will not confide their true needs to the real estate agent who has the listing on the property offered for sale. Do not always believe the reason the agent gives as the seller's motivation. The agent may not know the full story.

Make a list of what you can offer a property seller in return for his selling to you. Your list might include:

Cash down payment

Personal property—auto, boat, RV (recreational vehicle), furniture, appliances

Personal services—carpentry, plumbing, wiring, legal services, dentistry, or whatever else you can do

Payment of seller's debts—this can often be done at a discount by contacting the seller's creditors (with his permission after you have a binding sales contract to buy the property)

Cash raised from borrowing on your present properties or on the property to be acquired

Offering the seller a mortgage secured by property you already own

Trading property you already own for the property you want to acquire

You can probably think of many other creative benefits to offer to a property seller for the down payment. For example, recently a professional property investor told me he bought an out-of-town property for nothing down from a seller who did not want to sell to local buyers. "Saving face" is another seller motivation, and it is often very easy for a creative buyer to satisfy this need.

When you spot a property you would like to own, try to find out what will motivate the seller to sell to you on your terms. Although many realty agents try to prevent it, often there is no other way to learn the seller's true motivation than to sit down, face to face, with him to get acquainted. While I prefer to let the listing agent do my negotiating, if this fails, I do not hesitate to suggest a meeting with the seller to learn if I can offer him something which will meet his needs. At this point, if the traditional method of keeping the buyer and seller apart does not work, *there is nothing to lose and everything to gain* by having the buyer and seller meet each other.

Often the seller's needs can be satisfied with something other than cash. For example, I have purchased several rental houses from elderly sellers who were selling so they could move closer to their children. These sellers, I learned, did not need large amounts of cash. What they wanted was security. By offering them a small cash down payment and a first or second mortgage on the property they were selling to me, I satisfied their security needs in the form of monthly income payments (paid by my tenant's rent).

One elderly seller told me the monthly payment I send her of over $1,000 per month is more money than she ever earned in her life. That payment will provide her with more than adequate retirement income, so she will not be dependent on her children for living expenses.

HOW TO LOCATE THE RIGHT PROPERTY FOR YOU

Now that you have (1) analyzed your financial position so you know how much you can afford to spend and maintain your property purchase and (2) decided what you can offer to induce property sellers to sell to you, you are ready to start the property selection process.

Hopefully, by now you have decided what kind of property you want to seek. If you are looking for condominiums, for example, do not waste time looking at single-family homes for sale. Similarly, if you want to invest in apartments, save time by not investigating office buildings, warehouses, or vacant land.

There are several property-locating techniques which work well for different buyers. Depending upon your personal inclinations and time available for the search, you may want to use one or all of these suggestions.

THE BEST PLACE TO START

Most property buyers start their searches in the newspaper classified want ads. This is a highly efficient marketplace for sellers and buyers to get together. If possible, check more than one newspaper in your area. The smaller papers, especially the weekly community papers, often have special bargain ads by do-it-yourself sellers who are too cheap to place a want ad in the more expensive city daily newspapers.

Each community usually has one leading newspaper which carries most of the real estate want ads. This is usually the best source, but do not overlook the smaller papers with cheaper ad rates that most other realty buyers may not be checking.

As you read the want ads, remember why those ads were placed there. If the advertiser is a realty agent, the purpose is twofold. One motive is to sell the advertised property. But the second motive, often more important, is to make the realty agent's phone ring.

Most realty agents have many listed properties that they are not advertising. The properties that get advertised often are the ones that are (a) overpriced, (b) seriously deficient in some respect, (c) listings about ready to expire, or (d) owned by sellers who pester the agent to advertise their property.

When phoning a realty agent on a want ad, if the advertised property turns out not to be what you want to buy, be sure to ask the agent if he has another listing which better meets your requirements. The best agents who have "floor duty" time answering "cold calls" will have prepared a "switch sheet." A switch sheet lists alternative listings similar to the advertised property, usually in the same price range. The properties on the agent's switch list are often better bargains than the advertised properties.

But if it turns out the agent you talk to does not have any alternative listings, be sure to leave your name and phone number. Some agents are so lazy you will have to force them to write down your name and phone number. If you are lucky, and if you tell enough agents what you want to buy, eventually an agent will phone you when he learns of a property meeting your requirements.

For example, recently an agent I met four months ago at a Sunday open house phoned me about her new listing that she hopes I will buy. Unfortunately, this agent did not take good notes as to what financing I want, but at least she has not forgotten my buying interest. The more people you tell of your buying desire, the greater your chances of finding exactly the right property for you. Property buying is not easy, so widen your chances of success.

IS IT BEST TO DEAL WITH ONLY ONE REAL ESTATE AGENT?

While we are talking about real estate agents, the question often is asked whether it is best to deal with only one real estate agent. When looking for a personal residence, I find it is best to start out dealing with just one agent. Let that agent know you are relying on him (or her) to find you a perfect home to live in. Give the agent plenty of time to produce results. One to two months, however, should be adequate.

If the agent you select to deal with exclusively has not come up with suitable property within a month or two, however, do not hesitate to start dealing with other agents. The problem is if one agent knows you are dealing with that agent exclusively, the agent tends to become lazy. Competition does wonders to bring out the best in realty agents. But if your agent is doing a first class job, deal with that agent exclusively because many agents uncover "insider deals" that they present only to their best, exclusive clients.

ANOTHER WAY TO LOCATE GOOD REALTY AGENTS

In addition to the newspaper want ads, another good way to find realty agents with listings that meet your requirements is to write letters. I recall once writing to all the realty agents listed in San Francisco, describing the particular type of property I wanted to buy. Out of several hundred letters, less than a dozen agents bothered to contact me. However, one of those agents had a bargain property that I immediately bought. It had been listed over six months, but the agent was too cheap to advertise it.

OTHER METHODS OF FINDING BARGAIN PROPERTIES

In addition to using the want ads, and writing or phoning realty agents, another profitable technique is to "cruise." That means drive around neighborhoods where you would like to buy property. Jot down the addresses of any properties with "for sale" signs and phone the agent (or owner if it is a "for sale by owner" FSBO). Better yet, jot down addresses of properties that look like they might be for sale. Telltale signs include need for paint, vacant-looking windows with no shades or curtains, overgrown lawns, and other signs of absentee ownership. Then check the ownership at the court house or other local place where the owner's name can be easily obtained. In my county, I find the tax collector's office offers the easiest access to owner's names and addresses, but you may find a better place where you live.

One technique used by a friend of mine is he buys a master list of property owners in the area where he wants to buy properties. About four times a year he sends mass mailings to all owners of appropriate properties asking if they might like to sell "on flexible terms." He tells me each mailing usually produces lots of flakey phone calls but at least a dozen serious sellers who want to sell but have not yet listed their properties for sale with an agent. Although this technique takes time and organization, the results can be very profitable, especially since you have no competition. To locate a source for a master list of property owners in your area, check with local title insurance companies, realty agents, or real estate attorneys.

THE MULTIPLE LISTING TECHNIQUE

Still another technique for finding good properties for sale is to borrow a local realty agent's multiple listing book. Once you get to know an agent well, he or she will usually agree to loan you the current multiple listing book overnight. Better yet, ask the agent to give you last week's multiple listing book so you can study the listings. Although giving the multiple listing book to a nonmember technically violates the multiple listing service's monopolistic rules, it is done all the time. If your agent will not give you access to a current or recent multiple listing book, find an agent who will.

Once you have the current or recent multiple listing book, go through it carefully. Note the properties that interest you. Drive by them. Check recent sales prices for neighborhood homes (recent comparable sales prices are often in the back of the multiple listing book). Then make many offers (through the agent who gave you the multiple listing book, of course), contingent upon your inspecting the properties.

Many professional realty investors make purchase offers before they inspect the property. This saves many hours of inspection time. Of course, such purchase offers are contingent upon inspection and approval of the property. One investor I know bought a $2,000,000 industrial property this way, sight unseen. First he works out the purchase price and terms. Then he spends time inspecting the property to see if it as good as the listing agent says it is.

OTHER BARGAIN-FINDING TECHNIQUES

Ways of finding realty bargains are virtually unlimited. One friend of mine, a social climber who goes to lots of cocktail parties, is constantly asking people he meets "Have you got any property you want to sell?" He is a medical doctor, and he even asks his patients. Although he misses some great bargains advertised in the newspapers and available through realty agents, this doctor probably makes more money from his realty investments than from his medical practice, thanks to his technique of asking people what they own and want to sell.

Another technique for locating bargain properties is to run a newspaper want ad under "Real Estate Wanted" or similar title. I have tried this method and was bombarded with phone calls from flakey people. Only one serious seller surfaced in the month I ran my ad. But this method works if you run your ad long enough and can put up with all the unusual phone calls. Many real estate agents buy properties or get listings this way. One local realtor runs a productive ad reading "I'll buy your property, any condition, within 48 hours." He has been running this ad for years so it must pay off. Of course, the ad does not say that the realtor will buy the property at his price and on his terms.

Still another property-finding technique is to phone owners who have placed newspaper want ads under "for rent." To illustrate, if you want to buy a house, phone advertisers trying to rent houses. First, find out over the phone where the house is located and what the rent is. If you would like to live there, make an appointment to inspect it *with the owner*. Once you see the house, if you like it and would really like to own it, ask the owner if he would lease to you with an option to buy. If so, you have found yourself a bargain.

Why? Because today it is cheaper to rent a house than it is to buy it (unless you make a huge cash down payment to reduce the mortgage payments). But an owner can afford to lease to you, with an option to buy, because he probably bought the house years ago, and his mortgage payments are less than you would incur if you buy today.

Many owners of rental houses would like to sell. But when the house becomes vacant, instead of listing it for sale with all the inconveniences of selling, the owner decices to rent it because that is usually much easier. It is surprising how often an owner will sell when he receives an unsolicited purchase offer. Owners of empty rental houses are especially good candidates for this technique.

DISTRESS SALES

Another fruitful source of property bargains is distress sales. This category includes properties in what I call "special situations." Examples include probate or estate sales, foreclosures, property tax sales, divorces, deaths, bankruptcies, out of town owners, and sheriff's or marshall's sales. Checking these sales takes considerable time and large amounts of cash, but the competition from other buyers is practically nil. Cash talks. If you have lots of cash with which to buy properties, look into local procedures for distress property sales. Most of these sales will be advertised in legal notices published in local newspapers. Your county clerk or other local official can show you which newspapers carry these notices, and there is also usually a bulletin board at the courthouse where notices of such sales are posted. It takes considerable time and work to follow these distress property sales, but if you work faithfully at it, you will soon discover shortcuts. Further details on buying distress properties are in Val Cabot's excellent book *Goldmine in Foreclosure Properties* (Impact Publishers).

STILL MORE SOURCES OF BARGAINS

Wherever you go, if you want to buy good properties, talk about real estate. Do not be afraid to bring up the subject. You will be surprised to find it is one topic on which most people freely share their knowledge. People who especially like to talk about real estate include your attorney, banker, and barber or beautician. They often know who wants to sell or who has to sell. Let everyone you know understand that you are buying real estate. Within a few weeks or months, you will have so many properties offered to you that you cannot possibly buy them all.

But if you sit back and wait for the bargains to come to you, you will be waiting forever. Get busy. Make contacts, starting with the newspaper want ads. You will be surprised how much fun finding and buying property can be.

WHAT TO LOOK FOR IN A BARGAIN PROPERTY

Smart investors not only know the sources of bargain properties, but they know how to recognize one when they see it. A big problem with novice investors is they faithfully look for properties to buy, but they never actually buy. Novice buyers have a list of criteria, such as good location, good structural condition, and good financing. Rarely will all the requirements be met in one property. THERE IS NO SUCH THING AS A PERFECT PROPERTY. EVERY PROPERTY HAS SOMETHING WRONG WITH IT. The secret of buying the right property is to *avoid incurable defects*. An incurable defect is a drawback that is offensive to a majority of property buyers.

It is true there is a buyer for every property. But that buyer will buy at his price and on his terms. If the price and terms do not match those acceptable to the seller, no sale takes place.

Examples of incurable defects include (1) bad neighborhood (such as one with high crime rate, poorly maintained neighboring properties, or heavy street traffic), (2) poorly planned physical layout (such as a home with its bathroom located off the living room), (3) defective physical characteristics (such as a defective foundation or drainage toward the building rather than away from it), (4) economic or social obsolescence (factors outside the property that affect its usefulness, such as a home located downwind of a smelly sewerworks), and (5) high maintenance costs (such as an uninsulated building in North Dakota that can be insulated only at great cost).

Although defects such as these are called incurable defects, they really are curable. But the cost is so great that it is uneconomic. To illustrate, a beautiful home located adjacent to a noisy highway has an incurable defect. But if you had enough money, you could pay to relocate the highway or build sound barriers along the highway to cut down the noise. The cost of such corrective action, however, is beyond its worth to the homeowner.

In addition to avoiding incurable defect properties, smart investors buy only in good locations. Please notice I did not say "best locations." Usually the greatest real estate profits are made in locations other than the very best ones. For example, if your town has a (1) wealthy neighborhood, (2) a middle-class neighborhood, and (3) a lower-class slum neighborhood, the greatest realty profits can probably be earned by buying in the middle-class neighborhood. Money can be made in the wealthy neighborhood too, but it often takes more cash to invest there and the returns per dollar invested may not be as great as in the middle-class neighborhood. Of course, stay away from the lower-class slum neighborhood because it is considered a "poor location."

WHAT IS A GOOD LOCATION?

Every book on real estate investments says to buy only well-located property. That is true. But those books do not tell what a good location is. The truth is a good location depends on the people who use or can use the property. Good locations either already exist or can be created by the property owner. Bad locations usually already exist and are obvious, but they occasionally are created (such as when a new highway is built, thus chopping up adjoining land parcels and creating lower property values due to heavy noise or traffic congestion).

Is it wise to buy cheap, poorly located property for improvement so it can be profitably resold? NO! Unless you have a vast fortune and can buy up all the properties in a bad location and redevelop the neighborhood, stay away from bad locations. They are too costly to try to improve. Of course, if you see a well-established neighborhood trend developing, such as Chicago's famous Old Town area, buy in the bad location before everyone else realizes what is happening. Smart investors buy in such improving locations only (1) with high leverage (small cash down payments) and (2) if they can afford to lose their small investment if things do not turn out as expected.

Good locations are those that are highly useful or are considered desirable by the majority of people in the community. That does not mean those people live or work in those good locations. But they consider good locations to be where they want to live or work. Consider, for example, your town's busiest commercial intersection. It is called a "100 percent location" because it is the most desirable in town. The value of real estate at that intersection is probably also the most expensive in town too. Since most investors cannot afford to buy there, they buy in lesser locations which are still considered "good" by most people in the community.

In fact, the largest real estate profits are usually not made by purchasing property at a 100 percent location. The biggest realty profits are made buying in lesser locations and creating value by improving the property. This is called "forced inflation." An example would be buying a run-down house in a middle-class neighborhood, fixing it up, and reselling it at a profit. Doing the same thing in a bad location, such as a slum neighborhood, probably would not produce any profit because smart investors do not buy in bad locations no matter how attractive the property is made to appear.

SUMMARY

Summing up this chapter on how to locate good properties involves three key ingredients. (1) Use many sources to locate desirable properties. (2) Avoid buying properties with incurable defects. (3) Buy only in good locations; avoid neighborhoods which are not considered desirable by a majority of the people in the local community.

QUESTIONS AND ANSWERS

HOW TO FIND PROPERTY BARGAINS

Q. How do you find bargain properties? You make it sound so easy.
—*Bill M.*

A. My major source of property bargains is knowing many top real estate agents who contact me when they find properties meeting my requirements. Although I am a real estate broker, I never split a sales commission with these agents. The commission is all theirs to keep. As a result, they bring me their best bargains.

But if my "bird dog agents" do not produce enough property bargains, and I am desperate to buy a property, I (1) check newspaper want ads daily in several local newspapers, (2) phone agents advertising property that sounds interesting (I always ask about their unadvertised listings which are often better bargains than those advertised), (3) get to know many realty agents and make sure they know my property desires and do not forget me, and (4) drive around neighborhoods where I would like to own property, noting addresses of neglected-looking property, and then contact the owners to see if they would like to sell. Lastly, when I see a property I like that meets my buying criteria, I make a purchase offer immediately before someone else beats me out of the bargain.

HOW ZONING CAN HELP OR HURT PROPERTY'S VALUE

Q. We own a vacant lot on a busy street. The city is proposing to rezone from commercial to residential apartment house district. Some of the neighbors oppose this change, others favor it. Will it hurt or help the value of my property?—*Susan A.*

A. Commercially zoned property is usually worth more than a similar residentially zoned parcel. In the residential zoning category, apartment zoning is generally more valuable than single-family zoning.

But these are general rules of thumb which may not apply to your situation. The fact that your lot is vacant might indicate there is not much demand for it as commercial property. Yet if the zoning is changed to apartment zoning, you might find your lot is in great demand for apartment or condominium construction.

Go to the public hearings on the proposed zoning change. Listen to the arguments on both sides. If you feel strongly one way or the other, voice your opinion at the hearing. Zoning changes are generally made by local zoning or planning boards only after careful consideration of all viewpoints.

REINSPECT PROPERTY PURCHASE
JUST BEFORE CLOSING SETTLEMENT

Q. My husband says we should insist in reinspecting our home purchase a day or two before the closing settlement. Is this necessary?
—Mary Ann T.

A. While reinspection is not necessary, it is a very smart idea. Let the seller know you plan to reinspect before the sale closing. You will be pleasantly surprised at how much cleaner the house will be, and the seller will not try to play games, such as switching light fixtures and substituting cheap items for those that were in the house when you first inspected it. You have maximum leverage over the seller before the sale closes. After closing, when the seller has received his money, he could care less.

AVOID INCURABLE PROPERTY DEFECTS

Q. My cousin has agreed to sell us his home for $79,000. We like the location, but the floor plan is bad. There are three bedrooms, but to get to one bedroom you have to walk through another bedroom. While this would be all right for our two children, when we want to sell I think this would be a drawback. If my cousin was selling to us at a bargain price, I would buy in a minute. But he's asking top dollar for our town. Do you think we should buy in spite of the bad floor plan?—*Roger D.*

A. I think you have already answered your question. Bad floor plans are known as incurable defects or incurable obsolescence. I suspect your cousin is having trouble selling his home, and that is why he is being so generous in offering it to you.

Of course, even though your cousin is not offering a bargain price, if he is offering special terms, such as a small down payment and seller financing, then you might wish to buy the home in spite of its defects. But if you can do just as well buying another house, buy the other house. Sometimes it does not pay to make business transactions a family affair.

BUY INADEQUATE, WELL-LOCATED HOME
RATHER THAN GOOD, POORLY LOCATED ONE

Q. The last four weekends we have been looking at homes for sale. After we got over the shock of today's prices, we realized we'll either have to buy a home we like in a "not so good" location or a less-than-adequate home in a better, close-in location. Which do you think is the better home to buy?—*Martin E.*

A. Always go for the well-located home. The reason is that when you want to resell your home in the future, location will be a big part of its value. A "perfect" home in a bad location will always suffer in value. It usually will not go up in value as fast as the well-located home. A more expensive home in a good location is almost always a better buy than one in a second-rate location.

Remember, most home buyers stay in the home an average of less than seven years before selling. Even if you buy that "less-than-adequate" home in a top, close-in location, you probably will not be living there the rest of your life. Chances are you will sell it in a few years and buy a home that more closely meets your needs.

That technique is called "home pyramiding." Young couples use it to buy a small cottage where they live a few years before moving up to a better home. Older people use it to buy a second or third home that is their "dream home." Elderly people use this method to buy their retirement home, often in a community offering special amenities such as golf courses, swimming pools, or other extras. But whatever home you buy, always choose one that is favorably located in a popular resale area.

HOW TO FIND PROPERTY FORECLOSURE BARGAINS IN YOUR MAILBOX

Q. On the ABC-TV program "20/20," they recently showed how some properties are being bought in Los Angeles just before they go into foreclosure. But the details weren't shown. While I don't want to operate the way the people were shown on that TV program, I would like to learn where to find out about foreclosure sales. It seems to me that bargains can be bought, and the owners can be paid a fair price for their properties before they lose them by foreclosure.—*Roy A.*

A. Most of the properties on which foreclosure notices are filed never go to foreclosure sale. The reason is smart buyers contact the defaulting owners and buy out their equity before the sale. This gives the financially troubled owner some cash with which to get started again, and it gives the buyer a bargain purchase.

I do not approve of the techniques shown on that "20/20" telecast. But investors who contact defaulting owners can often perform valuable services in buying their homes. These defaulting borrowers often have no other way to save their equity.

To learn about foreclosures in your area, contact the county clerk or other local official who records notices of mortgage default. You can check the records to find out which lenders have filed notices against which borrowers. In many urban areas you can have information on these defaults delivered to your mailbox by subscribing to a local public recording summary service. The county clerk or recorder, title insurance firm, or realty office can tell you if such a service exists in your area.

THE CHEAPEST WAY TO BUY YOUR NEXT HOME

Q. We don't have very much cash for a down payment on a home. Just about $4,500. We talked to an old-time real estate agent. She suggested we buy a home on a lease with option to purchase. It just happened she had a home available on a lease-option. The way the deal works, she says, is we put up $4,000 "consideration for the option." It is to be a three-year option at purchase price agreed upon today. We would pay $550 per month rent, half of which applies to the option purchase price. But we are to pay all maintenance and property taxes on the house. We're wondering if there is some "catch?"—*James M.*

A. Consider yourself fortunate to find a smart real estate agent who understands lease-options. Many do not, so they discourage potential buyers from even thinking about lease-options. Grab that "good deal" before someone else like me does.

For the buyer, lease-option advantages are (1) you lock up the home's purchase price today, (2) it is usually cheaper to pay rent than to make mortgage payments, (3) you will benefit from the appreciation in market value between now and the time of option exercise, (4) it takes little cash to get into a lease-option, and (5) if you decide not to buy, the option can be assigned (sold) unless prohibited by its terms.

For the seller, lease-option advantages are (1) tax-free use of the option consideration money until either the option is exercised or it expires unused, (2) monthly rent payments cover the payments on the existing mortgage, (3) tenant pays the maintenance and property taxes, thus reducing or eliminating the negative cash flow problem, (4) with a substantial option consideration payment, you can consider the house sold, and (5) tax advantages of a delayed sale and installment sale taxation of the profit.

I have used lease-options for many years. They work out very well. However, I have found realty agents resist them because they often have to wait for all or part of their sales commission until the option is exercised. But as you found out, smart agents suggest lease-options to increase their sales and to provide for future commission income.

MAKE AN OFFER, ANY OFFER, IN TODAY'S BUYER'S MARKET

Q. Recently you said we're in a "buyer's market" for home sales. Please explain further. Do you mean this is a good or bad time to buy a home? I ask because my wife and I are waiting to buy a home until mortgage interest rates come down.—*Conrad C.*

A. A "buyer's market" means there are more homes listed for sale than there are active buyers seeking a home to purchase. Although I do not have exact statistics, I estimate in most communities there are four or five homes listed for sale for each one which has sold in the last month.

This means it is a terrific time to buy a home. While you probably will not get much of a price reduction from the seller, you will find home sellers are now very flexible on terms they are offering. Low down payments, low interest rates, and low monthly payments are not uncommon today if the seller is motivated and will help finance the sale.

Start making offers. Do not get discouraged. Provide for seller financing in your offers. Forget about getting a new mortgage because they are too expensive. Buy only if the seller will finance your purchase.

There are so many ways to buy homes today on terrific seller-financed terms I cannot list them all. Work with a good realty agent who understands creative finance so the terms can be tailored to your circumstances.

Ideas to consider include lease with option to buy later, land contracts, wrap-around mortgages, deferred down payments, and trading unwanted cars, boats, RVs, or land as your down payment. The important things to remember when buying a home today are (1) think creatively and (2) make offers.

IS TODAY A BAD TIME TO BUY REAL ESTATE?

Q. My parents have what I call "depression mentality." They never take any chances, and they keep warning me not to take any either. But I don't want to wind up like them. They are retired, barely existing on social security and a tiny pension. Dad worked thirty-four years for the same company. All he got was a handshake and a gold watch when he retired. I am twenty-eight, a bachelor. It seems to me real estate is the safest and potentially most profitable investment. Do you think today is a bad time to buy real estate? I'm considering buying a condominium apartment. Is this wise today?—*Morrow T.*

A. Unless you want to wind up like your parents, barely one step away from welfare, plan ahead. Investing in good real estate can be your retirement security. When you are young, buy sound, well-located property. When you are old, sell it and take back mortgages for retirement income. Today is a great time to buy because fantastic seller financing terms are available.

Condominiums can be excellent first investments. But check the particular condo complex very closely. Ask current residents if they would buy there again.

Find out from the residents and your realty agent the recent annual percentage increase in market value of the condominiums. If this annual increase in value has been less than the inflation rate, maybe you should buy elsewhere. Also, ask current residents if there are any drawbacks, such as poor soundproofing or bad management.

After you buy your home, then start buying investment property. I like small residential income property such as rental houses and apartments.

Other investors favor commercial and industrial buildings. To learn more about investment property, take real estate courses at a nearby college. Also, read every real estate book you can so you will understand the tax, income, and other benefits of owning real estate.

TO MAXIMIZE PROPERTY PROFITS, AVOID "RED RIBBON DEALS"

Q. I inherited about $45,000 that I want to invest in real estate as I think it offers the best inflation hedge and income tax benefits. But I am undecided whether to buy income property that is in good shape or should I buy "fix up" buildings?—*Hilda P.*

A. If you buy buildings in perfect condition, called "red ribbon deals," your profits come only in the form of possible future market value appreciation. When you are selling, of course, offer a "red ribbon deal" because that is what most naïve buyers want to buy. They are willing to pay top dollar for "red ribbon" property in top condition.

But if you buy run-down property and fix it up, then your profit opportunities are much greater. The reason is you benefit from both increased value due to the improvements and increased value due to inflation. The property thereby acquires a double profit potential.

THE FOUR-WAY CHECKLIST FOR BUYING YOUR NEXT HOME

Q. Do you have a checklist of things to look for when buying a home? We are first-time home buyers who are worried we'll make a bad buy.—*Marlis A.*

A. Fortunately, real estate is a forgiving investment. If you should make a "bad buy," inflation will probably bail you out. But to prevent making a mistake, here are the most important home-buying considerations.

1. *Neighborhood.* Before buying any home, inspect at least ten houses in various locations throughout your community. Of course, do not waste your time looking at $200,000 homes when your budget can afford only a $75,000 home. Buy in a stable or improving neighborhood, never in a declining one. Also, be sure the particular house does not have incurable location defects such as adjacent railroad tracks, smells, or freeways.
2. *School quality.* Never buy in an area where the public schools are bad. If you buy in an area with poor public schools, good quality middle-class families will not buy a home there, thus limiting your resale market to singles and people without school-age children.
3. *Financing.* Before you inspect a house, ask the realty agent "What financing is available on this house?" In today's market, try to find

a home where the seller will carry all or most of the financing at a reasonable interest rate. This is far cheaper than getting a new mortgage at a bank or savings and loan association.

4. *Physical condition.* Unless you or your husband are construction experts, provide in your purchase offer for an inspection clause. In termite-infested areas, insist on a termite inspection report, with the seller to pay for any necessary repairs.

Better yet, include an offer contingency such as "This offer contingent upon buyer's inspection and approval of the property." Then hire a professional building inspector if you have doubts. Also, try to get the seller to pay for a one-year home warranty (available through most realty agents) for repairs to built-in appliances, plumbing, wiring, and furnace.

COMPETITIVE MARKET ANALYSIS
AVOIDS OVERPAYING FOR PROPERTY

Q. How can I be sure I'm not paying too much when I buy a house or investment property?—*Julius M.*

A. Your first profit from a property is earned by buying it for the right price. To avoid overpaying for a property, before you make your purchase offer, ask your realty agent to prepare a "competitive market analysis" for you.

This is a written summary of (1) recent sales price of similar nearby properties, (2) other comparable properties now for sale that have not sold yet, and (3) properties that were recently listed for sale but which did not sell.

Your agent can easily prepare such a written analysis from records available at the local Board of Realtors, title insurance companies, or mortgage lenders. Only by analyzing such a comparison of similar properties can you be sure you are not offering too much for a property.

If you are buying investment property, such as apartments or commercial buildings, to avoid paying too much ask your agent to find the "capitalization rate" (that is net income divided by the sales price) for similar nearby properties which sold recently. Then apply that "cap rate" to the investment property you are considering buying. Make your purchase offer at that indicated market value.

DO REALTY AGENTS BUY UP ALL THE GOOD PROPERTIES?

Q. We've decided real estate is the best place to invest our money. But we're having trouble making our first income property purchase. It seems all the real estate brokers buy up the bargains. Do you think I should get my real estate sales license so I can learn of the best buys when they first come on the market for sale?—*Hugo L.*

A. It is true that real estate brokers and salespeople do invest in many of the best properties which come up for sale. But realty agents cannot possibly buy all the good properties.

If your only reason for getting a real estate sales license is to get first crack at good properties, I would not bother getting a realty sales license. A better approach is to get to know a dozen or more realty agents who specialize in the type of property you want to buy. Let them know you will act fast when they notify you of a "hot" new listing. You should not have to wait long before you will be buying your first investment property.

IS IT WISE TO BUY A LESS-THAN-IDEAL HOME?

Q. For some time we've read and enjoyed your articles on why it pays to buy a home. But my husband is still in college. So our only income is from my job as a bank loan officer. We both hate paying our $325 per month apartment rent as we know that money is wasted. So we've been trying to find a home we can afford to buy. The best we can find is a tiny three-room cottage which is in, shall we say, less than the best neighborhood. But the cottage is in perfect condition even though it was built in 1932. The original owner is the seller. He will let us buy for only a 10 percent down payment and he will carry the mortgage for ten years. Should we buy?—*Joanne G.*

A. Unless there is something very bad about the neighborhood, it usually pays to buy just about any home rather than continuing to waste money on apartment rent. Even if the cottage does not appreciate much in market value, you will have the income tax savings from mortgage interest and property taxes.

But ninety-nine out of a hundred homes go up in market value at least as fast as the inflation rate.

You probably will not spend the rest of your lives in that three-room cottage. But it can be an excellent starter home until your husband graduates and starts earning an income. By then your cottage may have gone up in market value 10 or 20 percent, perhaps more. Buy now before prices go higher. The seller's attractive easy financing is another reason to buy that cottage.

HOW TO BEGIN BUYING PROPERTY

Q. We have about $2,000 for the down payment on a home. I earn about $24,000 per year. Can I afford to buy a home?—*Steve R.*

A. Yes. Start reading the newspaper want ads. Sooner or later you will find a home for sale advertising "low down payment" or "no down payment," or other attractive terms. Phone the agent on every ad that remotely interests you and tell him your situation.

Most realty agents know of at least one "starter home" that can be bought for little cash. The sooner you buy, the sooner you will start building equity so you can eventually sell and buy a better home. The important thing is to buy your first home now before prices go higher.

6.

Secrets
of Financing
Property Purchases

There is an old real estate maxim, never truer than today, that says "If you can't finance it, you can't sell it." Adapting that truism to today's real estate market changes it to "If you can't finance it creatively, you can't buy it."

Although it is important to understand the tax and leverage benefits of owning real estate, financing is the key to opening the real estate door. Without a firm understanding of financing opportunities, chances of successful real estate investing are nil.

Some real estate buyers, especially older people, think the best way to buy property is with all cash. This was correct when annual inflation was only 2 or 3 percent. But paying all cash is downright stupid in today's highly inflationary economy. Borrowing other people's money (OPM) is vital to profitable real estate purchases. If you cannot stand to borrow money, change your thinking, because borrowing money is the prime profit method in real estate.

At the other extreme from the 100 percent cash buyers (who are few and far between, by the way) are realty buyers who think the best way to buy is with 100 percent financing and little or no cash investment of their own money. While this goal is attainable and is being achieved every day, 100 percent financing is not desirable for every situation. If something goes wrong with a property in which the owner has little or no equity, he is too easily tempted to walk away and let the mortgage holder foreclose. Thousands of FHA and VA home loan foreclosures are testimony to the risks, for the lender, of financing with little or zero cash down payment.

THE TRUTH ABOUT
REAL ESTATE MONEY LENDERS

Most real estate lenders hate to foreclose. When they must, if the owner does not make his loan payments, the lender has failed in his primary job

121

of maximizing profits. Realty lenders are usually very good at making big profits by lending money. But, next to bank trust departments, lenders are usually the poorest property managers you can find. That is why they are so cautious making real estate loans. *Most realty lenders never, never, never want to end up owning the property, by foreclosure, on which they loan money.*

But lenders must make loans to earn profits. Never forget that. Although real estate lenders often lead loan applicants to believe otherwise, if lenders do not loan money, they soon have big trouble with declining profits. The recent huge losses of eastern savings banks and many savings and loan associations are due in large part to lack of new loan volume and mortgage loan fees charged to borrowers.

NEVER FORGET THAT LENDERS NEED BORROWERS, JUST AS BORROWERS NEED LENDERS

Persistence is the key to successful real estate financing. Arranging financing terms for any property, from a small cottage to a multimillion dollar high-rise building, is like shopping for groceries. To find the best terms and price (interest rate), *you have to shop around.* Call it "comparison shopping" or whatever you like, but realty lenders are not all the same.

Most lenders do not advertise their loans vigorously, so it is usually necessary to phone or visit realty lenders to find which one is offering the best terms at the moment if you need financing money.

For example, one bank or savings and loan association may offer terrific terms on improvement loans (which are extremely profitable for lenders, by the way) but high interest rates and short terms on first mortgage loans. It is obvious such a lender wants one type of loan business, but not the other. The only way to find out the facts of life in real estate financing is to shop around and make many contacts with loan officers at different loan sources.

DO NOT BE SURPRISED IF YOUR LOAN REQUEST IS REJECTED

The most successful real estate investors have had dozens of their loan applications rejected by lenders. It happens to the best people! They just do not happen to fit the lender's loan formula. Those formulas change constantly and will even vary between loan officers working for the same lender, depending upon the loan officer's authority and willingness to bend the rules. I recently heard of a successful realty developer in my area who was turned down by twenty-one banks, savings and loan associations, and insurance companies before the twenty-second lender agreed to finance his new office complex! Persistence pays.

THE FIRST STEP TO SUCCESSFUL REALTY FINANCING

All lenders ask, before they make a loan, (1) will it be profitable, (2) what will the money be used for, and (3) where will the funds come from to repay the loan. Once the lender is satisfied with the answers, the loan is approved.

But even if the answers to questions two and three are not satisfactory, many lenders will still approve the loan if there is sound security for its repayment. These "equity lenders" loan on the security of the real estate rather than the borrower's apparent financial ability to repay the loan. Many second mortgage brokers are "equity lenders," whereas banks and savings and loan associations are more conservative and look at both the equity and the borrower. These "credit lenders" loan primarily on the borrower's income.

So if your credit or income is not the greatest, borrow from an "equity lender." The cost will be higher, but the inquiry into your ability to make the payments will be less probing.

The security for a real estate loan, of course, is a mortgage, deed of trust, land contract, or other security device on the property. Unsecured loans can be made by banks, but other lenders insist on security of some type, most often the property itself.

As we have seen, *the first step to successful real estate financing is satisfying the lender.* One way or another, the lender gets his answers to his "big three" questions before a loan is approved. Even though the property is the security for real estate loans, lenders qualify borrowers for trouble-free repayment. Old-time lenders looked solely at the mortgaged property for repayment in the event of default. But they learned in the Great Depression of the 1930s that the borrower's financial status is often more important than the property securing the mortgage. That is why today most lenders look at both the property and the borrower closely.

WHERE DO YOU STAND TODAY FINANCIALLY?

In Chapter 5 you prepared your asset-liabilities and income-expense statements. If you have not completed those financial surveys, do it now.

Even if you are not planning to apply for any loans today, it is sound financial planning to prepare your financial balance sheet and earnings statement at least twice a year, preferably on January 1 and July 1. Comparisons can be made each six months to see how your financial position is improving. If it is not getting better, corrective action should be taken.

It is easy to prepare a financial statement. Use the format shown in

Chapter 5. A good place to keep your financial reports is in a notebook where you can compare your progress each six months. Some lenders will accept a neatly typed copy of your financial statement, but others insist it be transferred to their own loan application forms. Below each category on your personal balance sheet enter the details, such as name of the bank that has your savings account. You may think of assets you had long forgotten about.

Here is a sample of how a typical financial report might look. It is important to know how to prepare such a statement because most lenders require you to prepare one. The only exceptions are (1) some equity lenders who loan on just the security of the property and (2) some property sellers who finance the sale of the property without inquiring closely into the buyer's finances.

YOUR BALANCE SHEET

NAME	John and Mary Investor		DATE	January 1

Assets	
Cash in checking and savings accounts	3,900
Accounts Receivable	1,150
Mortgages owned	14,000
Marketable securities owned	6,600
Cash surrender value of life insurance policy	400
Real estate owned (today's market value)	54,000
Automobiles owned (today's market value)	1,500
Personal property (today's market value)	2,000
Other assets	$1,150
TOTAL ASSETS	$84,700

Liabilities	
Accounts payable within thirty days	800
Notes payable beyond thirty days (installment contracts total)	4,500
Income taxes payable (state and federal)	1,000
Loans on life insurance policy	0
Mortgages of liens on real estate	36,450
Other debts and liabilities	450
TOTAL LIABILITIES	43,200
NET WORTH*	$41,500
TOTAL (Must equal total assets)	$84,700

*Net worth equals Assets minus Liabilities

The totals at the bottom of the asset and liabilities columns must agree.

If they do not, any lender sees a red flag that he is dealing with a novice borrower.

No matter how good your personal balance sheet looks to a lender, he also wants to see an equally important financial report—your income statement. Be sure to show current income information. Last year's earnings might be substantially different from this year's. If both husband and wife are employed steadily, show the earnings of each separately. Lenders must accept total annual earnings of both spouses, even if the wife is pregnant and expects a baby next week. Include income from all sources in your family total.

YOUR INCOME STATEMENT

ANNUAL EARNINGS

Job salary (husband's and wife's) gross employment income	$16,000
Interest income and dividends	450
Rental income (net after expenses and mortgage payments)	1,425
Fees or commissions	0
Alimony, child support, separate maintenance	0
Other income	0
TOTAL ANNUAL INCOME	$17,875

If a significant part of your income comes from self-employment, most lenders want to see a copy of your income tax returns for the latest one or two years. Although such information may be irrelevant to your current year's income, lenders use this method to verify self-employment income. Often just the front and back pages of IRS Form 1040 will satisfy most lenders. But some nasty ones insist on seeing all the supporting schedules too. Frankly, much of the information on your tax returns is not the lender's business, but if you want the loan, you have to play by their rules.

Wage earners on a salary should bring a copy of their W-2 form when applying for a loan. This verification will speed the loan approval since many employers will no longer give employment earnings verifications to lenders. Some employers will not even verify employment status unless the employee makes a written request. Smaller employers are usually more cooperative with lenders who seek to verify employment and earnings status.

In addition to providing a potential lender with your balance sheet and income statement, many lenders will ask four key questions you should be prepared to answer:

1. Do you have any contingent liabilities as endorser or guarantor, any taxes past due, any damage claims against you not covered by insurance, or any other lawsuits against you?

2. Have you ever filed bankruptcy or compromised a debt?
3. Are any assets shown on your financial statement the separate property of one spouse?
4. What assets are pledged other than those shown on your statement?

TYPES OF REAL ESTATE FINANCING

Now that you have a good picture of your financial status and ability to repay loans, it is time to look at the different types of real estate financing available.

Traditionally, the mortgage (or deed of trust in some states) is the most frequently used real estate finance device. Most property buyers use some type of realty financing that is secured by a mortgage or trust deed. Very few pay 100 percent cash for real estate because of the tax and leverage drawbacks of doing so. Even if you can afford to pay all cash for a property, don't (unless you get a huge price discount for your cash payment).

The most common formula for buying real estate is to make a cash down payment of 5, 10, 15, or 20 percent of the sales price, plus a first mortgage for the balance of the purchase price. A second mortgage may be used to fill any finance gap between the amount of the down payment and the first mortgage amount.

But there are many alternatives to this traditional finance formula. However, before discussing these alternatives, let us take a quick look at the two basic types of mortgage financing used today.

INTERIM OR CONSTRUCTION FINANCING

Construction financing is usually a temporary loan to finance costs of erecting a building. It may or may not include the cost of buying the land. Payments are made periodically by the lender, often a bank, to the contractor, or the materialmen may be paid directly by the construction lender. The security for the construction loan is the value of the underlying land plus the increasing value of the building under construction. Today most construction loans have a floating interest rate, such as the prime rate (the bank's best interest rate for unsecured loans to its best customers) plus two or three points (each point equals one percent of the amount borrowed).

Sometimes a riskier type of loan is used where the construction loan is converted by the lender, after construction completion, into a long-term permanent mortgage. Costs of a construction loan, due to the high interest rate, are usually much greater than for the permanent mortgage, which involves no lender problems with mechanic's liens, cost overruns, or uncompleted work.

Because of the risky nature of construction loans, many Real Estate Investment Trusts (REITs) specializing in this high-risk, high-earnings type of loan are today either bankrupt or far from healthy. The importance of having a permanent mortgage loan commitment to take out (pay off) the construction lender cannot be overemphasized for the safety of the lender.

DEVELOPMENT FINANCING

This really is a variation of the construction loan. Here a mortgage is used to finance purchase of a tract of land where a builder plans to construct homes or, perhaps, a commercial development. A lender takes a mortgage on the entire project and then releases individual parcels from the loan as they are sold to buyers.

For example, upon payment of an agreed sum to the lender (the money comes from the parcel buyers), the development lender releases his mortgage on that parcel sold. A major disadvantage of this type of financing is the developer has his profits tied up in the project until the last parcels are sold. The profits are not fully realized until these last, sometimes difficult-to-sell parcels are finally sold (which may take years). Needless to say, development loans are expensive, due to the high risk for the lender.

PERMANENT FINANCING

The first mortgage or deed of trust is the most common form of real estate financing. This loan is secured by a particular property. It is often used to finance the buyer's purchase of that property. Or it may be used to refinance an existing loan or loans already against the property.

Due to increasing property values, many property owners refinance their mortgage loans every four or five years to take tax-free money out of their property for other uses.

Second mortgages are another form of permanent mortgage financing. Because they have secondary claim against the property in the event of default by the borrower, they are riskier than first mortgages. Upon foreclosure, the first mortgage is paid off; any remaining money realized at the foreclosure sale is paid toward the second mortgage.

To compensate for this greater risk, the interest rate on second mortgages is usually 1, 2, or 3 percent (sometimes more) higher than that of the first mortgage, depending upon state usury laws.

Second mortgages are often carried back by the seller of the property. Such a loan is called a "purchase money mortgage." Many individual investors and finance companies make "hard money" second mortgage loans because of the high interest rate they usually yield. To further maximize their return, second mortgage investors often buy existing second mortgages at substantial discounts off the balance due from individuals who wish to sell their second mortgages to raise cash. Returns on invested dollars of 15 percent to 20 percent or more are not unusual when buying discounted second mortgages.

THE HIGHER THE INTEREST RATE, THE HIGHER THE RISK

In real estate lending, the maxim "The higher the interest rate, the higher the risk" applies. Since second mortgages are usually riskier than first mortgages, they usually carry a higher interest rate to compensate the lender for his risk.

LENDING STANDARDS

All mortgage lenders (called mortgagees) have lending standards. Some are more conservative than others. The interest rate charged varies with the lender's risk, the borrower demand for loan funds, and the lender's loan standards.

Lenders usually charge the lowest interest rate on single-family home loans. Higher rates are usually charged on income property loans, such as apartments and stores. Construction loans have the highest interest rates because of the high lender risks during construction.

The lender's appraisal of a property's fair market value is the key to the decision to make or reject a loan application. Without the underlying value of the property to secure the mortgage loan, a lender will not risk his funds. Most lenders also consider the borrower's ability to repay the loan, as discussed earlier, but there are some "equity lenders" who do not even run a credit report on the borrower. They look strictly to the property for their loan security.

SECURITY—THE ABSENCE OF RISK

Security is defined as the absence of risk. If a loan is 100 percent secure, it is riskless. An example would be a loan secured by the cash in your bank savings account. But if you think carefully about it, even a loan secured 100 percent by cash is a risky loan for a lender today. The reason is inflation.

Today it is impossible to have a 100 percent riskless loan because of the loss of purchasing power caused by inflation. The major cause of our high inflation rate, of course, is government deficit spending. Nobody knows how high the inflation rate will go. As a result, long-term lenders demand high interest rates to compensate for their risk of high future inflation rates.

Mortgages are regarded as relatively safe investments if the appraised value of the property security does not decline (as it rarely does). The major factors considered by all mortgage lenders in evaluating their risks are:

1. Location of the property—the community and the specific neighborhood.
2. Building activity, stability, or expected growth in the area, or lack of growth.
3. The subject property—its condition of repair, its cost of reproduction, and the suitability of the improvement for the neighborhood.
4. Loan to value ratio (percentage of the loan balance to the property's market value).
5. Borrower's credit history and his financial ability to repay the loan.
6. Income property: stability of its income and ability of the property to repay the loan from income rentals.
7. Operating expenses of the subject property and if increases can be passed along to tenants.
8. Term of the loan in years, its amortization schedule, and ability of the lender to compensate for inflation (variable rate loans).

Various lenders apply their own lending standards to each loan request. Even though a lender may have written guidelines for its loan officers, these guidelines are often violated, especially for good customers. Exceptions are also made if the property security is outstanding.

For example, a real estate broker friend of mine contacted seventeen banks, mortgage brokers, and savings and loan associations for financing the sale of a well-located downtown office building. All turned him down because the building was about forty years old. But when his buyer opened a large savings account with one of the S&L lenders that had previously said no, the answer suddenly changed to yes.

KNOW YOUR MAJOR SOURCES OF REAL ESTATE LOANS

Today there are more sources of real estate loans than ever before. But much of this money is ultraexpensive. It pays to shop carefully for the best financing source. Saving just one percentage point on a long-term mortgage can save thousands of dollars.

THE BEST MORTGAGE SOURCE OF ALL

Usually the reason a mortgage is being sought is to finance the purchase of a property. Too often the buyer and real estate agent overlook the best and most obvious finance source of all—the seller. Especially in the home sale market, the individual seller is the cheapest and best source of a mortgage loan. Especially good sources are "motivated sellers" who are anxious to sell and will do anything reasonable to get the property sold.

To tap this financing source, a few guidelines will help. (1) If the realty agent says something like "The seller won't carry a first or second mortgage," do not believe it until you have made a written purchase offer which the seller has rejected. (2) Before making a purchase offer, find out the seller's true motivation for selling (this will help you tailor your purchase offer to meet the seller's needs). (3) Make your purchase offer on terms you can live with, such as a low interest rate, deferred payments, and long term. Beware of "short fuse" mortgages, such as a one- or two-year mortgage carried by the seller, that just postpone your finance problem. (4) Do not get discouraged if your first seller finance offer is rejected; there are thousands of other properties for sale, and many of them can be bought with seller financing.

More about the important area of seller-finance techniques will be explained later. For now, it should be regarded as the most important and best finance source of all.

SAVINGS AND LOAN ASSOCIATIONS

Until recently savings banks and savings and loan associations made about 60 percent of all conventional home mortgage loans in the United States. But due to their financial problems brought on by high interest rates, which most mortgage borrowers cannot afford, S&Ls have cut their loan volume substantially. But they will continue to be an important finance source, especially for home loans. They can make a limited number of commercial property mortgage loans too, but most of their loans are secured by single-family houses.

Nationwide, there are over 6,000 S&L offices and they invest about 85 percent of their assets in mortgages. Maximum loan-to-value ratios go up to 95 percent of the appraised value of single-family homes. However, on amounts over 80 percent of the property's market value, most S&Ls insist on "private mortgage insurance" (PMI). These high-ratio home loans are often called "magic loans" because of the initials of the largest private mortgage insurer, Mortgage Guaranty Insurance Corporation of Milwaukee.

Most home loans are made for 75 percent to 80 percent of the house's appraised value at the time of a sale. For refinancing of existing mortgages, S&Ls tend to be more conservative, often making loans up to 75 percent of their appraised value.

MUTUAL SAVINGS BANKS

There are about 500 mutual savings banks which function like savings and loan associations. Only eighteen states allow mutual savings banks. Both mutual savings banks and S&Ls, as well as banks and mortgage brokers, make FHA and VA insured home loans, although they jump in and out of the FHA-VA market depending upon yields available.

COMMERCIAL BANKS

Banks in some communities are a major factor in real estate finance, especially for commercial and construction mortgage lending. But their role in home mortgage financing fluctuates wildly, depending upon yields available and if the loans can be sold. Banks like to originate home loans and then sell them to other lenders, but they retain the servicing for which they earn a fee of about ¼ percent.

Many banks make home mortgage loans only to their customers who have established accounts. Surprisingly, the nation's largest home mortgage lender is a bank, Bank of America. But as a general rule, banks tend to be very conservative on home loans, and they are usually not an outstanding home loan source.

INSURANCE COMPANIES

Insurance companies used to be major lenders on home mortgages. Today, because other investments offer higher yields, few insurance companies make direct home loans. Some, however, will buy packages of home loans originated and serviced by other lenders, such as banks and savings and loan associations.

Since insurance companies are less regulated than banks and S&Ls, they can be more flexible in financing special or unusual real estate properties. But their interest rates are usually higher than mortgages from banks or S&Ls. That is because the risk is usually higher, and the insurance company may be the only available financing source, so they charge what the traffic will bear.

Many insurance companies want a share of the project's gross or net income (called a "kicker"). Insurance companies usually make their loans through mortgage brokers, known as "correspondents." Their loan processing time is often long, as compared to banks and S&Ls which make loan decisions in a few days. Some correspondents demand the loan fee be paid at the time the insurance company loan is requested. If the mortgage broker requests the advance fee, the borrower should obtain written evidence the fee is fully refundable if the mortgage loan is not approved as requested. Be especially aware of crooked mortgage brokers who request advance loan fees for "shopping the loan application" because it is these brokers who often are unable to refund the loan fee if their loan source search is unsuccessful. Any mortgage broker who demands a nonrefundable loan fee should be avoided.

PENSION AND TRUST FUNDS

Although they control billions of dollars of long-term money, the pension and trust funds have been slow to invest in real estate mortgages. These lenders operate much like insurance companies in mortgage lending. They usually arrange their loans through mortgage brokers, or they buy existing mortgages originated by mortgage bankers. As these huge pension and trust funds diversify their investments for safety, and as they realize the high and safe yields available in first and second mortgages, more pension and trust fund money is becoming available for mortgages.

But these lenders have high-minimum loans, usually at least $1,000,000. They are not interested in home mortgages, except to occasionally buy packages of home loans originated and serviced by the original lender such as a bank, mortgage broker, or savings and loan association.

MORTGAGE LOAN BROKERS AND BANKERS

Mortgage loan brokers are often the local correspondents for insurance companies, pension or trust funds, and out-of-state S&Ls or banks. Mortgage bankers, however, use their own funds (often borrowed from a bank) to originate mortgage loans which are then sold to institutional mortgage investors such as insurance companies.

Loan fees of mortgage bankers and brokers tend to be the highest of all the lending sources listed. But these people are often the only source of mortgage money for difficult-to-finance loans. To cut expenses, some S&Ls now make all their loans through mortgage brokers.

INDIVIDUAL LENDERS

Every town and city has individuals who will make mortgage loans. They make such loans for a variety of reasons such as (1) high return on invested dollars, (2) opportunity to participate in project profits, and/or (3) profits from occasional foreclosures. These individuals often buy first or second mortgages at large discounts to further enhance their return on investment. Some seek security of investment with a low loan-to-value ratio. Others want a higher interest rate in return for a higher loan-to-value ratio.

Many individual lenders become involved in mortgage financing by carrying back the first or second mortgage when they sell their property to a new owner. Some individual lenders make direct loans to borrowers. But most work through a mortgage loan broker who collects a loan fee from the borrower for arranging the loan. Such mortgage brokers often service the loan, usually a second mortgage, without charge and handle any delinquent loan collection problems or foreclosures.

Newspaper want ads frequently carry notices of individual lenders who have funds to loan. Loans for sale are also often advertised in the want ad pages of newspapers, especially in larger cities.

OTHER MORTGAGE SOURCES

There are many other sources of mortgage money. They vary in each community. Some include finance companies (a big factor now in the second mortgage market), credit unions, and cash-by-mail personal property brokers. State usury laws that regulate maximum interest rates often determine whether or not these secondary real estate loan sources do business in a particular state.

THIRTY WAYS TO FINANCE VIRTUALLY ANY PROPERTY

There is no limit to the creative methods which can be used to finance the acquisition and operation of real estate. The major methods are often combined and adjusted to meet the requirements of the parties to the transaction. When using these methods, *think creatively.* There is no such thing as an impossible realty financing situation. Keep an open mind. Seek help from real estate finance specialists in your community. Listen, learn, and prosper by understanding the basic and advanced methods of financing real estate.

1. The Traditional First Mortgage

All of the loan sources listed above will make first mortgage or deed of trust loans. By being well prepared when approaching your most logical lender for the type of property you want to finance, you will save lots of time and work. Even though it pays to search several sources for the best loan terms and interest rates, do not become known among mortgage lenders as a "shopper."

A "shopper" is a borrower who plays one lender off against another lender. Lenders do not like this. Even though it pays to shop and compare for the best mortgage finance terms, do not tell the lenders you are doing this.

When you find reasonable terms on a firm mortgage commitment, *take it!* Don't fool around and run the risk of losing a choice loan commitment. Real estate brokers and agents, working to finance their sales, often know the best local mortgage sources so encourage them to assist you as part of their service when purchasing a property. But double-check with other lenders to be sure you are actually getting the best terms, not just the easiest loan.

Of course, when purchasing a property, always provide in your initial purchase offer bid for the seller to finance your purchase. Even if the agent says this is impossible, insist the agent write up your offer providing for seller financing. In the last four years, with only one exception, all my property purchases have been seller-financed. On most of them, the agent was as surprised as I was when the seller accepted my offer. The worst that can happen is the seller will make a counteroffer that requires outside financing. If you can't get seller-financing, avoid the new adjustable rate mortgages. Insist on a fixed interest rate loan instead.

2. Second, Third, Fourth, etc., Mortgages

The same rules apply here as when seeking a new first mortgage. If you cannot arrange a large enough first mortgage, or if you are buying "subject to" or "assuming" an existing first mortgage, a second mortgage can fill the finance gap between your down payment and the first mortgage.

In some situations, the second mortgage can take up *all* the slack and make 100 percent financing (no down payment) possible. Of course, the further down a mortgage is on the chain of priority, the higher the risk for the lender. Naturally, the interest rate on a second or third mortgage will be higher than on a first mortgage. The seller is usually the best source for second, third, or fourth mortgages (because he does not actually have to advance any cold, hard cash) although outside individuals and mortgage brokers often make or arrange these secondary mortgages too. Again, shop carefully among local hard money lenders because interest rates and terms vary widely. Depending upon local loan conditions, sources of secondary "hard money" mortgages include banks, S&Ls, finance companies, credit unions, and mortgage brokers.

A WORD ABOUT A COMMON MISUNDERSTANDING

It is important, while considering second mortgages, to explain a common misunderstanding regarding the safety of such loans. In the Great Depression of the 1930s, many second mortgage holders were wiped out when a first mortgage lender had to foreclose because the borrower did not make his loan payments. In those days a second mortgage lender had to pay off the entire first mortgage balance to protect his second mortgage from being wiped out when the first mortgage lender foreclosed.

These laws have been changed. Today if a borrower defaults on *either or both* a first and/or second (or third, fourth, etc.) mortgage, *only the missed payments* need be paid up by the secondary lender to protect his mortgage. No longer are large amounts of money needed to protect a secondary mortgage in the event of foreclosure by a prior mortgage lender in the chain of priority. Even today many potential secondary mortgage lenders do not understand this important fact of mortgage life. Many homesellers refuse to carry back a second mortgage due to misunderstanding this mortgage concept.

To summarize, if you hold a second mortgage and the borrower defaults on either your mortgage or the first mortgage, or both, to protect your loan from being wiped out at a foreclosure sale by the first mortgage lender, you must make up any missed payments on the first loan. Then you can declare a default and begin foreclosure on your second mortgage. But do not wait to do so. If a borrower falls behind on his loan payments, begin foreclosure immediately, otherwise keeping up the payments on the prior mortgages may become a financial burden.

Of course, any amounts advanced by a second mortgage lender on behalf of the borrower to make up missed payments on a prior mortgage are added to the balance owed on the second mortgage.

3. Purchase-Money Mortgages

Although we have just discussed first, second, third, etc., mortgages, special attention must be directed toward such a mortgage that is financed by the property seller at the time of sale. These are called "purchase-money mortgages," whether they are a first, second, third, etc.

In some states, such as California, purchase-money lenders cannot collect any deficiency loss from the borrower if, after foreclosure, the property does not bring enough foreclosure sales proceeds to pay off the debt owed to the lender. Anti-deficiency laws vary from state to state, so secondary mortgage lenders should check with their attorneys as to local law.

But foreclosure deficiencies are rarely important unless property values drop below the amount owed on the mortgage at the time of foreclosure. Sellers who carry back purchase-money mortgages usually get higher sales prices for their property than if they demand 100 percent cash from the buyer.

Although the seller does not get all-cash if he helps finance the sale, he can earn excellent return on his loan to the buyer. In most states, except where barred by usury laws, yields of at least 10 percent to 15 percent are possible on purchase-money mortgages. Some state laws, such as California, have no interest rate usury limit on purchase-money mortgages from the property seller. Purchase-money mortgages not only give the seller excellent interest income, but they also qualify the sale for deferred-payment installment-sale tax savings.

But a word of caution is in order. If the seller does not want the property back in the event of the borrower's default and foreclosure, he should insist on a substantial cash down payment. This is called "protective equity." But if the seller would not mind receiving the property back someday, so he can sell it for another profit, a low or no down payment sale could be advantageous. Of course, the lower the down payment, the greater the amount of loan money at risk for the seller and the greater the interest income he will receive.

4. Special FHA and VA Home Mortgage Programs

The Federal Housing Administration (FHA) and the Veteran's Administration (VA) have many special home loan programs that require no or a minimum cash down payment. While these insured or guaranteed mortgage programs involve lots of government red tape delays, the low down payment can make the frustrations worthwhile. Loan processing has been greatly improved in recent years so the drawbacks aren't as severe as formerly.

For the latest information on FHA and VA home loans, check with your local approved FHA-VA lender such as a bank, S&L, or mortgage broker. As of this writing, VA no-down-payment loans are generally available up to $110,000. VA mortgages above this amount usually require a 25 percent down payment, but the lender has considerable flexibility on VA loan terms.

As of this writing, FHA home loans are available up to $67,500, but there are higher loan amounts available in high-cost communities. The cash down payment required is 3 percent of the first $25,000 plus 5 percent of the balance.

With both FHA and VA mortgages, the home buyer can pay more than the loan amount in cash, but second mortgages are not allowed at the time of FHA or VA mortgage origination (except VA will allow a fully amortized second mortgage).

The big drawback of VA home loans is the government sets the maximum interest rate. Usually this interest rate is below the prevailing open market interest rate that lenders can obtain on conventional home loans. Since lenders are not fools, they charge "loan fees" or "discount points" to raise their yield on VA mortgages. A one-point loan fee equals 1 percent of the amount borrowed. For each one-point loan fee charged, the lender raises its true yield about ⅛ percent. To illustrate, if the government-set VA interest rate is 12 percent and a lender charges a three-point loan fee, the lender really earns 12⅜ percent yield.

Unfortunately, by law the VA borrower cannot pay his own loan fee (as do borrowers obtaining conventional home mortgages from lenders such as banks and S&Ls). Since the buyer cannot pay the loan fee, that leaves the seller the "opportunity" to pay the loan fee. Many home sellers refuse to pay their buyer's loan fee. Some will pay only if they can raise their sales price by a corresponding amount. When this is done, however, the home may not appraise at a market value including the inflated loan fee added on.

Many realty agents have had unfortunate incidents with FHA and VA home loan appraisers who tend to be very conservative in their appraisals. If you do offer to buy a home contingent upon obtaining a VA or FHA home loan, be sure your realty agent accompanies the VA or FHA fee appraiser and points out to him recent comparable sales prices of similar neighborhood homes that reflect true market value.

5. Trade-ins and Exchanges

There is no law saying the down payment to purchase real estate must be in cash. It can be just about anything the seller is willing to accept.

Typical real estate trade-ins and exchanges involve autos, boats, motor homes, other real estate such as lots, cabins, and houses, corporate stocks or bonds, and just about anything of value the owner wants to get rid of. Many realtors offer guaranteed trade-in plans or guaranteed sales programs so a potential home buyer can be sure of the minimum price he will receive for his old home.

Exchanges involving investment property, such as a trade of a vacant lot for an apartment house, are frequently arranged to avoid paying income tax on the profitable disposal of the smaller property. A direct trade is necessary to defer the tax on the trade up (with the exception of Starker and Biggs "indirect exchanges" which are discussed in Chapter 10). But after the swap is completed, the owner of the larger property who accepts the smaller property as a down payment often sells the smaller property for cash. Such a trade is then called a three-way exchange because there are three parties, the up trader, the down trader, and the cash-out buyer.

When disposing of one personal residence to buy another, however, it is not necessary to go through the "exchange game." As discussed in Chapters 2 and 3, an owner must defer paying his profit tax when selling his principal residence and buying a more expensive one within eighteen months before or after the sale.

6. Assigned, Transferred, and Assumed Mortgages

Another method of paying for property to be acquired is to assign, transfer, or assume an existing mortgage. There are important differences in the meaning of these terms.

An assigned mortgage is one that you already own. In other words, someone owes you money, and your security is a mortgage on a property which can be foreclosed if the debt is not paid to you as agreed. You could assign this mortgage, as your down payment, to the seller of the realty you want to acquire. Another example of a mortgage assignment occurs when a construction lender, after the building is completed, assigns the construction loan to a permanent lender thereby converting the mortgage into long-term financing. This saves considerable escrow and recording fees. However, there may be tax aspects to consider on a mortgage assignment, so check with your tax adviser.

A transferred mortgage changes the borrower but keeps the original lender. This is frequently called a mortgage assumption if the new borrower assumes the legal obligation to make the loan payments and the lender releases the previous borrower from further liability. If the buyer merely takes over the loan payments, without any formal arrangement with the lender, this is called buying the property "subject to" the mortgage. Problems can develop with "subject to" mortgages if the loan contains a legally enforceable "due on sale clause." This is a hot real estate topic now as the legal enforceability of due on sale clauses differs in each state.

7. Hypothecated Mortgages

If you hold a mortgage on a property now and want to acquire a property, but the seller will not accept a mortgage assignment, hypothecate instead.

Hypothecate means to pledge as security or borrow against. For example, I held a seven-year second mortgage at 7 percent interest on an apartment house I sold. As there has not been much of a demand from investors to buy 7 percent mortgages, and I did not want to sell the mortgage because the discount would be at least 50 percent, I borrowed on it instead. The $15,000 mortgage was collateral for a loan of $7,500 at 10 percent interest. Sure, I took a 3 percent interest rate loss on the $7,500, but when the $15,000 loan paid off in seven years, I then used $7,500 to pay off my hypothecated loan. Hypothecation is a great way to obtain tax-free money secured by a mortgage you will not want to sell at a big discount.

8. Blanket Mortgages

There are many ways to use blanket mortgages, including buying property with little or no cash down payment. However, to use this finance technique, you must already own one or more properties.

Lenders love to get the maximum security for their mortgage loans. Often a bank or S&L will suggest you give a blanket mortgage on two or more properties you own as security for their mortgage loan. If the properties are in poor repair or in undesirable locations, the lender wants to spread the risk over as many properties as possible.

To illustrate, a friend of mine owns several duplexes in a not-so-hot neighborhood, a run-down hotel, and a small office building. He wanted to raise cash by refinancing his mortgages on these properties. But no lender desired to loan on these marginal properties. However, a lender would make a blanket mortgage on all of them. If my friend does not make the payments, the lender can then foreclose on all the properties. Without a blanket mortgage it would be next to impossible to borrow on these properties.

Another use for blanket mortgages is for buying property. Suppose you find a house for sale where the elderly seller does not need a cash down payment, but he or she wants secure monthly income. So you offer to buy the house, take over its existing first mortgage, and give the seller a blanket mortgage for the balance of the purchase price (no cash down payment). The blanket mortgage would be secured by the property you are buying as well as another property you already own. The blanket mortgage lets you acquire another property for no cash and gives its seller the security he or she seeks.

9. Lease With Option to Buy

This is such a powerful finance method for buyers and sellers, it is a special topic in the next chapter about short- and long-term lease-options. In the last year there has been considerable interest from my newspaper readers in this creative finance technique. The next chapter includes explanations and sample forms for this special finance method that can accomplish many real estate goals.

10. Tax-Deferred Single-Payment Mortgages

One of the most powerful finance techniques is the tax-deferred single-payment mortgage. It really means the buyer makes no payment until the balloon payment, including both principal and interest, becomes due in perhaps ten years. In the meantime the buyer has no monthly payments and the interest is accruing for the seller.

For example, in 1982 I bought a rental house investment with a partially tax-deferred mortgage. I wanted the seller to carry back a twelve-year $60,000 third mortgage at 12 percent interest with all interest accruing. In twelve years the balloon payment would be $146,400. But the seller insisted on a $150 monthly interest payment with the $450 remaining interest accruing tax-deferred. I agreed because this method held my monthly payments down to an affordable total.

11. Sale-Leasebacks

This finance method often produces 100 percent financing for the buyer. The property seller sells the property, usually business property, to an investor, such as a pension trust fund or an insurance company, at the fair market value. Often there is an option to repurchase the property when the lease expires, sometimes before.

By using the sale-leaseback method, the lessee-seller obtains cash and can now deduct his rent payments for a building he may have owned many years and fully depreciated before the sale. Stores, banks, factories, apartments and many other types of commercial properties are suitable for sale-leasebacks. But a tax adviser should be consulted because the tax require proper structuring of the sale-leaseback transaction.

12. Land Contract, Contract of Sale, Contract for Deed, and Agreement of Sale

All these names refer to the same type of transaction. Using this finance method, the property's seller retains legal title to the property until all or an agreed part of the sale price is paid by the buyer to the seller. This method is often used where the buyer makes no or a very small cash down payment. The seller feels more secure in such a transaction if he still holds the deed to the property.

But in the event of the buyer's default on the payments, the seller may have problems getting back possession of the property or clearing up the title. The status of land contract sales varies in each state, and an attorney should be consulted before using this technique. Although land contracts are used to finance otherwise "impossible transactions," they can be risky if not properly structured to protect both buyer and seller.

Another land contract sale problem can occur after the buyer has made all his payments and is entitled to receive the deed from the seller. Legally the seller is required to convey marketable title to the buyer at this time. But what if he cannot? Of course, the buyer can sue the seller for damages, but this can be costly and nonproductive. Many attorneys suggest, to avoid title problems, that the seller's deed should be held in escrow or a trust until the buyer completes his payments.

13. Commercial Loans
14. Chattel Loans
15. Personal Loans

Any one or a combination of these loan types can be used to finance the cash portion required for a down payment to buy a property. If the realty to be acquired needs immediate improvements, part of the money can be used to make those improvements. If you have built up a good credit history, you can probably borrow $5,000 to $20,000 from a bank or finance company on your signature alone. Sometimes the lender will record a lien on your household goods as security, but this is just to meet lending requirements and you can be 99 percent sure the lender never wants to foreclose on your furniture if you default on the loan.

16. Improvement Loans

An often overlooked finance source is the improvement loan. It can be either on property you already own or on the property you want to acquire. One of the first loans I ever obtained was a home improvement loan. The friendly old-time banker was extremely successful making these loans. He knew the money was not going to improve the property, and he did not care. All he wanted was good security for his loan in case of default.

Today, some lenders are sticky about improvement loans and want to see how the money will be spent to improve the property. Others do not care as long as there is sufficient equity in the property which secures the loan.

Since banks and S&Ls no longer play games and now make second mortgage loans readily, there really is not much need to call such loans improvement loans anymore. Improvement loans are really second mortgages. As bankers change their thinking and loan on the security of the property rather than on the borrower's credit, expect to see more second mortgages from banks and S&Ls and fewer improvement loans. Of course, if the owner lacks sufficient property equity to justify a second mortgage, and if the money really is going to finance improvements that will increase the property's value, then an improvement loan solves the problem. In such a situation, the lender will make sure the money really is spent on improvements which will increase the market value of the property.

17. Wrap-around mortgages

Another way to finance property acquisition is by use of a wrap-around mortgage. Such a loan is really a second mortgage. It can be either "hard money" (actual cash obtained from a mortgage lender) or "soft money" (loaned by the property seller to the buyer without cash actually changing hands). This finance technique can be good for buyers and sellers. But it is badly misunderstood and is often used in the wrong circumstances. Along with lease-options, wrap-around mortgages are fully discussed in the next chapter.

18. Syndication of Limited Partnerships

Often you will locate excellent investment property that is beyond your financial ability to buy and maintain. This is the time to consider forming a partnership with other investors. There are thousands of investors who want to invest in real estate but who lack the time and ability to find and buy properties. Examples include wealthy doctors, dentists, and lawyers who can better use their time making money than renting to tenants.

Many successful realty investors started out, as I did, investing with partners. This combination can work out very successfully if it is clearly understood, in a written partnership agreement, that the general partner will manage the property and will consult the investors (limited partners) only on major decisions such as selling or refinancing the property.

My first partnership ended by my buying out my partner. When we got our first vacancy, I wanted to fix up the unit so it could command higher rent. But my partner wanted to milk the property and take out as much cash as possible by putting in minimal maintenance. This fundamental clash of management philosophy should have been ironed out before buying the property. Thankfully, my partner was willing to sell out to me without any hassle, but it could have been a sticky problem if he had resisted.

A limited-partnership syndication should be entered into only after consultation with an attorney who should draw up the documentation. Investors should invest in such partnerships only if they will not need their investment money for the agreed number of years of the partnership's life. Some major stockbrokers offer huge limited-partnership offerings, based mostly on tax shelter benefits, but the "front end" load fees of such offerings diminish the limited-partner profit potential. Before investing in any limited partnership, check the general partner's experience and track record as that is some indication of probable future results too.

Frankly, I would never invest in the large, nationwide, partnership offerings. The tax shelter and investment returns are better, I find, on local properties that I can see, touch, and smell.

19. The Equity Release Technique

There are thousands of homeowners and other property owners who have idle equity in their properties. For example, if your home is worth $100,000 and you have a $60,000 mortgage on it, you have $40,000 of idle equity that is doing you absolutely no good just sitting there. It produces no income, no tax shelter, and no other benefits.

Equity is the difference between a property's fair market value and the amount owed on that property. To illustrate, suppose your home is worth $75,000 and it has a $25,000 first mortgage and a $10,000 second mortgage. The difference between the $75,000 value and the $35,000 total loans is the $40,000 idle equity that can be fully or partially used to buy more realty.

To release this idle equity, the property owner simply creates a promissory note, secured by a mortgage or trust deed on the property owned.

EXAMPLE:

Home's Current Market Value	$95,000
Old First Mortgage Balance	$40,000
New Second Mortgage Created	$40,000
Owner's New Equity in Home	$15,000

This homeowner can now go shopping for another property to buy, knowing he can use his $40,000 created second mortgage for his down payment. If he adds a little cash to "sweeten" the transaction for the seller of the property the homeowner wants to buy, his chances of getting a "good deal" are appreciably enhanced. To illustrate, suppose this homeowner finds a $200,000 apartment house he wants to buy. The financing might look like this:

Purchase Price	$200,000
Existing First Mortgage	$100,000
Buyer's Down Payment Created Second Mortgage on Home	$40,000
New Second Mortgage Taken Back by Seller	$60,000

However, this buyer should be careful to structure the payments on the second mortgage created on his home and the second mortgage to the seller secured by the apartments. If the payments exceed the rents minus operating expenses, a negative cash flow results. To avoid this problem, perhaps one of the second mortgages can be structured to allow interest to accumulate, with no monthly payments and a balloon payment due in five or ten years.

20. The Life Estate Finance Method

Many older homeowners would like to (1) sell their homes to produce cash or monthly payments and (2) remain in their homes until they die or are physically unable to care for themselves. Although these desires are conflicting, they occur very frequently among elderly homeowners. The solution can be the life estate finance method.

A life estate allows a property user to retain use of a property as long as he or she is alive. For example, it is common for a husband in his will to provide a life estate for his surviving widow in the family home, but at her death the home is to go to the children.

When an investor buys a home subject to a life estate for the seller, it means the seller is guaranteed the privilege of living there for the rest of his or her life. If the property is being sold by husband and wife, the life estate can be for their joint lives.

The buyer-investor in such a house, which is subject to a life estate in the seller, would agree to pay the life tenant an agreed monthly payment based on that person's life expectancy at the time of the sale to the buyer-investor. This buyer will, of course, need an outside source of funds for these payments, such as purchasing an annuity based on the seller's life expectancy.

Advantages for the seller: Small cash down payment plus monthly income for living costs so occupancy of the home can be retained for life.

Advantages for the buyer: Little cash required. The property is bought at today's market value which will surely increase with inflation.

Disadvantages for the seller: Cannot will the property and may die before receiving the property's full value in payments from the investor-buyer.

Disadvantages for the buyer: Seller may outlive the life expectancy tables; resale or refinance of property subject to a life estate is very difficult so such property should not be bought with the thought of quick resale.

EXAMPLE: Investor wants to buy a $50,000 house owned by an elderly lady. He offers her $1,000 down payment and agrees to pay her $300 per month for life. To finance his purchase, the investor could get an open-end mortgage, adding to the mortgage balance periodically as need for funds arise. Or the buyer could purchase an annuity that would pay $300 per month for the seller's life, but this could be very expensive.

21. Foreclosures Purchased From the Lender—Buying Wholesale

Although this is not a finance device, because of the seller's unique position, REO (real estate owned) foreclosures bought from lenders such as banks and savings and loan associations offer special financing terms.

Mortgage lenders do not like to admit it, but they make mistakes occasionally. These mistakes are called foreclosures. After the lender becomes the owner of a foreclosed property (if there are no cash bidders at the foreclosure sale), it is called REO property. Most banks, real estate investment trusts, savings and loan associations, and insurance companies own REO property which they would love to sell.

To get rid of these REOs (never call them foreclosures when talking to the lender because they do not like it known they make mistakes), 90 percent, 95 percent, and even 100 percent mortgage loans are made by the lender "to facilitate the sale." It is called "basket money." Such REO properties can be located in two ways. One is to phone all the S&Ls and banks in your area and ask to speak to the lender's officer in charge of real estate owned. If that person says the lender does not have any REOs at the present time, that may be the truth. Leave your name, address, and phone number. Better yet, follow up your phone conversation with a short typewritten letter on your letterhead reinforcing your buying interest. If you are lucky, when an REO comes available, the lender's REO officer may phone you.

The second method is to get a copy of the lender's latest quarterly financial statement. On that report you will see an item headed "real estate bought in settlement of loans" or some similar, misleading asset title. That is REO property. Regulated lenders want to get rid of this property because they have to set aside special reserves for such property. If you see that item on a lender's financial statement, you will know they have REO property to sell. Then contact the lender to find out what the property is, and then decide if you are interested in it.

But do not be misled! If the item on the lender's financial report statement says something like "Real estate held for investment," that is not REO property, and the lender may not want to sell it.

Lastly, keep checking back with lenders monthly to see if they have any new REO property. The best bargain property I ever bought was an REO sold by a large S&L that was so desperate to sell it they had even listed it with a real estate broker. Most lenders will not list REOs with realty agents because they do not want to play favorites, and they do not want to pay a sales commission. I found out about the REO from the realty broker, but I probably could have bought it cheaper before he got the listing if I had bought direct from the lender and if I had regularly phoned the lender for new REO offerings.

22. The Sandwich Lease

This finance technique is much like the lease-option method to be discussed in the next chapter. But it is even better. Its application is usually limited to commercial properties, but it could also be used on apartment houses.

An example will illustrate how a sandwich lease works. Suppose there is a vacant supermarket building in your town. Due to competition from newer stores, it is no longer suitable for a supermarket. But the building is basically sound. It is most likely being leased by a major supermarket chain that has several years remaining on its lease, plus an option to renew.

This abandoned supermarket might be a terrific location for several small shops—perhaps a "Farmer's Market" of restaurants, such as Chinese, Italian, German, Mexican, fast-food, and pizza, for example. So you go to the supermarket chain's real estate manager and obtain (1) a master lease on the store and (2) maybe, an option to purchase the property if the supermarket's lease contains such a purchase option. Frankly, the option is not important.

Suppose you master lease the store for $10,000 per month. You then divide it into perhaps ten smaller stores renting for $1,500 per month each ($15,000 total monthly rent). You will then have a $5,000 per month profit for being "sandwiched" between the owner and the shopkeepers. Your investment is minimal, unless you agree to make the improvements (for which higher rent can be charged, of course). Ideally, when you negotiate your master lease with the supermarket chain, you will have an option to purchase the building, so if the project is very successful, the property's value will appreciate. If it does not, you don't have to exercise the purchase option.

23. The Option

The cheapest yet potentially most profitable finance technique is the bare, naked option. Six- to twelve-month options often can be bought for 1 to 5 percent of the market value of a property. If the option expires but you have not exercised your purchase option, you lose your option money. But hopefully by the time the option is ready to expire, you have found a buyer who will purchase the property from you for a substantial profit. Or you may decide to buy the property to hold it as an investment.

To convince a property owner to sell you an option to buy his property, be sure to point out the tax advantages to the owner. Your option payment, perhaps $10,000, is nontaxable to the property owner until either (1) you exercise the purchase option or (2) the option expires unexercised. Either way, the property owner has the tax-free use of the option money. If the option is exercised and the option money is applied toward the purchase price, that option money becomes long-term capital gain to the seller. If the option expires unexercised, the option money is ordinary income to the seller. But until one of those events happens, the seller can use the option money as he pleases without any tax consequences.

24. Tax-deferred Exchanges

If you already own property held for investment or for use in your trade or business, your equity in that property can be used to trade toward a larger such property. In such an exchange, the tax on your profit is deferred if you meet the simple conditions of Internal Revenue Code Section 1031. The details on tax-deferred exchanges are explained in Chapter 10.

25. The Deferred Down Payment Method

When you are ready to buy a property, with lots of cash in your bank account, may not be the time when a property meeting your requirements is for sale. What often happens is you will hear of a property you would like to own, but at the time you do not have available cash for a down payment. Unless the seller is willing to sell for no down payment (such a seller is highly motivated and not easy to find), you may have difficulty buying that property.

But here is an idea which may convince the seller to sell to you now with little or no cash down payment. It is called the deferred down payment. The method of deferral can take several forms.

If you can afford high monthly payments to the seller, provide in your purchase offer for such high payments on the second mortgage the seller takes back to finance your purchase. In other words, your monthly payments will consist of interest on the unpaid principal plus abnormally high principal payments (your deferred down payment).

Another approach, if you are expecting to receive a large amount of cash in a few months, is to use a "short fuse mortgage" which has its balloon payment due in six or twelve months. But this can be dangerous if your expected source of the balloon payment does not materialize as expected. So be very careful before committing yourself to a short fuse mortgage for the deferred down payment.

Still another variation of the deferred down payment is to provide in your purchase offer for 100 percent financing to the seller but with prepayment of the first six monthly payments at the time of the closing.

To illustrate, suppose you find a $100,000 investment property that has a $60,000 existing assumable mortgage. You might offer the seller his full $100,000 asking price if he will finance your purchase with a $40,000 second mortgage. Most sellers will not accept such an offer. But if you pay the first six month's payments on that $40,000 second mortgage at the time of closing (which would be a $2,400 payment if it was a 12 percent interest-only second mortgage), that might sweeten the deal for the seller. Better yet, offer to prepay the entire year's monthly payments at the close of escrow.

The happy result for the buyer of this variation of the deferred down payment is the entire "down payment" becomes tax deductible interest.

26. Borrow the Realtor's Commission

Sometimes the buyer does not have enough cash for the down payment and he has no readily available source for borrowing that money such as a bank, S&L, cash-by-mail company, or "plastic money" from credit cards.

The last hope for the buyer may be the realty agent. Although they like to be paid their sales commission in cash, many real estate agents will loan their buyers all or part of their commission to finance the purchase.

To protect the agent, the promissory note should be secured by a mortgage or deed of trust either on the property being purchased or on other property owned by the buyer. Smart agents realize it is wise to take sales commission notes because this evens out the peaks and valleys of cyclical real estate sales commission income. If an agent builds up a portfolio of secured commission notes, he does not have to worry where his next dollar is coming from.

But a word to realty agents is in order. Never, never, never loan your sales commission to a buyer without getting adequate security. I recall selling a large apartment house where the seller did not have enough cash out of the sale to pay all the debts he owed on the building. He asked the two agents involved to loan him $7,000 so the sale could close. Although we were glad to make the loan (we got the rest of our commission in cash), we did not have time before the closing to check the seller's title on the property he offered as security. Unfortunately, he did not have clear title to it, so we wound up with an unsecured $7,000 commission note. When it came due in six months, the seller was now broke and either could not or would not pay us. We had to sue on the unsecured promissory note, get a court judgment, and then try to collect. We are still looking for assets to attach. Does anybody want to buy an unsecured $7,000 promissory note?

27. Refinance Before or During the Sale

If you find a property you want to buy, and the seller absolutely must have more cash from the sale than you have available, provide in your purchase offer for either (1) seller to refinance the mortgage before the sale or at the time of sale, or (2) at the time of sale you will take over payments on the existing first mortgage, obtain a new "hard money" second mortgage to give the seller the cash he needs, and seller will take back a third mortgage for the balance of the purchase price (thus giving you a no down payment purchase).

Last year I used this technique to acquire a rental house for practically no down payment. The seller said he needed $30,000 down payment. That was more than I wanted to invest in the house, which was worth about $115,000. So my purchase offer provided the following: (1) seller to refinance his $45,000 existing first mortgage for $80,000 and (2) seller to take back a second mortgage for the balance of the purchase price. The seller counteroffered that I was to make a $5,000 cash down payment, and I accepted. The happy result was a highly leveraged purchase, maximum tax shelter for me, and the seller got the cash he needed (to buy another house).

The same result could have been obtained by leaving the old first mortgage intact, adding a new "hard money" second mortgage, and the seller could have carried back a third mortgage for the balance of the sales price.

28. Borrow on Something You Already Own

In many property purchases there is often no adequate substitute for cash from the buyer to the seller. To raise this cash, consider what you already own (but do not want to sell) and can raise cash from. Examples probably include your auto, summer home, boat, common stocks, bonds, house, condominium, or furniture. By borrowing on the security of these items from your bank or finance company, you can acquire the necessary cash for the down payment on the real estate you want to acquire. Of course, be sure you can make the total payments on all your loans, otherwise this could be foolish borrowing.

29. The Right Day of the Month to Buy Income Property

Smart buyers of income property cut down the cash needed to finance their purchases by closing their purchase on the right day of the month.

What is that day? It is the day after the rents are due. For example, if you are buying a ten-unit apartment house where each tenant pays $250 per month rent on the first of the month, if you close the sale on the second of the month, you will receive a prorated rent credit for $^{29}/_{30}$ (assuming it is a thirty-day month) of $2,500 which is $2,416.66. In addition, you will be credited at the closing settlement with the amount of the tenant's security deposits. Depending upon state law, you may or may not be able to use the security deposits to reduce your cash needed to close the purchase. In most states, you can use the security deposits, and they do not have to be held in separate trust accounts for the tenants.

Of course, as the new owner you must be prepared to refund tenant security deposits when the tenant moves out. But since you will soon be renting to a new tenant who will pay a new security deposit, the money to return the old tenant's security deposit, in essence, comes from the new tenant.

30. Other Creative Ways to Finance Your Purchase

There are dozens of other creative, innovative methods of financing your property purchase. Examples include using the cash value of your life insurance policy (the cost is usually only 5 percent or 6 percent); giving the seller prepaid rent so he can remain in the property, free, for an agreed period in return for a no or low down payment purchase; selling part of the property acquired to raise cash for the down payment (works very well if the property can be split into two or more lots); or taking in a rich partner who puts up the down payment cash in return for a 50 percent or 75 percent of the property you found and will manage.

The key to financing real estate today is to think positively and do not be afraid to innovate. Of course, do not take unnecessary or unreasonable risks. Your reputation is extremely important. Do not do anything to tarnish it. Be sure you can meet your payments on time because if you once default, it harms your credit and your future ability to finance property acquisitions creatively.

Listen to other real estate investors. Attend meetings of your local property owner's association, which is usually very inexpensive to join. Spend money attending real estate seminars. Buy books on real estate investments. An excellent one on creative finance is Robert G. Allen's *Nothing Down,* published by Simon and Schuster.

There is no real estate finance technique that will work in every situation on every property. Although the traditional buying formula of a 20 percent cash down payment and an 80 percent new mortgage is not gone, it is dying fast. Those buyers who understand innovative finance will be the ones who prosper in real estate. But buyers and their realty agents who do not understand the new finance methods will miss profit opportunities. You will be a winner if you keep up with the changes in real estate finance and adapt to changing conditions.

QUESTIONS AND ANSWERS

SELLER CAN NAME OWN PRICE
IF HE WILL CARRY THE MORTGAGE

Q. We are selling our home so we can move to a condominium we have already purchased in south Florida. As we are retiring, income will be very important to us. I want to maximize my retirement income. Does this idea make sense? Our home should sell for about $125,000. It presently has a $24,000 FHA mortgage at 8 percent interest. I would like to sell for $20,000 cash down payment and take back a $105,000 "wrap-around mortgage" at 10 percent interest only (no principal payments). This would give me $875 monthly income without touching the principal. What do you think?—*Joseph M.*

A. I think you have got an outstanding idea. More sellers should follow your suggestion. Sellers who are willing to carry the purchase-money mortgage for their buyers can practically name their own price in today's market. By offering easy financing, you should be able to get a sales price higher than for similar recent home sales in your neighborhood.

Be sure to have your attorney draw up that wrap-around mortgage to be sure it does not violate any usury law in your state, however.

WHY FHA AND VA MORTGAGES
DO NOT APPEAL TO MANY SELLERS

Q. We own a rental house in a low income part of town. It is listed for sale with a nearby real estate agent. He brought us a purchase offer from a GI buyer who wants to get a 100 percent VA home loan. That's fine with us, but the agent says if we accept the purchase offer we must pay the buyer's loan fee. This sounds stupid to me. Why should I, the seller, pay the buyer's loan costs? The agent says the law prohibits the buyer from paying such loan fees. Is this true or is the agent lying?—*Ed R.*

A. The agent is telling the truth. I agree with you that it is a stupid law which prohibits VA mortgage borrowers from paying the loan fee on their own home loan. Borrowers using conventional mortgages pay their own costs, why cannot VA borrowers do so too?

Lenders are charging high loan fees on VA mortgages now because the government-set interest rate on these loans is below that lenders can get on conventional home mortgages. You are not alone in refusing to pay those outrageous loan fees for the buyer.

IS BUYING "SUBJECT TO"
OR "ASSUMING" OLD EXISTING MORTGAGE BETTER?

Q. Our real estate agent has shown us several homes that have large existing mortgages. She said we can either take title "subject to" these mortgages or "assume" them. I'm not clear on the difference. Which is better for us?—*Bruce R.*

A. Buying "subject to" an existing mortgage means the buyer takes title to the property and takes over the payments on the old mortgage. But he does not legally assume any liability on that mortgage. Of course, if he does not keep up the payments, he loses the property by foreclosure.

Assuming an existing mortgage means the buyer takes title to the property and legally assumes the responsibility for paying the mortgage. The lender will then usually release the original borrower from further liability on that mortgage. However, some lenders blackmail buyers into paying an increased interest rate when they assume the old mortgage. Or they rewrite a fixed interest rate mortgage as a dangerous adjustable rate mortgage. But FHA and VA loans can be assumed without change of interest rate or terms.

IS VARIABLE INTEREST RATE MORTGAGE
GOOD FOR BORROWER?

Q. I know you dislike variable interest rate mortgages. But with mortgage interest rates so high today, don't you think they will come down in six months or so? We have just been transferred here and must buy a home quickly. Should we request a variable interest rate mortgage? —*Moses S.*

A. That is a difficult question. Please understand that interest rates on variable rate mortages (VRMs) will drop only if the lender's cost of funds drops. While that cost is near all-time peaks today, there is no guarantee it will drop. It could go up further if we have hyperinflation.

Canada, for example, has had high interest rates for many years. Maybe we are due for a similar period of long-term high interest rates.

Even if interest rates drop on mortgages, that does not mean the lender's cost of funds will drop, thereby reducing the interest rate on VRMs already existing. With lenders under extreme pressure to raise interest rates paid to savers, I see little hope of lender fund costs dropping much if any.

In spite of what you read in the newspapers, fixed interest rate mortgages are still available if you shop hard enough. For example, as of this writing FHA and VA fixed rate thirty-year mortgages are readily available. Considering their advantages, and their assumability by a subsequent buyer, that fixed-rate mortgage is far more attractive than a VRM.

HOW SOME MORTGAGE LENDERS USE
PREPAYMENT PENALTY RIP-OFFS

Q. We are trying to sell our home. Our mortgage, from a savings and loan association, has a prepayment penalty which is 4 percent of our $74,000 balance. That's $2,960. In our area, most lenders waive the prepayment penalty if the new buyer gets his mortgage from the same lender. Our house sold for $136,000, subject to the buyer's getting a new mortgage for $100,000. But our present lender refuses to make the loan to the new buyer, even though it only means a $26,000 increase and a raise in the interest rate. I'm told this lender has a policy of wanting to collect the prepayment penalty, and it rarely makes new loans for buyers of properties on which it has existing loans. What can we do to save the $2,960 prepayment penalty?—*George P.*

A. You have encountered a classic mortgage lender rip-off practiced by many savings and loan associations. I have been a victim of it twice from lenders in my area. Of course, I will not do business with those lenders again, but there was nothing I could do, other than not sell.

It is highly unethical for a lender to refuse to make a new loan to your buyer, but there is no law violation unless the lender is illegally redlining or discriminating. Many unscrupulous lenders refuse to make loans to property buyers where that lender already has the loan because the lender knows the prepayment penalty must be paid if the loan is obtained elsewhere.

Prepayment penalties add millions of dollars to lender earnings. In addition, prepayments wipe out old, low interest rate mortgages so that money can be reloaned to another borrower at today's higher interest rates. Unfortunately, it is all prefectly legal.

WATCH FOR MORTGAGE GIMMICKS ON NEW HOMES

Q. My wife and I are trying to find a home to buy. We've looked at several brand new home projects where the mortgage interest rates are about 10 percent. But realtors tell us mortgage money to buy an older house costs at least 12 percent in our area now. Why the big difference? Do the builders have some secret source of cheap money we can tap?—*Simon U.*

A. Those below-market interest rates on new homes are gimmicks. The builders, months ago, bought mortgage commitments from lenders for their entire project. The cost may have been one to five points (each loan point equals 1 percent of the amount borrowed), which, you can be sure, is passed along to buyers in the form of inflated home costs.

Although you will only pay the advertised interest rate on the new homes, lenders make their profit on such loans up front when the builder pays the loan commitment fee.

P.S. Watch out for below-market interest rates which only prevail for the first year or two, with the interest rate then reverting to market levels.

HOW TO TAKE THE SHOCK OUT OF HIGH MORTGAGE INTEREST RATES

Q. I am a worried real estate agent. My fear is the high mortgage interest rates will dry up the market for home sales, and I won't make any commissions. So far I've managed to keep up my sales volume using "creative finance" ideas such as wrap-around mortgages, land contracts of sale, and lease-options. How long do you think these high interest rates will last or should I look for another job?—*Lottie M.*

A. I share your concern.

When mortgage interest rates substantially decline, be ready for buyer demand to soar. So will home prices because there will only be a limited supply of homes for sale then.

To take the shock out of high mortgage interest rates, point out to your buyers their true after-tax mortgage cost. To illustrate, suppose a home buyer gets a new mortgage at 12 percent interest. If he is in a 30 percent income tax bracket (combined state and federal taxes), his tax dollar savings for the interest deduction are about 30 percent of 12 percent which is 3.6 percent. Twelve percent minus 3.6 percent is 8.4 percent. Considering that the home is probably appreciating in value at least 8 percent per year, that mortgage is virtually cost-free for the buyer. If more buyers understood this, they would not wait to buy, even if interest rates drop a little in the next few months.

TIME AND INFLATION RULE OUT BIG HOME CASH DOWN PAYMENT

Q. Like many apartment dwellers, we are saving for the down payment on a home of our own, probably a condominium. So far we've saved about $6,000. But it seems at our rate of saving, prices of houses and condos are going up faster than we can save. We were hoping to make a 25 percent cash down payment to hold down the monthly mortgage payments. Do you think we're doing the right thing?—*Elizabeth D.*

A. No. It is smart to save up for your down payment, but time and inflation are against you. Buy as soon as you can, so you will benefit from inflation instead of being its victim.

You probably realize your $6,000 sitting in a savings account or money market fund is costing you lost purchasing power due to inflation. Since prices of houses and condos usually go up at or faster than the inflation rate, the sooner you buy a home the sooner you will participate in the appreciation in market value of your home. That's why real estate is such a great inflation hedge.

A $6,000 down payment will not buy a very fancy home or condo, but it is enough to buy a "starter home." By use of creative finance ideas, you can buy a home now. Your benefits will include income tax savings for mortgage interest and property tax deductions, protection from rising rents, and the joy of building equity in your own home instead of helping your landlord buy his building. Work with a good realty agent to find and finance the right home for you.

ARE MORTGAGE PRINCIPAL PAYMENTS TAX DEDUCTIBLE?

Q. Is it true that mortgage interest, but not principal, payments are tax deductible?—*Fred D.*

A. Yes, it is true. Mortgage principal payments are never itemized income tax deductions for home owners or property investors.

HOW TO BUY A HOME IF YOU HAVE GOT BAD CREDIT

Q. Two years ago we went through bankruptcy. Since then, we have paid our bills and obligations on time. We talked to a loan officer at the bank where we have our savings account. She said we would have a hard time getting a home mortgage, even though we now have up to $9,000 for the down payment. Is there any way we can buy a house with our poor credit?—*Pat E.*

A. Yes. Your credit history should be no problem if you buy a home that the seller will finance. Many home sellers, especially retirees, want to carry back a first or second mortgage since this will give them safe, profitable interest income. Work with a good real estate agent. Explain your problem so the agent can concentrate on finding a seller-financed home for you.

FINANCING IS THE KEY TO REAL ESTATE SUCCESS

Q. I am a new real estate salesman and am mystified by all the property finance methods you discuss. Wrap-around mortgages, land contracts, and purchase money mortgages are some of the terms I don't understand. Is there any way to simplify home financing?—*Nathan E.*

A. Basically there are only five ways to finance property sales. (1) All cash (highly undesirable for buyers, due to inflation), (2) buyer "assumes" or takes title "subject to" an existing mortgage already on the property, (3) seller takes back a first or second mortgage or trust deed, or sells on a land contract, wrap-around mortgage, lease-option, or other innovative finance method, (4) buyer borrows on a new conventional, FHA, or VA mortgage from a bank, S&L, or mortgage broker, and (5) any combination of the above methods.

Financing is the key to real estate success. Learn all you can about real estate finance so you will prosper in real estate sales good times and bad. One good way to learn quickly is to take evening classes in real estate finance at a nearby college. Another good way is to read books on real estate finance, available at your local bookstore or library.

HOW TO PAY OFF HOME MORTGAGE BALLOON PAYMENT

Q. The seller of the house we are considering buying will help finance our purchase with a second mortgage. But he wants the payments to be "interest only" for six years at which time the entire balance of $24,000 will be due. Is this safe for us?—*Evan G.*

A. Yes. When that balloon payment comes due in six years, the balance on the first mortgage will probably be much lower than it is today. That first mortgage can probably then be refinanced to give you the cash to pay off the second mortgage's balloon payment. You may even have leftover tax-free cash from the refinancing.

Another alternative, in six years, would be to leave the old first mortgage alone and get a new second mortgage from an outside lender to pay the second mortgage balloon payment.

But a word of caution is in order. A six-year mortgage is safe, but large short-term second mortgages with balloon payments can be dangerous. For example, if your $24,000 second mortgage has its balloon payment due in only two years, then you might not be able to refinance the first mortgage or get a new second mortgage to produce the necessary $24,000 cash. If you cannot pay the balloon payment, of course, you lose the property by foreclosure.

As for the "interest-only" feature of the proposed second mortgage, that is good for you because all your payments will be tax-deductible interest. Although the interest only mortgage keeps your loan at a constant balance, you will be building equity due to the probable market value appreciation of the home.

TAKING OVER OLD HOME MORTGAGE
CAN HOLD DOWN COSTS

Q. We're in the process of buying a home, but we think the seller is taking advantage of us. When we made our purchase offer, it said we are to take title "subject to" the existing mortgage, and the seller was to give us a second mortgage to help finance the sale. The seller accepted in writing. Then about two weeks ago, the realty agent told us we'll have to "assume" the old mortgage as the seller wants to be released from liability on it. This will involve extra fees and the lender wants to increase the mortgage's interest rate. What do you advise?—*John G.*

A. See your attorney. Find out if the old mortgage has a legally enforceable "due on sale clause." If it does, when title to the property is transferred, the lender can demand full payment and foreclosure if you do not pay off the loan. When you assume such a mortgage, the lender can charge an assumption fee and raise the interest rate. Frankly, it is a lender's rip-off—also known as "legalized blackmail." After you assume the mortgage, the lender will probably agree to release the seller from further liability on the mortgage.

But if the old mortgage does not have an enforceable "due on sale clause" (FHA and VA mortgages do not), then you can take title "subject to" the old mortgage at its old interest rate and without a big assumption fee.

When a property buyer takes title "subject to" an old, existing mortgage, the seller remains liable on that loan if the buyer defaults. If you did not agree to assume the old mortgage in the sales agreement, however, it would appear the seller cannot require you to do so now. Be sure your attorney is up to date on the latest court decisions in this area as "due on sale clauses" are a hot real estate topic throughout the nation today.

FIFTEEN WAYS TO FINANCE HOME PURCHASE WITH LITTLE OR NO CASH

Q. My husband and I earn about $20,000 total per year. But we only have around $450 in our savings account. Any ideas how we can buy a home without waiting to save up a down payment?—*Tammie R.*

A. Yes. To build up your down payment savings account, always deposit your paychecks in your savings account, never in your checking account. Withdraw only for necessary living costs. Cut the frills. Then start looking for a home to buy. Keep making purchase offers until a motivated seller accepts one. Here are fifteen ways to buy a home with little or no cash. Your realty agent can probably suggest more.

(1) Lease a home with an option to buy it in twelve months, (2) VA no down payment mortgage, (3) FHA low down payment mortgage, (4) 90 percent or 95 percent PMI (private mortgage insurance) mortgage from over 22,000 banks and S&Ls, (5) buy a foreclosed FHA or VA home from HUD, (6) borrow the down payment from relatives, (7) borrow the down payment on your car or other personal property from a bank or finance company, (8) get seller to finance the sale on a first or second mortgage with minimal cash down payment, (9) buy an REO (real estate owned) foreclosed home from a bank or S&L, (10) "equity squeeze" by creating a down payment second mortgage on property you already own, (11) get a group of friends to form a limited partnership syndicate to buy your home and give you an option to buy it for a higher price from them in a few years, (12) buy an option on a home, (13) buy out the owners' equity in a

home that he is about to lose through foreclosure, (14) borrow the down payment on an unsecured loan at your bank (if your credit is good), and (15) buy on a land contract with little or no cash down payment.

7.

How to Avoid Mortgage Due on Sale Clause Problems

Today's high mortgage interest rates have made if difficult for prospective home buyers and real estate investors to obtain and make the monthly payments on a new mortgage. So smart property buyers search for properties for sale with existing mortgages that can be taken over at the old existing low interest rate.

The big problem is there are not enough properties with existing assumable mortgages at low interest rates. But the smart buyers know how to take over virtually any existing mortgage at its old interest rate, thus saving thousands of dollars of interest each year. A special procedure should be followed when buying a property with an attractive low interest rate existing mortgage. Here are the steps that should be followed.

GET A COPY OF THE EXISTING MORTGAGE OR TRUST DEED AND THE PROMISSORY NOTE

The first step to taking over an existing mortgage at its old interest rate is to get a copy of both the mortgage (or trust deed) and the promissory note. Check to see if it contains a due on sale clause. FHA and VA home loans do not contain such clauses; a buyer can assume such a mortgage at its old low interest rate for about $50 in costs.

Many S&L, bank, and mortgage company loans lack due on sale clauses. There is no substitute for reading these loan papers to see if such a clause exists. The realty agent or the property seller should have a copy of these important documents. Or the agent can get them for you.

If the mortgage lacks a due on sale clause, when writing your purchase offer specify that the buyer is to purchase "subject to" the existing mortgage. Never, never, never use the words "Buyer to assume existing mortgage" (except for VA and FHA mortgages which cost about $50 for the buyer to assume).

The reason for not using the word *assume* is that if the buyer obligates himself to legally assume the old mortgage (with a release of the seller's liability on that loan), then the lender can demand assumption fees and an increased interest rate. Worse yet, the mortgage lender might require rewriting the old mortgage from fixed interest rate terms to a variable or adjustable rate loan.

When looking for the due on sale clause in an existing mortgage, check first at "Clause 17." Most "Fannie Mae" (Federal National Mortgage Association) and "Freddie Mac" (Federal Home Loan Mortgage Corporation) loan forms have the due on sale clause in Clause 17.

WHAT TO DO IF YOU FIND A DUE ON SALE CLAUSE

If the existing mortgage contains a due on sale clause and the loan was originated by a federal savings and loan association, the Garn-St. Germain Depository Institutions Act of 1982 says such a due on sale clause is legally enforceable when title to the property is transferred. The loan's date of origination is immaterial.

However, if the S&L converted to federal status but did not hold a federal charter at the time the loan was originated, the Garn Law makes clear that the due on sale clause is not enforceable under the federal S&L exception. For example, several large California S&Ls such as World, Great Western, American, and Imperial recently converted from state to federal charters. They have backed down trying to enforce due on sale clauses in some of their loans made under state charters.

When a due on sale clause is found and the loan was not originated by a federal S&L, then the question of the due on sale clause's legal enforceability becomes important. A real estate attorney should be consulted in the state where the property is located because the rules differ in each state.

THE LOAN WINDOW

If the existing loan was originated by any nonfederal S&L lender, such as a bank, finance company, individual lender, or mortgage company, and the loan has a due on sale clause, in some states a buyer can take over that old loan on its original terms if the loan was made during certain "window periods."

However, the dates of these window periods are not always clear. For example, in California most mortgage lenders feel the loan window opened on August 25, 1978 (the date of the famous California Supreme Court decision in *Wellenkamp* vs. *Bank of America*). That means a mortgage made on California property between August 25, 1978, and October 15, 1982 (the date President Reagan signed the Garn Law) can be taken over "subject to" by a new buyer of the property and the mortgage lender cannot enforce the due on sale clause. But some lawyers argue the California loan window period opened for loans made after 1974 (the date of the *Tucker* vs. *Lassen Savings and Loan Association* court decision). Still other California lawyers argue the California loan window period opened for mortgages originated after 1872, the date California Civil Code 711 barring unreasonable restraints on property transfers was passed by the California legislature.

Here are some loan window period opening dates, as supplied by Fannie Mae. They are subject to court interpretation in each state, so check with a local real estate attorney.

ARIZONA: Loan may be assumed on existing terms if originated after March 13, 1978 (*Patton* vs. *First Federal Savings and Loan Association,* 578 Pac.2d 152).

CALIFORNIA: Loan may be assumed on existing terms if originated after August 25, 1978 (*Wellenkamp* vs. *Bank of America,* 581 Pac.2d 970); some lawyers argue 1974 or 1872 were the loan window opening dates.

COLORADO: Loan may be assumed with one percent (1%) increase in the existing note's interest rate (July 1, 1975, Colorado Revised Statutes, Article 38-60-65).

GEORGIA: Loan may be assumed with one percent (1%) increase in the existing note's interest rate if a request for release of liability is made and approved by the lender (limited to one rate increase each twenty-four months), (July 1, 1979, Georgia Code Ann., 67-3002).

IOWA: Loan may be assumed on existing contract terms (July 1, 1979, Iowa Code Ann. 535.8).

MICHIGAN: Loan may be assumed on existing contract terms (January 5, 1977, *Nichols* vs. *Arbor Federal Savings and Loan Association,* 250 N.W. 2d 804).

MINNESOTA: Loans made between June 1, 1979, and May 8, 1981, may be assumed on existing contract terms, but for any loan made between May 9, 1981, and October 15, 1982, the note rate shall be increased to the greater of the existing note rate or the "most recently published monthly index of the Fannie Mae auction yields'' (June 1, 1979, Minnesota Statutes Ann. 47.20).

NEW MEXICO: Loan may be assumed on existing contract terms (March 15, 1979, N.M.S.A. 48-7-11 through 48-7-14).

UTAH: Loan may be assumed with one percent (1%) increase in the existing note interest rate and an additional one percent (1%) increase five years later (May 12, 1981, Utah Code Ann. 57-15-1 et seq.).

WASHINGTON: Loan may be assumed on existing contract terms (August 19, 1976, *Bellingham First Federal Savings and Loan Association* vs. *Garrison,* 553 Pac. 2d 1090).

In these states it is clear that a loan made between the date given and October 15, 1982, can be assumed without the lender changing the loan terms except as noted above even if the loan contains a due on sale clause.

THE TITLE TRANSFER WINDOW

If the mortgage was originated during the state's loan window period, then the due on sale clause cannot be enforced if the property title is transferred between October 15, 1982, and October 14, 1985. The Garn Law, however, allows for possible extension of this title transfer window period by action of the state legislature.

WHAT IF THE MORTGAGE HAS A DUE ON SALE CLAUSE BUT THE LOAN WAS NOT ORIGINATED DURING THE STATE'S LOAN WINDOW PERIOD?

If a mortgage containing a due on sale clause wasn't originated during the state's loan window period, or if the state has no window period because the state's courts or legislature never acted on this issue, the due on sale clause is legally enforceable for title transfers after October 15, 1982. The issue then becomes one of how to avoid enforcement by the lender of the due on sale clause.

Contrary to popular belief, it is not illegal to thwart a mortgage lender from enforcing a due on sale clause. Smart real estate investors do so every day because they want to enjoy the benefits of an old low interest rate mortgage. Here are several methods to consider using, depending on the facts of the transaction. Of course, always consult an experienced real estate attorney to adapt each method to your specific situation.

A. THE FRIENDLY FORECLOSURE METHOD

This method is the simplest, yet the most daring, of all the methods of avoiding enforcement of a mortgage's due on sale clause. It involves the property buyer loaning the seller the amount of the buyer's down payment, secured by a mortgage on the property, the seller's deliberate failure to make any payments, and the buyer's foreclosing on the seller. At the foreclosure sale, the buyer-lender takes title by foreclosure "subject to" the old, existing low interest rate first mortgage which, in most states, the first lender is powerless to call.

> EXAMPLE: Suppose you want to buy a $100,000 house. It has an existing $75,000 first mortgage at 8 percent interest, but this mortgage contains a legally enforceable due on sale clause. Naturally, you want the benefits of this beautiful old mortgage. Therefore, you agree with the seller to "loan" him $25,000 (the amount of your down payment) on a thirty-day mortgage that the seller never intends to pay. After your balloon payment mortgage comes due in thirty days you foreclose and take possession of the house subject to the old first mortgage. In most states, a buyer at a foreclosure sale takes title subject to any senior mortgages and those lenders cannot enforce a due on sale clause after a foreclosure sale.

However, watch for several possible pitfalls. At the foreclosure sale an outsider might bid more than your $25,000 opening bid (the amount of your loan to the seller) in the example above. The worst that could happen is you wind up with your $25,000 back, plus interest. To avoid this tragedy, you could get the seller to give you a deed in lieu of foreclosure. Such a deed should give you the same legal right to take title subject to any senior liens (mortgages), but the law in most states is not crystal clear on this issue.

The big advantage of this method is the buyer gets title to the property in a relatively short time. With the other methods suggested below, title is held in a name other than that of the true property owner. However, consult your title insurance company about this method to be sure they will insure the title acquired by foreclosure. Some title companies want to wait six to twelve months before insuring such titles.

B. THE TRUST TECHNIQUE

One of the specific exceptions to the Garn Law due on sale clause enforcement provision occurs when a property owner conveys title into an inter vivos (living) trust. A mortgage lender cannot enforce a due on sale clause when such a trust is created.

This simple trust method involves the seller transferring title into an inter vivos trust. The trustee can be any qualified trustee such as an attorney, bank, trust company, title or escrow company (in some states), or an individual. Title companies often call these trusts "holding agreements." Then after the trust is created, a copy of the simple trust can be sent to the lender. Later, the beneficial interest in the trust in transferred to the property buyer. Such a trust transfer is not recorded. Legal title remains in the trustee's name.

The fire insurance policy will be in the name of the trustee. Most lenders learn about title transfers when they receive a new fire insurance policy, but that is no problem when using this method.

The only way the lender might discover the sale, within the trust, is by obtaining a court order to disclose the off-record transfer of beneficial interest under the trust from the original owner to the buyer. It is highly unlikely the lender would get such a court order without proof of the trust beneficiary change.

C. THE PARTNERSHIP TECHNIQUE

Another way to thwart a mortgage lender from enforcing a mortgage due on sale clause is to have the seller(s) form a partnership and the buyer(s) then acquires the seller's interest in the partnership.

EXAMPLE: Sam and Sara Seller transfer title to their property to the "Sam and Sara Seller Partnership." The lender probably won't object to such a transfer, especially if the sellers gladly send the lender a copy of the partnership agreement. Then Sam and Sara Seller later transfer their partnership interests to Bob and Betty Buyer, but the legal title remains in the name "Sam and Sara Seller Partnership."

As mentioned above, the only possible drawback of this method is there has been a title transfer from Sam and Sara Seller to the "Sam and Sara Seller Partnership."

D. THE CORPORATION TECHNIQUE

A related method of avoiding the due on sale clause is for the seller to form a corporation to hold title to the property.

EXAMPLE: Suppose Otto Owner is the legal owner of a property he desires to sell. It has an attractive low interest rate first mortgage with a legally enforceable due on sale clause. So Otto transfers legal title to the Otto Owner Corporation. Although such a transfer could trigger the due on sale clause, it is highly unlikely. Then Otto sells his shares to Paula Propertyowner, the buyer. But the legal title will remain in the name of Otto Owner Corporation.

One drawback of this method, however, is that in most states it costs money to incorporate and to pay annual income tax fees (even if the corporation has no taxable income). But these small fees are usually far less than it would cost to get a new high interest rate mortgage.

By the way, consult your tax advisor when using the partnership or corporation method to structure the transfer into the corporation as a non-taxable event.

E. THE LAND CONTRACT

This method is *not* recommended as a way to thwart the due on sale clause, but it is mentioned here because it has been widely used in the past. However, current mortgage due on sale clauses usually allow the lender to call the loan if a land contract sale is used to change ownership.

This method, known by at least twenty different names in various states (such as contract for deed, agreement for sale, contract of sale, and uniform land purchase installment contract), involves the seller retaining legal title until the buyer makes all his payments or an agreed number of payments to the seller.

In other words, the buyer pays the seller, who keeps making monthly payments to the original mortgage lender. The result is the lender doesn't learn of the sale. However, if the buyer records his land contract (as he should), the lender can learn of the sale and call the mortgage.

Other drawbacks of the land contract involve problems in getting rid of a defaulting buyer. Eviction is just one difficulty. In many states the buyer must be given a full or partial refund of his equity before a court will order title quieted in the seller's name after the buyer's default.

From the buyer's viewpoint, land contract problems can develop if the seller can't deliver good title to the property after the buyer faithfully makes his monthly payments to the seller and becomes entitled to the property deed.

F. THE WRAP-AROUND MORTGAGE

The wrap-around or all-inclusive mortgage is another method *not* to be used to thwart enforcement of a due on sale clause. Wrap-arounds can be very profitable for sellers if the underlying existing mortgage lacks a legally enforceable due on sale clause. But it is not a way to avoid the due on sale clause, because title is transferred to the property buyer, thus allowing the lender to enforce the due on sale clause.

EXAMPLE: Suppose you want to buy a $100,000 home that has an existing $60,000 first mortgage at 8 percent interest. You have $10,000 for the down payment. The seller could take back a $30,000 second mortgage at, perhaps, 12 percent interest to fill the finance gap. But if the seller takes back a $90,000 wrap-around mortgage at 12 percent interest instead, the seller's yield will be much higher. The seller will earn the same 12 percent on the $30,000 "at risk" ($3,600 per year) plus a 4 percent differential on the $60,000 underlying first mortgage ($2,400 per year). The $6,000 total annual interest ($3,600 plus $2,400) is a 20 percent yield on the seller's $30,000.

The wrap-around mortgage works fine if the old underlying mortgage lacks a legally enforceable due on sale clause. But it should not be used if the old loan's due on sale clause can be enforced. If the lender calls the old loan, the wrap-around lender could be wiped out by foreclosure.

What Is a Wrap-around Mortgage?

Wrap-around mortgages (WAM) have been used in Canada for over thirty years where they are called "blanket mortgages." (Do not confuse this with the U.S. useage of blanket mortgages which refer to a mortgage secured by two or more parcels of real property.) Wrap-around mortgages have been used in the U.S. since the 1930s, but they have achieved most of their popularity since 1960. They periodically become very popular as a method of overcoming our cyclical "credit crunches" when mortgage money becomes very expensive and hard to find.

It is impossible to use a WAM if the property involved does not already have an existing first mortgage on it. Of course, there can be an existing second and/or third mortgages too, in which case the WAM wraps around those old mortgage too. Any existing mortgage(s) on the property remain undisturbed.

The WAM, also called an all-inclusive mortgage, a hold-harmless mortgage, or an overriding mortgage, is really a second mortgage. It is the security device for a promissory note that states the debt owed by the borrowers to the lender. In many states, trust deeds are used instead of mortgages to secure the debt which is evidenced by the promissory note. Whether a trust deed or mortgage is used, the result is the same, although the details of mortgages and trust deeds differ slightly from a legal viewpoint.

The face amount of the WAM's promissory note is the *total* of the existing first (and second, and third, and fourth, etc.) mortgage *plus* the cash or equity loaned by the lender to the borrower. The interest rate of the WAM must equal or surpass the interest rate on the underlying old mortgage which remains undisturbed when the WAM is placed on the property. In other words, the WAM wraps around the old mortgage(s) already secured by the property.

A WAM borrower makes one mortgage payment monthly, quarterly, or annually to the WAM lender. That WAM lender then uses part of the borrower's payment to keep up payments on the old underlying mortgage(s). The leftover cash is the WAM lender's net payment.

EXAMPLE: Sam wants to retire in Arizona and sell his home in Illinois for $60,000. It now has a 7 percent FHA mortgage with a $25,000 balance. Sam wants to finance the sale for his buyer to (1) make an easy quick sale for top dollar and (2) provide extra interest income with excellent safety for his retirement years. Of course, Sam could take back a traditional second mortgage, but he wants the higher yield and simplicity offered by a WAM.

Sam sells his home for $60,000, taking a $9,000 cash down payment from his buyer. He also receives a $51,000 WAM at 10 percent interest. He decides on a twenty-five-year amortization payback schedule to keep the buyer's payments competitive with conventional mortgages, but he insists on a balloon payment of the unpaid balance due in ten years.

Because Sam takes back a WAM instead of a second mortgage, he earns 10 percent interest on his $26,000 loan ($51,000 minus the $25,000 existing FHA mortgage) to the buyer, plus the 3 percent interest differential on the underlying old $25,000 FHA 7 percent loan, which remains undisturbed.

This WAM is good for both the buyer (where else can he borrow so cheaply?) and for seller Sam (who earns a 12.8 percent total yield on his $26,000 net loan—$2,600 annual interest at 10 percent plus the 3 percent interest differential of $750 on $25,000 is $3,350 total yield which is 12.8 percent return on the $26,000 "at risk"). The buyer can pay the balloon payment in ten years by refinancing with a new conventional first mortgage if Sam will not extend the loan then.

This is a classic example of when a WAM should be used. It is much easier for a buyer to understand a $60,000 sale with $9,000 down payment and a $51,000 mortgage at 10 percent interest than it is to understand a $9,000 down payment, assumption of a $25,000 first mortgage, and the seller will carry back a $26,000 second mortgage at 12.8 percent. The result is exactly the same for the buyer and seller, but a WAM's simplicity makes the sale easy to understand.

Sam's sale was an example of a "soft money" WAM. It is called soft money because Sam did not physically loan the buyer any cold, hard cash. The entire transaction took place on paper. But WAMs can also be used for hard money loans too. In fact, many smart lenders are making hard money WAM loans instead of loaning on new conventional first mortgages.

EXAMPLE: Aaron owns a small shopping center worth $300,000. It has a $150,000 first mortgage at 7 percent from Friendly Insurance Company. This mortgage has a big prepayment penalty if Aaron pays it off early to refinance with a bigger new mortgage from another lender.

Aaron can secure a new AAA-rated tenant for his shopping center, but he must make $50,000 of improvements to obtain this new tenant. So Aaron goes to the local First National Bank to get a new hard money WAM for $225,000 at 12 percent (slightly below the "going rate" on such loans). The bank will earn their 12 percent interest on the $75,000 actual cash loan ($225,000 minus $150,000) plus a 5 percent interest differential on the underlying old $150,000 insurance company mortgage, which remains untouched.

The bank's total yield will be about 22 percent. Twelve percent is earned on the $75,000 cash loan ($9,000 per year) plus 5 percent on the $150,000 (about $7,500 per year) for which the bank advanced zero cash, a total interest income to the bank of $16,500 per year. This is a 22 percent annual return on the $75,000 "at risk" loan. This WAM is a "good deal" for both Aaron and the First National Bank.

When Should a Wrap-around Mortgage Be Used?

The WAM can be used in many mortgage situations, but not in every case. The major circumstances when it can and should be used include (1) a purchase-money mortgage where the seller carries or takes back a WAM on the property being sold (as Sam did in the example above), (2) refinancing of the mortgage on a property with a commercial hard money lender (such as the First National Bank in the example above), and (3) purchase-money supplied by a third-party hard money lender, such as a bank or individual, to aid a buyer in purchasing property.

Wrap-around Mortgage Features and Pitfalls

Although there are many WAM advantages for lenders and borrowers, there are pitfalls to watch for. In situations where these drawbacks are present, a WAM should not be used.

THE "DUE ON SALE CLAUSE" TRAP

Always be certain the existing first or other mortgage around which the

WAM is wrapping does not contain a legally enforceable "due on sale clause." Such a clause means the existing first or other mortgage's balance is due in full if the property title is transferred without the lender's approval (such approval is usually granted if the buyer assumes the old mortgage's legal obligation and agrees to pay a higher interest rate than was originally written on the old mortgage).

The law is still developing on this topic, and consultation with an experienced real estate attorney is advised if the mortgage to be wrapped contains a due on sale clause that may be enforceable. If the existing first mortgage is from a federal savings and loan association (a S&L with the word "federal" in its name), watch out. These lenders are especially militant in trying to enforce due on the sale clauses.

If the old existing mortgage contains a legally enforceable due on sale clause, do not risk using a WAM. The reason is if that lender decides to enforce the due on sale clause and "call" the loan because property title was transferred without the lender's approval, the WAM lender is then in a bad position. He then must pay off the underlying first or other mortgage to protect his WAM. But he cannot go out and get a replacement underlying first or other mortgage because he is not the title owner of the property.

Special Note: FHA and VA home mortgages do not contain due on sale clauses. They are freely assumable by the new owner upon payment of a modest assumption fee. FHA and VA mortgages therefore are excellent candidates for WAMs.

THE BALLOON PAYMENT TRAP

If the existing first or other existing mortgage on the property contains a balloon payment due in a few years, the WAM should provide for payoff of that balloon payment. The WAM should specify the borrower is to either pay off the WAM or come up with the cash to make the balloon payment on the old underlying mortgage. If this is not done, and the lender on the underlying mortgage forecloses, the WAM could be wiped out, since it was recorded after the underlying mortgage.

THE PREPAYMENT PENALTY TRAP

If the WAM is obtained from a commercial lender, such as a bank or insurance company, its terms often bar prepayment for ten or fifteen years. A penalty is often imposed for early repayment thereafter. The reason is a WAM lender wants to discourage early repayment. The WAM lender earns the maximum yield on its invested dollars after the underlying existing lower interest rate mortgage is paid down (if it is an amortizing loan). The longer the WAM exists, the higher the lender's yield rises.

Although the exact terms of WAMs are open to negotiation between the lender and the borrower, there are now preprinted standard forms for WAMs in most states. However, those forms should be carefully read to be sure they do not conflict with the terms of the transaction as the lender and borrower understand those conditions.

THE PURCHASE-MONEY TRAP

When a mortgage lender makes a mortgage loan to enable a buyer to purchase a property, it is called a "purchase-money mortgage." It can be a first, second, third, or a WAM. Some states, such as California, have laws barring a purchase-money mortgage lender from collecting any foreclosure loss deficiency from the borrower after default. In other words, the property is the sole security for a purchase-money mortgage in some states.

A seller who finances a purchase-money mortgage for the buyer, especially if the buyer makes a very low down payment, should be aware of this limitation in some states. In the low down payment situation, a land contract or a lease-option (where the seller retains legal title) might be a better alternative to a sale using a WAM.

THE TITLE INSURANCE TRAP

A few ultraconservative title insurance companies will not insure WAMs. But most title insurance firms insure WAMs like second mortgages. A WAM lender should check to be sure title insurance will be available and to see if any special WAM drafting requirements must be met to obtain title insurance for the lender.

THE USURY TRAP

The interest rate on the face of the WAM promissory note cannot exceed the applicable state usury interest rate. The usury problem arises with WAMs because, although the interest rate on the face of the WAM note must be below the legal usury limit, the lender's effective or actual total yield often exceeds the state's usury maximum allowable interest rate. This is due to the differential earned on the underlying old mortgage.

A second problem with usury is a WAM may run afoul of state laws prohibiting collection of interest on interest.

Almost every state has usury law affecting mortgage loans. Many exclude certain lenders, such as banks, S&Ls, corporations, and mortgage brokers. Others have differing tests for usury. Some calculate interest on the basis of actual dollars received by the borrower. For example, see *Mindlin* vs. *Davis,* a 1954 Florida case (74 So.2d 789) that held interest received by a lender is to be measured against the lender's net dollar investment in the loan, rather than on the face amount of the WAM note.

The unhappy result was the lender's total yield exceeded the state's usury limit at the time.

But there is considerable doubt if this reasoning would apply to a purchase-money WAM financed by a property seller if no cash funds are actually advanced to the buyer (a soft money loan). Since many states are now changing their usury laws to meet the realities of today's high inflation rate, consultation with a real estate attorney is advised to avoid usury problems when using a WAM.

Many commentators feel usury laws do not apply to purchase-money WAMs because most usury laws apply to "loans or forebearances" and not to sales of real property. For example, this is the California view. In court decisions dating back to at least 1927, the California Supreme Court repeatedly has held that since a buyer and seller are free to adjust their sales price and terms to give the seller his desired return, the usury laws do not apply to purchase-money mortgages or credit sales of real property.

The theory is a sale or loan of credit in the form of a purchase-money "soft" mortgage is outside the usury laws because no cash is actually loaned. It seems the usury laws are to protect the penniless, desperate borrower, not an affluent property buyer. But this purchase-money mortgage exception from usury laws does not apply to third-party hard money cash lenders who make loans in excess of the applicable state usury limit.

By the way, this usury problem does not occur with Canadian WAM loans because Canada's usury law only prohibits "unconscionable interest."

G. THE TWO TYPES OF LEASE-OPTIONS

There are two types of lease-options, the short- and long-term lease-option. The primary purpose of the short-term lease-option is to sell an otherwise "difficult" property. But a secondary short-term lease-option purchase is for a buyer to acquire a property with very little cash. However, the owner-seller retains the income tax benefits until the option is exercised.

The purpose of the long-term lease-option is quite different. Its purpose is to avoid lender enforcement of a mortgage due on sale clause. The long-term lease-option is really an installment sale, giving the buyer all the income tax benefits of ownership. The only thing the buyer lacks is the deed to the property which he can obtain at any time, thereby however triggering the old mortgage's due on sale clause.

THE MOST OVERLOOKED
REALTY FINANCE TECHNIQUE

Today's buyers and sellers, and their real estate agents, are innovating as never before to create finance techniques for the sale of real estate. The high cost of traditional first mortgage financing has neccessitated this result.

Probably the cheapest and most overlooked real estate finance technique, which is now coming out of the closet to meet a financing need, is the lease-option. There are two primary types of lease-options, the long-term lease-option of thirty years or more, and the short-term lease-option.

THE SHORT-TERM LEASE-OPTION

My favorite method of buying and selling single-family rental houses is the short-term lease-option. The reason it is the most underused home finance technique is real estate agents hate lease-options and discourage their use. There are two reasons for this: (1) most agents do not fully understand the short-term lease-option and (2) the agent does not receive his full sales commission until the purchase option is exercised in the future.

Lease-options are a great way to control property when buying. But they are also advantageous during ownership by (1) cutting or eliminating negative cash flow, (2) renting houses quickly in two hours or less, (3) assuring top quality tenants who treat the house as their own, and (4) giving the owner tax-free option money.

HOW THE SHORT-TERM LEASE-OPTION WORKS

A lease-option is simply a combination of a lease (usually for one to three years) and an option for the tenant to buy the property during the lease term. Although the lease conditions are the same as for a regular lease, the option terms can be as creative as the owner and tenant desire.

An outstanding lease-option form is available from Professional Publishing Corporation, 122 Paul Drive, San Rafael, California 94903. A copy of that form is on pages 178–181. Please note that the first page is basically a lease.

The reverse side contains the purchase option, with plenty of blank space to type in the conditions of the option.

The exact purchase terms of the option must be spelled out in the lease-option. Leave nothing to future doubt or negotiation. This is a key point to remember when creating a lease-option.

WHY USE A SHORT-TERM LEASE-OPTION?

There are many reasons for using a short-term lease-option. Usually the buyer wants to buy the property, but he is not yet in a position to do so. By use of the short-term lease-option, he "ties up" the property while he gets his finances in order so the purchase can be completed before the purchase option expires.

The circumstances of my purchase of my current home on a lease-option are probably typical. Before I sold my old residence I wanted to be sure I would be able to purchase a larger home. Yet, like many prospective sellers, I did not want to put my old home up for sale until I had the new one tied up.

The lease-option was the answer. With the aid of an outstanding realtor who never quit negotiating with the seller, Mrs. Betsy White of J. M. Tayler Company in Burlingame, California, a lease-option was negotiated that met my needs as a buyer, and it met the needs of the seller too.

Most sellers, and their realty agents, never think of a lease-option. But it can create those extra sales and purchase which otherwise would not occur. By giving the buyer time to arrange his financing, the lease-option practically assures the seller that the option will be exercised. More important, the short-term lease-option enables a buyer to buy a property he probably could not finance by any other method.

Another reason for using a short-term lease-option is for a property owner to collect immediate rental income, often at an above-market rate, while waiting for the tenant-buyer to purchase. Many rental house investors use lease-options to obtain high rentals while giving the tenant maximum incentive to properly maintain the property because he eventually plans to purchase it.

Still another reason for use of a short-term lease-option is to "sell" property which has been on the market a long time without any buyer materializing. As will be explained later, the lease-option makes property purchase easy. Once the potential buyer sees, feels, and smells the property (usually by living in it), he wants to own it. The lease-option gives him this opportunity.

THE HARDEST PART OF USING A SHORT-TERM LEASE-OPTION

The most difficult part of creating a lease-option is setting the purchase price of the property. When I purchased my home on a lease-option, it was not too difficult because the lease term was only six months. But we agreed on the home's purchase price at the time of the lease-option signing. While there is not much danger of a seller selling too cheaply on a six-month lease-option, a one-, two-, or three-year lease-option is another matter.

From experience, I have learned to set the purchase price on one-year lease-options at least 5 percent above today's fair market value of the property. Of course, this estimate would depend on the owner's expectations of future property price increases in the local market, usually based on price trends over the last few years in the neighborhood.

I once tried marketing a home on a lease-option that said "Purchase price to be determined by appraisal at the time of option exercise." While dozens of prospective buyers were interested in the house, they definitely wanted to pin down the future purchase price at the time of signing the lease-option.

Unfortunately, I have usually been too conservative when setting the purchase price. But a built-in sale profit, even though it turns out to be slightly less than the property's actual value in the future, is better than no sale.

In addition to setting the purchase price, a lease-option should also spell out the purchase terms. If the seller will carry back a first, second, third, or wrap-around mortgage, put those terms in the lease-option so nothing is left to doubt at the time of option exercise. However, I will not permit my lease-options to be recorded (only one tenant-buyer ever asked) because such recording clouds the title if the tenant does not exercise the purchase option.

LEASE-OPTION ADVANTAGES TO RENTAL HOUSE OWNERS

If you invest in rental houses, as I do, the short-term lease-option is ideal for both "buying" such property and for renting it to tenants.

To illustrate how the short-term lease-option advantages work for the owner (as well as for the tenant-buyer), let me use as an example a house I purchased in August of 1980 for investment. It cost me $135,000 with $13,500 down payment. The seller financed the $121,500 balance at 11 percent interest only for five years, payable at $1,113.75 "or more" per month. By the way, when buying property with seller financing, be sure those magic words "or more" are used on the promissory note as this gives the borrower the automatic right to prepay the note at any time.

This house rented within a week for $750 per month. The tenant is a sharp real estate broker who recognized a bargain when he saw it. Normal rent for this house would be about $650 or $675, but lease-option tenants are willing to pay a high rent in return for the lease-option. This house was advertised in the newspaper "$1,650 MOVES YOU IN—OPEN SUN-DAY 1–3 PM." In less than two hours, it was rented on a lease-option with two back-up applications.

Although my primary purpose for renting houses on lease-options is to get above-market rent from good quality tenants, some tenants will exercise their purchase options, others will sell them, some will ask for extensions (at a higher rent and purchase price, of course), and some just walk away at the end of their lease term without exercising their purchase option. If I wanted to assure a sale, I would require a large up-front "consideration for the option" such as $5,000 or $10,000.

I have found the one-year lease-option works best. But on this particular house in this example, I wrote a three-year lease-option with an escalating purchase price.

It is important to give lease-option prospects an information sheet spelling out the details. They usually will not understand your explanation, so it is important for them to have something in writing. The next illustration shows the information sheet I used on this house in the example.

This particular house can be bought in the twelfth month of the lease for the option purchase price of $158,500 with a rent credit of $4,500 for one-half of the year's rent paid. Thus, $154,000 becomes the net purchase price. This is approximately 15 percent more than my purchase price paid for the house one year earlier. The option price goes up approximately 15 percent per year for the next two years (although I found the three-year lease-option is too complicated and I would not use it again, I am using it here for illustration).

To exercise the purchase option, the buyer can either obtain his own financing, or I will finance the purchase if the buyer makes a $20,000 cash down payment. Although I only invested $13,500 in this house, the extra $6,500 more than covers the negative cash flow. It is vital to spell out the purchase terms exactly in the lease-option because these terms are a major consideration for the tenant-buyer. Of course, he can obtain his own financing if he can do better elsewhere.

It is also important to spell out some lease-option conditions for the protection of the landlord. These are detailed on the information sheet as well as on the lease-option signed by the tenant and the owner.

While there are many variations of the short-term lease-option, it is an effective technique for (1) minimizing negative cash flow from a rental property and (2) selling a property that is otherwise hard to sell. If the owner's purpose for using a short-term lease-option is to get the property sold, he should require a reasonable "consideration for the option" such as $5,000 or $10,000 to practically assure that the tenant will exercise the purchase option.

AVAILABLE FOR RENT or LEASE WITH AN OPTION TO PURCHASE

Well-maintained two-bedroom home with living room, dining area, bathroom, two-car garage, kitchen with gas stove and refrigerator, kitchen breakfast area, fenced backyard with fruit trees and beautiful flowers. Forced air heat. Fresh paint in living room, bedrooms, and hallway. Hardwood floors in bedrooms. Drapes and curtains included. Rear view toward open space scenic hills. Underground sprinklers.

RENT: $650 per month, plus $1,000 refundable security deposit ($1,650 total)   OR

LEASE WITH OPTION TO PURCHASE: $750 per month rent on a 36-month lease, plus $900 refundable security deposit ($1,650 total to move in). One-half rent paid is applicable toward the purchase price if you wish to buy this home. The option purchase price is $158,500 if bought between the 12th thru 18th month of the lease, $173,500 if bought between the 19th thru 30th month, and $190,500 if bought between the 31st and 36th months of the lease.

EXAMPLE #1: $158,500 -- Option purchase price if bought in 12th month
              -4,500 -- ½ credit for rent paid for 12 months
              $154,000 -- Net Purchase Price
   TERMS: If desired by tenant-buyer, with a $20,000 cash down payment, the seller will finance the $134,000 balance at 11% annual interest, payable $1,228.33 per month (interest only) or more, mortgage loan balance due June 1, 1985 (at which time the buyer must refinance to pay off the $134,000 balance).

EXAMPLE #2: $173,500 -- Option purchase price if bought in 24th month
              -9,000 -- ½ credit for rent paid for 24 months
              $164,500 -- Net Purchase Price
   TERMS: If desired by tenant-buyer, with a $20,000 cash down payment, the seller will finance the $144,500 balance at 11% annual interest, payable $1,324.58 per month (interest only) or more, mortgage loan balance due June 1, 1985 (at which time the buyer must refinance to pay off the $144,500 balance).

EXAMPLE #3: $190,500 -- Option purchase price if bought in 36th month
              -13,500 -- ½ credit for rent paid for 36 months
              $177,000 -- Net Purchase Price
   TERMS: If desired by tenant-buyer, with a $20,000 cash down payment, the seller will finance the $157,000 balance at 11% annual interest, payable $1,439.17 per month (interest only) or more, mortgage loan balance due June 1, 1985 (at which time the buyer must refinance to pay off the $157,000 balance).

CONDITIONS OF THE LEASE WITH OPTION TO BUY

1--Rent must be paid each month no later than 3 days after the due date or the purchase option becomes void and the ½ rent credit toward the purchase price is forfeited.
2--The purchase option is assignable and can be sold without the landlord's permission.
3--The lease cannot be assigned or sublet without the owner's permission (which will not be unreasonably withheld).
4--The tenant may cancel the lease (thereby cancelling the option) at any time.
5--Owner extends the special financing terms above only to the original tenant and he reserves the right not to extend these terms to any sublessee or assignee.
6--When the purchase option is exercised, the property is to be sold in its then "as is" condition, with no warranties or representations by the seller. Owner shall pay for routine maintenance until the time of option exercise.
7--Tenant shall receive a copy of the August, 1980 termite pest control clearance report.

For further information, please call Bob Bruss

DIFFERENT PURPOSES OF THE LONG-TERM LEASE-OPTION

The purposes of the long-term lease-option are entirely different from the short-term lease-option. A long-term lease-option should be used, in my opinion, only if the existing mortgage(s) on a property have a legally enforceable due on sale clause and if the buyer wants to retain the advantages of the old financing.

I have been using long-term lease-options since 1970 and have never yet had a lender try to accelerate. Some mortgage forms give the lender the right to enforce the due on sale clause if a lease-option is created, but I have never heard of a lender trying to do so and am not aware of any court decisions upholding the lender's claimed right to do so. As a practical matter, the lender would have great difficulty proving a lease-option exists unless the buyer-tenant records the lease-option. Some buyer-tenants record a memorandum of the long-term lease-option, but I recommend recording either (1) a one sentence "Memorandum of Purchase Option" or (2) a trust deed or mortgage from seller to buyer for a guaranty of seller's faithful contractual performance (no monetary amount is given).

An advantage of using such a trust deed or mortgage is the tenant can take title by foreclosure if the seller should default on the long-term lease-option in any way. If the tenant is living on the property, he is there to give notice to anyone of his ownership rights. Even if the seller was crooked and tried to sell the property twice, the rights of the lease-option buyer would predate the second buyer's, and the second buyer would take subject to the first buyer's rights. In my opinion, a long-term lease-option should be recorded only if the buyer-tenant is not occupying the property. Consultation with a real estate attorney is suggested for more information on this recording vs. nonrecording issue.

The best way to illustrate a long-term lease-option is to go through an actual transaction. Each long-term lease-option will differ, primarily because the existing financing is always unique. A real estate attorney should draw up the lease-option, but a regular purchase offer can be made when the "buyer" offers to buy the property on a lease-option. Such a purchase offer would contain words such as "This purchase offer contingent upon buyer and seller approving the final draft of the lease-option to be written by Larry Lawyer, Esq."

Here is an actual long-term lease-option, with only the names and address changed to protect the privacy of the parties.

LEASE WITH OPTION TO PURCHASE

This lease with option to purchase is between SAM SELLER, hereafter called Lessor, and BOB BUYER, hereafter called Lessee.

1. Description of Premises

Lessor agrees to lease to Lessee and Lessee hires from Lessor, as herein provided, the premises located at 1234 Easy Street, a single-family house, including any fixtures, window and floor coverings, built-in appliances, draperies including hardware, shades, blinds, window and door screens, awnings, outdoor plants, trees, and other permanently attached items now on the premises, in the County of Washington, State of California, City of Prosperity, and more particularly described as follows:

(The legal description should be inserted here.)

BEING also known as Assessor's Parcel number 123–456–7890.

2. Term

The term of this lease shall be for thirty (30) years beginning January 1, 1981 and ending December 31, 2010. Possession of premises is to be given to Lessee on January 1, 1981.

3. Consideration for Granting This Lease

Lessee agrees to pay to Lessor the sum of $5,000 as consideration for granting this lease with option to purchase.

4. Rent

The monthly rent payments shall be made payable to Sam Seller, P.O. Box 111, Retirement City, California 99999 or to such person or at such place to be designated by Lessor in the future. Such rent payments are to be paid by the first day of each month, with a ten (10) day grace period.

Lessee to pay a late charge of ten (10) percent if the monthly rent is not received by the tenth day of each month. Failure of Lessee to make any rent payment within thirty (30) days of due date, including any late charge, shall terminate this lease and purchase option.

Lessor shall be paid as rent the sum of the following monthly payments:

a. The principal balance of the existing promissory note and deed of trust to Greedy Federal Savings and Loan Association recorded February 2, 1976 in Book 999, at Page 21, Official Records of the County of Washington, payable as follows:

Date: January 1, 1981

Principal Balance: $53,425.01

Interest Rate: 9.5 percent

Payable: $463.00 per month

b. Balance of the purchase price shall be Lessee's promissory note to Lessor secured by this agreement; said note attached as Exhibit A:

Date: January 1, 1981

Principal Balance: $71,574.99

RESIDENTIAL LEASE WITH OPTION TO PURCHASE

RECEIVED FROM John and Jane Jones .... hereinafter referred to as Tenant,

the sum of $ 100.00 ...... (ONE HUNDRED——————————————————————————DOLLARS),

evidenced by personal check ...., as a deposit which, upon acceptance of this Lease, the Owner

of the premises, hereinafter referred to as Owner, shall apply said deposit as follows:

	RECEIVED	PAYABLE PRIOR TO OCCUPANCY
Rent for the period from January 15, 1983 to February 14, 1983	$ 100.00	$ 650.00
Last .... month's rent	$	$ 800.00
Security Deposit	$	$
Key Deposit	$	$
Cleaning charge	$	$
Other	$	$
TOTAL	$ 100.00	$ 1450.00

In the event that this agreement is not accepted by the Owner or his authorized agent, within 3 days, the total deposit received shall be refunded.

Tenant hereby offers to lease from the Owner the premises situated in the City of San Mateo ., County of San Mateo. State of Calif., described as #9 Westchester Place. ....

and consisting of a five-room house, including gas stove, refrigerator, washer, dryer & window coverings upon the following TERMS and CONDITIONS:

TERM: The term hereof shall commence on January 15, ..., 1983 , and continue for a period of 12 months thereafter.

RENT: Rent shall be $ 750.00 .... per month, payable in advance, upon the 15th day of each calendar month to Owner or his authorized agent, at the following address: 251 Baldwin Avenue, San Mateo, California 94401 or at such other places as may be designated by Owner from time to time. In the event rent is not paid within five (5) days after due date, Tenant agrees to pay a late charge of $10.00 plus interest at 10% per annum on the delinquent amount. Tenant agrees further to pay $5.00 for each dishonored bank check.

UTILITIES: Tenant shall be responsible for the payment of all utilities and services, except: none ...., which shall be paid by Owner.

USE: The premises shall be used as a residence with no more than 2 adults and 2 children, and for no other purpose, without the prior written consent of the Owner.

PETS: No pets shall be brought on the premises without the prior consent of the Owner.

ORDINANCES AND STATUTES: Tenant shall comply with all statutes, ordinances and requirements of all municipal, state and federal authorities now in force, or which may hereafter be in force, pertaining to the use of the premises.

ASSIGNMENT AND SUBLETTING: Tenant shall not assign this agreement or sublet any portion of the premises without prior written consent of the Owner which may not be unreasonably withheld.

MAINTENANCE, REPAIRS OR ALTERATIONS: Tenant acknowledges that the premises are in good order and repair, unless otherwise indicated herein. Owner may at any time give Tenant a written inventory of furniture and furnishings on the premises and Tenant shall be deemed to have possession of all said furniture and furnishings in good condition and repair, unless he objects thereto in writing within five days after receipt of such inventory. Tenant shall, at his own expense, and at all times,

ENTRY AND INSPECTION: Tenant shall permit Owner or Owner's agents to enter the premises at reasonable times and upon reasonable notice for the purpose of making necessary or convenient repairs, or to show the premises to prospective tenants, purchasers, or mortgagees.

INDEMNIFICATION: Owner shall not be liable for any damage or injury to Tenant, or any other person, or to any property, occurring on the premises, or any part thereof, or in common areas thereof, unless such damage is the proximate result of the negligence or unlawful act of Owner, his agents, or his employees. Tenant agrees to hold Owner harmless from any claims for damages no matter how caused, except for injury or damages for which Owner is legally responsible.

POSSESSION: If Owner is unable to deliver possession of the premises at the commencement hereof, Owner shall not be liable for any damage caused thereby, nor shall this agreement be void or voidable, but Tenant shall not be liable for any rent until possession is delivered. Tenant may terminate this agreement if possession is not delivered within .... 5 .... days of the commencement of the term hereof.

DEFAULT: If Tenant shall fail to pay rent when due, or perform any term hereof, after not less than three (3) days written notice of such default given in the manner required by law, the Owner, at his option, may terminate all rights of Tenant hereunder, unless Tenant, within said time, shall cure such default. If Tenant abandons or vacates the property, while in default of the payment of rent, Owner may consider any property left on the premises to be abandoned and may dispose of the same in any manner allowed by law. In the event the Owner reasonably believes that such abandoned property has no value, it may be discarded. All property on the premises is hereby subject to a lien in favor of Owner for the payment of all sums due hereunder, to the maximum extent allowed by law.

In the event of a default by Tenant, Owner may elect to (a) continue the lease in effect and enforce all his rights and remedies hereunder, including the right to recover the rent as it becomes due, or (b) at any time, terminate all of Tenant's rights hereunder and recover from Tenant all damages he may incur by reason of the breach of the lease, including the cost of recovering the premises, and including the worth at the time of such termination, or at the time of an award if suit be instituted to enforce this provision, of the amount by which the unpaid rent for the balance of the term exceeds the amount of such rental loss which the tenant proves could be reasonably avoided.

SECURITY: The security deposit set forth above, if any, shall secure the performance of Tenant's obligations hereunder. Owner may, but shall not be obligated to, apply all or portions of said deposit on account of Tenant's obligations hereunder. Any balance remaining upon termination shall be returned to Tenant.

DEPOSIT REFUNDS: The balance of all deposits shall be refunded within two weeks from date possession is delivered to Owner or his Authorized Agent, together with a statement showing any charges made against such deposits by Owner.

ATTORNEYS FEES: In any legal action brought by either party to enforce the terms hereof or relating to the demised premises, the prevailing party shall be entitled to all costs incurred in connection with such action, including a reasonable attorney's fee.

WAIVER: No failure of Owner to enforce any term hereof shall be deemed a waiver, nor shall any acceptance of a partial payment of rent be deemed a waiver of Owner's right to the full amount thereof.

NOTICES: Any notice which either party may or is required to give, may be given by mailing the same, postage prepaid, to Tenant at the premises or to Owner at the address shown below or at such other places as may be designated by the parties from time to time.

HEIRS, ASSIGNS, SUCCESSORS: This lease is binding upon and inures to the benefit of the heirs, assigns and successors in interest to the parties.

TIME: Time is of the essence of this agreement.

HOLDING OVER: Any holding over after expiration hereof, with the consent of Owner, shall be construed as a month-to-month tenancy in accordance with the terms hereof, as applicable. No such holding over or extension of this lease shall extend the time for the exercise of the option unless agreed upon in writing by Owner.

Appliance Repairs: Owner makes no warranties or representations as to the condition of the appliances (Stove, refrigerator, washer, dryer). If repairs should become necessary, owner will NOT be responsible for the cost of such repairs.

CONTINUED ON REVERSE SIDE

OPTION: So long as tenant is not in substantial default in the performance of any term of this lease, Tenant shall have the option to purchase the real property described herein for a PURCHASE PRICE OF $.130,000.00 ....(.ONE..HUNDRED..THIRTY..THOUSAND------------------------------- DOLLARS), upon the following TERMS and CONDITIONS:

1--Purchase option can be exercised anytime during the term of the lease.

2--Full credit for rent paid to be given toward the down payment if purchase option is exercised.

3--Owner agrees to extend the following purchase terms to tenants, if desired by them:

A--$130,000 Purchase Price

B--$ 9,000 Less: Full credit for rent paid in 12 months toward down payment

C--$121,000 Net Purchase Price in 12 months

D--$ 10,000 Cash Down Payment

E--$111,000 Balance will be financed by owner-seller for tenant at 13% annual interest, payable $1202.50 per month (interest only) or more, loan balance due December 15, 1986. Monthly payment does not include property taxes or insurance which are buyer's responsibility.

4--The purchase option, with full credit for rent paid, is assignable by tenant to another buyer.

5--The lease cannot be assigned or a sublease created without owner's written permission (which will not be unreasonably withheld).

6--The provisions of paragraph #3 above are extended only to the tenant and not to any assignee or subtenant.

7--Rent must be paid each month no later than 3 days after the due date or this purchase option becomes void.

8--When the purchase option is exercised, the property is to be conveyed in its then "as is" condition with no warranties or representations by the seller.

9--Tenant is aware of the most recent termite inspection clearance report by Terminex Termite Company, dated January 5, 1983 and takes subject to that report without further liability by the owner-seller.

10-Upon exercise of this purchase option, buyer to receive a grant deed and pay normal escrow and closing costs.

ENCUMBRANCES: In addition to any encumbrances referred to above, Tenant shall take title to the property subject to: 1) Real Estate Taxes not yet due and 2) Covenants, conditions, restrictions, reservations, rights, rights of way and easements of record, if any, which do not materially affect the value or intended use of the property.

The amount of any bond or assessment which is a lien shall be ☒ paid, ☐ assumed by ..seller..

EXAMINATION OF TITLE: Fifteen (15) days from date of exercise of this option are allowed the Tenant to examine the title to the property and to report in writing any valid objections thereto. Any exceptions to the title which would be disclosed by examination of the records shall be deemed to have been accepted unless reported in writing within said 15 days. If Tenant objects to any exceptions to the title, Owner shall use all due diligence to remove such exceptions at his own expense within 60 days thereafter. But if such exceptions cannot be removed within the 60 days allowed, all rights and obligations hereunder may, at the election of the Tenant, terminate and end, unless he elects to purchase the property subject to such exceptions.

EVIDENCE OF TITLE: Evidence of Title shall be in the form of ☒ a policy of title insurance, /☐ other:................. from Founder's Title Company,...........to be paid for by.....buyer..

CLOSE OF ESCROW: Within ____30____ days from exercise of the option, or upon removal of any exceptions to the title by the Owner, as provided above, whichever is later, both parties shall deposit with an authorized escrow holder, to be selected by the Tenant, all funds and instruments necessary to complete the sale in accordance with the terms and conditions hereof.

PRORATIONS: Rents, taxes, premiums on insurance acceptable to Tenant, interest and other expenses of the property to be prorated as of recordation of deed. Security deposits, advance rentals or considerations involving future lease credits shall be credited to Tenant.

EXPIRATION OF OPTION: This option may be exercised at any time after ____January 15, 1983____, and shall expire at midnight ____January 14____, 19_84_, unless exercised prior thereto. Upon expiration Owner shall be released from all obligations hereunder and all of Tenants rights hereunder, legal or equitable, shall cease.

EXERCISE OF OPTION: The option shall be exercised by mailing or delivering written notice to the Owner prior to the expiration of this option and by an additional payment, on account of the purchase price, in the amount of

$__10,000.00_____ (__TEN THOUSAND_____DOLLARS)
for account of Owner to the authorized escrow holder referred to above, prior to the expiration of this option.

Notice, if mailed, shall be by certified mail, postage prepaid, to the Owner at the address set forth below, and shall be deemed to have been given upon the day following the day shown on the postmark of the envelope in which such notice is mailed.

In the event the option is exercised, _____percent from the rent paid hereunder prior to the exercise of the option shall be credited upon the purchase price.

The undersigned Tenant hereby acknowledges receipt of a copy hereof.

Suzy Saleslady .... Agent

DATED ____January 10, 1983____

John Jones .... Tenant
John Jones

Jane Jones .... Tenant
Jane Jones

By ....
Suzy Saleslady

Broker ____Coldwell Banker____

.... Address

.... Phone

.... Address

.... Phone

ACCEPTANCE

The undersigned Owner accepts the foregoing offer.

BROKERAGE FEE: Upon execution hereof the Owner agrees to pay to ____Coldwell Banker____,
the Agent in this transaction, the sum of $__540.00__ (6%) (_Five Hundred Forty_____DOLLARS)
for leasing services rendered and authorizes Agent to deduct said sum from the deposit received from Tenant. In the event the option is exercised, the Owner agrees to pay Agent the additional sum of $_5,000.00___ (_Five Thousand_____DOLLARS).
This agreement shall not limit the rights of Agent provided for in any listing or other agreement which may be in effect between Owner and Agent. In the event legal action is instituted to collect this fee, or any portion thereof, the Owner agrees to pay the Agent a reasonable attorney's fee and all costs in connection with such action.

The undersigned Owner hereby acknowledges receipt of a copy hereof.

Dated ____January 12, 1983____

Robert J. Brugs .... Owner
Robert J. Brugs

.... Owner

.... Address

.... Phone

Interest Rate: 12 percent

Payable: $715.75 per month (interest only) or more. The interest rate on this note can be adjusted by Lessor on January 2, 1986, 1991, 1996, 2001, and 2006 to the interest rate then being charged by Greedy Federal Savings and Loan Association, or its successor, for single-family home loans made on those dates.

5. *Use of Premises*

The premises are leased to Lessee for use as a residence and Lessee agrees to restrict its use to such purposes, and not to use or permit the use of the premises for any other purpose without first obtaining the written consent of Lessor.

6. *No Use That Increases Insurance Risk*

Lessee agrees not to use the premises in any manner, even in his use for the purposes for which the premises are leased, that will increase risks covered by insurance on the building where the premises are located, so as to increase the rate of insurance on the buildings where the premises are located, or to cause cancellation of any insurance policy covering the building. Lessee further agrees not to keep on the premises, or permit to be kept, used or sold thereon, anything prohibited by the policy of fire insurance covering the premises. Lessee agrees to comply with all requirements of the insurers applicable to the premises necessary to keep in force the fire and public liability insurance covering the premises and building at Lessee's expense.

7. *Insurance*

Lessor agrees to procure and maintain in force during the term of this lease fire, extended coverage, public liability, and any other insurance requested by Lessee, adequate to protect against fire damage not less than ONE HUNDRED THOUSAND DOLLARS ($100,000). Lessor to procure public liability insurance coverage in a minimum amount of ONE HUNDRED THOUSAND ($100,000) DOLLARS for each person insured, and THREE HUNDRED THOUSAND ($300,000) DOLLARS maximum for any one incident. Such insurance policies shall provide coverage for Lessor's and Lessee's contingent liability on such claims or losses. The policies shall be subject to Lessor's and Lessee's mutual inspection and approval. The insurance premium for such policies procured by Lessor are to be paid by Lessee within thirty (30) days after receipt of a statement therefor. If unpaid within such time, Lessor may procure such insurance, pay the premium therefor, and such premium shall be repair to Lessor as additional rent for the month following the date on which such premiums are paid. Failure to pay such insurance premiums is a default in this lease that will cause it to be terminated.

8. No Waste, Nuisance, or Unlawful Use

Lessee shall not commit, or allow to be committed, any waste on the premises, or nuisance, nor shall he use or allow the premises to be used for any unlawful purpose.

9. Repairs and Maintenance

Lessee shall maintain the premises and keep it in good repair at his own expense. Lessee shall make any alterations and changes that he deems advisable in the operation of the property providing such changes shall not decrease the inherent value of the premises. Lessee to pay for any such costs of repairs and maintenance.

10. Payment of Utilities, Property Taxes, and Operating Expenses

The property taxes for the current year ending June 30, 1981 and insurance acceptable to Lessee as specified above, rents, and other current expenses of the premises shall be prorated to January 1, 1981, the date of commencement of this lease. After transfer of possession to Lessee, Lessee shall pay for all utilities, property and other taxes, and other operating expenses of the property including gas, water, garbage, and all necessary and customary expenses of operating the property.

11. Delivery, Acceptance, and Surrender of the Premises

Lessor represents that the premises are in fit condition for use as residential property. Lessee agrees to accept the premises upon possession as in a good state of repair and in sanitary condition. Lessee agrees to surrender the premises at the end of the lease term to the Lessor in substantially the same or better condition than when he took possession, except for damage by acts of God, unless Lessor shall have exercised the purchase option prior to termination of this lease.

Lessee agrees to take possession of the premises subject to any month-to-month thirty (30) day rental agreements to its residents that exist as of January 1, 1981.

Lessee agrees to accept the property in its current condition with no warranties or representations by Lessor both at time of accepting possession and at time of future exercise of the purchase option.

12. Nonliability of Lessor for Damages

Lessor shall not be liable for liability or damage claims for injury to persons, including Lessee or his agents or employees, or for property damage from any cause, related to Lessee's occupancy of the premises, including those arising out of damages or losses occurring on sidewalks or other areas adjacent to the leased premises, during the term of this lease. Lessee hereby covenants and agrees to indemnify Lessor and to save him harmless from all liability, loss, or other damage claims or obligations because of or arising out of such injuries or losses.

13. Lessee's Assignment, Sublease, or License for Occupation by Other Persons

Lessee agrees not to assign or sublease the premises leased, any part thereof, or any right or privilege connected therewith, without first obtaining Lessor's written consent, or to allow any other person, except Lessee's agents and employees, to occupy the premises or any part thereof, without first obtaining Lessor's written consent. However, this shall not be construed to prohibit Lessee from normal operation of the property, including renting or leasing the property for use as a residence. The term of such rentals shall not exceed one year, although such rentals may be renewed at the end of each year.

Lessee's unauthorized assignment, sublease, or license to occupy shall be void, and shall terminate the lease at Lessor's option.

14. Lease Breached by Lessee's Receivership, Assignment for Benefit of Creditors, Insolvency, or Bankruptcy

Appointment of a receiver to take possession of Lessee's assets (except a receiver appointed at Lessor's request as herein provided), Lessee's general assignment for benefit of creditors, or Lessee's insolvency or taking or suffering action under the Federal Bankruptcy Act is a breach of this lease which shall terminate it.

15. Lessor's Remedies Upon Lessee's Breach of This Lease

If Lessee breaches this lease, Lessor shall have the following remedies in addition to these other legal rights and remedies in such event:

a. *Reentry.* Lessor may reenter the premises immediately and terminate Lessee's occupancy of this premises.

b. *Termination.* After reentry, Lessor may terminate this lease by giving ten (10) days written notice of such termination to Lessee, the reason for such termination, and giving Lessee the opportunity to correct any breach of this lease specified in such notice of termination within twenty (20) days after notice to lessee. Reentry alone will not terminate this lease.

c. *Appointment of a Receiver.* After reentry, Lessor may procure the appointment of a receiver to take possession and collect rents and profits of Lessee's operation of the property. If necessary, the receiver may continue to operate the property without compensating Lessee therefor. Proceedings for appointment of a receiver by Lessor, or the appointment of a receiver and conducting by him of Lessee's operations, shall not terminate this lease unless Lessor has given Lessee written notice of such termination as provided herein.

d. *Rights*. Upon termination of this lease for breach of any of its conditions and terms the Lessee shall relinquish all rights, privileges, and financial considerations including the equity buildup, appreciation in market value of the property, and moneys spent for improvements. Lessee agrees to vacate the premises upon such breach and termination of this lease.

16. Arbitration of Disputes

Lessor and Lessee agree that any disputes under this lease, unless resolved by the parties, shall be arbitrated in accordance with the arbitration laws of the state of California, as supplemented by the rules then obtaining of the American Arbitration Association. Judgment on the arbitration award rendered may be entered in any court having jurisdiction of the parties.

17. Manner of Giving Notice

Notices given pursuant to the provisions of this lease or necessary to carry out its provisions shall be in writing and delivered by first class mail with return receipt to the person to whom the notice is to be given. For such purposes, Lessor's current mailing address is P.O. Box 111, Retirement City, California 99999 and Lessee's current mailing address is 1234 Easy Street, Prosperity City, California 88888.

18. Lease and Purchase Option Applicable to Successors

This lease and its terms, covenants, and conditions apply to and are binding on the heirs, successors, executors, administrators, and assigns of the parties thereto.

19. Time of Essence

Time is of the essence to this agreement. Dates and time limits specified in this agreement may not be waived without the written consent of both parties.

20. Effect of Eminent Domain Proceedings

Eminent domain proceedings resulting in the condemnation of part of the premises leased herein that leave the remaining portion usable by Lessee for purposes of operating the property will not terminate this lease. The effect of such condemnation will be to leave this lease in effect as to the remainder of the premises. All compensation awarded in the eminent domain proceeding as a result of such condemnation shall belong to Lessee.

Lessor hereby assigns and transfers to Lessee any claim he may have to compensation for damages as a result of such condemnation. In the event that eminent domain proceedings result in condemnation of the premises so it cannot be operated as residential property, Lessee shall be entitled to any compensation awarded and the provisions of paragraph twenty-one (21) below shall become operative as an exercise of the option to purchase. Any disputes in such case are to be decided by arbitration as specified above.

21. Option to Purchase the Premises

Lessor grants to Lessee an option to buy the leased premises at any time Lessee may elect before December 31, 2010, provided Lessee shall have performed the terms of this lease and made all payments required hereby to that time of exercise of such purchase option. In the event of the exercise of this option, Lessor agrees to convey said property to Lessee by grant deed free and clear of all encumbrances except property taxes and assessments that under this lease are to be paid by Lessee.

Lessor hereby agrees not to further encumber the leased premises. Any encumbrances now existing against the property created by or on the account of Lessor may, however, remain until time of exercise of this purchase option. Lessor agrees to protect and defend Lessee and the property against foreclosure or loss by reason of any encumbrances created by or through the Lessor and now existing against the property.

The obligations of Lessee under the lease shall cease after the exercise of this option and completion of said transfer of title to Lessee or his designate.

Whenever Lessee shall desire to exercise this purchase option before its expiration, Lessee shall give Lessor written notice thereof. Lessor will within thirty (30) days after receipt of such notice deliver to Lessee a preliminary title search report by the Talented Title Company of Prosperity City, California. Defects in title, if any, shown by such report shall be remedied by Lessor within thirty (30) days after notice to him of such defects and he shall deliver to Lessee at the time of closing of escrow an unconditional grant deed to the property.

The purchase shall, in any event, be completed by conveyance of the property and payment of the outstanding purchase obligations within thirty (30) days from the delivery by Lessee of notice of intent to exercise this option. If said notice is not given by Lessee before December 31, 2010, then this purchase option shall be null and void. The consideration for granting this purchase option shall be the FIVE THOUSAND DOLLARS ($5,000.00) specified in paragraph three (3).

22. Exercise of the Purchase Option

To exercise the purchase option referred to in paragraph twenty-one (21), in addition to giving notice to Lessor of intent to exercise this option as stated above, Lessee must also:

a. Arrange to pay, assume, or take title "subject to" the encumbrance to Greedy Federal Savings and Loan Association, referred to in paragraph four A (4a), and either (1) pay the promissory note referred to in paragraph four B (4b) to Lessor or (2) secure that promissory note to Lessor referred to in paragraph four B (4b) by a second deed of trust against the property.

1. In the event Lessee exercises the purchase option and is unable to assume the existing loan from Greedy Federal Savings and Loan Association and is required to obtain financing elsewhere, then Lessee shall obtain financing to pay off the then existing balance of the existing first loan to Greedy Federal Savings and Loan Association, together with any prepayment penalty and other charges, and the balance of the purchase price owed under the promissory note to Lessor.

2. Should the proceeds of such new loan be insufficient to pay off the full remaining balance owed to Lessor, Lessor then agrees to accept a promissory note in the form of the note attached and marked Exhibit A and secured by a second deed of trust in the standard form for said balance, said note and deed of trust to be payable to Lessor on the same terms as the original promissory note referred to in paragraph four B (4b), with the unpaid balance due December 31, 2010.

b. Pay the title insurance and normal escrow and transfer costs for acquisition of property in the County of Washington, City of Prosperity.

22. Acceleration Clause

Lessee acknowledges being advised that the deed of trust to Greedy Federal Savings and Loan Association contains a provision for acceleration of the indebtedness in the event of a sale or transfer of the property. If purchase of this property is consummated, or if and when there is deemed to be or have been a purchase, then Lessee shall assume and agree to pay any charges or prepayment penalties to Greedy Federal Savings and Loan Association. In such event, both Lessor and Lessee agree to carry this purchase option agreement into effect.

23. Tax Consequences of This Lease Agreement

It is the intent of the Lessor and Lessee to eventually consummate a sale of the leased premises to the Lessee. Therefore, for income tax purposes, this transaction shall be treated by Lessor and Lessee as if the Lessor had sold the property to the Lessee as of January 1, 1981. The Lessee shall be entitled to all normal income tax duties and benefits of real estate ownership, including depreciation of the property improvements and deduction of operating expenses and interest paid on the loan obligations to the Lessor and to Greedy Federal Savings and Loan Association, as allowed by the Internal Revenue Code. Lessor shall treat payments received under this agreement as if a deferred payment installment sale of the property has occurred, as provided for by the Internal Revenue Code.

24. Recordation of Option to Purchase

A memorandum of the option to purchase the premises may be recorded by Lessee in the Official Records of the County of Washington at any time. Lessor agrees to sign such memorandum before a Notary Public at any reasonable time when requested by Lessee.

25. Modification

This lease and option to purchase may be modified only by a written agreement signed by both parties.

26. Acceptance

This lease with option to purchase shall be deemed to have been accepted by both Lessor and Lessee when:

a. A signed copy is delivered by Lessor to Lessee and Lessee signs and returns that original copy to Lessor, and

b. Lessee pays to Lessor FIVE THOUSAND DOLLARS ($5,000.00) consideration for the purchase option referred to in paragraph twenty-one (21).

c. Lessee pays to Lessor the following additional amounts:

1. Rent of ONE THOUSAND ONE HUNDRED SEVENTY-EIGHT AND $^{75}/_{100}$ ($1,178.75) DOLLARS for the month of January, 1981, plus

2. Prorated fire insurance and public liability insurance premium of $195.39 ($211.00 annual premium less credit of $15.61 at .578¢ per day for 27 days; policy expires December 3, 1981; Lessee acknowledges receipt of a copy of this insurance policy).

3. Less any security deposits or other credits due to the current tenants of the property.

4. Total of ONE THOUSAND THREE HUNDRED SEVENTY-FOUR AND $^{14}/_{100}$ ($1,374.14) DOLLARS.

This offer by Lessor to Lessee shall remain valid until acceptance by Lessee but not later than December 21, 1980. Upon acceptance by

Lessee, Lessor agrees to pay to ABC Realty a commission of FOUR THOUSAND DOLLARS ($4,000).

This offer to lease is made December 5, 1980.

ACCEPTED:
　　　　　　　　　　　　　　　　　　　　　　─────────────────────
　　　　　　　　　　　　　　　　　　　　　　SAM SELLER

　　　　　　　　　　　　　　　　　　　　　　─────────────────────
　　　　　　　　　　　　　　　　　　　　　　BOB BUYER

NOTARY PUBLIC ACKNOWLEDGMENT

This long-term lease-option form is presented for illustration purposes only. It should not be used for actual transactions without consultation with a real estate attorney who can either adapt it to the particular circumstances of the sale or draft another lease-option form that meets the needs of the parties. There are no standard long-term lease-option forms, so the services of a real estate attorney are essential for each such transaction.

The reason for using a thirty-year term is that such a lease, which includes a purchase option, is acceptable to the IRS as the equivalent of a sale. IRS Revenue Ruling 60–4, now superseded by Revenue Ruling 72–85, leads to this result. There is a long chain of tax cases holding that for income tax purposes, where the lessee is treated like an owner, a sale will be recognized. See *Oesterreich* v. *IRS,* 226 F.2d 798, IRC Regulation 1.1031 (a)-1-C, and *Lichtman* v. *U.S.,* T.C. Memo 1982-630.

For emphasis, it is worth repeating that the primary reason for using a long-term lease-option is to avoid a lender enforcing a "due on sale clause." If this condition is not present, a long-term lease-option is of little value to the buyer and seller.

One final footnote. Most mortgage lenders learn of a title transfer when they receive a new fire insurance policy that shows a new insured's name. The long-term lease-option overcomes this problem because the fire insurance policy remains in the name of the lessor so the lender will not learn of the transaction from the insurance agent. In states where a due on sale clause in a mortgage is legally enforceable, the long-term lease-option makes it virtually impossible for the mortgage lender to learn of the sale. Thus the buyer retains the benefit of the old low interest rate mortgage.

QUESTIONS AND ANSWERS

Q. You often say a wrap-around mortgage is better than a second mortgage. I don't understand why. If I sell my house, which has a VA mortgage of about $38,000 at 8 percent interest, for $100,000 with a $10,000 down payment, would I be better off with a $90,000 wrap-around mortgage or a $52,000 second mortgage?—*Adrian M.*

A. You will be better off with a wrap-around mortgage. Suppose you charge 10 percent interest on the $90,000 wrap-around mortgage. That is about $9,000 annual interest. But you will have to keep up the VA loan payments (using part of the money your borrower pays you). Your interest cost on $38,000 at 8 percent will be about $3,040, leaving you net annual interest earnings of about $5,960. On the $52,000 you will have "at risk," this is a return of 11.46 percent.

You could earn the same return on a $52,000 second mortgage by charging 11.46 percent interest. But that is usurious in some states and is less acceptable to most buyers than would be a wrap-around mortgage with a 10 percent interest rate.

Before using a wrap-around mortgage, however, check with your attorney as to the maximum interest rate which can be charged in the state where your property is located.

WHY WRAP-AROUND MORTGAGES ARE SO GOOD

Q. Please explain more details about wrap-around mortgages. (1) Why would a seller or buyer want one? (2) Where can they be obtained? —*Margo M.*

A. Suppose you sell your home for $50,000, and it has an existing FHA $25,000 first mortgage at 7 percent interest. The buyer offers you $10,000 cash down payment, asks you to carry a $15,000 second mortgage at 9 percent interest, and agrees to assume the existing $25,000 FHA mortgage, which remains undisturbed. You would earn about $1,350 annual interest (9 percent of $15,000).

But a $40,000 wrap-around mortgage at 9 percent interest would be better for you. You would take in about $3,600 interest, pay out about $1,750 interest on the old mortgage, and keep about $1,850 interest ($3,600 minus $1,750). That is a 12.33 percent yield on your $15,000 "at risk" loan.

(1) Such a loan maximizes the seller's total yield and still lets him qualify for installment sale tax benefits (installment sale details are in Chapter 8). Wrap-around all-inclusive mortgages are good for buyers too, since the interest rate is usually below conventional mortgage interest rates.

(2) Property sellers are the most common sources of wrap-around mortgages. But some banks, finance companies, and individual lenders now make "hard money" wrap-around mortgage loans too. Shop around among local lenders in your community to see which lenders make wrap-around mortgage loans.

HOME LEASE-OPTION DIFFERS FROM LEASE-PURCHASE

Q. Some time ago you said your favorite creative finance method is the lease-option. I recently contacted a real estate agent about buying a home, and she suggested a "lease-purchase plan." Is this different from a lease-option?—*Ginny S.*

A. Yes. A lease-purchase means the buyer temporarily leases the home now but agrees to purchase it later, presumably when mortgages are more readily available than today. The tenant-buyer is obligated to complete the purchase. If he does not, he loses his deposit and may incur a penalty too.

But a lease-option gives the buyer the option of deciding if he wants to buy the property before the option expiration date. The lease-option is good for both the tenant and the landlord-seller.

Tenant advantages of a lease-option include (1) full or partial credit toward the purchase price for rent paid, (2) opportunity to try the home before buying, (3) no obligation to the landlord-seller if the purchase option is not exercised, (4) knowing the sales price and terms in advance, and (5) having a big incentive to save up the down payment to use to exercise the purchase option.

Lease-option advantages for the seller include (1) practically being assured of a sale, since few people walk away from a large rent credit toward the purchase price, (2) rental income to pay mortgage and other payments, (3) tax advantages, (4) lease-option tenant usually takes good care of the property, and (5) option consideration is not taxable until tenant either exercises the option or lets it expire.

DO NOT FORGET LEASE-OPTION HOME-BUYING TECHNIQUE

Q. We must buy a home soon before my wife and I wind up in a mental hospital. At present we live with our two children, ages four and two, in a two-bedroom apartment where we are about to go crazy. But with the difficulty of getting a home loan, we wonder if we can buy a home at all. I earn about $21,000 per year, including overtime. My wife works Saturdays and Sundays at a supermarket where she earns about $5,000 per year. One agent found us an ideal house on which we could have easily afforded the mortgage payments. But the lender said we would have to have $38,000 annual income to qualify for a loan. Please help us. —*Craig M.*

A. You and thousands of other prospective home buyers are having the same problem of qualifying for a mortgage in today's market. The truth is, and lenders will not tell you this, they do not want to make new mortgage loans today. So they have raised the interest rates so high few people can qualify. From a public relations viewpoint, this is better than telling loan applicants the lender is out of money.

If you want to buy a home today, you will have to buy without getting a new mortgage. It is not really so hard. My favorite technique is the lease-option where you lease a house for twelve or twenty-four months with an option to buy during the lease term at a price agreed upon today. By then, mortgage financing should be more affordable. But in case it is not, be sure the lease-option provides for alternative seller financing.

Other home finance possibilities for you include (1) making a down payment, taking over payments on the existing mortgage, and getting the seller to take back a second mortgage for any balance, and (b) getting the seller to finance the sale on a wrap-around (all-inclusive) mortgage. Work with a good real estate agent who understands that creative finance is the key to successful home buying today.

LEASE-OPTION PERFECT FOR HOME BUYERS WITH $1,500

Q. We are a young couple, both college graduates, with total annual income of about $23,000. It's so low because we are teachers. We have saved close to $1,500 but are very discouraged by every real estate agent we talk to about buying a home. They claim we need 10 percent to 20 percent cash down payment to qualify for mortgage money. How should we proceed?—*Robert and Susan F.*

A. I have rented many homes to young couples in situations like yours. The lease-option is perfect for honest, employed, reliable people like you.

Look in the newspaper want ads under "houses for rent." Make appointments to visit those which interest you. When you find one you like, ask the landlord if he would consider a lease with option to buy. Many will.

Offer to put up your $1,500 as "consideration for the option."

Try to structure the lease-option so all or part of your lease rent payments are credited toward the purchase price. Owners of dumpy, run-down houses are especially good candidates for lease-options.

However, do not include me in that category, as my rental houses are in top condition. Ask my tenant-buyers. By the way, you will rarely find a lease-option available through real estate agents because the agent does not get his commission until the purchase option is exercised, usually in twelve to twenty-four months. Realty agents like to be paid now.

READER TELLS HOW TO BEAT MORTGAGE "DUE ON SALE CLAUSE"

Q. Our house has been for sale several months with no buyer. The old mortgage is not assumable because it has a "due on sale clause." Since the lender wants a stiff assumption fee and wants to raise the interest rate for a buyer, the house hasn't sold. But I found a real estate lawyer who told me how to get my house sold. He drew up an option contract, and the buyer recorded a "memorandum" of this option. The buyer paid $20,000 "consideration for the option" (which was the down payment). He must make regular monthly payments to me to keep the option in force. I use part of this money to keep up the payments on the old mortgage. The rest goes to pay off what the buyer owes me, gradually reducing the buyer's option purchase price. It's like a wrap-around mortgage. Since there has been no title transfer, the lender can't enforce the due on sale clause and is stuck with its old 9 percent mortgage. My lawyer says the IRS recognizes this as a sale for tax purposes. Just thought you'd want to know there's a way to beat the nasty lenders.—*Elmer G.*

A. The "due on sale clause" issue is a very controversial one with lenders, especially federal savings and loan associations. A valid "due on sale clause" allows a mortgage lender to "call" a loan when the property is sold.

However, there is one possible flaw in your lawyer's option idea. From the buyer's viewpoint, how does he know he will receive good title? It is possible to buy title insurance on options, but this does not assure your buyer that the title will remain good until he exercises his purchase option and obtains the deed from you. This is a "gray area" of real estate law so a real estate attorney should be consulted.

8.
How to Maximize
Your Profits
at Resale Time

Smart investors not only make good profits while owning property, but they maximize their profits at resale time. This resale profit maximization starts at the time of purchase. By purchasing only property which is well-located, in sound condition, and with good financing, the investor then is in a position to gain the maximum potential from the property.

Unfortunately, many home buyers and investors in other properties buy the wrong way. Profit maximization begins the day the property is bought.

Assuming the property is in a reasonable location and in sound physical condition, the other key to getting the most from the property is its financing. The last few chapters have discussed various finance methods which can meet your needs when buying a property. When financing your acquisition, always ask the key question *"How can I best finance this property to buy it now and to eventually resell it in the future with a maximum profit?"*

To illustrate, think of all the retirees who sold their homes up north, received a bundle of cash from the sale, and bought a retirement home in the south or west. Most of those people paid all cash. But when they want to resell today, perhaps because of illness or changed family circumstances, they are finding that it is hard to resell for all cash. The reason is the potential buyers, today's new retirees, are having trouble selling their old homes for cash. But if those homes had been financed with assumable mortgages, they would be easy to resell today (although the seller would probably have to help out by carrying a second mortgage).

In other words, when you buy a property, finance it so it can be sold easily. This means *mortgage it to the hilt* at the time of purchase. The bigger the mortgage, the easier it will be to resell that property in the future.

Even if you can afford to pay all cash, or make a big cash down payment, DON'T! Like every good rule, however, this one has an exception. The only time to pay all cash or make a big cash down payment

194

is if that cash will gain you a substantial discount off fair market value. A "substantial discount" means at least 20 percent below fair market value.

Just as financing is the key when buying property, it is the key to success when selling property too. But there is more to maximizing resale profits than just offering good financing. When getting ready to sell a property, there are two additional considerations: (1) the physical aspects and (2) the income tax aspects. Both are important. Smart investors consider both when they decide to dispose of a property they no longer want to own.

Although the next section deals with selling your principal residence, most of the comments also apply to the sale of investment property too. Further suggestions for maximizing resale profits of investment properties are in the installment sale section, toward the end of the chapter.

THE "RED RIBBON DEAL"

Selling your home, whether it is a single-family house, a condominium or cooperative apartment or townhouse, or perhaps a houseboat or mobile home, can be a very rewarding and profitable experience. Or, it can be financial disaster.

To earn the greatest net profit from your property sale, *after taxes,* requires taking a series of steps, one at a time. The sales process is really quite simple. But do not risk selling your property until you fully understand every step of the sales procedure.

Selling your property, especially your home, is one of the greatest profit opportunities you will ever have—DON'T MESS IT UP! One mistake can easily cost thousands of dollars in low profit or taxes paid unnecessarily. It is far cheaper to pay fees for expert advice than to make a mistake that costs far more.

Here are the easy steps to maximizing your profit and minimizing the tax when selling your residence.

GET YOUR HOME IN TOP PHYSICAL CONDITION

To get top dollar for any home, it must be C-L-E-A-N! That means really clean. If necessary, paint it inside and outside. *Paint is the cheapest and most profitable improvement you can make.* Be especially certain the entrance has been recently painted and all outside trim is in top condition.

Clean the yard, basement, and garage thoroughly. A neat, clean home brings full market value, but similar dirty homes repel buyers from making any purchase offer. You may be accustomed to the dirt, dog smells, cooking odors, and other personality traits of your home, but potential buyers are not. It is the rare buyer who can overlook sloppy housekeeping, poor maintenance, and dirt. Those buyers who will buy such a house expect to buy at a rock bottom price. If you are buying, and can find a messy property which the seller will not get into top condition before sale, that is your opportunity to buy for a bargain price because you will have little or no competition from other buyers.

So *do not even think of putting your residence up for sale until you have cleaned and fixed it up.* Your home may not be the Taj Mahal, but it can be as neat and clean as if it were. Spending $1,000 or $2,000 on cleaning and painting can return many times that small cost in the form of a higher sales price.

INCOME TAX SAVINGS FOR FIX-UP COSTS

If you are buying a replacement principal residence, many expenses to fix-up your old home, which normally have no tax consequence, take on tax aspects. Examples of such fix-up costs include painting, cleaning, and repairing.

Such expenses, to be subtracted from your home's gross sales price, must be incurred within ninety days before the date of signing the sales agreement, and they must be paid for within thirty days after the close of the sale.

The net tax result will be no tax saving if you are buying a qualifying, more-expensive replacement principal residence (because all your tax is deferred anyway), but it will be a greater tax deferral if you are buying a less-expensive replacement. When buying a less-expensive replacement principal residence, the sale profit from your old home is only taxed up to the difference in the two prices. The fix-up costs reduce this difference.

To illustrate, suppose you sell your old home for $100,000 with $2,000 of fix-up costs, and buy a replacement for $80,000. Normally, your profit would be taxed up to the $20,000 price difference. But because you spent $2,000 on fix-up costs, only $18,000 of your sale profit will be taxed.

This fix-up rule only applies to costs of preparing your home for sale. Items of a major capital improvement nature, such as installing a new air conditioner, new built-in appliances, or a new roof, should be capitalized and added to the cost basis of your residence. Be sure to save the bills for both capital improvements and home sale fix-up costs.

Money spent fixing up your home for sale is money well spent. But of course do not go overboard and overimprove your house for its neighborhood. For example, installation of a swimming pool in a neighborhood of working-class tract subdivision homes probably will not increase the home's market value by the cost of the new pool.

PRICE YOUR HOME CORRECTLY

After your home is in top physical condition and ready for sale, then it is time to determine its market value. "Market value" is defined as the price a willing buyer agrees to pay to a willing seller, neither being under pressure to buy or sell, with the property given exposure to the marketplace for a reasonable period of time.

Nothing is worse than for a home seller to overprice his residence. After all, if the local real estate agents and their potential buyers find out it is overpriced, they will avoid the house like the plague. The reason is they figure the seller is not serious about selling, so why waste time?

Buyers often will not even make offers at an overpriced home's true market value because there are too many other homes available for sale, so why beg a seller to sell an overpriced home for its true value? But smart buyers do make purchase offers on overpriced homes, after the houses have been on the market for sale a long time. By then, other buyers and their agents have lost interest in the overpriced house, and the seller is often so desperate he will accept a below-market purchase offer.

The market value of a home depends on recent sales prices (and terms) of similar residences in the immediate neighborhood. Home prices are *not* based on (1) how much the seller thinks his home is worth, (2) what he needs to get for it to make a good profit, (3) how much he has invested in the house, or (4) how much he needs to pay off his debts.

For example, although your three-bedroom home is different from the three-bedroom home next door in appearance, floor plan, and physical condition, if the house next door sold for $75,000 last month, yours is probably worth about $75,000 too, with price adjustments up or down for any major differences in features and condition.

By comparing recent sales prices of several homes in your neighborhood, you will soon arrive at a good approximation of your home's fair market value. Not to be overlooked, of course, is the effect of mortgage financing terms available. If "easy financing" is available, buyers will often pay more than if the seller is demanding 100 percent cash.

HOW TO FIND COMPARABLE PROPERTY SALES PRICES

Real estate sales agents, through their local board of realtors or multiple listing service, usually have easy access to comparable home sale prices. When you talk with several realty agents about possibly listing your home for sale with them, find out what the agent estimates your home will sell for *and why*. The top agents will prepare written "competitive market analysis" forms for you. These forms show recent sales prices of similar nearby homes, as well as current asking prices of other homes for sale now (your competition).

Before listing your home for sale with any agent, however, check with at least three active local agents before deciding on your asking price. Set your price too high, and you discourage potential buyers (and more importantly, their agents who have *other* buyers). Set your price too low, and you have lost a big part of your profit. If you set your price too high, to test the market, it often takes a big price reduction to rekindle any interest in the property, since it has been "shopped around" too long.

It is OK to set your asking price 3 percent to 5 percent above what you expect to accept for the residence, but do not set it so far above market value that you price yourself out of the local market. Once you do that, you are wasting valuable time that costs you (and your agent) money. If you really want to sell, and you have overpriced your home, you will eventually have to reduce your price to fair market value, or below. Why not save time, money, and hassle by pricing your home right from the start?

TO MAKE THE BIGGEST PROFIT, OFFER THE BEST TERMS

If an automobile dealer tells his prospective auto buyers who walk into his showroom "You'll have to pay all cash or arrange your own financing to buy any car we sell here," he would soon be out of business. Whether we like it or not, credit is a way of life in the U.S. for almost every car buyer. CREDIT IS EVEN MORE A WAY OF LIFE FOR VIRTUALLY EVERY HOME BUYER. When was the last time you heard of a buyer paying all cash for a house? It rarely happens.

Circumstances may require that you receive 100 percent cash when you sell your residence. If so, that usually means your buyer has to put up a cash down payment of at least 20 percent of the home's sale price. The balance is often paid with an 80 percent conventional mortgage from a bank, S&L, or mortgage broker. Or the buyer may want a low down payment FHA or VA mortgage (govermment-backed mortgages are discussed later). Another possibility is a PMI (private mortgage insurance) mortgage for 90 percent or 95 percent of the home's sale price.

The better the "built-in financing," the better the home seller's chances of selling his home for top dollar. You suddenly increase the number of potential buyers who can afford to buy your home if you will agree, at the time of listing the home for sale, to help finance the sale. The greater the seller's participation in the sale financing, the greater the number of potential buyers for that home.

However, at the time a new VA, FHA, or PMI loan is made to sell a home, there can be no secondary financing. But when the home is resold in the future and the second buyer purchases "subject to" an existing VA or FHA mortgage, second mortgages are allowed.

So be flexible about taking back a first or second mortgage to make your home appeal to the largest number of potential buyers. In fact, if you want to really get your home sold quickly when you list it, include on the listing the exact financing you will accept, such as 10 percent down payment, buyer to assume existing mortgage, and seller will carry back a second mortgage for the balance of the sales price (then spell out the terms you want on that second mortgage).

Suppose two similar homes are for sale in the same neighborhood on these terms:

No. 1. THREE-BEDROOM HOME
$95,000—All cash to seller

No. 2. THREE-BEDROOM HOME
$100,000—Financing Available
$15,000—Cash Down Payment (15%)
$75,000—1st Mortgage, 12%, 29 years
$10,000—2nd Mortgage, 10%, 10 years
$772—1st Mortgage monthly payment
$100—2nd Mortgage monthly payment
$872—Total monthly mortgage payments

Which home will have the most potential buyers? Which terms would you, as a buyer, prefer? Which house is likely to sell first? Assuming both sellers have the same cost and sell for their full asking price, which seller will earn the largest total profit? In addition to earning $5,000 more profit on his sales price, which seller will earn $1,000 in annual interest income on the second mortgage he carried back?

House No. 2, of course. By now you probably have the general idea that to get the best possible sales price when selling your residence, it is very important to (1) offer it in top condition, (2) at the right asking price, and (3) on the best possible sales terms.

But do not go overboard by offering terms that are too good, such as *no* down payment. Be sure the buyer has sufficient equity in the residence so he will not be tempted to walk away from it if he loses his job or becomes sick and unable to work.

No down payment purchases make it too easy for the buyer to abandon the house if he cannot make the monthly payments or if it suddenly needs expensive repairs. Let the FHA and VA mortgage loan programs take care of the high risk buyers. You cannot afford to. Every home seller, before he will consider taking back all or part of the financing on a first or second mortgage, deed of trust, or land contract, should insist on a cash down payment of at least 10 percent of the sales price, plus a credit history check on the buyer.

However, like every good rule, *there is an exception.* If a buyer offers you a small cash down payment (and you do not need more cash), that can be safe for the seller *if* the buyer will give adequate security. To illustrate, suppose a buyer offers you a 5 percent down payment with you to finance the sale on a first or second mortgage. Normally, that is dangerous for you, the seller, because the buyer has so little equity. But if the buyer secures his promissory note to you with a first or second mortgage on the property you sell him *plus* a first or second mortgage on other property he owns, then you have got a safe loan. If the buyer defaults, then you can foreclose on both the property you sold him and also on the second property he gave you as security. But be sure you receive title insurance on both properties for your first and second mortgage. Title insurance is the only safe protection to be sure the buyer really owns the second property he is offering as security.

BEWARE OF 110 PERCENT FINANCING

Occasionally home sellers who are willing to help finance the sale are confronted by offers that look like this. Suppose your home is for sale at $100,000. A buyer offers you full $100,000 price, contingent upon his getting a new first mortgage for $75,000 from a S&L. His offer further provides you will receive a second mortgage on the house for $35,000. This means that of the $75,000 cash from the new first mortgage, the buyer gets $10,000! In other words, when the smoke clears you will get $65,000 cash (from the new first mortgage) plus a $35,000 second mortgage. The buyer gets $10,000 cash.

This is dangerous for the seller. It is good for the sharp buyer because he walks away from the purchase with $10,000 cash. If he is a crook, he may keep walking and never make any payments either to you on your second mortgage or to the first mortgage lender.

The reason this is so risky for the seller is if the buyer defaults, the original seller forecloses on his second mortgage and will probably get the property back (there are not likely to be many bidders at the foreclosure sale of a second mortgage for 100 percent of the property's market value). But when you get the house back, you will owe the first mortgage lender $75,000, of which you only received $65,000.

However, this can be turned into a perfectly safe transaction for the seller, and the buyer still gets his 110 percent financing. By securing that second mortgage with both the property being sold and other property the buyer already owns, the second mortgage holder (seller) has more than adequate security if the buyer defaults. But be sure the buyer has plenty of equity in the second property and that title insurance is obtained on the second lien on it.

This 110 percent finance scheme is being used nationwide by shrewd buyers who take advantage of naïve sellers. If you know how to handle such an offer, you can benefit from it. In fact, you may want to go out and buy property this way. But to protect the seller, be sure there is adequate equity security in two or more properties for the amount of the second mortgage to the seller.

OFFER THE BEST SALE TERMS
FOR BOTH THE BUYER AND SELLER

Most home buyers (and buyers of investment property too) want to buy with the lowest possible cash down payment (if they can comfortably afford the resulting monthly mortgage payments). In fact, it is downright smart to buy with the smallest down payment possible. Reasons include (1) mortgage repayment in cheaper, inflated dollars worth less than today, (2) maximum income tax deduction for mortgage interest, (3) cash conservation for emergencies and other investments, and (4) easy resale if the property has a big assumable existing mortgage.

But from the seller's viewpoint, if the buyer cannot afford a 10 percent or 15 percent cash down payment, that buyer might not be a good risk if the seller is considering helping finance the sale. The FHA, VA, and PMI loan programs are available for these low down payment, high risk buyers.

But unless you have no other way to finance the sale of your home, try to avoid selling to a buyer who wants to get a FHA or VA mortgage. Reasons include (1) the seller usually must pay "loan points" (one point equals one percent of the amount borrowed) for the buyer to get a new VA home loan because the VA will not allow their buyers to pay the loan fee, (2) FHA and VA appraisals are often lower than those of conventional lenders, (3) FHA AND VA appraisers often require minor repairs to be made before they will approve the loan, (4) red tape bureaucratic delays frequently prolong the closing time for FHA and VA home sales to sixty or ninety days, sometimes longer, and (5) second mortgages are not allowed with new FHA and VA mortgages, thus reducing your profit potential for earning extra income from interest on an installment sale.

Fortunately, it is usually possible to match the most desirable sales terms from both the buyer's and seller's viewpoints to minimize the seller's tax on the sale, thus maximizing his profit. When structuring the sale terms, consider the tax aspects closely. There are four major tax breaks to consider when planning the sale of your personal residence.

1. The "Over-55 Rule" $125,000 Home Sale Tax Exemption

As discussed in Chapter 3, the "over-55 rule" benefits many home sellers who are fifty-five or older. If you meet the easy requirements, then you have little or no tax to be concerned about when planning the sale of your residence. To review the three requirements of this rule, they are (1) one or more co-owners must be fifty-five or older on the title transfer date, (2) the seller must have owned and lived in the principal residence three of the last five years before its sale, and (3) the seller cannot have used this tax exemption before (any unused portion of the $125,000 profit tax exemption cannot be saved for future use).

EXAMPLE: Larry and Mary, husband and wife, paid $13,500 for their house many years ago. They sell it for $75,000 so they can enter a life-care retirement home. If either Larry or Mary is at least age fifty-five on the title transfer date and that spouse holds a title interest in the home, the entire $61,500 profit ($75,000 minus $13,500) is tax-free if they lived in the house as their principal residence any three of the last five years before the sale. But the unused $39,500 of their $125,000 possible tax exemption cannot be saved for future use.

2. The Principal Residence Replacement Rule

In Chapter 3, this tax deferral rule was thoroughly explained. But it bears repeating that this rule is available to taxpayers of any age who (1) sell their principal residence and (2) buy a replacement principal residence within eighteen months before or after the sale (an additional six months is allowed if a new home is constructed).

However, this tax break results in 100 percent profit tax deferral only if a more expensive replacement is bought. If the replacement costs less, then the profit is taxable up to the difference in the prices of the two residences.

EXAMPLE: Howard, age sixty, sells his principal residence for $95,000 and buys a condominium in Florida for $120,000. Although he qualifies for the "over-55 rule," he should save it for future use since his profit tax is deferred anyway using the replacement residence rule.

EXAMPLE: Evan and Ellen, ages fifty-six and fifty-four, sell their principal residence for $90,000, earning a $40,000 profit. They buy a $75,000 condominium. Since their replacement costs $15,000 less than the sale price of their old residence, $15,000 of their $40,000 profit is potentially taxable. But if they meet the requirements of the "over-55 rule," they can use their $100,000 exemption to avoid paying tax on this $15,000 profit.

By the way, purchase of life-care in a retirement home does *not* qualify as a principal residence replacement under the "replacement residence rule" of Internal Revenue Code section 1034, discussed next.

3. The Installment Sale Tax Deferral Method

If the sale qualifies for neither the "over-55 rule" nor the "residence replacement rule," then an installment sale should be considered. Most property sellers who use installment sales (available on any sale, whether the property is your principal residence or owned as an investment or for use in your trade or business) do so (1) to minimize their profit tax by spreading out the payments received from the buyer (and the tax on those payments) into future years, (2) to maximize their profit from interest income and from a higher sales price due to a lower cash down payment required from the buyer, and (3) to provide for future income security with a first or second mortgage, deed of trust, or land contract on their former property.

> EXAMPLE: Ann, age fifty, decides to sell her home for $100,000. Her cost was $44,000. Thus her profit will be $56,000 ($100,000 minus $44,000). She owns the home free and clear (this is not an installment sale requirement, however). A buyer offers Ann a $15,000 cash down payment on an installment sale. Ann agrees to take back the $85,000 mortgage at 12 percent interest for 25 years. Each month she will receive $874.58 from the buyer. The interest portion of each payment will be taxed as ordinary income. Of the principal part of each payment, 56 percent ($56,000 divided by $100,000) is taxed as long-term capital gain at the lowest tax rates available. The other 44 percent ($44,000 divided by $100,000) is tax-free return of Ann's initial $44,000 cost basis in the home. Over the next twenty-five years, Ann will receive a total of $262,374 in payments, of which $177,374 is interest and $85,000 is principal. It is like getting two profits from the sale of one house.

HOW THE INSTALLMENT SALES LAW
CAN INCREASE YOUR REALTY PROFITS

One of the few major accomplishments of the 96th Congress was passage of the 1980 Installment Sales Revision Act. This law opened new opportunities to real estate profits. But it also created some new pitfalls to avoid.

Property sellers with large profits are always anxious to eliminate or at least minimize their income tax on their profit. If the property and the seller both qualify for the "residence replacement rule" of Internal Revenue Code Section 1034 or the "over-55 rule" $100,000 home sale tax exemption of Internal Revenue Code Section 121 (both rules apply *only* to the sale of the taxpayer's principal residence), then profit tax can be either completely eliminated or deferred.

But many property sales do not qualify for these two tax breaks. Even those sales that do qualify can be structured to use the installment sale principles to maximize the seller's total profit. Installment sales can be used on *any* property sale. Not only do installment sales defer the seller's profit tax payment, but they also usually lower the total tax too. This is done by avoiding a boost of the taxpayer into a high tax bracket in the year of the property sale, as would occur if he receives all his profit in the sale year.

WHAT IS AN INSTALLMENT SALE?

An installment sale is any real or personal property sale where the buyer's payment of the sales price is not fully received in the tax year of the sale. Until 1980, the definition of an installment sale also required that not over 30 percent of the gross sales price be received by the seller in the year of sale and payments must be made by the buyer to the seller in two or more tax years. Both of these limiting rules were repealed by the 1980 Installment Sales Revision Act.

In other words, an installment sale is simply a sale where the buyer's payments to the seller are deferred over a period of time. The seller pays his profit tax as he receives those payments, rather than paying the entire tax in the year of the property sale.

WHY USE AN INSTALLMENT SALE?

There are many reasons for structuring a property sale as an installment sale. Some of the major reasons include:

1. *Facilitate the sale and improve the sales price and terms.* If the seller assists the property buyer in obtaining easy financing, the buyer will be willing to pay a higher purchase price or offer more generous terms to the seller.

The usual security for the buyer's installment debt to the seller is a mortgage, deed of trust, land contract (called a contract for deed in some states), or a long-term lease-option. In tight mortgage markets, an installment sale may be the only practical way to get a property sold because seller financing may be all that is available.

2. *Deferral of profit tax over the years in which the buyer pays for the property.* Since the seller waits for the buyer's deferred payments, it is only sensible for the seller to postpone tax payment until the buyer's payments are received. The 1980 Installment Sales Revision Act encourages this tax result by making all deferred payment sales *automatically* installment sales with deferred tax payment.

3. *An installment sale can defer tax payments into future tax years when the seller expects to be in a lower tax bracket.*

EXAMPLE: Lucy will retire next year from her job. Her taxable income then will drop by about 50 percent. But she has an excellent offer today to sell her four-family apartment house. The buyer may not be interested next year. By using an installment sale, Lucy can finalize the sale now, get either no or a small cash down payment this year, and begin getting installment payments next year. The interest income on the buyer's unpaid balance to Lucy will supplement her retirement pension and social security. Although interest income is taxed as ordinary income, Lucy's profit portion of each installment sale principal payment received will be taxed at the lower long-term capital gain tax rates if she owned the property over twelve months before selling.

4. *Deferral of a capital gain into a future tax year can offset an expected loss from other sales, such as sale of common stock at a loss.*

5. *Avoidance of a boost into a high tax bracket in the year of a property sale maximizes profit by saving tax dollars.* By spreading out the buyer's payments over several years, the taxpayer can avoid being thrown into a high tax bracket in the year of sale. For example, if a taxpayer is normally in a 20 percent tax bracket, if he makes a property sale of his farm for all cash, he could easily be thrown into a 40 percent or 50 percent tax bracket. An installment sale can avoid this bad result by spreading out the buyer's payments over several tax years.

6. *Safe, secured interest income increases the seller's annual earnings and makes them more predictable.* Retirees especially like installment sales because the interest income, secured by a mortgage, deed of trust, land contract, or long-term lease-option on the property sold adds to their retirement income. Although this interest income is taxed as ordinary income, since most retirees are in low tax brackets, the tax bite on the interest is not of major importance to them.

The general rule is that a deferred payment or installment sale of real or personal property defers the tax on the seller's profit until the money is received from the buyer. Each payment received has three parts: (1) interest on the buyer's unpaid balance (taxed as ordinary income), (2) nontaxable return of the seller's capital investment in the property, and (3) taxable profit (taxed as long term capital gain if the property was owned over twelve months before sale).

Interest must be charged on installment sales. From time to time the IRS adjusts the minimum interest rate required. If it were not for this interest requirement, property sellers would raise the price (since most profits are taxed at the lower long-term capital gains rates) and lower the interest (taxed as ordinary income). Congress is considering new legislation on this topic, so watch for changes in the minimum interest rate which must be charged on installment sales.

After July 1, 1981, the IRS will impute interest to installment payments received by a property seller if at least 9 percent interest is specified in the installment sale obligation of the buyer. The IRS can impute interest at 10 percent if a rate lower than 9 percent is contained in the installment contract.

RULES FOR INSTALLMENT SALES

The 1980 Installment Sales Revision Act made several important installment sale rule changes. Here is a summary of the major changes.

1. *Elimination of the 30 percent year of sale maximum payment.* The old installment sale rules disqualified many taxpayers from deferring their profit tax over the years of receiving the buyer's payments. A slight miscalculation could cause income tax disaster by making the full profit tax due in the year of sale if over 30 percent of the gross sales price was received in the sale year.

The simple new rule says tax is owed on the sale profit in the tax year it is received by the seller. Each principal payment the seller receives is split in the normal way between tax-free return of capital investment and taxable profit (long-term gain if the property was owned over twelve months before its sale).

But a word of caution is in order. If the property seller refinanced the mortgage before selling, and if that mortgage exceeds the seller's adjusted cost basis (book value) for the property sold, the amount of excess mortgage counts as a payment received in the year of sale.

To illustrate, suppose you sell your property for $100,000 with $10,000 cash down payment. If your adjusted cost basis is $25,000, the buyer assumes or takes title "subject to" your old $40,000 refinanced first mortgage, and the buyer gives you a second mortgage for the $50,000 balance of the sales price, your $15,000 "excess mortgage" over adjusted cost basis ($40,000 minus $15,000) is partly taxable in the year of the sale.

The reason the excess mortgage amount is taxable when a property is sold is an excess mortgage balance over the property's adjusted cost basis is the same as if the seller had received that amount as part of the cash down payment. In fact, the seller did receive that excess mortgage money in cash at the time he refinanced the mortgage. This excess mortgage taxable result is the same as under the old installment sale law.

Elimination of the 30 percent year of sale maximum payment limit applies to installment sales made after January 1, 1980.

2. *Two payment rule abolished.* Another major change was elimination of the old minimum two payment installment sale rule. The old law required at least two installment payments in two separate income tax years. Now it is possible to sell a property for no down payment in the sale year and still qualify for installment sale benefits.

For example, suppose a property seller has had a very good income year. In November he receives an excellent offer to sell his property. But if he sells this year, it will boost him into a sky-high income tax bracket. Frankly, he does not need any more income this year. So he makes an installment sale with the payment for the property due in January of next year.

This provision is retroactive to installment sales made after January 1, 1980.

3. *Automatic installment sale election.* As mentioned earlier, the new law requires taxpayers to use installment sale tax deferral benefits unless they elect not to do so. This election is now automatic for installment sales made after October 19, 1980.

Occasionally a property seller wants to pay his entire profit tax in the year of the property sale, even though he will not receive all his payments from the buyer until future years. Such a taxpayer must now "unelect" his automatic installment sale election.

4. *Special rules for sales to relatives and controlled corporations.* One of the most complicated provisions of the 1980 Installment Sales Revision Act involves property sales to relatives and closely controlled corporations. Oversimplified, the new law says the original seller will owe tax on any resale profit if the installment sale buyer resells the property within two years after the original installment sale. But this only applies to persons related to the original seller if they resell within two years.

The purpose of this new provision is to control intrafamily property sales which are motivated by tax purposes. Such sales made after May 14, 1980, are affected. If the profitable resale is made within two years after the original sale, before installment sale payments to the original seller are completed, the resale profit is taxed to the original seller.

But there are numerous exceptions to this two-year resale "relate back" rule. One applies if there is no tax motivation for the sale. Another applies to sale of marketable securities, trust funds, and mutual fund shares. Still another applies if the second sale was after the death of either the original installment sale seller or the related purchaser, or if the second sale was due to an involuntary conversion.

For purposes of this rule, "related purchasers" are defined as spouse, child, grandchild, or parent (brother and sister are NOT on the list), controlled corporations, partnerships, and trusts and estates.

5. *"Like-kind" tax-deferred exchanges can now be installment sales too.* The installment sale law now says a trade of a "like-kind" property in an Internal Revenue Code Section 1031 tax-deferred exchange (discussed in Chapter 9) will not be treated as a payment when it is received with an installment obligation. In other words, installment sale benefits can now be combined with a tax-deferred exchange.

To illustrate, suppose you trade your property with a $400,000 basis for "like-kind" property worth $200,000, plus an installment note for $700,000, plus $100,000 cash paid in the year of trade. In other words, you are trading down and receiving "boot" (boot is personal property, rather than real property). Under the old law, the contract price is $1,000,000 ($200,000 + $700,000 + $100,000) with a $600,000 gross profit ($1,000,000 minus $400,000 basis). This is a 60 percent ratio of $600,000 profit divided by $1,000,000. The old law would require taxation on 60 percent of $300,000 ($100,000 cash plus the $200,000 value of the "like-kind" property received) which is $180,000.

But the new law excludes value of the "like-kind" real property received even though it is a "down trade." The contract price is now $800,000 ($700,000 + $100,000) with a $600,000 gross profit ($1,000,000 minus $400,000). The gross profit ratio now is 75 percent ($600,000 divided by $800,000) so the reportable gain in the year of sale is 75 percent of $100,000 cash payment received, or $75,000. Gain reportable in future tax years is 75 percent of the $700,000 installment note, which is $525,000. Total gain on the sale is $600,000, the same as under the old law.

This exchange applies to sales closed after October 19, 1980.

6. *Open-end contingency sales now qualify for installment sales.* Open-end property sales, where either price or terms of the sale remain to be determined after the sale closing, now can qualify for installment sale benefits. This portion of the new law applies to sales closed after October 19, 1980.

This new provision, however, will eliminate use of the "cost recovery method" whereby a taxpayer first recovered his cost basis in the property before he incurred any tax liability on the contingency sale. Now payments received are taxed on a pro rata basis, using the maximum sales price to determine the contract price and gross profit ratio in the normal installment sale manner (described later).

However, if the maximum sale price is later reduced in a future tax year, such as when a performance mortgage's rental income from the property does not meet expectations, then installment sale figures must be recomputed. Congress left it up to the IRS to issue regulations implementing this complicated part of the new law.

WHICH PAYMENTS ARE TAXABLE IN AN INSTALLMENT SALE?

1. *Buyer's down payment.* Part of the buyer's cash down payment represents profit to the seller and will be taxable. A portion is tax-free return of capital investment. The taxability ratio is determined according to the method discussed later in this chapter. Also taxable would be the profit portion of any noncash down payment made by the buyer, such as transferring to the property seller common stocks, bonds, personal

property (such as a car or boat), or any other payment made to a third party on behalf of the seller (such as buyer's payment of seller's debt to a finance company).

However, payments made by the buyer on a debt secured by an existing lien (such as a mortgage or deed of trust) on the property are not taxable to the seller (except an excess mortgage, of course).

2. *Buyer's principal payments to seller in year of sale.* Any principal payments made by the buyer to the seller on the installment obligation in the year of sale are partly taxable according to the taxability ratio.

EXAMPLE: Craig sold his land for $100,000 and received a $40,000 cash down payment from the buyer. But in the year of sale the buyer also paid $2,000 of principal on the installment sale second mortgage Craig carried back to finance the sale. The $42,000 total received by Craig in the year of sale is partly taxable to him as profit.

3. *Excess mortgage over seller's basis (book value).* If the existing first mortgage (plus a second, third, etc., mortgage) that the buyer assumes or takes title "subject to" exceeds the seller's adjusted cost basis in the property, the excess mortgage amount becomes partly taxable to the seller in the year of sale.

4. *Option payments.* If the buyer paid consideration for an option to buy the property, in the tax year the purchase option is exercised the option money becomes partly taxable to the seller.

5. *Rental payments.* Similarly, if the buyer made prior rent payments that are credited toward the purchase price, the rent paid becomes partly taxable unless the seller already reported that rental income on his prior year income tax returns. This might occur, for example, when a tenant has a lease with option to buy the property.

SPECIAL INSTALLMENT SALE PROBLEMS AND HOW TO HANDLE THEM

1. *Buyer's debt to the seller.* The buyer's obligation to the seller, usually secured by a first, second, or third mortgage, trust deed, or land contract on the property, is *not* taxable in the year of sale. It does not matter whether or not the buyer's obligation is secured or unsecured. The buyer's obligation becomes taxable to the seller only when the buyer actually pays the seller on that debt obligation.

2. *Existing obligations secured by the property sold.* Any existing mortgage or trust deed obligations already secured by the property sold are *not* taxable to the seller in the year of the sale, even though the buyer makes payments on those obligations to a third-party lender. It does not matter whether the buyer takes title "subject to" or assumes those liens. The only exception, of course, is an "excess mortgage" where the mortgage balance exceeds the seller's adjusted cost basis for the property.

Such excess mortgage amount is taxable to the seller in the first year of an installment sale.

> EXAMPLE: Don sold his land for $70,000. The buyer made a $10,000 cash down payment and assumed Don's existing $30,000 first mortgage. Don took back a $30,000 second mortgage from the buyer. The land cost Don $25,000. This is his book value or adjusted costs basis. The $5,000 excess mortgage over Don's $25,000 adjusted cost basis represents partially taxable profit in the year of the sale. In other words, Don pays profit tax on the profit portion of the $10,000 cash down payment plus the $5,000 excess mortgage exceeding his basis.

3. *Proceeds of seller's sale of buyer's obligation.* After the sale is closed, the seller may find he needs cash. To raise cash, he may sell his mortgage, trust deed, or land contract received from the buyer. The cash received from the sale of the note and security is a separate transaction from the property sale. But part of the proceeds will be taxable as if payments were made on the buyer's promissory note.

> EXAMPLE: Lenny sold his home for $100,000. The buyer paid $10,000 cash down payment. Lenny took back a $60,000 first mortgage for 25 years and a $30,000 second mortgage. Later, Lenny sold his second mortgage for $22,000 cash. The $22,000 received from the sale of the second mortgage is partly taxable as capital gain profit. The rest is nontaxable return of capital investment.

4. *Buyer's payments on existing loans.* The payments the buyer makes toward the principal reduction on any existing loans secured by the property before the sale (which were assumed or taken "subject to" by the buyer) are *not* taxable to the seller.

5. *Seller's refinancing of existing loans before the sale.* If the seller refinanced an old loan or put on a new mortgage before selling the property, the money raised from the refinance is *not* taxable unless a portion is an excess mortgage (discussed earlier).

> EXAMPLE: Benny desires an installment sale of his apartment house that has an adjusted cost basis of $32,000. His old mortgage is paid down to $15,000. Before the installment sale, Benny refinances for $32,000 and then sells the apartments on an installment sale for a $100,000 adjusted sales price. Since the refinanced mortgage does not exceed Benny's adjusted cost basis, he does not owe any tax on the $17,000 cash proceeds ($32,000 minus $15,000) from the mortgage refinance. But if the refinanced mortgage exceeded Benny's adjusted cost basis (book value), then he would owe capital gains tax on the profit portion of that excess mortgage.

HOW TO CALCULATE TAXABILITY OF
INSTALLMENT SALE PAYMENTS RECEIVED

Whether received in the year of sale or in a later tax year, a percentage of each principal dollar received by the seller from the buyer toward payment of the principal balance on the installment sale debt is taxable profit.

Interest received is taxed as ordinary income, of course. The remainder of each dollar of principal received is nontaxable return of capital investment.

NET GAIN (profit) is the "adjusted sales price" (gross sales price minus sales expenses such as realty sales commission and transfer costs) minus the "adjusted cost basis" (purchase price plus capital improvements added during ownership, minus any depreciation and casualty losses deducted during ownership).

CONTRACT PRICE is the gross sales price minus any existing liens or mortgages taken over by the buyer (whether he assumes or takes "subject to"), plus the excess (if any) of any existing mortgages over the property's adjusted cost basis to the seller.

$$\frac{\text{NET GAIN}}{\text{CONTRACT PRICE}} = \text{Percent of each principal dollar which is taxable}$$

EXAMPLE:

Gross sales price	$100,000
Existing mortgages, trust deeds, or liens	$40,000
Seller's adjusted cost basis	$50,000

CONTRACT PRICE:

Gross Sales Price	$100,000
Minus: Existing Mortgages, Trust Deeds, etc.	$−40,000
	$60,000
Plus: Excess mtg. over adjusted cost basis	$+0
Contract Price	$60,000

NET GAIN

Gross Sales Price	$100,000
Minus: Selling expenses	$−6,000
Adjusted Sales Price	$94,000
Minus: Adjusted cost basis	$−50,000
Net Gain (Profit)	$44,000

$$\frac{\text{NET GAIN}}{\text{CONTRACT PRICE}} = \frac{\$44,000}{\$60,000} = 73.3 \text{ percent}$$ of each principal dollar received is taxable long-term capital gain profit

When a property sale is made with tax-deferred installment sale payments, the seller's questions then become "How much of each payment I receive is taxable?" and "How much is tax-free return of my capital investment?"

Of course, before these questions can be answered, the interest portion of each payment received must be subtracted to get the amount of principal received. Interest is taxed as ordinary income. As the loan is amortized, this interest portion of each payment will decline, and the principal portion will increase.

As mentioned earlier, interest must be charged on installment sales. The IRS can impute interest if the taxpayer-seller failed to charge the buyer a reasonable interest rate. This minimum changes from time to time. As of this writing if at least 9 percent interest is not charged on the unpaid installment sale balance, the IRS can impute interest at 10 percent.

HOW TO MAXIMIZE SALE PROFITS WITH AN INSTALLMENT SALE

Suppose you sell your property for $100,000 on an installment sale with a $15,000 cash down payment from the buyer, and you take back an $85,000 installment sale mortgage at 10 percent interest from the buyer for a 30-year term. The monthly payments will be $745.95. Over the 30-year mortgage term, total payments will be $268,542, including the $85,000 principal. The happy result is you, the seller, double the amount you receive from the property by taking back an installment sale mortgage. The extra profit comes in the form of the interest income earned on the buyer's unpaid balance owed to you.

But in these days of high inflation rates, the installment sale seller should protect himself by providing for periodic interest rate adjustments every three or five years. This will guard the installment sale seller against hyperinflation. Provision in the promissory note and the mortgage for interest rate adjustment to the national average mortgage index rate every three or five years is fair to both the seller and the buyer.

COMPREHENSIVE EXAMPLE OF AN INSTALLMENT SALE

Since all deferred payment real estate sales now qualify for installment sale tax deferral benefits, it is important for property sellers and real estate agents to understand how to compute the taxable and tax-free portions of each principal payment received (after the interest portion of each payment is first subtracted.) These computations apply only to the principal, *not* to the interest part of each payment received.

Gross sales price	$100,000
Buyer's cash down payment	20,000
Existing mortgages or trust deeds	30,000
Installment sale second mortgage or trust deed to seller	50,000
Sales expenses (realty commission and transfer costs)	7,000
Seller's adjusted cost basis (depreciated book value)	60,000

Calculation of taxability of principal payments:

A—NET GAIN:

Gross sales price	100,000
Minus: Sales expenses	$ – 7,000
Adjusted sales price	93,000
Minus: Adjusted cost basis *(depreciated book value)*	– 60,000
Net gain (profit)	$33,000

B—CONTRACT PRICE:

Gross sales price	$100,000
Minus: Existing mortgage or trust deed	– 30,000
Payments made or to be made by buyer	$70,000
Plus: Excess of mortgages over adjusted cost basis	+ 0
Contract price	$70,000

TAXABLE PERCENTAGE OF EACH PRINCIPAL PAYMENT RECEIVED:

$$\frac{\text{NET GAIN}}{\text{CONTRACT PRICE}} = \frac{\$33,000}{\$70,000} = 47.1 \text{ percent}$$

The result is 47.1 percent of each principal payment received by the seller, including the buyer's cash down payment of $20,000, is taxable (as long-term capital gain if the property was owned over 12 months before the sale). Installment payment long-term capital gains received after October 31, 1978 (the effective date of the 1978 Tax Act) are taxed at the new, lower long-term capital gains rates (basically, 40 percent of the long-term capital gain is taxable, 60 percent is tax-free).

4. Income Averaging

Regardless of the tax method you qualify for when selling your property, if your taxable income jumps drastically in any one tax year, consider income averaging. Taxpayers using installment sales or receiving other long-term capital gains can qualify for income averaging.

Real estate profits, whether ordinary income or long term capital gain (if the property was owned over twelve months or, over six months if acquired after June 22, 1984), qualify for income averaging to cut the income tax on the sale profit. If your taxable income, including long-term capital gains, exceeds by 40 percent your average taxable income for the last three years, it will usually pay to use income averaging.

Although the income averaging computations can be long and difficult, the tax savings are worth the extra effort to be sure you pay the lowest possible tax. An experienced tax adviser's services are essential for this complicated tax calculation. It is especially advisable to use a tax preparer with access to a computer tax program to assure accurate calculations. The tax savings of income averaging can often be very dramatic.

SUMMARY

All of the above methods of maximizing your profit from the sale of your home or other real estate can be used alone or in combination with other tax breaks, if you qualify. For example, you can combine the "over-55 rule" and the "residence replacement rule" when selling your large old house and purchasing a less expensive condominium replacement principal residence.

The purpose of this chapter is to highlight how to maximize sale profit at the time of disposing of property. The next chapter, probably the most profitable in the book, explains how to use tax-deferred exchanges to legally avoid tax payment on investment properties. It is another technique for maximizing your benefits from owning real estate.

QUESTIONS AND ANSWERS

Q. Our home has been for sale several months. The agent has presented us with two purchase offers, but both provided for us to carry back a large second mortgage for the buyers. We couldn't do that since we need $40,000 cash for another house we have already contracted to buy. Our existing VA mortgage is assumable. How can we get a cash sale? —*Lannie O.*

A. Few all-cash home sales are being made today. It is much easier to make a sale with seller financing. Even though mortgage interest rates have dropped a little, it is still difficult for most potential home buyers to qualify for a new mortgage.

Although you did not give the price of your home, if it is below $125,000, you might consider advertising it with GI financing. You would have to pay the loan fee for the buyer's new VA home loan, but it would give you an all-cash sale.

To get your home sold, you have got to make it a "red ribbon deal." That means make your home an attractive package, both physically and financially, for the buyer. Here is another idea to consider.

Suppose your home is worth $100,000. Have your agent advertise it as follows: (1) seller to obtain a new refinanced first mortgage for $75,000, (2) buyer to pay $15,000 cash down payment, and (3) seller to take back a $10,000 second mortgage. Of course, be sure the new first mortgage is not due upon sale. The cash from the mortgage refinancing, plus the buyer's down payment, will probably give you the $40,000 cash you need.

You may be able to use that small second mortgage as part of your down payment on the house you are buying. If necessary, you can probably sell it at a discount to raise more cash. To get your home sold, work with a creative real estate agent who understands innovative finance because that is how homes are sold today.

HOW SELLER FINANCING RELATES TO INSTALLMENT SALES

Q. Recently you mentioned "installment sale tax benefits." Please give more details.—*Palmer MacD.*

A. Installment sale tax deferral can be a major benefit of selling property. The big advantage is the seller's profit is spread out over future tax years, thus avoiding a boost into a high tax bracket in the year of sale.

Other installment sale advantages include (1) easy, quick sale (since no outside financing need be obtained by the property buyer), (2) top dollar sales price due to the built-in financing offered to the buyer, and (3) excellent, safe income for the seller at a high interest rate, secured by a first, second, or third mortgage on the property being sold.

To qualify for installment sale tax deferral benefits, the seller can accept any amount of payment in the year of sale. The old 30 percent limitation has been abolished.

Only the profit portion of the buyer's down payment, his principal payments on the installment sale note to the seller, and any "excess mortgage" over the seller's adjusted cost basis (due to refinancing) get taxed in the year of sale. For further details, consult your tax adviser.

HOW TO COMBINE WRAP-AROUND MORTGAGE
WITH INSTALLMENT SALE

Q. I am considering selling a house where I used to live. It is now rented to tenants. Its mortgage is an assumable loan from a bank. My idea is to sell on an installment sale to spread out the profit tax and give me some extra interest income. But after reading your article about wrap-around mortgage benefits, I'm wondering if it would be possible for me to use both an installment sale and a wrap-around mortgage?—*Hugh E.*

A. Yes, installment sales and wrap-around mortgages make a great combination.

For example, suppose you sell the house for $100,000 with a $15,000 cash down payment. If your first mortgage is $40,000 at 8 percent interest, you might take back an $85,000 wrap-around mortgage at 12 percent (assuming that does not exceed the usury limit in the state where the house is located). You will earn 12 percent on the top $45,000 "at risk" plus the 4 percent differential on the underlying $40,000 first mortgage, which remains undisturbed. This totals about $7,000 annual interest ($5,400 plus $1,600) for a yield of 15.5 percent.

Using a wrap-around mortgage, the buyer makes one monthly payment to you. You then use part of that payment to keep up payments on the old first mortgage, which remains undisturbed.

As you can see, a wrap-around mortgage is a "good deal" for the buyer. Where else can he borrow at 12 percent interest with no loan application or other red tape? And it is a good deal for you, the seller, too because you will earn high yield secured by a mortgage on your old house.

Thanks to the 1980 Installment Sale Revision Act, any deferred payment sale now qualifies for tax deferral. The tax will be automatically spread out over the years the buyer makes his wrap-around mortgage payments to you. Your tax adviser can explain further.

SHOULD SEVENTY-FOUR-YEAR-OLD HOME SELLER FINANCE HOME SALE FOR THIRTY YEARS?

Q. I am selling my home and moving to a retirement home. I am seventy-four. A buyer offered to pay my full asking price, with a $10,000 down payment, if I will carry the mortgage on a 30-year term, payable at $1,640 per month. I want to accept, but my children say I am foolish to do so since I probably won't live thirty years. When I die, the payments will go to my children until the loan is paid off. If I should live thirty years, I'll have good income. What do you think?—*Olive P.*

A. I think you should listen to your children. The thirty-year amortization schedule is fine, but insist on a five- or ten-year "balloon payment" due date on that mortgage. When the balance comes due in five or ten years, you can either extend the loan or have the buyer pay off the balance. High inflation rates make long-term lending unsound. P. S. By financing the sale on deferred payments, you will make your home easy to sell and assure yourself of excellent retirement income. That is the right way to "package" your home for maximum sale profit.

"OVER-55 RULE" AND INSTALLMENT SALE CAN BE COMBINED

Q. The cost of my home was $35,000 and it is worth at least $135,000 if I sell it today. I qualify for that "over-55 rule" $125,000 home sale tax exemption, so I have the potential of receiving the entire $135,000 tax-free. If I sell on an installment sale, in what order do I report the payments received? Can I wait until I receive the full $135,000 and then start reporting the interest to the IRS? Neither my CPA nor the local IRS people can answer my question.—*Lorenz N.*

A. Your situation shows how to combine use of the "over-55 rule" with the installment sale principle.

In the year you sell your principal residence, file IRS Form 2119 with your income tax returns. Use this form to elect use of the "over-55 rule" $125,000 home sale tax exemption. The result will be that your future payments received from the buyer will be free of capital gains tax if your sale profit does not exceed $125,000. If it does, you pay tax on the capital gain profit as you receive it from the buyer.

The IRS requires (as of this writing) at least 9 percent interest be charged on any unpaid installment sale balance. If you don't charge at least 9 percent interest on each payment, the IRS can impute interest at 10 percent.

The interest portion of each installment payment received is taxable as ordinary income. Interest is first deducted from each payment received. The balance is then credited to principal reduction. If your CPA was not aware of this, perhaps you need to find a new tax adviser.

DELAY HOME SALE TO MAXIMIZE TAX SAVINGS

Q. My wife's doctor urges us to move to Arizona for her health. The problem is neither of us is yet fifty-five, and if we sell our home now, we will have a big profit, probably about $85,000. I am fifty-four and my wife is fifty-two. But I don't think we can wait a year to sell. We would like to rent in Arizona for a year or two to see if we like living there. Any ideas for saving tax if we sell our home now?—*David C.*

A. Yes, do not sell now. To qualify for the "over-55 rule" $125,000 home sale tax exemption, at least one co-owner spouse must be fifty-five or older on the day of title transfer. In addition, the principal residence must have been owned and occupied at least three of the five years before sale. So you will maximize your net profit by waiting to sell your home until you are at least fifty-five.

But you can rent your present home for up to two years (assuming you have owned and lived in it the last three years) before closing the sale.

An especially good way to offer your home would be to have your agent advertise it on a "lease with option to buy." Tenants who have a purchase option usually take remarkably good care of the home. With a substantial "consideration for the option" of perhaps several thousand dollars, then you can consider the house practically sold. By waiting to close the sale until you are fifty-five, you will avoid paying tax on that $85,000 profit. Your tax adviser can explain further.

9.

How to Legally Pyramid Your Wealth Without Paying Income Taxes

In Chapter 4 the concept of tax avoidance by ownership of depreciable real estate was explained. If you own enough such properties, you can shelter all your income from taxation.

But most of us do not want to stand still, just owning our current real estate holdings. We would like to increase our real estate wealth, preferably without paying income taxes as we do so.

The good news is it is possible to pyramid your wealth in real estate from a small investment to as many properties as you would like to own— all without paying income tax as you do so.

HOW TAX-DEFERRED PROPERTY EXCHANGES CAN PYRAMID YOUR WEALTH

Real property has unique tax advantages most other investments do not have. Already explained were the "residence replacement rule" and the "over-55 rule" which apply to the sale of your principal residence. This chapter concentrates on the greatest wealth-building technique of all—the tax-deferred exchange.

Internal Revenue Code Section 1031(a) says no profit or loss is recognized (that means taxed) when one property *held for investment or for use in a trade or business* is exchanged for another "like-kind" property.

This unique tax rule applies to just about any property *except* your personal residence. For simplicity, *keep your personal residence out of any tax-deferred property exchange.* The reason is your personal residence is' "unlike property" because it is not held for investment or for use in your trade or business.

EXAMPLE *of a Tax-Deferred Exchange:* George owns rural vacant land worth $200,000. But it produces no income with which to pay the

218

property tax and mortgage payments. George's cost for this land was $150,000. Instead of selling his land and paying tax on his $50,000 profit, George makes a tax-deferred trade of it for a $400,000 apartment house. The tax on George's $50,000 profit is deferred indefinitely until he sells the apartment house since George is trading up and receiving no "boot" (unlike property such as cash or net mortgage relief). If George wishes, he can later trade the apartments for a larger "like-kind" property and continue his tax-deferred exchange pyramid chain endlessly. In this example, George (1) improved his cash flow and (2) had his full $50,000 equity to trade, without income tax erosion. It is almost always better to defer paying tax than to pay it now because tomorrow's dollar will be worth less than today's, due to inflation.

WHAT IS A "LIKE-KIND" REAL ESTATE EXCHANGE?

Property which is eligible for a tax-deferred exchange is any real property, fixtures, and leaseholds of at least thirty years, held for investment or for use in a trade or business. Although this definition excludes your personal residence, it does not exclude a house which you rent to tenants (because such a house is trade, business, or investment property).

Nonqualifying property is called "boot" which means "unlike property." Examples of boot include cash, promissory notes from third parties, personal property such as cars, boats, and trailers, property held primarily for sale (such as a builder's supply of new homes for sale), your personal residence, and net mortgage relief (when the mortgage on the property traded exceeds the mortgage on the property acquired). Boot received in a property exchange is taxable, up to the amount of the profit on the property being relinquished.

Therefore, a tax-deferred property exchange usually requires a property trade up from a smaller to a larger property. The "down trader" in such an exchange will usually pay tax on his profit, to the extent "boot" is received. But, as mentioned in Chapter 8, tax on this boot can now qualify for installment sale tax benefits.

WHY TRADE INSTEAD OF SELLING?

Many real estate owners desire to sell their investment property and use their proceeds to acquire a larger investment property. But a sale, followed by a purchase of other investment property, means the profit on the property sold will be taxed. Paying profit tax on such a sale, followed by a purchase, erodes the net equity available for acquisition of the larger property.

It is not normally possible to sell one investment property, use the proceeds to buy another such property and avoid paying profit tax. However, if you plan ahead, you can come pretty close by use of the new

"Starker" and "Biggs" delayed-exchange techniques, discussed later.

However, if both properties are your principal residences, you can sell your old home and buy a more expensive replacement within eighteen months before or after the sale (take up to twenty-four months after the sale if you build a new residence) and defer paying the property tax. This "residence replacement rule" was discussed in Chapter 3.

The primary reason for use of a tax-deferred exchange is tax deferral. But another major reason is the ability to pyramid wealth, without paying profit taxes, from a small nest egg into substantial holdings. Two well-known investors who have done this are William Nickerson, author of *How I Turned $1,000 into $5 Million in Real Estate in My Spare Time* (Simon and Schuster, 1980) and Albert J. Lowry, author of *How You Can Become Financially Independent by Investing in Real Estate* (Simon and Schuster, 1982).

SIX MAJOR REASONS
FOR USING TAX-DEFERRED EXCHANGES

There are at least six major reasons why it is important to understand tax-deferred exchanges. Although tax avoidance is a major motivation, there are others too. Some are nonfinancial reasons.

AVOIDANCE OF TAX EROSION

By deferring paying of tax on his sale profit, an investor using a tax-deferred exchange has more cash available with which to acquire a larger investment property. Depending upon the investor's income tax bracket, tax conserves 5.6 percent to 20 percent of his total profit. This is a big benefit for putting up with the slight inconvenience of making a tax-deferred exchange instead of a sale followed by purchase of a larger property.

AVOIDANCE OF RECAPTURE OF ACCELERATED DEPRECIATION

For income tax purposes, tax-deferred property exchanges are viewed as one continuous investment from the date the first property was acquired. For this reason, there is no need to be concerned about the twelve-month holding period for long-term capital gains taxation. Similarly, since there is no "sale," any accelerated depreciation deducted that exceeds the straight line depreciation rate (normally "recaptured" and taxed if there is a sale) is not taxed as ordinary income as it would be if a sale took place.

However, the depreciation recapture rules of Internal Revenue Code Section 1250 apply to an exchange unless the value of the property received by the taxpayer equals or exceeds the value attributable to the depreciable realty given up on the exchange. To illustrate, if you traded your depreciable building for raw nondepreciable land, recapture could occur.

DISPOSAL OF OTHERWISE UNSALABLE PROPERTY

Taxpayers can often trade a property that is unsalable, except at a loss to the owner, for one that is either more easily salable or more profitable to retain. This result is possible since price tags are often not used when making property trades. The owners of the two parcels suddenly avoid the need to "save face" when the dollar amounts become insignificant.

SOLUTION TO TIGHT MONEY MORTGAGE FINANCE PROBLEMS

When property buyers do not have cash, and mortgages are not easily available, an exchange of equity in an already-owned property can substitute for cash. Cash or a mortgage taken back by one of the traders can be added to balance the equities in the exchange.

INCREASED DEPRECIABLE BASIS

An exchange can increase the up trader's basis for depreciation deductions, such as a trade of land with a rental house on it for a commercial office building offering substantial improvements to depreciate. The basis of the larger property acquired in the trade will usually be the up trader's book value for the old property plus the value of any additional encumbrances (mortgages) on the acquired property. Perhaps a simpler way of computing basis for the up trader on his acquired property is to subtract from its trade value (usually the same as market value) the amount of the untaxed profit on the property relinquished in the trade up.

TAX-DEFERRED EQUITY PYRAMIDING

Tax-deferred exchanges offer the only method of pyramiding one's investment into larger holdings without paying profit tax along the way. For the down trader, an exchange can be a way to dispose of property without being boosted into a high tax bracket in the year of sale.

The down trade can be combined with an installment sale to spread out the tax over several years and to increase the down trader's profit from the interest earnings on the unpaid balance owed to the down trader on the larger building acquired by the up trader.

Another aspect of equity pyramiding involves consolidating several properties into one large property. Many investors, for example, start out by acquiring one or two investment properties per year. Eventually all these little properties become a management headache. So the investor can combine them all into a trade and exchange for a large investment building that is efficient to manage.

Still another angle to equity pyramiding involves fixing up run-down property, thereby increasing its market value by more than the cost of the improvements, and then trading up to a larger "fix up" property. This is the principle that Nickerson and Lowry advocate in their formula of fortune building.

REQUIREMENTS FOR TAX-DEFERRED EXCHANGES

To comply with the simple requirements of Internal Revenue Code Section 1031 is quite easy. In the last few years these rules have become easier to meet by virtue of liberal court decisions, including the well-known Starker cases and the new Briggs ruling.

TRADING UP TO A LARGER PROPERTY

Exchanges are tax-deferred only for the party trading up from a smaller to a larger property if no boot is received by the up trader. To qualify, it must be a direct trade or a delayed "Starker" or "Biggs" exchange. The up trader cannot first sell his property and then use the proceeds to buy a larger property without owing tax on his sale profit (unless a Starker-type delayed exchange is documented).

Frequently, however, the "seller" of the larger property in the trade does not want to keep the smaller building. After the exchange is completed, the party receiving the smaller property in the exchange can sell it to a third-party cash buyer in a "cash out sale." This will not affect the up trader's tax deferral. Such an exchange is called a "three-way" or "cash out" trade.

EVEN EXCHANGES

Sometimes two taxpayers will make an even exchange of one property for another, with no cash or mortgages used to balance the equities. This is done most frequently by businesses seeking property more suitable for their business needs. Or it may be done by individuals seeking property of a different type.

EXAMPLE: Tom owns a lot that is zoned for apartments. Mark, a contractor, has just completed a fourplex apartment house that Tom would like to own. Mark would like to own Tom's lot on which he can build another apartment house for profit. Mark's equity in the apartment house (because it has a large mortgage on it) equals Tom's free and clear equity in the lot. So an even exchange can be made. However, Mark is the down trader and he will owe profit tax on his boot (net mortgage relief) received. As a builder, this does not bother Mark because he expected to pay tax on his profit. A down trader such as Mark should be aware of this profit taxation problem whenever boot is received in an exchange.

DOWN TRADES DISPOSE OF PROPERTY EQUITY

Each tax-deferred property exchange usually involves an up trader (who defers paying tax on his profit since he receives no boot) and a down trader (who owes tax on his profit since he receives boot). Boot (unlike property), of course, is taxable.

But trading down can be an excellent way to liquidate holdings which may otherwise be too large to sell. Another advantage of trading down is it can be a great way to dispose of property very profitably, pay tax on that profit, and defer the rest of the tax by liquidating gradually instead of all in one tax year.

> EXAMPLE: Mary wishes to retire and be free to travel if she can sell her $600,000 apartment house. Her depreciated book value is only $100,000, which is approximately the value of the nondepreciable land. In other words, Mary has run out of depreciation deductions. If Mary sells for cash, however (assuming a cash buyer can be found), she will owe tax on a $500,000 long-term capital gain.
>
> Len owns a parking lot, free and clear, worth $300,000, which is leased to a trucking company. He wants to acquire income property that will give him tax shelter from depreciation tax loss (but with positive cash flow).
>
> Mary agrees to accept Len's parking lot $300,000 equity in trade on her apartment house. Len gives Mary a mortgage on the apartment house for the $300,000 balance. Since this is a trade down for Mary, she will owe tax on the boot (the $300,000 mortgage) received. But Mary's tax on this boot profit will be taxed as an installment sale as she receives the payments from Len in future years. Mary accomplishes her desire of gradual liquidation and freedom from property management so she can travel. Len acquires the depreciable building he wants so both traders are happy.

The same result could have been attained whether or not these properties had mortgages on them before the trade. If Mary should need tax-free cash before Len pays off the $300,000 mortgage, she can probably hypothecate her mortgage at her bank and borrow on the security of that mortgage. Or Mary could mortgage the parking lot, tax-free, if she prefers since loan proceeds are not taxable.

HOW TO CALCULATE BASIS
FOR THE PROPERTY ACQUIRED IN A TRADE

Basis from a property traded in a tax-deferred exchange carries over to the property acquired in the trade, with several important adjustments. These adjustments to basis are made only if boot is received or gain is recognized (basis is reduced by boot received and increased by gain recognized, that is, taxed, in the exchange).

ADD:

A—Original purchase price or basis, including any mortgage, land contract, or trust deed to finance the original purchase

B—Capital improvements made during the ownership period

C—Boot or other property paid to acquire the property traded up to

D—Special assessments paid (e.g. sidewalks, sewers, streets)

E—Recognized (taxed) gain on which tax was paid

MINUS:

A—Boot received (cash or other "unlike" property) in the trade

B—Any mortgage or trust deed remaining after the trade (net mortgage relief)

C—Depreciation deducted during ownership on the property traded

D—Any casualty loss deducted from basis during the ownership period

RESULT:

Basis for the property acquired in the exchange

But a much easier way to arrive at the basis of the property received in an up trade is to subtract from its market value the amount of deferred gain traded as down payment. This is then the up trader's basis for the property acquired in the exchange.

EXAMPLE: Robert's basis in a rental house is $33,000. It is worth $45,000 market value. Subtracting a realtor's commission of $2,000, he has $10,000 net profit. Robert trades this rental house for a $100,000 apartment building. Robert's new basis in the apartment house will be $100,000 minus his $10,000 deferred gain, which is $90,000.

To avoid receiving taxable boot, usually cash or net mortgage relief, in an exchange, the taxpayer trading up should refrain from refinancing the larger property as part of the exchange. Any refinancing should wait until after the exchange is completed. Or its "seller" can refinance before the trade if he needs cash. If the refinance is part of the exchange, the mortgage on the property being traded may be classified as boot. By exchanging the two properties "subject to" their existing mortgages and not refinancing in the trade, this problem is avoided.

A SUCCESSFUL FOUR-WAY TAX-DEFERRED EXCHANGE

As explained earlier, the primary motivation for tax-deferred exchanges is to defer profit tax on the smaller property being traded up for the larger one. But another major motivation for an exchange can be to dispose of difficult-to-sell property which the owner no longer wants. Here is an actual trade which satisfied the property needs of four traders.

OWNER #1 (George) wanted to retire. He owned an apartment house worth $415,000. For two years he tried to find a buyer for it. He was even willing to accept a 10 percent cash down payment and take back a large secondary mortgage for the balance. But due to the location in a low-income area, buyers with $41,500 chose to invest in better neighborhoods.

OWNER #2 (Alice) had $20,000 cash, plus $40,000 free and clear equity in a vacant city lot which cost her money for property taxes, weed clearing, and trash removal. The lot produced no income and was difficult to sell because of its location in a low-income neighborhood. Alice wanted income.

So she offered to trade her $60,000 ($20,000 cash plus $40,000 lot equity) "down payment" for George's $415,000 apartment house. Owner #1, George, accepted the exchange offer, subject to a "cash out sale" of the lot for $40,000 cash. For Alice this will be a tax-deferred exchange up. For George, it will be a down trade, and he will owe tax on the $60,000 cash boot he eventually received in the exchange and subsequent cash out sale. George will have an installment sale on the remainder of his profit as Owner #2, Alice, pays off the mortgage to him on the $415,000 apartment house.

OWNER #3 (Vic) wants to buy the vacant lot which is zoned for light industry. Vic wants to build a small industrial building for his growing kitchen cabinet manufacturing business. But Vic has no cash with which to buy the lot. However, he does have about $45,000 equity in a six-unit apartment house in a city about fifty miles away.

Vic offers to trade his equity in the six-unit apartment house for the lot. George accepts, contingent upon cash out sale of the six apartments to produce not less than $40,000 cash after paying the realty agent's commission. A cooperating realty broker in the distant city is given the listing, and within a month, he decides to personally buy the six apartments for $40,000 cash down payment.

RESULTS. All four parties are happy (and so are the realty agents who split over $25,000 of sales commissions). Owner #1, George, got rid of his apartment house so he could retire. Owner #2, Alice, got rid of her vacant lot and obtained an income-producing property. Owner #3, Vic, acquired a lot on which to construct his manufacturing building. Owner #4, the realty broker, acquired a six-unit apartment house that he later profitably resold.

As a sidelight, Alice was a seventy-three-year-old widow acquiring her first apartment house. Three years later she sold the large apartment building for $550,000 for $20,000 cash down payment on an installment sale which produces for her (or her heirs) about $1,600 monthly net income for the next twenty years.

DELAYED TAX-DEFERRED PROPERTY EXCHANGES—STARKER AND BIGGS CASES

In April, 1975, Judge Gus J. Solomon of the Oregon Federal District Court rendered his landmark Starker I decision (75–1 USTC 87142). That decision held that a tax-deferred exchange occurs even if the up trader does not yet own the second property to be acquired in the trade. This case adds to Revenue Ruling 75–291 which approves nonrecognition (nontaxation) of loss or gain even if the property to be acquired in the up trade is specifically bought for the purpose of exchanging it. The holding of Starker I, in other words, was that trading of the properties in a tax-deferred exchange need not take place simultaneously.

In Starker I, Bruce and Elizabeth Starker received a purchase offer for their Oregon timber land from Crown-Zellerbach and Longview Fibre Company. The Starkers agreed to the transaction, but they directed the buyers to hold the money in trust until the Starkers could locate a second property for Crown-Zellerbach and Longview to buy and then trade to the Starkers to complete the tax-deferred exchange.

Crown-Zellerbach and Longview were directed by the Starkers to buy eight parcels between 1968 and 1972. The IRS disallowed this transaction as a tax-deferred exchange. But Judge Solomon ruled it qualified for tax deferral under IRC 1031. The IRS, after originally filing an appeal, dropped the appeal for some unexplained reason.

But in May 1977, serious doubt was cast on the precedent value of Starker I. Judge Solomon rendered a contrary opinion in Starker II, involving Bruce's father, T. J. Starker (77–2 USTC 87675, 432 Fed. Supp. 864). But Judge Solomon's ruling in Starker II was reversed on appeal by the U.S. Court of Appeals for the Ninth Circuit (602 F.2d 1341). In Starker II, the appeals court approved the result of Starker I and allowed T. J. Starker to rely on it as precedent.

The facts of Starker II are important to understanding the new "delayed-exchange" concept. In 1967 T. J. Starker received an offer from Crown-Zellerbach Corporation to buy his 1,843 acres of Oregon timberland. Because Starker did not want to sell, but C-Z needed his land, C-Z agreed to find Starker other suitable properties and to trade these at a later date for the timberland that they immediately acquired. C-Z promised to hold the $1,502,500 timberland money in trust until Starker could find properties for C-Z to buy and then trade to Starker to complete the tax-deferred exchange. In addition, C-Z agreed to add a 6 percent annual "growth factor" to the value. By 1969 when Starker located all the properties, his credit had grown to $1,577,387.91.

In the Starker II decision, Judge Goodwin of the Court of Appeals for the Ninth Circuit ruled this "delayed exchange" qualified as a tax-deferred exchange under Internal Revenue Code Section 1031. But he said the 6 percent growth factor was taxable as interest in the year received.

However, Goodwin ruled this was not a tax-deferred trade as to two properties acquired by C-Z at Starker's direction, since he ordered them conveyed to his daughter, Jean Roth, instead of to Starker. But Goodwin ruled that tax-deferral applied to the other ten properties acquired by C-Z and then conveyed to Starker to complete the exchange.

STARKER OPENS NEW TRADING OPPORTUNITIES

Although the Starker cases open new trading opportunities, certain cautions apply. Of course, a real estate attorney should always be used to draft the documents that follow guidelines outlined in the Starker cases.

1. The contract must boldly express the taxpayer's desire for a tax-deferred exchange, not to receive cash for the purchase of his property.
2. If an interest or "growth factor" is charged on the proceeds being held in a trust arrangement, that looks like a sale rather than an exchange.
3. If the up trader has a right to receive the cash paid for his property instead of finding other property to complete the exchange, then the IRS auditor would have strong grounds for denying a tax-deferred trade. Leaving the money in an escrow, where the up trader has a right to claim his money at any time, clearly will not qualify. Some type of trust arrangement is required so the money is beyond the up trader's reach. Although this was not necessary because Crown-Zellerbach could be trusted to keep the money in the Starker cases, most traders are not dealing with such high-caliber buyers.
4. The seller's contract rights should be nonassignable (to block the IRS argument the transaction was really a sale rather than an exchange).
5. The 1984 Tax Act added the requirements that (a) the property to be acquired must be designated within 45 days after selling the old property and (b) it must be acquired within 180 days of the old property's sale.

Starker "delayed" exchanges are a rapidly developing new area of tax-deferred exchange law that makes exchanges easier than ever. The philosophy behind Starker exchanges is (a) a buyer wants to acquire a property now, (b) he is offering a good price and terms, (c) if the seller does not immediately accept the purchase offer, the buyer may not wait until the seller can find another property for a direct tax-deferred exchange, (d) it is better to attempt a Starker "delayed" exchange than to pay tax on an outright sale.

THE UNIQUE BIGGS CASE

In December 1980, the Court of Appeals for the Fifth Circuit (with authority in Alabama, Florida, Georgia, Louisiana, Mississippi, and Texas) ruled in the tax-deferred exchange case involving *Franklin B. Biggs* (632 F.2d 1171). Upholding the tax court's approval of a tax-deferred exchange, the appeals court further liberalized the exchange concept.

The facts in the Biggs case, greatly simplified, involved a Maryland tract of land that Biggs wanted to exchange for a Virginia parcel. Biggs had a buyer for the Maryland land, Mr. Powell. But Powell apparently either would not or could not acquire the Virginia land to trade to Biggs for the Maryland land. So Biggs loaned the Shore Title Company money to acquire the Virginia land, which was then traded to Biggs for his Maryland land. After the trade, the Maryland land was deeded to Powell (who then immediately resold the Maryland land at a substantial profit).

The issue was whether this qualified as a tax-deferred exchange because (a) Powell never had title to the Virginia land, and (b) Biggs supplied the cash with which the Virginia land was purchased by Shore Title so it could be traded to Biggs.

Frankly, the documentation was very sloppy in this case because the wording used terms of "sale" rather than "exchange." A few commentators feel this case means "anything goes" as long as it looks like an exchange after the smoke clears. But more rational commentators believe the Biggs case (a) means indirect deeding in an exchange is all right, (b) it must be clear that the exchanger at no time had a right to receive cash proceeds from the exchange, and (c) advance of funds by the exchanger to a fourth party to acquire the property to be acquired in the trade is all right.

At the least, the Biggs case strengthens the Starker concept of a delayed tax-deferred exchange. Simultaneous, direct deeding of the properties is clearly no longer required to qualify for a IRC 1031 tax-deferred trade. Although Biggs was successful in deferring his profit tax, future exchangers are cautioned to use careful documentation prepared by a real estate or tax attorney to make sure an exchange can be proven, if necessary, to the IRS.

SUMMARY

Tax-deferred exchanges are the only way for owners of investment, trade, or business property to dispose of one property and acquire another such "like-kind" property without paying tax on their profit. Such trades have become more flexible since the Starker and Biggs court decisions, but the requirements of Internal Revenue Code Section 1031 must still be met. In this area of real estate transactions, assistance of an experienced real estate or tax attorney is essential to avoid adverse tax consequences.

QUESTIONS AND ANSWERS

Q. You've said the best way to avoid paying tax when disposing of investment property is to make a "tax-deferred exchange" for a larger such property. As we own a four-family apartment building with about $40,000 equity, how can we use such a trade to get a bigger apartment house without paying tax on our profit of about $25,000?—*Gwinn A.*

A. Virtually the only way to dispose of investment or business property without paying profit tax is to make a tax-deferred exchange as authorized by Internal Revenue Code Section 1031.

For example, suppose your apartment building is worth $100,000 and you owe $60,000 on the mortgage. Your equity is therefore $40,000. If you sell outright, you would pay tax on your $25,000 profit. But if you trade your $40,000 equity as down payment on a larger "like-kind" investment property, you defer the tax until the acquired property is sold without trading again.

As you can see, exchanging is an excellent way to pyramid a small equity into a fortune, all without any tax erosion along the way. However, you cannot take any "boot" out of the trade. Boot means "unlike property," such as cash or net mortgage relief.

If you trade for a larger property owned for investment or use in your trade or business (called an "up trade"), it should be tax-deferred for you. The down trader, however, will owe tax on all or part of his profit. Work with a good realty exchange specialist who can show you how to make your exchange work, usually by use of a three-way (three-party) trade where a third-party cash buyer purchases your property after you make the tax-deferred exchange.

HOW TO PYRAMID YOUR PROPERTY PROFIT
WITHOUT PAYING TAX

Q. We own some farmland for which we have received an excellent purchase offer. But the tax on our profit would be huge. I recall your saying it is possible to exchange properties without paying any tax. Please explain how that might work for us. We would like to acquire some property that would produce tax shelter and income, such as a small shopping center or maybe apartments.—*Bennie S.*

A. You are an excellent candidate for a tax-deferred "like-kind" property exchange. For example, suppose your farmland is worth $500,000. You can make a tax-deferred trade of it for any other property, except a personal residence, worth $500,000 or more if you do not take any "boot" out of the trade. Boot includes personal property such as cash or net mortgage relief.

Your exchange would work like this. You trade your farmland for, perhaps, a small shopping center of equal or greater value. But your farmland would be traded subject to the purchase offer you have for it. One minute after your tax-deferred exchange is completed, the other trader can sell your farmland for cash to the third-party buyer you already have lined up. It is called a three-way exchange because there are three parties involved.

By means of tax-deferred trades, you can pyramid your farmland equity into a fortune without having your profit eroded by income taxes. See your tax adviser for details.

HOW TO FIND REALTY AGENTS
WHO LIKE TO TRADE PROPERTIES

Q. I've enjoyed your explanations of tax-deferred exchanges. As I own a two-family rental house that I would like to trade, tax-deferred, for a larger income property, where can I find a realty agent who understands exchanging? I've talked to several, and they tell me exchanging isn't done here.—*Wendy T.*

A. Tax-deferred property trades are made in large and small towns throughout the country. Some realty agents are afraid of exchanges because they have not bothered to educate themselves about them. A sale is much easier, of course. But wise agents prefer exchanges because two commissions are involved.

One way to find local property exchange specialists is to phone your local board of realtors for a roster of their exchange club members. Another way is to contact real estate brokers who specialize in commercial properties; these firms usually have real estate exchange specialists.

NO TIME LIMIT ON STARKER EXCHANGE TIME LAG

Q. Your report on the new Starker "delayed-exchange" concept was very educational. What is the time limit from the day the first property is sold until the second property must be acquired to complete the tax-deferred Starker exchange?—*Betty W.*

A. The 1984 Tax Act set a 180-day maximum time limit. Basically, the Starker decision of the Court of Appeals for the Ninth Circuit held it is possible to defer profit tax when selling one property if the proceeds of that sale are held in a trust arrangement beyond the reach of the seller. The trustee can then be directed by that seller to buy a second property with that money and deliver the title to the up trader.

The Starker exchange time lag is only 180 days. But both properties must be held for investment or for use in a trade or business. Keep your personal residence out of such exchanges. Your tax adviser can explain further.

HOW TO BUILD YOUR PYRAMID OF TAX-DEFERRED REAL ESTATE PROFITS

Q. At a dinner last week, the man next to me said it is possible to "pyramid" real estate profits, tax-free, by trading up from a small property into larger ones. He tried to explain the concept to me, but I don't understand. You explain real estate so well; please explain realty pyramids to me.—*Sonnie M.*

A. Internal Revenue Code Section 1031 encourages tax-deferred, "like-kind" real estate exchanges. The basic idea is to trade your equity in a small property as down payment on a larger one. After the second property's equity grows, often due to improvements that increase value more than they cost, then the second property can be traded for a larger investment property. The profit tax can again be deferred. It is called pyramiding. There is no limit to the number of times this tax concept can be used in a chain of tax-deferred exchanges.

Advantages of tax-deferred property trades include no income tax erosion, increased tax deductions from depreciation of larger properties, and tax-deferred estate building.

To qualify for a "like-kind," tax-deferred exchange, both properties must be held for investment or for use in your trade or business. In other words, your personal residence and personal property cannot qualify. Trades are usually tax-deferred for the "up trader" if he receives no "boot," such as cash or net mortgage relief. Your tax adviser or realty exchange specialist can give you further details.

HOW CAN I TRADE MY HOME FOR APARTMENTS?

Q. You wrote that a tax-deferred exchange applies only to "like-kind" properties, such as apartments and commercial buildings. Is there any way I can trade the equity in my home, about $65,000, for income property? —*Corla S.*

A. Yes. Your personal residence is "unlike property," which cannot qualify for a tax-deferred exchange if you wish to acquire investment or business property.

But you can convert your home into "like-kind" property by (1) moving out and (2) renting it to tenants. The law does not specify how long you must rent it to tenants. Just to be safe, six to twelve months should be adequate. Then trade your home for the income property you want to acquire. If you trade up to more-expensive investment or business property, without receiving any taxable boot in the exchange, it will be a tax-deferred exchange for you.

10.

How Realty Brokers Can Help Accomplish Your Real Estate Goals

Real estate agents have the best job in the world—and they know it. They have the opportunity for unlimited earnings, freedom to work as hard or as little as they want, flexible working hours, and nonroutine work. But there are drawbacks too, such as peaks and valleys in their commission earnings (also called feast or famine), frequent evening and weekend working hours, and intense competition with other agents.

The quality of real estate agents has vastly improved in the last few years. Real estate sales attracts the finest people you will ever meet. But it also attracts some of the sleaziest characters too, probably because it is possible to earn a handsome income without working too hard. Real estate, due to its financial structure, opens doors to all types of "innovative finance," some of which is not completely honest.

In other words, do not put blind trust in a real estate agent. Make them back up their statements unless they are just expressing their opinions, such as "I think this is the best neighborhood in town." But if the agent says "This house is in perfect condition," that is a statement you should have in writing signed by the agent and the seller, just in case it is not true.

REAL ESTATE AGENTS ARE THE PROPERTY INVESTOR'S BEST FRIENDS

By virtue of their daily contacts, realty agents know who is buying and selling. The top agents keep files of buyers and sellers of specialized properties. It is not unusual for a good agent, when he learns of a new listing, to sell it within twenty-four hours to a buyer he knows will buy that type of property. A quick sale like that can save the seller hundreds, sometimes thousands of dollars, in carrying costs.

Buying through real estate agents costs the buyer no more than if he purchased direct from the seller. The reason is the market value of a property is determined from recent sales prices of similar nearby properties. Since the buyer is going to pay market value anyway, he might as well get all the extra services provided by a realty agent.

To understand better how to work with realty agents, let us view the situation from the perspective of a home seller. Later, tips on how buyers can effectively work with realty agents will be explained.

HOW TO SELL YOUR HOME WITH OR WITHOUT A REAL ESTATE AGENT

Selling your residence, whether it is a single-family home, condominium, mobile home, or even a houseboat is the greatest profit opportunity you will probably ever have. But home sellers must be careful not to make costly mistakes that can cut into their resale profit. Thousands of dollars can be lost when selling property if it is not done right.

GETTING YOUR HOME READY FOR SALE

When you go to your job each day, or when you go out for a special event such as a party or dinner, you prepare. You probably take a bath, brush your teeth, and put on clean clothes. Getting your home ready for sale is a similar process that also requires preparation. The goal is to present your home at its best. Just as an actor or actress wants to show his or her talent in a play or movie, your home should give its best appearance when you present it for sale to prospective buyers.

Painting and cleaning a home for sale is the cheapest, yet most profitable, step to take before putting your home on the market for sale. Get it in top condition. Perhaps even invite your mother-in-law or other supercritical person to inspect it and to make suggestions for fixing it up for sale.

Home buyers have remarkably little imagination. They often cannot visualize how desirable a home can look after it is painted and fixed up. That is why you, the seller, must make the home look its best to help the buyer visualize how desirable your home can be.

Even though the buyer may not like your choice of colors, and will probably repaint shortly after buying your home, having your home appear at its best will command top sales price and terms. A home that is in bad condition invites buyers to look for defects, thus hurting your negotiating power on sale price and terms. Many potential buyers will not even make purchase offers on a home that is in less than first class condition.

The idea is to make your home physically so attractive that its condition will not be objectionable to any buyer. *If you do not fix up your home before sale, it will appeal to only a very limited market of buyers.*

Those buyers are the bargain hunters—also known as the forty thieves!

They buy only at rock bottom prices. But if the home is dirty and in bad condition, these are the only buyers it will appeal to.

Within reason, correct all significant defects in your home before putting it up for sale. For example, new gutters make buyers confident of the home's structural integrity. But leaky gutters cast doubt on the building's entire condition by indicating the owner probably has not maintained the home very well.

BUT DON'T GO OVERBOARD! Overimprovement for the level of homes in the neighborhood will not pay off. To illustrate, adding a $20,000 swimming pool to a home in a working-class area of two-bedroom, one-bathroom homes in the $75,000 price range probably will not produce a high enough additional sales price to even pay for the pool's cost.

FIX-UP COST TAX BENEFITS

In Chapter 3, the "residence replacement rule" and the home sale fix-up cost myth were explained. Just for emphasis, it should be remembered that costs of fixing up your principal residence for sale, contrary to popular myth, never qualify as itemized income tax deductions. The only tax benefit for fix-up costs (home cleaning, painting, and repairing costs that normally have no income tax significance because they are personal living expenses) occurs when selling your old principal residence and buying a less-expensive replacement within eighteen months before or after the sale.

Home sale fix-up costs, as emphasized in Chapter 3, will never eliminate any profit tax. But they can postpone the time of tax payment if a less-expensive replacement principal residence is purchased. If a more-expensive replacement is bought, the tax is postponed anyway, with or without the fix-up cost expenses. Such fix-up expenses must (a) be incurred within ninety days before signing the home sale agreement (not the listing but the sales contract) and (b) be paid for within thirty days after the sale closing.

Of course, capital improvement costs, such as for a new furnace, new roof, or new wall-to-wall carpets, should be capitalized and added to your home's purchase price cost basis. Save the receipts forever!

HOW TO DETERMINE YOUR HOME'S FAIR MARKET VALUE

After your home is all spruced up, looking its best, and ready for sale, the issue becomes "How much is my home worth?"

The answer is determined from the local real estate market. Recent sales prices for similar homes in your neighborhood determine the price at which a willing buyer will buy your home, assuming you are under no urgent pressure to sell for less than its fair market value. Generally, homes need to be exposed to the marketplace for at least ninety days.

They should sell within this time at their true market value.

Home prices are based on fair market value, as determined by recent sales prices of comparable neighborhood homes. Your home's value is *not* based on (1) how much you think it is worth, (b) how much you need to get to make a good profit, (3) how much you have invested in the home, or (4) how much you need to get from the home to pay your other expenses.

For example, although the home next door to yours is different, if both your home and the one next door have three bedrooms, two bathrooms, and six rooms, and the one next door sold last month for $100,000, your home is probably worth about the same amount, with adjustments higher or lower for any significant differences in features or condition.

There are two excellent methods of determining your home's fair market value.

A. Professional Appraisal of Fair Market Value

An appraisal of a home's fair market value is an expert appraiser's opinion of its probable sales price, based on recent sales prices of similar neighborhood homes (or your home's replacement cost, minus depreciation, if it is of unusual design and there are no comparables available).

Professional appraisals cost from $100 to $200 for an average home and are especially recommended for home sellers considering selling without the professional services of a real estate agent. Local banks and savings associations can usually recommend experienced residential appraisers. Be sure to select an appraiser with home appraisal experience.

But remember that an appraisal is only an expert's opinion of your home's value, so be sure to hire an appraiser familiar with recent residential sales in your area. Be sure to tell the appraiser you want a thorough, written appraisal that you can show to prospective buyers and real estate agents.

B. Comparative Market Analysis

Another method of determining your home's market value is to invite several active local real estate agents to give you their listing presentation. Most realty agents will be happy to prepare a free written "comparative market analysis" showing recent neighborhood home sales prices, including the home's size, sale price, and terms. Of course, they hope to get your listing by doing this work for you. Any agent who does not prepare such a written analysis should probably be dismissed from your listing competition.

A comparative market analysis will show not only recent sales prices (not listing prices), but also current asking prices of unsold homes available for sale (your competition).

THE ASKING PRICE SETTING PROCEDURE

Setting the asking price for a home is critical. Set it too low, and you have lost part of what could have been profit. Set it too high, and your home will remain unsold for a long time. Costs of holding an unsold home add up quickly, especially if you have already bought another home and are making payments on two homes at the same time.

Home buyers are not dumb. They are hard to fool. That is because they know home values by comparative shopping. Many potential buyers have been looking for months and have inspected dozens of homes for sale. Some know more about market value of local homes than do realty agents who do not keep up with recent sales prices.

Although it is considered good practice to set your home's asking price a little above the price you expect to accept (to allow room for negotiation on terms), setting the price too high repels buyers who will not even inspect an overpriced home. Setting the asking price about 5 percent above the price you expect to accept will not normally discourage buyers from inspecting your home and making a purchase offer if they like it.

HOW TO DECIDE WHETHER OR NOT TO HIRE A REAL ESTATE AGENT TO MARKET YOUR HOME

Most home sellers are confronted with the question of whether or not to use a real estate agent to market their home. The main reason for not using an agent, of course, is to save the sales commission. On a typical home sale at $75,000, for example, the average 6 percent sales commission saving is $4,500. Or is it?

Nationwide, home mortgage lenders report an average of eleven mortgage loans made on sales arranged by realty agents for every mortgage on a "for sale by owner" (FSBO) home sale. There must be reasons why eleven out of twelve home sellers use real estate agents. Yet there are some home sellers who have no need to use a real estate agent to market their home. Consider the pros and cons of hiring an agent or not.

SETTING THE SALES PRICE

Even if you obtained a professional appraisal of your home's market value, it pays to double-check it. The appraiser may not have been fully aware of a rapidly appreciating or declining local market which even the best real estate agents, frankly, have difficulty anticipating.

Therefore, every home seller should invite at least three local realty agents to evaluate his home's value, using the "comparative market analysis" approach. Select agents whose "sold" signs or newspaper advertising in your area attracted your attention. Do not, however, be "snowed" by the fancy ads of some nationwide franchise organizations that, after all, depend on locally owned independent offices and the services of their local realty agents.

Invite these three or more agents to "bid" on listing your home. Tell them frankly you are undecided about listing your home with an agent. Explain that you want their opinion of your home's market value *and why!* Any agent who cannot or will not explain how your home's estimated sales price was computed should not be seriously considered further. That means disregarding any agent who does not give you a written market value analysis.

Ask about the marketing services each agent will offer if he or she gets your listing. Ask for references of at least three previous clients from each agent and check them out by phone. Ask the client references "Would you list your home for sale again with this agent?" Do not be afraid of young or new agents—sometimes they are very eager to succeed and will work twice as hard as a salesperson who has been very successful in realty sales and who now is taking life easy.

After interviewing at least three realty agents, and checking their client references, then decide (a) if you can handle the sale of your home without a realty agent, and (b) if you elect to list with an agent, list with the best (not necessarily the agent who estimates the highest sales price). Here are the factors to consider in making your decision whether or not to hire an agent:

A. Advertising

Are you prepared to write newspaper want ads about your home? How much will the advertising cost? Who will answer the phone? What information will be given out on the phone? What time will inspections be allowed? Will you have to take off work to accommodate a prospective buyer who wants to see your home? Will you hold weekend open houses? Are you familiar with Regulation Z (Truth in Lending) limitations on advertising finance terms, such as down payment, interest rate, mortgage amount, and other finance conditions? Are you going to have a lawn "for sale by owner" (FSBO) sign? How can you effectively compete with the many homes agents have in the multiple listing service since you have only one home to sell?

B. Financing

Are you familiar with current available mortgage finance terms? FHA? VA? State mortgage programs? Installment sale benefits? Purchase-money mortgage terms to be included in any seller financing? Land contract benefits and pitfalls? Existing mortgage payoff and prepayment penalty, if any? How large should the earnest money deposit be? Should the current mortgage be assumed or should the house be sold "subject to" its existing mortgage?

C. Can You Write a Legally Binding Contract?

Are you prepared to negotiate the sale price and terms in face-to-face negotiations with the buyer? Do you or other family members become upset easily, especially when involved in financial matters? Are you aware how many bargain-hunters prey on "for sale by owner" (FSBO) sellers? Can you draw up a legally binding sales contract? Do you have an attorney who has advised you on essential terms to include? Can you qualify your buyer to be sure he can really afford to buy your home and is not wasting your time?

D. Sale Terms and Conditions

Are you able to negotiate with a buyer regarding sales terms, such as financing, who pays title insurance, transfer tax, escrow fee, attorney fee, fire insurance premium, and other negotiable costs? What about property tax proration, move-in date, rental for hold-over occupancy, personal property items included and excluded, hidden defects in the home that buyer must be told about, and title transfer date?

E. Urgency

Is a rapid sale necessary to avoid paying for two homes at the same time, or due to an out-of-town job transfer?

F. Security

Can you screen out potential troublemakers and even thieves from the serious buyers? Can the home be shown at any time or only when you are not at work? How can you know if the person ringing the doorbell for an inspection is a serious buyer or a curiosity seeker?

G. Closing the Sale

Are you familiar with local title settlement closing procedures? Is an attorney necessary? Will the lender require title insurance? An abstract? Escrow? How will the documents be recorded, loan papers processed, old loans paid off, and liens cleared?

A FINAL WORD ON SELLING YOUR HOME ALONE

Lawyers have a motto: "He who is his own lawyer has a fool for a client." That same wisdom may apply to home sellers who try to sell their own home without professional marketing help from a real estate agent. One costly mistake can cost a home seller far more than the sales commission he thought he was saving by selling his own home.

HOW TO MARKET YOUR INVESTMENT PROPERTY

Selling a home is easy compared to marketing investment or business property. The reason is smart investors do not sell their property, they exchange it to avoid having to pay tax on their profit.

As emphasized in Chapter 9, tax-deferred exchanges are much easier to make than they previously were. No longer are direct, simultaneous exchanges required. Delayed "Starker exchanges" and "Biggs exchanges" are now available. But they require the assistance of a real estate or tax attorney who know how to document delayed exchanges. Such exchanges also require the services of a real estate agent who understands the mechanics of Starker and Biggs exchanges.

Frankly, finding these experts for the legal and marketing aspects of tax-deferred exchanges is not easy. Realty agents who handle residential sales are not qualified, in most cases, to handle tax-deferred exchanges, but they can often recommend exchange specialists who understand the procedures for both direct and delayed tax-deferred exchanges.

Locating a real estate or tax attorney to handle the documentation can be equally difficult because most attorneys have never heard of Starker or Biggs exchanges. One good method for finding such an attorney, in addition to asking for recommendations from realty agents and exchange specialists, is to check with local universities and community colleges offering real estate law or taxation courses. The instructor of those classes is usually a part-time instructor and a full-time real estate or tax attorney who thoroughly understands tax-deferred exchanges.

Real estate agents can accomplish miracles for property owners and buyers in the investment field. But investment or commercial specialists are a different breed from the typical residential salesperson. If you are involved with investment property, such as apartments, offices, and other commerical property, it is best to work with a specialist in that field because most residential sales agents are not qualified to handle commercial sales too.

QUESTIONS AND ANSWERS

BE CAREFUL OF REALTY AGENT'S OPINION STATEMENTS

Q. Were we swindled? We bought a house that the realty agent said was "in tip-top condition?" After we moved in, we found the cement foundation had a bad crack which cost us over $4,000 to have rebuilt. Do you think we should sue the agent for his misrepresentation?—*Eve C.*

A. See your attorney. Remarks by real estate agents, such as "This is the best house on the block" are usually just opinion statements that carry no legal liability. But if the agent misrepresents the house intentionally, then the agent is liable for resulting damage.

For example, if the agent says "This house has all copper pipes," and it doesn't, the agent is liable for damages. But if he says "I think the plumbing is in good condition," that is probably just an opinion statement which incurs no legal liability.

ARE LISTING CANCELLATION FEES NORMAL?

Q. We want to cancel the listing on our home as we've decided not to sell after all. Our agent says there is a $400 "cancellation fee" for his expenses and time. I recall several months ago you told another reader to just let her listing quietly expire when she changed her mind about selling. Do we have to pay the cancellation fee?—*Alan A.*

A. No. Some realty brokers charge listing cancellation fees to discourage sellers from changing their minds. But if you take my suggestion and quietly let your listing expire, you owe nothing to the listing agent.

Of course, if he brings you a purchase offer which exactly meets the listing terms and if you do not accept that offer, then you will owe the agent the full sales commission. But this is highly unlikely. Ask your attorney to explain further.

REALTY SALES COMMISSION SAVING CAN CAUSE NET LOSS

Q. As I was reading your article about the benefits of selling a home with a real estate agent's help, I thought of my former neighbor who felt she saved the realty commission by selling her home without any agent. Her attorney handled the whole transaction for a fee of about $700, she told me. Although I didn't say anything, I know my neighbor sold her home for at least $7,000 below the going rate for neighborhood homes at the time. Your explanation does an excellent job of laying out the pros and cons of selling one's home without any agent.—*Scottie M.*

A. Thank you for the compliment. People who sell their property without a realty agent, of course, save the real estate sales commission. But that saving often results in a net loss, as you emphasize, because they sell too cheaply. There are many other pitfalls of selling without professional marketing help, especially in today's unusual real estate sales market.

WHY SOME LAWYERS ARE KNOWN AS "DEAL KILLERS"

Q. Do you think we should have a lawyer advise us on the sale of our home? The realty agent who will be getting our listing strongly advises against also hiring a lawyer. We told her we wanted our lawyer to advise us. I had the feeling the agent was trying to keep us away from our lawyer's office. Do we need a lawyer?—*Ken L.*

A. Lawyers can perform valuable services in advising on the legal aspects of a property sale. But be sure your lawyer advises only on the law, not on the marketing aspects of the sale, or you will get into a hopeless conflict with your realty agent.

Unfortunately, unless a lawyer specializes in real estate law, he may not have kept up to date on changes in realty law and customs. Another problem is that some of my fellow lawyers give low priority to real estate sales transactions since the "big money" is in other fields such as personal injury and business law. Lastly, a few lawyers feel they must justify their fees, so they nit-pick and find minor objections which result in the sale not closing.

If you have a lawyer who understands real estate law, he or she can be of great assistance in a realty transaction. To test the lawyer on his real estate knowledge, ask for an explanation of how a "Starker exchange" and a "Biggs exchange" works. If the lawyer cannot explain those important cases to you in simple language in less than five minutes, find another lawyer.

HOW TO AVOID OVERPRICING
OR UNDERPRICING YOUR HOME FOR SALE

Q. We want to put our home up for sale. There is a nice real estate lady who stops by about once a month with a little real estate newsletter. We are thinking of giving her our listing. Last time I saw her I asked how much she thought our house was worth. She says she's sure she can get us at least $97,000. How can I be certain this price isn't too low?—*Sara I.*

A. The best way to avoid overpricing or underpricing your home is to invite at least three active local realty agents to give you their listing presentations. A major part of their explanation should be a written "comparative market analysis" prepared by each agent.

This form will show you in black and white the recent sales prices of similar nearby homes and the selling terms. Each agent will then help you add or subtract value, depending on your home's advantages and drawbacks, to arrive at an estimate of its current market value. Only by having at least three of these market analysis forms from different agents can you be sure each agent used the most recent and accurate sales price data.

Another approach is to hire a professional appraiser to estimate your home's current market value.

When you talk to the agents, be sure to ask for client references of previous sellers. Before listing with any agent, phone those previous sellers to ask "Would you list your home with that agent again?" and "Were you in any way unhappy with the agent's service?"

WILL RECESSION MEAN FALLING HOME PRICES?

Q. Do you think home sales prices will drop soon? I ask because we are considering selling our present home and buying a larger one for our growing family. If you think prices will drop, maybe we should sell now and wait until prices drop to buy a new home. In the meantime, we could rent.—*Kevin T.*

A. In the 1974–1975 recession, home prices did not drop in most communities. Due to continuing demand for homes, especially from the forty-two million new potential home buyers who will reach age thirty in the 1980s, plus the rapidly increasing numbers of single-person households, I do not expect any significant home sale price decreases now.

If mortgage interest rates drop a little, buyers will come out of the woodwork. This increasing demand, with a limited supply of homes for sale, especially in areas where home-building volume has dropped, should result in rising prices for homes.

To summarize, buy now before prices go higher. You should be able to get a good price for your home if you "package" it right with affordable financing for your buyer.

HOW TO FIND THE SECOND-BEST REALTY AGENT IN TOWN

Q. I want to sell my former home in the city where I used to live. As I only know one real estate agent there, I'm wondering the best way to go about the sale. My friend works for a tiny realty brokerage. I really don't have much confidence in her sales ability as she only works part-time. How should I select a real estate agent to sell my old home, which is now rented to a tenant?—*Wes M.*

A. Before you list your home for sale, ask your tenant if he would like to buy. He is your most logical buyer.

But if he does not want to buy, phone your agent friend. Ask her to inspect your house and give you a written "comparative market analysis" of its value. Then ask her for the names of the second- and third-best real estate salespeople in town.

Phone them and ask them to also give you a market analysis showing your home's value and why you should list it for sale with them. Ask all three agents for reference names of former sellers. Then phone those clients to inquire if they would list with their agent again.

Spending a few dollars on phone bills is a cheap way to select the best agent to sell your old home. By the way, do not be suckered by the agent who estimates the highest sales price. Select the agent with the best success record. All things being equal, steer away from part-time realty agents as they usually cannot give you first class service on your listing.

LISTINGS CREATE SPECIAL DUTIES FOR REALTY AGENTS

Q. About four months ago, we listed our home for sale with a real estate agent we thought was reputable. Since then we have hardly heard from her, except just before the listing was about to expire. Then she held two weekend open houses and advertised our home in the newspaper twice. We have been very disappointed. Through a friend we heard our agent discouraged several prospects from making offers on our home. We now realize our asking price is a little high, but we followed our agent's advice on this. What should we do to get our home sold?—*Vivian M.*

A. When you signed that listing with your real estate agent, special duties were created by that contract. Your agent undertook to use "due diligence" to find a buyer for your home. She also undertook to inform you of all "material facts" which develop during the listing term.

Material facts include purchase offers that prospective buyers wish to make. Ask your agent about those alleged offers. All offers, no matter how ridiculous, must be presented to sellers during the listing term. Failure to present all offers is a violation of the principal-agent listing contract and grounds to revoke the agent's license.

But a listing is a two-way contract. You, the seller, have a duty to keep your agent informed of all material facts that develop, such as change in the home's condition or your desire to reduce the asking price.

It is possible the agent overestimated your home's market value. Perhaps she was using old data of comparable sales prices of nearby similar homes. Or maybe the local market was rising, and she anticipated a further price rise which did not materialize.

While 99 percent of all real estate agents do a satisfactory job for their clients, it appears your agent is doing less than her best. When your listing expires, switch to a better agent. But check that agent's client references thoroughly. Before listing, ask the new agent's last three sellers if they would list their home for sale with that agent again.

READER SHOUTS PRAISES FOR MULTIPLE LISTINGS

Q. Why don't you ever mention all the benefits of multiple listings? We listed our home for sale last spring with a realty agent who has several offices. She said she doesn't like to use the multiple listing exchange because her firm has so many salespeople it sells most of its listings within the company. But our house didn't sell. When the listing expired we switched to another agent who works in a small office of only four salespeople. He put our exclusive listing into the multiple listing exchange, and within a week another agent from another realty company sold our home to his buyer. You ought to tell people about the benefits of using the multiple listings which didn't cost us anything extra.—*Grace M.*

A. Many times I have encouraged home sellers to insist their realty agent use the multiple listing service. The multiple listing exchange distributes listings to all member realty agents who may have buyers waiting to buy particular types of properties.

The reason a few realty agents are reluctant to use the multiple listing service is they earn a bigger share of the sales commission if the sale is made by two salespeople who work for the same firm. I believe this is not in the best interests of the seller because nonuse of multiple listings limits the seller's market exposure of the home, as you found out. Thanks for your letter telling of your good results from using the multiple listing service.

REALTY AGENTS MUST PRESENT EVEN RIDICULOUS OFFERS

Q. You're always telling home buyers to "make an offer." That's what we've been trying to do as we badly want to buy a home. Two realty agents who showed us homes we wanted to buy have refused to write up the purchase offers we wanted to make. One said he knew the seller wouldn't accept our offer, as she had turned down a better one. The other agent said the seller had to have more cash than we were offering. Isn't there some law about this?—*Marcos M.*

A. Yes. Real estate agents represent the property seller. To carry out their agency relationship, all offers must be presented to the seller, no matter how ridiculous the offer may appear to that agent.

Just last week a real estate saleswoman told me of a ridiculous offer she presented to a home seller. The buyers, a young couple with very good jobs but little cash for a down payment, offered $1,000 down payment on a house priced just over $100,000. Their offer provided for seller financing with monthly payments of $2,000 per month (which the couple can afford). Guess what happened? The seller accepted. The realty agent agreed to take a promissory note, secured by a third mortgage on the house, for her sales commission payable at $200 per month.

If that agent had not written up and presented that offer, nothing would have happened. But the happy result was a house was sold, the buyers bought their first home, and the realty agent will have a steady commission income until her note is paid in full.

Insist your purchase offer be written and presented to the seller. If the agent refuses, report the incident to the state real estate commissioner who may revoke the agent's license for failure to properly represent the seller.

IS THE REALTY AGENT THE SELLER'S OR BUYER'S AGENT?

Q. In a recent article you said "most realty sales involve two salespersons, one representing the seller and one representing the buyer." I disagree. In the usual transaction, the real estate broker who takes the listing from the owner becomes the agent of the owner. This also applies to salespersons working for that broker as well as cooperating brokers and salespeople (who become subagents). Unfortunately, too many agents give the impression they represent the buyer when, in truth, they are the seller's agent and owe their primary loyalty to him.—*Paul M.*

A. You are absolutely correct. I did not intend to imply otherwise. Real estate brokers are agents of the property owner who lists the property for sale. The owner is the principal, and the broker is the agent. Cooperating brokers and their salespeople who have a buyer for the property, as you emphasize, are subagents for the seller.

The status of the buyer, however, is unclear. Some courts have held him to be a third-party beneficiary of the principal-agent listing contract. Others simply say the realty broker and any subagent owe the buyer the same duty of honesty and full disclosure that is owed to the seller.

Since this can lead to conflicts of interest, some realty brokers have a policy of never allowing the same salesperson to work on behalf of both buyer and seller in a transaction.

To summarize, the realty broker is the property seller's agent. Cooperating brokers and salespeople who may have a buyer for the property are subagents of the listing broker. But these subagents must be just as honest with the buyer as they must be with the seller.

SHOULD REALTY AGENTS SNOOP INTO HOME BUYER'S FINANCES?

Q. We've just started looking for a home to buy. Every realty agent we talk to starts out by asking "How much to you want to invest?" Our reply is "As little as possible." Then the agent usually says something like "How much do you earn?" or "How much can you afford for monthly mortgage payments?" Isn't this pretty snoopy? Or is this customary for realty agents to probe this personal information?—*Dave N.*

A. Those snoopy real estate agents are trying to save your time and theirs. In the "good old days," realty agents used to waste time showing prospects homes they could not afford to buy. Today, wise realty agents cut the preliminaries and get down to business fast.

Chances are you cannot afford to buy the type of home you really want. Agents probe your financial situation, so that you will be shown only houses you can afford to buy.

Be honest with your agent. Tell him or her what you earn and how much you have to invest in the down payment. If you are short of cash for a down payment, do not hide this fact from your agent. There are dozens of ways to buy a home with little or no cash. Not every home can be bought this way, of course, but smart agents know which listings are good candidates for low or no down payments.

A probing realty agent also wants to find out if you are eligible for special home finance programs such as VA, FHA, or special state and federal mortgage programs. Asking questions is the only way the agent can learn this information. Some agents may seem snoopy, but they are just trying to help.

GET REALTY AGENT'S PROMISES IN WRITING

Q. We recently bought a condominium apartment that we like very much. The location, size, and price are ideal. Our problem is the salesman promised us things like new kitchen appliances, new carpets, and fresh paint. As we were in a hurry to move in, he said these things would be arranged later. It has been seven months since we moved in, and the work hasn't been started. The salesman has moved away, but the seller is still around. He says he knows nothing about these promises. What can we do to get these promised improvements?—*Cornelia G.*

A. See your attorney. Misrepresentations are hard to prove without some written agreement. If the seller's salesman made promises, those promises may be binding on the seller if you can prove the details.

Were there any witnesses? If not, you may have a tough time convincing a judge or jury. Next time, get all promises in writing as if you expect to wind up in court. If you are well prepared, then everything usually turns out fine.

COOPERATION AMONG REALTY AGENTS MEANS MORE PROPERTY SALES

Q. I am a novice real estate saleswoman, as I've had my license only four months. When I signed up with my broker, he told me the firm belongs to the multiple listing exchange, which it does. Although I've already brought in three new listings, my broker won't let me put them in the multiple listings. He says we earn more money if the sale is made within the firm. He even refuses to cooperate with other agents who phone to inquire about our ads for these houses. I'm pretty discouraged as my listings haven't sold yet. Am I working for a crooked broker?
—*Agnes D.*

A. Cooperation among real estate brokers from different firms means maximum total earnings for everyone. In most towns the local multiple listing service distributes listings to member brokers to get the widest market exposure so the best price and terms can be attained for the seller.

It is shortsighted policy for a broker to refuse to cooperate with other local realty agents. Although some large firms have this policy, those brokers eventually find other local agents will not cooperate with them either. Although the broker and salespeople earn higher fees on "in-house sales," I feel a noncooperation policy results in lower sales volume than would be attainable by cooperating fully with other local realty agents. Perhaps you should consider switching to a broker who is more progressive about use of the multiple listing service.

HOW TO SELECT THE BEST REALTY AGENT TO SELL YOUR PROPERTY

Q. We understand it is difficult to sell homes now, but we must sell ours in the next few months. What is the best procedure for selecting the best realty agent who can get our home sold without cutting the price? —*Mr. A. F.*

A. In today's market it is more important than ever before to select the best real estate agent to professionally market your home. Many of the inferior realty agents are being forced out of the market, due to lack of commission earnings, but the top agents will survive and prosper.

Never select a real estate agent on the basis of his commission rate or estimated sales price of your home alone. Choose the agent who will do the best job marketing your home on the terms you specify. Of course, base your asking price and terms on current market conditions in your area. The realty agent can help you make these decisions.

Before listing your home for sale, invite at least three active local agents to discuss the listing (separately of course). Ask your friends for recommendations or select them from names of agents who advertise often in the newspaper or who have "sold" signs on homes near yours. When you talk to these agents, ask about their commission rates, probable sales price of your home, and anything else you want to know.

Disregard any agent who does not prepare a written "competitive market analysis" showing how he arrived at the estimate of your home's probable sales price. Before listing with any agent, phone his client references, then select the agent you feel will do the best job.

WILL CUT-RATE REAL ESTATE BROKERS SURVIVE?

Q. I am a new real estate broker. My office has just been open about four months and it isn't breaking even yet. I am considering switching to cut-rate and charging only a 4 percent sales commission. Our area had a cut-rate broker, but he only lasted about ten months before he closed. Do you think cut-rate real estate brokers will survive the current mortgage credit crunch?—*John B.*

A. Cut-rate realty brokers, who charge less than the 6 percent or 7 percent customary sales commissions, are prospering in some towns and starving in others.

As you know, real estate sales commissions are fully negotiable between the seller and agent. In the past, realty brokers were reluctant to cut their commission schedule, but some brokers are now doing so, especially on the higher-priced properties.

The biggest problem for cut-rate brokers is the lack of cooperation with other local brokers who may have buyers for their listings. Cooperating brokers have been reluctant to show listings of the cut-rate brokers because each agent then earns such a small sales commission.

If your commission is 4 percent of the sales price, for example, you would earn only 2 percent and the cooperating broker would earn 2 percent. It is almost impossible to pay expenses with such a small commission.

However, if you represent both the buyer and seller, then you can probably survive on a 4 percent commission if you have a high enough sales volume. Perhaps you should provide in your listings for a 4 percent commission if you represent both buyer and seller but a 6 percent commission if a cooperating broker represents the buyer. At least 50 percent of all residential sales involve two cooperating brokers, so you cannot afford to overlook them if you want to succeed.

WHY AN OPEN LISTING IS NO WAY TO SELL A HOME

Q. My husband's boss, who is quite knowledgeable about real estate, suggested we sell our home on an "open listing" with several real estate brokers. So we prepared a little flyer about the house's features, property taxes, insurance, and mortgage details. This was mailed to about twenty local realty brokers. The result has been lots of activity from these brokers, not so much to get our home sold but to get an exclusive listing from us. What should I do to get the brokers to sell my house instead of pestering me for an exclusive listing?—*Anne M.*

A. Your first mistake was to send that open listing flyer to the twenty brokers. A better approach would have been to list your home exclusively with one agent who would then cooperate with other local brokers, usually through the local multiple listing exchange, who may have a buyer.

An open listing is really no listing at all. That is because if you find a buyer for the house, the brokers earn nothing. The result is most good realty brokers work on open listings only on rainy days when they have nothing better to do.

Rarely will brokers advertise or spend much time trying to sell open listings, as you found out. The reason is open listings are a race between you and the brokers to find a buyer. Since the brokers lack control over your property, they prefer to work on selling their exclusive listing properties.

TO GET YOUR PROPERTY SOLD, WRAP IT IN AN ATTRACTIVE PACKAGE

Q. Our home has been listed for sale several months in a town that has too many homes for sale. I blame this problem on the home builders who built too many homes, many of which are unsold. We have an excellent realty agent who tells us to be patient. She says there are about five homes listed for sale for every home which sells. What can we do to get our home sold as we've already bought another?—*Sue Ann C.*

A. To sell your home for top dollar, in good or bad times, wrap it in an attractive package. First, look at your home's physical condition. Be sure it is in top condition. Look at it critically to see if it needs painting, cleaning, or repairing. If so, get the work done.

Next, look at your home's financing package. If you are expecting an all-cash sale, you will be waiting a long time in today's market. To get your home sold, offer special finance terms, such as taking back a second mortgage at a reasonable interest rate for at least three to five years.

There are plenty of buyers for "red ribbon deals," like this, that combine an attractive home with affordable financing. Make your home stand out from the crowd of listed homes for sale.

For example, price your home at its full market value, maybe even a little higher. But offer to carry back a second mortgage at 10 percent interest. I guarantee that will get attention in today's market. It is much cheaper for you to cut the interest rate a little on that second mortgage than it is to have an unsold home.

WHY HOME SALE PRICES WILL NOT FALL

Q. I am a real estate saleswoman. Lately many of my prospective buyers have said they think home sale prices will drop soon. So they are holding back selling their old homes and buying larger ones. Do you think home sale prices will drop if we have a recession?—*Janet A.*

A. No. The volume of homes sales, of course, dropped in 1980, 1981, and 1982 from previous years, due to the high cost of mortgage money. Many buyers can't qualify for new mortgages at today's high interest rates. In some communities, the median home sale price has dropped too. But do not be fooled. What is happening is the less-expensive homes are selling in greater volume than are the more-expensive ones, thus dropping the median sales price.

Although we are still in a "buyer's market" as of this writing, since there are more homes for sale than buyers looking for homes to buy, prices are generally not dropping. But they are rising more slowly than they did in 1979.

Except in communities where there is an oversupply of new homes for sale, sellers are holding firm on prices. But they are becoming very flexible on sales terms, thus creating some terrific bargains for buyers.

Owning a home or other good property is not a speculative investment like gold, silver, or common stocks where the value fluctuates beyond the owner's control. If a real estate owner cannot get the price he wants, he just waits until he can. Have you ever heard of a realty owner selling for less than he paid for a property? It rarely happens in real estate, but it happens every day to owners of gold, silver, bonds, and common stocks.

In other words, the great benefit of real estate investing is the property owner controls the destiny of his property. Tell your buyers to buy now before mortgage interest rates drop substantially. When that happens, buyers will be out in droves and home sale prices will rapidly escalate because there will be a shortage of new and resale homes for sale.

11.

How Real Estate
Can Give You
Lifetime Income

The last chapter of a book is supposed to tie everything together. Well, this chapter will not let you down. But it will do more. Since you got this far in the book, you are now saying to yourself either (1) this real estate investing is hard work, and it is not for me, or (2) real estate is the best investment I have heard of, and I can hardly wait to get started.

Lazy people will have made the first choice. For them, investing in passive investments is probably best. While the risk is much greater in such investments, little work is required. The rewards can be spectacular, such as picking a common stock which goes up in value, but the losses can be disastrous because the passive investor has no control over what happens to his investment. That is why the New York Stock Exchange is known as the world's largest casino. It is a pure gamble. Of course, it is possible to lessen the risk by careful study before making passive investments, but all the research in the world will not assure a profit. Just talk to the bond investors who now have huge losses. The only way they can come out ahead is to hold their bonds to maturity, but those dollars they then collect will have depreciated in purchasing power by 5 percent to 15 percent *per year*. If you own a twenty-year bond, at maturity it will pay off in full, but those dollars will be virtually worthless.

But if you have concluded that real estate offers the best investment opportunities, you have made the right choice. However, I hasten to point out that real estate is not the perfect investment. There is none, so stop searching.

THE BIGGEST DISADVANTAGE
OF REAL ESTATE INVESTING

Management time is the biggest drawback of investing in real property. Real estate is not a passive investment. If you invest in real estate (with the possible exception of raw, vacant land), it requires management time to (1) locate the right property to buy, (2) negotiate with the seller for its purchase, (3) find tenants to pay the rent, (4) collect the rents, (5) handle necessary repairs and improvements, and (6) prepare your income tax returns to maximize your tax shelter benefits from the property.

Somehow, around April 15 each year, that last time-consuming requirement does not seem bothersome at all because it is always a pleasure to see how many income tax dollars do not have to be paid to Uncle Sam because of my property ownership. Although someone has to pay income taxes, let it be another person. Congress wrote the tax laws to encourage real estate investment because this policy results in more housing, commercial prosperity, and individual reward. Of course, the tax benefits of investing in real estate are a major incentive, but property should never be bought for the tax gimmicks alone.

THE BIGGEST ADVANTAGE OF REAL ESTATE INVESTING

Time is the biggest drawback of real estate investing. But the biggest advantage is its inherent, basic value if it is (1) well-located and (2) of basically sound construction. That is why good real estate does not lose value. In fact, in recent years most good properties have appreciated in market value at least at the pace of the inflation rate and usually faster.

While that is nice to know, and it means good real estate is a safe place to invest as an all-cash buyer, real estate is even more profitable for the highly leveraged buyer. To illustrate, suppose you buy a $100,000 property with $10,000 cash down payment. If that property appreciates in market value at an inflation rate of about 5 percent, a year from now that property will be worth $105,000. But as a percentage return on your $10,000 investment, that $5,000 value increase is 50 percent. Not many alternative investments offer this leverage advantage available in real estate. How many other investments do you know of offering such high returns to keep pace with inflation?

The nice thing about real estate is if you buy depreciable income property, such as apartments, rental houses, or commercial income property, the rent from the tenants usually pays the carrying costs while you make these profits. If the purchase is properly structured, there will be little or no negative cash flow. Larger properties produce substantial cash flow. Even if there is a negative cash flow in the early years of ownership, as rents increase with inflation, after a few years the negative cash flow is usually wiped out by rising rents.

THE SECOND-BIGGEST ADVANTAGE OF REAL ESTATE INVESTING

Inherent basic land value is real estate's greatest advantage. In other words, its usefulness will not be wiped out overnight (as can happen with stocks, bonds, commodities, and other investments).

But the second-greatest advantage of real estate investing is it can provide lifetime income for the owner. The variations of how good real estate can provide income to the owner are limitless.

Many owners who have owned income property for a long time live off the net rental income. Although it is difficult in most communities to buy property today with a high net income, the longer you own the property the greater its net income usually becomes. While the owner waits for the rent income to increase with inflation, he enjoys the income tax savings from the depreciable property's tax shelter. Another way of saying this is, buy all the income property you can when you are young, so you can live off its income when you are old.

Another way rental property can provide income to its owner is by periodic refinancing. As the market value of your property holdings rises, refinance the mortgage every few years. I have one property that I have refinanced three times. That cash produced from refinancing is tax-free to be spent with no strings attached by Uncle Sam. Hopefully, if the refinance cash is not needed for living expenses, it will be invested in more good-income property.

Still another method of income production from real estate occurs when the owner decides it is time to dispose of a property, pay Uncle Sam his long-term capital gain tax on the profit, and cash monthly installment sale checks from the buyer. Many retirees do this. When they retire from their jobs, they sell their properties, carry the financing for the buyer on an installment sale mortgage, and enjoy the income from those monthly checks.

Recall Alice in the chapter on tax-deferred exchanges. She sold her apartment house because she grew tired of its management. Now she receives a nice monthly check from the buyer. Her only work is endorsing that check and depositing it in her bank account. If the buyer should fail to make the payments, Alice can foreclose and either (a) get paid off in cash by the buyer at the foreclosure sale or (b) get the property back to resell it for another profit.

To summarize, real estate offers the best of all worlds. During ownership, investment property can offer (a) tax shelter, (b) net income cash flow, (c) tax-free refinance cash, and (d) inflation hedge protection as the property appreciates in market value. When the owner eventually decides to dispose of the property, this can be done on an installment sale to minimize resale profit tax and to provide retirement income.

A footnote, however, is in order. If the owner does not sell his investment property during his lifetime, when he dies, there is no capital gain tax on what would have been profit if the property was sold before the owner's death. To illustrate, suppose you own property with an adjusted cost basis of $100,000. If its market value on the date of your death is $300,000, the $200,000 difference between market value and adjusted cost basis escapes capital gain tax. Of course, the $300,000 value will be included in your estate for federal estate tax and state inheritance tax purposes.

But if you had sold that property the day before your death, then the $200,000 capital gain profit would be taxable on your last income tax return. So even death offers tax shelter from profit taxes, but it is a rather extreme and irreversible way to get out of paying capital gains taxes. By the way, if you have been making tax-deferred exchanges in a chain of trades, all those deferred taxes are forgiven at death too. The same applies to any deferred profit taxes using the "residence replacement rule" on the sale and replacement of your residences.

Thanks to the magic of our tax laws, it is not only possible to legally avoid paying income taxes during the real estate owner's lifetime, but that same property's "profits" escape capital gains tax on accumulated profits at the time of death. So whether the owner dies while still owning real estate, or if he sells it and lives off the installment sale income, good real estate investments provide the best tax advantages of any investment.

QUESTIONS AND ANSWERS

IS TODAY A GOOD TIME TO INVEST IN VACANT LAND?

Q. I know of some terrific bargains in land for sale about a mile away from a just completed subdivision tract of homes. When home construction starts up again when mortgage interest rates come down, this land will be ideal for a builder to buy. I can get it for only $45,000 down payment. Do you think now is a good time to buy it?—*Ramos M.*

A. No. Even professional home builders do not want to own land ahead of the time they can build homes on it. Holding land is very costly for property taxes, mortgage interest, and other carrying costs. Just to break even, the land value must appreciate at least 25 percent each year (inflation eats up purchasing power, mortgage interest will cost at least 10–12 percent, property taxes are 1–3 percent of market value, realty agent's sales commission is 5–10 percent, and miscellaneous costs run 1–? percent per year).

Unless you are very wealthy, I doubt you have the "staying power" to hold the land for several years.

Professional builders, rather than buy land, now purchase options to buy it. Options are far cheaper, often just 1 percent to 3 percent of the purchase price, depending on the length of the option term. The option holder controls the land, even though he has only a small amount of option money at stake. Rather than buying that land, get an option on it so you will not lose much if things do not go as you expect. Many fortunes have been made speculating in land, but far more have been lost. You should be a winner, not a loser, so do not get tied up in land speculation that produces no tax shelter and no immediate ownership benefits.

SHOULD FORMER HOME BE SOLD OR RENTED?

Q. We recently bought a new home. Fortunately, the builder had a mortgage commitment at a low interest rate. Our question involves the wisdom of selling or renting our old home. Some friends say we should sell it, but others say we should keep it for the tax advantages. What do you suggest?—*Bruce H.*

A. The more real estate you own, the better protected you are against inflation. Keep your old home. Today is not an especially good time to sell a house unless you must, due to the high cost of mortgage money.

By keeping your old home, you will also gain some tax advantages. You will be able to depreciate the lower of (a) your basis for the house (excluding the value of the nondepreciable land) or (b) its market value on the date of conversion to rental status.

The result of this noncash depreciation deduction should be to shelter all of the rent income and some of your other orindary income, such as job salary, from income taxes.

Another advantage of keeping your old home is that when you eventually retire, you can sell the house on an installment sale to provide extra retirement income. Or if you have children to send to college, you can sell the house and use the payments to pay your children's college tuition. In the meantime, you will enjoy your old home's tax shelter for some of your ordinary income.

HOW TO CREATE YOUR REAL ESTATE MONEY MACHINE

Q. I recently read a book about real estate that suggested that people buy one rental property per year for investment. The author said that after a few years, the property would go up in market value due to inflation and the mortgage could be refinanced to produce tax-free cash to buy more properties. This sounds too good to be true. If it is true, would it be possible to keep doing this and then retire by selling one or two properties each year and take back the mortgage financing to provide retirement income?—*Becker M.*

A. Yes. I suspect you are referring to Robert G. Allen's terrific book *Nothing Down* (Simon and Schuster, 1984). It is true that money produced by refinancing is tax free. The plan is a sound one.

It is like creating your own "money machine" each time you buy an investment property. That property not only should produce tax-sheltered income for the owner, but when it is refinanced, the money produced is tax-free.

Of course, when investment property is eventually sold, Uncle Sam is waiting to collect his capital gain tax. But an installment sale can be used to spread out this tax bite over future years, thus avoiding a boost into a high income tax bracket in the year of sale and also providing safe retirement income.

The hard part, however, is buying your first investment property and then keeping on buying one more property each year. But when you see all the income tax advantages on April 15 as you pay little or no income tax, that should provide sufficient motivation to keep buying more properties.

TEN-YEAR TAX-FREE REALTY TRUST PAYS CHILDREN'S COLLEGE TUITION

Q. My lawyer suggests I set up a "ten-year trust" to pay for my children's college tuition costs. He says the money I contribute to the trust can go to buy good real estate, with the net income accumulating tax-free. Is this a good idea?—*George T.*

A. Yes. Such a trust, called a "Clifford Trust," must be for at least ten years plus one day.

You can transfer either property now owned or newly acquired property to the trust. The net income is reinvested in the trust. At the end of the trust period, the assets can be used to fund your children's college expenses.

Such a trust will not cost you any after-tax dollars. If paid out before your child is twenty-one, the accumulated trust assets are tax-free. You still retain the normal dependency income tax deductions for your children while the trust assets are growing, tax-free, in market value. It sounds like you have got a smart attorney who understands tax planning. Real estate can be the vehicle to help you achieve your goals with the ten-year trust for your children.

INHERITED PROPERTY NOT TAXABLE TO HEIRS

Q. My late uncle left me a duplex worth about $100,000. Will I have to pay tax on it?—*Tom R.*

A. You may owe state inheritance tax, but this is usually paid by the estate's executor before you receive the property. However, you will not owe any capital gains tax.

Even though your late uncle probably had a lower book value for the duplex, your basis will be its $100,000 market value on the date of your uncle's death. If you sell it for $110,000, for example, only your $10,000 profit will be taxed (as a long-term capital gain, by the way).

But there is no capital gain tax to pay on the difference between the duplex's market value on the date of your uncle's death and his book value for the property. If he had sold the duplex the day before he died, he would have owed capital gain tax. But upon his death, all capital gain tax liability is forgiven. Your tax adviser can explain further.

HOW TO CASH IN YOUR CHIPS

Q. Over the last ten years my ex-wife and I have bought four rental houses in which we now have about $200,000 total equity. We want to "tap out" and use the proceeds for semiretirement. What is the best game plan to maximize the dollars available after selling these houses while minimizing our tax bite? I'm in a 44 percent income tax bracket and my ex-wife is in a 20 percent tax bracket.—*Mr. C. K.*

A. Installment sales would be ideal for you. The security is a first or second mortgage on the property sold.

Advantages to you and your ex-wife include (1) high-interest income on the buyer's unpaid balance, (2) safe investment secured by a second mortgage on the houses, (3) spreading out your profit tax into future years when your retirement income will be low, and (4) easy quick sale for top dollar due to the built-in financing. Ask your tax adviser to further explain installment sale tax advantages.

HOW PROPERTY INVESTMENTS CAN CREATE
LIFETIME INCOME

Q. At present I invest the maximum in a Keogh Retirement Plan. But considering the taxes I will owe when I withdraw that money after retirement, I figure I'm barely keeping up with inflation. Would I be better off investing my money in good real estate, such as land, instead? Then when I retire, I could sell off the land for my retirement income and take back mortgages.—*Edwina R.*

A. While your basic idea is sound, it needs some refinement. The major advantage of Keogh and IRS retirement programs is the money contributed is tax-exempt until you withdraw it. Another advantage is the compounding of interest if the money is well invested.

While real estate can match the interest compounding benefits, due to the advantages of realty leverage, the money you invest in real estate will not be tax-deferred unless you find a Keogh Plan trustee who will invest in land for you. Many will not.

Another aspect of your plan that needs thought is your idea of investing in vacant land. While land can be an excellent investment, it often does not go up in value fast enough to cover its carrying costs and inflationary loss of the dollar's purchasing power. Good income property often does much better.

Before you switch retirement plan strategies, talk to an estate planning attorney or other specialist. While real estate can provide secure retirement income, its acquisition must be carefully planned for maximum benefits. There is a right and wrong way to use real estate for your retirement planning. It does not appear you have found the right way yet.

HOW REAL ESTATE CAN PROVIDE YOUR RETIREMENT SECURITY

Q. We look forward to your newspaper articles, especially the questions about investment properties. For the last twelve years my husband and I have bought at least one property per year. At first it was a struggle to save for the down payment. But now we just refinance one or two of the properties to give us cash to buy another. In September, my husband will retire at age fifty-five, thanks mostly to the security our investment properties give us. We plan to keep refinancing our properties, perhaps selling one occasionally on an installment sale mortgage. Keep telling your readers that investing in good income properties is the best way to beat inflation. Another big advantage is we haven't had to pay any income taxes for many years thanks to the tax shelter of the depreciation deductions.—*Gertrude J.*

A. Thank you for sharing your success story. It will convince more people of the merits of real estate investing than I can. Real estate is definitely the most tax-favored investment available, probably because so many member of Congress invest in real estate.

Your letter pointed out three primary reasons why investors buy real estate: (1) for a hedge against inflation, (2) income tax shelter for ordinary income, such as job salary, and (3) retirement security. Of course, there are other advantages too, such as leverage benefits, tax-free refinancing cash, long-term capital gains upon resale, and safety of investment. No other investment offers all the advantages of real estate.

FOR FURTHER READING

There are many excellent real estate books which should be read for further information on the various advantages of real estate investing. New real estate books are being published constantly so watch for new offerings. For further reading, here is a list of the best real estate books currently available at larger libraries and bookstores. Real estate is a field where investors and salespeople never stop learning better methods of investing in and selling property.

1. *Nothing Down,* by Robert G. Allen (Simon and Schuster, 1984), a classic book explaining creative finance methods for acquiring property with little cash.
2. *Double Your Money in Real Estate Every Two Years,* by Dave Glubetich (Impact Publishing, 1980), an outline of how to create profits in real estate by investing in single-family rental houses. This book is the sequel to Glubetich's earlier classic on how to invest in single-family rental houses, *The Monopoly Game* (Impact Publishing), now in its fourth edition.
3. *How I Turned $1,000 into Five Million in Real Estate,* by William Nickerson (Simon and Schuster, 1980), a revision of the classic textbook on how to pyramid profits in real estate by buying rundown property, improving it to increase its market value, and exchanging for larger property. The unfortunate aspect of this new edition is it was not completely updated from earlier editions, and it uses outdated information which is no longer accurate for today's investors. But the book is still a classic real estate guidebook.
4. *How You Can Become Financially Independent by Investing in Real Estate,* by Albert J. Lowry (Simon and Schuster, 1982), follows in the footsteps of Nickerson's basic book. This best-seller adds new information to Nickerson's principles and is well worth reading.
5. *Landlording,* third edition, by Leigh Robinson (Express Publishing, 1980), a practical, humorous guide to property management by a pro who emphasizes the profit aspects of managing for maximum return from income realty.
6. **Landlording, third edition, by Leigh Robinson (Express Publishing, 1980), a practical, humorous guide to property management by a pro who emphasizes the profit aspects of managing for maximum return from income realty.**

Index

Index

ABOUT THE AUTHOR

Robert Bruss writes the nationally syndicated "Real Estate Mailbag" question and answer newspaper column, the "Real Estate Notebook" newspaper feature on real estate trends, "Real Estate Law and You" articles about new court decisions affecting real estate, and "Real Estate Book Review" features. Tribune Media Services distributes these features to several hundred newspapers.

Originally from Minneapolis, Minnesota, Bruss graduated from Northwestern University's School of Business Administration in Evanston, Illinois, in 1962. He received his J.D. law degree from the University of California's Hastings College of the Law in San Francisco in 1967. He was admitted to the California Bar the same year. In 1968, he received his California real estate broker's license.

Bruss has been and is involved in ownership of investment properties, primarily houses, apartments, and commercial buildings. He gained much of his practical how-to-do-it real estate sales and management insight as investment manager with Grubb & Ellis Company in San Francisco. Grubb & Ellis Company is one of California's largest statewide real estate brokerages. Bruss also has taught real estate practice and real estate law courses at the College of San Mateo and for the continuing education division of the University of Southern California. He serves as a director of the National Association of Real Estate Editors.